Journal of Ancient Egyptian Interconnections

Volume 37

March 2023

Egypt and the Mediterranean World from the Late Fourth through the Third Millennium BCE

Proceedings of the
Conference Held
18–27 May 2021,
Amman, Cairo, Jerusalem, Sydney

edited by
Karin Sowada and Matthew J. Adams

EgyptianExpedition.org

FRONT COVER: Royal fleet returning with captured Asiatics. Detail from the mortuary temple of Sahure at Abusir, Fifth Dynasty. Neues Museum, Berlin (CC BY-SA 4.0, Osama SM Amin FRCP (Glasg), commons.wikimedia.org/wiki/File:Royal_fleet,_returning_ship_with_captured_West_Asiatics._Detail_of_a_wall_panel_from_the_mortuary_temple_of_Sahure_at_Abusir,_Egypt._25th_century_BCE._Neues_Museum.jpg).

Journal of Ancient Egyptian Interconnections, new series, volume 37

Cover design by Noreen Doyle

Library of Congress Cataloging-in-Publication Data
Beyond Egypt: Relations and Imaginations of the Ancient Past
ISBN-13: 979-8-9878754-0-7

Journal of Ancient Egyptian Interconnections

Volume 37
March 2023

Table of Contents

Journal of Ancient Egyptian Interconnections

About This Journal

The *Journal of Ancient Egyptian Interconnections* (*JAEI*) is an online scholarly publication integrating Egyptian archaeology with Mediterranean, Near Eastern, and African studies—providing a dedicated venue for this growing field of interdisciplinary and inter-area research. The journal has a wide geographical and temporal range while continuing to specialize in all aspects of interaction between ancient Egypt and its neighbors. This extends to environmental, reception, and other types of studies, including the application of new methodologies, the history of Egyptology, the development and curation of Egyptian collections, "Egyptomania," and broadly related topics.

JAEI publishes full-length articles, short research notes, and reviews of published works, each of which has been peer-reviewed in a double-blind screening process by at least one Egyptologist and a specialist from the area or field of interaction, as well as reports and announcements of relevant conferences and symposia.

The editors are assisted by an international editorial board composed of distinguished experts in the cultures of ancient Egypt's neighbors or aspects of their interaction with Egypt. In this way, *JAEI* is well equipped to provide a solid publication platform for an area of study with true focus yet wide application within Egyptology and general historical studies.

The *Journal of Ancient Egyptian Interconnections* is published four times a year, with occasional additional volumes.

Subscription instructions and contributor guidelines are available elsewhere in this volume and at egyptianexpedition.org/announcements/.

Editorial and subscription questions should be sent to the journal staff at jaei@egyptianexpedition.org.

Journal of Ancient Egyptian Interconnections

Journal of Ancient Egyptian Interconnections

Guide for Contributors

Topics for Contributions

The *Journal of Ancient Egyptian Interconnections* is a scholarly, peer-reviewed online journal that will consider potential contributions on any aspect of interaction (one- or two-way) between ancient Egypt and other cultures of the ancient world. Normally, these other cultures are ones directly or closely surrounding Egypt in Africa, the Near East, and the Mediterranean world, although demonstrable interactions between Egypt and more distant regions are also acceptable. Posited interactions between Egypt and the New World will not be considered. Topical interconnections will be considered (e.g., the ancient environment, application of new or novel scientific methods to Egyptological subjects).

Types and Lengths of Contributions

The *JAEI* publishes three types of studies: full-length articles, short research notes, and reviews. Articles should be of a length commensurate with that of articles in printed journals. Contributors should check with the editor before submitting an unusually long contribution. There is no minimum length for short research notes as long as these clearly make a significant point. Reviews may be of any length, depending on the significance and size of the work reviewed. For more specific guidelines, contributors are advised to consult with the editor.

Spelling and Punctuation

For submissions in English, United States spelling and grammar conventions are preferred. British spellings will be accepted, but either the British or the U.S. convention must be used consistently (exclusive of quotations, which must retain their original spellings). The *UCLA Encyclopedia of Egyptology* should be followed for preferred spellings of transliterated place names and personal names unless the argument of the contribution requires alternatives that are explained in the contribution itself (https://uee.cdh.ucla.edu/spelling/). Only American punctuation conventions will be used (e.g., period or comma inside the closing quotation mark; superscript number for endnote always after punctuation; period after abbreviated titles such as "Dr."). Use of the serial comma (a.k.a. "Oxford comma") is preferred. Do not use superscript for ordinals (e.g., 18th, *not* 18th). For a range of numbers, such as pages or dates, use an en-dash (–), not a hyphen (-).

Dates

The *JAEI* does not publish calendar dates, ranges, or estimates (e.g., for dynasties, reigns, or events) predating 664 BCE (the beginning of the Late Period) unless dates are material to the argument of the contribution. All dates are to be designated "BCE" or "CE." The *UCLA Encyclopedia of Egyptology* "Preferred

Chronology" should be followed for general chronological matters and associated terminology (https://uee.cdh.ucla.edu/chronology/).

Format of Contributions

The preferred language for submissions is English; French and German contributions are also acceptable. All contributions must be submitted in MS Word format (.doc, .docx). Submissions with special fonts must include a note naming the font and a PDF or hardcopy of the text. If a font is not available to the author, they may transliterate Egyptian in the standard Manual de Codage (ASCII) style. The typesetter will then employ an appropriate font.

Normally, texts in ancient languages should be in transliteration. If it is important to show the actual script (hieroglyphic, hieratic, cuneiform, etc.), these texts should be submitted as digital image files noting their intended placement in the text of the manuscript. Such images must be high quality and must remain legible at small size.

The first page of the manuscript should carry the title of the article, with the name and affiliation of the author, followed by a short abstract (not more than 150 words) and then the main text. If the text includes figures or tables, the positions of these should be indicated by captions. Note that the typesetter might need to vary this placement for logistical reasons.

Tables and figures must be submitted as separate documents, not embedded in the manuscript with the main text. Authors may suggest placement within the paper, but the typesetter will make final decisions in this regard. To conform to the style and/or general appearance of the *JAEI*, the typesetter may typeset tables provided by the author.

A list of keywords (a minimum of three; no maximum) must also be provided.

Submission Procedures, Publication, and Copyright

Contributions should include a cover letter with the 1) author's name, 2) affiliation, 3) email, 4) mailing address, and 5) **a list of three potential referees with email addresses**. Contributions may be sent to the editor at jaei@egyptianexpedition.org, transmitted via an online file download site, or mailed on a USB drive (other media will not be accepted) to: Journal of Ancient Egyptian Interconnections, PO Box 18656, Tucson AZ 85731, USA.

Because the *JAEI* is a scholarly, peer-reviewed publication, contributions to the journal are not automatically accepted and may be declined if editorial reviewers do not support their publication. The *JAEI* is published quarterly; if accepted by the journal, submissions will normally appear within a few months of receipt. Copyright of submitted material remains with the contributor. Submissions may be freely shared by their authors in other venues six months after their publication in the *JAEI*.

Permissions and Illustrations

Authors must obtain permissions for the reproduction of copyrighted images or material used in their submissions. The *JAEI* cannot research or obtain permissions for its contributors.

Images (photographs [color or black and white], line art, etc.) to illustrate submissions should be sent in separate, individual digital files (not printed on paper). Images may be submitted in compressed format (jpg/jpeg), provided that they are of sufficient size and quality to allow clear screen display and printing. At least 300 dpi is preferred. Large image files should be submitted via an online file-download site rather than as email attachments. Authors wishing to include more than 10 images in an article should clear this with the editor. All figures must be numbered consecutively; maps are considered figures.

References to figures in the main text are to be given as, for example: Fig. 1, Figs. 3–7; Figs. 2, 5, 9. Captions should begin with Figure 1: (note the colon) and include a photo/illustration credit or other citation. (See below for citation style.) Captions may not contain endnotes.

Notes and Citations

A reference list of all cited works must be provided, following the guidelines below. (Given names may be provided in full or as initials.) Online citations must include a full URL and information regarding author, page title, website, and so forth. URLs will be checked for accuracy and updated or removed if necessary.

Do not include hotlinks in the manuscript.

References and other notes must be given as endnotes indicated by superscript numbers at relevant places in the text. The *JAEI* does not use footnotes. Standard Egyptological abbreviations (e.g., *JAEI*, PM; *KRI*, *Wb.*, etc.) are not generally used. If the author does choose to employ bibliographic and related abbreviations in the reference list, endnotes, main text, captions, or tables, these must be provided as list placed before the reference list.

Endnotes cannot be placed in the title, byline, abstract, or captions. (An acknowledgments section, between the main text and the reference list, may be used to offer information commonly placed in title or byline foot/endnotes.) Citations in tables must be kept within the table itself, that is, not incorporated among the endnotes of the text. They must be either in-text citations or footnotes given as superscript lower-case letters. Table footnotes will be typeset in a designated footnote row at the bottom of the table. If the author provides a camera-ready table, they must similarly keep any footnotes within the body of the table.

Note that, in the reference list, inclusion of series data is optional; if included, it must be spelled out in full (i.e., no abbrevations). See the second example below, under "Edited Volume."

EXAMPLES FOR REFERENCE LIST:

Journal Article

Koch, Ida, Sabine Kleiman, Manfred Oeming, Yuval Gadot, and Oded Lipschits. 2017. "Amulets in Context: A View from Late Bronze Age Tel Azekahs." *Journal of Ancient Egyptian Interconnections* 16: 9–24.

Article or Chapter in Book

Shinnie, Peter L. 2001. "Meroë." In Donald B. Redford (ed.), *The Oxford Encyclopedia of Ancient Egypt* vol. 2, 283–284. Oxford: Oxford University Press.

Book

Wengrow, David. 2006. *The Archaeology of Early Egypt: Social Transformation in North-East Africa, 10,000–2650 BC.* Cambridge: Cambridge University Press.

Edited Volume (with series data)

Bietak, Manfred and Ernst Czerny (eds.). 2004. *Scarabs of the Second Millennium BC from Egypt, Nubia, Crete and the Levant: Chronological and Historical Implications.* Denkschriften der Gesamtakademie/Österreichische Akademie der Wissenschaften 35; Contributions to the chronology of the Eastern Mediterranean 8. Vienna: Verlag der Österreichischen Akademic der Wissenschaften.

Edited Volume (without series data)

Bietak, Manfred and Ernst Czerny (eds.). 2004. *Scarabs of the Second Millennium BC from Egypt, Nubia, Crete and the Levant: Chronological and Historical Implications.* Vienna: Verlag der Österreichischen Akademic der Wissenschaften.

Online Source (note: do not *make the URL a hyperlink/hotlink in the manuscript)*

Muhlestein, Kerry. 2008. "Execration Ritual." In Jacco Dieleman and Willeke Wendrich (eds.), *UCLA Encyclopedia of Egyptology*. Los Angeles: eScholarship. < escholarship.org/uc/item/3f6268zf >, accessed 17 April 2021.

Metropolitan Museum of Art. n.d. "Relief Fragment with a Ship Under Sail, ca. 2465–2458 B.C." *The Met.* < metmuseum.org/art/collection/search/543894 >, accessed 17 April 2021.

EXAMPLE CITATIONS TO WORKS IN THE REFERENCE LIST *(note: do* not *use "ibid.," "op. cit.," and similar abbreviations)*

Koch et al. 2017, 13 fig. 6; Shinnie 2001; Wengrow 2006, 115–132; Bietak and Czerny 2004; Muhlestein 2008, 3; Metropolitan Museum of Art n.d.

Journal of Ancient Egyptian Interconnections

SUBSCRIPTION INSTRUCTIONS

The *Journal of Ancient Egyptian Interconnections* is published in digital format at least four times a year on a subscription basis. Login-based individual and IP-based institutional annual subscriptions are available. Both types of subscriptions include electronic access to all current and past issues of the journal.

INSTITUTIONAL SUBSCRIPTION: **$160/year**

Access is provided by IP addresses. There is no limit to the number of IP addresses that can be assigned to an institutional subscription. Institutional subscriptions can also be configured to use a domain rather than a set of IP addresses or IP ranges. For this option, only one domain is permitted per subscription account.

The institution, or its payment agency, must provide the IP addresses at the time of the subscription. Payment may be made by check (made payable to "Journal of Ancient Egyptian Interconnections") sent to the address below. Subscriptions can also be paid by credit card or wire transfer. For information, visit egyptianexpedition.org/register/ or e-mail the journal at jaei@egyptianexpedition.org.

INDIVDUAL SUBSCRIPTION: **$45/year**

An individual subscription provides access for one user. Payment may be made by check (made payable to the "Journal of Ancient Egyptian Interconnections") and mailed to the address below, or by credit card (or PayPal) at egyptianexpedition.org/register/. Upon payment, our system will send an e-mail with instructions for how to set your password.

Journal of Ancient Egyptian Interconnections
PO Box 18656
Tucson AZ 85731
USA

For further information about use of IP ranges, terms longer than one year, or any other questions regarding subscription procedures and access, please contact the journal staff at jaei@egyptianexpedition.org.

Updated September 2021

Journal of Ancient Egyptian Interconnections

EGYPT AND THE MEDITERRANEAN WORLD
FROM THE LATE FOURTH THROUGH THE THIRD MILLENNIUM BCE
CONFERENCE 18 - 27 MAY 2021 AMMAN - CAIRO - JERUSALEM - SYDNEY

Egypt and the Mediterranean World from the Late Fourth through the Third Millennium BCE

Matthew J. Adams
W.F. Albright Institute of Archaeological Research

Karin Sowada
Macquarie University

Introduction

The first iteration of the Egyptian state emerged in the late fourth millennium and survived into the late third millennium BCE. This first pharaonic state, however, was not monolithic. During this period, Egypt experienced ongoing complex developments in social and political organization that impacted all levels of Egyptian society. These changes are most evident in the transition to the pyramid-building society of the 3rd and 4th Dynasties, but periods of far-reaching change can also be detected throughout the Early Dynastic Period (1st–2nd Dynasties), the later Old Kingdom (5th–6th Dynasties), and the First Intermediate Period. So too did Egypt's relationships with the outside world change across this first millennium of state-level organization.

As one of the earliest state-forming societies whose reach can be seen across the Mediterranean world, Egypt's interaction with its neighbors has been of great interest to scholars inside and outside of Egyptology for more than a century. Over the last 15 years, new textual evidence has emerged, while the application of archaeological sciences has given new life to legacy data. Importantly, recent developments in the absolute chronology of the third millennium coupled with new archaeological data from all parts of the Mediterranean, have started a new wave of reassessment of the synchronisms, nature, and intensity of Egypt's relationships with its northern neighbors.

Given these developments, it was timely to convene a cross-disciplinary dialogue through an international conference showcasing the latest research on interactions between Egypt, the Levantine and Aegean worlds in the late 4th–3rd millennium (Late Early Bronze I – EB IV/Intermediate Bronze Age). Each region was represented by a different institutional partner which hosted invited papers related to the questions of Egypt's interaction with that region. The conference was held in a fully online format that allowed for global participation in real time.

The Conference

The conference was conceived of and organized by the editors and institutional partners including the Centre for Ancient Cultural Heritage and Environment (CACHE) at Macquarie University hosting online from Sydney, The W.F. Albright Institute of Archaeological Research (AIAR) hosting online from Jerusalem, the *Journal of Ancient Egyptian Interconnections* (*JAEI*) hosting online from Amman, and the American Research Center in Egypt (ARCE) hosting online from Cairo. The authors represented their respective institutions, while Dr. Pearce Paul Creasman represented *JAEI* and Dr. Louise Bertini represented ARCE.

Over four days—20 May, 24 May, 27 May, and 2 June 2021—32 invited papers were presented, representing 50 contributors from seventeen countries. Participants included PhD candidates, early and mid-career researchers, and senior scholars. Overall, 635 people attended the conference free of charge, representing 39 countries and the dedicated Twitter account amassed 310 followers in a short space of time. The abstracts of papers presented during these sessions are in the Appendix below.

Overall, *Egypt and the Mediterranean World* was a ground-breaking event, and we sincerely thank everyone who supported the conference and participated in many and various ways. It brought together archaeologists, historians, and scientists working across Egypt and the eastern Mediterranean to present and discuss data and broad themes that crossed geographical and disciplinary boundaries. The Zoom webinar format enabled people from politically disparate locations to meet and share their work in a free and neutral environment.

The Publication

This volume collects sixteen papers that ultimately derived from the presentations and discussion during the conference. They are all significant contributions to wider debates on state formation and the role and impact of trade in the emergence of complex societies. Each provides new historical, archaeological, and scientific data uniquely drawn from across the region by a wide range of specialists, and helps develop the rich mosaic of interconnections between Egypt and its Mediterranean neighbors.

In his paper, Matthew J. Adams focuses on the three temples *in antis* of Stratum XV Megiddo, offering an updated interpretation that derives from the data collected by the excavations of the Tel Aviv University Megiddo Expedition from 1993–2010. He argues for an Intermediate Bronze Age date for the complex, traditionally dated to the Early Bronze Age III, on the basis of stratigraphy and finds. His conclusions go further, offering a new understanding of the complex in a broad Northern Levantine context and demonstrate its connections with Egypt during the late 3rd millennium. Overall, his reassessment offers a new cutting-edge perspective on this phase of the cultic complex of Megiddo and opens the door to new research paths on southern Levantine networks to the north and Egypt to the south during this period.

Samuel Atkins and Yuval Yekutieli review Egypto-Levantine connectivity in the EB I based on new data from excavations at two sites in the Negev. They convincingly show Egyptian trading connections deep into the Negev Highlands during the EBI through the analysis of ceramics at Erani, Mitzpe Sde Hafir and Yeroham-Nahal Avnon. The presentation is the initial publication of material from Mitzpe Sde Hafir.

Whereas the focus often falls on Byblos, Maria Eugenia Aubet presents the results of her recent excavations at the Early Bronze Age site of Tyre, a remarkable site on a rocky island with no arable land. The data presented paint a picture of an island citadel with a protected harbor and storage facility, which imported everything it needed, but also played a significant role in the international sea trade of the period. The paper also underscores the likelihood of fresh Early Bronze Age data from Tyre, including Egyptian material and combed two-handled ceramic jars, possibilities that further nuance local and interregional relationships.

Maria Giovanna Biga builds on important work she began with P. Steinkeller on the identification of "Durugasu" in the Ebla archives as Egypt or a place in the Egyptian Delta. It summarizes the findings of that ground-breaking work, and provides new discourse on a hitherto unknown trade in live animals from Egypt to Ebla in the form of monkeys. The question of an exchange in live animals across the eastern Mediterranean region is only now the subject of academic debate, into which this paper delivers historical sources of previously unseen animal movements.

Marta D'Andrea takes as her task the reassessment of the contacts between Egypt and the Southern Levant in the Early Bronze Age IV (Intermediate Bronze Age), specifically noting the lack of chronological resolution for this period. The paper seeks to expose assumptions in scholarship on this subject and to take a fresh look at the evidence. It illustrates well the chronological / stratigraphic problems of defining the EB IV, its subphases, and the dates thereof. Clearly this period is not well understood, especially since the new Levantine chronology has given it a longer chronological horizon. Furthermore, these issues highlight the problems of anchoring radiocarbon dates between sites.

Michel de Vreese and Kamal Badreshany examine the EB III settlement landscape of Byblos, bringing many new insights to the study of urban neighborhoods, while providing a satisfying context for the major changes noted in the study of the near hinterland to Byblos's north. The paper is a significant new contribution to the archaeology and role of Early Bronze Age Byblos. Many have tried over the years to make sense of the early excavations and this paper takes the reader into a fresh space with a holistic assessment of the promontory as a ritual precinct, with the additional reflections based on new excavations in the region.

Hermann Genz and Alexander Ahrens offer an overview of the importance of Tell Fadous-Kfarabida on coastal Lebanon, along with an insightful discussion of objects likely from Egypt found at the site. Evidence from EB III Tell Fadous-Kfarabida demonstrates connections with Egypt within the context of Byblos as the primary trade node in the region. The nature and main features of the site are outlined and discussed, along with evidence for administrative systems and the importance of its 10km proximity to Byblos itself. Importantly, the work presents the likelihood of perishable exports which do not easily survive in the archaeological record.

Haskel Greenfield and Eleuterio Sousa address the question of the role of metallurgy in the rise of complex society through the analysis of cut marks on animal bones. The paper compares archaeological and zooarchaeological data from EB Egypt and the southern Levant, differentiating between flint/ stone tool cut marks with those made by copper tools, using various forms of microscopy. The paper offers observations about elite and every-day use of metal and stone tools, trade, and highlights the evidence from zooarchaeology as an additional analytical tool.

Mathilde Jean and Kamal Badrashany team up to present an important overview of the state of research on Levantine ceramics imported into early Egypt. The paper aggregates the existing published data from Egypt starting with Cemetery U at Abydos and proceeding through to the Early Dynastic Period at Helwan. The authors present a convincing case that embraces morphology, surface finish, petrography, and geoscience for a zone of production in the central Levant. Comparisons are then made with petrography from broadly parallel phases in the central Levant in order to clarify the origin of a corpus of imports in Egypt.

Johannes Jüngling and Felix Höflmayer offer a detailed critique of the bases for the historical chronology of the 3rd and 4th Dynasties, adding a brief update on the radiocarbon situation on correspondences with the Levant. Their focus on a range of historical sources for the number, order, and regnal years of 3rd Dynasty kings reminds the reader of the on-going historical uncertainty of this period. They further consider the issue of the biennial cattle count for the 4th Dynasty. A radiocarbon summary then rounds out the contemporary picture in a holistic way.

The Tale of Sinuhe forms the basis of Anna-Latifa Mourad-Cizek's contribution. Mourad interrogates the well-known tale from the Middle Kingdom to examine the experience of Egyptians associated with foreign expeditions as described in texts from the Old and Middle Kingdom. The question is raised as to whether the Old Kingdom experience of travelers abroad formed source material for the later classic work.

Itzak Paz revisits the ongoing debate about the nature of the Egyptian presence in the southern Levant during the late EB IB / Dynasty 0. The approach taken interrogates theoretical models against the archaeological evidence, in particular highlighting the spatial differences of Egyptian patterns of occupation, residence, and engagement at a "household" level in the region. The conclusions suggest a somewhat antagonistic and unwelcome Egyptian presence, underscoring earlier interpretations that the Egyptian presence was a hostile move on the part of the emerging Egyptian state.

Metoda Peršin presents an examination of little-studied applied potmarks on ceramic vessels from Lebanon and imported vessels from Egypt. Her work reveals the benefits of a contextual analysis of these potmarks to further understand their function(s) and enhance knowledge of exchange practices. Different marks in their combinations represent a specific graphic system understood in Lebanon, but likely not comprehended by the Egyptian recipients of jars. With potmarks applied at the point of manufacture, the author contends that they represented a form of local brand of location or content.

Maura Sala presents *aegyptiaca* and egyptianising material from EB II Tell el-Farah North and Jericho that had not been previously published, providing fresh insights into the material. With particular focus on these sites, she examines exchange between Egypt and the Levant, noting that Egyptian and south Levantine relations in the EB II requires a significant reassessment in the light of new data and scientific analyses.

The team of Karin Sowada, Wilma Wetterstrom, Geraldine Jacobsen, Fiona Bertuch, and Margaret Serpico tackle the nature and preservation of contents from a corpus of imported combed jars found in Giza tombs, now housed in the Museum of Fine Arts, Boston. The archaeology of the jars is examined to assess questions of royal patronage, ancient use and reuse, residue preservation and the impact of modern interventions. The work includes an examination and radiocarbon case-study of the contents of one jar to help answer the question of why, surprisingly, so few visible residues are found inside the jars from this corpus.

Rounding off the contributions, Valentina Tumolo and Kamal Badrashany present a dataset of combed ware vessels from Khirbet ez-Zeraqon in the northern reaches of the southern Levant and measure its regional importance in light of ceramic studies from other sites. Thin-section petrography is used to demonstrate the same shift in raw materials evident in the northern Transjordan and central Levant, adding to our understanding of regional technological change and the *chaîne opératoire* from the perspective of a single site.

Acknowledgements

We wish to thank all of the host institutions for their participation in this project and especially, Pearce Paul Creasman and Louise Bertini for facilitating their cooperation. Pearce Paul is further to thank for taking on the task of publishing the papers resulting from the conference herein.

The Conference was held free of charge for presenters and participants, but relied on financial contributions behind-the-scenes to ensure its success. CACHE provided funding for web hosting the event, ticketing and the administrative support of Dr. Alice McClymont. The Center for the Mediterranean World (American Archaeology Abroad) provided on-line technology support and editing services, while the Australian Research Council Future Fellowship Grant FT170100288 'Pyramids, Power and the Dynamics of States in Crisis' held by Dr Karin Sowada funded the graphic support provided by Mr. Anthony Dakhoul and other elements of the Conference.

Finally, we are extremely grateful to Viviana Moscovitch of The Center for the Mediterranean World for the hard work of copy editing and formatting of the final articles.

Appendix: Abstracts of Papers Presented

Egypt, Byblos, and Megiddo in the EB IV

Matthew J. Adams (W.F. Albright Institute of Archaeological Research}

The Stratum XV Triple Temple Complex at Megiddo has been the subject of debate concerning its date since it was first uncovered by the University of Chicago in the 1930s. Generally, an Early Bronze Age III date became the status quo interpretation, but several problems with this date are apparent. First, there was already significant EB III stratigraphy at the site consisting of a well-planned palace, elite quarter, and temple complex. The construction of the triple temple complex completely put this EB III palatial phase out of commission. Therefore, if an EB III date for the temples is preferred, then a completely new urban plan was envisioned within that period – a phenomenon not seen elsewhere at EB III palatial centers. Second, it leaves a significant gap in architectural occupation at the site during the EB IV / Intermediate Bronze Age, a period for which Megiddo has produced a significant amount of material culture. A solution presented itself with the Tel Aviv University Megiddo Expedition's discovery of a cache of Egyptianized pottery below the temple complex. Originally thought to have come from underlying EB IB strata, ongoing excavation at the site and a refinement of the stratigraphy of the cultic area lead the present author to argue that the pottery cache was a foundation deposit associated with the Stratum XV Triple Temple Complex, and that typologically the cache fits well Egyptian foundation deposits from the late Old Kingdom/ First Intermediate Period, in turn supporting an EB IV/IB date for the construction of the Megiddo Triple Temple Complex.

This paper returns to this this issue to place the architecture of the Triple Temple Complex properly into its Northern Levantine EB IV world as temples in antis, and to consider Northern Levantine and Egyptian contacts from the unique perspective of Megiddo.

Contact between Egypt and Crete in the 3rd/4th Dynasty: An Early Minoan II Vessel from Mendes, Egypt

Matthew J. Adams (W.F. Albright Institute of Archaeological Research), Christopher Hale (O.P. Jindal Global University), and Peter Tomkins (University of Leuven)

Of the varied projects of the Pennsylvania State University excavations at Mendes excavation project, one focused on an extensive stratigraphic sondage through a mound upon which the New Kingdom temple was built (Field AJ). The mound was shown to be a tell of its own comprised of the Old Kingdom temple complex, adjacent domestic and production buildings, and provincial cemetery. At present, the stratigraphic sondage has revealed continuous remains from the early First Dynasty through the First Intermediate Period. One of the phenomena observed at the site is the construction of a large mudbrick platform in the 5th Dynasty, understood to be the base for the temple of the Banebdjed, around which grew a large provincial cemetery (Field AJ, Phase III). The entire site was dramatically destroyed, and the tombs looted in the late 6th Dynasty.

In the remains of a building preceding the construction of the temple (Field AJ, Phase IV), dated to the 3rd/4th Dynasty, a vessel was discovered bearing a number of Cretan typological and technological features indicative of an Early Minoan II date. In this paper, we present the context of this unique vessel, review Aegean parallels, consider issues of chronological synchronization, and initiate a broader discussion of Egyptian and Aegean contact in the mid Third Millennium BCE.

Multi-Proxy Residue Analysis of Levantine Combed Vessels from the Early Old Kingdom

Sophia Aharonovich (Macquarie University), Ailish Schneider (University of Sydney), and Karin Sowada (Macquarie University)

Flat-based ceramic jars with vertical loop handles and a 'combed' exterior surface, are a well-known type associated with Levantine commodity exchange (Thalmann, Sowada 2014). Based on petrographic results from samples of 4th Dynasty Combed jars from Giza, Sowada, Ownby & Wodzinska (2019) concluded that the vessels originated in the Byblos region. The jars probably arrived in Egypt from Byblos by maritime trade routes (Sowada 2009). However, the original commodities transported to Egypt from the Levant are not known with certainty. In this paper, we present preliminary results of multi-proxy analysis of organic and botanical residues from the jars sampled in the petrographic study.

Ten sherds from different vessels were analysed in Macquarie University laboratories. To detect and identify pollen grains, diatoms, and phytoliths, we utilized Scanning Electron Microscope (SEM) images. For residue analysis, we used Gas Chromatography-Mass Spectrometry (GC-MS). In six sherds we did not detect traces of botanical residue using SEM images. Four other samples suggest the presence of *Olea Europaea* (Olive), *Ziziphus* sp. (Jujube), and *Salvia Sativa* (Sage) pollen grains. The data also show detectable levels of various n-alkanes and fatty acids, indicating that the major source of the organic residue derives from plant origins.

Sowada, K., 2009. *Egypt in the Eastern Mediterranean during the Old Kingdom: An archaeological perspective*. Saint-Paul.

Sowada, K., Ownby, M., Wodzińska, A., 2019. The petrography of imported Levantine Combed vessels from early Old Kingdom Giza. Levant, 1-18. https://doi.org/10.1080/00758914.2019.1664197

Thalmann, J.-P., Sowada, K., 2014. Levantine "combed ware", *Associated Regional Chronologies for the Ancient Near East and the Eastern Mediterranean: ARCANE Interregional* Vol. I: *Ceramics*. Brepols, 355-378.

Correlating Egypto-Levantine Connectivity in Ceramic Assemblage Profiles between Tel Erani and the Negev Highlands

Samuel Atkins (Ben-Gurion University of the Negev)

The role of nomadic pastoral tribes in the Egypto-Levantine interaction sphere of the late 4th millennium southwestern Levant has been often acknowledged, but rarely examined in detail. New data on the subject has been acquired from recent excavations by Ben-Gurion University at Mitzpe Sde Hafir and by the Israel Antiquities Authority excavations at Yeroham – Nahal Avnon, two late EB I sites in the Western Negev and Central Negev Highlands respectively. The study of the new data has revealed two zones of complex and transformational nomadic encounters with sedentary societies at a pivotal phase of Egypto-Levantine connectivity. A comparative multivariate statistical analysis of ceramic assemblage profiles from these two desert sites along with phases of Egypto-Levantine colonial relations at Tel Erani has revealed unexpected correlations, with consequent chronological and social-evolutionary implications. Viewed within a holistic frame that considers the overall material morphology of these sites, the interplay between Nomadic agency and Egyptian socio-economic and cultural influence in the region was evidently stimulative in the formation of new structures of desert-sown interaction.

Tyre: An Intermediate Harbour in Interregional Trade

Maria Eugenia Aubet (Universidad Pompeu Fabra)

The founding of a small, fortified center on the island of Tyre in the Early Bronze Age cannot be explained without hypothesizing the complicity of a continental center on the nearby coast. The island is rocky with no arable land, however, the Early Bronze Age settlement there has provided a notable volume of combed storage jars as well as remains of cereals, olive pits and grapes. As a maritime outpost of a continental center controlling a fertile plain, the island was ideally situated along the navigable Mediterranean current coming from the Nile Delta up the coastal Levant and in an excellent intermediary position between the southern Lebanese coast, the Bay of Akko and Egypt.

Status of Race and Syro-Palestinian Combed Ware in the Fifth and Sixth Dynasty

Miroslav Bárta (Charles University, Prague)

In this paper, I explore the phenomenon of the status of race in connection with imported and/or imitated Syro-Palestinian ceramic wares in the Fifth and Sixth Dynasty. Several Old Kingdom tombs from Abusir feature well-preserved genuine imported as well as imitated pottery jars in the burial chambers of their respective owners. The social status of these persons as reflected through their individual titles and the reasons behind their decision to include these vessels in their burial chambers will be discussed and interpreted.

Crafting Communities into Contact: Investigating the Production and Uses of Stamp Seals in Egypt and Crete during the Third Millennium BCE

Nadia Ben-Marzouk (Tel Aviv University)

Eastern Mediterranean exchange networks of the third millennium BCE saw the movement of goods and people, as well as the development of new practices. One such practice to gain prominence in Egypt and on Crete is the use of stamp seals. Though miniature in size, glyptic provides a window into the construction of new practices and identities in a community. This paper critically investigates the stamp seals in Egypt and on Crete during the third millennium, seeking to better understand the appearance of similarities and differences in each corpus. While previous research has debated the extent to which each regional assemblage was influenced by the other, this paper builds on a prior proposal that glyptic specialists from Crete were in direct contact with individuals in Egypt, suggesting similarities were more than superficial. Production techniques, form, iconographic motifs, and consumption practices will be surveyed, as well as non-glyptic material engaged in order to provide a more nuanced understanding of the nature of contact between communities. It is argued that these regional assemblages may have evolved alongside one another, reflecting local participation in an interregional community of exchange during the late third millennium. The implications of such contact will be explored.

The Relationships between Egypt and Syria in the 24th cent. BC according to the Texts of the City of Ebla, Syria

Maria Giovanna Biga (Università degli Studi "La Sapienza" di Roma)

In a number of articles that appeared between 2012 and 2017, Maria Giovanna Biga, studying the types of materials that were exchanged between the kingdom of Ebla and that of Dugurasu, hypothesized that Dugurasu could be identified as a place in the Delta of Egypt. This proposal was positively received by a number of scholars. Archi (A. Archi, Egypt or Iran in the Ebla Texts, *Orientalia* NS 45 (2016), pp. 1-49) questioned this hypothesis, arguing that Dugurasu is none other than the land of Turkish which, according to him, is to be sought in northwestern Iran.

This issue is of importance for the history of relationships of Syria and Egypt, and the nature of international trade during the late third millennium BC.

For this reason, M.G. Biga and P. Steinkeller recently offered in the Journal of Cuneiform Studies a systematic examination of the data bearing on the question of Dugurasu's identity and location. They studied in detail the materials traded between Ebla and Dugurasu. In addition, the city of DUlu was identified as an intermediary between Ebla and Dugurasu, with all the data pointing to an identification of DUlu with the city of Byblos. This presentation will discuss in detail the materials traded, presenting the results of the Biga-Steinkeller study, in addition to some new texts.

Deconstructing the Putative Egyptian Colonial System in Southern Levant at the End of the Fourth Millennium BC

Marcin Czarnowicz (Jagiellonian University in Kraków) and Eliot Braun (W.F. Albright Institute of Archaeological Research, Jerusalem)

Since the first traces of a 4th-millennium-BCE Egyptian settlement were found in southern Levant at Tel Erani by Shmuel Yeivin, various scholars have suggested interpretations of the nature of relations between the two regions. Presently, the most popular interpretation assumes that a newly born Egyptian state tried to establish a colony in the region in order to exploit its resources. Copper, olive oil and wine were exported to Upper Egypt via localities in the Delta region to fulfill a demand by the local nobility for luxury goods. The hypothesis states that Tell es-Sakan was the center of the colony directly controlled the southern coastal plain, the northern Negev and the southern Judean Shephela (piedmont).

Although the nature of the relations between Egypt and southern Levant has been at the center of scholarly debate for almost seven decades, the theoretical foundations of this relationship has not been thoroughly discussed. In this paper we discuss the definition of "colonization" within the context of that time and place. We suggest a new methodological background for understanding the Egyptian presence in southern Levant at the end of 4th millennium BCE which suggests a much reduced "colonial" experience.

Contacts between Egypt and the Southern Levant in the Early Bronze IV Period: An Open Question

Marta D'Andrea (Università degli Studi "La Sapienza" di Roma, Dipartimento di Scienze dell'Antichità)

According to revised absolute chronologies (increasingly accepted, though not yet unanimously), the Early Bronze Age IV in the southern Levant spans from ca. 2500 BCE to ca. 1920/1900 BCE, a period corresponding to the late Old Kingdom, First Intermediate Period, and the very beginning of the Middle Kingdom in Egypt.

Earlier, scholars assumed that Egyptian raids during the late Old Kingdom played a role in the demise of southern Levantine fortified settlements of the Early Bronze III period. Later, contacts between the two regions were framed within the hypothesis of commercial contacts related to trade of southern Levantine copper with the late Old Kingdom Egypt with virtually no evidence of contacts afterwards until the early Middle Kingdom. But what do we really know about southern Levantine-Egyptian interconnections in the Early Bronze IV period? How much does the lack of chronological resolution in the sub-phasing of the EB IV impact are current ability to understand these contacts?

This paper briefly reviews textual, pictorial, and archaeological evidence traditionally considered as evidence for southern Levantine-Egyptian interactions in the EB IV, outlining the current state of research. Taking the view from the southern Levant, it re-examines the local developmental trajectory to discuss how recent archaeological research may reenvision the way we understand this non-urban era. Moving from these insights, it discusses how the archaeological evidence may fit into newly proposed interpretations of Levantine-Egyptian contacts during this period.

The Negev and Surrounding Deserts during the Late 3rd Millennium BCE: An Update from the South

Zachary C. Dunseth (Brown University)

This paper summarizes the results of the nearly decade-long Negev Highlands Research Project, an interdisciplinary study of the desert settlement phenomena of the fourth and third millennium BCE at the macro- and microscale. Using a battery of geoarchaeological methods, this work has focused on identifying subsistence strategies, evaluating desert metallurgical activities, establishing a high-resolution radiocarbon framework, and reconstructing settlement patterns at four sites: two central sites, Ein Ziq and Mashabe Sade, and two smaller sites, Nahal Boqer 66 and Nahal Nizzana 328. In parallel to our work, other researchers in the southern deserts of the Negev, Jordan, and Sinai have contributed much to the understanding of the period, including the study of desert waterscapes, iconography, and copper sourcing. Altogether, the results of these studies enable a new discussion about desert societies and the role of the larger economies of Egypt and Syria in the arid south during the long 3rd millennium BCE.

The *ẖkr nswt* and the Role of Luxuria in Egyptian Diplomacy in the Levant during the Late Old Kingdom

Andres Diego Espinel (CCHS CSIC)

The aim of this paper is to offer a new interpretation of the Egyptian term *ẖkr-nswt,* proposing its connection to Egyptian diplomatic practices in the Levant. This expression, usually translated as "royal ornaments" or "royal insignia", seems to refer more precisely to both the most precious items intended for the royal consumption and the institution devoted to their elaboration, management and keeping. Prosopographical evidence indicates that the *ẖkr-nswt* was tightly connected to the Egyptian Treasury (*pr-ḥḏ*) and was related to either exotica collected in foreign regions or luxuria crafted in/for the royal palace, as is the case of some textiles, gold jewels or unguents.

Maria Giovanna Biga's recent identification of the toponym Dugurasu with Egypt in some Eblaite tablets offers new insights on the diplomatic and trading connections between Egypt and its Levantine neighbours during the late Old Kingdom (6th Dynasty). According to data from the Ebla state archive, different products were sent by the court of Dugurasu/Egypt to Ebla as payment and/or recognition of the giving by Ebla of materials such as lapis lazuli and tin, among others. The bulk of the Egyptian gifts comprised some of the main items that formed the *ẖkr-nswt*: textiles, gold and other luxury materials (e.g., semi-precious stones).

Considering the Eblaite data connected to the products given by Dugurasu/Egypt and other pieces of evidence coming from Egypt, Syria and Mesopotamia during the Early and Middle Bronze Ages, it is possible to suggest that the main, if not all, diplomatic gifts were managed by the Egyptian State as *ẖkr-nswt* items. On the other hand, these gifts fit well within Near Eastern diplomatic practices attested during the 3rd millennium BCE, pointing toward the integration of Egypt into the diplomatic procedures of the region.

In the Shadow of Byblos: The Aegyptiaca from Tell Fadous-Kfarabida

Hermann Genz (American University of Beirut) and Alexander Ahrens (German Archaeological Institute, Damascus Branch)

During the Old Kingdom, Byblos emerged as one of the main ports of trade between Egypt and the Levant. This is not only suggested by textual references in the Egyptian record, but also by a surprisingly large number of Egyptian objects dating to the Old Kingdom from Byblos. However, various chronological and contextual problems hugely diminish the value of the aegyptiaca from Byblos for the reconstruction of the relations between Egypt and the Levantine coast.

Excavations at Tell Fadous-Kfarabida undertaken between 2004 and 2016 help establish a more secure chronology for the Early Bronze Age in Byblos. As the site is only 12 km north of Byblos, it certainly must have been in the economic and political orbit of Byblos. In this paper the few aegyptiaca from Tell Fadous-Kfarabida are presented, and the relationship to Byblos is discussed. As Fadous-Kfarabida lacks a good natural harbor, it is very likely that the aegyptiaca retrieved reached the site via Byblos.

The Adoption of Quotidian Metallurgy in Egypt and the Levant: A Comparative Zooarchaeological Perspective

Haskel J. Greenfield (University of Manitoba and St. Paul's College) and Eleuterio (Luther) Abreu De Sousa (Macquarie University)

Most studies of the spread of copper and bronze metallurgy across the Near East have relied upon the relatively few metal finds that have survived. Further, most of these are from mortuary contexts and indicate little about daily life activities. In recent years, a new method that circumvents the biased metallurgical record has been developed using microscopic groove analysis on zooarchaeological remains. In this paper, we present and compare our data from the southern Levant and Egypt to begin assessing the nature of the spread of metallurgy between the two regions. The paper will present the method, followed by a presentation of the data from the southern Levant, and finally from Old Kingdom Egypt. The results allow an initial assessment of the relative importance of stone versus metal tools in different parts of the eastern Mediterranean for quotidian activities, such as meat processing.

Early Dynastic / Old Kingdom Egypt and the Early Bronze Age Levant: Ancient History and New Radiocarbon Dates in Dialogue

Felix Höflmayer (Austrian Academy of Sciences), Johannes Jüngling (Austrian Academy of Sciences), Roman Gundacker (Austrian Academy of Sciences)

Radiocarbon dating and Bayesian analysis have revolutionized our perspective on Early Dynastic and Old Kingdom Egyptian interconnections with the Early Bronze Age (southern) Levant. A short Early Bronze II duration and the early end of (most) urbanized sites around 2500 BCE (instead of 2300/2200 BCE) has called for renewed analyses of the mechanisms behind the rise and fall of early urbanism during the first half of the 3rd millennium BCE.

This paper summarizes and updates previously published radiocarbon models for the Levant and Egypt using the most up-to-date IntCal20 radiocarbon calibration curve, recent improvements in understanding of (limited) regional offsets, and new understandings of Egyptian reign lengths during the Old Kingdom. Based on this coherent chronological framework we outline the history and development of Egyptian-Levantine interactions during the 4th and early 3rd millennia BCE.

The Northern Levant, a Commercial Partner of Ancient Egypt? A Petrographic View

Mathilde Jean (Université Paris 1 Panthéon-Sorbonne)

Contacts between Ancient Egypt and the Levant have been a main issue of archaeological research in the eastern Mediterranean for decades. Pottery is an essential tool to investigate this question, as many Levantine ceramics were discovered in Egyptian contexts (both in Upper and Lower Egypt). Recent research aims at determining the provenance of those Levantine imports: southern or northern Levant? From which region or site?

This paper focuses on the identification of northern Levantine imports to Egypt during the third millennium BCE. The study is based on pottery assemblages from 7 northern Levantine sites: Tell Arqa (reference site), Tell Bseise and Tell Laha (Akkar plain), Enfeh and Byblos (Lebanese coast), Ras Shamra and Qatna (western Syria). Petrography is the main analytical method, along with technological, typological and chronological comparison.

The results of northern Levantine analyses are compared to published data on Levantine imports in Egypt. Several hypotheses on provenance and chronology of Levantine imports in Egypt are then set forth in order to offer new insights on trade relations between the northern Levant and Egypt during the third millennium BCE.

Tales of Destruction and Disaster: The End of Third Millennium BC in the Central and Northern Levant and its Regional Impact

Melissa Kennedy (The University of Western Australia)

Scholars have frequently described the end of the 3rd millennium BC as an era of 'collapse' and settlement disruption. In the southern Levant, this horizon is distinguished by the disintegration of the walled-town culture of the Early Bronze Age II–III (ca. 3200–2600/2500 BCE) and a return to small-scale ruralism during the Early Bronze Age IV (ca. 2600/2500–2000 BCE). Whilst in the northern Levant settlement continued relatively unchanged. A variety of differing hypotheses have been posited to account for these changes—with aridification, earthquake and population movements all cited to account for the decline of the southern Levantine Early Bronze Age. This paper will focus on the destructions of settlements in the central and northern Levant (the Lebanese coast and western inland Syria) at the end of the 3rd millennium

BCE, exploring the potential causes, as well as the wider regional impact these destructions had on the surrounding regions, such as Egypt and the southern Levant.

Imported Combed Ware from the Abydos Tombs of Weni the Elder and His Family

Christian Knoblauch (Swansea University, Wales & University of Michigan Middle Cemetery Project) and Karin Sowada (Macquarie University)

A 2010 article reported on a corpus of supposedly imported Combed Ware vessels found in contexts of the late Fifth and Sixth Dynasties in the Abydos Middle Cemetery. At the time, apart from some unique finds from sites like Elephantine, Edfu and Meydum, the 11 vessels described in that paper were the largest group of Combed Ware vessels of this date found outside the Memphite region, increasing by approximately one-third the total number of true imports recorded from Egypt for this period. In the decade since the publication, a number of important new studies on Combed Ware in both Levantine and Egyptian contexts have appeared. At the same time, work on the Abydos material has continued and the corpus has grown to more than 20 vessels. The current paper evaluates the Abydos corpus in light of this new work with the goal of identifying the likely origin of the vessels, Combed ware workshop traditions, and the nature of late Old Kingdom foreign relations at the end of the Early Bronze Age.

'There's No Place Like Home'? Travels, Travelers, and Tropes from the Old to the Middle Kingdom

Anna-Latifa Mourad (Macquarie University)

The Tale of Sinuhe is one of the most frequently attested pieces of literature that has survived from the Pharaonic Period. Its exploration of Sinuhe's encounters with courtly affairs, border crossers, and Levantine lands and peoples, has been well-studied. However, how novel was the tale in its representation of travel to the northeast? This paper focuses on travel and travelers, as mainly preserved in Old to Middle Kingdom textual material relating to Egyptian-Near Eastern relations. Examining similarities and differences across time, it questions whether Old Kingdom transregional agents and activities, as well as their representations, influenced the emergence of tropes on border transgression and foreign entities. It further discusses how periods of increased connectivity may have impacted concepts of travel, distance, geography, and cross-border social relations, and whether such concepts were temporally transmitted in spite of the political shifts in Egypt from the late 3rd to the early 2nd Millennium BCE.

Early Dynastic and Old Kingdom Copper in Egypt: Latest Data, Open Questions

Martin Odler (Charles University, Prague), Jiří Kmošek (Academy of Fine Arts, Vienna), Marek Fikrle (Academy of Sciences of the Czech Republic), and Yulia V. Erban Kochergina (Czech Geological Survey)

Recent years have brought to light the first substantial corpora of data on the provenance of ancient Egyptian copper of the Early Dynastic and Old Kingdom periods (Kmošek et al. 2018; Odler and Kmošek 2020; Rademakers et al. 2018). Besides establishing Sinai and the Eastern Desert as the major sources of copper in ancient Egypt at this time, the corpora also opened new questions, commented upon already by Ben-Yosef 2018. We would like to frame these datasets into the wider context of the statistical population (i.e. total counts) of all known Early Dynastic and Old Kingdom copper artefacts, and the limited subset of data already analysed (and data published on the ore sources), raising the question of the statistical representativeness of the available information. Some published and unpublished case studies of particular artefacts will clarify our main argument: currently, a patchwork of data is available, representing a few odd pieces of a giant mosaic. Although the systems of the Early Bronze Age were scaled down in comparison to the trade and exchange systems of the Late Bronze Age, supra-regional exchange of precious materials must have existed already in fourth millennium BC, including metals. Application of the techniques of natural sciences is vital in uncovering these "invisible connections", especially in the Chalcolithic and Early Bronze Age, specifically as detailed sources such as the Amarna Letters or the annals of Amenemhat II are lacking. The possibilities and limits of the natural sciences on the one side, and on the other the limitations of the historical and archaeological evidence, must be realized and accounted for in truly interdisciplinary research.

Ben-Yosef, Erez. 2018. "Provenancing Egyptian Metals: A Methodological Comment." *Journal of Archaeological Science* 96: 208–15. https://doi.org/10.1016/j.jas.2018.06.001.

Kmošek, Jiří, Martin Odler, Marek Fikrle, and Yulia V. Kochergina. 2018. "Invisible Connections. Early Dynastic and Old Kingdom Egyptian Metalwork in the Egyptian Museum of Leipzig University." *Journal of Archaeological Science* 96: 191–207. https://doi.org/10.1016/j.jas.2018.04.004.

Odler, Martin, and Jiří Kmošek. 2020. *Invisible Connections: An Archaeometallurgical Analysis of the Bronze Age Metalwork from the Egyptian Museum of the University of Leipzig*. With Chapters by Katarína Arias, Veronika Dulíková, Lucie Jirásková. Archaeopress Egyptology 31. Oxford: Archaeopress.

Rademakers, Frederik W., Georges Verly, Luc Delvaux, and Patrick Degryse. 2018. "Copper for the Afterlife in Predynastic to Old Kingdom Egypt: Provenance Characterization by Chemical and Lead Isotope Analysis (RMAH Collection, Belgium)." *Journal of Archaeological Science* 96: 175–90. https://doi.org/10.1016/j.jas.2018.04.005.

Prestige and Petrography: Reexamination of Tomb U-j Jars

Mary F. Ownby (University of Arizona) and Ulrich Hartung (German Archaeological Institute, Cairo)

The Abydos cemetery tomb U-j is well-known in Egyptology and its contents have been thoroughly studied. However, the imported vessels, though examined chemically and petrographically, remained an enigma. A reexamination, utilizing the more complete understanding of Levantine raw materials achieved over the past 30 years, has suggested the jars are true imports. Most appear to derive from a number of places in Palestine, with some also possibly from Lebanon. The high diversity of fabrics could indicate jars were acquired from many places in order to fulfill the Egyptian "order". Further, some vessels that do not have good Levantine parallels may also represent potters creating jars to fulfill the request. While the exact nature of early trade between Egypt and the Levant remains unclear, it seems likely that being buried with foreign jars of many shapes, indicating the ability to acquire vessels from throughout the Levant, conferred some amount of prestige on the tomb owner. Finally, these results can now be put into a fuller context in relation to later imported jars, whose petrographic study suggests Lebanon became a prime trade partner for goods.

A Note on Some Theoretical, Cultural and Spatial Aspects of the Egyptian Presence in Southern Levant during the late 4th Millennium BC

Yitzhak Paz (Israel Antiquities Authority)

The Egyptian presence in the Southern Levant in the late 4th millennium BCE has been intensively studied for several decades with researchers covering every aspect of material culture, relative and absolute chronology, socio-political and economic implications, and more. The nature of the physical Egyptian presence at the southern Levant has been characterized by scholars in various scales that from maximal (military and/or colonial occupation, focusing on the establishment of Egyptian enclaves within local settlements) to minimal (purely commercial activity with almost no physical presence of Egyptians). The geography-based tripartite scheme in which the Egyptian presence in the land of Israel is reconstructed according to the analysis of spatial distribution of Egyptian finds seems to best reflect the situation to date.

The current paper focuses on the nature of the Egyptian presence in the late 4th millennium BCE by pointing out some theoretical, cultural, and spatial aspects, based on old and new finds from sites like Tel Lod, Al-Maghar and 'En Esur. The study of various settlements located north of the Besor basin (in which Egyptian physically resided) may point towards a short-time foreign presence that had no dramatic influence on local population and did not change the nature of local "Canaanite" settlements.

Applied Potmarks between Lebanon and Egypt in the Bronze Age

Metoda Peršin (Freie Universität Berlin)

Although potmarks have been discovered at many archaeological sites in the Near East and Egypt, interpretations of their functions vary. Despite the diversity of techniques used in making potmarks (e.g. incised, painted, impressed, applied), applied potmarks have been especially neglected. It is mostly the so-called "ram's head" applications that have previously attracted some attention, however, these have often been considered as decorative elements rather than potmarks. A recent systematic study of potmarks from Bronze Age contexts in Lebanon has revealed not only that applied marks do exist, but that they appear frequently and come in a variety of forms and sizes. Contacts between the Levant and Egypt in the Bronze Age are confirmed by both written sources and analyses of archaeological materials, including ceramic vessels, that were exported to Egypt. Some of these vessels bear applied potmarks. This paper aims to integrate the data obtained on applied potmarks from sites in Egypt, as well as other information concerning the connections between Egypt and the Lebanese coast to better understand the function of applied potmarks in the Early Bronze Age Lebanon.

There and Back Again: A Preliminary Discussion about the Presence of Imported Artefacts in Elite Tombs of the Egyptian Early Dynastic Period

Olivier P. Rochecouste (Macquarie University)

For over 4000 years, ancient Egypt has conveyed its ability to conduct and maintain foreign relations with a variety of cultural groups based within the Fertile Crescent, Arabia, Sub-Saharan Africa and the Mediterranean regions. Evidence of these relations have been known from textual sources such as the Palermo Stone recounting maritime trade with Lebanon and pictorial reliefs depicting representations of expeditions to Punt within Hatshepsut's funerary temple of Deir el-Bahari. However, questions have been asked as to how these relations originated, how they transformed Egypt's social complexity and benefited its people, especially during the Early Dynastic period (c. 3100-2700 BCE) when the first royal rulers emerged to commence the age of Dynastic Egypt.

Information about Egypt's foreign relations and understanding how foreign trade was conducted during this time is limited, but the information we have mostly comes from the study of imported artefacts from Egyptian tombs, especially the royal tombs within the Umm el-Qa'ab cemetery at Abydos. These artefacts come in the form of pottery, stone vessels and semi-precious stones like lapis lazuli, which have been sourced from faraway lands. However, such items are not exclusive to the royal tombs and have been found amongst First Dynasty dated elite tombs in Tell el-Farkha, Saqqara, Helwan and Abu Rawash.

This presentation will discuss what the presence of these artefacts signified for elite and / or non-royal tomb owners during the Early Dynastic period, and how tomb owners may have acquired such foreign provisions. Did they acquire them through the royal administration or through independent means? These are important questions to ask, especially given that an apparent quantitative decline in foreign mortuary objects is noticed amongst elite tomb assemblages from the 2nd Dynasty onwards. On the other hand, royal tombs gain more notoriety in their mortuary provisions, culminating in the construction of the Step Pyramid of Djoser of the 3rd Dynasty.

Reconsidering Egyptian-South Levantine Interaction: Neglected Evidence from EB II contexts at Tell es-Sultan and Tell el-Far'ah North

Maura Sala (Facoltà di Teologia di Lugano)

Interactions between Egypt and the southern Levant in the late Fourth / early Third millennium BCE have been reconsidered variously in recent scholarly literature. Following the growing identification of Egyptian material at key sites (e.g. Tel Yarmuth, Tell Abu al-Kharaz, Bet Yerah), evidence of a more articulated two-way relationship between First Dynasty Egypt and the south Levantine communities during the Early Bronze II has begun to emerge. While a complete reassessment of First Dynasty-EB II relations is beyond its scope, this paper seeks to review key evidence from Tell es-Sultan and Tell el-Far'ah North. Tell es-Sultan is a key site in Egyptian-Levantine exchange because of its proximity to essential raw materials of the Dead Sea basin; Tell el-Far'ah North is the leading centre in the area between the central hills and the Jordan Valley. The analysis confirms the existence of a branched network of commodity trading between Egypt and the southern Levant which was operational at the dawn of the earliest urbanization in the region. This paper considers the amount, range, and find context of Egyptian materials in order to assess the nature and intensity of the relationships between Egypt and these EB II south Levantine communities; and what role may they have played in the development of the first urban-centered society in the region.

The Curious Contents of Combed Ware Storage Jars from Giza

Margaret Serpico (University College London), Richard Newman, (Museum of Fine Arts, Boston), Karin Sowada (Macquarie University)

Over the years, there has been considerable speculation on the likely contents of Levantine two-handled Combed Ware storage jars imported into Egypt in the Early Bronze Age. Most often, oils and resins, notably coniferous resin, have been suggested as possible commodities, but apart from analysis by Alfred Lucas in the 1950's, little scientific research has been carried out on the vessels themselves.

As part of a wider investigation of these vessels (led by Dr Karin Sowada, Macquarie University), it has been possible to sample and analyse the contents of a selection of jars from Reisner's excavations at Giza, now in the Museum of Fine Arts, Boston. However, during study of the jars, it quickly became apparent that the contents had been disturbed both in ancient and modern times, presenting a number of challenges for scientific analysis and interpretation of the results. This paper discusses the complex mixtures identified in these jars within the framework of this complicated life-cycle.

This work dovetails with ongoing botanical and pollen analyses of the jar contents; study of their archaeological contexts; and petrographic and chemical examination of the clays used in their manufacture. The aim is to provide a wider picture of the Egyptian-Levantine liquid commodities trade during this time, the exchange of valuable natural products, and the role of the jars themselves as symbols of status.

Social History of Cultural Interaction from Non-Elite Context: Paleoethnobotanical and Isotopic Evidence

Amr Khalaf Shahat (University of California, Los Angeles)

The study of cultural interaction between Egypt and other cultures in the Near East and East Mediterranean has been of increasing interest to archaeologists. Meanwhile, the main reliance on textual and iconographic evidence from Egypt has a caveat that is limiting our understanding to elite contexts. Cultural interactions from non-elite contexts (settlements and graves), where textual, iconographic, and lavish material cultures are limited, continues to be less understood, especially in the predynastic. This study presents unpublished datasets of ancient archaeobotanical food remains from the predynastic site of Nag ed Deir and the New Kingdom site of Deir el Ballas in Egypt to address diachronic and regional variation in Egyptian history of cultural interaction. This research also presents a new application of interdisciplinary methods combining stable isotope and nano-archaeology on ancient desiccated botanical remains to answer questions on cultural interaction from the lens of food as an active agent in the formation of society, economy, and cross-regional relationships. The data will also help future research applying stable isotope in Egyptian archaeology by providing an isotopic baseline for the reconstruction of diet and environmental history. The goal is to contribute to the broader social history of Egyptian cultural interactions with the ancient Near East and Eastern Mediterranean, specifically from under-researched non-elite contexts.

The Archaeology and Re-Use of Combed Jars from Old Kingdom Giza

Karin Sowada (Macquarie University) and Wilma Wetterstrom (Ancient Egypt Research Associates & Harvard University)

Many imported Combed jars were found by George Reisner in and around tombs of the Egyptian elite during the 1907–42 Harvard University-Boston Museum of Fine Arts Expedition on the Giza plateau. The Museum of Fine Arts (Boston) holds the largest number of such jars outside Egypt, which have been the subject of intensive study for the last three years as part of a wider project examining trade and foreign relations during the Old Kingdom.

Over the decades, many assumptions have been made in the literature about the contents of the jars, with wine, olive oil and cedar or coniferous resins proposed. Very limited scientific analysis has been conducted. Yet to date, these questions are not resolved, owing to the ephemeral nature of what remains inside the vessels. Many jars retain no signs of contents visible to the naked eye, while others contain only a small amount of loose material.

This paper discusses the archaeology of the jars and their contents, arguing that although they were status markers for elite burials, jars were used more than once prior to deposition. Moreover, the quality of the data inside the vessels has been affected by multiple post-excavation interventions. A case study of the contents of one jar, MFA 47.1662, is presented to highlight the problematic nature of the archaeological data. As a result, techniques of micro-analysis using GC-MS and examination of phytolith and pollen samples offer the most promising opportunities for unravelling this complex story.

Khirbet ez-Zeraqon in its Regional Context: A Reappraisal of the EB II-III Evidence in Light of Recent Studies

Valentina Tumolo (Durham University) and Kamal Badreshany (Durham University)

Following a recent stratigraphic re-evaluation of the site of Khirbet ez-Zeraqon made in light of new radiocarbon data, the archaeological evidence from the site further delineates the characteristics of the Early Bronze Age II–III transition in northern Transjordan.

This paper presents an overview of the settlement transformations and the changes in material culture that occur through the EB II and III at Khirbet ez-Zeraqon, with a particular emphasis on the organisation of pottery production and the development of a large repertoire of Combed Ware storage and transport vessels. Data will be presented that demonstrates the integration of the site within the wider phenomenon of Levantine Combed Ware pottery production and the developing exchange networks of the eastern Mediterranean world during the Early Bronze Age. The evidence from Khirbet ez-Zeraqon offers additional insights for investigating the socio-economic changes that affected the Southern Levant in this period. In turn, this will contribute to a greater understanding of dynamics underpinning the relationship between Egypt and the Levant during the Early Bronze Age.

Toward a New Understanding of Early Bronze Age Developments on the Lebanese Coast: Putting Together Old and Recent Discoveries

Michel de Vreeze (Durham University) and Kamal Badreshany (Durham University)

In this paper we reexplore the relationship between Egypt and the Lebanese coast during the Early Bronze Age in light of evidence from recent excavations as well as of new work on artifact assemblages in the region. The role of Byblos as hub for Egyptian activity in Lebanon during the Bronze Age is well-known, but new data further illuminates the nature of these early interactions. We aim to contextualize the significance of Byblos-Egypt interactions within the wider EB settlement landscape of the Lebanese coast. We argue that the influence of Byblos grew, in part, due to longstanding mutually beneficial exchange networks with Egypt where were centered around Byblos's temples. Despite changing economic fortunes in the region, the key cultic role of Byblos continued into later periods with the site remaining a focal point for local communities and for Egyptian attention.

Presence of the Imported Combed Ware at Heit el-Ghurab: Use and Importance

Anna Wodzińska (University of Warsaw)

The settlement of Heit el-Ghurab is located at Giza directly south of a massive Wall of the Crow. The site has been extensively investigated since 1989 by Mark Lehner (Ancient Egypt Research Associates), revealing a large settlement with clearly divided sections with groups of people responsible for different activities inhabited the various settlement quarters (the gallery system, so-called Eastern and Western Towns, etc.). The material culture associated with the settlement shows differential wealth among its inhabitants, however, the presence of some "luxurious" artefacts does not necessarily mean "luxurious" use. Among many Egyptian ceramics, fragments of imported Combed Ware jars have been identified, including a large krater of Lebanese origin. Complete imported vessels are known from the tombs of prominent people buried in Giza and elsewhere during this period and their value in Egypt seems to be well-documented. However, the Heit el-Ghurab settlement tells a different story. This paper describes the types of imported vessels found at the site and seeks to address the role they have there in relation to other sites where such pots were found. The paper show the fragments of imported vessels, their exact context and discusses their use at the site and general importance.

Egyptian-Southern Levantine Interaction on the Fringe of the Desert: A View from the Negev Highlands

Yuval Yekutieli (Ben-Gurion University of the Negev)

Surveys, excavations, and rock-art research carried out by BGU teams in the Northwestern Negev Highlands have revealed substantial activities bearing witness to interconnections between the region's local population and Egypt during the Fourth and Third millennia BCE. These interconnections demonstrate what we propose to understand as two different patterns: exchange activity focused on products and crops produced within the area, and trade routes that crossed the region, along which products made in other regions were transported.

The first pattern existed in the region during the Fourth millennium BCE (Early Bronze 1b), while it was inhabited by a local population that traded with agents from the Egyptian colony located further north, towards the Mediterranean coast. This was most dramatically evidenced in our survey and excavations at the site of Mitzpe Sde Hafir, which probably served as a regional barter trade center.

The second pattern occurred during the Third millennium BC (Intermediate Bronze Age - IBA), when copper shipments from Feinan to Egypt passed through the region. New indications for this activity—beyond the already known IBA sites in the region—are rock-art scenes and icons carved along the routes and some pottery scatters.

Journal of Ancient Egyptian Interconnections

The Three Temples *in antis* at Megiddo

Matthew J. Adams
W.F. Albright Institute of Archaeological Research

Abstract
The date of the Stratum XV Triple-Temple Complex at Megiddo has been the subject of debate since it was first uncovered by the University of Chicago in the 1930s. Generally, an Early Bronze Age III date became the status quo interpretation, but several problems with this date are apparent. First, there was already significant EB III stratigraphy at the site, consisting of a well-planned palace, elite quarter, and temple complex. The construction of the Triple-Temple complex completely put this EB III palatial phase out of commission. Therefore, if an EB III date for the temples is preferred, this infers that a completely new urban plan was envisioned within that period – a phenomenon not seen elsewhere for EB III palatial centers. Second, it leaves a significant architectural gap at the site during the EB IV/Intermediate Bronze Age, a period for which Megiddo produced a significant amount of material culture. The solution presented itself when the Tel Aviv University Megiddo Expedition discovered a cache of Egyptianized pottery below the temple complex. Originally thought to have come from underlying EB IB strata, ongoing excavation at the site and refinement of the stratigraphy of the cultic area led the present author to conclude that the pottery cache was a foundation deposit associated with the Stratum XV Triple-Temple Complex. The cache, fitting well, typologically, with Egyptian foundation deposits from the late Old Kingdom/First Intermediate Period, supports, in turn, an EB IV/IB date for the construction of the Megiddo Triple-Temple Complex.

This paper returns to this issue to properly place the architecture of the Triple-Temple Complex into its Northern Levantine EB IV world as temples *in antis* and to consider Northern Levantine and Egyptian contacts from the unique perspective of Megiddo.

Keywords
Megiddo, Early Bronze Age, Byblos, Intermediate Bronze Age

Introduction

The three temples *in antis* at Megiddo were uncovered in the 1930s by the University of Chicago's Oriental Institute (OI) expedition., who attributed the temples to their Stratum XV, dated to the Intermediate Bronze Age.[1] Loud characterized Stratum XV as "a period of massive building," which included the three large Temples 4040, 5192, and 5269, Altar 4017, retaining Wall 4114 to their east, and the large Building 3160 featuring two monumental stairways at the edge of the mound (Fig. 1).[2]

Of note is the fact that Area BB was excavated differentially by the OI. After a probe revealed the Middle Bronze and Late Bronze Age Temple 2048 (sitting roughly above Temple 4040, Altar 4017, and Wall 4114), the area east of this temple was first excavated down to bedrock during the 1935/1936, 1936/1937, 1937/1938 seasons. Stratum XV was first reached in the 1936/1937 season, revealing Building 3160 and the monumental staircases (Fig. 1). At this time, the western portions of the stratum, including Wall 4114, Altar 4017, and the three Stratum

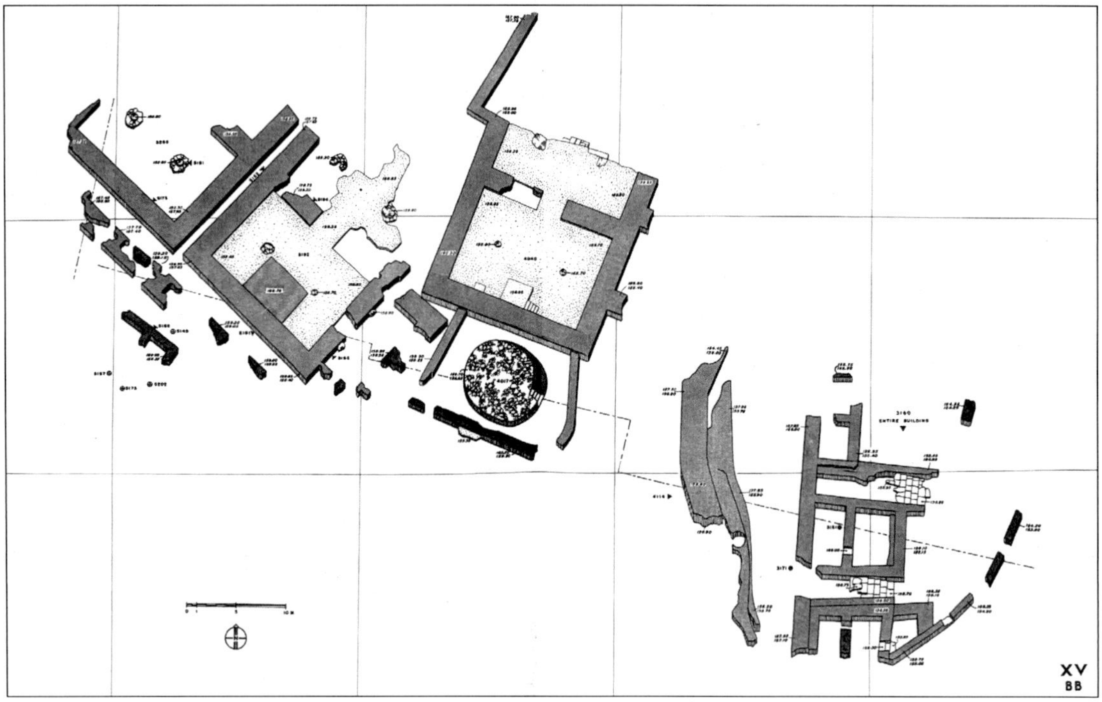

Figure 1: Stratum XV as presented by Loud (1948, fig. 395).

XV temples were still unexcavated beneath the ongoing work clearing and removing the Middle/Late Bronze Age Temple 2048. Only in the 1937/38 Season had Temple 2048 finally been cleared away and the central portion of Area BB, beneath its footprint, excavated to Stratum XV. Temple 4040 and Altar 4017 were also revealed during this effort, but nothing was uncovered farther west. Finally, in the last season at Megiddo, in 1938/1939, Area BB was expanded to the west, beginning from the Late Bronze Age layers located at the top of the mound, revealing Temples 5192 and 5269 by the end of the season. Ultimately, Stratum XV was revealed over four seasons in three chunks.[3] The largest contiguous exposure, the three temples, was the last stratum exposed in the area's central and western sections; only Building 3160 enjoyed excavation of strata above and below the structure. Hence, without the excavation of strata beneath the Triple-Temple Complex itself, the temples' stratigraphy and chronology would remain questionable.

After the OI expedition ended, the questions of whether the three temples were built together or in a particular sequence and their Intermediate Bronze Age dating were heavily debated.[4] Most of these discussions depended on reinterpreting the evidence presented by Loud, though the arguments of Dunayevski and Kempinski did result from additional on-site fieldwork,[5] and those of Mirsoschedji from novel metrological analyses.[6] These studies attempted to stratify Temple 4040 back into Strata XVII–XVI (Early Bronze Age II–III), thus becoming the first of the three temples to which Temples 5192 and 5269 were later added. By the 1990s, this proposal had become the status quo understanding of the three temples.[7]

From 1992 to 2010, the Tel Aviv University Megiddo Expedition (TAU) conducted renewed excavations in the area, renamed Area J (Fig. 2), refining much of the stratigraphic determinations made by Loud (Table 1).[8] This paper focuses on the results of the TAU excavations vis-à-vis OI Stratum XV (i.e., TAU Level J-7). In doing so, the remains of Strata XVI–XVII (TAU Levels J-5–6) beneath the Triple-Temple complex and those of Stratum XIV (Levels J-8–9) above the complex will be summarized. Because the new data renders many of the earlier studies moot, they will be only engaged as needed.[9]

OI Strata XVII–XVI (TAU Levels J-5–J-6)

The overall shape of Megiddo's upper and lower eastern terraces was determined in the Early Bronze Age I with the construction of the Great Temple of Stratum XVIII (Level J-4; Fig. 3).[10] The Great

FIGURE 2: Aerial view of Area J (Area BB) after the TAU 2008 Season. Courtesy of the Megiddo Expedition.

Level	Loud 1948 Stratum	Description	Absolute Dates	Period
J-10	XIIIA/B	Domestic area with proto-palace		MB I
J-9	XIVA	Domestic area with repurposed Temple 4040		MB I
J-8	XIVB	Domestic area with repurposed Temple 4040		MB I
J-7	XV	Triple temples in antis (4040, 5192 and 5269)		IB
J-6a	XVI	Palace Compound and Palace 3177	2700–2600/2500 BCE	EB III
J-6b	XVII	Palace Compound and Palace 3177	2800–2700 BCE	EB III
J-5	XVII	Palace Compound and Palace 3177	2850–2800 BCE	EB III
J-4a		Sporadic activity within the otherwise abandoned Great Temple.	3020–2850 BCE	EB II
J-4	XVIII	Great Temple complex	3090–2920 BCE	EB Ib
J-3	XIX	Temple 4050		EB Ib
J-2	Undetected	Temple beneath 4050 and Picture Pavement		EB Ib
J-1	XX+	Carved bedrock and associated structures		EB I

TABLE 1: Current Early Bronze to Middle Bronze I stratigraphy of Megiddo Area BB/TAU Area J (after Adams 2013b). Absolute dates are only included if known from radiocarbon samples from the site (n.b. maximum ranges are given, hence the apparent chronological overlap of some phases; Regev et al. 2014).

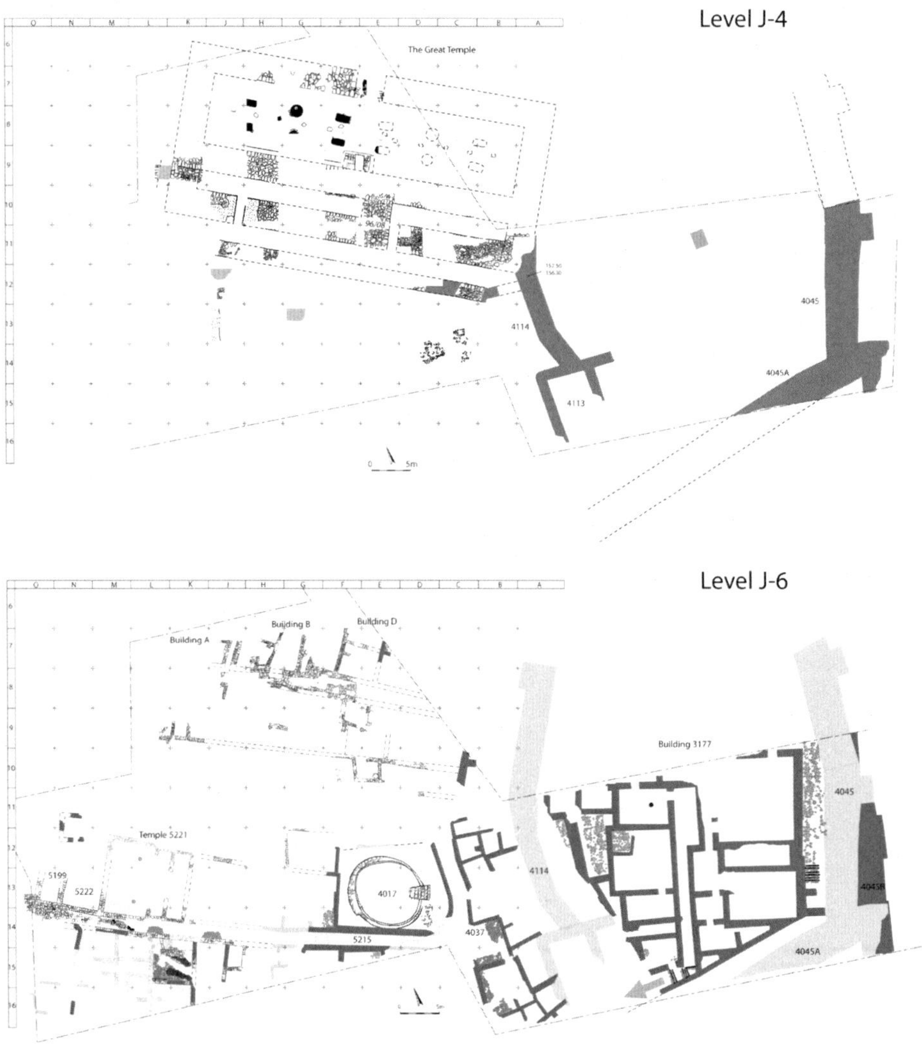

FIGURE 3: The Level J-4 EB Ib Great Temple (top), with the Level J-5/6 composite plan (below) showing reused terraces.

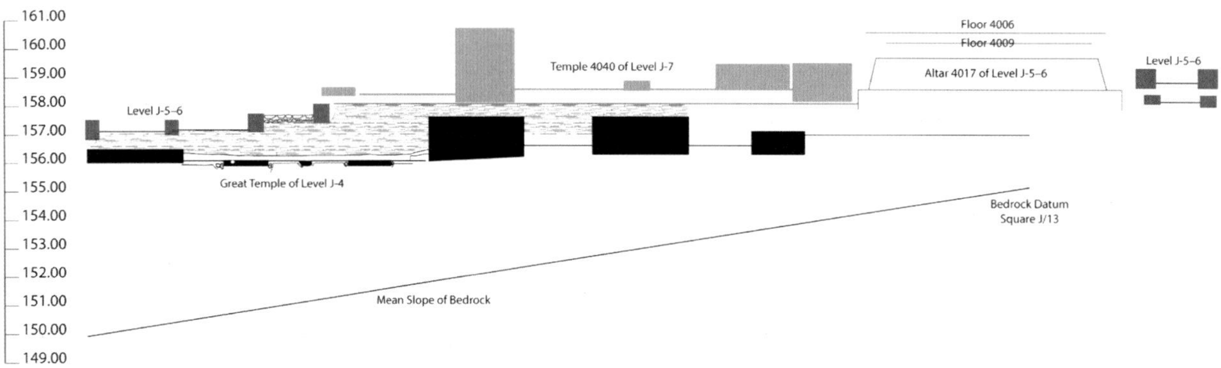

FIGURE 4: A schematic north–south (right–left) section showing sloping and terraced structures in Levels J-4 (black), J-5–6 (dark gray), and J-7 (light gray).

Temple was built to maximize the east–west width of a bedrock spur, with a temenos/retaining wall immediately to its west and its eastern wall serving as a terrace wall bonded to Terrace Wall 4114.[11] To the east, a lower terrace was formed by Wall 4045, some 30+ m downslope.[12] To the south of the Great Temple, a large exterior space is terraced up to higher ground. Succeeding strata would contend with this topographic arrangement well into the Middle Bronze Age (OI Stratum XII) when major terraforming activities took place in the cultic area.

Strata XVII–XVI (TAU Levels J-5–J-6) are best understood as a single cohesive stratum with multiple subphases and rebuilds (FIG. 3). The OI detected two subphases (Strata XVII and XVI); TAU found that in most areas excavated, three phases could be identified (hence Levels J-5, J-6b, and J-6a). It should be noted that most of the architecture uncovered by the OI in this stratum was on the lower eastern terrace, with only some exposure on the upper terrace, while the TAU excavations exposed significant remains from the upper terrace only. The OI dated this stratum to the Early Bronze Age, and subsequent commentators and the TAU excavations have confirmed this general date with a more specific attribution to the EB III.[13] Radiocarbon models for samples taken from these strata indicate that the three subphases can be dated, according to their maximum extremes, from 2850 to 2600/2500 BCE.[14]

Strata XVII–XVI (TAU Levels J-5–J-6) consist of a large building (3177) occupying the lower eastern terrace, which the original excavators interpreted as a Palace due to its layout of courtyards and rooms paved variously with pebbles and plaster, an interpretation still generally agreed upon in the literature today (FIGS. 3–4).[15] The upper terrace was laid out in an orthogonal grid of streets that continued the general orientation of Palace 3177. The buildings on the upper terrace step down from south to north, with each of the east–west streets acting as a terrace (FIGS. 3–4). The streets slope down dramatically from east to west, and near the westernmost section of Street 5215, a series of steps control the downward slope. The central terrace, occupying much of the center of the exposed area, was obliterated by the construction of the later Stratum XV Triple-Temple Complex. Of note in this regard is the better-preserved northern street and associated buildings, which survived destruction because they were lower than the foundations of the temples, and the better-preserved Street 5215 and the buildings to the south, which were higher but not cut by the later Stratum XV foundations (see below).

A prominent feature of the central terrace is Altar 4017, already exposed by the OI, found surrounded with the remains of animal sacrifice.[16] To the west, the OI excavation revealed a part of Building 5221, which was reinvestigated by the TAU excavations. This well-built structure featured a white plastered floor and walls, and a finely carved pillar base similar to those in Building 3177.[17] Based on the renewed work, the excavator suggested that these were the remains of the Strata XVII–XVI (TAU Levels J-5–J-6) temple.[18] Indeed, this proposal solves the issue of the 'missing' temple for this period. In addition, it is supported by the fact that the building is similar to the temples at Khirbet ez-Zeraqon, which are also in the proximity of a round altar.[19]

Between Temple 5221 and Altar 4017 was found much evidence of cultic activity. Locus 98/J/152 in Square J/13 consisted of a highly burnt ash and bone accumulation on a floor located just before the temple's entrance.[20] The accumulation included pottery items such as a cult stand.[21] In the adjacent Square G/13, a large, amorphous plaster installation with grooves was also surrounded by ash and bone deposits.[22] The overall impression of this material is of an open cultic activity space situated between the temple and the altar.

While Building 3177, on the eastern lower terrace, does appear to have palatial characteristics,[23] the Upper Terrace is more difficult to characterize. Clearly, there is an altar that can be linked to sacrificial remains and an adjacent temple. Both, however, are integrated into a well-planned orthogonal system that would seem characteristic of a 'city' plan: streets with buildings serving a variety of functions, including elite households and other public structures. However, this is a far-from-clear way to define the space. First, there is a clear overarching plan with streets terraced to create leveled spaces, yet there are no distinct stand-alone buildings, as one might expect when dealing with private houses. All the structures, if these can even be defined as separate structures, share walls. The finds from the various rooms are also difficult to discern. Indeed, there is evidence of so-called domestic activities in some rooms, such as hearths and grinding installations. However, several of the rooms yielded quite specialized finds, including

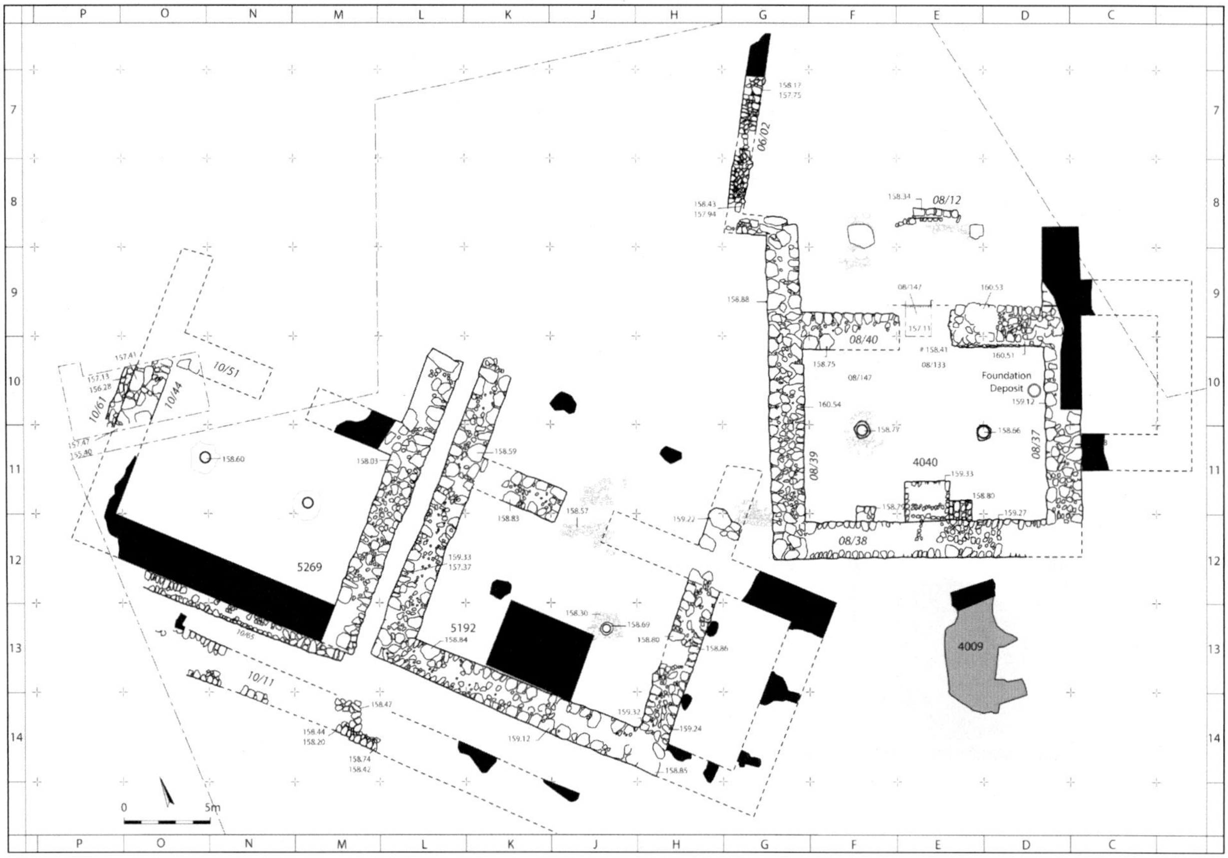

FIGURE 5: Plan of Level J-7 after the TAU excavations. Elements planned in the field by TAU appear as stone-by-stone, while elements seen by Chicago but not replanned appear in black.

mace heads,[24] an Egyptian cylinder seal,[25] abundant specialized lamps,[26] pebbled floors similar to those in Building 3177,[27] and a room paved with imported red-burnished pottery.[28] Overall, the impression is of a highly integrated architectural unit that comprised both the upper and lower terraces and featured consistently specialized finds centered on the more obviously cultic Altar 4017 and Temple 5221.

OI Stratum XV (TAU Level J-7): The Triple-Temple Complex

The renewed excavations' broadening of the Strata XVII–XVI (TAU Levels J-5–J-6) exposure on the upper terrace made it clear that the strata ended at the same time and that Stratum XV (Level J-7) was a distinct and new stratum across the site (Fig. 5). Attempts to see Temple 4040 being constructed already within the life of Stratum XVI,[29] cannot be sustained by the coherency of the newly revealed architecture and stratigraphic subphases now known to be beneath it. In addition to the internal stratigraphic coherency of both Stratum XVI and XV, constructional aspects of the Triple-Temple Complex demonstrate the seeming contemporaneity of some elements of the Stratum XVI plan with the Stratum XV temples is an artifact of mistakes in the original excavation, as shall be seen below.

The topography of the Stratum XVI compound sloped from south to north on terraces formed by each of its streets (Figs. 3–4). The compound also sloped down dramatically from east to west. Those responsible for the Triple-Temple Complex had to take this into consideration, as reflected in the foundations of each of the temples; each wall from east to west was founded progressively deeper such that the western wall of Temple 5269 is more than 2.5m deeper than the eastern wall of 5192 (Fig. 6). Despite this dramatic slope, the builders intended the floors of each of the three temples to be at the same level, so each wall of each temple was effectively a terrace wall, with the western

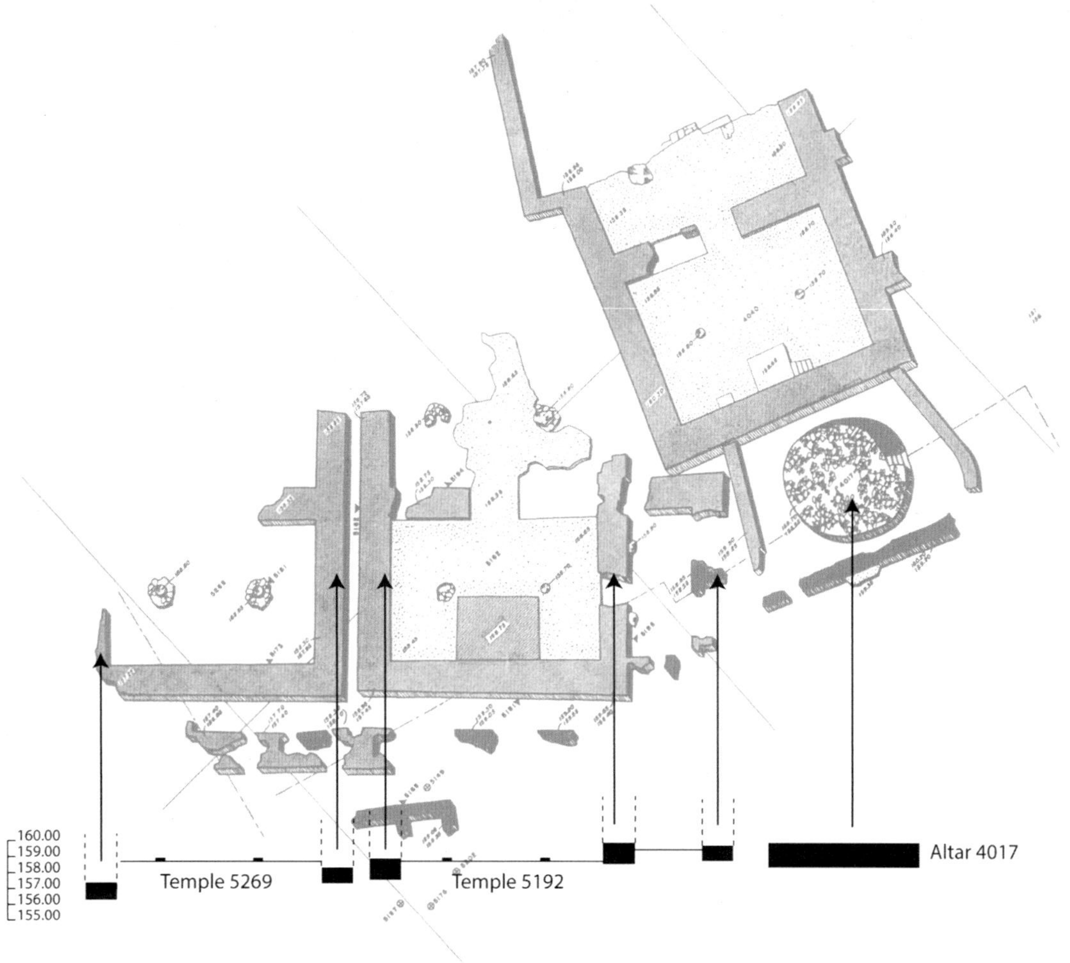

Figure 6: Plan and schematic section of the Triple Temple Complex looking north showing the dramatic east–west slope and the progressively deeper foundations required in that direction.

wall of 5269 supporting the entire complex on the western side. Indeed, a stone revetment (Wall 10/J/61) was added to the foundation's outer face at some point (Fig. 5). This western expansion of the upper terrace is a process that can be seen in each successive stratum from as far back as the EB Ib at least; throughout the EB and MB, new terraces were constructed farther and farther west to extend the acropolis.[30]

The south–north slope was also a feature with which the Stratum XV builders had to contend. However, in this direction, their approach was different; they did not adjust the foundations to accommodate the slope but instead created a flat space by cutting down the higher areas of the mound to the south at precisely the planned location of the back walls of each temple. This was done with some precision, indicating that the temples had been laid out in their location ahead of time, and diggers were assigned the task of cutting the mound (and the strata within) at the determined spot. This can be clearly seen behind temples 5192 and 5269 in both plan and section (Figs. 4; 7–8). The foundations cut right through Stratum XVI at the back of the temple wall. In the case of 5192, the cut and the location of the temple's back wall were so precise that the walls of the underlying J-6 appear to abut the later temple. The cut for Temple 5269 was too large, and the Stratum XV builders filled in the extra gap with stones, Wall 10/65 (Figs. 5, 7–8). Behind the Triple-Temple Complex, Stratum XV remains did exist, but on a higher level (the level from which these foundations were cut). Behind Temples 5192 and 5269, a thick wall (Wall 10/11) was built at a level at least 60 cm higher than the base of the temple walls (Figs. 5, 8).

Figure 7: Plan of Level J-6, showing the cutting of the Level J-7 architecture.

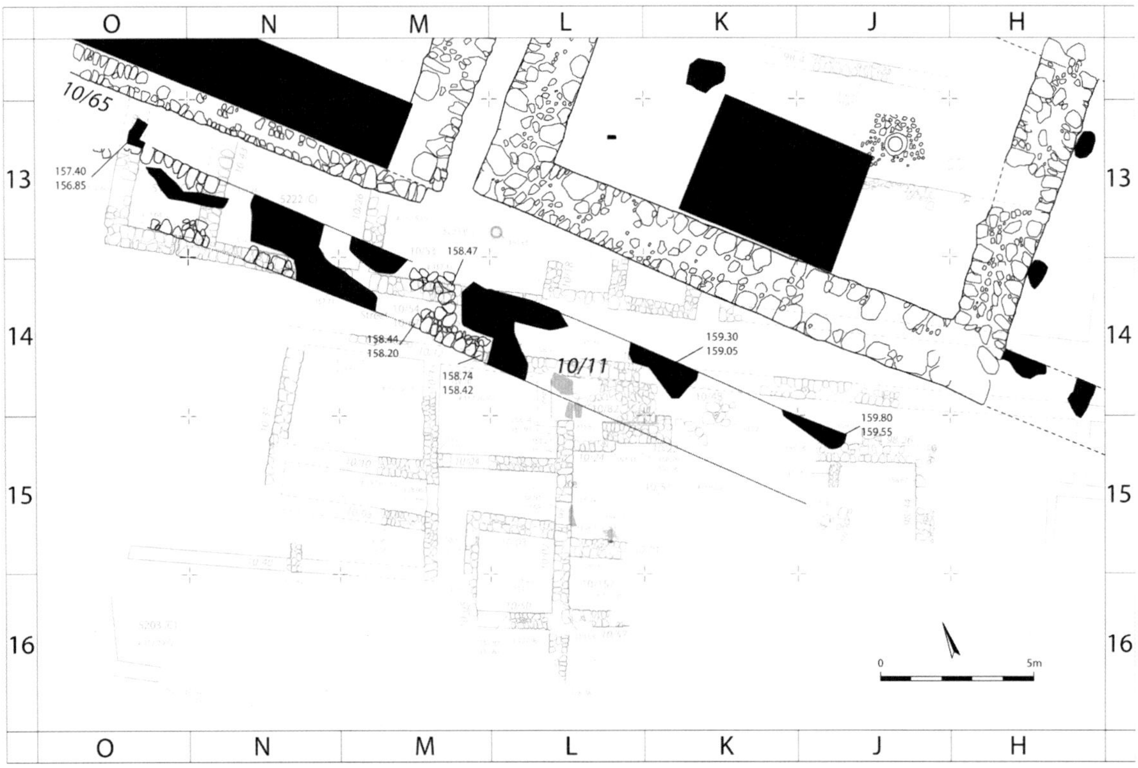

Figure 8: Plan of Level J-7, showing the underlying cut architecture of Level J-6.

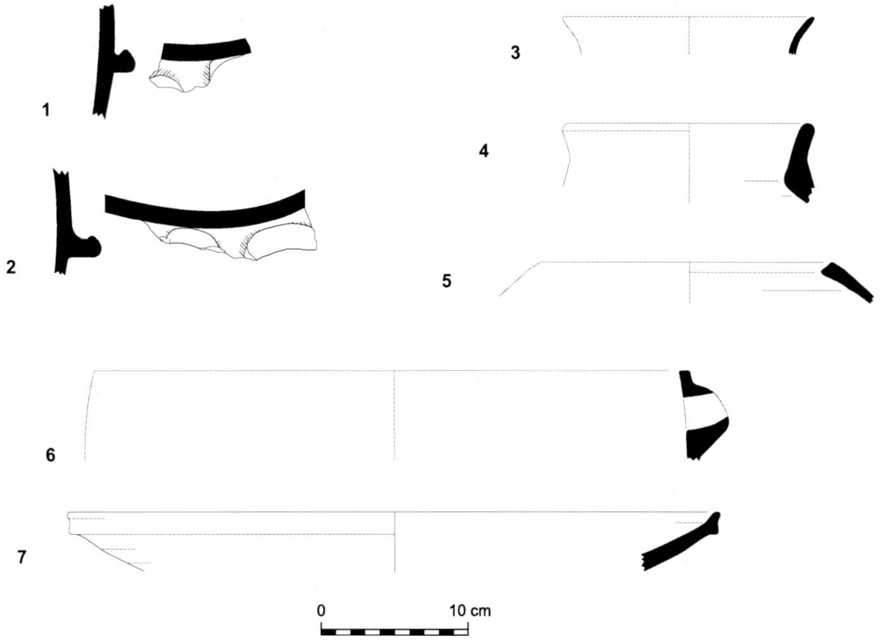

Figure 9: Ceramics from the threshold's foundation trench of Temple 4040. Courtesy of the Megiddo Expedition.

Turning to Temple 4040, when the same principles are applied, walls that the excavators considered abutting Temple 4040's foundations now appear to be cut by the structure. These include the 'fence' walls of Altar 4017, all belonging to Stratum XVI.[31] The actual contemporary walls and surfaces behind Temple 4040 are higher and appear on the XIIIB plan by the OI (i.e., Locus 4009) (Figs. 4–5).[32] It should be recalled here that Temple 4040 and Altar 4017 were excavated the season prior to Temples 5192 and 5269, so the realization of the cutting down of these temples was not apparent until later. Further, Wall 10/11 behind Temples 5269 and 5192, which overlays the Level J-6 walls, rises dramatically from west to east such that the easternmost preserved fragment is nearly as high as the top of Altar 4017.

In sum, the Triple-Temple complex was constructed on a flat surface cut into the underlying stratigraphy. The Level J-6 architecture, including Altar 4017, was already buried by the time of the construction, but due to the sloping nature of the underlying strata, appeared to the original excavators as contemporary with the Level J-7 temples. The architecture contemporary with Level J-7 behind Temples 5192 and 5269 is represented by Wall 10/11. The architecture behind and contemporary with Temple 4040 can only be the remains found directly above Altar 4017, which the OI placed on the Stratum XIIB plan (i.e., Locus 4009) (Figs. 4–5), to which we shall return below.

Other than the Triple Temple Complex itself, the large, monumental staircase to the east is worth recalling. These stairs, built on the lower terrace of Stratum XVI, provided access to the area south of the temple complex, demonstrating that Megiddo in Stratum XV was more than just a cultic area, perhaps a larger town occupying much of the later footprint of the modern tell.

Finds from and Date of Stratum XV (Level J-7)

Finds from the newly reconstituted Stratum XV (Level J-7) present a unified picture dating these buildings to the Southern Levantine Intermediate Bronze Age.

TAU excavations in the threshold of Temple 4040 exposed the remains of the continuous foundation trench of its front closing wall sealed by the original floor of the temple (Fig. 5).[33] Pottery from the foundation trench included items paralleling "post-Khirbet-Kerak" phases from sites in the Galilee and several forms clearly associated with Intermediate Bronze Age types. The latter include two ledge-handles (Fig. 9:1–2) of the flattened 'envelope' type, which are characteristic of the period (=EB IVB).[34] The thin flaring rim (Fig. 9:3) and the thick flaring rim with an interior ridge at the joint of neck and shoulder (FIG. 9:4) are characteristic of the bag-shaped jars and amphoriskoi of the Intermediate Bronze Age.[35] The holemouth cooking-pot with a thickened rim and ridged lip (FIG. 9:5) has Intermediate Bronze Age parallels at Jebel Qa'aqir.[36] The open bowl with the exterior grooved rim (FIG. 9:7) has its best parallels from the Intermediate Bronze Age single-period site of Ḥorvat Qishron, where there are several permutations of this style of bowls and 'cooking bowls,' characterized by the grooved exterior rim, wheel finish and sooted exteriors associated with cooking.[37] Examples with affinities to this open bowl can also be found at Bet Yeraḥ BS local phase 5 (Period F [MB I]),[38] and may represent the continuation of the form into the MB I. It is also possible that the bowls from Ḥorvat Qishron and the sherd from Megiddo anticipate the traditional MB I open bowl forms with profiled rims.[39] Overall, the latest ceramics from the foundation trench of Temple 4040, which was sealed by the plaster floor of the temple, are of an Intermediate Bronze Age date.

The TAU renewed excavations also discovered a foundation deposit associated with Temple 4040.[40] The unique cache was located just before the entrance to the eastern side chamber of Temple 4040 in a pit beneath the plastered floor of the temple (FIGS. 5, 10) (i.e., the cache was placed in the pit during the building's construction process – hence a foundation deposit.[41] It consisted of 16 vessels of local production, but Egyptian in form and manufacture (i.e., straw tempered; Goren 2000). The forms of the vessels are peculiar, hence the difficulty of earlier commenters on the vessels to date them typologically (FIG. 11).[42] In fact, the typology of these vessels is unique to their function as foundation deposits, and the best parallels for both the individual forms and the assemblage come from the foundation deposits of Mentuhotep (11th Dynasty) at Deir el-Bahari (FIG. 12).[43] The four deposits shown in Fig. 12 comprise nearly the same repertoire forms of the Megiddo cache (FIG. 11), including large and medium flaring bowls, small saucers (not lids, *contra* Ilan and Goren),[44] tall U-shaped bowls, and tall drop-shaped bottles with a narrow opening. Small–medium flaring bowls and drop-shaped bottles with a narrow opening are also well-known from other First Intermediate Period assemblages, for example, at Mendes in the T-A Vaults cemetery (FIG. 13).[45] Many of these forms are not part of a standard domestic assemblage and are unique to

FIGURE 10: Excavation beneath the floor of Temple 4040, looking north. The pit for the Foundation Deposit is on the right, covered with stone capping (black arrow) and cutting through earlier Level J-6 surfaces. Courtesy of the Megiddo Expedition.

foundation deposits of the Late Old Kingdom and First Intermediate Period. The Megiddo cache also contains two beer jars ('Rolled Rim Storage Jar' according to Joffe),[46] which are classic Old Kingdom forms.

The significance of the Mentuhotep foundation deposits is that they give a *terminus ante quem* for the Megiddo cache. During the reign of Mentuhotep, foundation deposits underwent a typological change that can be documented within the development of the Deir el-Bahari complex itself.[47] In the later architectural developments of the complex, a new type of deposit was introduced that included a wider variety of objects, including plaques with the ruler's name, a feature that would become standard for foundation deposits to the end of the Pharaonic period. The parallels to the Megiddo cache, however, fit into the earlier deposits

Figure 11: Egyptianized Foundation Deposit of Temple 4040. Courtesy of the Megiddo Expedition.

Figure 12: Eleventh Dynasty foundation deposits from the tomb of Mentuhotep II at Deir el-Bahari (from Arnold 1979 pl. 32). (a) pottery from the northeast deposit, M3C 264; (b) pottery from the southeast deposit, M3C 262; (c) pottery from the southwest deposit, M3C 263; (d) pottery from the northwest deposit, M3C 265.

at Deir el-Bahari, which typify foundation deposits from the later Old Kingdom (6th Dynasty) such as those from Hierakonpolis.[48] Foundation deposits from the earlier Old Kingdom (i.e., 5th Dynasty and earlier) are typologically different from those of the later Old Kingdom[49] and are not parallel to the Megiddo cache. Perhaps providing a *terminus post quem* is the foundation deposit from the mortuary complex of Raneferef at Abu Sir, which has a quite different ceramic assemblage.[50]

Locus 4009, the paved structure above Altar 4017, argued above to belong to Stratum XV, yielded several finds dating to the Intermediate Bronze Age (Fig. 14).[51] These include an Intermediate Bronze Age jar (Fig. 14.1),[52] typical IB cups (Fig. 14:2–4),[53] a "Nahariya lamp" (Fig. 14:5);[54] an axe (Fig. 14:5),[55] and a copper-alloy double axe (Fig. 14:7).[56] The double axe is of Minoan or Anatolian origin.[57]

In the subsequent Stratum XIV (Level J-8), dating from the early Middle Bronze Age I, Temple 4040 was remodeled into a condensed shrine with an adjacent platform of standing stones.[58] A small room was prepared within the larger room, with the space in between filled with debris. Within this debris was a copper-alloy fenestrated axe (Fig. 14:6).[59] The axe is of a "transitional" type dated to the Intermediate Bronze Age.[60]

Figure 13: Mendes T-A Vault #3 showing medium flaring bowls and tall drop-shaped bottles as a burial assemblage of the First Intermediate Period. Courtesy of the PSU Expedition to Mendes.

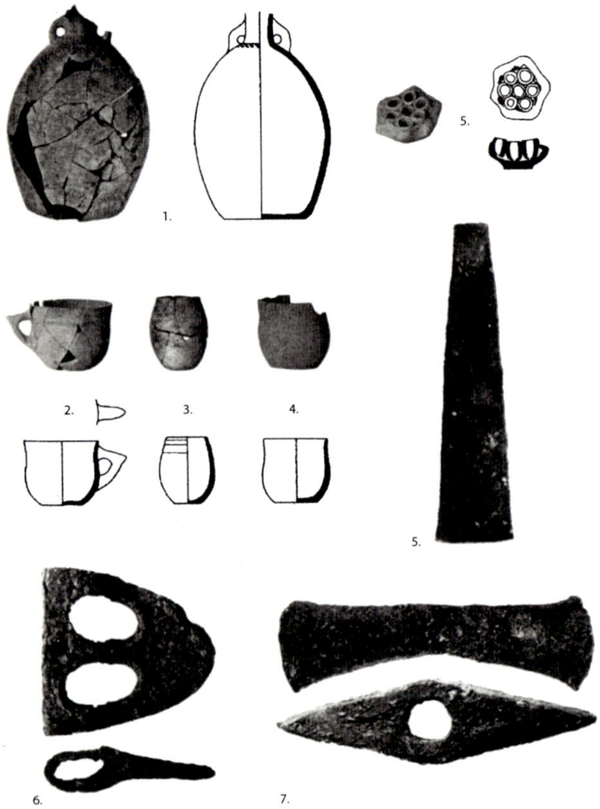

Figure 14: Finds from Locus 4009 (compiled from Loud 1948).

Discussion

The data gathered above provides an unexpected dimension to late 3rd-millennium Megiddo, and several discussion points are in order.

The date of the temples can be determined from various strands of evidence. First, the ceramics sealed beneath the floor of the threshold of Temple 4040 clearly date to the Intermediate Bronze Age. Second, the Egyptianized foundation deposit has a specific typological window of time dating from the 6th Dynasty to the reign of Montuhotep II at the latest. In absolute dates, this is approximately 2400–2050 BCE, squarely within the local Intermediate Bronze Age.[61]

We should also consider another Intermediate Bronze Age assemblage from Megiddo, the Black Wheel-Made Ware (BWMW). More than fifty tombs from the Intermediate Bronze Age were excavated on the east slope, many of which contained pottery connected with northern traditions, especially large quantities of BWMW pottery;[62] thus, Megiddo appears to be the southernmost large site within its distribution range.[63] This assemblage became a hallmark of the northern pottery tradition of the Intermediate Bronze Age, known as "Megiddo Ware".[64] Subsequently, BWMW has been identified at several sites in northern Israel, particularly in the Jezreel Valley and Hula Valley, most numerously at Hazor.[65] One important aspect of BWMW pottery is that it is a style imported from the north,

Lebanon and Syria, where it defines the Syrian Calceiform Culture.[66] Bechar's typological study of BWMW compared to parallels in Syria and Lebanon demonstrated southern Levantine BWMW contemporary with the later styles in Syria dating from the local EB IVb, c. 2300–2000 BCE.[67] These dates were further supported by the radiocarbon study of the Intermediate Bronze Age levels at Tel Hazor, where the largest assemblage of BWMW was found. The samples provided a modeled date range of 2300–2200 BCE (2σ), synchronous with the beginning of the EB IVb in the northern Levant.[68]

It is also to the northern Levant that we must look for parallels to the architectural form of the Triple-Temple Complex. These temples fit well into the Syrian temples *in antis*. Many are known from Syrian sites such as Tell Bi'a, Tell Chuera, Tell Rawda, Tell Halawa A and B, Tell Kabir, Ebla, and so on.[69] The closest parallel to the Megiddo Triple-Temple Compound is the "Temple en L" and the "Chapelle Orientale" at Byblos, of *Piqueté* I–III,[70] especially in the "Temple en L," where the temple form appears in triplicate, like the Megiddo Triple-Temple Complex.[71] These temples are dated to the northern Levantine late EB III and mostly to the EB IV, that is, after 2500 BCE and the end of the southern Levantine EB III.[72]

A Note on the Typological Sequence of Temples in Third Millennium Megiddo

The sequence of temples at Megiddo shows several typological changes throughout the Bronze Age. The earliest temples at Megiddo are the three Early Bronze Age IB ones (Levels J-2–J-4), which are broad-room in shape and feature tables within the sanctuary—"Broad-room Table Temples"—culminating in the enormous Great Temple which dominated the upper terrace (Fig. 3).[73] A significant change was introduced to the cultic complex in the EB II–III (OI Strata XVII–XVI), with the introduction of a palatial compound at the center of which was round Altar 4017 and at least one temple (5221) of smaller dimensions and a different architectural plan than those preceding it. While still broad or square in *cella*-shape, this temple can be reconstructed with two column bases within the *cella* and a partially enclosed porch, also presumably supported by columns (Fig. 3). The only other regional parallel for both this temple form and its proximity to a round altar is from Khirbet ez-Zeraqon, where Temples B.04 and B.05 match the symmetry, column bases, and enclosed porch of the Megiddo Strata XVII–XVI temple.[74] Bietak has classified this type "Broad-room Temples with Pseudo-antae."[75]

Before the current stratigraphic realization that the Megiddo Altar 4017 does not belong to the Triple-Temple Complex but solely to the Level J-5–J-6 compound, scholars often compared the ez-Zeraqon temples with the Triple-Temple Complex based primarily on the presence of the round altars.[76] This comparison did not sit well with D'Andrea, who argued that they were from two distinct traditions from different influences in Syria and Lebanon.[77] We agree that the comparison is inappropriate, especially since we can now show that the Level J-7 Triple-Temple Complex is significantly later in date than the ez-Zeraqon complex and that we have identified a temple of a "Broad-room Temple with Pseudo-antae" type in Level J-5–J-6 with more concrete parallels at ez-Zeraqon. Megiddo and ez-Zeraqon represent an EB II–III development; whether local or imported remains to be determined.

The Megiddo Triple-Temple Complex of Stratum XV should be seen as a distinct temple type bearing only superficial comparison to the earlier Megiddo Level J-5–J-6 and ez-Zerqaqon compounds. The closest parallel to the Megiddo Triple-Temple Compound is the "Temple en L" and the "Chapelle Orientale" at Byblos, of *Piqueté* I–III,[78] especially in the "Temple en L." where the temple form appears in triplicate like the Megiddo Triple-Temple Complex. It appears that the Stratum XV temples are directly influenced by the architecture and the cult from the north-central Lebanese coast, centered in Byblos.[79]

Summary and Conclusions

During the EB III, Megiddo featured a large palatial complex with a "Broad-room Temple with Pseudo-antae" (5221) and Altar 4017 at its core (Strata XVII–XVI; Levels J-5–J-6; Fig. 3). The settlement was abandoned around 2500 BCE along with many of the other major centers of the EB III in the southern Levant. The tell was resettled in Stratum XV (Level J-7) with the construction of the Triple-Temple Complex and the monumental staircase to its east—it was a large undertaking that emerged fully formed, not through a slow process of resettlement (Figs. 1, 5). Further to the east, beyond the edges of the town, a cemetery was founded on the bedrock slope.

The Triple-Temple Complex introduced a new style of architecture to the region, that of Temples *in antis*, a style that emerged in the northern Levant and Upper Euphrates in the local late EB III and EB IV, equivalent to the southern Levantine Intermediate Bronze Age. Finds from the TAU excavations beneath the floor of Temple 4040 yielded Intermediate Bronze Age pottery (FIG. 9) and OI Locus 4009, a built surface overlaying Altar 4017, also provided restorable pottery dated to the Intermediate Bronze Age (FIG. 14). The eastern cemetery also yielded tombs of the Intermediate Bronze Age, several comprising Black Wheel Made Ware, a style from EB IV Syria, whose presence in the Hula and Jezreel Valleys was dated at Hazor by radiocarbon to the 23rd century BCE. Further, two calibrated radiocarbon dates from IB contexts at Megiddo have returned dates of 2334–2149 calBCE and 2200–2060 calBCE (unmodeled), further supporting the dating of IB activity at the site to the later part of this time.[80] Overall, the dates for Stratum XV and its cemetery place it firmly in the 23rd–22nd centuries BCE, that is, the second half of the Intermediate Bronze Age, equivalent to the northern EB IVb.

One peculiar feature of the Triple-Temple Complex is the presence of a clearly Egyptian-style foundation deposit discovered beneath the floor of Temple 4040 (FIGS. 10–12). The typology of the deposit matches well deposits in Egypt from the 6th–11th Dynasties, paralleled most strongly by the early deposits of Montuhotep II at Deir el-Bahari, which also provide a *terminus ante quem* for this foundation deposit type. According to the latest radiocarbon study of Dynastic Egypt, this period would range from c. 2400 BCE to c. 2050 BCE.[81] This period matches well the dates provided by the temple *in antis* parallels in Syria and Lebanon and the relative and absolute dates provided by the BWMW.

Stratum XV appears to have ended in abandonment, only to be resettled in the Middle Bronze Age I (Stratum XIV; Level J-8). For the most part, domestic structures were built over the Triple-Temple Complex;[82] however, Temple 4040 was reconfigured into a small shrine with an adjacent open-air space with standing stones.[83] Radiocarbon studies from the earliest MB I levels at Megiddo date these levels to the early 20th century BCE.[84]

With new data and updated stratigraphic analysis, the Megiddo Stratum XV Triple-Temple Complex can be better understood within the broader scope of the late 3rd-millennium Levant. Stratum XV at Megiddo stands out as enigmatic only when it is considered in light of the southern Levantine Intermediate Bronze Age. This is an era generally understood as an age of post-urban collapse, village-level society, and pastoral nomadic subsistence. The suggestion that a monumental city such as Megiddo Stratum XV could exist in this context would immediately cause incredulity and disdain. Indeed, that is what basically happened. The re-attribution of the Triple-Temple Complex from the Intermediate Bronze Age, as suggested by the excavators, to the Early Bronze Age III by Dunayevsky and Kempinski, de Miroschedji, and others, was based on the seeming impossibility of Intermediate Bronze Age southern Levantines to build cities and monumental architecture.

However, Stratum XV Megiddo does not seem so enigmatic when considered in light of the northern Levantine EB IV. It would hardly stick out on the Lebanese coast, in the Orontes plain, or in the upper Euphrates. We need to change our perception to understand that Megiddo (and perhaps Hazor), in the second half of the Intermediate Bronze Age, is within the cultural sphere of the northern Levantine EB IV and represents the southernmost sprawl of the northern Levantine culture.

In this regard, Megiddo Stratum XV can be understood alongside some of the better-known historical scenarios known from that time. Stratum XV dates roughly to the 23rd–21st centuries BCE, EB IVB in the north, and, in Egyptian Chronology, the 6th–11th Dynasties. I believe the Egyptian connection helps to pare down the date range. The Egyptian-style foundation deposit is uniquely Egyptian in manufacture and suggests the presence of actual Egyptians, probably with state sponsorship. It seems unlikely that this could have been achieved during the bulk of the First Intermediate Period. On the bookends of the chronology, however, during the 6th Dynasty or the reign of Montuhotep, it is entirely plausible that an Egyptian expeditionary force could visit Megiddo;[85] in the 6th Dynasty, especially during the reign of Pepi I and Merenre, when Iny and Weni carried out several expeditions to locations in the Levant, including Byblos.[86]

REFERENCES

Adams, Matthew J. 2013a. "Area J, Part I: Introduction." In Israel Finkelstein, David Ussishkin, Eric H. Cline, Matthew J. Adams, Eran Arie, Norma Franklin and Mario A.S. Martin (eds.), *Megiddo V: The 2004–2008 Seasons,*

21–27. Sonia and Marco Nadler Institute of Archaeology Monograph Series 31. Winona Lake, IN: Eisenbrauns, for the Institute of Archaeology of Tel Aviv University.

———. 2013b. "Area J, Part III: The Main Sector of Area J" [The Early Bronze Age, Stratigraphy and Architecture]. In Israel Finkelstein, David Ussishkin, Eric H. Cline, Matthew J. Adams, Eran Arie, Norma Franklin and Mario A.S. Martin (eds.), *Megiddo V: The 2004–2008 Seasons*, 47–118. Sonia and Marco Nadler Institute of Archaeology Monograph Series 31. Winona Lake, IN: Eisenbrauns, for the Institute of Archaeology of Tel Aviv University.

———. 2013c. "The Early Bronze Pottery from Area J." In Israel Finkelstein, David Ussishkin, Eric H. Cline, Matthew J. Adams, Eran Arie, Norma Franklin and Mario A.S. Martin (eds.), *Megiddo V: The 2004–2008 Seasons*, 295–334. Sonia and Marco Nadler Institute of Archaeology Monograph Series 31. Winona Lake, IN: Eisenbrauns, for the Institute of Archaeology of Tel Aviv University.

———. 2017a. "Egypt and the Levant in the Early/Middle Bronze Age Transition." In F. Höflmayer (ed.), *The Early/Middle Bronze Age Transition in the Ancient Near East. Chronology, C14, and Climate Change*, 493–515. The University of Chicago Oriental Institute Seminars, 11. Chicago: Oriental Institute.

———. 2017b. "Djehutihotep and Megiddo in the Early Middle Bronze Age." *Journal of Ancient Egyptian Interconnections* 13: 1–11. https://journals.uair.arizona.edu/index.php/jaei/article/view/19858.

———. 2017c. "The Egyptianized Pottery Cache from Megiddo's Area J: A Foundation Deposit for Temple 4040." *Tel Aviv* 44 (2): 141–164. http://dx.doi.org/10.1080/03344355.2017.1357272. (Reprinted in Israel Finkelstein and Mario A.S. Martin (eds.), *Megiddo VI: The 2010–2014 Seasons*, 1779–1797. Sonia and Marco Nadler Institute of Archaeology Monograph Series. Winona Lake, IN: Eisenbrauns, for the Institute of Archaeology of Tel Aviv University.

———. Forthcoming. The Cult Spaces of Megiddo in the Middle Bronze Age: New Data and New Hypotheses.

Adams, Matthew J. and James M. Bos. 2013. "Part IV: Sub-Area Upper J" [The Middle and Late Bronze Ages, Stratigraphy and Architecture]. In Israel Finkelstein, David Ussishkin, Eric H. Cline, Matthew J. Adams, Eran Arie, Norma Franklin and Mario A.S. Martin (eds.), *Megiddo V: The 2004–2008 Seasons*, 119–142. Sonia and Marco Nadler Institute of Archaeology Monograph Series 31. Winona Lake, IN: Eisenbrauns, for the Institute of Archaeology of Tel Aviv University.

Adams, Matthew J. and Melissa S. Cradic. 2022. "The Middle Bronze Age Burials from Area J." In Israel Finkelstein and Mario A.S. Martin (eds.), *Megiddo VI: The 2010–2014 Seasons*; 187–223. Sonia and Marco Nadler Institute of Archaeology Monograph Series. Winona Lake, IN: Eisenbrauns, for the Institute of Archaeology of Tel Aviv University.

Adams, Matthew J., Israel Finkelstein and David Ussishkin. 2014. "The Great Temple of Early Bronze I Megiddo." *American Journal of Archaeology* 118/2: 285–305.

Adams, M.J., Z. Dunseth, A. Yasur-Landau and I. Finkelstein. Forthcoming. "The Early Middle Bronze Age I at Megiddo."

Albright, Wiliam F. 1949 "Review of Megiddo II: Seasons of 1935–39." *American Journal of Archaeology* 53(2): 213–215.

Amiran, Ruth. 1970. *Ancient Pottery of the Holy Land; from Its Beginnings in the Neolithic Period to the End of the Iron Age*. New Brunswick, NJ: Rutgers University Press.

Arnold, Dieter. 1979. *The Temple of Mentuhotep at Deir el-Bahari*. New York: Metropolitan Museum of Art, Egyptian Expedition.

Bechar, Shlomit. 2015. A Reanalysis of Black Wheel-Made Ware of the Intermediate Bronze Age." *Tel Aviv* 42: 27–58.

Bietak, Manfred. 2019. "The Spiritual Roots of the Hyksos Elite: An Analysis of their Sacred Architecture, Part I." In Manfred Bietak and Silvia Prell (eds.), *The Enigma of the Hyksos, Volume* I, 47–67. CAENL 9. Wiesbaden: Harrassowitz.

Blockman, Noga and Benjamin Sass. 2013. "The Small Finds." In Israel Finkelstein, David Ussishkin, Eric H. Cline, Matthew J. Adams, Eran Arie, Norma Franklin and Mario A.S. Martin (eds.), *Megiddo V: The 2004–2008 Seasons*, 866–929. Sonia and Marco Nadler Institute of Archaeology Monograph Series 31. Winona Lake, IN: Eisenbrauns, for the Institute of Archaeology of Tel Aviv University.

Braemer, Frank. 2002. "La Céramique du Bronze Ancien en Syrie du Sud." In Michel Al-Maqdissi, Valérie Matoïan and Christophe Nicolle, (eds.), *Céramique de l'Âge du Bronze en Syrie, I: La Syrie du Sud et le Vallée de l'Oronte.* 9–21. Bibliothèque Archéologique et Historique 161. Beirut: Publications de l'Institut français du Proche-Orient.

Braemer, Frank and Jean-Claude Échallier. 2000. "A Summary Statement on the EBA Ceramics from Southern Syria, and the Relationship of this Material with that of Neighbouring Regions." In Graham Philip and Douglas Baird (eds.), *Ceramics and Change in the Early Bronze Age of the Southern Levant*, 403–410. Sheffield: Sheffield Academic Press.

Brandl, Baruch. 2013. "Cylinder Seals." In Israel Finkelstein, David Ussishkin, Eric H. Cline, Matthew J. Adams, Eran Arie, Norma Franklin and Mario A.S. Martin (eds.), *Megiddo V: The 2004–2008 Seasons*, 993–1010. Sonia and Marco Nadler Institute of Archaeology Monograph Series 31. Winona Lake, IN: Eisenbrauns, for the Institute of Archaeology of Tel Aviv University.

Bronk Ramsey, Christopher, Michael W. Dee, Joanne M. Rowland, Thomas F.G. Higham, Stephen H. Harris, Fiona Brock, Anita Quiles, Eva M. Wild, Ezra S. Marcus and Andrew J. Shortland. 2010. "Radiocarbon-Based Chronology for Dynastic Egypt." *Science* 328(5985): 1554–1557. DOI: 10.1126/science.1189395.

Bunimovitz, Shlomo and Greenberg, Raphael. 2004. "Revealed in their Cups: Syrian Drinking Customs in Intermediate Bronze Age Canaan." *BASOR* 334: 19–31.

———. 2006. "Of Pots and Paradigms: Interpreting the Intermediate Bronze Age in Israel/Palestine." In Seymour Gitin, J. Edward Wright and J.P. Dessel (eds.), *Confronting the Past—Archaeological and Historical Essays on Ancient Israel in Honor of William G. Dever*, 23–31. Winona Lake, IN: Eisenbrauns.

Castel, Corinne 2008. "Al-Rawda, a Town in the Steppe (Central Syria, Early Bronze Age IV)." In Hartmut Kühne, Rainer Maria Czichon, and Florian Janoscha Kreppner (eds.), *Proceedings of the 4th International Congress of the Archaeology of the Ancient Near East. 29 March–3 April 2004, Freie Universität Berlin. Volume 2: Social and Cultural Transformation: The Archaeology of Transitional Periods and Dark Ages. Excavation Reports*, 301–312. Wiesbaden: Harrassowitz.

———. 2010. "The First Temples in antis: The Sanctuary of Tell Al-Rawda in the Context of 3rd Millennium Syria." In Jorg Becker, Ralph Hempelmann and Ellen Rehm (eds.), *Kulturlandschaft Syrien. Zentrum und Peripherie. Festschrift für Jan-Waalke Meyer*, 123–164. Alter Orient und Altes Testament 371. Münster: Ugarit-Verlag.

Cline, Eric H. 2020. *Digging up Armageddon. The Search for the Lost City of Solomon*. Princeton, NJ: Princeton University Press.

Cooper, Lisa. 2006. *Early Urbanism on the Syrian Euphrates*. New York and London: Routledge.

Covello-Paran, Karen. 2009. "Socio-economic Aspects of an Intermediate Bronze Age Village in the Jezreel Valley." In Peter J. Parr (ed.), *The Levant in Transition : Proceedings of a Conference Held at the British Museum on 20-21 April 2004*, 9–20. Leeds: Maney.

D'Andrea, Marta. 2020. "The Religious Complexes of Megiddo and Khirbet ez-Zeraqon and the Early Bronze Age Interregional Connectivity." *Studia Eblaitica* 6: 1–39.

Dunayevsky, Immanuel and Aharon Kempinski. 1966. "Notes and News: Megiddo. *Israel Exploration Journal* 16: 142.

———. 1973. The Megiddo temples. *Zeitschrift des Deutschen Palästina-Vereins* 89: 161–187.

Esse, Douglas. 1991. *Subsistence, Trade and Social Change in the Early Bronze Age Palestine*. Studies in Ancient Oriental Civilization 50. Chicago: Oriental Institute of the University of Chicago.

Finkelstein, Israel, David Ussishkin and Jennifer Peersmann. 2006. "Area J (The 1998–2000 Seasons)." In Israel Finkelstein, David Ussishkin, and Baruch Halpern (eds.), *Megiddo IV. The 1998–2002 Seasons*, 29–53. Sonia and Marco Nadler Institute of Archaeology Monograph Series 24. Tel Aviv: Emery and Claire Yass Publications in Archaeology.

Genz, Hermann. 2002. *Die frühbronzezeitliche Keramik von Ḫirbet ez-Zeraqōn mit Studien zur Chronologie und funktionaler Deutung frühbronzezeitlicher Keramik in der südlichen Levante.* Abhandlungen des Deutschen Palästina-Vereins 27/2; Deutsch-jordanische Ausgrabungen in Ḫirbet ez-Zeraqōn 1984–1994, Endberichte 5. Wiesbaden: Harrassowitz Verlag.

Gitin, Seymour. 1975. "Middle Bronze I 'Domestic' Pottery at Jebel Qa'aqir: A Ceramic Inventory of Cave G23." *Eretz-Israel* 12: 46*–62*.

Goren, Yuval. 2000. "Technology, Provenience and Interpretation of the Early Bronze Age Egyptian Ceramics." In Israel Finkelstein, David Ussishkin and B. Halpern (eds.), *Megiddo III: The 1992–1996 Seasons*, 496–501. Monograph Series of the Institute of Archaeology of Tel Aviv University 18. Tel Aviv University: Emery and Clare Yass Publications in Archaeology.

Greenberg, Raphael. 2006. "Notes on the Early Bronze Age Pottery (The 1998–2000 Seasons)." In Israel Finkelstein, David Ussishkin, and Baruch Halpern (eds.), *Megiddo IV. The 1998–2002 Seasons*, 149–165. Sonia and Marco Nadler Institute of Archaeology Monograph Series 24. Tel Aviv: Emery and Claire Yass Publications in Archaeology.

Greenberg, Raphael, Emanuel Eisenberg, Sarit Paz and Yitzhak Paz. 2006. *Bet Yeraḥ: The Early Bronze Age Mound. Volume I: Excavation Reports, 1933–1986*. IAA Report 30. Jerusalem: Israel Antiquities Authority.

Greenhut, Zvi. 1995. "EB IV Tombs and Burials in Palestine." *Tel Aviv* 22(1): 3–46.

Guy, Philipp L.O. and Robert M. Engberg. 1938. *Megiddo Tombs*. Chicago: University of Chicago Press.

Helms, S. 1989. "An EB IV Pottery Repertoire at Amman, Jordan." *BASOR* 273: 17–36.

Ibrahim, M. and S. Mittmann. 1994. "Excavations at Khirbet ez-Zeraqon, 1993." *Newsletter of the Institute of Archaeology and Anthropology, Yarmouk University* 16: 11–15.

Ilan, Ornit and Yuval Goren. 2003. "The Egyptianized Pottery Vessels of Early Bronze Age Megiddo." *Tel Aviv* 30: 42–53.

Joffe, Alexander H. 2000. "The Early Bronze Age Pottery from Area J." In Israel Finkelstein, David Ussishkin and Baruch Halpern (eds.), *Megiddo III: The 1992–1996 Seasons*, 161–185. Monograph Series of the Institute of Archaeology of Tel Aviv University 18. Tel Aviv University: Emery and Clare Yass Publications in Archaeology.

Kamlah, Jens. 2012. "Temples of the Levant – Comparative Aspects." In Jens Kamlah and Henrike Michelau (eds.), *Temple Building and Temple Cult. Architecture and Cultic Paraphernalia of Temples in the Levant (2.–1. Mill. B.C.E)*, 507–534. Abhandlungen des deutschen Palastina-Vereins, 41. Wiesbaden: Harrasssowitz Verlag.

Kempinski, Aharon. 1989. *Megiddo. A City-State and Royal Centre in North Israel*. Materialien zur Allgemeinen und Vergleichenden Archäologie, Band 40. Munich: Verlag C.H. Beck.

Kenyon, Kathleen M. 1958. "Some Notes on the Early and Middle Bronze Age Strata of Megiddo." *Eretz Israel* 5: 51*–60*.

Langgut, Dafna, Matthew J. Adams and Israel Finkelstein. 2016. "Climate, Settlement Patterns and Olive Horticulture in the Southern Levant during the Early Bronze and Intermediate Bronze Ages (ca. 3600–1950 BCE)." *Levant* 48(2): 1–18. http://dx.doi.org/10.1080/00758914.2016.1193323.

Lauffray, J. 2008. *Fouilles de Byblos, Tome VI. L'urbanisme et l'architecture. De l'époque proto-urbaine à l'occupation amorite (de l'Énéolithique à l'âge du Bronze II)*. Bibliothèque archéologique et historique 182. Beirut: Institut français du Proche-Orient.

Lev, Ron, Shlomit Bechar and Elisabetta Boaretto. 2021. "Hazor EB III City Abandonment and IBA People Return: Radiocarbon Chronology and its Implications." *Radiocarbon* 63(5): 1453–1469.

Loud, Gordon. 1948. *Megiddo II: Seasons of 1935–39*. Chicago: University of Chicago Press.

Marcolin, Michele and Andrés Diego Espinel 2011. "The Sixth Dynasty Biographic Inscriptions of Iny: More Pieces to the Puzzle." In Miroslav Bárta, Filip Coppens and Jaromír Krejãí (eds.), *Abusir and Saqqara in the Year 2010 /1*, 570–615. Prague: Czech Institute of Egyptology, Faculty of Arts, Charles University in Prague.

Marquet-Krause, Judith. 1935. "La Deuxième Campagne de Fouilles a Ay (1934)." *Syria* 16: 325–345.

Matthiae, Paolo. 2015. "Cult Architecture at Ebla between Early Bronze IVA and Middle Bronze I: Continuity and Innovation in the Formative Phase of a Great Tradition. An Evaluation." *Studia Eblaitica* 1: 75–109.

Mazar, Amihai and Pierre de Miroschedji. 1996. "Hartuv, an Aspect of the Early Bronze I Culture of Southern Israel." *BASOR* 302: 1–40.

Miron, Eli. 1992. *Axes and Adzes from Canaan*. Prähistorische Bronzefunde, Abt. 9, 19. Stuttgart: Steiner.

Miroschedji, Pierre de. 1988. *Yarmouth I. Rapport sur les trois premières campagnes de fouilles à Tel Yarmouth (Israël) (1980–1982)*. Paris: Éditions Recherche sur les Civilisations.

———. 2001. "Notes on Early Bronze Age Metrology and the Birth of Architecture in Ancient Palestine." In Samuel R. Wolff (ed.), *Studies in the Archaeology of Israel and Neighboring Lands in Memory of Douglas L. Esse*, 465–491. SAOC, 59. Chicago: Chicago Oriental Institute.

Nigro, Lorenzo. 2008. *Khirbet al-Batrawy II: The EB II City-Gate, the EB II–III Fortifications, the EB II–III Temple. Preliminary Report of the Second (2006) and Third (2007) Seasons of Excavations*. Rome "La Sapienza" Studies on the Archaeology of Palestine and Transjordan, 6. Rome: Università degli studi di Roma "La Sapienza."

Palumbo, Gaetano. 1990. *The Early Bronze Age IV in the Southern Levant: Settlement Patterns, Economy, and Material Culture of a 'Dark Age.'* Contributi e Materiali di Archeologia Orientale 3. Rome: University of Rome.

Palumbo, Gaetano and Glen Peterman. 1993. "Early Bronze Age IV Ceramic Regionalism in Central Jordan." *BASOR* 289: 23–32.

Prag, Kay. 1974. "The Intermediate Early Bronze-Middle Bronze Age: An Interpretation of the Evidence from Transjordan, Syria and Lebanon." *Levant* 6: 69–116.

———. 1986. "The Intermediate Early Bronze-Middle Bronze Age Sequences at Jericho and Tell Iktanu Reviewed." *BASOR* 264: 61–72.

Rast, Walter E. and R. Thomas Schaub. 2003. *Bâb edh-Dhrâ': Excavations at the Town Site (1975–1981). Part 1: Text*. Winona Lake, IN: Eisenbrauns.

Redford, Donald B. 2010. *City of the Ram-Man. The Story of Ancient Mendes*. Princeton, NJ: Princeton University Press.

———. 2020. "The T-A Vaults." In. Donald B. Redford and Susan Redford (eds.), *Excavations at Mendes, Volume 2. The Dromos and Temple Area*. Leiden: Brill.

Regev, Johanna, Pierre de Miroschedji, Raphael Greenberg, Eliot Braun., Zvi Greenhut and Elisabetta Boaretto. 2012. "Chronology of the Early Bronze Age in the South Levant: New Analysis for a High Chronology." *Radiocarbon* 54(3–4): 525–566.

Regev, Johanna, Israel Finkelstein, Matthew J. Adams and Elisabetta Boaretto. 2014. "Wiggle-matched 14C Chronology of Early Bronze Megiddo and the Synchronization of Egyptian and Levantine Chronologies," *Egypt and Levant* 24: 243–266. (Reprinted in Israel Finkelstein and Mario A.S. Martin [eds.]. 2022. *Megiddo VI: The 2010–2014 Seasons*, 1391–1415. Sonia and Marco Nadler Institute of Archaeology Monograph Series. Winona Lake, IN: Eisenbrauns, for the Institute of Archaeology of Tel Aviv University.

Richard, Suzanne. 1980. "Toward a Consensus of Opinion on the End of the Early Bronze Age in Palestine-Transjordan." *BASOR* 237: 5–34.

Sala, Maura. 2015. "Early and Middle Bronze Age Temples at Byblos: Specificity and Levantine Interconnections." *BAAL Hors-Série* X: 5–32.

Schaub, R. Thomas. 1973. "An Early Bronze IV Tomb from Bâb Edh-dhrâ." *BASOR* 210: 2–19.

Schumacher, Gottlieb. 1908. *Tell el-Mutesellim; Bericht über die 1903 bis 1905 mit Unterstützung Sr. Majestät des deutschen Kaisers und der Deutschen Orient-Gesellschaft vom Deutschen Verein zur Erforschung Palästinas veranstalteten Ausgrabungen Vol. 1*. Leipzig: J.C. Hinrichs'sche Buchhandlung.

Smithline, Howard. 2002. "An Intermediate Bronze Age Site at Horbat Qishron." In Z. Gal (ed.), *Eretz Zafon: Studies in Galilean Archaeology*: *20–*46. Jerusalem: Israel Antiquities Authority.

Thompson, Thomas L. 1970. "The Dating of the Megiddo Temples in Strata XV–XIV." *ZDPV* 86: 38–49.

Ussishkin, David. 2015. The Sacred Area of Early Bronze Megiddo: History and Interpretation. *BASOR* XX: 69–104.

———. 2018. *Megiddo-Armageddon. The Story of the Canaanite and Israelite City*. Jerusalem: Israel Exploration Society.

Verner Miroslav, Miroslav Bárta and Český. 2006. *Abusir IX: The Pyramid Complex of Raneferef: The Archaeology*. Prague: Czech Institute of Egyptology.

Wapnish, Paula and Brian Hesse. 2000. "Mammal Remains from the Early Bronze Sacred Compound." In Israel Finkelstein, David Ussishkin and Baruch Halpern (eds.), *Megiddo III: The 1992–1996 Seasons*, 429–462. Monograph Series of the Institute of Archaeology of Tel Aviv University 18. Tel Aviv University: Emery and Clare Yass Publications in Archaeology.

Ward, William. 1971. *Egypt and the East Mediterranean World, 2200–1900 B.C.: Studies in Egyptian Foreign Relations during the First Intermediate Period.* Beirut: American University of Beirut.

Weinstein, James M. 1973. "Foundation Deposits in Ancient Egypt." Ph.D. Diss., University of Pennsylvania. Philadelphia.

Wightman, Greg J. 1988. "An EB IV Cemetery in the North Jordan Valley." *Levant* 20: 139–159.

Yasur-Landau, Assaf. 2015. "From Byblos to Vapheio: Fenestrated Axes between the Aegean and the Levant." *BASOR* 373: 139–150.

———. 2020. "Notes on the Anatolian or North Syrian Axes in the Southern Levant." In Barış Gür and Semra Dalkılıç (eds.), *Anadolu Prehistoryasina Adanmiş Bir Yaşam: Jak Yakar'a Armağan / A Life Dedicated to Anatolian Prehistory: Festschrift for Jak Yaka,* 479–485. Kızılay Ankara: Bilgin Kültür Sanat Yayınları.

Notes

1 That is, their "Middle Bronze Age I," as it was known in contemporary terminology; Loud 1948, 5. In consultation with Albright, he also attributed it to Tel Beit Mirsim I–H; Loud 1948, 5; Albright 1949, 2151. Wright (1950), Kenyon (1958), and Thompson (1970) made similar attributions.

2 Loud 1948, 78–84.

3 Cline 2020, *passim.*

4 For the details and references to these debates, see Ussishkin 2015, 95. In light of the new data presented here and elsewhere (Adams 2013b; 2017a; 2017c), much of this debate remained purely academic.

5 They carried out small soundings over a few days in 1965; Dunayevsky and Kempinski 1966; 1973; Kempinski 1989.

6 de Miroschedji 2001.

7 Esse 1991.

8 The main stratigraphic results are discussed in Adams 2013a; 2013b; Adams and Bos 2013. For additional relevant data and studies, see Adams 2017a; 2017b; 2017c; Ussishkin 2015; 2018; and the present paper.

9 The reader is directed to summaries of these earlier studies in Ussishkin 2015.

10 Adams, Finkelstein and Ussishkin 2014. The temple is dated by the excavators to EB Ib (ESL 3 according to the ARCANE terminology based on ceramics, radiocarbon, and stratigraphy).

11 Adams 2013b, 71–72.

12 Adams 2013b, 72–74.

13 Loud 1948; Joffe 2000; Greenberg 2006; Adams 2013c. There is some discussion about whether or not there is any EB II occupation at the site, which is outside the scope of this paper.

14 Regev et al. 2014. The less-precise end date of 2600/2500 BCE results from the fact that no radiocarbon samples from the succeeding Stratum XV (Level J-7) were available for the study and were thus not included in the model to constrain the date of the last sample beyond the $\pm 1\sigma$ range of the latest sample, which could date from as early as 2600 or as late as c. 2500 BCE.

15 Loud 1948; Ussishkin 2015; 2018.

16 Finkelstein, Ussishkin, and Peersmann 2006; Wapnish and Hesse 2000.

17 Loud 1948, fig. 393 (Square N/12). Cf. Loud 1948, fig. 393 (Square N/14); Loud 1948, fig. 174.

18 Adams 2013b, 117.

19 Ibrahim and Mittmann 1994; Genz 2002; D'Andrea 2020.

20 Finkelstein, Ussishkin and Peersmann 2006, 42 fig. 3.22.

21 Greenberg 2006 fig. 10.2: 12, erroneously attributed to Level J-4.

22 Finkelstein, Ussishkin and Peersmann 2006, 42 fig. 3.22.

23 E.g., Miroschedji 2001.

24 Blockman and Sass 2013, 889, No. 407, fig. 15.9.

25 Brandl 2013, 993–1000, figs. 18.1–2.

26 Adams 2013c, 305–324.

27 Loud 1948, figs. 177, 393; cf. Loud 1948, figs. 172–175.

28 Adams 2013c, 324–327, table 8.1; Greenberg 2006.

29 E.g., Kempinski, 1989; de Mirsoschedji, 2001.

30 See Adams and Bos 2013, 120, 125–126, fig. 2.82; Schumacher 1908, 39–40.

31 This includes the fragment of a wall originally used by Dunayevsky and Kempinsky (1973) ("Wall A") to suggest that Temple 4040 predated Temples 51129 and 5269. They understood this wall as bonded to the foundations of Temple 4040 and going under the adjacent Temple 5129. The TAU excavations also rechecked this wall and found the description of Wall A as 'bonded' to be overstated, with no clear point of contact between that wall and Temple 4040 (more than 15 cm between them). As we can see now, all the

cut walls of the earlier Strata XVI–XVII appear to be bonded because the foundations for the triple-temple complex were so precisely cut.

32 Loud 1948, Fig. 369.

33 Adams 2013b, 96–99; 2013c, 328–329.

34 Guy and Engberg 1938, 148; Richard 1980, 13 fig. 1:2, 3, 7; Prag 1974, 1986; Wightman 1988; Helms 1989, 19–20, fig. 7: a–d; Palumbo 1990, fig. 47; Palumbo and Peterman 1993, figs. 1–2; Covello-Paran 2009, fig. 9.

35 Guy 1938, e.g., pls. 20, 21; Amiran 1970, pls. 22–23; Schaub 1973, fig. 6.2.

36 Gitin 1975, figs. 2.3–2.4.

37 Smithline 2002, figs. 10.8, 13.4–13.5, 13.7; see especially his discussion of cooking bowls and parallels, p. 30; examples also known from the IB at 'Ein el-Hilu.

38 Greenberg et al. 2006, fig. 5.100, especially No. 2.

39 See, for example, Amiran 1970, pl. 25.

40 Adams 2017a, 2017c.

41 see detailed discussion in Adams 2017c, 156–158.

42 Joffe 2000; Ilan and Goren 2003.

43 Arnold 1979, 49–57, pls. 28–32.

44 Ilan and Goren 2003, 44.

45 Redford 2010, fig. 4.18, 21; Redford 2020.

46 Joffe 2000.

47 Arnold 1979; Weinstein 1973.

48 Weinstein 1973, 32.

49 Weinstein 1973, 30.

50 Verner, Bárta and Český 2006, 48.

51 Loud 1948, 176.

52 Loud 1948, pls. 16:8, 117:5.

53 Loud 1948, pls. 16:16–18; 117:8–10.

54 Loud 1948, pls. 16:21; 117:11. These lamps are usually associated with the early MB I, so they might be out of place here or represent an early version of these cultic lamps.

55 Loud 1948, pl. 182:8.4

56 Loud 1948, pl. 182:7.

57 Miron 1992, 80, 85; Yasur-Landau 2015, 146; 2020. In general, quite a large number of Intermediate Bronze Age finds are associated with OI Loci affiliated with Strata XV–XVI, which probably originate in Stratum XV. See Loud 1948, *passim*; Guy and Engberg 1938, *passim*.

58 Adams, forthcoming. Stratum XIV has traditionally been dated to the Intermediate Bronze Age (see, e.g., Ussishkin 2015; 2018), primarily on the conceptual basis that such an "ugly" reuse of the Stratum XV Temple 4040 could only be the product of the Intermediate Bronze Age people. The current excavations uncovered parts of Stratum XIV in Area J (Adams and Bos 2013), demonstrating that the stratum unequivocally dates to the early Middle Bronze Age I and represents the re-establishment of settlement at Megiddo in that Period. This will be dealt with in detail in Adams, forthcoming.

59 Loud 1948, pl. 182:3; Kempinski 1989, fig. 26:15; Miron 1992, pl. 15:231; Yasur-Landau 2015, 146–147.

60 Miron 1992, 58; Ussishkin 2018, 164–166.

61 Bronk Ramsey et al. 2010; Regev et al. 2012; 2014.

62 Guy and Engberg 1938, 148–149.

63 Welton and Cooper 2014, fig. 1; Bechar 2015.

64 Amiran 1970.

65 Bechar 2015.

66 Guy and Engberg 1938; Ussishkin 2015, 166–170; Bechar 2015; Bunimovitz and Greenberg 2004; 2006. It should also be noted that Intermediate Bronze Age plain ware ceramics from northern Israel, Syria, and Lebanon show strong affinities with each other as well; for example, with envelope ledge handles, as seen in the foundation trench of Temple 4040 (Braemer and Échallier 2000; Braemer 2002, 12–15). Megiddo Tomb types with IB pottery are also recognized to have inspiration in Syria (Greenhut 1995).

67 Bechar 2015, 49–54.

68 Lev, Bechar, and Boaretto 2021.

69 see Castel 2008; Castel 2010; Cooper 2006.

70 Lauffray 2008, 331–353.

71 Lauffray 2008, 331; Sala 2008, 190–201.

72 Castel 2010.

73 See discussion of this classification in Adams, Finkelstein and Ussishkin 2014, 298–299, fig. 9. To this architectural tradition, one can assign the Stratum II sanctuary at Hartuv (Mazar and Miroschedji 1996), the Acropolis Temple at 'Ai (Marquet-Krause 1935), Sanctuary B at Bab edh-Dhra (Rast and Schaub 2003), Temple F1 at Khirbet al-Batrawy (Nigro 2008), and the Bâtiment Blanc at Yarmut (Miroschedji 1988).

74 Genz 2002. Recently, what appears to be another example of a round altar has been excavated at Qiryat Atta (Assaf Kleiman, personal communication).

75 Bietak 2019. M. D'Andrea has suggested that this type should be traced to the Tell Halawa B

in *Bau* II and the "Latest Temple" at Al-Rawda in north Syria (D'Andrea 2020), though this hypothesis does not yet have wide acceptance.

76 Kamlah, 2012; Sala 2015; Ussishkin 2015.

77 D'Andrea 2020.

78 Lauffray 2008, 331–353. D'Andrea (2020, 4) makes a distinction between broad vs. long temples *in antis*, in this particular case paralleling the Megiddo Triple-Temple Complex only with the earlier EB III strata (*Piqueté* I). While in the long run, a trend from broad to long rooms does seem to be the case (see Matthiae 2015 for Ebla), I am not convinced that this feature of temples *in antis* has, by itself, a significant typological meaning or any chronological decisiveness, especially in this relatively narrow window of time during which the transition toward a long-room form is occurring differentially across space and time.

79 D'Andrea 2020, 16. However, she saw this as two influences occurring at the same time from different directions, whereas we can now see it as a chronological shift—from the Euphrates in the EB II–III (Megiddo J-5–6; ez-Zeraqon) to Lebanon in the Intermediate Bronze Age (Megiddo Stratum XV).

80 Adams et al. forthcoming.

81 Bronk Ramsay et al. 2010.

82 Adams and Bos 2013; Adams and Cradic 2022.

83 The re-urbanization of Megiddo in the MB I, and in particular, the ongoing development of the cultic compound during that time, is addressed in Adams, forthcoming.

84 Unmodeled; Adams et al., forthcoming.

85 Several texts from the reign of Montuhotep II allude to a campaign and trade in that direction. Redford 1993, 69–70; Ward 1971.

86 Marcolin and Espinel 2011.

Journal of Ancient Egyptian Interconnections

Egypto-Levantine Connectivity between the Shephelah and the Negev Highlands: New Insights from Ceramic Assemblage Profiles at Tel Erani, Mitzpe Sde Hafir, and Yeroḥam—Naḥal Avnon

Samuel Atkins
Institute of Archaeology, Hebrew University, Jerusalem

Yuval Yekutieli
Ben-Gurion University of the Negev, Beer Sheva

Abstract
Investigation of new data from recent Ben-Gurion University excavations at Mitzpe Sde Hafir and Israel Antiquities Authority excavations at Yeroḥam—Naḥal Avnon, two late EB I sites in the Western Negev and Central Negev Highlands, respectively, has revealed two zones of complex and transformational nomadic encounter with sedentary society at a pivotal phase of Egypto-Levantine connectivity during the late 4th millennium BCE. A comparative multivariate statistical analysis of ceramic assemblage profiles from these two desert sites and phases of Egypto-Levantine colonial relations at Tel Erani revealed unexpected correlations with chronological and social-evolutionary implications. Viewed within a holistic frame that considers the overall material profiles of these sites, the interplay between nomadic agency and Egyptian socio-economic and cultural influence in the region was evidently stimulative in the formation of new structures of desert-sown interaction.

Keywords
Early Bronze Age; EB I; pottery; interactions; contact zone

Introduction
In the last forty years, anthropological and ethnographic research has pivoted toward a view of nomadic pastoral society as essentially integrated within broader socio-economic systems and developmental trajectories. Archaeological researchers are increasingly cognizant of this shift and the importance of what has often been viewed as 'fringe' societies with low material visibility in ancient contexts. A growing body of data from diverse cultural milieus around the globe is demonstrating with clarity that ancient mobile societies are eminently traceable and that localized shifts in their internal structure and external relations are key considerations in formulating accurate projections of ancient social environments, as well as regional and interregional transformations over time.[1] This paper takes an integrated systemic approach to new datasets that shed light on the Negev Highland pastoral nomad society of the late 4th millennium BCE, investigating its connectivity within the context of Egyptian involvement in the southwest Levantine interaction sphere. During this phase, southwest Levantine society underwent a major intensification of contact with Nilotic society (or perhaps socie*ties*) of Lower and Upper Egypt.[2]

Toward the end of the 4th millennium BCE, there was an apparent sudden incursion of Egyptian communities into the coastal plain of the southwestern Levant. Large quantities of Naqadan ceramics appear in archaeological strata dating from the final phase of Early Bronze I (hereafter EB Ib2)

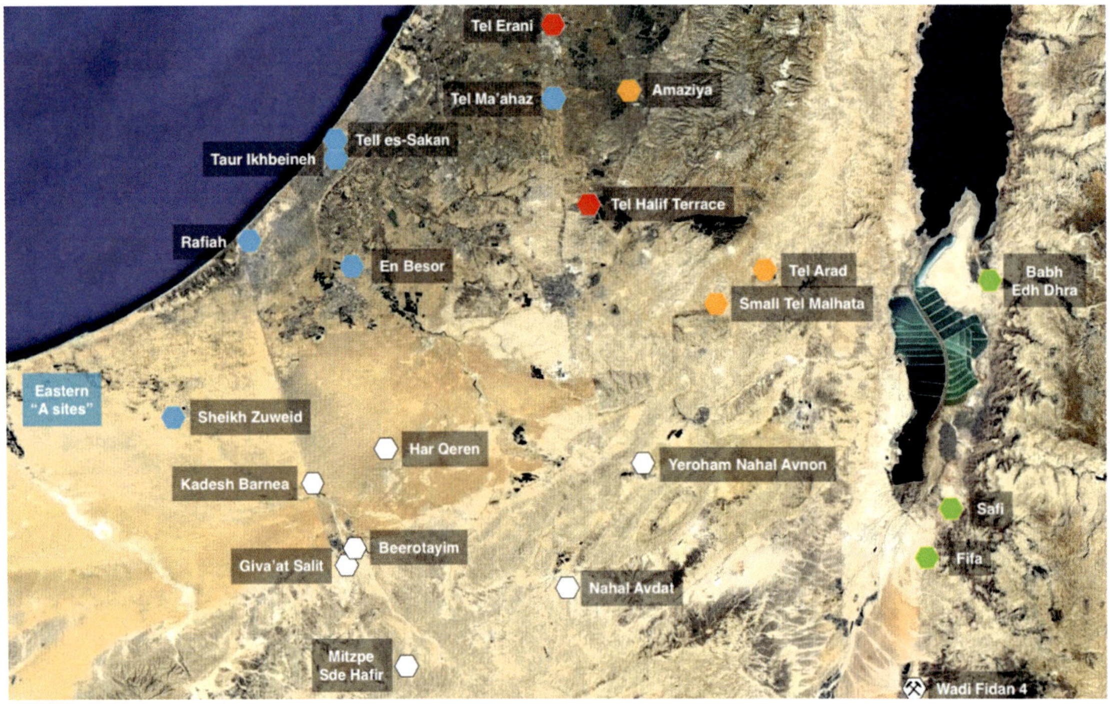

Figure 1: Map of the study region with marked mentioned key sites: sites of Egyptian character in blue, Negev desert/South Jordan/Sinai pastoral nomadic sites in white, Levantine sites in orange, Dead Sea plain sites in green, and sites where Egyptians and Levantines lived side-by-side in red. Base Map Data: Google, Landsat/Copernicus.

at Levantine centers alongside new foundations of expressly Egyptian character, and most scholars agree that evidence of Egyptian presence seems to fade in scale with distance from three core sites: Tel es-Sakan, En Besor, and Tel Ma'ahaz.[3] At sites in close proximity to these are local sedentary sites where Egyptian permanent habitation seems to have existed alongside the local population.[4] The paraphernalia of Egyptian everyday life has been identified at these latter sites, perhaps most characteristically, by the presence of Egyptian baking bowls used in bread production, sometimes in situ in hearths typologically identical to those identified at sites in Egypt.[5] Phenomena such as these may be characterized as Egyptian "home away from home" in the southwestern Levant, in what has been interpreted as enclaves and collectively—by both Yekutieli and de Miroschedji—as a regional contact zone.[6]

The Egypto-Levantine 'Contact Zone' and Evidence for Nomadic Contact

Neither Yekutieli's nor de Miroschedji's concept of a regional contact zone is explicitly defined or presented as a systematized framework, and it is in many ways difficult to test for its hard to define. Pratt defined contact zones as "social spaces in which cultures meet, clash, and grapple with each other."[7] According to Pratt's definition, contact zones are strange and uncomfortable spaces of seemingly indefinite 'struggle' in an environment of cultural encounters. They are conflicted and yet dynamic places of innovation, creation, and social and psychological generation. Ultimately, all participants in such encounters are expected to be transformed socially and psychologically by the encounter in complex ways. Pratt's definition, and the many scholarly discussions which have elaborated upon her ideas, have tended to view contact zones as the actual locales of sustained encounters between distinct cultural spheres.[8] Turner's notion of 'liminal spaces' has recently been attached in formulation to the contact zone construct to clarify and specify its usage to the 'thresholds' of encounter.[9] In these arenas of liminality, structures of order and interpretation undergo dissolution and regeneration, where new negotiated meanings are framed. This definition assumes the sustained presence of both cultural spheres within a single bounded geographic locale as a prerequisite to liminality. Thus, to propose this concept more precisely for the late 4th millennium, the Egypto-Levantine framework should entail a close examination of the exact contexts of sustained and transformative encounters.

Such sustained encounters are clearly demonstrable archaeologically in just a few cases. Egyptian enclaves were established at Tel Erani, Tel Halif Terrace, and possibly also Tel Lod, yet the 'contact zone' of Egypto-Levantine encounter, as framed by both Yekutieli and de Miroschedji, included a southern branch of interaction and encounter that extended into the Negev Highlands, based on the testimony of a few Egyptian artifacts returned from EB I nomadic campsites.[10] These finds include a fragment of a Naqada IIIa juglet with an outward folded rim from a site near Moshav Nitsane Sinai (Moshav Kadesh Barnea upon publication), and a Naqada II–III bifacial flint knife and three additional sherds of Predynastic storage jars from among scatters of structures and pens near Giv'at Salit.[11] Similar evidence for contact with Naqada II–III Egyptian society has been uncovered in excavations at Rogem Be'erotayim, a nomadic campsite near modern Ezuz, in the form of a rim sherd of an Egyptian wine jar, with imported parallels at several sites in Israel's coastal plain in the EB Ib2 and in the North Sinai, including one example dated to the EB Ib1.[12] This modicum of material testifies to an undeniable link, direct or indirect, between the nomadic pastoral society of the mid-late EB I and the edge of a developing Egyptian interaction sphere in the southern Levant.

New light on Nomadic Connections with the Egypto-Levantine Interaction Sphere

Two new datasets from recent excavations have offered fresh opportunities for exploration of the form and extent of Negev desert nomadic involvement in the late 4th-millennium Egypto-Levantine interaction sphere to the north:

1. Mitzpe Sde Hafir is an EB I site with clear Egyptian material connections located in the heart of the Negev Highlands at roughly the southern extent of the Egyptian contact corridor projected by both Yekutieli and de Miroschedji. The site was identified by Lior Schwimer of Ben-Gurion University of the Negev (BGU) and is the subject of an ongoing project directed by Yuval Yekutieli and conducted by a multidisciplinary team of researchers from the Archaeology division at BGU since 2017.
2. The EB I site of Yeroḥam—Naḥal Avnon, excavated by the Israel Antiquities Authority from 2013 to 2015 under the direction of Ron Be'eri and Emil Aljem, is situated on the northern edge of the Negev Highlands, apparently within the socio-economic spheres of both nomadic pastoralist and settled agricultural societies, including a late 4th millennium BCE Egyptian cultural component in its ceramic assemblage.

The profiles of the ceramic assemblages from both desert sites were analyzed in comparison to late EB I layers at Tel Erani, Area D3-H, where an Egyptian community apparently lived alongside the local population. Tel Erani was selected as the frame of reference for Egypto-Levantine interaction forms due to its complex stratigraphy, prolonged Egyptian habitation alongside a local Levantine population, and evident evolution in the form relations between these groups over time and across archaeological layers. Variance in ceramic assemblages from different stages of Egypto-Levantine interaction at Tel Erani was employed to model signatures of various forms of cultural contact between Egyptians and Levantines. These signatures were then used as a chrono-cultural yardstick by which to compare interaction dynamics at Mitzpe Sde Hafir and Yeroḥam—Naḥal Avnon.[13]

Ceramic Coding and Assemblage Profiles

The ceramic coding system applied by Yekutieli to EB I datasets of North Sinai was developed and expanded.[14] Every vessel from a sample of 9279 sherds, representing 1955 vessels (henceforth MNV, i.e., minimum number of vessels) from Tel Erani, and the entire ceramic assemblages of the two desert case studies, were assigned a six-letter code incorporating key descriptive elements: function, form, plastic decoration, fabric composition by visual identification, surface decoration, and manufacturing technique. Such that the code "SWEMCA" referred to a "Large storage jar (S) with an inward-inclined neck (W) and an outward-folded, sharpened rim (E), made of clay with crushed calcium carbonate temper (M), hand-smoothed exterior (C) and wheel trace on interior (A)." The first half of the code, indicating vessel function and

cal. BC	Stratum	Layer	Chronology: Southern Levantine terminology	Chronology: Egyptian terminology (Naqadan chronology)	Important features
-	I	1	Topsoil (modern)	-	
-	II	2	EB II - EB III (?)	-	Wall 106 only
ca. 3050 - 2920	III	3	EB IB2 to EB II transition	Naqada IIIC/Dynasty 1	No imports
ca. 3050 - 3150	IV	4	EB IB2	Naqada IIIC	Small amount of imports
		5			Imports and some locally made Naqadan types (mostly jars) including baking bowls
	V	6	EB IB2	Naqada IIIB	Presence of imports, locally made Naqadan pottery as well as baking bowls in situ in ovens; imported flint material
		7			
		8			
ca. 3200 - 3150	VI	9	EB IB2 (post-'Erani C)	Naqada IIIB (?)	A few imports. Prior to Egyptian presence (?)
Unexplored					
ca. 3500 – 3250 (?)	At least two strata	Several layers	EB IA2 – IB1	Naqada IIC – IIIA	Fortifications in Areas P/Q and N Pillared building in Area D

Figure 2: Tel Erani chronology and characterization of strata and layers. Adapted from a table by Marcin Czarnowicz (Czarnowicz *et al.* 2016, Table 1).

form, allows the quantification of typological and cultural features, while the second half, signifying vessel technology and decoration, provides access to the subtleties of cultural transference. In this manner, the constructed database allows us to generate complex statistical queries and quantitative multivariate analyses of traditionally qualitative archaeological parameters. More specifically, the database will provide approximations for the degree of hybridization. It will do so, for instance, by tracing the occurrence of straw-tempered (an Egyptian technique) Levantine vessels or wheel-thrown (a primarily Levantine technique) Egyptian vessels across layers.

Establishing Ceramic Assemblage Profiles at Tel Erani

Five seasons of collaborative excavations from 2013 to 2019 by BGU and the Jagiellonian University, Krakow, at Tel Erani revealed a multi-phase sequence of Egypto-Levantine encounter in Area D3-H, from the beginnings of the Egyptian incursion at the site to the Early Bronze Age (EB) II period.[15] The stratigraphy of Area D3-H was divided into six archaeological strata (Fig. 2), which refer to major cultural horizons such as the sudden appearance of much Egyptian material and its equally sudden disappearance, and layers, sub-units which refer to smaller-scale changes in architectural layout and repairs. The deepest of these, Stratum VI, corresponds to a destruction layer that contained mostly local ceramic types that can be dated to the late EB Ib1 'Erani C' phase at the site. The four layers (8 to 5) of Strata IV and V are the principal ones associated with the Egyptian colony, in which imported and 'hybrid' ceramic types reach a peak proportion within the entire assemblage. Stratum III is not well understood, based on only fragmentary remains which survived in the western part of Area D3-H.[16]

An assemblage of several thousand indicative sherds was recovered from the above strata. For the purposes of this study, a large ceramic sample (9279 sherds) from selected loci was sorted and classified according to the above outlined coding system. Loci were selected from what have been interpreted as internal and adjacent external areas associated with the main architectural complex in Squares J11 and J12 as well as the balk J12/K12, which underwent at least three major construction phases throughout the duration of the Egyptian colony.[17] Preference was given to a selection of the main living floors associated with each layer, while a few representative loci were taken from various depths of the destruction layer in Square J12. Fig. 3 shows the quantities of vessels (MNV) classified by layer in the internal and external areas. Following collation of the database, statistical queries have been performed related to functional distributions,

	Exterior Space MNV	Interior Space MNV
5	403	164
6	222	249
7	108	122
8	188	301
9	81	117

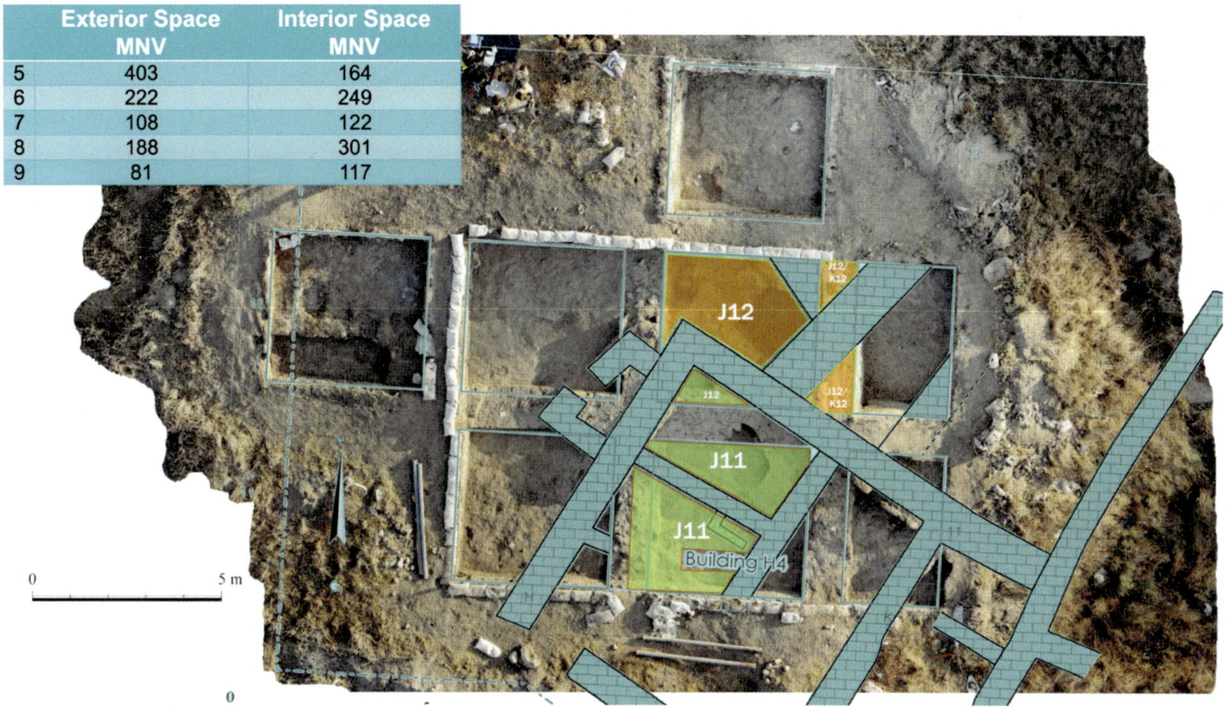

Figure 3: Area D3-H at the end of the 2015 BGU-JU excavation season, with sampling information: internal space in green and external space in orange; MNV counts for layers in each space included in the table. Aerial photography by Marcin Czarnowicz.

material compositions, technological change, and spatial considerations regarding cultural provenance and the extent of hybridization. The results of these queries were analyzed against a range of possibilities for the form of colonial enterprise at the site and the nature of the encounter between Egyptians and locals in Area D3-H.

Results of the ceramic-coding statistical analysis convey a clear narrative for the development of engagement between Egyptians and Levantines in colonial encounters at Tel Erani:

Layer 9, the deepest layer in the sequence, prior to sustained Egyptian habitation at the site, contained a meager ratio of Egyptian material and almost no hybridity in forms, fabric composition, decoration, or manufacturing process.

Layer 8 showed a sudden dramatic increase in Egyptian material in both the internal and external areas, accompanied by hybridity across the spectrum of ceramic traditions, including the transferral of wheel manufacturing and white wash decoration.

Layer 7 returned an unexpected result in that hybridity suddenly diminished to almost complete elimination, perhaps suggesting a phase of tension and social anxiety.

Layer 6 was accompanied by new social divisions, with a clear functional division of space between the internal areas dominated by serving and storage and external areas oriented towards cooking. Also, the Levantine vessels significantly decreased in the internal space while dramatically increasing in the external area. Hybridity seems to have increased dramatically in this phase to more than double proportionally to that of Layer 8. The most convincing explanation for the rise in hybridity in this layer is that establishing clear social and spatial boundaries between Levantines and Egyptians caused a flourishing of relations.

Layer 5 corresponds to the end of the Egyptian colony, but the ratio of Egyptian vessels in the assemblage remained high and witnessed even greater hybridity levels, which increased overall by roughly 30%. It is my suggestion that fragmenting definitions of social relations and possibly also systems of control in this phase brought out much creativity and innovations.

The variation in ceramic assemblage profiles for the external and internal areas at Tel Erani D3-H revealed not only a clear trajectory of developmental change in the pattern of relations (Fig. 4), but it established expected signatures in the ceramic

Trajectory		
IV	5	Flexible (fragmenting?) relations
	6	Social/functional division of space
V	7	Clear demarcation of social boundaries
	8	Flexible relations
VI	9	Egyptian Arrival

Figure 4: Developmental trajectory of Egypto-Levantine colonial encounter at Tel Erani.

database for these forms of relations for comparison with the desert zone sites examined here.

1. Mitzpe Sde Hafir

The site of Mitzpe Sde Hafir is impressive in scale among desert sites of the period, contained within 2–3 ha of a rocky hillside on a ridge at the southwestern edge of the fertile plateau of Sde Hafir in the Western Negev highlands around 10 km south of the modern-day village of Ezuz. Local vegetation is Irano-Turanian steppe type, and the immediate vicinity of Sde Hafir is particularly fertile; undoubtedly a strategic location for nomadic tribes of the region, providing opportunities for pasture, hunting, and foraging. To the west lies Nahal Horsha and Nahal Ezuz, with Har Ezuz to the southwest. Directly south of the site is Har Hamran, and to the north, the many streambeds of the hills and valleys surrounding Sde Hafir meet Nahal Nitsana as the Negev highlands descend into the area of sand dunes beyond Nitsana and Moshav Nitsane Sinai. The site is carved through its middle by a wadi draining into the fertile plateau of Sde Hafir immediately to the east, which is well irrigated by the many other streambeds feeding down from the surrounding hillside (Fig. 5). At the north end of the site, a small network of structures is in what seems to be a typical pen-and-room formation common among nomadic pastoralists of the Negev highlands during the 5th–3rd millennia BCE. Three rock-art panels are carved into the surface of large iron-rich stones in the cluster of boulders located at the lower central and south-eastern edge of the site, behind which the scatter of collapsed structures and tumuli rise like a theatre across the hillside. The orientations of the rock-art panels seem to carry semiotic significance suggestive of the possible designation of a 'precinct' of social or cultic function. That the location was a center of funerary activity at some stage and evidently in multiple phases over time adds to the impression that the site can be identified as a gathering place of an unusual scale for nomadic groups of the Western Negev. The relative quantity and scale of non-domestic features suggest that primary functions at the site diverge from the typical activities of pastoralist groups of the 4th–early 3rd millennium BCE.

Survey and Excavations, 2017–Present

Following surveys at the site that yielded several EB I sherds, including an Egyptian component, excavations were conducted in two main sub-areas of the site: an area of pen-and-room type structures (Area H1) and an area to the north of the structures (Area H2) adjacent to a locus where much flint debitage and some tools had been identified on the surface. The structures yielded meager finds, but unusually rich deposits were identified in the latter area , including a stratigraphic construction sequence and activity layers, an installation, burnt areas, and local and imported ceramics (with an Egyptian component, flint tools, and caprid bones).

Excavations were conducted to almost a meter at the deepest point, with a sequence of occupation layers around a main architectural feature of undetermined function constructed of at least five courses of fieldstones organized along a very straight line on the northern face and with the non-linear side of the stones facing south. The feature resembles a terrace construction, but it is as yet unclear if this was indeed its function. Carbon samples from both sides of the structure were taken with two dates from the southern side, returning dates clearly within the EB Ib range, and one date from the northern side of the main wall returning a late Chalcolithic date.[18] This latter result is somewhat problematic as ceramic finds both above and below correspond to the EB I, with both local and Egyptian sherds, and may result from the so-called "old wood effect."

Ceramic Typology

Most of the ceramic material from the Mitzpe Sde Hafir were non-indicative body sherds, which only gave an impression of vessel size without further particular stylistic characteristics. Internal surface treatments showed, in most cases, whether a vessel was closed or open, and the rough, poorly fired and highly friable holemouth jars characteristic of EB

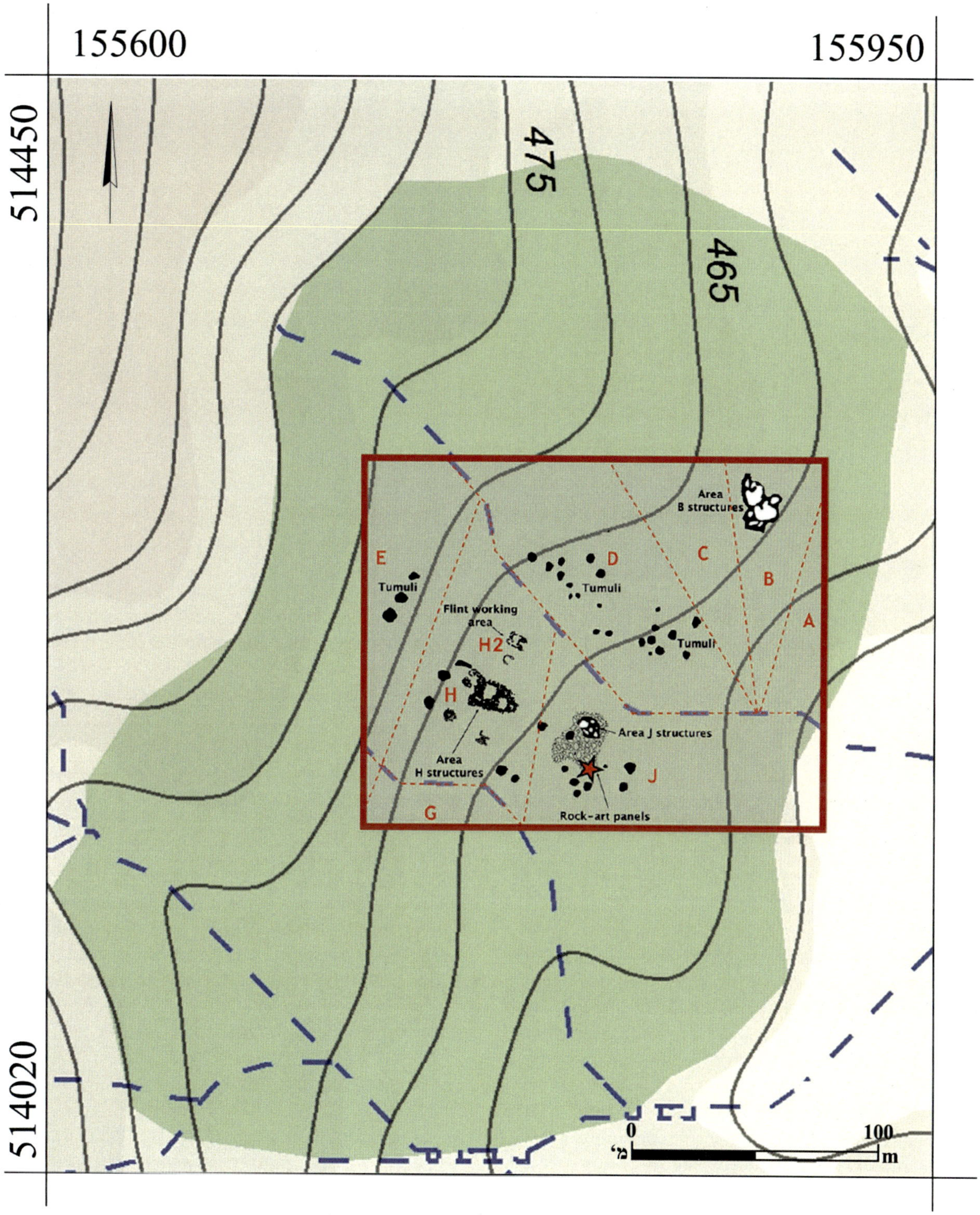

FIGURE 5: Plan of Mitzpe Sde Hafir survey and excavation areas. Map created by Eli Cohen-Sasson.

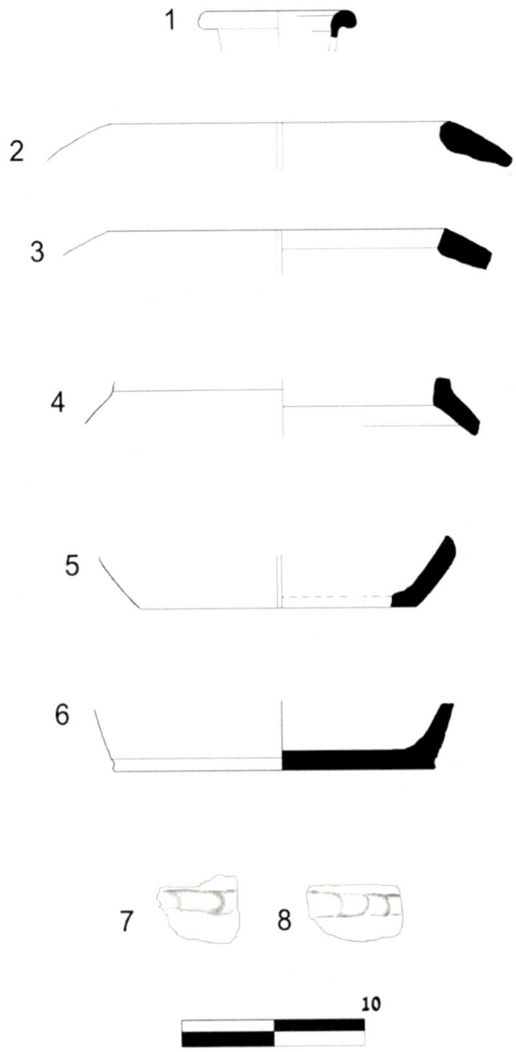

FIGURE 6: Sample of indicative sherds collected from Mitzpe Sde Hafir. Illustrated by Eli Cohen-Sasson.

desert sites were easily distinguishable from body sherds alone. The range of indicative sherds is shown in FIG. 6. The range of types is fairly limited, with the culturally characteristic Levantine assemblage made up mainly of holemouth jars that may have been made locally in the Negev and storage jars with unpreserved rims. Base diameters indicate that a number of the storage jars were of considerable size. A few rope-decorated body sherds were located, most clearly belonging to holemouth jars, but two examples belonging to storage jars composed of well-fired fabrics with calcite and grog inclusions and well-levigated clay probably originated in the Shephelah region.

FIGURE 7: Sample of Egyptian sherds from Mitzpe Sde Hafir. Photography by Yevgeny Ostrovsky.

The sherds of Egyptian pottery (FIG. 7) belong almost entirely to medium- and large-sized closed storage vessels, although rims are not preserved, except in the case of one small juglet, probably drop-shaped, although only the rim was found (FIG. 6:1). Interestingly, although this vessel is typologically characteristic of the Naqada III period, it seems to have been made using clay local to the Shephelah region, indicating a connection with Egyptians living in the southwestern Levant during the late 4th millennium BCE.

The same coding system applied to the ceramic assemblage retrieved from a sample of loci in Area D3-H at Tel Erani was applied to the entire ceramic assemblage from all surveys and excavations carried out at Mitzpe Sde Hafir to date, totaling around 324 sherds in total, among which 67 distinct vessels (MNV) were identified.

FUNCTIONAL DISTRIBUTION ANALYSIS AND REGIONAL COMPARISONS

The proportional functional distribution of vessel types at Mitzpe Sde Hafir is unlike other desert sites, which usually have an extremely dominant cooking component of coarse holemouths (FIGS. 8-9).[19] The substantial storage feature at Mitzpe Sde Hafir corresponds more closely to that of sedentary sites and particularly those involved in intensive trade

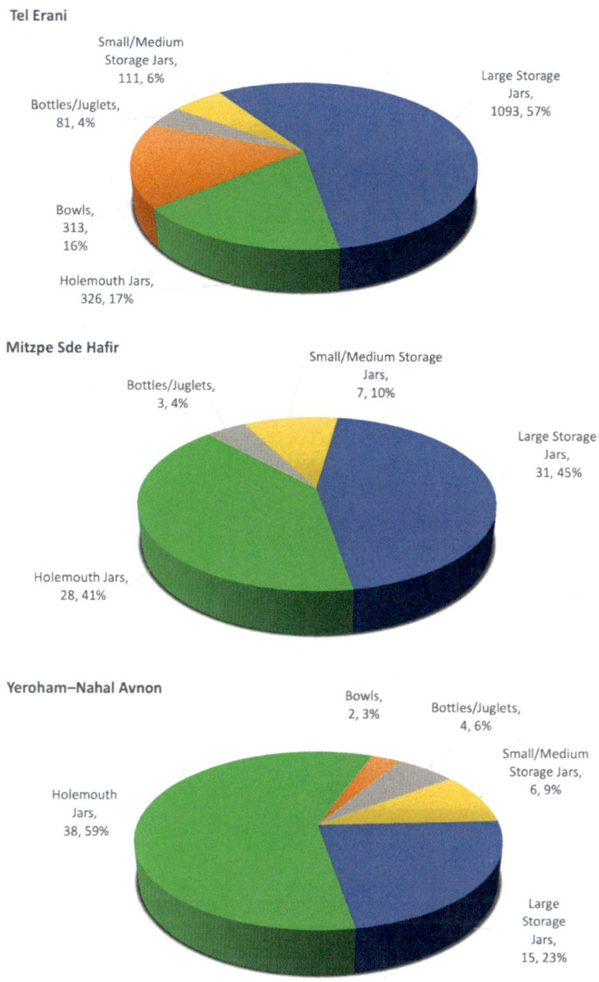

Figure 8: Comparison of the functional distribution of the entire Tel Erani ceramic sample and the ceramic assemblages from Mitzpe Sde Hafir and Yeroḥam—Naḥal Avnon.

mechanisms such as Tel Erani and Tel Arad in the EB I. The storage component even proportionally exceeds that of Tel Arad Stratum IV (Fig. 9).[20] It is lower than that of EB I north Sinai sites, which were evidently trading stations (Fig. 9).[21] The imported Egyptian and Shephelah/Judean Hills pottery classes at Mitzpe Sde Hafir are entirely composed of storage vessels indicating a clear exchange economy at the site. Likewise, there are very few examples of storage vessels composed of fabrics that could have been obtained locally in the Negev (Fig. 10). The large number of storage vessels indicates imports exceeding those that could have been transported by EB I Negev Highland nomadic groups under normal circumstances, with implications for both the mobility of the groups utilizing the site at Mitzpe Sde Hafir, and their connectivity.

Fabric Distribution Analysis

Four main fabric groups identified at Mitzpe Sde Hafir, with considerable variation in the use of temper, were confirmed petrographically with the help of Yarden Pagelson and Prof. Yuval Goren's microarchaeology lab at BGU.[22] These groups show diverse links with four regions beyond the immediate environs of the Negev Highlands: Egypt, the sedentary Levantine spheres of the Shephelah and the Judean Hills, as well as the Arava (probably in the region of Faynan). The latter group was made up mostly of fabrics with arkose sand inclusions, a granitic temper well known from the site of Wadi Fidan 4.

Red painted pottery from the sedentary Levantine zone was also identified with Motza dolomitic clay fabric, indicating clear connections with this region.[23] Red painted pottery and vessels composed of Motza clay fabric were both small but consistent components in the Tel Erani assemblage in all layers.[24]

The total quantity of pottery retrieved from the small archaeological exposure at Mitzpe Sde Hafir is highly unusual for a site within the desert sphere, and the ratio of imported pottery is especially remarkable. Vessels from Egypt and Jordan total more than one-third of the MNV (see Fig. 11), and, if the Shephelah/Judean Hills component is included, imported fabrics make up over half of the ceramic assemblage. As with the functional analysis, these results seem to support the impression of a desert site with an emphasis on connectivity and exchange.

Decoration Distribution Analysis

There is a strong similarity between the distributions of exterior decoration types between the local and Egyptian components of the Mitzpe Sde Hafir assemblage and those of Tel Erani Layer 9, with close comparability to those of Layer 8 (Fig. 12). Plain-smoothed vessels are predominant, followed by red- and white-slipped, accompanied by a few red-painted vessels. The Egyptian vessels in both Miẓpe Sede Ḥafir and Tel Erani Layer 9 also manifest the same pattern: Most of them are plain-smoothed, while the remainder is red-slipped. The same is largely true in Layer 8, especially for the Levantine vessels.

Layer 9 in D3-H at Tel Erani was a phase of probably relatively intensive trade with Egypt, as indicated by the presence of a significant quantity of imports. The extreme dominance of plain-smoothed

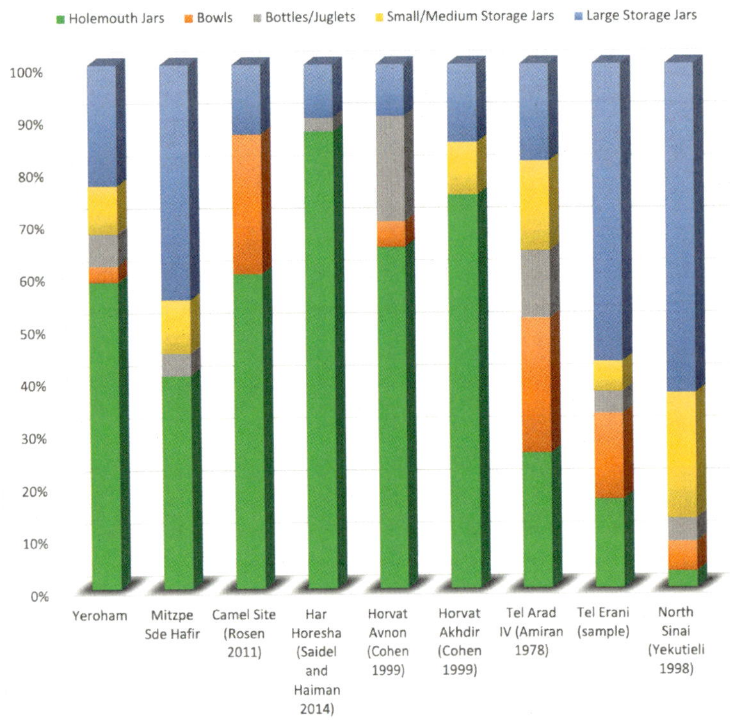

Figure 9: Multi-site comparison of ceramic assemblage functional distributions. Data taken from published excavations. A random sample of 70 vessels was selected from Tel Arad, Stratum IV, and 150 vessels from EB I sites in the North Sinai survey.

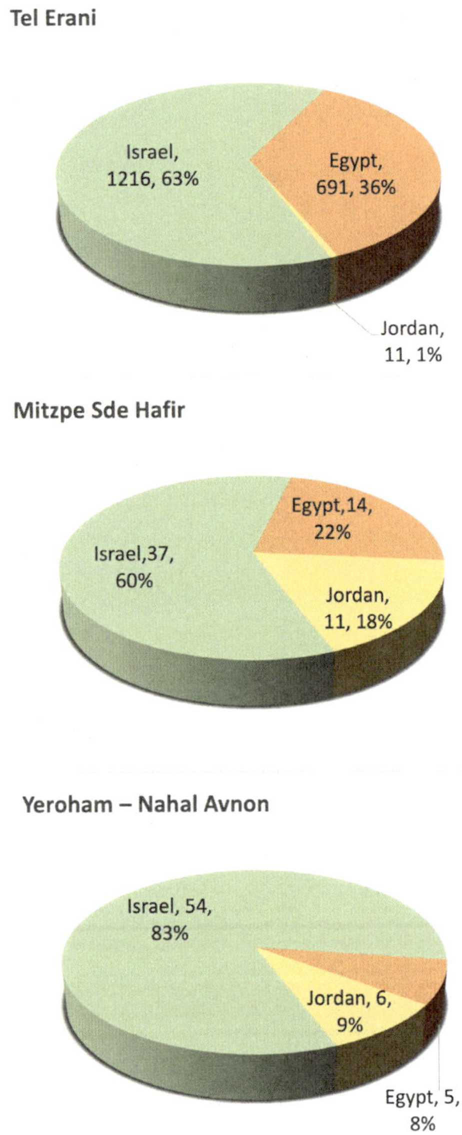

Figure 11: Comparison of fabric origins/traditions distribution in ceramic assemblages from Tel Erani (entire sample), Mitzpe Sde Hafir, and Yeroḥam—Naḥal Avnon.

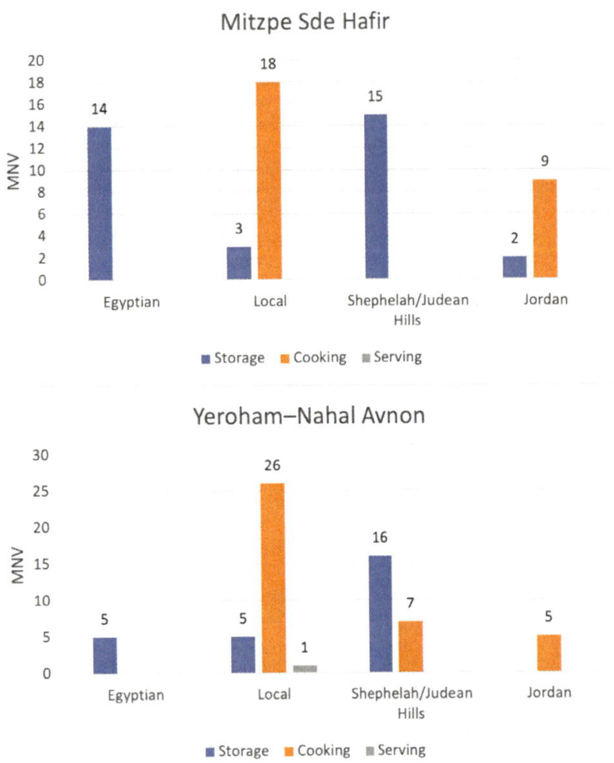

Figure 10: Ceramic assemblage functional distribution by fabric origin/tradition at Mitzpe Sde Hafir and Yeroḥam—Naḥal Avnon.

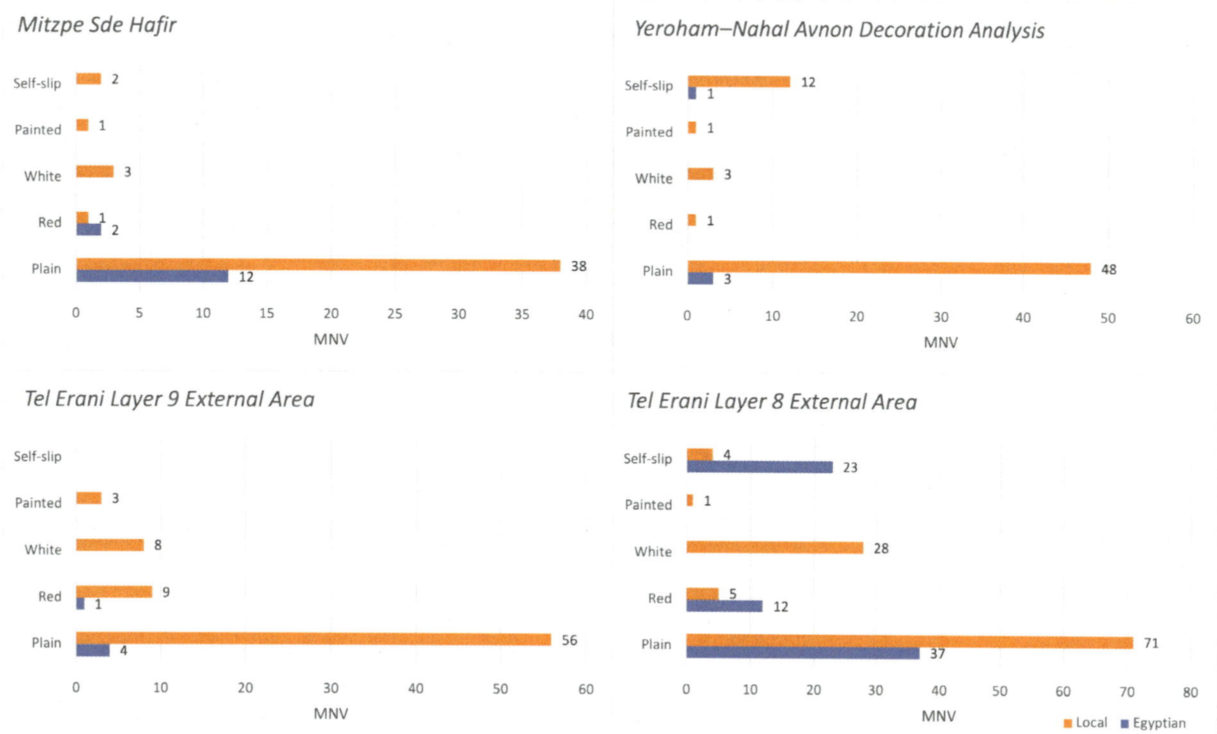

FIGURE 12: Comparison of decoration-type distributions in ceramic assemblages from Mitzpe Sde Hafir, Yeroḥam—Naḥal Avnon, and Tel Erani Layers 9 and 8.

vessels probably reflects this economic rather than stylistic orientation in manufacturing practice. The layer may predate the arrival of the Egyptian community that settled at the site, although to date, it was only investigated in a small exposure in Area D3-H, and its stratigraphic boundary with Layer 8 has not yet been clearly defined. Layer 9 exhibited almost no hybridity limited to Egyptian-type vessels made using local fabrics. The similarity of the decoration distributions between Mitzpe Sde Hafir and Tel Erani D3-H Layers 8 and 9 seems to indicate that similar kinds of relations with Egyptians were at play, complemented by the very high ratio of Egyptian imports (not hybridized). In fact, the overall ratio of Egyptian imports in the Mitzpe Sde Hafir assemblage far exceeds that of Tel Erani layer 9 and may bear a closer comparison to Layer 8. The most likely scenario is that the correspondence with both layers indicates contemporaneity with at least the foundational stages of the colony at Tel Erani.

Other Relevant Finds

In addition to the ceramic dataset, the flint assemblage from the excavated areas, mostly made up of ad hoc blades and small amounts of debitage, also contained some noteworthy elements. Almost all loci contained at least one item that could be said to belong to the family of tabular or fan scrapers (FIG. 13). There is remarkable variation in size, shape, and material selection within these forms, ranging from less than 3.5cm to 12cm in length. Unusual among the chipped stone assemblage is the presence of three Canaanean blade fragments (Fig. 14), a small quantity but very significant considering the modest archaeological exposure, testifying to connections with the sedentary zone to the north.[25] Ground stone tools, probably for processing agricultural products, were also present in surface finds and excavated areas.

Overall Characterization

The ceramic assemblage from Mitzpe Sde Hafir contains an unusually large quantity of EB I pottery for a Negev desert site of this period and especially unusual quantities of Egyptian (Naqada II–III) pottery. The archaeological stratigraphy for an EB I desert site is also unusually substantial, as yet mostly unexplored. There are phenomenological indications that the site functioned as a 'gathering place' for Negev desert communities of the region. A clear storage orientation in ceramics and a tentative interpretation of architectural storage units may indicate a focus on exchange/redistribution. There are also possible indications of small-scale agricultural activity at the site in chipped and ground stone tool assemblages, including glossy Canaanean blades imported from the Shephelah region and grinding stones. Overall, it seems that activities at Mitzpe Sde Hafir represent a diverse desert economy.

Regarding the scale and form of Egyptian contact, correspondence with Tel Erani Layer 9 vessel-decoration ratios in both Egyptian and local components and the functional distribution and quantities of Egyptian imports are indicative of regular, systematic trade links with Egyptians via the Egyptian colony. The functional distribution of Egyptian and Shephelah/Judean Hills pottery components indicates bulk exchange, probably exceeding the amount that could be transported by EB Ib Negev pastoralist groups, leading to the conclusion that Egyptian traders actually arrived at the site from the Egyptian colony in the coastal plain for the purpose of exchange. The site's clear links with Jordan, demonstrated petrographically, offer a possible indication of a role in the trade of copper and/or tabular scrapers that the Egyptians may have sought to acquire.

Figure 13: Range of tabular/fan scraper forms recovered from Mitzpe Sde Hafir. Photography by Yevgeny Ostrovsky.

Figure 14: Canaanean blade fragments from Mitzpe Sde Hafir. Photography by Yevgeny Ostrovsky.

2. Yeroḥam—Naḥal Avnon

Yeroḥam—Naḥal Avnon is situated north of the modern town of Yeroham at the northern edge of the Negev highlands. The site was identified by Yigal Israel in surveys conducted in 1992, prior to the expansion of the modern town. Small-scale initial archaeological inspections were conducted at the site in 2013–2014 by Emil Alajem, with larger-scale salvage excavations held in 2015 under the direction of Ron Be'eri and Emil Alajem. The site spreads over an area of 900 m2 on a low hill and adjacent slope around 490 m above sea level and roughly 5 m above the surrounding plain, next to the dry wadi bed of Naḥal Avnon that flows into the Yeroḥam basin. The region is arid, receiving approximately 90 mm of rainfall per annum, and there is no reliable natural water source or pasture grounds in the surrounding area.

Interaction on the Desert Fringe in Late EB I

Excavations revealed a site that was clearly not permanently occupied during the Early Bronze Age, with also no evidence for the practice of agriculture of any kind. It certainly does not fit the profile of typical campsites of Timnian pastoralists of the 4th and 3rd millennia BCE, lacking animal pens or faunal remains. It is composed of a complex of industrial installations and domestic structures (Fig. 15) that seems to have been occupied on a semi-permanent basis during these periods. No remains of substantial stone-built architecture were identified, and it is reasonable to suggest that the low stone walls acted as bases for temporary shelters built from local brush vegetation. Most of the

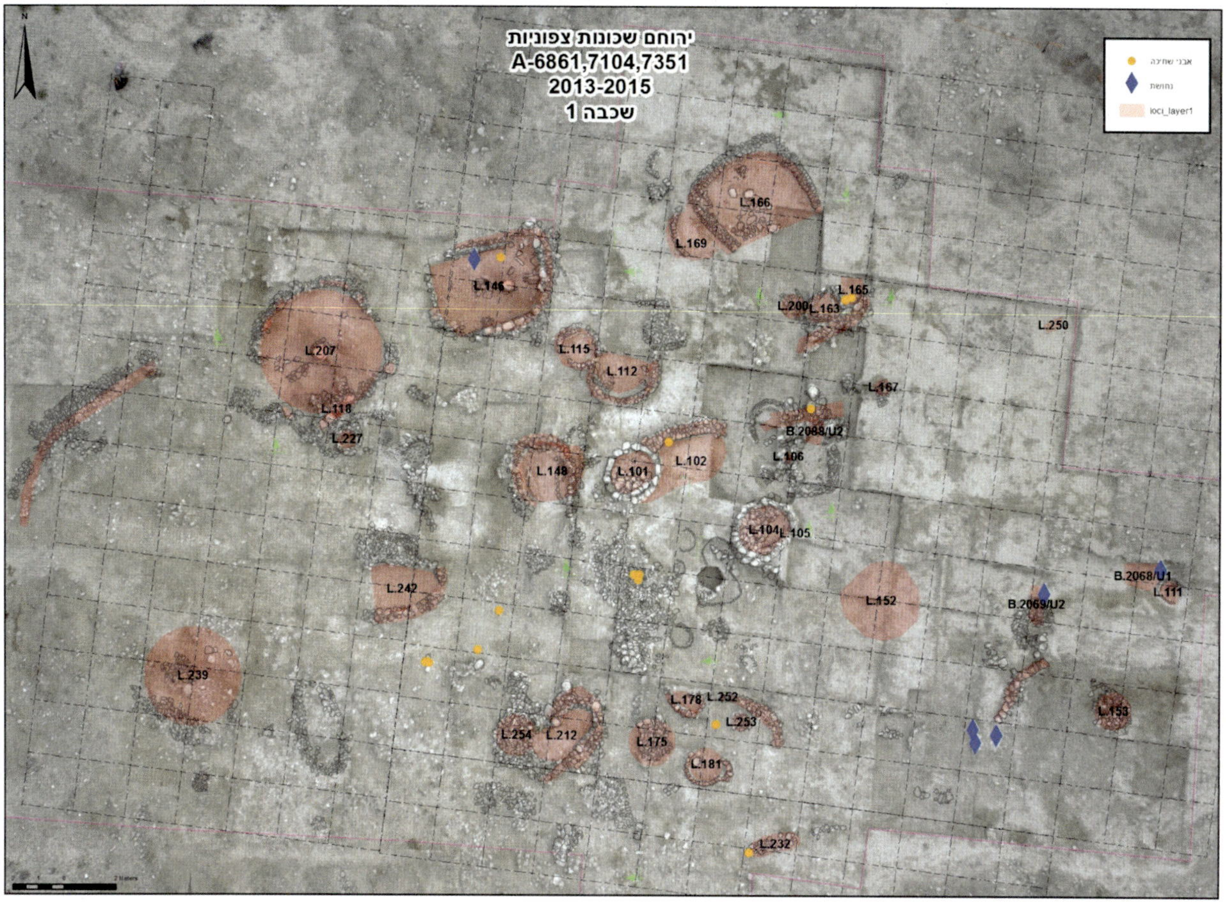

Figure 15: Aerial photo and plan of Yeroḥam Layer 2 (EB I) post-excavation. Courtesy of the Israel Antiquities Authority.

ceramic material is of an EB I–II date, mostly local, including a very small 'Erani C' component and some imported Naqada III vessels. One structure where much EB I–II pottery was found is almost rectilinear, perhaps an early form of the 'Aradian' type found at many sites in the Negev and Sinai and generally dated to the EB II period.

Four radiocarbon dates taken from areas of installations all fall early within the EB Ib, around 3300 BCE, but there are hints of copper processing in the same areas of the site during later periods with the retrieval of a copper ingot of a type typical of those from Jordan during the Intermediate Bronze Age (henceforth, IBA).[26] Due to the abundance of EB I material and the early Carbon 14 results, as well as clear connections with Nilotic society and Levantine sedentary society of the coastal plain during the EB I, the site offers an unusual insight into connectivity during a developmental stage of 'multi-resource' nomadism in connection with the settled zone.[27] Its location situated far from natural water sources along a natural route from the northern Arava to the coastal plain region of En Besor via the Yeroham basin, as well as the abundant quantities of locally manufactured grinding stones retrieved from the site, indicate that trade and perhaps industry were the principal motivations for the site's establishment.

The Ceramic Assemblage

A total of 83 indicative sherds belonging to a minimum number of 66 distinct vessels were recovered from loci dated to the EB I phase at Yeroḥam—Naḥal Avnon. The general character of the majority of the ceramic assemblage is coarse, hand-smoothed wares with poorly sorted sand inclusions, although more well-levigated wares also constitute a significant component. All the EB I material was analyzed after full completion of fieldwork at the site and following preliminary on-site sorting by excavators Ron Be'eri and Emil Alajem. The assemblage contained an extremely high ratio of holemouth cooking pots. However,

FIGURE 16: Egyptian bottle fragment. Courtesy of the Israel Antiquities Authority.

FIGURE 17: Egyptian globular jar fragment. Courtesy of the Israel Antiquities Authority.

imports from the Shephelah and Judean Hills identified typologically show clear connections with the southwest Levantine sedentary zone, including a loop-handled juglet and larger storage jars, some examples with wavy ledge handles. Five Egyptian vessels were identified, including a bottle (FIG. 16), a small jar with an incomplete rim (FIG. 17), two medium storage jars, and one large storage jar. All were composed of Nile clay, confirmed petrographically as true imports rather than locally manufactured wares.[28]

FUNCTIONAL DISTRIBUTION COMPARATIVE ANALYSIS

The functional distribution of vessels at Yeroḥam—Naḥal Avnon fits more the standard profile of desert campsites with around 60% cooking pots (FIGS. 8-9). Its closest parallel proportionally is the Camel site. However, the proportion of imported storage jars exceeds almost all desert sites, as reflected by petrographic analysis and the visual examination of fabrics in the entire assemblage detailed below. As with the case of Mitzpe Sde Hafir, the large number of storage vessels implies that exchange was essential to the economy of the site and, by extension, its function.

Examination of functional distribution by fabric class confirmed that the vast majority of storage jars were imported from the Shephelah and Judean Hills regions, suggesting that the site possessed strong ties to the Levantine sedentary economic sphere. Also noteworthy is the presence of holemouths apparently imported from the Judean Hills regions. The overall distribution by fabric class seems to indicate a closer connection with the culture of the sedentary Levantine zone and connections also in daily life practices such as cooking, if perhaps not serving (FIG. 10).

FABRIC DISTRIBUTION ANALYSIS

Five main fabric groups were identified in the assemblage showing links with Shephelah, Judean Hills, Jordan, and Egypt, as well as vessels probably manufactured locally. Imports from the Shephelah and Judean Hills show clear connections with the southwest Levantine sedentary zone (FIGS. 10-11). The five Egyptian vessels, as mentioned above, were composed of Nile clay.[29] The lack of hybridization in form or fabric defines these vessels as true imports, possibly received via down-the-line mechanisms through contacts in the Levantine sedentary sphere. In this sense, the composition of the Egyptian element corresponds most closely to Tel Erani D3-H Layer 7, which is interpreted as a period of tension between Levantines and Egyptians, with no hybridity and clearly established boundaries between cultures.

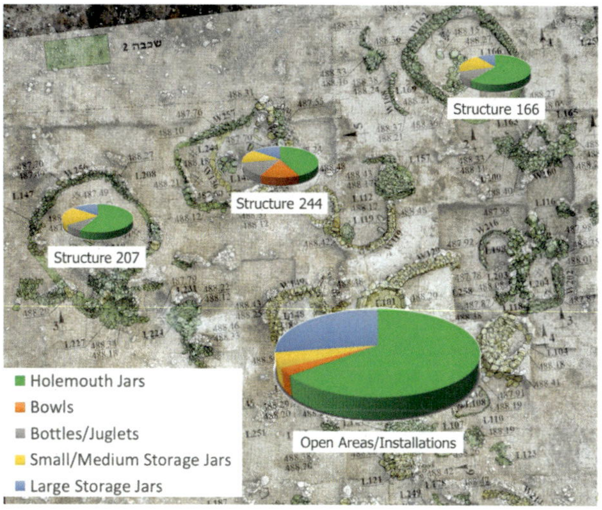

FIGURE 18: Intra-site vessel distribution.

As with the case of Mitzpe Sde Hafir, the fabric distribution shows a clear link with the eastern side of the Arabah valley and specifically the region of Faynan, establishing a possible driving force for the economic connections between this site situated clearly within the desert economy but strongly connected to the sedentary world. The IB layer at Yeroḥam—Naḥal Avnon contained a few copper artifacts, and it is possible that the site may have also played a role in copper exchange during the EB I period.

Ceramic Coding to Reveal Spatial Functions and Divisions

Due to the comprehensive fieldwork carried out at Yeroḥam—Naḥal Avnon, with the site excavated almost in its entirety, it was possible to perform more detailed spatial queries using the ceramic database for the EB I phase. Essentially, proportional distribution of function, cultural provenance, and material composition could be considered across different areas of the site, revealing implied divisions of functional and social space.

A comparative analysis was conducted on the percentage distribution of vessel types in the three main structures of Layer 2 (Structures 166, 207, and 244) and the surrounding open areas and installations (Fig. 18). The results support the interpretation of the three structures as the domestic hub of the site during the EB I phase, with a much greater ratio of serving wares and small/medium storage vessels (31%). Vessels from surrounding open areas and installations were almost exclusively holemouth jars (64%) and large storage jars (38%), supporting the interpretation of the function of these spaces as areas of industrial activities, waste disposal, and cooking.

Most imported vessels were located within or immediately adjacent to the three structures, and all the Egyptian vessels were found in the vicinity of Structures 207 and 244, possibly indicating a functional division of external relations with the domestic spaces. Structure 166 may have been preserved as a purely 'local' and 'domestic' environment, while business was conducted with outsiders in Structures 207 and 244. The site's overall layout with the three domestic structures at the northeastern edge, enclosing the scatter of installations and pits between them and the dry wadi bed opposite, may have a protective significance. The domestic structures were positioned on the edge of the site, closest to the Egypto-Levantine interaction sphere to the northeast with which the site apparently conducted an exchange relationship, perhaps further indicating a certain amount of social anxiety in these exchanges. The notion of explicit definitional division of spaces and the indications of social anxiety lend further credence to the concept suggested above, that is, that relations between desert groups at Yeroham and the Egypto-Levantine interaction sphere to the north existed on a similar basis to Egypto-Levantine interactions in Tel Erani Layer 7.

Decoration Distribution Analysis

The range of exterior surface decorations at Yeroḥam—Naḥal Avnon in the Levantine cultural component is notably similar to Tel Erani Layer 8, with a possible chronological implication in the stages of stylistic development (Fig. 12). This early period in the Egyptian colony would also fit well with radiocarbon dates obtained from Yeroḥam—Naḥal Avnon. The comparison also reveals a clear alignment between the cultural and particularly stylistic spheres of Yeroḥam—Naḥal Avnon and the Shephelah region of Tel Erani. These sites were undoubtedly connected, if not directly, then certainly as part of the same social system.

General Summary and Implications

It is clear from the above results that Yeroḥam—Naḥal Avnon was a site embedded in the desert economy, although, as with Mitzpe Sde Hafir, it does not fit the typical profile of EB I–II pastoral nomadic encampments of the Negev. With no evidence of stabling of herds, very few animal bones, an absence of sickle segments suggesting no agricultural practice, and a geographical situation remote from the nearest water sources, the economy and subsistence of the site remain an enigma. It is certainly evident that only periodic use of the site was possible, although it also seems clear that it did not function as a pastoral camp. There is evidence of industrial activity at the site, including grinding stones, a few copper fragments, and various poorly defined installations, and its focus is at present obscure.

Agricultural goods were evidently processed for consumption at the site in food-preparation areas, and storage jars from Israel's southern coastal plain and Judean Hills indicate that the site played an important role in the exchanges between nomadic and Levantine settled communities. The relatively small Egyptian component may be best explained by indirect exchange mechanisms. Limestone grinding stones, probably manufactured in Makhtesh Ramon offer a hint as to the substance of exchange, alongside typological and material links with Jordan in the pottery assemblage. The site may have played some role in the exchange of copper or the bitumen trade.

Based on the above evidence, the most likely explanation seems to be one of two possibilities: the site was either founded by groups from the settled zone for the purpose of exchange with nomadic tribes or represents an early example of an emergent intermediary class from within the nomadic world. The above-described factor of social anxiety in encounters, expressed in the spatial organization of domestic structures and apparently directed towards the settled zone, seems to lend more weight to the latter suggestion that the site was a foundation, an emergent nomadic social sector engaged primarily in desert-sown exchanges. This phenomenon has many known ethnological parallels, such as among the Basseri of South Persia[30] or the Shammar of North Arabia,[31] situations in which elites emerged from nomadic societies as a result of wealth accumulation born out of exchanges with sedentary societies. For these groups, their ability to traverse both worlds became social currency.

Such a developmental trajectory for pastoral nomadic populations has been posited for EB II pastoral nomads of the Negev and Sinai, with Arad framed as the sedentarization of an elite sedentary merchant sector specializing in trade with regions to the north.[32] The archaeological evidence, both from Arad itself and 'Aradian' outposts in the Negev and Sinai, seems to reflect a reverse process of southward intrusion of sedentary society into the desert regions.[33] However, that does not preclude the possibility that a small elite class may have emerged as intermediaries either in the desert zone itself or in a permanent sedentary role at Arad. A similar process has also been proposed for nomadic sedentarization in the Negev Highlands during the IBA.[34] Yeroḥam—Naḥal Avnon may represent a precursor to these later processes.

Two "Zones" of Nomadic Contact During the EB Ib Period

The analysis of the two desert zone case studies and their comparison of their ceramic assemblages with layers of Egypto-Levantine interactions at Tel Erani revealed two distinct arenas of connectivity with separate regional and perhaps also chronological associations (Fig. 19). The site of Mitzpe Sde Hafir seems to be situated at the southernmost extent (as far as is presently known) of a contact corridor stretching from the Egyptian colony in the Mediterranean littoral and northeastern Sinai into the Western Negev Highlands. Yeroḥam—Naḥal Avnon seems conversely more integrated with the Levantine sedentary economy while apparently socially remaining situated within the sphere of Negev desert pastoral nomadic tribes. These are both claims which demand further explanation and elaboration.

Western Negev Highlands

Based on the very high ratio of Egyptian pottery uncovered in the small archaeological exposure of Mitzpe Sde Hafir, as well as the presence of an Egyptian style vessel made using local Shephelah region clays, it seems clear that Mitzpe Sde Hafir was connected to the core region of Egyptian activity in the Mediterranean littoral and/or sites of primarily Egyptian character in northeastern Sinai. Furthermore, the apparently large volumes of products implied by the dominance of the storage component among the imports suggest that Egyptians probably had arrived at Mitzpe Sde Hafir. The interpretation of a "contact corridor" by which expeditions of Egyptian traders would have arrived at Mitzpe Sde Hafir further explains the scattering of small quantities of Egyptian materials at sites in

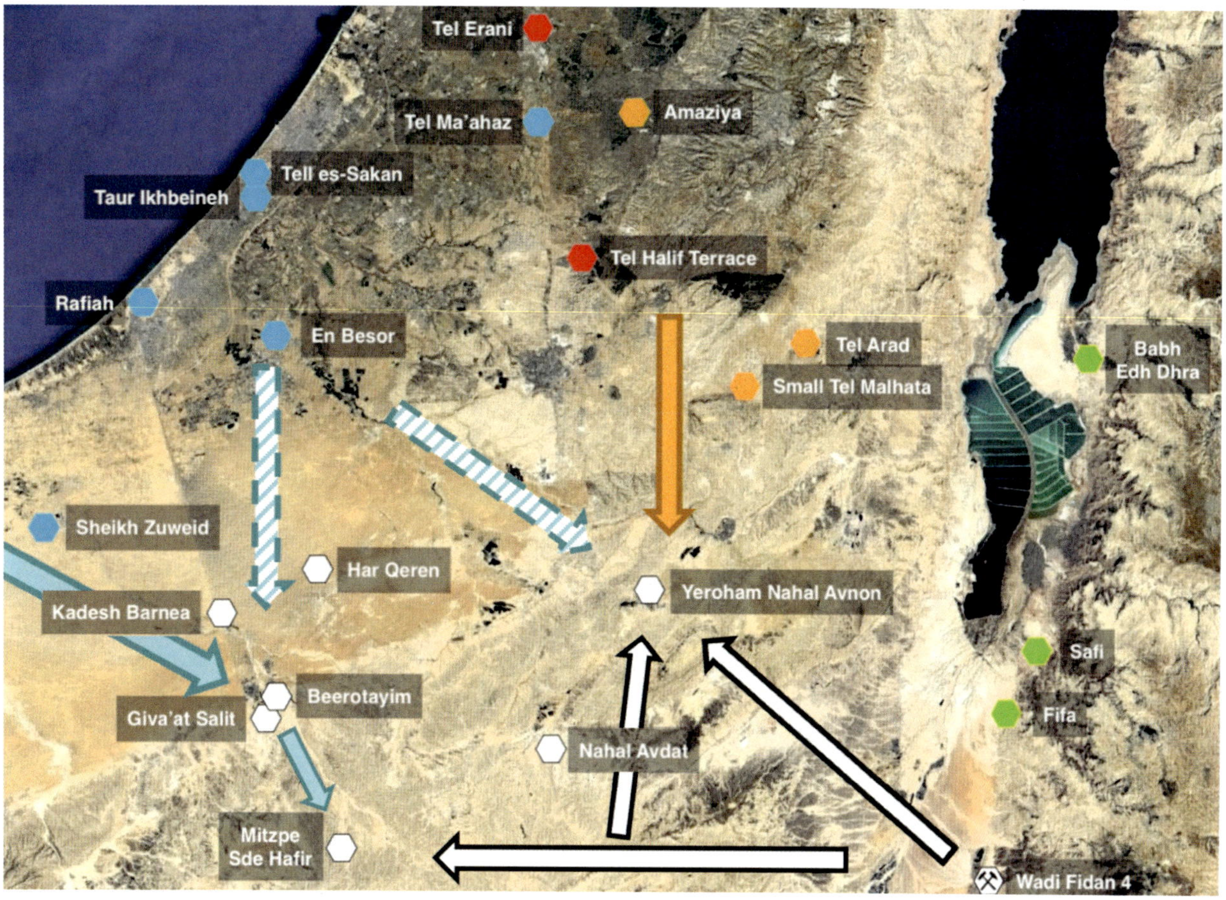

Figure 19: Model for two zones of nomadic connectivity in the Negev desert. Blue arrows show Egyptian access to desert products (striped, blue arrows are potential additional access routes). Orange arrows show a Levantine sedentary access route to desert products at Yeroḥam—Naḥal Avnon. White arrows show probable movements of desert products within the Timnian sphere.

the intervening region: Be'erotayim, Giv'at Salit, and Kadesh Barne'a.[35]

Based on evident contacts with South Jordan in the region of Faynan, it seems likely that desert products, perhaps including copper and tabular scrapers, were the motivation for Egyptian demand. Copper exchange is not well understood in the EB Ib, but Negev nomadic involvement in copper trade has been convincingly discussed for the Chalcolithic–EB Ia and the EB II.[36] The level of contacts at Mitzpe Sde Hafir, as expressed in the ceramic assemblage profile, most closely resemble Layer 9 or 8 at Tel Erani, with a high number of Egyptian imports and low levels of hybrids. These layers at Tel Erani are the phases immediately prior to and immediately following the establishment of Egyptian permanent habitation at the site and were most likely phases of intercultural negotiation, and conceptual and material exchange.

Mitzpe Sde Hafir has a unique functional profile, represented both by the high ratio of imported storage vessels in the ceramic assemblage, implied secondary agricultural practices with sickle segments and grinding stones, an unusual overall layout, and a high ratio of tabular scrapers in the chipped stone assemblage, as well as the notable absence of certain elements typical of campsites, such as arrowheads and burins. In this sense, this site might fit the concept of a 'negotiated periphery,' with its potential for reordering and restructuring social norms and value standards.[37] In contexts of complex encounters between highly disparate cultures, and considering the inherent flexibility of nomadic lifeways, it would be expected to see considerable socio-cultural transformation or the order that might ultimately shape the unique profile of a site such as Mitzpe Sde Hafir, unparalleled in its diverse archaeological elements among contemporary desert sites. As such, the complexity of features at Mitzpe Sde Hafir, in the context of direct contacts and exchanges with Egyptian groups conducted at the site, implies a form of relations that might be suitably characterized as a "contact zone," with its accompanying features of social struggle and restructuring.

Taken together, the symbolic elements at the site, including complex iconography in the rock-art panels, the theatre-like phenomenology of the layout, and the large quantities of tabular scrapers, which have been interpreted to exhibit ritual associations in other contexts, suggest that Mitzpe Sde Hafir was a site of considerable local significance.[38] The extent of Egyptian contact at the site further implies that the site's importance extended well beyond the nomadic sphere.

Central Negev Highlands

A complex impression is conveyed by the data processing and analysis of finds from Yeroḥam—Naḥal Avnon. As stated above, the site does not fit the profile of a pastoral nomadic campsite in its location (distant from water sources), scarcity of animal bones, absence of stabling pens, absence of any signs of agricultural practice, and its array of typologically obscure installations. However, the ceramic assemblage shows clear alignment with desert assemblages with a majority of coarse, poorly fired holemouths. Concurrently, the remainder of the assemblage shows diverse connections with Egypt, Jordan, and Levantine sedentary society, mostly large storage vessels that imply an exchange economy.

Most of the imported storage vessels originate in the Shephelah and Judean Hills and indicate that the site's main economic partners can be traced to these regions. The additional factor of a modicum of serving wares also from the Shephelah or Judean Hills suggests a further level of socio-cultural relations beyond simply materialist exchange. These data lead to the natural conclusion that the site was a dedicated locus for barter exchange of desert products for agricultural goods from the sedentary zone. The complex array of installations may have been engaged in the processing of a diversity of materials from the desert regions, including grinding stones and perhaps copper, with clear links to Faynan demonstrated in the ceramic assemblage.

The Egyptian component, represented by a small number of imports of Nile clays, is best explained as having arrived at the site indirectly via exchanges with Levantine sedentary trading partners. As such, the indirect relations with permanent Egyptian settlements in the region, carried out via second-hand economic mechanisms, were probably socio-culturally non-transformative. However, the overall integration of desert communities within local sedentary economic processes, which may in large part have catered to and been accelerated by Egyptian demand, seems to have been highly transformative for nomadic lifeways in the region.

The unusual function of Yeroḥam—Naḥal Avnon, apparently catering in some as yet undefined capacity to external exchange demands and apparently lacking any infrastructure to support pastoral nomadic subsistence, is suggestive of nomadic groups whose main occupation was commercial. As such, the case of Yeroḥam—Naḥal Avnon may represent the early emergence of an intermediary trading class from within the nomadic world, which would later reach full expression in partial settlement of a sub-sector of nomadic society at EB II Arad and the institution of a systematic exchange system. Processes of social stratification and institution of "parasocial" elites resulting from nomadic pastoral integration with sedentary economics are well documented in ethnographic contexts such as among the Yomut Turkmen, the Basseri of South Persia, and the Shammar tribes of North Arabia.[39] This model seems to provide an explanation for the overall dataset from Yeroḥam—Naḥal Avnon. Indications of social anxiety in exchanges with the outside world, identified in the spatial distribution of imports and the layout of domestic structures at the site, are further indication that the form of relations between the emergent nomadic traders and sedentary society was still in formative stages of negotiation and institution of shared orders of value.

Notably, while radiocarbon dates place Yeroḥam—Naḥal Avnon early within the EB Ib2, a comparative assessment of the ceramic assemblages from the site and layers at Tel Erani revealed a strong parallel in the distribution of vessel decoration types in the Levantine component with that of Layer 8 of D3-H, providing apparent typological support to specific phasing early in the phase of Egyptian permanent habitation in the southwestern Levant. The contemporaneity of the Egyptian arrival in the region and the emergence of the nomadic intermediary exchange activities at Yeroḥam—Naḥal Avnon is unlikely to be coincidental, with new Egyptian demands in the region likely acting as an economic stimulant for exchanges between the desert and sown.

Conclusions

Overall, Egyptian involvement in the region seems to have been highly stimulative (both directly and indirectly) to the transformation of the Negev nomadic society and the acceleration of its integration with sedentary economic systems, with additional implications for social stratification among nomadic groups. The extent of direct contacts at Mitzpe Sde Hafir also indicates that the desert economy was a far more serious motivation for Egyptian colonial enterprise in the region than has previously been appreciated. Ceramic coding is a useful means of investigating and comparing culture contact mechanisms through the construction of local and regional ceramic variation databases, processing complex statistical queries to situate datasets in relation to one another, and observing variation at multiple levels (intra-site, inter-site, regional, interregional). This methodology acts as a fertile ground for the emergence of unusual and unexpected correlations and correspondence.

Examination of the two desert sites above adds to the huge variance that is becoming visible in late 4th-millennium Egypto–Levantine encounters, even at relatively localized levels. In examining such interaction contexts, relations should be expected to change over time, even at the intra-site level, but especially across regions. The study of these kinds of relations demands the pursuit of diverse and inventive theoretical modeling, new hypotheses, and multi-level contextualization in local and regional trajectories, in which the actions and responses of individual agents are informed by the entirety of the structures and systems of which they are a part.

Acknowledgments

We express our sincere thanks to all the members of the Mitzpe Sde Hafir research team: Lior Schwimer, Dr. Eli Cohen-Sasson, Roy Galili, Yarden Pagelson, and Roi Shavit. We also thank Dr. Masatoshi Yamafuji and Dr. Taichi Kuronma for their collaboration in developing a coding system for EB I ceramics, and Dr. Ron Be'eri for his collaboration on Yeroḥam—Naḥal Avnon. We further extend our gratitude to the Israel Science Foundation for their financial support of our work at Tel Erani and Mitzpe Sde Hafir.

References

Al-Rasheed, Madawi. 1987. "The Process of Chiefdom-Formation as a Function of Nomadic/Sedentary Interaction: The Case of the Shammar Nomads of North Arabia." *The Cambridge Journal of Anthropology* 12(3): 32–40.

Amiran, Ruth. 1969. *Ancient Pottery of the Holy Land. From Its Beginnings in the Neolithic Period to the End of the Iron Age.* Jerusalem: Massada Press.

———. 1978. *Early Arad I. The Chalcolithic and Early Bronze City: First–Fifth Seasons of Excavations, 1962–1966.* Jerusalem: Israel Exploration Society.

Andelkovic, Branislav. 1995. *The Relations between Early Bronze Age I Canaanites and Upper Egyptians.* Belgrade: The University of Belgrade.

Atkins, Samuel. 2017. "A New Inter-Regional Trajectory for Interactions between Northeast Africa and the Southwest Levant during the 4th Millennium BCE." *Strata: Bulletin of the Anglo-Israel Archaeological Society* 35: 135–164.

———. 2021. *The Role of Negev Highland Pastoral Nomadic Societies in Interactions Between Nilotic and South-West Levantine Groups During the 4th and Early 3rd Millennia BC.* Ph.D. Diss. Ben Gurion University of the Negev. Beer Sheva.

Bar-Adon, Pessah. 1989. "Excavations in the Judean Desert." *Atiqot* 9: 1–91 (Hebrew).

Barth, Fredrik. 1961. *Nomads of South Persia: The Basseri Tribe of the Khamseh Confederacy.* Boston: Little Brown.

Bates, Daniel G. 1973. *Nomads and Farmers: A Study of the Yörük of Southeastern Turkey.* Anthropological Papers 52. Ann Arbor: Museum of Anthropology, University of Michigan.

Beeri, Ron, Emil Aladjem, Yael Abadi-Reiss, Katia Zutovski, Samuel Atkins, Anat Cohen-Weinberger, Johanna Regev, Elisabetta Boaretto, Omri Yagel, Yehudit Halavan and Erez Ben-Yosef. *Forthcoming* 2022. "Sites from the Early Bronze Age I and Intermediate Bronze Age Sites of Yeroḥam—Naḥal Avnon." *Atiqot.*

Beit-Arieh, Itzhaq and Ram Gophna. 1999. "The Egyptian Protodynastic (Late EB I) Site at Tel Ma'aḥaz: A Reassessment." *Tel Aviv* 26(2): 191–207. DOI: 10.1179/tav.1999.1999.2.191.

Brandl, Baruch. 1989. "Observations on the Early Bronze Age Strata of Tel Erani." In Pierre de Miroschedji (ed.), *L'urbanisation de la Palestine à l'âge du Bronze ancien: bilan et perspectives des recherches actuelles. Actes du colloque d'Emmamüs (14–20 Octobre 1986)*, 357–388. Oxford: British

Archaeological Reports.

Braun, Eliot. 2011. "Early Interaction Between Peoples of the Nile Valley and the Southern Levant." In Emily Teeter (ed.), *Before the Pyramids: The Origins of Egyptian Civilization*, 105–124. Chicago: The Oriental Institute.

———. 2014. "Reflections on the Context of a Late Dynasty 0 Egyptian Colony in the Southern Levant: Interpreting Some Evidence of Nilotic Material Culture at Select Sites in the Southern Levant (ca. 3150 BCE – ca. 2950 BCE)." In Agnieska Mącynszka (ed.), *The Nile Delta as a Centre of Cultural Interactions between Upper Egypt and the Southern Levant in the 4th Millennium BC. Proceedings of the Conference Held in the Poznan Archaeological Museum, Poznań, Poland, 21–22 June 2013*, 37–56. Studies in African Archaeology 13. Poznán: Poznań Archaeological Museum.

Ciałowicz, Krysztof, Yuval Yekutieli, and Marcin Czarnowicz (eds.). 2016. *Tel Erani I: Preliminary Report of the 2013–2015 Excavations*. Krakow: Wydanictwo Alter.

Cohen, Rudolph. 1999. *Ancient Settlement of the Central Negev* Vol. 1, Jerusalem: Israel Antiquities Authority (Hebrew).

Dunseth, Zachary C., Israel Finkelstein, and Ruth Shahack-Gross. 2018. "Intermediate Bronze Age subsistence practices in the Negev Highlands, Israel: Macro- and microarchaeological results from the sites of Ein Ziq and Nahal Boqer 66." *Journal of Archaeological Science* 19: 712-726.

Finkelstein, Israel. 1990. "Early Arad—Urbanism of the Nomads." *Zeitschrift des Deutschen Palästina-Vereins* 106: 34–50.

———. 1995. *Living on the Fringe: The Archaeology and History of the Negev, Sinai and Neighbouring Regions in Bronze and Iron Ages*. Sheffield: Monographs in Mediterranean Archaeology 6.

Finkelstein, Israel, Matthew J. Adams, Zachary C. Dunseth, and Ruth Shahack-Gross. 2018. "The Archaeology and History of the Negev and Neighbouring Areas in the Third Millennium BCE: A New Paradigm." *Tel Aviv* 45: 63–88.

Frachetti, Michael D. 2008. *Pastoralist Landscapes and Social Interaction in Bronze Age Eurasia*. Oakland, CA: University of California Press.

Czarnowicz, Marcin, Yuval Yekutieli, Agnieszka Ochał-Czarnowicz, and Martin Pasternak. 2016. "The Excavation of Area D-3." In Krzysztof M. Ciałowicz, Yuval Yekutieli, and Marcin Czarnowicz (eds.), *Tel Erani I: Preliminary Report of the 2013–2015 Excavations*, 27–44. Krakow: Wydanictwo Alter.

Gophna, Ram. 1990. "The Egyptian Pottery of 'En Besor." *Tel Aviv* 17: 144–162. DOI: 10.1179/tav.1990.1990.2.144.

Haiman, Mordechai. 1996. "Early Bronze Age IV Settlement Pattern of the Negev and Sinai Deserts: View from Small Marginal Temporary Sites." *BASOR* 303: 1–33.

Ilan, Ornit, and Michael Sebbane. 1989. "Copper Metallurgy, Trade and the Urbanization of Southern Canaan in the Chalcolithic and Early Bronze Age." In Pierre de Miroschedji (ed.), *L'urbanisation de la Palestine à l'âge du Bronze ancien. Bilan et perspectives des recherches actuelles*, 139–162. BAR International Series 527. Oxford: British Archaeological Reports.

Irons, William. 1971. "Variation in Political Stratification among the Yomut Turkmen." *Anthropological Quarterly* 44(3): 143–156. DOI: 10.2307/3316935.

———. 1974. "Nomadism as a Political Adaptation: The Case of the Yomut Turkmen." *American Ethnologist* 1(4): 635–658. DOI: 10.1525/AE.1974.1.4.02A00040.

Kansa, Eric C. 2001. *Smitten by Narmer: Ethnicity, Economy and Trade in the 4th Millennium BCE Egyptian Presence in the Southern Levant*. Ph.D. Diss., Harvard University.

Kansa, Eric and Thomas E. Levy. 2002. "Ceramics, Identity, and the Role of the State: The View from Nahal Tillah." In Edwin C.M. van den Brink and Thomas E. Levy (eds.), *Egypt and the Levant. Interrelations from the 4th through the Early 3rd Millennium B.C.E*, 190–212. London: Leicester University Press.

Kardulias, P. Nick. 1999. "Preface." In Paul Nick Kardulias (ed.), *World-Systems Theory in Practice: Leadership, Production, and Exchange*, xvii–xxi. Boulder: Rowman and Littlefield.

———. 2007. "Negotiation and Incorporation on the Margins of World-Systems: Examples from Cyprus and North America." *Journal of World-Systems Research* 13: 55–82. DOI: 10.5195/jwsr.2007.359.

Kardulias, P. Nick (ed.). 2015. *The Ecology of Pastoralism*. Boulder: University of Colorado Press.

Kempinski, Aharon and Itzhik Gilead. 1991. "New Excavations at Tel Erani: A Preliminary Report of the 1985–1988 Seasons." *Tel Aviv* 18: 164–192.

Khalil, Lufti, and Klaus Schmidt. 2009. *Prehistoric Aqaba*. Leidorf: Rahden/Westf.

Knabb, Kyle, Steven A. Rosen, Sorin Hermon, Jakob Vardi, Liora K. Horwitz, and Yuval Goren. 2018. "A Middle Timnian Nomadic Encampment on the Faynan-Beersheba Road: Excavations and Survey at Nahal Tsafit (Late 5th/Early 4th Millennia B.C.E.)." *Bulletin of the American Schools of Oriental Research* 380: 27–60.

Lehmkuhl, Ursula, Hans-Jürgen Lüsebrink, and Laurence H. McFalls (eds.). 2015a. *Of 'Contact Zones' and 'Liminal Spaces': Mapping the Everyday Life of Cultural Translation*. New York: Waxmann.

Lehmkuhl, Ursula, Hans-Jürgen Lüsebrink, and Laurence H. McFalls. 2015b. "Spaces and Practices of Diversity: An Introduction." In Ursula Lehmkuhl, Hans-Jürgen Lüsebrink, and Laurence H. McFalls (eds.). *Of 'Contact Zones' and 'Liminal Spaces': Mapping the Everyday Life of Cultural Translation*, 7–27. New York: Waxmann.

Levy, Thomas E., David Alon, Yorke Rowan, Edwin C. M. van den Brink, Caroline Grigson, Augustin Holl, Patricia Smith, Paul Goldberg, Alan J. Witten, Eric Kansa, John Moreno, Yuval Yekutieli, Naomi Porat, Jonathan Golden, Leslie Dawson, and Morag Kersel. 1997. "Egyptian-Canaanite Interaction at Nahal Tillah, Israel (ca. 4500- 3000 B.C.E.): An Interim Report on the 1994–1995 Excavations." *Bulletin of the American Schools of Oriental Research* 307: 1–52. DOI: 10.2307/1357702.

Milevski, Ianir. 2011. *Early Bronze Age Goods Exchange in the Southern Levant: A Marxist Perspective*. London: Equinox.

de Miroschedji, Pierre. 2002. "The Socio-Political Dynamics of Egyptian-Canaanite Interaction in the Early Bronze Age." In Edwin C.M. van den Brink and Thomas E. Levy (eds.), *Egypt and the Levant. Interrelations from the 4th through the Early 3rd Millennium B.C.E.*, 39–57. London and New York: Leicester University Press.

———. 2015. "Les relations entre l'Égypte et le Levant aux IVe et IIIe millénaires à la lumière des fouilles de Tell es-Sakan." *Comptes rendus des séances de l'Académie des Inscriptions et Belles-Lettres* 159(2): 1003–1038.

Morris, Ian. 1999. "Negotiated Peripherality in Iron Age Greece: Accepting and Resisting the East." In P. Nick Kardulias (ed.), *World-Systems Theory in Practice: Leadership, Production, and Exchange*, 63–84. Boulder: Rowman and Littlefield.

Oren, Eliezer and Yuval Yekutieli. 1992. "Taur Ikhbeineh: Earliest Evidence for Egyptian Interconnections." In Edwin C.M. Van den Brink (ed.), *The Nile Delta in Transition: 4th–3rd Millennium B.C.: Proceedings of the Seminar Held in Cairo, 21.–24. October 1990, at the Netherlands Institute of Archaeology and Arabic Studies*, 361–384. Tel Aviv: The Israel Exploration Society.

Pratt, Mary Louise. 1991. "Arts of the Contact Zone." *Profession* 91: 33–40.

Rosen, Steven A. *An Investigation into Early Desert Pastoralism: Excavations at the Camel Site, Negev.* Monograph 69. Los Angeles, CA: Cotsen Institute of Archaeology Press.

———. 2017. *Revolutions in the Desert: The Rise of Mobile Pastoralism in the Negev and the Arid Zones of the Southern Levant*. London: Routledge.

Rowton, Michael B. 1974. "Enclosed Nomadism." *Journal of the Economic and Social History of the Orient* 17: 1–30. DOI: 10.2307/3596248.

Saidel, Benjamin A. 2011. "The Pottery from the Camel Site." In Steven A. Rosen (ed.), *An Investigation into Early Desert Pastoralism. Excavations at the Camel Site, Negev*, 67–80. Monograph 69. Los Angeles: Cotsen Institute of Archaeology Press.

Saidel, Benjamin A., Tali Erickson-Gini, Jacob Vardi, Steven A. Rosen, Edward Maher, and Haskel Greenfield. 2006. "Test Excavations at Rogem Be'erotayim in the Western Negev." *Journal of the Israel Prehistoric Society* 36: 201–229.

Saidel, Benjamin A. and Mordechai Haiman (eds.). 2014. *Excavations in the Western Negev Highlands: Results of the Negev Emergency Survey 1978–89*. BAR International Series 2684. Oxford: Archaeopress.

Saidel, Benjamin A. and Eric J. van der Steen. 2007. *On the Fringe of Society: Archaeological and Ethnoarchaeological Perspectives on Pastoral and Agricultural Societies*. BAR International Series 1657. Oxford: Archaeopress.

Spooner, Brian. 1973. *The Cultural Ecology of Pastoral Nomads*. Reading, MA: Addison-Wesley.

Szuchman, Jeffrey (ed.). 2009. *Nomads, Tribes, and the State in the Ancient Near East: Cross-disciplinary Perspectives*. Oriental Institute Seminars 5. Chicago: The Oriental Institute.

Turner, Victor W. 1964. "Betwixt and Between: The Liminal Period in *Rites de Passage*." In M. E. Spiro (ed.). *Symposium on New Approaches to the Study of Religion*, 4–20. Seattle: American Ethnological Society.

———. 1998. "Liminalität und Communitas." In A. Belliger and D. J. Krieger (eds.), *Ritualtheorien. Ein einführendes Handbuch*, 251–264. Opladen: Westdeutscher Verlag.

Wodianka, Stephanie and Christoph Behrens (eds.). 2017. *Chaos in the Contact Zone: Unpredictability, Improvisation and the Struggle for Control in Cultural Encounters*. Bielefeld: Transcript Verlag.

Yeivin, Shmuel. 1960. "Early Contacts between Canaan and Egypt." *Israel Exploration Journal* 10: 193–203.

Yekutieli, Yuval. 1998. *The Early Bronze Age I of North Sinai-Social, Economic and Spatial Aspects*. Ph.D. Diss., Ben Gurion University of the Negev (Hebrew).

———. "The Desert, the Sown and the Egyptian Colony." *Ägypten und Levante* 14: 163–171. DOI: 10.1553/AEundL14s163.

Yekutieli, Yuval, Samuel Atkins, Eli Cohen-Sasson, Lior Schwimer, Roy Galili, Yarden Pagelson, and Roi Shavit. *Forthcoming* 2022. "An Early Bronze Age I gathering place of interregional significance: initial results from surveys and excavations at Mitzpe Sde Hafir in the Negev Highlands." *Levant*.

NOTES

1 Saidel and van der Steen 2007; Frachetti 2008; Szuchman 2009; Kardulias 2015.

2 For a recent overview of this subject, see Atkins 2017, 135–164.

3 The concept of a core region of Egyptian presence fading with distance has been proposed by many scholars but is most extensively elaborated upon by de Miroschedji 2002, 39–57; de Miroschedji 2015, 1003–1038; Yekutieli 2004, 163–171; and Braun 2011, 105–124.

4 Sites with clear evidence of a permanent presence of Egyptian communities during the late EB I: 1) Tel Erani –Yeivin 1960, 193–203; Brandl 1989, 357–388; Kempinski and Gilead 1991, 164–192; Ciałowicz, Yekutieli, and Czarnowicz 2016; Andelkovic 1995, 39–47; 2) Tel Halif Terrace – Levy et al.; Kansa 2001; Kansa and Levy 2002; 3) Lod –Braun 2014.

5 E.g., at Tel Erani, Czarnowicz et al. 2016.

6 Yekutieli 2004; de Miroschedji 2015.

7 Pratt 1991.

8 See especially Lehmkuhl, Lüsebrink, and McFalls 2015a; and Wodianka and Behrens 2017.

9 Turner 1964; Turner 1998; for the application of Turner's concept of liminality to the thresholds of cultural encounter, see especially Lehmkuhl, Lüsebrink, and McFalls 2015b.

10 See notes 4 and 6.

11 Yekutieli 2004.

12 For the sherd of an Egyptian wine jar from Rogem-Be'erotayim, see Saidel et al. 2006, fig. 6.13. For parallels from sites in the coastal plain: 1) Tel Erani, Czarnowicz 2016, fig. 6; 2) En Besor, Gophna 1990, fig. 9; 3) Tel Ma'ahaz, Beit-Arieh and Gophna 1999, fig.10. For an EB Ib1 parallel from North Sinai, see Oren and Yekutieli 1992, fig. 9; and Yekutieli 1998, 149.

13 The research at Mitzpe Sde Hafir and Tel Erani was conducted as part of a more comprehensive project funded by a grant from the Israel Science Foundation (ISF no. 1321/17) to examine Egyptian interactions with Southwest Levant at the end of the EB I.

14 See Yekutieli 1998 for the original coding system. The coding system was later with the assistance of Dr. Masatoshi Yamafuji and Dr. Taichi Kuronoma of the Japan Institute for Cultural Properties, who also assisted with some of the preliminary analyses of ceramic materials from Tel Erani, Area D3-H.

15 Ciałowicz, Yekutieli, and Czarnowicz 2016. Renewed excavations at Tel Erani were conducted under the direction of Dr. Yuval Yekutieli, Prof. Krysztof Ciałowicz, Dr. Eli Cohen-Sasson, and Dr. Marcin Czarnowicz.

16 For a full discussion of Area D3-H stratigraphy, see Atkins 2021, 127–128.

17 Ciałowicz, Yekutieli, and Czarnowicz 2016 define the architectural complex as belonging to building phases H5–H1.

18 For C14 results, see Yekutieli et al. 2022.

19 Data collected from the Camel Site (Saidel 2011); Har Horesha (Saidel and Haiman 2014); and Ḥorvat Akhdir and Ḥorvat Avnon (Cohen 1999).

20 Sample taken from published ceramic data from Arad (Amiran 1978).

21 Sample taken from Yekutieli 1998.

22 The petrography study was carried out by Yarden Pageson (not yet published).

23 Parallels are known from Jericho (Amiran 1969, pl. 13:9, 11) and Arad (Amiran 1978, pl. 11).

24 The ceramic assemblage from Tel Erani has not yet been published but was analyzed by the author in collaboration with Yuval Yekutieli, Masatoshi Yamafuji, and Taichi Kuronuma.

25 For a discussion of production and distribution zones of Canaanean blades in the EBA, see, for example, Milevski 2011, 94–98.

26 For C14 results, see Beeri et al. 2022.

27 The beginning of the EB II is characterized by Rosen (2017, 199) as the beginning of "multi-resource nomadism" in the Negev.

28 The petrography study was conducted by Anat Weinberger-Cohen (not yet published).

29 See note 22.

30 Barth 1961.

31 Al-Rasheed 1987.

32 Finkelstein 1990, 67–86; 1995; Finkelstein et al. 2018.

33 For discussion and references, see Atkins 2021, 62–65.

34 Haiman 1996; Dunseth et al. 2018.

35 See notes 11 and 12.

36 For the Chalcolithic, see, for example, Knabb et al. 2018; for the EB Ia, see Khalil and Schmidt 2009; for the EB II, see, for example, Ilan and Sebbane 1989.

37 For detailed elaboration on the concept of a "negotiated periphery," see Kardulias 1999, xvii–xxi; Kardulias 2007; Morris 1999.

38 For the ritual association of tabular scrapers, see mainly Bar-Adon 1989.

39 For examples of the emergence of "parasocial leaders" in various social contexts, see the sites of Yomut Turkmen (Irons 1971; Irons 1974; Bates 1973; Spooner 1973); Basseri of South Persia (Barth 1961; Rowton 1974); and Shammar of North Arabia (Al-Rasheed 1987).

Journal of Ancient Egyptian Interconnections

Tyre: An Intermediate Harbor in Interregional Trade

María Eugenia Aubet
Universidad Pompeu Fabra, Barcelona

Abstract
The founding of a small fortified center on the island of Tyre in the Early Bronze Age cannot be explained without the complicity of a continental center on the nearby coast. Although it is a rocky island with no arable land, it has nonetheless provided an important volume of Combed Storage Jars, cereals, olive pits, and grapes. As an outpost in the sea of a continental center controlling a fertile plain, the island was at an excellent intermediate position between the southern Lebanese coast, the Bay of Akko, and Egypt. Here, we present the preliminary results of the 2019–2020 excavation seasons in Tyre.

Keywords
Insular center; economic autonomy; processing of agricultural resources; local metallurgy; close relationship with the mainland

The area on the ancient island where the new project presented here is carried out, the so-called "acropolis," lies between the famous Crusader cathedral and the sectors excavated in the early 70s of the 20th century by Bikai.[1] This area coincides with the highest and central point of the ancient island (Fig. 1). Here, during the excavation of a large surface area with Byzantine, Roman, Hellenistic, and Iron Age structures, at 5 m above sea level, we discovered part of an old sounding (Fig. 2), whose record and results remain unknown to us. It seems that this sounding was done at the end of the 60s by Maurice Chehab and never published (Aubet 2020).

First, the west section of that sounding was cleaned to verify its extension, characteristics, morphology, and depth. Samples of organic remains and geological sediments were collected for analysis and radiocarbon dating. The resulting section, slightly over 5 m in depth, produced a comprehensive sequence of the history of Tyre (Fig. 3), spanning from its very origins in the Early Bronze Age to the last stages of the Iron Age.[2]

Among other aspects, it was observed that the Late Bronze Age levels rested directly upon an almost 0.5 m thick layer of fine sand (Fig. 3). This sandy stratum, of Eolic origin, did not produce any organic remains or archaeological evidence, clearly representing a rather long occupational break in human settlement during the Middle Bronze Age, during which the island shows no sign of permanent human occupation.

Underneath, the Early Bronze Age stratigraphic sequence was unexpectedly rich and complex. Although the study of the materials is still ongoing, we can say that EB III is very well documented at the site, with the possible presence of an EB II horizon in the lower strata directly above the bedrock, at 1 m above sea level. The Early Bronze Age in Tyre ended

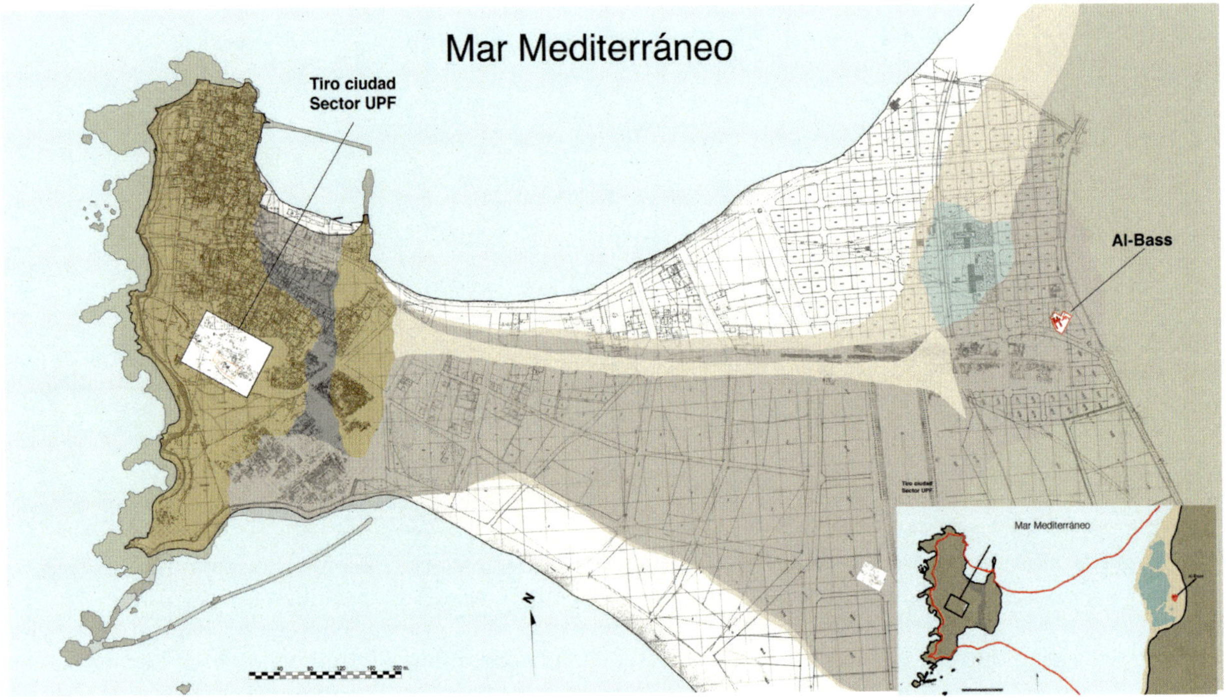

FIGURE 1: Map of Tyre with the location of the 2019 excavation area and the island of Tyre before the Hellenistic period.

FIGURE 2: The acropolis of Tyre with the Crusader cathedral (left) and the excavation area (right).

Figure 3: Chehab's sounding in 2019 and the western section.

in a stratum of destruction and fire, associated with a possible fortification, which provided some EB IV pottery.

Several layers corresponding to the Early Bronze Age appeared underneath this layer of sand and directly above the bedrock. They contained some clearly differentiable horizons and solid buildings. These levels produced typical Early Bronze Age materials, such as Combed ware of domestic type and storage jars (Fig. 4), as well as sherds displaying cylinder seal impressions (Fig. 5), pot marks (Fig. 6), and the so-called pattern burnished ware. It should also be noted the presence of non-local materials, undoubtedly imports, such as a black stone bowl and a faience sherd (Fig. 6).

Three aspects should, however, be taken into account regarding the EB of Tyre:

1. First, the regularity and monumentality of some structures, with clear indications of imprints of wooden pillars on stone supports.
2. Second, a local and developed lithic industry, based on the carving of flint and quartz cores inside some buildings, at a domestic level; the abundance and presence of cores show an intensive local and self-sufficient production of lithic tools (Fig. 7).
3. And last, the presence of crucibles with remains of copper slags to melt tools for local use, such as fishing hooks and needles (Fig. 8); that is, activities typical, once more, of a small-scale local and self-sufficient metallurgy production that indicates some degree or will of permanence, autonomy, or stability on the island.

Thus, the founding of Tyre in the EB can only be understood if considered an offshore projection of a continental site, probably of the Paleo-Tyros or Ushu from the written tradition, mainly the Amarna Letters. Its founding was most certainly a response to new strategic needs: having a protected and safe anchorage for maritime navigation and interregional trade.[3]

However, the large buildings of the EB III occupation levels at Tyre and the local flint and metal production suggest a deliberate choice toward permanence on a small rocky islet to serve as an outpost for a nearby center on the mainland. Given its characteristics, the density of its stratified deposits, and its location in a fertile plain, all signs point to the tell of el-Rachidiyeh, located on the coast just 4 km southeast of the island of Tyre and close to the important freshwater springs at Ras el 'Ayn (Fig. 9).[4] The Amarna Letters[5] mention that, during the Late Bronze Age, drinking water and wood were regularly transported in boats from Ushu, on the mainland, to the island of Tyre.

Figure 4: A domestic area near the bedrock and Combed ware.

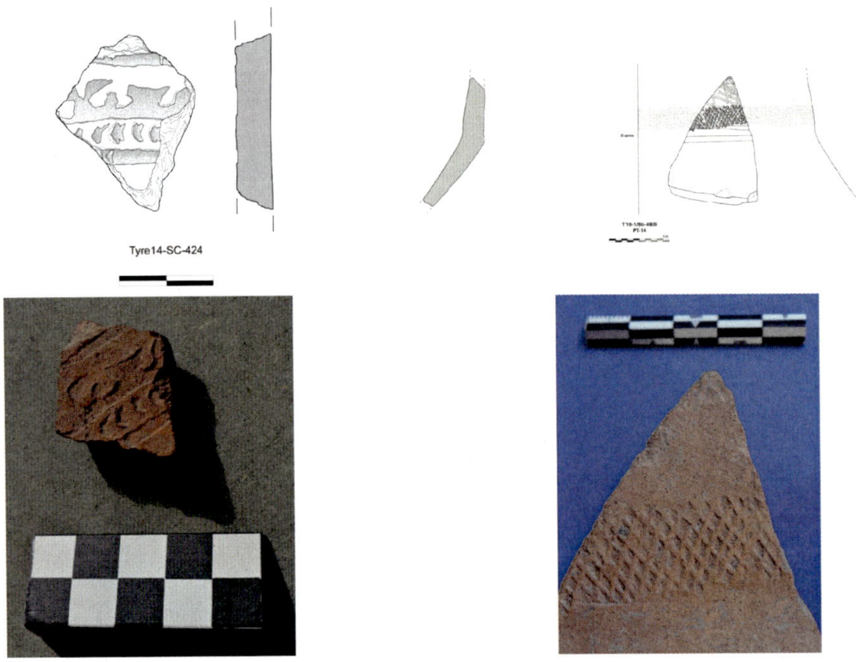

Figure 5: Cylinder seal impressions.

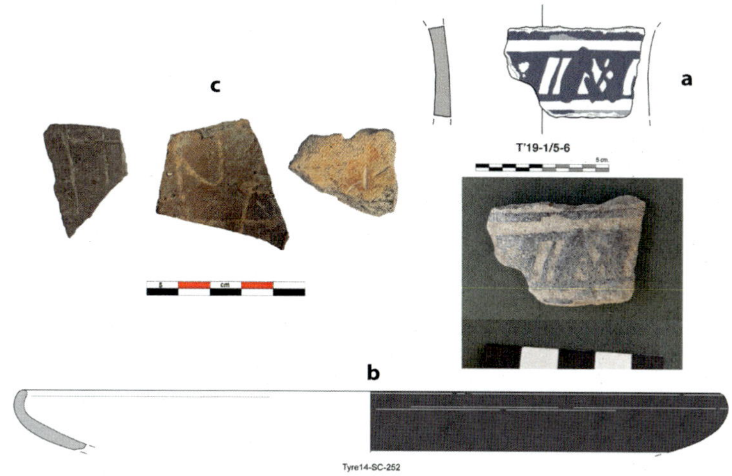

Figure 6: Pot marks, a faience sherd, a stone bowl, and a pattern burnished jug.

Figure 7: Quartz core and flint industry.

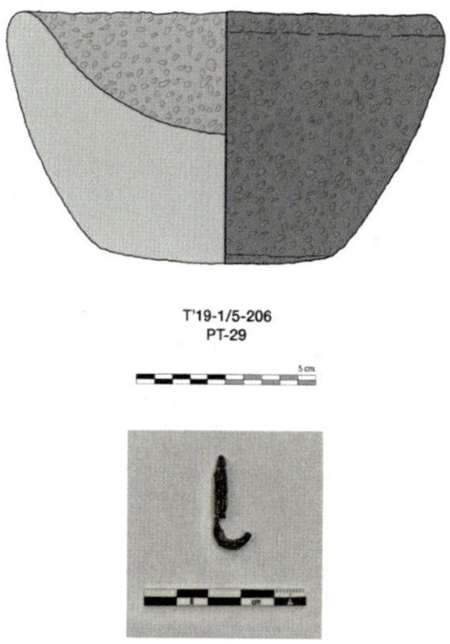

Figure 8: Basalt crucible and copper fishing hook.

The island also served as a citadel where agricultural resources—olives, grapes, cereals—from the mainland and planned for exporting overseas were probably processed and stored (Fig. 10). Products, natural resources, and raw materials found on the island depended on a fertile and well-communicated hinterland during a period when urban centers with public structures and fortifications were thriving on the Lebanese coast.[6]

One wonders what specific circumstances forced the coastal population to establish a new fortified settlement on an island in the middle of the sea (a garrison?) with specialized functions: a protected harbor, a storage place, and certain autonomy. In this sense, we must not forget that from the third millennium BCE onward, almost the entire history of Tyre was that of a safe and inexpugnable site (Fig. 9).

Acknowledgments

We want to thank the close collaboration and technical support of the people who participated in field and registration work during these excavation seasons in Tyre: Ana M. Arruda, Ali Badawi, Amelie Beyhum, Patricia M. Bikai, Ramón Buxó, Hermann Genz, José M. Lopez Garí, Stefania Mazzoni, Alfredo Mederos, Ianir Milevski, David Montanero, Francisco Nuñez, Kosmas Pavlopoulos, Karin Sowada, Laura Trellisó, and Rami Yassine. We also thank the institutions that supported the project: the Ministry of Culture (Madrid), the Direction Générale des Antiquités du Liban (Beirut), the Palarq Foundation (Barcelona), and the Municipality of Tyre.

FIGURE 9: Map of Tyre and the mainland; ideal reconstruction of ancient Tyre.

FIGURE 10: Storage jar and seeds: cereals, olive pits (*olea*) and grapes (*vitis*).

References

Aubet, Maria Eugenia. 2020. "Tyre before Tyre: The Bronze Age Foundation." In Ayelet Gilboa and Assaf Yasur-Landau (eds.), *Nomads of the Mediterranean: Trade and Contact in the Bronze and Iron Ages. Studies in Honor of Michal Artzy*, 14–30. Leiden: Brill.

Aubet, Maria Eugenia, Ali Badawi and Francisco Nuñez. In press. "Some Remarks on the Stratigraphic Sequence of Tyre during the Bronze and Iron Ages." *Bulletin d'Archéologie et d'Architecture Libanaises* 19 (2019).

Badawi, Ali. 1997. "The Basins and Aqueduct of Ras-el-Ain near Tyre." *National Museum News* (Beirut) 5: 30–33.

Badreshany, Kamal, Graham Philip, and Melissa Kennedy. 2019. "The Development of Integrated Regional Economies in the Early Bronze Age Levant: New Evidence from 'Combed Jars'." *Levant*. DOI: 10.1080/00758914.2019.1641009

Bikai, Patricia M. 1978. *The Pottery of Tyre*. Warminster: Aris and Phillips Ltd.

Carayon, Nicolas, Nick Marriner, and Christopher Morhange. 2011. "Geoarcheology of Byblos, Tyre, Sidon and Beirut." *Rivista di Studi Fenici* 39(1): 55–66.

Genz, Hermann, Simone Riehl, Canan Çakirlar, F. Slim, and Alison Damick. 2016. "Economic and Political Organization of Early Bronze Age Coastal Communities: Tell Fadous-Kfarabida as a Case Study," *Berytus* 55: 79–119.

Moran, William L. 1987. *Les lettres d'El Amarna*. Paris: Le Cerf.

Sowada, Karin N. 2009. *Egypt in the Eastern Mediterranean during the Old Kingdom. An Archaeological Perspective*. Orbis Biblicus et Orientalis 237. Fribourg & Göttingen: Academic Press & Vandenhoeck & Ruprecht.

Thalmann, Jean-Paul. 2003. "Transporter et conserver: jarres de l'Âge du Bronze à Tell Arqa." *Archaeology and History in Lebanon* 17: 25–37.

Notes

1 Bikai 1978.

2 Aubet, Badawi and Nuñez 2019.

3 Sowada 2009; Carayon, Marriner and Morhange 2011.

4 Badawi 1997.

5 Moran 1987, EA nº 149.

6 Thalmann 2003; Genz et al. 2016.

Journal of Ancient Egyptian Interconnections

The Relationships between Egypt and Syria in the 24th century BCE according to the Texts of the City of Ebla, Syria

Maria Giovanna Biga
Sapienza Università di Roma

Abstract
While studying the types of materials exchanged between the kingdoms of Ebla and Dugurasu, Biga proposed (2012) that Dugurasu could be identified as a place in the Delta of the Nile. She also proposed to identify the city of DUlu— from which almost the same materials came to Ebla and had a role of intermediary between Ebla and Dugurasu— with Byblos, as already proposed by Pettinato at the beginning of Eblaite studies. These proposals, positively received by some scholars, were questioned by Archi, who argued that Dugurasu is to be sought in Iran and DUlu in Anatolia. These issues are important for the history of the relationships between Syria and Egypt; for this reason, Biga and Steinkeller recently (2021) offered a systematic examination of the data bearing on the question of Dugurasu's identity and location. The present paper presents a synthesis of the main points in Biga and Steinkeller's article. The recently proposed identification of the presence of monkeys among the goods arriving in Ebla solely from Dugurasu and DUlu is another strong point in favor of the proposed identifications. Thus, monkeys must be studied in much detail in the Ebla texts. This is the topic of a new article (Biga and Steinkeller, in preparation), with all the data pointing to the identification of DUlu with the city of Byblos.

Keywords
Lapis lazuli; tin, silver; Dugurasu; DUlu; linen; elephant ivory; hippopotamus ivory; monkeys

I. The Geopolitical Horizon of the Ebla Texts of the 24th century BCE and the Supposed Absence of Egypt

Clay tablets from the archives of the city of Ebla, present–day Tell Mardikh in northern Syria, about 60 km southwest of Aleppo, were found in the Royal Palace G, mainly in the years 1974–1976. Written in cuneiform writing and a previously undocumented Semitic language and dated to the 24th century BCE, they allowed to begin writing the political, diplomatic, economic, and commercial history of Syria in that period of the third millennium BCE, totally unknown before Ebla's discovery. In particular, the texts found in 1975 in the main archive revealed the relations of the Eblaite kingdom with a large number of other kingdoms of the time during a period of about 45 years. The texts documented that the city had been an important trade center in the region with an extensive commercial network (Archi 2015, 163–179; Biga 2015, 181–190; Michalowski 2020; Sallaberger-Schrakamp 2015, 96–104; Steinkeller 2021).

Ebla's relations with states both near and far were reconstructed after the texts were placed in their relative chronology (Biga 2003). The Eblaite kingdom had many political-diplomatic relations with some prominent contemporary kingdoms such as Mari, present-day Tell Hariri on the Middle

FIGURE 1: Map of sites mentioned in the text.

Euphrates; Nagar, the present Tell Brak in the Khabur river plain; and Kiš, an important Semitic kingdom in central Mesopotamia.

The reconstructed geopolitical horizon of the kingdom of Ebla went from Hamazi to the east of the Tigris river, Assur and Gasur in the Tigris area, and Erbil in present-day Iraqi Kurdistan. To the west, it reached Karkemiš on the Euphrates and Kharran (now in southern Turkey) and the Syro-Palestinian coast, with the center of Alalakh, now in southern Turkey, about 30 km from the Mediterranean coast. It also had many close relations with a series of kingdoms in upper Syria and along the river Euphrates: these are the kingdoms of Burman, Nirar, Dub, Ra'ak, Lumnan, Kakmium, Emar, the closest allies of Ebla, and many others. Except for Emar (identified with Tell Meskene on the Euphrates), all the other kingdoms are hard to identify with current *tells*. Some of them, such as Nirar, were possibly not too far from Ebla.

Even after 40 years of study, Egypt was the great absent entity within this vast geographic horizon, despite the fact that archaeological evidence from Ebla itself and other Syro-Palestinian cities such as Byblos demonstrated close relationships between Syria and Egypt already in the third millennium BCE. In the palace of Ebla, many Egyptian objects, including diorite and alabaster cups and vase jars, and especially two important pieces with the names of two great pharaohs, Chephren (fourth pharaoh of the Fourth Dynasty) and Pepi I (the third pharaoh of the Sixth Dynasty), were found (Scandone Matthiae 1979, 1981, 1997). The presence of a diorite oil lamp engraved with the title of Chephren has been considered by Scandone Matthiae as possibly resulting from the pillaging of a town, taking into account that we do not know the history of Ebla's relationships before the period of the archives. However, we cannot exclude the existence of relations between Ebla and Egypt already from the time of the fourth dynasty taking into account that relations between Egypt and Byblos flourished during that period. Perhaps at the time of the fourth dynasty, different diplomatic rules were applied, and the evidence should be considered as linking the brother of Chefren, Hardedef, to lapis lazuli (Luft 1973: 111–112).

Pepi I was undoubtedly a contemporary of the last king of Ebla, Išar-damu. A lid of an alabaster jar with the cartouche of Pepi I, commemorating his *sed*-festival, was found in the Royal Palace G of Ebla. It is admitted by Egyptologists that Pepi I himself sent these types of jars with ointments to his ruler friends. Thus, he sent a vase to king Išar-damu of Ebla and to the king of DUlu/Byblos since such vases have also been found there (Diego Espinel 2002: 110–112). Moreover, it becomes increasingly clear that Pepi I was a great ruler who had diplomatic relations with many regions (see below).

It is impossible to recognize in the Ebla texts a word indicating Egypt, probably because there was no word for Egypt used by Egyptians themselves at that time.

Egypt was the great absent, and the quotation of the city of Byblos as DUlu, proposed by Pettinato (Pettinato 1983, 107–118; Pettinato 1986, 245–250) at the beginning of Eblaite studies, had been considered improbable by some scholars and rejected by others.[1]

Byblos was an important city already closely related to Egypt from the early third millennium BCE; it was the major harbor where Egyptians came to buy precious wood, especially cedarwood and other products from Syria, Anatolia, and the east, for which Syria was an important trade center. In the archaeological excavations of Byblos were found many important and precious objects of the kings of the Third, Fourth, Fifth, and mainly the Sixth Dynasty. Pepi I is documented by a number of objects found at Byblos (Scandone Matthiae 1994, 37–48). It seems highly improbable that the kingdom of Ebla did not have any relationship with Byblos, undoubtedly very important at that time and not too far away. Thus, there is no better candidate for Byblos in the Ebla texts than DUlu, as suggested by Pettinato.

II. Lapis Lazuli in Ebla Texts and Archaeological Data from Ebla Palace G; the Biography of Iny

At the beginning of the 1980s, the present author collected, for years, references to lapis lazuli (and other stones of different colors) in the Ebla texts, because it was surprising to find several quotations of raw lapis lazuli—a precious stone that was surely imported from far away giving the fact that lapis lazuli mines are in Badakhshan, a region of Afghanistan. In the Royal Palace G of Ebla, at least 43 kg of raw lapis lazuli, mostly in small pieces roughly worked, were found by the excavators, who supposed that "most of the lapis was traded in preworked pieces of ca 1 mina" (Peyronel and Vacca 2013, 443).[2] They prove that Ebla was a commercial center for this stone. From the Ebla texts, it is evident that lapis lazuli arrived in Ebla via Mari, which was an important stop on the long route of lapis lazuli from Afghanistan to Babylonia and then to the Mediterranean. This stone was sent as a gift by Mari's royal court to the Ebla king and queen; it was brought to Ebla over several years by different stewards (heads of diplomatic delegations), especially by the steward Šugadu who for years came to Ebla with precious gifts of lapis lazuli and other objects (Archi 1999). It has been calculated (Archi 2017a, 38) that during the first thirteen years of Ibbi-zikir as vizier, the deliveries of lapis lazuli from Mari to Ebla amounted to 153.35 minas (72.184 kg). While collecting texts mentioning lapis lazuli, it was easy to realize that this precious stone was sent by Ebla as a gift only to one kingdom, that of Dugurasu. Although several gifts sent by the Eblaite court to different kingdoms are often mentioned, it is surprising that gifts of conspicuous quantities of lapis lazuli (as well as tin and silver) from the Ebla court were sent only to the king of Dugurasu, a king who never came to Ebla to swear allegiance in the temple of the god KUra.

In 2010, Marcolin published a very important inscription[3] that he joined from fifteen pieces he found in several museums and private collections in Japan, Spain, and the United States and that he recognized were all parts of the same text. In this text, a biographical inscription possibly from his mastaba originally in Saqqara, an Egyptian official named Iny, who was active during the reigns of the Sixth Dynasty's rulers Pepi I, Merenra I, and Pepi II, narrated his business trips to the Levant. He had come to Byblos by ship and, from there, had reached various places in Syria and Anatolia by land (Roccati 2015b), searching not for timber but lapis lazuli, tin, and silver, exactly the products that were sent from Ebla to Dugurasu. He went back to Egypt with lapis lazuli, tin, silver, bitumen, "Asiatic" men and women, and "Byblos" ships. This important text proves the existence of a direct trade relationship between Syria and Egypt at the time of the VIth Dynasty.

III.1. The Proposal Dugurasu=Egypt and DUlu = Byblos

The identity of the materials that Iny was seeking with those sent from Ebla only to the kingdom of Dugurasu was surprising. For this reason, considering the types of materials exchanged between Ebla and Dugurasu, an identification of Dugurasu with a city in Egypt, possibly in the Nile Delta, has been proposed; and the identification of DUlu with Byblos, already suggested by Pettinato, was put forth once again because DUlu was an intermediary trade center between Dugurasu and Ebla (Biga 2012).

In the appendix to Biga's article, Roccati tried to demonstrate that the city of *R-ḥ3t* from which Iny started his trips to Byblos could have been written in cuneiform as Dugurasu, and proposed an etymology as "the mouth(s) of the river (Nile)" (Roccati 2012a, 2015a); between 2012 and 2021, Biga continued to study the toponyms Dugurasu and DUlu in a number of papers.[4] Several scholars accepted both proposals, that is, Dugurasu=Egypt and of DUlu =Byblos.[5]

III.1.1. Archi's Reaction

Archi (Archi 2016a) rejected this proposal arguing that Dugurasu is the land of Tukriš, which, according to him, was located in "the mountainous regions east of the Tigris" in northwestern Iran (Archi 2016a, 30–33). He maintained his position in a number of subsequent publications (Archi 2017a, 39; 2017b, 167; 2020, 28). But he ignored, in fact, that in 2014 Steinkeller offered a very extensive study on Tukriš in which he demonstrated that mentions of Tukriš are essentially limited to literary and lexical sources of the Ur III period (2100–2000 BCE), of the Old Babylonian and Old Assyrian period (first half of the second millennium) into the first millennium BCE. These texts identify Tukriš as a distant exotic land, a source of lapis lazuli and gold; it is cited together with the exotic lands of Makkan, Meluhha, Marhaši, and Aratta, all of which were located east of Babylonia. In his article, Steinkeller examined all the other sources on Tukriš and hypothesized that Tukriš designates at least some components of the Bactria-Margiana-archaeological complex that must have extended as far as Tepe Hissar and Gorgan to the west.

The name Tukriš does not appear in the documentation from Babylonia and Iran before the beginning of the second millennium BCE.

In the Ebla texts, it would seem that, to the east, Ebla had many contacts with the Khabur Valley, and some contacts with Assur, Gasur, and Erbil; the most distant place to the east with which Ebla had at least one contact was Hamazi. Dugurasu and Tukriš were two different places. The similarity between these two words indeed is remarkable. One could envisage that Tukraš, the original third-millennium term for Egypt, had become a term (Tukriš) for another distant land famous for its precious materials, located in the east. Such terminological shifts are not uncommon: Meluhha, the third-millennium Babylonian designation for the Indus Valley, later and already in the el-Amarna correspondence, denotes Nubia. This observation has also been proposed by J.-M. Durand (personal communication).

III.2. Biga and Steinkeller's Article in the *Journal of Cuneiform Studies* 73 (2021)

The question of the contact between Egypt and northern Syria during the late third millennium BCE and the nature of international trade during that time is of great importance for the history of both the ancient Near East and Egypt. For this reason, Biga and Steinkeller, following Archi's article, decided to offer a systematic examination of the data bearing on the question of Dugurasu's identity and location and the location of the kingdom of DUlu, often mentioned with Dugurasu, studying in detail the materials traded between Ebla and Dugurasu.

The most important results of Biga and Steinkeller's study will be summarized here, with reference to the article and the bibliography cited in it for further details and the discussion of philological problems. Fifty-one mentions of Dugurasu in Ebla sources have been identified by Biga and Steinkeller (Archi cited forty-two of them), and another one has recently been found in a monthly account of deliveries of textiles. This new text mentioning Dugurasu will be studied together with the texts on DUlu and monkeys in a forthcoming article (Biga and Steinkeller, in preparation).

The exchanges of various precious materials between Ebla and Dugurasu are described by the Ebla scribes as "gifts" (nig$_2$-ba) or "deliveries" (mu-DU).

The data on the commercial contacts between Ebla and Dugurasu are insufficient to gather how often these exchanges took place. However, it is evident that while the exchanges between Ebla and DUlu were regular, occurring as many as four times in one year and documented from the beginning of the archives, those between Ebla and Dugurasu were fewer and irregular and began at the time of the penultimate king Irkab-damu of Ebla, increasing under his successor Išar-damu, particularly under his second vizier Ibbi-zikir.

The precious materials supplied by the ruler of Dugurasu to the ruler of Ebla and often to his queen and his queen mother were elephant and hippopotamus ivory, *kirnanu* linen textiles, beads of gemstones, gold, and copper. The Ebla texts do not offer much information about the transportation of Dugurasu goods to Ebla; in some instances, the goods were physically delivered by a Dugurasu emissary while, in other instances, the goods of Dugurasu were brought to Ebla by DUlu representatives together with the goods of DUlu. DUlu had an intermediary role in these exchanges. The emissaries to Ebla received some textiles as a gift.

III.2.1. Lapis Lazuli, Tin, Silver from Ebla to Dugurasu

The gifts sent by Ebla to Dugurasu consisted essentially of three materials: lapis lazuli, tin, and silver. The most important product sent by Ebla to Dugurasu was lapis lazuli, sometimes also sent to DUlu. The texts from Ebla leave no doubt that lapis lazuli was obtained from the kingdom of Mari (see II, above). Archaeological data from Ebla Palace G confirm that Ebla was a place on the long road of lapis lazuli from its ultimate source, the Badakhshan mines in Afghanistan, to the Mediterranean. From Afghanistan, in subsequent stops, lapis lazuli reached Mari.

Lapis lazuli was exceedingly coveted in ancient Egypt and was imported throughout its entire history, the usual suppliers being northern Syria and Babylonia. In his inscription, Iny explicitly says that he went to Byblos and then to three places, quite probably in Syria or Anatolia (Roccati 2015b), and obtained lapis lazuli and other goods.

The identification of Dugurasu with a place in Iran as proposed by Archi is quite unlikely; it is hard to suppose that Ebla exported lapis lazuli to a place fairly close to its origins (Afghanistan).

Tin was exported by Ebla to Dugurasu and DUlu. Information on the sources of Ebla tin is sparse and somewhat conflicting. In one instance, Ebla obtained tin from Mari; another tin supplier to Ebla was Kakkaban, a site located in the Khabur Valley. Both Mari and Kakkaban were intermediaries for tin originating in the east, either in Afghanistan or Central Asia (Steinkeller 2014, 2016). However, there are strong indications that an alternative source of tin existed in Anatolia. Two ancient mines of tin have been identified in the central Taurus. It is quite probable that tin was mined in Anatolia during the second half of the third millennium BCE.[6] Tin was not found naturally in Egypt and therefore needed to be imported.

Silver was delivered from Ebla to Dugurasu and also exported to DUlu. It was available in great quantities at Ebla, and all the data from these texts confirm that silver originated in Anatolia (Yener 2015; Steinkeller 2016; Archi 2017b).

From Ebla, silver was also exported to Mari, Nagar, and Kakkaban. Steinkeller (2016) emphasized the fact that prior to the Sargonic period, the Babylonians obtained most of their silver indirectly from Ebla via Mari.

Iny's inscription mentions these three examined materials exported by Ebla to Dugurasu because he went to Syria to look for these materials.

III.2.2. Goods Exported by Dugurasu to Ebla

The materials exported by Dugurasu to Ebla consisted of linen, elephant and hippopotamus ivory, gold, copper, bronze, an assortment of objects made of stone and other materials, and an animal called KA.MA. Except for elephant ivory and gold, all these items were also exported to Ebla by DUlu. The most common item sent regularly and in great quantities from Dugurasu and DUlu to Ebla were linen textiles; among them, the *kirnanu* textiles were the most valuable (Biga and Steinkeller 2021, 32).

Almost all the linen used in Ebla came from Dugurasu and DUlu. When linen textiles arrived in Ebla, they were distributed to the members of the court. Linen was the Egyptian product *par excellence* and in no other place in the ancient Near East was it used more extensively for garments, underwear, ship sails, bandages, and wrappings of all kinds. Egypt sent linen textiles to Babylonia in all periods, including the Amarna period. Archi's proposal that these linen textiles were produced in northwestern Iran (Archi 2016: 16) is most unlikely since there is no evidence of production of linen in Iran.

Another type of merchandise sent by Dugurasu to Ebla consisted of two types of animal teeth or tusks. The first is si:am, which may be identified as an abbreviated variant of the Sumerian zu_2-am-si, literally "the tooth of a horned wild bull," normally translated "elephant ivory." Ebla obtained elephant ivory only from Dugurasu. So far, eleven mentions of elephant ivory have been found in Ebla texts.

Despite the repeated claims that during the second and first millennium BCE, northern Syria and, in particular, the Ghab Valley north of Hama and the Euphrates region near Aleppo supported a native elephant population, there is no convincing proof from the archaeological data to the presence of these animals. The elephant tusks found somewhere in Syria might have been imported. The many Old Babylonian (first half of the second millennium BCE) sources from important sites of Syria like Mari, Terqa, Tell Leilan, and even Alalakh (a city situated in the middle of the Ghab Valley) do not mention elephants. No contemporaneous visual representations of elephants are known from that region either.

No mention of elephants or their ivory can be found in the Middle Babylonian (second half of the second millennium BCE) texts from Alalakh, Ugarit, Qatna, and Emar, and also in Hittite sources on the interactions of the Hittite empire with northern Syria and the Levant or the Amarna letters. If elephants had indeed lived in the Ghab Valley or the region of Aleppo, we would have had more references to their ivory in the Ebla texts, yet these references to ivory are extremely rare, and all refer to ivory sent to Ebla by the kingdom of Dugurasu. All these facts seem to signify that there were no native elephants in northern Syria and the Khabur Valley during the third millennium and the first half of the second millennium BCE. Later on, the Asian elephant was imported into Syria.[7]

For all these reasons, it can be concluded that all the elephant ivory mentioned in the Ebla texts as coming from Dugurasu came from Egypt/Africa. From the biography of Harkhuf, of the Egyptian VIth Dynasty, we learn that elephant ivory arrived in Egypt as a gift to it from Nubia (Roccati 1982: 205).

Teeth of another animal, zu_2-AN.A.ENGUR,[8] arrived in Ebla from both Dugurasu and DUlu. It was more easily obtained and also cheaper than elephant ivory; it was defined as "hippopotamus ivory," popular in the ancient Near East. Archaeological data from many places in the Mediterranean show that hippo ivory was used more often than elephant ivory. The attestations of zu_2-AN.A.ENGUR in Ebla sources are much more common than those of elephant ivory. This material is commonly mentioned as forming the decoration of "Amorite" daggers, sometimes made entirely of gold or decorated with gold, and with inlays for their handles or sometimes even to form the handle. It is well known that hippo ivory was used more commonly than elephant ivory in the ancient Near East and the eastern Mediterranean. In many museums (for example, in those of Heraklion in Crete and Aleppo in Syria), wonderful objects (and daggers among them) are decorated with hippo ivory; the inlays made of hippopotamus ivory were very common in Middle Bronze Ebla (Peyronel 2015, 191–192).

Archi considered the possibility that zu_2-AN.A.ENGUR meant hippopotamus ivory but rejected this, preferring a translation as "the longest teeth of the crocodile." (Archi 2016a, 25). This identification is most unlikely, and no mention of the use of crocodile's teeth is found in Egyptian texts. There is no ancient or modern evidence of the use of crocodilian teeth to inlay objects. From archaeological data, we know that extensive remains of hippopotamus bones were unearthed at sites such as Tell Qasile and Tel Dor in Palestine, but the evidence from northern Syria is much less convincing. The fact that no visual representation or textual references to hippopotami survive from ancient northern Syria argues strongly against the presence of native hippopotamus populations in that region.

All the evidence from the Ebla texts points to Egypt as the ultimate source of Ebla's zu_2-AN.A.ENGUR, considering the significant presence and importance of hippopotamus in Egypt.

Gold was also delivered from Dugurasu to Ebla but in small quantities; Ebla imported huge volumes of gold from Anatolia. Some Eblaite golden objects from Palace G have been analyzed, but, for several reasons, "any attempt to identify the provenance of gold should be discarded" (Felici and Vendittelli 2013, 351). Dugurasu also sent Ebla some amount of copper and a copper type or alloy called a-gar_5-gar_5, and some axes of bronze. From the data in the texts, it is certain that Ebla obtained most of its copper from Anatolia. Unfortunately, this conclusion cannot be confirmed by the archaeometric analysis of metal objects from the Royal Palace G conducted some years ago (Palmieri, Hauptmann 2000, 1259–1282; Felici and Vendittelli 2013, 347–356). Gold and copper were easily obtainable in Egypt. For this reason, we can suppose that some copper came to Ebla also from Egypt. There is no evidence of deliveries of copper from Iran.[9]

Dugurasu and DUlu supplied Ebla with an assortment of finished objects, including strings or necklaces of beads made of gemstones. Ebla obtained this type of jewelry only from Dugurasu and DUlu. Among the gemstones,[10] all difficult to translate, are :

- si_4, perhaps "carnelian;"
- $ŠE_3$.LI, a stone of green or bluish color that could be identified as "amazonite" or "turquoise." A green amazonite gemstone was excavated in the EBA IIIb palace at Khirbet al-Batrawy (Nigro *et al.* 2020, 7, 23; fig. 15). Egyptian turquoise was mined in the Sinai Peninsula. It is noteworthy that a turquoise mine was identified near the Dakhla Oasis in the Western Desert, where rock inscriptions record an expedition sent by Chephren (Roccati 2012b);
- nab-hu, for which an identification (far from certain) as "rock crystal" has been proposed, and other gemstones of different colors that come to Ebla only from Dugurasu/ Egypt and arrived in Egypt probably from Nubia; some of them are also known from the Eastern Desert areas of Egypt.

Ebla obtained from Dugurasu and DUlu several necklaces (gu) made of all these gemstones of different colors. These necklaces are described in some already published Ebla texts (Archi 2002; Biga 2018). It can be supposed that the necklaces looked like the necklace excavated in the EBA IIIb palace of Khirbet al-Batrawy in the southern Levant (Nigro 2012b); it is composed of 660 individual pieces of carnelian, olivine, transparent rock crystal, smoky quartz, and amethyst, copper, bones, frit, and seashell. From Dugurasu (and DUlu) arrived in Ebla also several other objects whose identities need further study.

III.2.3. Monkeys

Finally, among the items sent to Ebla by Dugurasu and DUlu, and only by these two kingdoms, there is an item called KA.MA. This word can be found in the texts detailing the deliveries to Ebla (mu-DU texts) and in some monthly accounts of deliveries of textiles, especially those of the period of the last sovereign, Išar-damu, and his last vizier, Ibbi-zikir; fabrics intended for someone defined as hi-mu-DU 1 KA.MA or hi-mu-DU 2 KA.MA appear.

The Eblaite term KA.MA has remained unexplained until recently. However, thanks to a brilliant recent guess by Steinkeller (Biga and Steinkeller 2021, 45), interpreting KA.MA and reading it as KA-$peš_3$, the translation of KA.MA as "monkey" and hi-mu-DU as "the handler" of one or two monkeys has now been proposed.

Steinkeller, studying the Early Dynastic lexical source "List of Animals B," in which KA.MA appears before az, "bear," and before ur, "dog," concluded that KA.MA denotes an animal, and that it is an Eblaite term for "monkey." It is likely that KA.MA, to be read KA-$peš_3$, is a variant of the later KA-peš, which likewise designates an animal. In a lexical list [K]A-peš-tur = *ḫu-um-bi-bit-tú*, "the one looking like Humbaba / the one of Humbaba."[11] The identification of KA-peš as *ḫumbabītu* is of particular interest because Humbaba is sometimes depicted with simian features and dancing, a representation that undoubtedly goes back to the Egyptian depictions of dancing dwarfs or pygmies. Moreover, Humbaba is associated with monkeys in Tablet V of the Gilgameš Epic, where a band of monkeys dances daily before Humbaba: "[monkey mothers] sing aloud, a young monkey shrieks, [like a band] of singers and drummers, daily they clamor in the presence of Humbaba" (Al-Rawi, George 2014, 76–77, ll. 24–26).

Steinkeller based this interpretation also on the fact that the KA.MA animals, as they appear in the monthly accounts of deliveries of textiles, are commonly associated with "dancers" (NE.DI) and "dwarfs" (ba-za), as well as other types of entertainers, such as "flute players" (lu_2-gi), singers (nar), and "acrobats" (HUB_2.HUB_2). Also, there are records of several Ebla individuals who appear to have been KA.MA handlers. Two of them were the dancers *Ir_3-am_6-ma-lik* and *Zi-kir(-ra)-a-ba_4*, designated in several sources as lu_2 KA.MA, "the one (in charge) of the KA.MA." These data strongly argue that the KA.MA were used as part of the merrymaking activities held at the court of Ebla.

Monkeys that danced to the sound of tambourines and flutes are well documented in various periods throughout the history of the ancient Near East. In the Mediterranean, in Egypt, and on the island of Thera[12] are figures of monkeys dancing and playing. Dancing monkeys are depicted in some tombs in Egypt. Some Egyptian texts, also of the Vth and VIth Dynasties, speak of monkeys and dwarfs who danced for the god Bes or the goddess Hathor. For Hathor, acrobats of different types, especially women, are also attested. The monkeys were trained to dance and play instruments and were an exotic element. They were funny and amused the court parties. Many centuries later, dwarfs and monkeys were still present in European and Italian courts as funny and exotic elements and appeared in several paintings of Tiepolo, Veronese, and Carpaccio.

The origin of the monkeys is not mentioned in the texts detailing deliveries of textiles but, in the texts of deliveries of goods to Ebla (mu-DU texts), they are quoted as coming only from Dugurasu and DUlu.

Biga and Steinkeller decided to collect further evidence of DUlu and monkeys in the unpublished Ebla texts and are preparing an article on this topic.

IV. DUlu/Byblos and Monkeys

The kingdom of DUlu was one of Ebla's most important political and trading partners and one of the most quoted in the Ebla texts during the whole period covered by the archives. It is also evident that DUlu was an intermediary between Ebla and Dugurasu.

Even if we do not have itineraries in the administrative documents because the scribes did not register the outgoing deliveries in geographical order, many texts always cite Dugurasu and DUlu one after the other, so it is quite probable that the two kingdoms were connected. The role of DUlu in the exchanges was very important. DUlu imported products from Dugurasu and then exported them to Ebla. DUlu merchants made trips to Dugurasu on their own: DUlu also traded directly with Ebla exporting merchandise obtained from Dugurasu.

The relationships between these two polities was cemented by at least one dynastic marriage (Biga 2014c), and several members of DUlu's royal family paid official visits to Ebla at different times.

Monkeys are very well documented archaeologically at Byblos. All the tributes to Middle Assyrian and Neo-Assyrian kings include monkeys coming from cities of the Mediterranean, including Byblos (Dunham 1985). Some scholars proposed that monkeys arrived in Mesopotamia also from the Indus Valley and Iran, but all the evidence from Ebla strongly supports a provenience of monkeys to Ebla from Egypt and Byblos, at least in the third millennium BCE. Cattle also came to the Levant from Egypt, as suggested by Sowada (Sowada 2016–2018).

Monkeys came from Dugurasu/Egypt to DUlu / Byblos, a city where many monkey-shaped objects from the third millennium BCE are attested. In fact, in the temple of the goddess Ba'alat Gubal in Byblos, monkey-shaped vases were preserved in far greater numbers than in other cities. Only in Byblos have so many vases and monkey-shaped objects been found. Monkeys were offered to the goddess of Byblos, who was assimilated to the Egyptian goddess Hathor (Diego Espinel 2002, 103–105).

As Pinnock (2018, 498 and nos. 13, 14,15) recently noted, some seals in *Karum* II of Kanish in Anatolia, dated to the beginning of Middle Bronze I (beginning of the second millennium BCE), have north Syrian characters and not Egyptian characters "con l'unica eccezione della presenza di figure di scimmie, sedute e con la zampa anteriore levata davanti al muso, in stretto collegamento con figure rilevanti nel partito figurativo. Tali immagini dovrebbero essere riconducibili alla presenza, a Biblo, di oggetti votivi con questa forma, inviati dalla corte menfita al santuario della Baalat Gebal." In no. 14, Pinnock notes that in the foundation deposit of the so-called *Temple Syrien* (as named by P. Montet) were found several alabaster vases in the shape of monkeys with their young dated to the Ancient Kingdom. The same deposit also contained a jar (Jarre Montet) with some monkey-shaped objects.

Thus, people from Egypt and Byblos came to the court of Ebla with their trained monkeys and made them dance or perhaps even play music to enliven the banquets at the court. This information strongly suggests that DUlu cannot be located in Anatolia, as Archi has proposed.

Archi (2016: 4) locates DUlu "at Titrish (approximately 45 km north of Urfa)" and thinks that it "must be located … in roughly the same geographical direction as Armi, *not the opposite direction*" (2016 28); "Dulu [located] at Titrish Höyük, about 30 km southwest of Samsat" (2020: 28).

The data in the texts, including those quoting monkeys, strongly suggest that DUlu is Byblos (or Gubla, as it was known in antiquity). The only reasons preventing from accepting this identification outright are philological considerations; the value gub of DU (which would permit a reading *Gub-lu*^{ki} of the toponym in question) is not otherwise attested in the Ebla syllabary, a problem still unresolved.

In a recent article (Biga and Roccati, 2022), Roccati studies the writing of the foreign name of the town of Byblos in Egyptian sources, showing a fundamental change, by the second millennium BCE, in favor of hieroglyphs closely corresponding with the cuneiform writing of DUlu.

As one might expect, relations between DUlu/Byblos and Ebla are much more frequent than those between Ebla and Dugurasu / Egypt. There are a few hundred attestations of relations between DUlu and Ebla, and many of them are in the still unpublished texts that Biga and Steinkeller are studying for their article "More on the Locations of Dugurasu and DUlu."

The city-state of Arhadu (*Ar-ha-du*) was undoubtedly close to that of DUlu/Byblos, taking into account that even if no itineraries are specified in the Ebla texts, when two cities are cited with the conjunction *wa* "and," they can be considered as close to each other, as is often the case with DUlu and Arhadu (DU-*lu wa Ar-ha-du*). The citations of Arhadu will also be studied in Biga and Steinkeller's forthcoming article (in preparation).

V. Conclusions

The textual and archaeological data from Ebla and Iny's inscription lead strongly to the conclusion that Dugurasu must be identified as Egypt and that at the time of the Ebla archives, northern Syria and Egypt were engaged in commercial exchanges, as already documented by the archaeological finds in the Levant (Sowada 2009).

Indeed, the toponym Dugurasu cannot be connected with any Egyptian term designating either Egypt itself or any of its provinces and cities. Therefore, we can assume that Dugurasu is an Eblaite exonym for Egypt, completely unrelated to the Egyptian self-designations. DUlu is Byblos. An alternative solution, yet improbable, would be that DUlu refers to some intermediate place between Egypt and Ebla that served as a transshipment point of the materials sent from Egypt to Ebla. There are some candidates from the coast of Palestine into the southern Levant, all important urban and commercial centers during the Early Bronze Age: Tell es-Sakan in the Gaza strip (de Miroschedji 2015); Tell Keisan, on the coast between Haifa and Akko; and Khirbet al-Batrawy to the east of the Jordan River, in Jordan (Nigro 2012a, 2012b, 2015; Nigro *et al.* 2020).

Ebla was located in a particularly strategic position at the crossroads of various commercial routes, which made it strategic for trade to and from the Mediterranean, as would occur later for the city of Aleppo, which is about 60 km from Ebla. For this reason, Ebla controlled the main trade routes of the region that led to Egypt (south), Anatolia (west), and Babylonia (east).

Acknowledgments

I wish to thank Karin Sowada and Matthew J. Adams very much for organizing the important conference on Egypt and the Mediterranean in the third millennium BCE; it must have been difficult to organize, with such a large number of participants from all over the world, and to coordinate them during this time of pandemia. It was, for all of us, a great occasion of discussion. Karin Sowada also helped with corrections to the present paper and suggested bibliographical references. I want to thank Piotr Steinkeller for all the suggestions he gave me as we worked together; I learned a lot from him, and I continue to learn. I must also thank Marta D'Andrea and Luca Peyronel for their help, especially with the bibliography on the analysis of Ebla metal objects. Finally, I would also like to thank the two anonymous reviewers of my paper; both offered interesting suggestions, and I followed their advice.

References

Al-Rawi, Farouk N. H., and Andrew R. George. 2014. "Back to the Cedar Forest: The Beginning and End of Tablet V of the Standard Babylonian Epic of Gilgameš." *Journal of Cuneiform Studies* 66: 49–90.

Archi, Alfonso. 1980. "Notes on Eblaite Geography." *Studi Eblaiti* 2: 1–16.

———. 1999. "The Steward and His Jar." *Iraq* 61: 147–158

———. 2002. "Jewels for the Ladies of Ebla." *Zeitschrift fuer Assyriologie und Vorderasiatische Archaeologie* 92: 161–199.

———. 2015. "The Chronology of Ebla and Synchronisms with Abarsal, Tuttul, Nagar and Nabada, Mari, Kish." In Walther Sallaberger and Ingo Schrakamp (eds.), *History and Philology*, 163–179. *ARCANE* III, Brepols ,Turnhout.

———. 2016a. "Egypt or Iran in the Ebla Texts?" *Orientalia Nova Series* 85: 1–49.

———. 2016b. "Ebla and Mari—Years 2381/2380–2369 BC." In Jacques Patrier, Philippe Quenet, and Pascal Butterlin (eds.), *Mille et une empreintes: Un Alsacien en Orient. Mélanges en l'honeur du 65ᵉ anniversaire de Dominique Beyer*, 1–16. Subartu 36. Turnhout: Brepols.

———. 2017a. "Lapis Lazuli and Shells from Mari to Ebla." In Çigdem Maner, Mara T. Horowitz, and Allan S. Gilbert (eds.), *Overturning Certainties in Near Eastern Archaeology: A Festschrift in Honor of K. Aslihan Yener*, 34–47. Leiden: Brill.

———. 2017b. "Metals in Third Millennium B.C. Standpoint Ebla." In Fikri Kulakoğlu and Goiko Barjamovic (eds.), *Movement, Resources, Interaction, Proceedings of the 2nd Kültepe International Meeting, Kültepe, 26–30 July 2015, Studies Dedicated to Klaas Veenhof*, 163–172. Subartu 39. Turnhout: Brepols.

———. 2019. "Ebla and the Cities of Northern Syria" in Doris Prechel and Hans Neumann (eds), *Beiträge zur Kenntnis un Deutung altorientalischer Archivalien. Festschrift für Helmut Freydank zum 80. Geburstag*, 1–17. Dubsar 6. Münster: Zaphon.

———. 2020. "Personal Names of Proto-Anatolian Indo-European-Speaking Populations East of the Euphrates (24th Cent. BC." In Michele Cammarosano, Elena Devecchi, and Maurizio Viano (eds.), *talugaeš witteš. Ancient Near Eastern Studies Presented to Stefano de Martino on the Occasion of his 65th Birthday*, 27–36. Kasion 2. Münster: Zaphon.

Archi, Alfonso, Paola Piacentini, and Francesco Pomponio. 1993. *I nomi di luogo dei testi di Ebla. ARES* 2. Rome: Missione Archeologica Italiana in Syria.

Biga, Maria Giovanna. 2003. "The Reconstruction of a Relative Chronology for the Ebla texts." *Orientalia Nova Series* 72: 345–366.

———. 2012. "Tra Egitto e Siria nel III millennio a.C." *Atti dell'Accademia delle Scienze di Torino, Classe di Scienze Morali, Storiche e Filologiche* 146, 17–36. Torino: Accademia delle scienze di Torino.

———. 2014a. "Encore à propos des rapports entre les royaumes de Mari et d'Ébla à l'époque présargonique." *Syria, Supplément* 2: 173–81.

———. 2014b. "Inherited Space—Third Millennium Political and Cultural Landscape." In Eva Cancik-Kirschbaum, Nicole Brisch, and Jesper Eidem (eds,), *Constituent, Confederate, and Conquered Space in Upper Mesopotamia: The Emergence of the Mitanni State*, 93–110. TOPOI Berlin Studies of the Ancient World 17. Berlin: De Gruyter.

———. 2014c. "The Marriage of an Eblaite Princess with the King of Dulu." In Salvatore Gaspa, Alessandro Greco, Daniele Morandi Bonacossi, Simonetta Ponchia, and Robert Rollinger (eds.) *From Source to History: Studies on Ancient Near Eastern Worlds and Beyond. Dedicated to Giovanni Battista Lanfranchi on the Occasion of His 65th Birthday on June 23, 2014*, 73–79., AOAT 412. Münster: Ugarit-Verlag.

———. 2015. "The Geographical Scope of Ebla: Commerce and Wars. Some Remarks." In Walther Sallaberger and Ingo Schrakamp (eds.), *History and Philology*, 181–190. ARCANE III. Turnhout: Brepols.

———. 2016. "La Syrie et l'Égypte au IIIe millénaire av. J.-C. d'après les archives d'Ebla." *Académie des Inscriptions et Belles Lettres, CRAI 2016, II (avril–juin)*: 691–711.

———. 2017. "Voies commerciales, ports et marchands de Syrie, Anatolie et Méditerranée orientale au IIIe millénaire av. J.-C." *Pallas* 104: 51–59.

———. 2018. "Gioielli per una fanciulla alla corte di Ebla." In Agnese Vacca, Sara Pizzimenti, and Maria Gabriella Micale (eds.), *A Oriente del Delta. Scritti sull'Egitto ed il VO antico in onore di Gabriella Scandone Matthiae*, 63–78. Contributi e Materiali di Archeologia Orientale 18. Rome: Scienze e Lettere.

———. 2021a. "Ebla kings, rivers, lakes, wells." In Aline Tenu and Marine Yoyotte (eds), *Le roi et le fleuve. Exemples d'usages pluriels de l'espace*, 45–56. Paris. Editions Khéops.

———. 2021b. "The Role of Syria in Inter-regional Exchanges in the Second Half of the Third Millennium BC: Some Remarks."in Marc Lebeau (ed.), *Identity, Diversity and Contact from the Southern Balkans to Kinjiang, from the Upper Palaeolithic to Alexander*, 297–305. ICE 1. Turnhout: Brepols.

———. In press. "La vita nelle corti egee e vicino-orientali." *Fs Mario Negri*.

Biga, Maria Giovanna, and Alessandro Roccati. 2022 "Eblaite, Egyptian, and Anatolian place names at the crossroads." *Orientalia* 91: 70–93.

Biga, Maria Giovanna, and Piotr Steinkeller. 2021a. "In search of Dugurasu." *Journal of Cuneiform Studies* 73: 1–70.

———. 2021b. "Feasting and Entertaining at the Royal Palace of Ebla: Dancers, Acrobats and Monkeys." Paper presented at the 67 RAI, Turin (12–16 July).

———. Forthcoming. "More on the locations of Dugurasu and DUlu."

Bonechi, Marco. 1993. *I nomi geografici dei testi di Ebla*. RGTC 12/1. Wiesbaden: Reichert.

———. 2016. "Thorny Geopolitical Problems in the Palace G Archives. The Ebla Southern Horizon, Part One: The Middle Orontes Basin." *Syria, Supplément* 4: 29–87.

Diego Espinel, Andrés. 2002. "The Role of the Temple of Ba'alat Gebal as Intermediary Between Egypt and Byblos During the Old Kingdom." In Hartwig Altenmüller (ed.), *Studien zur Altägyptischen Kultur* 30, 103–119. Hamburg: Helmut Buske Verlag.

———. 2015/16. "Bringing Treasures and Placing Fears: Old Kingdom Epithets and Titles Related to Activities Abroad." *Isimu* 18–19: 103–46.

Dunham, Sally. 1985. "The monkey in the middle." *Zeischrift* für *Assyriologie* 75: 234–264.

Durand, Jean-Marie. 2014. "Les plus anciennes attestations de la côte occidentale au Proche-Orient d'Ebla à Mari (XXIVe–XVIIIe av. J.C.)." In André Lemaire (ed.), *Phéniciens d'Orient et d'Occident:* Mélanges Josette *Elayi*, 1–12. CIPOA 2. Paris: Maisonneuve.

Felici, Anna Candida, and Margherita Vendittelli. 2013. "Archaeometrical Analysis of Metal Objects from Royal Palace G." In Paolo Matthiae and Niccolò Marchetti (eds.), *Ebla and Its Landscape. Early State Formation in the Ancient Near East*, 347–356. Walnut Creek, CA: Left Coast Press.

Luft, Ulrich. 1973. "Zur Einleitung der Liebesgedichte auf Papyrus Chester Beatty I 2° XVI 9 ff." *Zeitschrift für Ägyptische Sprache und Altertumskunde* 99: 108–116.

Marcolin, Michele. 2010. "Una nuova biografia egiziana della VI dinastia con iscrizioni storiche e geografiche." *Atti dell'Accademia delle Scienze di Torino. Classe di Scienze Morali, Storiche e Filologiche* 144: 44–79.

Marcolin, Michele, and Andrés Diego Espinel. 2011. "The Sixth Dynasty Biographic Inscription of Iny: More Pieces to the Puzzle." In Miroslav Bárta, Filip Coppens and Jaromir Krejci (eds.), *Abusir and Saqqara in the Year 2010, vol. 1*, 570–615. Prague: Czech Institute of Egyptology, Faculty of Arts, Charles University of Prague.

Matoïan, Valérie. 2016. "Les vases égyptiens en pierre de la fin du IVe et du IIIe millénaires av. J.-C. découvertes à Ougarit." In Valérie Matoïan and Michel Al-Maqdissi (eds.), *Études ougaritiques* IV, 167–187. RSO 24. Leuven: Peeters.

Matthiae, Paolo. 2018. "Doni faraonici alla corte di Ebla nell'antico regno: Una riflessione sul contesto storico." In Agnese Vacca, Sara Pizzimenti, and Maria Gabriella Micale (eds.), *A Oriente del Delta. Scritti sull'Egitto ed il VO antico in onore di Gabriella Scandone Matthiae*, 347–366. Contributi e Materiali di Archeologia Orientale 18. Rome: Scienze e Lettere.

Michalowski, Piotr. 2020. "The Kingdom of Akkad in Contact with the World." In Karen Radner, Nadine Moeller, and D. T. Potts (eds.), *The Oxford History of the Ancient Near East, Volume I: From the Beginning to Old Kingdom Egypt and the Dynasty of Akkad*, 686–764. New York, NY: Oxford University Press.

de Miroschedji, Pierre. 2015. "Les relations entre l'Égypte et le Levant aux IVe et IIIe millénaires à la lumière des fouilles de Tell es-Sakan." *Comptes rendus des séances de l'Académie des Inscriptions et Belles-Lettres* (CRAI) 159(2) (avril–juin): 1003–1038.

Moreno García, Juan Carlos. 2019. "Marketplaces and Hubs of Trade in Egypt at the End of the 3rd Millennium BC: Heracleopolis Magna in Context." In Lorenz Rahmstorf, Edward Stratford (eds), *Weights and Marketplaces from the Bronze Age to the Early Modern Period, Weight and Value* 1, 185–202. Kiel: Wachholtz.

Nigro, Lorenzo. 2012a. "Khirbet al-Batrawy: Rise, Flourish and Collapse of an Early Bronze Age City in Jordan." In Roger Matthews, John Curtis (eds), *Proceedings of the 7th International Congress on the Archaeology of the Ancient Near East, 12 April–16 April 2010, the British Museum and UCL, London*, 609–628. Wiesbaden: Harrassowitz.

———. 2012b. "An EB IIIb (2500–2300 BC) Gemstones Necklace from the Palace of the Copper Axes at Khirbet al-Batrawy, Jordan." *Vicino Oriente* 16: 227–44.

———. 2015. "The Copper Axes Hoard in the Early Bronze Age IIIb Palace of Batrawy, Jordan." In Karolina Rosinska-Balik, Agnieszka Ochal-Czarnowicz, Marcin Czarnowicz, and Joanna Debowska-Ludwin (eds.), *Copper and Trade in South-Eastern Mediterranean: Trade Routes of the Ancient Near East in Antiquity*, 77–154. BAR International Series 2753. Oxford: Archaeopress.

Nigro, Lorenzo, Elisabetta Gallo, Romeel Gharib, Francesco Mura, Michele Macrì, and Teresa Rinaldi. 2020. "An Egyptian Green Schist Palette and an Amazonite Gemstone from the "Palace of Copper Axes" at Batrawy, Jordan." *Vicino Oriente* 24: 1–26.

Palmieri, Alberto, and Andreas Hauptmann. 2000. "Metals from Ebla. Chemical Analysis of Metal Artefacts from the Bronze and Iron Ages." In Paolo Matthiae, Alessandra Enea,

Luca Peyronel, and Frances Pinnock (eds.), *Proceedings of the First International Congress on the Archaeology of the Ancient Near East: Rome, May 18–23 1998,* Vol. II, 1259–1282. Roma: Università degli studi di Roma "La Sapienza," Dipartimento di scienze storiche, archeologiche e antropologiche dell'antichità.

Pettinato, Giovanni. 1983. Le città fenicie e Byblos in particolare nella documentazione epigrafica di Ebla. *Studi Fenici* 16: 107–118.

———. 1986. *Ebla: Nouovi orizzonti della storia.* Milan: Rusconi.

Peyronel, Luca. 2012. "Resources Exploitation and Handicraft Activities at Tell Mardikh-Ebla (Syria) during the Early and Middle Bronze Ages." In Roger J. Matthews, John Curtis et al. (eds.). *Proceedings of the 7th International Congress of the Archaeology of the Ancient Near East, 12 April – 16 April 2010, the British Museum and UCL, London, Volume 1*, 475–496. Wiesbaden: Harrasowitz.

———. 2015. "The "Outer Town" of Ebla during the Old Syrian Period. A Preliminary Analysis of the Off-Site Survey 2010." *Studia Eblaitica* 1: 131–64.

———. 2016. "Bone and Ivory Manufacturing at Ebla (Syria) during the Early and Middle Bronze Age (c. 2500–1600 BC)." *Levant* 48: 148–96.

Peyronel, Luca, and Agnese Vacca. 2013. "Natural Resources, Technology and Manufacture Processes at Ebla: A Preliminary Assessment." In Paolo Matthiae and Niccolò Marchetti (eds.), *Ebla and Its Landscape: Early State Formation in the Ancient Near East*, 431–449. Walnut Creek, CA: Left Coast Press.

Pinnock, Frances. 1985a. "About the Trade of Early Syrian Ebla." *Mari* 4: 85–92.

———. 1985b. "A proposito del commercio del lapis lazuli tra Mari ed Ebla nel III millennio a.C." *Studi Eblaiti* 8: 21–34.

———. 1986. "The Lapis Lazuli Trade in the Third Millennium B.C. and the Evidence from the Royal Palace G of Ebla." In Marylin Kelly-Buccellati, Paolo Matthiae, and Maurice van Loon (eds.), *Studies in Honor of Edith Porada*, 221–228. BiMes 21. Malibu: Undena Publications.

———. 1988. "Observations on the Trade of Lapis Lazuli in the IIIrd Millennium B.C." In Hartmut Waetzoldt and Hans Hauptmann (eds.), *Wirtschaft und Gesellschaft von Ebla. Akten der Internationalen Tagung Heidelberg 4.–7. November 1986*, 107–110. HSAO 2. Heidelberg: Heidelberger Orientverlag.

———. 2006. "The Raw Lapis Lazuli in the Royal Palace G of Ebla. New Evidence from the Annexes of Throne Room." In Maria Elena Alberti, Enrico Ascalone, and Luca Peyronel (eds.), *Weights in Context. Bronze Age Weighing Systems of Eastern Mediterranean: Chronology, Typology, Material and Archaeological Contexts*, 347–357. *Studi e Materiali* 13. Rome: Istituto Italiano di Numismatica.

———. 2018. "Ancora sui rapporti tra Ebla e l'Egitto: Note a margine." In Agnese Vacca, Sara Pizzimenti, and Maria Gabriella Micale (eds.), *A Oriente del Delta. Scritti sull'Egitto ed il VO antico in onore di Gabriella Scandone Matthiae*, 495–520. Contributi e Materiali di Archeologia Orientale 18. Rome: Scienze e Lettere.

Roccati, Alessandro. 1982. *La littérature historique sous l'Ancien Empire égyptien.* Paris: Les éditions du cerf.

———. 2012a. "Appendice. DUGURASU=*rw-h3wt.*" *Atti dell'Accademia delle Scienze di Torino, Classe di Scienze Morali, Storiche e Filologiche* 146: 37–41.

———. 2012b. "Una miniera di turchese di epoca faraonica nel deserto occidentale egiziano." *Atti della Accademia delle Scienze di Torino* 146: 46–53.

———. 2015a. "DUGURASU = *rw-h3wt.*" In Alfonso Archi (ed.), *Tradition and Innovation in the Ancient Near East: Proceedings of the 57th Rencontre Assyriologique Internationale at Rome, 4–8 July 2011*, 155–159. Winona Lake: Eisenbrauns.

———. 2015b. "Iny's Travels." In Maria Giovanna Biga *et al.* (eds), *Homenaje a Mario Liverani, fundador di una ciencia nueva (I)*, 225–229. Madrid: Servicio de Publicaciones, Universidad Autónoma de Madrid.

Sallaberger, Walther and Ingo Schrakamp. 2015. "The Chronology of Ebla and Babylonian History." In Walther Sallaberger and Ingo Schrakamp (eds.), *History and Philology*, 96–104. ARCANE III. Turnhout: Brepols..

Scandone Matthiae, Gabriella. 1979. "Vasi iscritti di Chefren e Pepi I nel Palazzo Reale G di Ebla." *Studi Eblaiti* 1: 33–43.

———. 1981. "I vasi egiziani in pietra del Palazzo Reale di Ebla." *Studi Eblaiti* 4: 99–127.

———. 1994. "La cultura egiziana a Biblo attraverso le testimonianze materiali." In Enrico Acquaro, Federico Mazza, Sergio Ribichini, Gabriella Scandone, and Paolo Xella (eds.), *Biblo.*

Una città e la sua cultura. Atti del Colloquio Internazionale, Roma, 5–7 dicembre 1990, 37–48. Roma: Consiglio nazionale delle ricerche.

———. 1997. "The Relations between Ebla and Egypt." In Eliezer D. Oren (ed.), *The Hyksos: New Historical and Archaeological Perspective*, 415–427. University Museum Monograph 96. Philadelphia: University Museum of the University of Pennsylvania.

Schneider, Thomas. 2015. "The Old Kingdom Abroad: An Epistemological Perspective. With Remarks on the Biography of Iny and the Kingdom of Dugurasu." In Peter der Manuelian and Thomas Schneider (eds.), *Towards a New History for the Egyptian Old Kingdom: Perspectives on the Pyramid Age*, 429–455. Harvard Egyptological Studies 1. Leiden: Brill.

Sowada, Karin N. 2009. *Egypt in the Eastern Mediterranean during the Old Kingdom: An Archaeological Perspective*. OBO 237. Göttingen: Vandenhoeck & Ruprecht.

———. 2016–2018. "Hidden Exports: a Likely Bronze Age Exchange in Egyptian Cattle to the Levant." *The Bulletin of the Australian Centre for Egyptology* 26: 71–78.

Steinkeller, Piotr. 2014. "Marhaši and Beyond: The Jiroft Civilization in a Historical Perspective." In Carl C. Lamberg-Karlovsky and Maurizio Tosi (eds.). *'My Life is like the Summer Rose': Maurizio Tosi e l'Archeologia come modo di vivere, Papers in Honour of Maurizio Tosi for His 70th Birthday*, 691-707. BAR International Series 2690. Oxford: Archaeopress.

———. 2016. "The Role of Iran in the Inter-Regional Exchange of Metals: Tin, Copper, Silver and Gold in the Second Half of the Third Millennium BC." In Kazuya Maekawa (ed.), *Ancient Iran: New Perspectives from Archaeology and Cuneiform Studies. Proceedings of the International Colloquium Held at the Center for Eurasian Cultural Studies, Kyoto University, December 6–7, 2014*, 127–150. Ancient Text Studies in the National Museum vol. 2. Kyoto: Iran–Japan Project of Ancient Texts.

———. 2021. "International Trade in Greater Mesopotamia during Late Pre-Sargonic Times: The Case of Ebla as Illustrated by Her Participation in the Euphratean Timber Trade." In Lorenz Rahmstorf, Nicola Ialongo, and Gojko Barjamovic (eds.), *Merchants, Measures and Money. Understanding the Technologies of Early Trade in a Comparative Perspective: Proceedings of Two Workshops Funded by the European Research Council (ERC)*, 173–193. Weight & Value 2. Kiel Hamburg: Wachholtz Verlag.

Yener, K. Aslihan. 2015. "Silver for Assur: Kanesh, Acemhöyuk and Metal Wealth in the Taurus Mountains." *Anatolica* 41: 1–7.

Yener, K. Aslihan, and Pamela B. Vandiver. 1993. "Tin Processing at Göltepe, an Early Bronze Age Site in Anatolia." *American Journal of Archaeology* 97: 207–38.

Yener, K. Aslihan Yener, K. Aslıhan, Fikri Kulakoğlu, Evren Yazgan, Ryoichi Kontani, Yuichi S. Hayakawa, Joseph W. Lehner, Gonca Dardeniz, Güzel Öztürk, Michael Johnson, Ergun Kaptan, and Abdullah Hacar. 2015. "New Tin Mines and Production Sites near Kültepe in Turkey: A Third-Millennium BC Highland Production Model." *Antiquity* 89: 596–612.

Notes

1 Archi 1980, 3 rejected the identification of DUlu with Byblos proposed by Pettinato. Archi, Piacentini, and Pomponio (1993, 206–211) mention the possibility of such an identification but reject it. Bonechi (1993, 111–112) mentions it too without rejecting it altogether.

2 For the finds of unworked lapis lazuli at Ebla, see Pinnock 1985a,b, 1986, 1988, 2006; Peyronel and Vacca 2013, 442–443.

3 Marcolin 2010; Marcolin and Diego Espinel 2011; Diego Espinel 2015–2016; Diego Espinel, this volume.

4 Biga 2012; 2014a,b,c; 2016; 2017, 2021a,b.

5 Roccati 2012a; 2015a; Durand 2014, 1–5; Schneider 2015, 445–446; Miroschedji 2015, 1035; Diego Espinel 2015–2016, 125–126; Steinkeller 2016, 128; 2021; Peyronel 2016, 185; Bonechi 2016, 30 no. 3; Matoian 2016, 179 nos. 35 and 38; Matthiae 2018, 348 no. 2; Moreno Garcia 2019, 190.

6 Yener et al. 2015; For the analysis of Eblaite tin objects, see Palmieri-Hauptmann 2000, 1264–1265; Biga and Steinkeller 2021, 26–28 and no. 64.

7 For a complete discussion of these points and bibliography, see Biga and Steinkeller 2021, 33–36.

8 The item is written in various ways; for a discussion (by Steinkeller) of the word in the Eblaite lexical sources and its translation and

a possible explanation of its spellings, see Biga and Steinkeller 2021, 36–38 and note 103.

9 About Eblaite silver and gold, Peyronel and Vacca (2013, 441) wrote that "the two precious metals arrived in Ebla from different geographical areas … the silver coming from the Taurus mountains in eastern Turkey, and the gold from sources located either in Egypt or in Middle Asia (at the moment it is not possible to identify the provenance)."

10 For a discussion of these gemstones, see Biga and Steinkeller 2021, 39–45. These gemstones deserve a detailed study, which was not our purpose in the JCS article.

11 For ḫumbabītu / ḫumbibītu, see CAD U 234.

12 For monkeys playing instruments documented at Thera, see Biga, Fs M.Negri, in print.

Journal of Ancient Egyptian Interconnections

Contacts between Egypt and the Southern Levant in the late Early Bronze Age: An Open Question

Marta D'Andrea
Sapienza Università di Roma, Dipartimento di Scienze dell'Antichità

Abstract
The second half of the third millennium BCE is traditionally interpreted as a period of intense interactions between the southern Levant and Egypt. In past scholarship, interpretative frameworks for these activities have centered either on conflicts or commercial relations linked to the trade of southern Levantine copper with Egypt, both considered limited to the time of the Old Kingdom with virtually no evidence of contacts afterward until the early Middle Kingdom. However, nothing is virtually known about southern Levantine–Egyptian connections during this time span. This article reconsiders, from the southern Levant perspective, the impact of the lack of chronological resolution in the sub-phasing of the southern Levantine Early Bronze IV on this question and discusses how recent archaeological research may enhance our understanding of this phase in an interregional context.

Keywords
Southern Levantine–Egyptian connections, Early Bronze Age III, Early Bronze Age IV, absolute chronology, relative chronology, copper trade, connectivity, mobility

Introduction

The existence of intense contacts between the southern Levant and Egypt during the second half of the 3rd millennium BCE is traditionally considered a fact. Scholars have often assumed that Egyptian raids during the late Old Kingdom played a role in the end of the southern Levantine fortified settlements of Early Bronze III.[1] Alternatively, contacts between the two regions have been framed within the hypothesis of commercial relations linked to the trade of southern Levantine copper with the late Old Kingdom Egypt, with virtually no evidence of contacts afterward until the early Middle Kingdom.[2] However, this remains, in fact, an open question. Although it is believed that there were trade contacts between the late Old Kingdom Egypt and the southern Levant, by then no longer urban if one follows the revised chronology (discussed below), this is still virtually an entirely unattested argument.

This paper will address current issues in the study of the late Early Bronze Age in the southern Levant, in particular the demise of urbanism between Early Bronze III (c. 2850–2500 BCE) and Early Bronze IV (c. 2500–1950/1920 BCE), and developments in the non-urban Early Bronze IV. It will also propose a short overview of recent research results at Khirbet Iskander in Jordan that may enhance our understanding of the passage from the Early Bronze III to the Early Bronze IV in the eastern Dead Sea Plain. In fact, this latter area has been traditionally connected with the control over the exploitation of copper in the Faynan and 'Arabah regions, so critical to traditional interpretations of southern Levantine–Egyptian connections in the later Early Bronze Age. The analysis will not focus on material culture evidence of such contacts during the second half of the third millennium BCE, already addressed in past scholarship and admittedly very limited. Rather, the paper will discuss biases in the study of connections with Egypt in this time span resulting from still ill-defined ceramic and radiometric sub-phasing of the late Early Bronze Age in the southern Levant.

The Late Early Bronze Age and the Demise of Urbanism in the Southern Levant

The late Early Bronze Age in the southern Levant (Fig. 1) is concerned with the crisis of urbanism in this region. According to the most recent periodization of the third millennium BCE in this region, the period spanning from c. 2500 to 1920 BCE[3] is currently labeled by scholars as either Intermediate Bronze Age or Early Bronze IV. The second definition is used throughout this article. It is agreed that Early Bronze IV was a non-urban phase following the end of the archaic urbanization that developed locally during the Early Bronze II–III (c. 3100/3000–2500 BCE).[4] Actually, the true urban nature of the Early Bronze II–III has been broadly discussed during the past three decades, with various scholars supporting different interpretative frameworks for the archaeological evidence, ranging from the city-state model to scalar versions of urbanism up to the refusal of urbanization in favor of models centering on heterarchy, corporate society, or similar non-hierarchical socio-political organizations.[5]

Lately, fresh research has increasingly produced solid evidence that the southern Levant as a whole was involved in a trajectory towards archaic urbanism all through the Early Bronze II–III. Archaeological correlates of this phenomenon can be seen in 1) the nucleation of often massively fortified sites within a hierarchically organized pattern of settlements that encompassed proper cities, towns, and rural villages, as well as active interactions with the pastoral components; 2) the appearance of temples and "non-residential" or "public buildings" with evidence for the concentration of staples and wealth of goods (often called "proto-palaces" and palaces); and 3) the concentration of production activities (e.g., crops processing, olive oil production, and pottery production) within these compounds.[6]

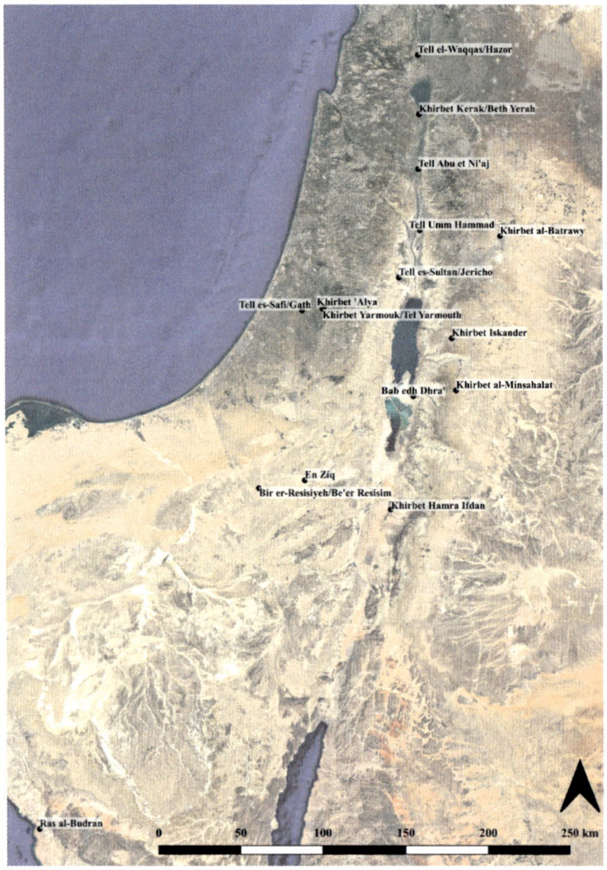

Figure 1: Location map of the sites mentioned in the text (map by Luca Volpi).

Moreover, it is becoming increasingly clear that these correlates can be found, during the first half of the third millennium BCE/Early Bronze II–III, not just in the southern Levant but also in the northern and central Levant, the regions corresponding to present-day Syria and Lebanon.[7] This suggests that a similar and broadly contemporaneous trend (with regional variations) toward urban complexity might have developed across the whole Levant during this time,[8] before various regions within this larger area developed otherwise in the second half of the third millennium BCE/Early Bronze IV. In fact, during the Early Bronze IV, the northern Levant saw continued urbanism and even archaic state formation (although with alternate fortunes at various sites, as well as with important changes in socio-political and socioeconomic balances), whereas the southern Levant reverted to a non-urban/rural economy and society.[9]

In general, recent research showed that the transition, in the southern Levant, from an Early

Absolute BCE dates	Southern Levant / Traditional periodization	Soutern Levant / Revised periodization	Northern Levant
2700 2600 2550	First half of Early Bronze III (Early Bronze IIIA)	Later Early Bronze III (starting ca. 2850 BCE)	Early Bronze III
2500/2450 2400	Second half of Early Bronze III (Early Bronze IIIB)	Early Bronze IV / Intermediate Bronze Age	Early Bronze IVA
2300 2200 2100	Early Bronze IV / Intermediate Bronze Age / Middle Bronze I (up to the 1990s)		Early Bronze IVB
2000 1950 1900	Middle Bronze I / Middle Bronze IIA*	Early Middle Bronze I	Early Middle Bronze I

TABLE 1: Differences between the traditional and the revised absolute dates associated with archaeological periods for the time span relevant to this article.
*Up to the 1990s, Middle Bronze IIA was used for the southern Levant and Middle Bronze I was used for Early Bronze IV; it has more rarely been used later too, up to the early 2000s.

Bronze III archaic (and unstable) urbanism to an Early Bronze IV ruralism and agropastoralism was a multifaceted process across the whole area. This might have resulted from diversified regional responses to a crisis starting already during the last Early Bronze III phase; in fact, the later Early Bronze III seems characterized differently at various sites throughout the Levant.[10]

At different sites, the later Early Bronze III phase appears as either the climax of archaic urbanization followed by abandonment (e.g. Khirbet Yarmouk/Tel Yarmouth), destruction (e.g. Tell es-Sultan/Jericho), or abatement/decline followed by abandonment (Khirbet Kerak/Beth Yerah),[11] or as part of a longer trajectory of resilience and reorganization that bridges between the late Early Bronze III and the Early Bronze IV occupation (Khirbet Iskander).[12] Such diverse processes happening around 2500 BCE, or rather, perhaps, with differentiated timings across the region from 2600 to 2400 BCE, may have involved changes in settlement patterns within the southern Levant, and, in some cases, movements across the region both during Early Bronze III and in the passage to Early Bronze IV.[13] This suggestion seems reinforced by the increasing evidence of a discrete archaeological *facies* identified in several one-phase sites associated with radiocarbon dates clustering around the 25th century cal BCE, as discussed below.

This phase of changes and transformations seems to have happened in the wake of either crisis or resilience scenarios, depending on the various trajectories of individual sites, the latter scenario being seemingly the case of Khirbet Iskander, in central Jordan (FIG. 2). Moreover, this phase seems to have been followed by an initial phase of reorganization and restructuring at the beginning of the Early Bronze IV. In the long term, this developmental path may have allowed for new growth in the following phases of the Early Bronze IV. In fact, it is increasingly evident that, despite the non-urban social structure, during Early Bronze IV there were complexity, connectivity, and technological developments and progress that would gradually pave the way for the regeneration of urbanism during the following Middle Bronze Age.[14]

CHRONOLOGY, STRATIGRAPHY, MATERIAL CULTURE, AND THE EVIDENCE FROM KHIRBET ISKANDER (JORDAN) AT THE EARLY BRONZE III–IV TRANSITION

During the past ten years, there has been a revision of the absolute chronology of the southern Levantine Early Bronze Age (see Table 1, indicating differences between the traditional and revised absolute dates associated with archaeological periods for the time span relevant to this article).[15] In particular, the local Early Bronze III is now dated to circa 2850–2500 BCE instead of c. 2700–2300 BCE, and the Early Bronze IV is now dated from c. 2500–1950/1920 BCE instead of 2300–2000 BCE. There are two most significant consequences to this change for interregional synchronisms, analyzed in several recent papers and books.[16] First, the southern Levantine non-urban Early Bronze IV phase, would coincide with the florescence of urbanism and state formation in the northern Levant during the local Early Bronze IVA (c. 2500–2000 BCE).[17] Second, the non-urban Early Bronze IV in the southern Levant

FIGURE 2: Khirbet Iskander, Jordan; aerial view of the site, looking northwest, with the excavation areas (photo: copyright APAAME, APAAME_20141013_REB-0161.jpg, photographer Rebecca Banks; edits by Marta D'Andrea for this article).

would not just coincide with the "problematic" First Intermediate Period in Egypt, but with a longer time span stretching from the late Old Kingdom to the early Middle Kingdom in the latter region.[18]

Although the revised chronology is increasingly accepted,[19] a universal scholarly consensus has not yet been reached, as there are some relevant exceptions.[20] It is the opinion of the author that there are some advantages in the revised chronology for the southern Levantine Early Bronze Age. Realigning Early Bronze III and IV in the northern and southern Levant, for instance, may allow us to get a better grasp of contacts between these two areas throughout most of the third millennium BCE.[21] What is still problematic in the new chronological scheme is that we do not yet seem to have enough stratified data from the southern Levant to fit into such a longer Early Bronze IV. In general, radiocarbon dating of different subphases of the southern Levantine Early Bronze IV is still at the beginning and, in some respects, problematic. There are virtually no long Early Bronze IV sequences that are radiocarbon-dated. One exception is Tell Abu en-Ni'aj in the northern Jordan Valley, though even the radiocarbon date series from this site are not framed within a continuous Early Bronze III–Early Bronze IV–Middle Bronze I sequence, and do not bridge over the end of the third millennium BCE.[22] Obviously, this general situation affects our current ability to define the upper and lower boundaries of the Early Bronze IV absolute chronology. This problem increases moving toward the central and later phases of this time, which are well characterized in the stratigraphic sequences of regional key sites (e.g., Tell Umm Hammad, Tell es-Sultan/Jericho, and Khirbet Iskander)[23] but are not yet radiocarbon-dated.

An archaizing material culture looking more like an impoverished, or rather, a vestigial Early Bronze III tradition than an Early Bronze IV one proper is attested at a few sites with different individual trajectories: Sites with previous Early Bronze III occupation (Phase Sultan IIId1 at Tell es-Sultan/Jericho, and Phase 1 in Area C Khirbet Iskander); one-phase sites with short-lived occupation (Elevation Point–167, Khirbet el-'Alya Northeast, and Khirbet al-Minsahalat); sites resettled after long-term abandonment (Stage 5 at Tell Umm Hammad); and villages established *ex-novo* (Phase 7 at Tell Abu et Ni'aj).[24]

The available radiocarbon dates associated with the ceramic assemblages fall either within the 25th

century BCE, with short intervals, or, more rarely, within roughly the third quarter of the third millennium BCE, with larger intervals.[25] At most of these sites, this chronological and material culture horizon may have equal chances to correspond to either an initial Early Bronze IV or to a terminal Early Bronze III phase or, more generally, to an Early Bronze III/IV transitional phase.[26] As discussed in the following section, the case of Khirbet Iskander (like the case of Jericho) in that the earliest Early Bronze IV phase is clearly nestled between the latest Early Bronze III and the middle Early Bronze IV levels within a long and continuous Early Bronze III–IV stratigraphic sequence.[27]

As said above, the exact date for the end of the Early Bronze IV is still unknown because of the lack of radiometric dating. Generally, there are few radiocarbon dates spanning the last centuries of the 3rd millennium BCE (Hazor,[28] Bab edh-Dhra',[29] and a few sites in the Central Negev[30]) or with intervals bridging the 3rd and 2nd millennia BCE; again, the ones that are available are neither associated with a long Early Bronze IV sequence[31] nor with continuous Early Bronze IV–Middle Bronze I sequences. Therefore, as suggested in previous works, we do not know if the later Early Bronze IV phases with transitional Middle Bronze I traits attested at certain sites overlapped with the archaic Middle Bronze I phases with conservative Early Bronze IV traits identified at other settlements, or if the two phases evolved from one another or how much time elapsed between them[32]. As we shall see in the following sections, the blurring definition of the upper and lower chronological boundaries of the Early Bronze IV also affects our understanding of contacts between the southern Levant and Egypt during this phase.

To determine unambiguously the beginning and the end of the Early Bronze IV within multi-period continuous stratigraphic sequences at individual sites, it would be necessary to anchor radiocarbon dates with short intervals to stratigraphic phases associated with discrete material culture assemblages. As an example of a work in progress on a continuous and imposing Early Bronze III–IV stratigraphic sequence of a southern Levantine site, I will shortly discuss the results of the most recent archaeological research at Khirbet Iskander in central Jordan. On the one hand, this is relevant to the issue of correlating stratigraphy and chronology for the southern Levantine Early Bronze III–IV. On the other hand, due to its "proto-urban" characteristics in the non-urban phase (including "non-residential" architecture and the reuse or even the reconstruction of fortifications[33]), the site has been often evoked in reconstructions of southern Levantine–Egyptian connections as linked to the exploitation of the Faynan copper mines in southern Jordan during Early Bronze IV.[34]

Khirbet Iskander may offer an example of a work on correlations between stratigraphy, phased pottery assemblages, and radiocarbon dates at a site spanning the Early Bronze III and IV. The recent discoveries in Area C at Khirbet Iskander, in the southwest sector of the site, may be connected to the evidence for multiphase Early Bronze III and IV strata excavated previously also in Area B, on the northeast edge of the site, where the remains of a multilayered Early Bronze III settlement with imposing fortifications, enhanced and rebuilt several times, were uncovered.[35] As the importance of the Early Bronze III occupation in Area C became apparent during the 2019 season,[36] this is now being investigated more deeply. However, Khirbet Iskander's complex stratigraphic sequences in both areas constitute altogether one of the longest continuous Early Bronze III–IV occupations identified thus far at a southern Levantine archaeological site (Fig. 3).

It seems clear that after a destruction around the middle Early Bronze III, identified previously in Area B[37] and seemingly found also in Area C at the end of the 2019 season,[38] the site saw continuous domestic occupation during Early Bronze III and into Early Bronze IV. During the 2019 excavation campaign, we clearly isolated the last phase in this long Early Bronze III sequence (Fig. 4) and the associated pottery (Fig. 5). This was immediately followed and directly overlain by the earliest Early Bronze IV phase (Fig. 4), with its ceramic assemblage clearly discrete though showing strong continuity with the Early Bronze III tradition because of the presence of new traits with a definite Early Bronze IV "feel" (Fig. 6). This evidence of possible Early Bronze III–IV residential continuity is still being investigated.

However, for the time being, Suzanne Richard, Jesse Long, and the present author explain it as the outcome of a possibly long episode of resilience starting already during later Early Bronze III (after the destruction) and paving the way for what seems to be a phase of stability already in the earlier Early

FIGURE 3: Khirbet Iskander, Jordan; general view of the multi-layered Early Bronze III–IV remains in Area C (Squares C8 and C6, from north to south), from the top, end of 2019 season (© Archaeological Expedition to Khirbat Iskandar).

a

b

FIGURE 4: Khirbet Iskander, Jordan; architectural remains of the last Early Bronze III phase in Squares C8 (top, looking south) and C6 (bottom, looking east) uncovered in the 2019 season in Area C. Note the Phase 1/earlier Early Bronze IV phase walls sealing the remains of the previous Early Bronze III occupation (© Archaeological Expedition to Khirbat Iskandar).

Bronze IV phase.[39] This earliest Early Bronze IV phase at Khirbet Iskander with its well-made walls and plaster floors, and its associated pottery with a "transitional" Early Bronze III/IV flavor seems much more substantial in terms of architecture and planning than the contemporary occupation attested at other sites in the region and mentioned before.[40]

This archaic Early Bronze IV phase was followed by other two major Early Bronze IV phases that eventually saw the gradual transformation of this domestic area into a public multifunctional complex interpreted as a monumental gateway to the inner sector of the site.[41] This long Early Bronze IV stratigraphic sequence has allowed S. Richard to isolate well-phased pottery assemblages associated with each phase.[42]

Some radiocarbon dates are available. A few dates associated with the destruction in the middle of Early Bronze III in Area B place this event in the interval between c. 2900 and 2700 cal BCE but are still unpublished. Recently, modeled radiocarbon dates were obtained for the Early Bronze III sequence in Area C, placed between 2600 and 2500 BCE, with the Early Bronze III/IV transition in Area C falling at or slightly before 2500 cal BCE (2515–2496 cal BCE in the 1-sigma range).[43]

Radiometric dating of Area C Phases 2 and 3 is still challenging. Phase 2, which is the middle Early Bronze IV phase in this sector of the site according to stratigraphy, yielded a radiocarbon range that falls in the interval spanning the entire first half of the Early Bronze IV.[44] This is too broad for fine-tuning the internal sub-phasing of the latter. Other recent dates obtained from Phases 2 and 3 are too high, yielding ranges like those of Phase 1 and the preceding phases and must, therefore, be considered

FIGURE 5: Khirbet Iskander, Jordan; selected pottery sherds associated with the last Early Bronze III phase in Area C (© Archaeological Expedition to Khirbat Iskandar).

FIGURE 6: Khirbet Iskander, selected pottery sherds from the earlier Early Bronze IV phase in Area C (after D'Andrea 2014a, Vol. 2, Pls. I, III; © Archaeological Expedition to Khirbat Iskandar).

problematic.[45] Accordingly, Khirbet Iskander's long Early Bronze IV sequence now awaits series of radiocarbon dates to be associated with the stratigraphy and the pottery assemblages of each phase. This might allow us to answer questions concerning Early Bronze IV in connection with the current difficulty to bridge the gap between stratigraphy and material culture, especially for the advanced Early Bronze IV phases and the Early/Middle Bronze nexus.[46]

The above re-examination of current chronological issues in the study of the second half of the third millennium BCE in the southern Levant has set the framework for reconsidering the question of possible south Levantine–Egyptian contacts during this period within the current state of research. In fact, as discussed in the following section, evidence of intense contacts between Egypt and the southern Levant during the second half of the third millennium BCE is virtually absent whether we use the traditional or the revised chronology.

Southern Levantine–Egyptian Contacts during the Early Bronze IV and the Question of Copper Trade

Written and iconographic records from this time (such as the autobiography of Uni/Weni dating from the Sixth Dynasty), used to define the nature of interactions between Egypt and the southern Levant within the framework of either commercial contacts or conflicts,[47] are somewhat problematic. There is no consensus whether toponyms mentioned in the inscriptions and other texts should be placed in the northern or southern Levant; it is even questioned whether it is possible to locate them at all. Likewise, there is no consensus whether the term *Wnt* refers to the southern Levantine fortified centers and if the word *ꜥ3mu*, traditionally translated as "Asiatics," refers to Levantine people in general, to southern Levantine people specifically, or to Bedouins settling the Sinai desert.[48] Since this issue has been discussed to some length, we bring only a few basic pieces of information, referring the readers to past scholarship.[49]

In general, for the late Old Kingdom texts and inscriptions, one-to-one correlations between geographic names and real places are uncertain, as is the correspondence between peoples' names and the inhabitants of the Early Bronze III fortified settlements of the southern Levant. For the following period, the First Intermediate Period, written records (mainly literary texts) are sometimes used to contextualize the lack of contacts between Egypt and the southern Levant within the framework of political instability in the former region and de-urbanization in the latter area, but their reliability may be impacted by their very propagandist nature.[50]

Besides the aspects discussed above, the dearth of Egyptian material in the southern Levant during Early Bronze III has been already pointed out by K. Sowada, who also suggested that the bulk of Egyptian finds from this region dates from the earlier Early Bronze III phase, many of them also possibly being heirlooms.[51] Likewise, Egyptian materials in the southern Levant during Early Bronze IV are limited to a few Meydum bowls and other sherds found at sites in the Central Negev and northwest Sinai.[52] Notwithstanding, the notion that copper mined in the Faynan and Arabah regions was traded to Egypt at this time has become a firm point, especially in studies that take the view from the arid regions of the southern Levant. In fact, it is widely held that copper mining and trading activities carried out at a large scale during Early Bronze IV would have been controlled by sites in the eastern Dead Sea plain, such as Bab edh-Dhra' and Khirbet Iskander.[53] Likewise, it is believed that copper trade would have prompted the flourishing of settlements in the Central Negev and the establishment of campsites in northwest Sinai.[54] This hypothesis has found a place also in conceptual frameworks using the revised absolute chronology.[55]

Recent scholarship has suggested that radiocarbon dates falling in the interval between the 26th and the 23rd century cal. BCE and associated with red-slipped pottery would attest for a major phase of occupation in the Central Negev and intense exploitation of copper mines in the Faynan and 'Arabah regions during the first half of the Early Bronze IV,[56] in continuity with the late Early Bronze III (which are, altogether, contemporaneous with the Old Kingdom in Egypt).[57] In this earlier non-urban phase, metallurgical activities would have been managed by desert people trading copper to the Late Old Kingdom Egypt.[58] This hypothesis would concur with the mention of *ꜥ3mu sṯt*, usually translated as "Asiatic copper," in the "Abusir Papyrus" dated to the Fifth Dynasty.[59]

According to a recent proposal,[60] this phase would have been followed by a smaller-scale occupation of the southern Levantine arid margins and limited copper mining for internal consumption between c. 2200 and 2000 BCE, in the second half of the Early Bronze IV.[61] This latter phase is characterized by the presence of pottery decorated with the wavy and horizontal combed motives typical of the south–central areas of the southern Levant at the Central Negev sites, at some of them also associated with a few later radiocarbon dates.[62]

This proposal is somewhat problematic when confronted with the extant datasets. Since 2012, the present author has called attention to the need to confirm beyond doubt that the already published red-slipped pottery from the Central Negev sites date from Early Bronze III, with parallels also in the corresponding assemblages from Khirbet Hamra Ifdan.[63] In fact, all the analogies at hand are sealed stratified assemblages whose date, the later Early Bronze III, is even secured by radiocarbon datings concurring with the revised chronology.[64]

To my knowledge, no single, published, later assemblage radiocarbon-dated to the 25th century BCE (by 14C dates with reasonably short intervals) shows pottery types and styles comparable to the published red-slipped and burnished ceramics found at En Ziq, Bir er-Resisiyeh / Be'er Resisim, and Khirbet Hamra Ifdan. Also, as discussed at length in previous works,[65] the older radiocarbon dates from these sites are by no means conclusive for dating the settlements in the Central Negev and the Faynan regions to the first half of Early Bronze IV. In fact, they are characterized by very large intervals that may equally encompass the late Early Bronze III, the Early Bronze III/IV transition, and the first half of Early Bronze IV, with no chances to further trim down the chronological range.

As suggested in previous works, the available evidence may point to the absence of sedentary occupation of these areas and a lack of evidence for significant exploitation of the copper mines in the earlier phases of Early Bronze IV.[66] This may suggest that copper mining and trading activities that were carried out there on a large scale during the urban Early Bronze III might have been halted or at least slowed down, reducing considerably at the beginning of Early Bronze IV following the demise of the local archaic urbanization and the associated socioeconomic structures. Alternatively, during the earlier Early Bronze IV phase, such activities might have been organized around a system that would not entail permanent settlements as in the previous (Early Bronze III) and in the following (middle-to-late Early Bronze IV) phases.

Large-scale copper mining and trading might have resumed only later, when band- and wavy-combed pottery is attested at sites in the Wadi Faynan and the Central Negev. However, as said before, the latter phase is not yet sufficiently well radiocarbon-dated within long Early Bronze IV stratigraphic sequences to place it within the new longer timeline of absolute dates for this time suggested by the revised chronology.

Considering the bulk of the published pottery from the 'Arabah, the Faynan, and the Central Negev, the latter assemblages with band- and wavy-combed pottery are the only ceramics from those sites that can be confidently ascribed to the Early Bronze IV. In fact, parallels for these vessel types and styles are available from well stratified, sealed assemblages from the advanced Early Bronze IV phases at Tell es-Sultan/Jericho and Khirbet Iskander.[67] In addition, radiocarbon dates with intervals falling in the last centuries of the third millennium BCE come from 'Ein Ziq in the Central Negev (2200 and 1980 cal BCE[68]), from 'En Yahav (1-sigma: 2030–1920 cal BCE; 2-sigma: 2140–1880 cal BCE), a copper smelting site in the 'Arabah,[69] and Khirbet Hamra Ifdan (2201–1884 cal BCE).[70]

The dates from 'En Yahav and Khirbet Hamra Ifdan, in particular, suggest that the 'Arabah and Faynan copper was exploited in this period. However, in general, the correlation between phased ceramic assemblages and radiocarbon dates is not yet sufficient for all these regions of the southern Levant (Dead Sea Plain, Judean foothills, Shephelah, Central Negev, and the Arabah and Faynan areas) to reconstruct a timeline of occupation and use in the second half of the third millennium BCE, either ceramically and/or radiometrically.

Of course, as suggested earlier, we cannot rule out that desert tribes that certainly kept settling the Negev, the Faynan and the Arabah regions might have exploited the copper mines to some extent in the earliest Early Bronze IV phases. Moreover, getting a firmer grasp on this and, more generally, on interactions of desert nomads with the resilient communities of the eastern Dead Sea Plain at that time—such as the one that may have continuously settled Khirbet Iskander throughout the Early Bronze III and IV—might be crucial for understanding if and how intense copper exploitation resumed later in Early Bronze IV.[71] Likewise, the hypothesis that southern Levantine copper was traded to Egypt during the third quarter of the third millennium BCE/the late Old Kingdom/the first half of the Early Bronze IV cannot be definitively ruled out until proven, on a solid basis, that it was not.[72] Also, the question of the "Asiatic copper" might need some reconsideration.

It is difficult to establish a one-to-one correspondence between the "Asiatic copper" mentioned in the Abusir Papyrus and the southern Levantine copper mined in the Faynan and the Arabah during Early Bronze IV. In fact, this identification remains speculative. Recent archaeometric analyses of Old Kingdom metal artifacts have suggested different sources of the copper used for the objects examined. Two studies led by two different research groups and published in 2018 have pointed, in most cases, to the Eastern Desert and southern Sinai as the most likely sources of copper used for the Egyptian metal objects from selected Old Kingdom contexts examined through lead isotope analyses.[73] Actually, Egyptian seasonal expeditions to southern Sinai for the procurement of copper and turquoise seem documented from the Third to the Sixth Dynasty, and it has been suggested that the fortress site at Ras al-Budran in the Wadi Maghara region may have served to secure it against Bedouins incursions.[74] On the one hand, even the latest information obtained from the chemical and physical characterizations of Old Kingdom metal objects from Egypt mentioned above and pointing to sources of copper different from the Faynan and Arabah regions may not be taken as a definitive proof that southern Levantine copper was not traded to Egypt in this period. In fact, Ben Yosef has proposed that, in contrast to the interpretations put forward in the two studies mentioned above and based on lead isotope analyses, the available data may support a connection between some Old Kingdom period metal artifacts and the 'Arabah copper.[75] It also has to be taken into consideration that the similarity between the geology of the Arabah and the Sinai might not always enable identifying copper chemically or geologically as clearly sourced from either region.

It is also likely that patterns of trade of southern Levantine copper during the Early Bronze IV included other possible recipients that could be sought in different regions. Actually, looking only to the southwest for potential entities interested in the southern Levantine copper trade would mean ignoring the wider Early Bronze IV interregional scenario. In fact, the growth of urbanism during the 25th century BCE and the formation of archaic states in the northern Levant from at least the 24th century BCE is seldom considered in recreations of possible patterns of distribution of southern Levantine copper during Early Bronze IV. However, the socio-political and socioeconomic dynamics accompanying developed urbanism and the formation of emergent states triggered interregional interactions of unprecedented scale for the procurement of goods, raw materials, and even livestock (see below in relation to Egypt), as well as high mobility of specialists in control of the necessary technological know-how for specific activities. In this conjunction, specialized animal breeding[76] and metallurgy stem out. In such a new interregional context, the quest for copper might have allowed the southern Levant to fuel northern demand for this metal, for example, from sites on the Lebanese coast that during Early Bronze IV might have been centers of metallurgical production.[77]

As suggested in earlier works, if we look at the spatial distribution of southern Levantine copper ingots in Early Bronze IV, different paths of circulation may be discernible. If the presence of such copper ingots at several Central Negev sites is any evidence of a west–east route pointing toward Egypt (?), a path of circulation pointing northward also emerges clearly, although from still limited evidence.[78] In fact, crescent-shaped copper ingots in the southern Levant have so far been found not only in some Central Negev sites but also in the Shephelah, in the Hebron region, at Tell es-Sultan/Jericho and at Tell el-Waqqas/Hazor.[79] In all these instances, the pottery associated with the finding contexts suggested a (relative) date in the second half of the Early Bronze IV (referring to traditional stratigraphic correlations, although, in the case of Hazor, the Early Bronze IV occupation is now also radiocarbon-dated to the second half of this era).[80] Hopefully, future research will shed more light on contacts between the most southerly regions of the southern Levant and the oasis of northwest Arabia that are increasingly coming into sharper focus as other potential major agents of interactions with the Levant, at least in the later Early Bronze Age and at the time of the Early/Middle Bronze transition.[81]

Conclusions: Some Thoughts for Future Answers to an Open Question

Based on the above, it certainly cannot be ruled out that contacts existed between the southern Levant and Egypt during the late third millennium BCE, despite how problematic the textual records and tenuous the archaeological evidence for them might be at present. Inconspicuous archaeological evidence of southern Levantine–Egyptian connections is not per se suggestive of a lack of contacts altogether or of the limited intensity or importance of contacts. On the contrary, different data sets should be used to reassess this question. In other words, attempts to stick to the longtime established interpretative frameworks of southern Levantine-Egyptian relations occurring out of a pharaonic interest for "Asiatic copper" mined in the 'Arabah and Faynan areas during the Late Old Kingdom may lead us to ignore more appropriate data sets to investigate interregional interactions. Therefore, reanalyzing this issue from different perspectives may bring out possible hidden connections to light.

For example, for the previous Early Bronze III, recent works have suggested that some types of mediums fueling interregional contacts at the time may be invisible macroscopically. Recent studies have showed evidence that livestock raised in Egypt was exported to the southern Levant during Early Bronze III, pointing to a different sort of intensive exchange between these two regions (although, for the time being, this was proved only in one direction). Through isotopic analyses of animal remains, Arnold and colleagues have discovered evidence that domestic (a goat) and draught/draft (a donkey) animals raised in the Nile Delta migrated to the site of Tell es-Safi/Gath in the Shephelah.

They used this study to suggest that the range of Egyptian–southern Levantine connections may have been multifaceted and more articulated than previously thought.[82] Likewise, Sowada, based on a reexamination of texts and iconographic records, has suggested that cattle raised in Egypt was exported to the southern Levant during the Early Bronze III.[83]

As for the Early Bronze IV, Sowada has suggested that "the continuous movement of domestic animals back and forth the Way of Horus (or by sea) during the third millennium BCE (...) is plausible,"[84] although, as she admits herself, this still has to be proved. Moreover, based on isotopic evidence, Stantis and colleagues suggested that "an influx of non-locals can be observed" in the Nile Delta starting from the Twelfth Dynasty, the beginning of which is now considered to be contemporary with the end of Early Bronze IV according to the revised chronology.[85] In this regard, it is worth noting that in her reexamination of the pictorial record of the early Middle Kingdom elite tombs at Beni Hasan, Mourad suggested that foreign people with different kinds of expertise, some of them of seemingly Levantine origin, crossed Egypt or even resided there at the time of the early Twelfth Dynasty, as well as possibly earlier in the Eleventh Dynasty.[86] This would be in a time span that may also cover the later part of the southern Levantine Early Bronze IV,[87] although, as said before, this still must be better assessed because of the current blurring lower absolute chronological boundary of the latter time.

In sum, albeit preliminary and patchy, residential mobility of animal and humans is being increasingly demonstrated through multiple lines of research for part of the third and the early second millennia BCE. As said before, for the Early Bronze IV, southern Levantine–Egyptian contacts

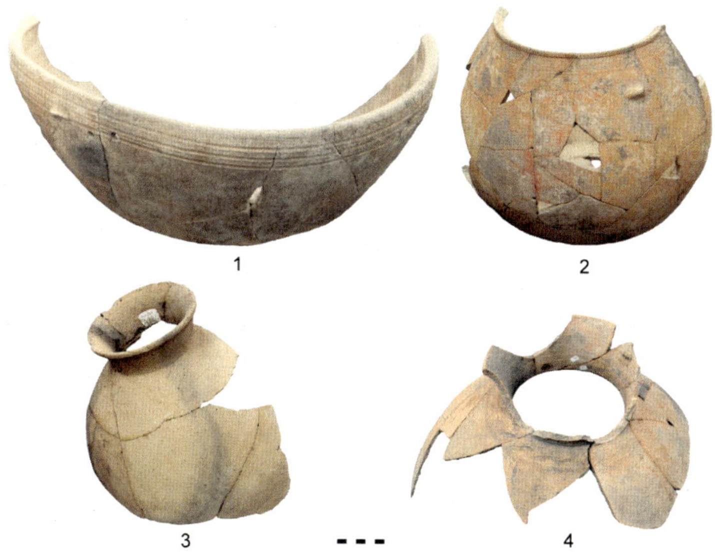

FIGURE 7: Khirbet Iskander, complete or restorable pottery vessels from Area B comparable to Early Bronze IV ceramics found at Khirbet Hamra Ifdan and the Central Negev sites (© Archaeological Expedition to Khirbat Iskandar) (Nos. 2–4 after D'Andrea 2014a, Pls. IX, XV:7; © Archaeological Expedition to Khirbat Iskandar).

are suggested by limited archaeological evidence of Egyptian materials in the southern arid regions of the southern Levant and by the distribution of campsites with mixed Egyptian and southern Levantine ceramics along the Way of Horus.

Therefore, it would be worth re-investigating the range of activities that might have triggered and sustained southern Levantine–Egyptian connections during the Early Bronze IV/ the second half of the third millennium BCE and may have been broader and differentiated and not just pivoting around trade of southern Levantine copper mined in the 'Arabah and Faynan areas to Egypt. In fact, it is not unlikely that, in the centuries that bridged the Early and the Middle Bronze Ages, livestock moved between the southern Levant and Egypt as also did people who were in control of different technologies and expertise that might have been required or prized in an interregional context.

Investigating if such interactions happened in the Early Bronze IV, to what extent and through what kinds of mediums, might allow us to reassess the otherwise quite puzzling presence of hundreds of campsites along the Way of Horus that yielded southern Levantine pottery and Egyptian sherds.[88] However, the chronology, contemporaneity and duration in time of these sites remains obscure until a time when it will be possible to trim down the chronological range to which we may ascribe the southern Levantine pottery found at the campsites. In fact, we are not yet able to refine the chronology of campsites distributed along the Way of Horus within the Early Bronze IV, since ceramic parallels for the published pottery are to be sought in later Early Bronze IV stratigraphic assemblages at multiphase sites of this

Figure #	Khirbet Iskander	Parallels
6:1	Area B, Phase B	Central Negev: Ein Ziq, Cohen 1999: fig. 102:5, 7, 10
6:2	Area B, Phase B	Faynan: Khirbet Hamra Ifdan, Fase 6: Adams 2001, fig. 21.9:8 Central Negev: Ein Ziq, Cohen 1999: fig. 110:1,7
6:3	Area B, Phase B	Central Negev: Ein Ziq, Cohen 1999: fig. 108:2
6:4	Area B, Phase B	Central Negev: Ein Ziq, Cohen 1999: fig. 108:1

TABLE 2: Parallels from sites in the Faynan and Central Negev for the Early Bronze IV pottery from Khirbet Iskander shown in Figure 6.

time, such as Jericho and Khirbet Iskander (FIG. 7, Table 2), that, as said before, are not yet associated with radiocarbon dates.

In conclusion, this article by no means intended to establish new paradigms, but rather aimed at calling attention to issues that may be faced not just when analyzing the records, but especially when trying to compare and combine our individual interpretations, each built on what may be both qualitatively and quantitatively different record types, into one coherent explanatory framework. There are hints to south Levantine–Egyptian connections lasting and intensifying during the following Middle Bronze Age being perhaps established during Early Bronze IV. However, their chronology, duration, evolution through time, as well as the types of activity and the agents of such interregional contacts must still be defined. We should establish our chronological grids—both relative and absolute—more clearly before we can suggest more appropriate conceptual frameworks for contacts between those two regions in the later 3rd millennium BCE. Work on the sequences of key sites has started but more cooperation among scholars working on different data sets, in different regions, and with varying professional backgrounds is needed.

ACKNOWLEDGEMENTS

This article is an extended version of a talk given at the international conference "Egypt and the Mediterranean World from the Late Fourth through the Third Millennium BCE" held in May 2021. The author wishes to thank deeply Karin Sowada and Matthew J. Adams for organizing this event and for their kind invitation to present her views in this venue, during the Amman session hosted by JAEI, for which also Pierce Paul Creasman deserves gratitude. The author also wishes to express her gratitude to Suzanne Richard for reading over several versions of this text and providing precious comments and suggestions, and to Paola Buzi for much appreciated advice. I am indebted with Luca Volpi for the map of the Levant used in the paper. Needless to say, any mistakes or omissions are solely the author's responsibility.

REFERENCES

Adams, Matthew J. 2013. "The Main Sector of Area J." In Israel Finkelstein, David Ussishkin, and Eric H. Cline (eds.), *Megiddo V: The 2004–2008 Seasons*, Vol. 1. Monograph Series of the Sonia and Marco Nadler Institute of Archaeology 31, 47–118. Eisenbrauns: Winona Lake, Indiana.

———. 2017a. "The Egyptianized Pottery Cache from Megiddo's Area J: A Foundation Deposit for Temple 4040." *Tel Aviv* 44 (2): 141–164.

———. 2017b. "Egypt and the Levant in the Early/ Middle Bronze Age Transition." In Felix Höflmayer (ed.), *The Early/Middle Bronze Age Transition in the Ancient Near East: chronology, C14, and climate change.* Oriental Institute Seminars 11, 493–515. Chicago: The Oriental Institute of the University of Chicago.

Adams, Russel B. 2000. "The Early Bronze Age III–IV transition in Southern Jordan: evidence from Khirbet Hamra Ifdan." In Graham Philip and Douglas Baird (eds.), *Ceramic and Change in the Early Bronze Age Southern Levant.* Levantine Archaeology 2, 379–402. Sheffield: Sheffield Academic Press.

———. 2006. "Copper trading networks across the Arabah during the later Early Bronze Age." In Piotr Bienkowski and Katharina Galor (eds.), *Crossing the Rift, Resources, Routes, Settlement Patterns and Interaction in the Wadi Arabah.* Levant Supplementary Series 3, 135–142. London: Council for British Research in the Levant and Oxbow Books.

Arnold Elizabeth R., Gideon Hartman, Hashkel J. Greenfield, Itzhaq Shai, Lindsay E. Babcock, and Aren M. Maeir. 2016. "Isotopic Evidence for Early Trade in Animals between Old Kingdom Egypt and Canaan." *PLoS ONE* 11/6: e0157650. https://doi.org/10.1371/journal.pone.0157650.

Avner, Uzi. 2006. "Settlement Patterns in the Wadi Arabah and the Adjacent Desert Areas: A View from the Eilat Region." In Piotr Bienkowski and Katharina Galor (eds.), *Crossing the Rift. Resources, Routes, Settlement Patterns and Interaction in the Wadi Arabah*. Levant Supplementary Series, 51–74. London: Council for British Research in the Levant and Oxbow Books.

Bar, Shay. 2020. "Khirbet el-Meiyiteh and Elevation Point-167: Evidence of Fortified and Rural Early Bronze IV Settlements in Eastern Samaria." In Suzanne Richard (ed.), *New Horizons in the Study of the Early Bronze III and Early Bronze IV in the Levant*, 347–364. University Park, PA: Eisenbrauns.

Ben-Yosef, Erez. 2018. "Provenancing Egyptian metals: A methodological comment." *Journal of Archaeological Science* 96: 208–215.

Ben-Yosef, Erez, Aaron Gidding, Lisa Tauxe, Uri Davidovich, Mohammed Najjar, and Thomas E. Levy. 2016. "Early Bronze Age Copper Production Systems in the Northern Arabah Valley: New Insights from Archaeomagnetic Study of Slag Deposits in Jordan and Israel." *Journal of Archaeological Science* 72: 71–84.

Burke, Aaron A. 2020. *The Amorites and the Bronze Age Near East: The Making of a Regional Identity*. Cambridge: Cambridge University Press.

Callaway, James A. 1978. "New Perspectives on Early Bronze III Canaan." in Peter R.S. Moorey and Peter J. Parr (eds.), *Archaeology in the Levant: Essays in Honor of Kathleen M. Kenyon*, 46–58 Warminster: Aris & Phillips.

Chesson, Meredith S., Cheryl Makarewicz, Ian Kuijt and Charlotte Whiting. 2005. *Results of the 2001 Kerak Plateau Early Bronze Age Survey*. Annual of the American Schools of Oriental Research 59, 1–62. Boston: Eisenbrauns.

Cohen, Rudolph. 1999. *Ancient Settlement of the Central Negev*, Vol. I: *The Chalcolithic Period, the Early Bronze Age and the Middle Bronze Age I*. Israel Antiquities Authority Reports 6. Jerusalem: Israel Antiquities Authority.

Cohen, Susan L. 2012. "Synchronisms and Significance, Reevaluating Interconnections between Middle Kingdom Egypt and the Southern Levant." *Journal of Ancient Egyptian Interconnections* 4(3): 1–8.

———. 2017. "Reevaluation of Connections between Egypt and the Southern Levant in the Middle Bronze Age in the Light of the New Higher Chronology." *Journal of Ancient Egyptian Interconnections* 13: 34–42.

———. 2018. "Continuity, Innovation, and Change. The Intermediate Bronze Age in The Southern Levant." In Assaf Yasur-Landau, Eric H. Cline, and Yorke Rowan (eds.), *The Social Archaeology of the Levant From Pre-history to the Present*, 183–198. Cambridge: Cambridge University Press.

———. 2019. "Not so Vile? Rhetoric and Reality in Egyptian–Levantine Relationships in Sinai during the Old and Middle Kingdoms." In: Jana Mynářová, Marwan Kilani, and Sergio Alivernini (eds.), *A Stranger in the House — the Crossroads III, Proceedings of an International Conference on Foreigners in Ancient Egyptian and Near Eastern Societies of the Bronze Age held in Prague, September 10–13, 2018*, 73–90. Prague: Czech Institute of Egyptology.

———. 2022. "The Negev in the Intermediate Bronze Age: Questions of Subsistence, Trade, and Status," *Journal of Ancient Near Eastern History* 9(2): 221–241. https://doi.org/10.1515/janeh-2021-0012.

D'Andrea, Marta 2012. "The Early Bronze IV Period in South-Central Transjordan: Reconsidering Chronology through Ceramic Technology." *Levant* 44(1), 7–50.

———. 2014a. *The Southern Levant in Early Bronze IV. Issues and Perspectives in the Pottery Evidence*, Vol. 1: *Texts*, Vol. 2: *Appendices and Plates*. Contributi e Materiali di Archeologia Orientale XVII. Roma: Scienze e Lettere.

———. 2014b. "Townships or Villages? Remarks on the Middle Bronze IA in the Southern Levant." In Piotr Bieliński, Michal Gawlikowski, Raphal Koliński, Dorota Ławecka, Arkadiusz Sołtysiak, and Zuzanna Wygnańska (eds.), *Proceedings of the 8th International Congress on the Archaeology of the Ancient Near East, 30 April–4 May 2012, University of Warsaw*, Vol. 1, 151–172. Wiesbaden: Harrassowitz Verlag.

———. 2016. "Pottery Production at Khirbat Iskandar, Jordan: Preliminary Results of the Technological Study of EB IV Pottery from the Site." In Rolf A. Stucky, Oskar Kaelin, and Hans-Peter Mathys (eds.), *Proceedings of the 9th International Conference on the Archaeology of the Ancient Near East, 8–14 June 2014 Basel*, Volume 3, 533–548. Wiesbaden: Harrassowitz Verlag.

———. 2018a. "The EB–MB Transition in the Southern Levant: Contacts, Connectivity and

Transformations." In Barbara Horejs, Christoph Schwall, Vera Müller, Marta Luciani, Mattias Ritter, and Monica Guidetti, Roderick B. Salisbury, Felix Höflmayer, and Teresa Bürge (eds.), *Proceedings of the 10th International Congress on the Archaeology of the Ancient Near East 25–29 April 2016, Vienna*, Volume 1, 81–95. Wiesbaden: Harrassowitz Verlag.

———. 2018b. "Le relazioni tra Egitto e Levante meridionale nella seconda metà del III millennio a.C.: Una visione d'insieme e un esame critico delle problematiche più recenti." In Agnese Vacca, Sara Pizzimenti, and Maria Gabriella Micale (eds.), *A Oriente del Delta. Scritti sull'Egitto ed il Vicino Oriente antico in onore di Gabriella Scandone Matthiae*. Contributi e Materiali di Archeologia Orientale XVIII, 195–222. Roma: Scienze e Lettere.

———. 2019a. "The periodization of Early Bronze IV in the Southern Levant: bridging the gap between stratigraphy and absolute chronology." In E. Gallo (ed.), *Conceptualizing Urban Experiences: Tell es-Sultan and Tall al-Ḥammām Early Bronze cities across the Jordan. Proceedings of a workshop held in Palermo, G. Whitaker Foundation, Villa Malfitano, June 19th 2017*. Rome «La Sapienza» Studies on the Archaeology of Palestine & Transjordan, 13), 61–78. Rome: Rome «La Sapienza» Expedition to Palestine & Jordan.

———. 2019b. "Before the Cultural *Koinè*: Contextualizing Interculturality in the "Greater Levant" during the Late Early Bronze Age and the Early Middle Bronze Age." In Manfred Bietak and Silvia Prell (eds.), *The Enigma of the Hyksos volume. I, ASOR Conference Boston 2017 – ICAANE Conference Munich 2018 – Collected Papers*. Contributions to the Archaeology of Egypt, Nubia and the Levant 9, 13–45. Vienna: Verlag der Österreichischen Akademie der Wissenschaften.

———. 2020a. "About Stratigraphy, Pottery and Relative Chronology: Some Considerations for a Refinement of Archaeological Periodization for the Southern Levantine EB IV." In Suzanne Richard (ed.), *New Horizons in the Study of the Early Bronze III and Early Bronze IV in the Levant*, 395–416. University Park, PA: Eisenbruans.

———. 2020b. "Ebla and the South: Reconsidering Inter-Regional Connections during Early Bronze IV." In Marco Iamoni (ed.), *Broadening Horizons 5. Civilizations in Contact. Volume I. From the Prehistory of Upper Mesopotamia to the Bronze Age Societies of the Levant*. West & East. Monografie 2, 201–222. Trieste: Edizioni Università di Trieste.

———. 2020c. "Some Thoughts on Early Bronze Age Religious Complexes at Megiddo and Khirbet ez-Zeraqon and Interregional Connections." *Studia Eblaitica* 6: 1–29.

———. 2021a. "Developing Connections and Changing Clusters: The Levant between c. 2600 and 1900 BCE." In Manfred Bietak and Silvia Prell (eds.), *The Enigma of the Hyksos Volume IV. Changing Clusters and Migration in the Near Eastern Bronze Age. Collected Papers of a Workshop held in Vienna 4th–6th of December 2019*. Contributions to the Archaeology of Egypt, Nubia and the Levant 12, 31–81. Wiesbaden: Harrassowitz Verlag.

———. 2021b. "Urbanism, Collapse and Transitions: Considerations on the EB III/IV and the EB IV/ MB I Nexuses in the Southern Levant." In William G. Dever and Jesse C. Long Jr (eds.), *Transitions, Urbanism, and Collapse in the Early Bronze Age. Essays in Honor of Suzanne Richard*, 43–66. Sheffield: Sheffield Academic Press.

D'Andrea, Marta, Long, Jesse C. Jr, and Richard, S. 2022. "New Insights about the Early Bronze Age Sequence at Khirbat Iskandar: The 2016 Excavations." In Fadi Balawi and Pearce Paul Creasman (eds.) *Studies in the History and Archaeology of Jordan XIV. Culture in Crisis Flows of People Artifacts, and Idea. Proceedings of the 14th International Conference on the History and Archaeology of Jordan, Florence, Italy, 21–25 January 2019. Part I*, 224-249. Department of Antiquities of Jordan: Amman: Department of Antiquities of Jordan 2022.

D'Andrea, Marta, Suzanne Richard, and Long, Jesse, C. Jr. 2020. "Khirbat Iskandar." *Archaeology in Jordan 2: 2018 and 2019 Seasons*: 89–91. https://publications.acorjordan.org/articles/khirbat-iskandar-2018-2019/.

D'Andrea, Marta and Agnese Vacca. 2015. "The Northern and Southern Levant during the Late Early Bronze Age: a Reappraisal of the "Syrian Connection." *Studia Eblaitica* 1: 43–74.

———. 2020. "Alike but Different. Drinking Vessels in the Eastern Mediterranean around 2500–2000 BC." In Stefano Valentini and Guido Guarducci (eds.), *Between Syria and the Highlands. Studies in Honor of Giorgio Buccellati and Marilyn Kelly-*

Buccellati. Studies on the Ancient Near East and the Mediterranean 3, 122–138. Roma: Arbor Sapientiae.

Dever, William G. 2014. *Excavations at the Early Bronze IV Sites of Jebel Qa'aqir and Be'er Resisim*. Harvard Semitic Museum Publications 6. Winona Lake, IN: Eisenbrauns.

Dever, William G. and Miriam Tadmor. 1976. "A Copper Hoard of the Middle Bronze Age I." *Israel Exploration Journal* 26: 163–169.

Dunseth, Zachary C., Andrea Junge, Markus Fuchs, Israel Finkelstein, and Ruth Shahack-Gross. 2016. "Geoarchaeological Investigation in the Intermediate Bronze Age Site of Mashabe Sade." *Tel Aviv* 43: 43–75.

Dunseth, Zachary C., Andrea Junge, Joanna Lomax, Elisabetta Boaretto, Israel Finkelstein, Markus Fuchs, and Ruth Shahack-Gross. 2017. "Dating Archaeological Sites in an Arid Environment: A Multi-Method Case Study in the Negev Highlands, Israel." *Journal of Arid Environments* 144: 156–169.

Dunseth, Zachary C., Israel Finklestein, and Ruth Shahack-Gross. 2018. "Intermediate Bronze Age subsistence practices in the Negev Highlands, Israel: Macro- and microarchaeological results from the sites of Ein Ziq and Nahal Boqer 66." *Journal of Archaeological Science: Reports* 19: 712–726.

Falconer, Steven E. and Patricia L. Fall. 2006. *Bronze Age Rural Economy and Village Life at Tell el-Hayyat, Jordan*. British Archaeological Reports – International Series 1586. Oxford: Archaeopress.

———. 2016. "A Radiocarbon Sequence from Tell Abu en-Ni'aj, Jordan and its Implications for Early Bronze IV Chronology in the Southern Levant." *Radiocarbon* 58/3: pp 615–647. DOI: 10.1017/RDC.2016.26.

———. 2017. "Radiocarbon evidence from Tell Abu en-Ni'aj and Tell el-Hayyat, Jordan and its implications for Bronze Age Levantine and Egyptian chronologies." *Journal of Ancient Egyptian Interconnections* 13: 7–19.

———. 2019. *Early Bronze IV Village Life in the Jordan Valley. Excavations at Tell Abu en-Ni'aj and Dhahret Umm el-Marar, Jordan*. British Archaeological Reports – International Series 2922. Oxford: Archaeopress.

Fall, Patricia L., Steven Falconer, and Felix Höflmayer. 2020. "New Bayesian radiocarbon models for Early Bronze IV Tell Abu en-Ni'aj and Middle Bronze Age Tell el-Hayyat, Jordan." *Radiocarbon* 63(1): 41–76. https://doi.org/10.1017/RDC.2020.104

Fall, Patricia L., Suzanne Richard, Suzanne E. Pilaar Birch, Elizabeth Ridder, Marta D'Andrea, Jesse C. Long Jr, and Steven Falconer. 2022. "New AMS chronology for the Early Bronze III/IV transition at Khirbat Iskandar, Jordan." *Radiocarbon*: 1–16. DOI: 10.1017/RDC.2022.22

Finkelstein, Israel, Matthew J. Adams, Zachary C. Dunseth, and Ruth Shahack-Gross. 2018. "The Archaeology and History of the Negev and Neighbouring Areas in the Third Millennium BCE: A New Paradigm." *Tel Aviv* 45, 63–88. DOI 10.1080/03344355.2018.1412054.

Gee, J. 2015. "Did the Old Kingdom Collapse? A New View of the First Intermediate Period." In Peter Der Manuelian and Thomas Schneider (eds.), *Towards a New History of the Egyptian Old Kingdom. Perspectives on the Pyramids Age*. Harvard Egyptological Studies 1, 60–75. Leiden and Boston: Brill.

Genz, Hermann, Simone Riehl, Canan Çakırlar, Francesca Slim, and Alison Damick. 2016. "Economic and Political Organization of Early Bronze Age Coastal Communities: Tell Fadous-Kfarabida as a Case Study." *Berytus* 55: 79–119.

Gidding, Aaron and Thomas E. Levy. 2020. "Manufacturing Copper in the Periphery: Radiocarbon and the Question of Urbanism during the Early Bronze III–IV Transition." In Suzanne Richard (ed.) *New Horizons in the Study of the Early Bronze III and Early Bronze IV in the Levant*, 312–326. University Park, PA: Eisenbrauns.

Greenberg, Raphael. 2017. "No Collapse: Transmutations of Early Bronze Age Urbanism in the Southern Levant." In Felix Höflmayer (ed.), *The Late Third Millennium in the Ancient Near East. Chronology, C14, and Climate Change*. Oriental Institute Seminars 11, 31–58. Chicago, IL: The Oriental Institute of the University of Chicago.

———. 2019. *The Archaeology of the Bronze Age Levant. From Urban Origins to the Demise of City-States, 3700–1000 BCE*, Cambridge: Cambridge University Press.

Greenberg, Raphael and Emanuel Eisenberg. 2006. "Area BS: the Bar-Adon excavations, southeast, 1951–1953." In Raphael Greenberg, Emanuel Eisenberg, Sarit Paz, and Yitzhak Paz (eds.),

Bet Yerah. The Early Bronze Age Mound. Volume I. Excavation Reports 1933–1986. Israel Antiquities Authority Reports 30, 117–234. Jerusalem: Israel Antiquities Authority.

Gundacker, Roman. 2017. "The Significance of Foreign Toponyms and Ethnonyms in Old Kingdom Text Sources." In Felix Höflmayer (ed.), *The Late Third Millennium in the Ancient Near East. Chronology, C14, and Climate Change*. Oriental Institute Seminars 11, 333–426. Chicago, IL: The Oriental Institute of the University of Chicago.

Haiman, Mordehai. 1996. "Early Bronze Age IV Settlement Pattern of the Negev and Sinai Deserts: View from Small Marginal Temporary Sites." *Bulletin of the American Schools of Oriental Research* 303: 1–32.

———. 2009. "Copper Trade and Pastoralism in the Negev and Sinai Deserts in the EB IV." In Peter J. Parr (ed.), *The Levant in Transition. Proceedings of a Conference Held at the British Museum on 20–21 April 2004*. Palestine Exploration Funds Annuals IX, 38–42. Leeds: Maney.

Hauptmann, Andreas, Sigrid Schmitt-Strecker, Thomas E. Levy, and Friedrich Begemann. 2015. "On Early Bronze Age Copper Bar Ingots from the Southern Levant." *Bulletin of the American Schools of Oriental Research* 373: 1–24.

Hausleiter, Arnulf, Marta D'Andrea, and Alina Zur (in collaboration with Mohammed Al-Hajri). 2018. "The EB–MB Transition from Early to Middle Bronze Age in Northwest Arabia: Bronze Weapons from Burial Contexts at Tayma, Arabia and Comparative Evidence from the Levant." *Zeitschrift für Orient-Archäologie* 11: 412–436.

Helms, Svend. 1986. "Excavations at Tell Umm Hammad, 1984." *Levant* 18: 25–49.

Höflmayer, Felix. 2014a. "Egypt and the Southern Levant in the Late Early Bronze Age." In Felix Höflmayer and Ricardo Eichman (eds.), *Egypt and the Southern Levant in the Early Bronze Age*. Orient-Archäologie 31, 135–141. Rahden/West: Marie Leidorf.

———. 2014b. "Dating catastrophes and collapses in the ancient Near East: The end of the first urbanization in the southern Levant and the 4.2 ka BP event." In Lorenzo Nigro (ed.), *Overcoming Catastrophes: Essays on disastrous agents characterization and resilience strategies in pre-classical Southern Levant*, Rome «La Sapienza» Studies on the Archaeology of Palestine & Transjordan, 117–140. Rome: Rome «La Sapienza» Expedition to Palestine & Transjordan.

———. 2015. "The Southern Levant, Egypt, and the 4.2 ka BP Event." In Harald Meller, Helge Wolfgang Arz, Reinhard Jung, and Roberto Risch (eds.), *2200 BC – Ein Klimasturz als Ursache für den Zerfall der Alten Welt? 7. Mitteldeutscher Archäologentag vom 23. Bis 26. October 2014 in Halle (Saale). 7th Archaeological Conference of Central Germany*. Tagungen des Landsmuseums für Vorgeschichte 12/I, 113–130. Halle (Saale): Landesamt für Denkmalpflege und Archäologie Sachsen-Anhalt.

———. 2017. "Introduction: The Late Third Millennium BC in the Ancient Near East and Eastern Mediterranean." In F. Höflmayer (ed.), *The Late Third Millennium in the Ancient Near East, Chronology, C14, and Climate Change*, 1–29. Oriental Institute Seminars 11. Chicago, IL: The Oriental Institute of the University of Chicago.

Holdorf, Paul, S. 2010a. "Quantitative Analysis of the Early Bronze IV Tell and Tomb Ceramic Assemblages." In Suzanne Richard, Jesse C. Long, Paul S. Holdorf, and Glenn Peterman (eds.), *Final Report on the Early Bronze IV Area C Gateway and Cemeteries*. American Schools of Oriental Research Archaeological Reports 14/ Archaeological Expedition to Khirbat Iskandar and its Environs, Jordan 1, 113 –132. Boston: American Schools of Oriental Research.

———. 2010b. "Comparison of EB IV radiocarbon results from Khirbat Iskandar and Bab adh-Dhra'." In Suzanne Richard, Jesse C. Long, Paul S. Holdorf, and Glenn Peterman (eds.), *Final Report on the Early Bronze IV Area C Gateway and Cemeteries*. American Schools of Oriental Research Archaeological Reports 14/ Archaeological Expedition to Khirbat Iskandar and its Environs, Jordan 1, 267 –270. Boston: American Schools of Oriental Research.

Kennedy, Melissa A. 2015. "Life and Death at Tell Umm Ḥammād, Jordan: A Village Landscape of the Southern Levantine Early Bronze Age IV/Intermediate Bronze Age." *Zeitschrift des Deutschen Palästina-Vereins* 131(1): 1–28.

———. 2016. "The End of the 3rd Millennium BC in the Levant: New Perspectives and Old Ideas." *Levant* 48(1): 1–32.

———. 2020. "Horizons of Cultural Connectivity North–South Interactions and Interconnections during the Early Bronze Age IV." In Suzanne Richard (ed.) *New Horizons in the Study of the Early Bronze III and Early Bronze IV in the Levant*, 328–346. University Park, PA: Eisenbrauns.

Kmošek, Jiří, Martin Odler, Marek Fikrle, and Yulia V. Kochergina. 2018. "Invisible connections. Early Dynastic and Old Kingdom Egyptian metalwork in the Egyptian Museum of Leipzig University." *Journal of Archaeological Science* 96: 191–207.

Kochavi, Moshe. 2009. "The Intermediate Bronze Age (IBA) in the Negev, Forty Years Later." In Peter J. Parr (ed.), *The Levant in Transition. Proceedings of a Conference Held at the British Museum on 20–21 April 2004*. Palestine Exploration Funds Annuals IX, 43–48. Leeds: Maney.

Lev, Ron, Shlomit Bechar, and Elisabetta Boaretto. 2021. "Hazor EB III city abandonment and IBA people return: Radiocarbon chronology and its implications." *Radiocarbon* 63(5): 1453–1469. http://doi.org/10.1017/RDC.2021.76

Lev, Ron, Ora Shalev, Joanna Regev, Yztak Paz, and Elisabetta Boaretto 2020. "Bridging the gap EBIII–IBA: Early Intermediate Bronze radiocarbon dates from Khirbat el-'Alya Northeast, Israel." *Radiocarbon* 62(6): 1637–1649. http://doi.org/10.1017/RDC.2020.83

Levy, Thomas E., Russell B. Adams, Andreas Hauptmann, Michael Prange, Sigrid Schmitt-Strecker, and Mohammed Najjar. 2002. "Early Bronze Age Metallurgy: A Newly Discovered Copper Manufactory in Southern Jordan." *Antiquity* 76: 425–437.

Long, Jesse C. Jr. 2010. "The Stratigraphy of Area C." In Suzanne Richard, Jesse C. Long, Paul S. Holdorf, and Glenn Peterman (eds), *Final Report on the Early Bronze IV Area C Gateway and Cemeteries*. American Schools of Oriental Research Archaeological Reports 14/ Archaeological Expedition to Khirbat Iskandar and its Environs, Jordan 1, 37–68. Boston: American Schools of Oriental Research.

Long, Jesse C. Jr., Suzanne Richard, and Marta D'Andrea. 2019. "Khirbat Iskandar." In *Archaeology in Jordan 1: 2016 and 2017 Seasons*, ACOR, Amman, 59–60, https://www.acorjordan.org/wp-content/uploads/2018/12/AIJ-2016-2017-High-Res.pdf.

Luciani, Marta. 2016. "Mobility, Contacts and the Definition of Culture(s) in New Archaeological Research in Northwest Arabia." In Marta Luciani (ed.), *The Archaeology of North Arabia: Oases and Landscapes. Proceedings of the International Congress Held at the University of Vienna, 5–8 December, 2013*. Oriental and European Archaeology 4, 21–56. Vienna: Austrian Academy of Sciences Press.

Mazar, Amihai. 2006. "Tel Beth-Shean and the Fate of Mounds in the Intermediate Bronze Age." In Seymour Gitin, J. Edward Wright, and J.-P. Dessel (eds.), *Confronting the past: archaeological and historical essays on ancient Israel in honor of William G. Dever*, 105–118. Winona Lake, IN: Eisenbrauns.

Mazar, Benjamin. 1968. "The Middle Bronze Age in Palestine." *Israel Exploration Journal* 18: 65–97.

Miroschedji, Pierre de. 2002. "The Socio-Political Dynamics of Egyptian–Canaanite Interaction in the Early Bronze Age." In Edwin C. M. van den Brink and Thomas E. Levy (eds.), *Egypt and the Levant. Interrelations from the 4th Through the 3rd Millennium BCE*. New Approaches to Anthropological Archaeology, 39–57. London and New York: Leicester University Press.

———. 2009. "Rise and collapse in the Southern Levant in the Early Bronze Age." *Scienze dell'Antichità* 15: 101–129.

———. 2012. "Egypt and Southern Canaan in the Third Millennium BCE: Uni's Asiatic Campaigns Revisited." In Mayer Gruber, Shmuel Aḥituv, Gunnar Lehmann, and Zipora Talshir (eds.), *All the Wisdom of the East. Studies in Near Eastern Archaeology and History in Honor of Eliezer D. Oren*. Orbis Biblicus et Orientalis 255, 265–292. Fribourg – Göttingen.

———. 2014 "The Southern Levant (Cisjordan) during the Early Bronze Age." In Margrete L. Steiner and Ann E. Killebrew (eds.), *Oxford Handbook of the Archaeology of the Levant*, 307–329. Oxford: Oxford University Press.

———. 2018. "The Urbanization of the Southern Levant in Its Near Eastern Setting." *Origini* XLII (= Marcella Frangipane and Linda R. Manzanilla [eds.], *Rethinking Urbanization and Its Living Landscapes from the Inspiring Perspective of a great "Maestro"*): 109–148.

———. 2019. "Early Bronze Age Palaces in the Southern Levant." In Manfred Bietak, Paolo Matthiae, and Silvia Prell (eds.), Ancient

Egyptian and *Ancient Near Eastern Palaces. Proceedings of a workshop held at the 10th ICAANE in Vienna, 25–26 April 2016*, Volume II. Contributions on Ancient Egypt, Nubia and the Levant 8, 159–179. Wiesbaden: Harrassowitz Verlag.

Mourad, Anna-Latifa. 2020. "Foreigners at Beni Hassan: Evidence from the Tomb of Khnumhotep I (No. 14)." *Bulletin of the American Schools of Oriental Research* 384: 105–132.

Mumford, Gregory. 2006. "Tell Ras Budran (Site 345): Defining Egypt's Eastern Frontier and Mining Operations in South Sinai during the Late Old Kingdom (Early EB IV/MB I)." *Bulletin of the American Schools of Oriental Research* 342: 13–67.

Nichols, John J. and Jill A. Weber. 2006. Amorites, Onagers, and Social Reorganization in Middle Bronze Age Syria. In Glenn M. Schwartz and John J. Nichols (eds.), *After Collapse: The Regeneration of Complex Societies*, 38–57. Tucson, AZ: University of Arizona Press.

Nigro, Lorenzo. 2003. "Tell es-Sultan in the Early Bronze Age IV (2300–2000 BC) Settlement vs Necropolis: a stratigraphic perspective." *Contributi e Materiali di Archeologia Orientale* IX: 1–38.

———. 2016. "The End of the Early Bronze Age in the Southern Levant Urban Crisis and Collapse seen from two 3rd Millennium BC-Cities, Tell es-Sultan/Jericho and Khirbet al-Batrawy." In Tim Cunningham and Jan Driessen (eds.), *Crisis to Collapse. The Archaeology of Social Breakdown*. Aegis. Actes de Colloques 11, 149–172. Louvain: Presses Universitaire de Louvain.

———. 2019. "Archaeological Periodization vs Absolute Chronology: What Does not Work with High and Low Early Bronze Age in the Southern Levant." In Elisabetta Gallo (ed.), *Conceptualizing Urban Experiences: Tell es-Sultan and Tall al-Ḥammām Early Bronze cities across the Jordan. Proceedings of a workshop held in Palermo, G. Whitaker Foundation, Villa Malfitano, June 19th 2017*. Rome «La Sapienza» Studies on the Archaeology of Palestine & Transjordan, 13, 1–46. Rome: Rome «La Sapienza» Expedition to Plestine & Transjordan.

———. 2020. "Tell es-Sultan/Jericho in the Early Bronze Age III: Apogee of an Unusual "Palatial Society" in Palestine." In Suzanne Richard (ed.), *New Horizons in the Study of the Early Bronze III and Early Bronze IV in the Levant*, 195–212. University Park, PA: Eisenbrauns.

Nigro Lorenzo, Lucio Calcagnile, Jehad Yasin Elisabetta Gallo, and Gianluca Quarta. 2019. "Jericho and the chronology of Palestine in the Early Bronze Age: A radiometric re-assessment." *Radiocarbon* 61(1): 211–241.

Oren, Eliezer D. and Yuval Yekutieli. 1990. "North Sinai during the MB I Period: Pastoral Nomadism and Sedentary Settlement." *Eretz Israel* 21: 6–22.

Palumbo, Gaetano. 1990. *The Early Bronze Age IV in the Southern Levant: Settlement Patterns, Economy and Material Culture of a "Dark Age."* Contributi e Materiali di Archeologia Orientale III, Roma: Sapienza University of Rome.

———. 2001. "The Early Bronze IV." In Burton MacDonald, Russel B. Adams, and Piotr Bienkowski (eds.), *The Archaeology of Jordan*. Levantine Archaeology, 233–269. Sheffield: Sheffield Academic Press.

———. 2008. "The Early Bronze IV." In Russel B. Adams (ed.), *Jordan: An Archaeological Reader*, 227–262. London: Equinox.

Philip, Graham. 1988. "Hoards of the Early and Middle Bronze Ages in the Levant." *World Archaeology* 20: 190–208.

———. 2008. "The Early Bronze Age I-III." In Russell B. Adams (ed.), *Jordan: An Archaeological Reader*, 161–226; London: Equinox

Prag, Kay. 2014. The Southern Levant during the Intermediate Bronze Age. In Margrete L. Steiner and Ann E. Killebrew (eds.), *Oxford Handbook of the Archaeology of the Levant*, 388–400. Oxford: Oxford University Press.

Priglinger, Elisa. 2019a. "One Ticket to Egypt Please!" Migration from Western Asia to Egypt in the Early Second Millennium BCE. In Manfred Bietak and Silvia Prell (eds.), *The Enigma of the Hyksos volume. I, ASOR Conference Boston 2017 – ICAANE Conference Munich 2018 – Collected Papers*. Contributions in the Archaeology of Egypt, Nubia and the Levant 9, 209–223. Vienna: Verlag der Österreichischen Akademie der Wissenschaften.

———. 2019b. "Different Aspects of Mobility and Migration during the Middle Kingdom." *Ägypten & Levante* 29: 331–353.

Rademakers, Frederik W., Georges Verly, Luc Delvaux, and Patrick Degryse. 2018. "Copper for the afterlife in Predynastic to Old Kingdom Egypt: provenance characterization by chemical and lead isotope analysis (RMAH collection,

Belgium)." *Journal of Archaeological Science* 96: 175–190.

Rast, Walter E. and R.Thomas Schaub. 2003. *Bâb edh-Dhrâ': Excavations at the Town Site (1975–1981). Part 1: Text, Part 2: Plates and Appendices*. Reports of the Expeditions to the Dead Sea Plain Jordan II. Winona Lake, IN: Eisenbrauns.

Regev, Johanna, Israel Finkelstein, Matthew J. Adams, and Elisabetta Boaretto. 2014. "Wiggle-Matched ^{14}C Chronology of Early Bronze Megiddo and the Synchronization of Egyptian and Levantine Chronologies." *Egypt and the Levant* 24: 243–266.

Regev, Johanna, Pierre de Miroschedji, and Elisabetta Boaretto. 2012. "Early Bronze Age Chronology: Radiocarbon Dates and Chronological Models from Tel Yarmuth (Israel)." In Elisabetta Boaretto and Noemi Rebollo Franco (eds.), *Proceedings of the 6th International Radiocarbon and Archaeology Symposium*, 505–524; *Radiocarbon* 54(3–4).

Regev, Johanna, Pierre de Miroschedji, Raphael Greenberg, Eliot Braun, Zvi Greenhut, and Elisabetta Boaretto. 2012. "Chronology of the Early Bronze Age in the Southern Levant: New Analysis for a High Chronology." In Elisabetta Boaretto and Noemi Rebollo Franco (eds.), *Proceedings of the 6th International Radiocarbon and Archaeology Symposium;*, 525–566; *Radiocarbon* 54(3–4).

Richard, Suzanne. 2010. "The Area C Early Bronze IV Ceramic Assemblage." In Suzanne Richard, Jesse C. Long Jr, Paul S. Holdorf, and Glenn Peterman (eds.). 2010. *Khirbat Iskandar. Final Report on the Early Bronze IV Area C "Gateway" and Cemeteries*. American Schools of Oriental Research Archaeological Reports 14/ Archaeological Expedition to Khirbat Iskandar and its Environs, Jordan 1, 69–112. Boston: American Schools of Oriental Research.

———. 2013. "Khirbat Iskandar Tall, Tombs, and Bab adh-Dhra': A Multidimensional Quantitative Approach." In Fares al-Hmoud (ed.), *Studies in the History and Archaeology of Jordan* XI: *Changes and Challenges*, 783–791. Amman: Department of Antiquities of Jordan.

———. 2014. "The southern Levant (Transjordan) during the Early Bronze Age." In Margrete L. Steiner and Ann E. Killebrew (eds.), *The Archaeology of the Levant c. 8000–332 BCE*, 330–352. Oxford: Oxford University Press.

———. 2016. Recent Excavations at Khirbat Iskandar, Jordan. The EB III/IV Fortifications. In Rolf A. Stucky, Oskar Kaelin, and Hans-Peter Mathys (eds.), *Proceedings of the 9th International Congress on the Archaeology of the Ancient Near East*, Vol. 3, 585–597. Wiesbaden: Harrassowitz Verlag.

———. 2020. "New Vistas on the Early Bronze Age IV of the Southern Levant: A Case for "Rural Complexity" in the Permanent Sedentary Sites." in Suzanne Richard (ed.), *New Horizons in the Study of the Early Bronze III and Early Bronze IV in the Levant*, 417–453. University Park, PA: Eisenbrauns.

Richard, Suzanne and Jesse C. Long, Jr. 2007a. "Social Institutions at Khirbat Iskandar: An Argument for Elites in EB IV." In Fawwaz al-Khraysheh (ed.), *Studies in the History and Archaeology of Jordan* 9, 71–81. Amman: Department of Antiquities of Jordan.

———. 2007b. "Khirbet Iskander: A City in Collapse at the end of the Early Bronze Age." In Thomas E. Levy, P.M. Michele Daviau, and Randall W. Younker (eds.), *Crossing Jordan: North American Contributions to the Archaeology of Jordan*, 269–276. Aningdon: Taylor & Francis.

———. 2009. "Khirbet Iskander, Jordan and Early Bronze IV Studies: A View from a Tell." In Peter J. Parr (ed.), *The Levant in Transition. Proceedings of a Conference Held at the British Museum on 20–21 April 2004*. Palestine Exploration Funds Annuals IX, 90–100. Leeds: Maney.

———. 2010. "Summary and Conclusions." In: Suzanne Richard, Jesse C. Long, Jr, Paul S. Holdorf, and Glenn Peterman (eds.), *Khirbat Iskandar Final Report on the Early Bronze IV Area C 'Gateway' and Cemeteries*. American Schools of Oriental Research Archaeological Reports 14/ Archaeological Expedition to Khirbat Iskandar and its Environs, Jordan 1, 271–279. Boston: Eisenbrauns.

Richard, Suzanne, Jesse C. Long Jr., and Marta D'Andrea. In press. "Expedition to Khirbat Iskandar and its Environs: the 2019 Season." *Annual of the Department of Antiquities of Jordan*.

Richard, Suzanne, Jesse C. Long Jr, Marta D'Andrea, and Rikke Wulff-Krabbenhöft 2018. "Expedition to Khirbat Iskandar and its Environs: the 2016 Season." *Annual of the Department of Antiquities of Jordan* 59: 597–606.

Schneider, Th. 2017. "What Is the Past but a Once Material Existence Now Silenced?": The First Intermediate Period from an Epistemological Perspective." In Felix Höflmayer (ed.), *The Late Third Millennium in the Ancient Near East. Chronology, C14, and Climate Change*, 311–322. Oriental Institute Seminars 11. Chicago, IL: The Oriental Institute of the University of Chicago.

Segal, D. 1999. "Results of Carbon-14 Tests of Samples from Early and Middle Bronze Age Sites in Eretz-Israel and Neighboring Areas." In Rudolph Cohen (ed.), *Ancient Settlement of the Central Negev. Volume I. The Chalcolithic Period, the Early Bronze Age and the Middle Bronze Age I.* Israel Antiquities Authority Reports 6, 336–339. Jerusalem: Israel Antiquities Authority.

Shai, Itzhaq, Hashkel J. Greenfield, Joanna Regev, Elisabetta Boaretto, Adi Eliyahu-Behar, and Aren M. Maeir. 2014. "The Early Bronze Age remains at Tell es-Safi / Gath: an interim report." *Tel Aviv* 41(1): 20–49.

Sowada, Karin. 2009. *Egypt and the Eastern Mediterranean during the Old Kingdom.* Orbis Biblicus et Orientalis 237. Fribourg and Göttingen: Vandenhoeck & Ruprecht Verlage.

———. 2014, "Never the Twain Shall Meet? Synchronising Egyptian and Levantine Chronologies in the 3rd Millennium BC." In Felix Höflmayer and Richardo Eichmann (eds.), *Egypt and the Southern Levant in the Early Bronze Age.* Orient Archäologie 31, 293–314. Rehden - Westf.: Marie Leidorf.

———. 2016–2018. "Hidden Exports: A Likely Early Bronze Age Exchange in Egyptian Cattle to the Levant." *Bulletin of the Australian Centre for Egyptology* 26: 71–78.

———. 2020. "Perspectives on Egypt in the Southern Levant in Light of the High Early Bronze Age Chronology." In Suzanne Richard (ed.), *New Horizons in the Study of the Early Bronze III and Early Bronze IV in the Levant*, 149–168. University Park, PA: Eisenbrauns.

Stantis, Chris, Arwa Kharobi, Nina Maaranen, Geoff M. Nowell, Manfred Bieak, Silvia, Prell, and Holger Schutkowski. 2020. "Who were the Hyksos? Challenging traditional narratives using strontium isotope ($^{87}Sr/^{86}Sr$) analysis of human remains from ancient Egypt." *PLoS ONE* 15/7: e0235414. https://doi.org/10.1371/journal.pone.0235414.

Thalmann, J.-P. 2008. "Tell Arqa et Byblos: essai de correlation." In Manfred Bietak and Ernst Czerny (eds.) *The Bronze Age in the Lebanon: Studies on the Archaeology and Chronology of Lebanon, Syria, and Egypt.* Denkschriften der Gesamtakademie 50/Contributions to the Chronology of the Eastern Mediterranean 17, 61–78. Vienna: Verlag der Österreichischen Akademie des Wissenschaften.

Ussishkin, David. 2018. "Was the Egyptianized Pottery Cache from Megiddo a Foundation Deposit of Megaron Temple 4040? Response to Matthew J. Adams." *Tel Aviv* 45: 216–223.

Vacca, Agnese. 2014–2015. "Recherches sur les périodes pré et proto-palatiale d'Ébla au bronze ancien III–IVA1." In Paolo Matthiae, Mohammed Abdulkarim, Frances Pinnock, and Mohammed Alkhalid (eds), *Studies on the Archaeology of Ebla after 50 Years of Discoveries.* Les Annales Archéologiques Arabes Syriennes LVII–LVIII, 15–42. Damas: Ministère de la Culture, Direction Générale des Antiquités et des Musées.

———. 2015. "Before the Royal Palace G. The Stratigraphic and Pottery Sequence of the West Unit of the Central Complex: The Building G5." *Studia Eblaitica* 1: 1–32.

———. 2018. "Centralization Before the Palace. The EB III–IVA1 Sequence on the Acropolis of Tell Mardikh/Ebla." In Paolo Matthiae, Frances Pinnock and Marta D'Andrea (eds), *Ebla and Beyond Ancient Near Eastern Studies after Fifty Years of Discoveries at Tell Mardikh Proceedings of the International Congress Held in Rome, 15th–17th December 2014*, 35–73. Wiesbaden: Harrassowitz Verlag.

Vacca, Agnese and Marta D'Andrea. 2020. "The Connections between the Northern and Southern Levant during EB III, Re-evaluations and New Vistas in the Light of New Data and Higher Chronologies." In Suzanne Richard (ed.), *New Horizons in the Study of the Early Bronze III and Early Bronze IV in the Levant*, 120–145. Winona Lake, IN: Eisenbrauns.

Weinstein, James M. 2003. A new set of radiocarbon dates from the Town Site. In Walter E. Rast and R. Thomas Schaub, *Bâb edh-Dhrâ': Excavations at the Town Site (1975–1981). Part 1: Text, Part 2: Plates and Appendices.* Reports of the Expeditions to the Dead Sea Plain Jordan II, 638–648. Winona Lake, IN: Eisenbrauns.

Wilkinson Tony J., Graham Philip, Jennie Bradbury, Robert Dunford, Donald Donoghue, Nicolas Galiatsatos, Dan Lawrence, Andrea Ricci, and S.L. Smith. 2014. "Contextualizing Early Urbanization, Settlement Cores, Early States and Agro-pastoral Strategies in the Fertile Crescent during the Fourth and Third Millennia BC." *Journal of World Prehistory* 27: 43–109.

Yahalom-Mack, Naama, Yuval Gadot, Eliyahu Behar, A., Shlomit Bechar, Sana Shilstein and Istral Finkelstein 2014. "Metalworking at Hazor: A Long-Term Perspective." *Oxford Journal of Archaeology* 33(1): 19–45.

Yekutieli, Yuval. 2002. "Settlement and Subsistence Patterns in North Sinai during the Fifth to Third Millennia BCE." In Edwin C.M. van den Brink and Thomas E. Levy (eds.), *Egypt and the Levant. Interrelations from the 4th through the 3rd Millennium B.C.E.* New Approaches to Anthropological Archaeology, 422–433. London – New York: Leicester University Press.

Yekutieli, Yuval, Sana Shilstein, and Sariel Shalev. 2005. "ʿEn Yahav: A Copper Smelting Site in the ʿArava." *Bulletin of the American Schools of Oriental Research* 340: 1–21.

Notes

1 Mazar 1968; Callaway 1978; more recently Miroschedji 2019; Sowada 2020.

2 See, for instance, Ben-Yosef et al. 2016, 80, 82; Dunseth et al. 2016, 70; 2018, 723–724; Finkelstein et al. 2018, 63, 73–77; Cohen 2019, 78–79; 2022. Kochavi 2009 places southern Levantine–Egyptian interactions in the First Intermediate Period within the framework of the traditional chronology for the southern Levantine Early Bronze IV during the last quarter of the third millennium BCE.

3 Regev et al. 2012 ; Regev et al. 2014.

4 On this time, see the analysis in Palumbo 2008; D'Andrea 2014a; 2019a; 2020a; Cohen 2018; Greenberg 2019, 136–176; Richard 2020.

5 See discussions in Philip 2008; Richard 2014; Miroschedji 2018; Greenberg 2019, 128–131; D'Andrea 2021a; 2021b, all citing further references.

6 Miroschedji 2018; Richard 2014; Nigro 2016; 2020; D'Andrea 2021b, 28–36, 40–41. See also Greenberg 2019, 70–135.

7 Lebanon: Genz et al. 2016; western inland Syria: Vacca 2014–2015; 2015; 2018.

8 Vacca and D'Andrea 2020. See also Wilkinson et al. 2014, 85–86.

9 See recent comparative overviews in D'Andrea 2019b; 2021a.

10 See, although with different interpretations, D'Andrea 2014a, Volume 1, 265–272; 2021a; 2021b; Nigro 2016, 166 and Tab. 8.1; Greenberg 2017; 2019, 125–131, 144–148.

11 D'Andrea 2014a, Volume 1, 265–272; Nigro 2016; earlier see Mazar 2006.

12 D'Andrea, Richard and Long 2020.

13 For southern Jordan, this was already noticed by Adams (2006, 139), describing this phenomenon as intermittency within continuity. On earlier proposal of sustained Early Bronze III–IV continuity in the region see also Avner 2006, 64–65.

14 D'Andrea 2014a; 2020a; Richard 2020.

15 Regev et al. 2012; Regev et al. 2014a; Shai et al. 2014; Höflmayer 2017.

16 See, recently, D'Andrea 2020a; Kennedy 2020; Richard 2020.

17 See, for instance, the remarks in D'Andrea 2019b; 2020b; 2021a.

18 Höflmayer 2014a; 2015.

19 See, for instance, the various contributions in Richard ed. 2020, but also syntheses on this time, such as Prag 2014; Cohen 2018; Greenberg 2019, 136–176.

20 Nigro 2019; 2020; Nigro et al. 2019.

21 D'Andrea and Vacca 2015; 2020; D'Andrea 2018a; 2020b; 2021a; Vacca and D'Andrea 2020. See also Kennedy 2020.

22 Falconer and Fall 2016; 2017; 2019; Fall, Falconer and Höflmayer 2020.

23 For a regional discussion of the middle and advanced Early Bronze IV phases in the southern Levant, see D'Andrea 2012; 2014a, Volume 1, 187–221; 2016, 540–543, 545; 2020a, 401–405, 408–409 and figs 22.2–22.4, 22.5: 1–8; 2021b; for site-specific treatments of individual sites, see Helms 1986, 43–45, figs 17: 4–8, 10–14, 18: 4–9, 19: 2–11 (for ceramic phasing of the latter site, see also Kennedy 2015); Nigro 2003, 131–133 (Tell es-Sultan/Jericho); Long 2010, 40–67, and Richard 2010, 93–94, figs. 4.6–4.7 (Khirbet Iskander).

24 This phase has been analysed and discussed on a regional scale according to general characteristics of material culture and patterns of settlement in D'Andrea 2012, 21–25; 2014a,

Volume 1, 183–187, figs 5.16–5.18; 2016, 537, 544–545 and figs. 3, 5.8–18; 2019a, 64–67 and fig. 2; 2020a, 399–401, 405–406, 408, and fig. 22.1; 2021a; 2021b; see recently also Greenberg 2019, 138–139. For site-specific descriptions, see Helms 1986, 43, figs 17: 1–3, 18: 1–2, 19: 1; for ceramic phasing of the latter site, see also Kennedy 2015); Nigro 2003, 133–134 (Tell es-Sultan / Jericho); Greenberg and Eisenberg 2006, 151–157, fig. 5.96–5.99 (Khirbet Kerak / Beth Yerah); Long 2010, 37–40, and Richard 2010, 933, fig. 4.5 (Khirbet Iskander); Falconer and Fall 2019, 42–45, figs 6.1–6.6 (Tell Abu en-Ni'aj); Bar 2020, 358–360 and fig. 19.10 (Elevation Point 167); Lev et al. 2020 (Khirbet el-'Alya Northeast).

25 Khirbet al-Minsahalat: EGS-AQ244: 2840–2500 cal BCE; ISGS-AG245: 2565–2460 cal BCE; ISGS-A0247: 2618–2471 cal BCE (Chesson et al. 2005); Tell Abu en-Ni'aj Phase 7: 2524–2486 cal BCE (Falconer and Fall 2019, 72 and Tab. 5.2; Fall, Falconer and Höflmayer 2020, 27, Tab. 5, with slightly different ranges in earlier publications: Falconer and Fall 2016, 621 [2591–2486 cal BCE, 1-sigma]; Falconer and Fall 2017, Tab. 5 [2518–2483 ca. BCE]); Elevation Point 167: 2480–2240 cal BCE (Bar 2020, 359 and tab. 19.1); 2570–2460 cal BCE (2-sigma) Khirbet el-'Alya Northeast (Lev et al. 2020, 16422 tab. 1, 1643).

26 D'Andrea 2021a; 2021b.

27 D'Andrea, Richard and Long 2020, 90–91, fig. 2; Richard, Long and D'Andrea in press.

28 Lev et al. 2021.

29 Rast and Schaub 2003, 639–640: sample 134016: 2341–2139 cal BCE (1-sigma), 2462–2128 cal BCE (2-sigma); sample 134017: 2145–2013 cal BCE (1-sigma), 2211–1915 cal BCE (2-sigma); P-2573: 2290–2131 cal BCE (1-sigma), 2351–2026 calBC (2-sigma); sample SI-2872, 2342–2141 cal BCE (1-sigma), 2462–2128 cal BCE (2-sigma); sample SI-2875: 2039–1889 cal BCE (1-sigma), 2139–1753 cal BCE (2-sigma).

30 Segal 1999, 338; Avner 2006, 59, Tab. 5. R-2514 ('Ein Ziq): 2166–1951 cal BC; RT-1558: 2124–1744 cal BC (Har Dimon): Ben-Yosef et al. 2016, 82, Tab. 3.

31 While several scholars support the notion that there is a multi-phase EB IV occupation at Bab edh-Dhra' with three EB IV subphases (Palumbo 1990, Fig. 28; Rast and Schaub 2003; Holdorf 2010a; Richard 2013), the present author believes that the occupation attested in the three areas at the site was shorter (D'Andrea 2012, 28–29; 2014a, Volume 2, 156–158; 2020a, 398).

32 D'Andrea 2014b, 157 and fig. 9; 2019b, 70–72 and figs 4–5; 2020a, 408 –409; 2021, 55–57, 59–60, and figs. 16–17; Cohen 2017, 36–39.

33 Richard 2016, 585–586, 593–595; 2020, 427428, figs 23.4a–b, 23.5, citing earlier references; D'Andrea, Richard and Long 2020, 90 and fig. 1.

34 See, for instance, Goren 1996, 63, 67; Haiman 1996, 20; 2009, 40.

35 Richard, Long, D'Andrea and Krabbenhøft 2018, 603–604; Long, Richard and D'Andrea 2019, 90; D'Andrea, Long and Richard 2022, 227–230.

36 D'Andrea, Richard and Long 2020, 90; Richard, Long and D'Andrea in press.

37 Richard 2016, 586, 593; D'Andrea 2021b.

38 Richard, Long and D'Andrea in press.

39 D'Andrea, Richard and Long 2020; Richard, Long and D'Andrea in press.

40 D'Andrea 2021a, 42.

41 Richard and Long 2007a, 79 and fig. 7; 2009, 94–95 and fig. 4; 2020, 430, fig. 23.6a–c; Long 2010 (in particular pp. 50–67 for the stratigraphy and architecture of the "gateway"); Richard and Long 2010, 273.

42 Richard 2010; Holdorf 2010a; Richard 2013.

43 Fall et al. 2022. In particular, Sample UGAMS-53624 places the earliest Early Bronze IV, Phase 1, in the following intervals: 2511–2493 cal BCE (1-sigma), 2522–2475 ca BCE (2-sigma), with a median of 2502 cal BCE; sample UGAMS-53630 places the last Early Bronze III phase at the site in the following intervals: 2520–2498 cal BCE (1-sigma), 2576–2489 cal BCE (2-sigma), with a median of 2510 cal BCE; sample UGAMS-53623 gave the following results for the same Early Bronze III phase: 2519–2499 cal BCE (1-sigma), 2580–2489 cal BCE (2-sigma), and a median of 2510 cal BCE (Fall et al. 2022, Tab. 2 on p. 8 and Tab. 3 on p. 9).

44 Holdorf 2010b, Tab. 15.1 sample # 2: 2576–2277 (2σ, 91.7%), charcoal.

45 Fall et al. 2022, Tab. 2 on p. 7 and Tab. 3 on p. 9. UGAMS-53626 (Phase 3): 2471–2456 cal BCE (1-sigma), 2487–2409 cal BCE (2-sigma), 2464 cal BCE (median); UGAMS-53627 (Phase 3): 2471–2457 cal BCE (1-sigma), 2488–2408 cal BCE (2-sigma), 2464 cal BCE (median); UGAMS-53622 (Phase 3): 2472–2460 cal BCE

(1-sigma), 2491–2408 cal BCE (2-sigma), 2466 cal BCE (median); AA-50178 (Phase 3): 2474–2458 cal BCE (1-sigma), 2492–2408 cal BCE (2-sigma), 2466 cal BCE (median); Tübingen (Phase 2): 2491–2467 cal BCE (1-sigma), 2508–2456 cal BCE (2-sigma), 2479 cal BCE (median); UGAMS-53625* (Phase 2): 2661–2500 cal BCE (1-sigma), 2846–2491 cal BCE (2-sigma), 2603 cal BCE (median).

46 Hayyat cannot be used to assess this question, because Early Bronze IV architecture has not been identified at the site; the Early Bronze IV pottery ascribed to Phase 6 was found in a basal level and might have been no longer in a primary context, due to the construction works for the following Phase 5 temple (Falconer and Fall 2006, 33).

47 See, e.g., Miroschedji 2002; 2012.

48 See Sowada 2009, 13, fn. 13; Gundacker 2017, 349–355, 373.

49 D'Andrea 2018b.

50 Gee 2015; Schneider 2017.

51 Sowada 2009, 123–124; 2014, 296; 2020, 152.

52 See discussions of these materials in Sowada 2009; D'Andrea 2014a, Volume 1, 252 and fig. 6.11; 2018b. In addition to this, there is M. Adams's recent proposal (Adams 2017a; 2017b) to redate the cache of Egyptianizing vessels found at Tell el-Mutesellim / Megiddo and earlier associated with the Early Bronze IB temple to EB IV based on suggested parallels with pottery in the funerary temple of Menthuhotep I (Eleventh Dynasty / First Intermediate Period), and to understand it as a foundation deposit for Temple 4040. Some scholars have rejected this new dating (Ussishkin 2018; Nigro 2020, 208). The present author has presented elsewhere her considerations on the local pottery (D'Andrea 2020a, 404–405) published by Adams (2013, 328–330, fig. 8.17) as supporting evidence for an Early Bronze IV date of the temple, as well as on hints of a possible construction of the three temples in Early Bronze III and use during part of the Early Bronze IV (D'Andrea 2020c, 2–6).

53 See endnote 34.

54 See, for instance, Sowada 186–187 (SOWADA 2009?).

55 See, for instance, Burke 2020, 34–35. Further literature is discussed within the text and quoted below.

56 Dunseth et al. 2017, 166; 2018, 719.

57 Ben-Yosef et al. 2016, 80, 82; Dunseth et al. 2016, 70; 2018, 723–724; Finkelstein et al 2018, 63, 73–77; Gidding and Levy 2020, 322–323; Sowada 2009, 186–188; 2020, 155; Kennedy 2016, 17–18; Cohen 2019, 78–79. On the pottery see also Dever 2014, 220–222, 227.

58 Dunseth et al. 2017, 166–167; 2018, 723–724; Finkelstein et al. 2018, 75.

59 Sowada 2009, 187, citing earlier references; see also Sowada 2014, fig. 2.

60 Ben-Yosef et al. 2016, 82.

61 Ben-Yosef 2016, 82. See also Cohen 2022, 223.

62 Dunseth et al. 2018, 719.

63 D'Andrea 2012, 33, 36, and figs. 13:12–13, 14:12–16; 2014a, Volume 1, 126–128, Tab. 7; 2020a, 401. For the pottery of Khirbet Hamra Ifdan and its chronology, see Adams 2000; 2006.

64 Khirbet Yarmouk / Tel Yarmouth, Khirbet al-Batrawy, and Bab edh-Dhra': D'Andrea 2012, fig. 14:1–11 and Tab. 4:1–11. The article still refers to the traditional absolute dates, as it appeared right before the publication of the first proposals of a higher chronology for the southern Levantine Early Bronze III and IV. However, this has no impact on the attribution of the assemblages to Early Bronze III, which was based on stratigraphy and ceramic chronology. For radiocarbon dates: Khirbet al-Batrawy: Höflmayer 2014b, 129–132, figs. 3–4; Khirbet Yarmouk / Tel Yarmouth: Regev, Miroschedji and Boaretto 2012; Bab edh-Dhra': Weinstein 2003, 638, tab. 22.2.

65 D'Andrea 2019a; 2020a; 2021.

66 D'Andrea 2012, 44–47; 2014a, Volume 1, 127–129; 2021a, 42–43, 46, 48.

67 See endnote 64.

68 Samples RT-2514 and RT-1558 respectively: Segal 1999.

69 Sample RTT-4683 (EY 17): Boaretto in: Yekutieli, Shilstein and Shalev 2005, 19–20.

70 Sample Beta-143812: Levy et al. 2002.

71 D'Andrea 2021a, 43.

72 Based on a recent reappraisal of the radiometric evidence from Arad, Gidding and Levy (2020, 322) have suggested that "the Central Negev sites associated with the production of copper in the Faynan were continuously occupied following the rule of Narmer (c. 3100 BCE) through sometime during the latter half of the EB IV (c. 2300–2100 BCE).

73 Kmošek et al. 2018; Rademakers et al. 2018; but cf. Ben-Yosef 2018.

74 Mumford 2006, 54.

75 Ben-Yosef 2018, 210, 213.

76 For the northern Levant and wider interregional connections, see, for instance the case of the KUNGA, a specialized equid breed, and the case of onagers, whose rearing was apparently in the hands of Amorite groups (Nichols and Weber 2006). For a possible involvement of the southern Levant into activities connected with animal breeding (in this case, sheep and goats), see Wilkinson et al. 2014, 90–92, while the Kennedy's proposal to include the Central Negev into this scenario (Kennedy 2016, 16–18,) seems more problematic.

77 Thalmann 2008, 72–76, figs 8–9.

78 D'Andrea and Vacca 2020, 129; D'Andrea 2021a, 48 and fig. 9.

79 Dever and Tadmor 1976; Philip 1998; Hauptmann et al. 2015, citing earlier references; Yahalom-Mack et al. 2014.

80 Lev et al. 2021.

81 Luciani 2016, 25–26, 28–30; Hausleiter, Zur and D'Andrea 2018. For the question of copper, see further comments in Ben-Yosef 2018, 211.

82 Arnold et al. 2016.

83 Sowada 2016–2018.

84 Sowada 2020, 157.

85 Stantis et al. 2020. For the early second millennium BCE see also Priglinger 2019a and 2019b, considering residential mobility and migrations between the Levant and Egypt in the framework of commercial contacts, but also of environmental degradations in the arid margins of the Levant and of political shifts in the early twentieth century BCE.

86 Mourad 2020, 117–126.

87 For lower dates of the beginning of Middle Bronze I corresponding to the early Twelfth Dynasty see Cohen 2012; 2017.

88 Oren and Yekutieli 1990; Yekutieli 2002.

Journal of Ancient Egyptian Interconnections

Identity and Monumentality: The construction of an Early Bronze Age landscape on the Lebanese coast

Michel de Vreeze
Durham University

Kamal Badreshany
Durham University

Abstract
This article will discuss the role of monuments in the construction of the Early Bronze Age (EBA) landscape on the Lebanese coast. The discussion focuses on Byblos, where an extensively excavated EBA town plan shows evidence of at least seven temples and a monumental town wall. Nearby contemporary sites that followed markedly similar building activity phases during the period will also be examined. Finally, we will argue that the construction of these buildings and the communal activities they facilitated were integral to the social organization of groups along this part of the Lebanese coast.

Temples and related monumental architecture were the nexus of labor and social ties, integrating both the hinterland and participants in overseas and overland exchange networks, most visible in Egypt but also likely including Syrian, Mesopotamian, and Anatolian communities. We show that Byblos was composed of several neighborhoods built around temples, where people participated in events that served to integrate local communities while simultaneously providing a stage for competitive display. Further, we will present evidence that the temples served as venues for these social acts and stimulated contact with emerging powers such as Egypt, which delivered prestige and status to local elites fostering the development of political hierarchies apparent in the following periods.

Introduction
The emergence of densely settled 'Urban' landscapes consisting of numerous fortified sites is considered a hallmark of Early Bronze Age II–III Levant. For the central and southern Levant, numerous commentators have described this earliest experiment in urbanism and usefully summarized its characteristics.[1] There is broad agreement on the physical traits of these newly built fortified settlements, and several models for their socio-political and economic organization have been posited. Among the common models is that of hierarchically controlled city-states, where fortified cities control territories of varying size.[2] Traditionally, these models have been framed around economic organization and are underlain by evolutionary assumptions.[3] These tend to view urbanism as the natural outcome of a long-term process of settlement nucleation that began in the Neolithic and was underpinned by technological innovations and gradual agricultural intensification to cope with population growth and resource imbalance to manage risk. Others have proposed heterarchical models which view these communities as structured through kinship organization, taking forms such as corporate villages or house society models, among others.[4] Fewer attempts have been made to explain the process, causality, and pathways

to these new forms of complexity. Greenberg points out the lack of self-aggrandizing architecture and durable prestige goods during the EB II and argues that this may indicate a focus on community over individuals, seeing these developments as a reaction to the emergence of inequality late in the EB I.[5]

This paper proposes an alternative model for the causality, development, and organization of EB II–III Levantine 'urban' societies, emphasizing the role of ritual monumentality and managed agricultural production in the development of the EBA landscape and emerging socio-political hierarchies. Byblos and its surrounding region during the EB III will be used as a case study, though the question remains how distinctive the Lebanese coast is compared to the contemporary developments in the Southern Levant. The site represents one of the most extensively excavated for the period in the Levant and provides a nearly complete EB III settlement plan. Additionally, the surrounding area is one of the most intensely investigated in Lebanon, thanks to several recent excavations and survey projects that provide a new regional context within which the data from Byblos can be examined.

Our discussion is based on four interconnected themes. First, a comparison of architectural units at Byblos with those from the nearby sites of Tell Fadous-Kfarabida and Tell Koubba suggests that the development of the settlement landscape, within what might be termed the Byblos hinterland, emphasized monumental construction undertaken in pre-planned, large-scale, and near-simultaneous episodes at sites across the region, rather than reflect organic growth. Second, monumentality was primarily focused on ritual architecture (temples and associated structures), though administrative and defensive architecture were also important foci. Third, the EB III settlement of Byblos was composed of distinct neighborhoods, each comprising a temple and closely associated buildings. Finally, the overall organization of the settlement and the differential distribution of Egyptian objects suggest that neighborhoods represent distinct socio-political or kinship units with potentially varying regional and international interests. Byblos, and other major Levantine sites of the period, are often represented as single entities in hypothesized political structures and exchange networks. We argue for a more complex and possibly internally competitive socio-political structure at the site.

Monumentality and Sacred Architecture as Driving Mechanisms for Social Change

Monumentalization underpinning the formation and maintenance of social groups is a common theme, cross-culturally, and has been discussed as a feature of Near Eastern Societies since at least the Neolithic period.[6] Ritualized monument construction drives the development of cooperative labor parties and has been discussed as a strategy for reinforcing hierarchical structures in small-scale societies where power is temporary, fluid, and conferred by consensus of the larger group.[7] Similar frameworks have been drawn upon for the EBA Levant to explain the construction of Levantine EBA 'defensive walls.'[8]

Greenberg and Askhenazi argued that the cooperative labor investment of groups, organized around ritual (seasonal) gatherings, was essential to the Early Bronze economy and most visible through the building of defensive walls erected partly or entirely around settlements.[9] Although ritual architecture is not dealt with in depth in their work, they suggest that temples are important as entities around which the periodic labor needed to construct walls could be ritually sanctioned.[10] Building on this notion, the archaeological record of the EBA Southern Levant is full of examples that suggest that monumental building projects were equally if not primarily vested in sacred architecture, including at Khirbet ez-Zeraqon with its three temples, and at Megiddo, with its large temple built during the latter EB I.[11] Likewise, EB III Byblos, with at least *seven* contemporary temples distributed throughout the settlement, demonstrates that ritual monumentality was a primary driver of the formation of the Early Bronze Age Landscape on this part of the northern Lebanese coast, embodying and motivating social change. Another dimension relevant to our understanding of these themes, as evidenced by recent excavations at Tell Fadous-Kfarabida and Koubba, is the primary role of these sites in the management of large-scale systems of communal agriculture that very likely focused on olive and grape.[12] This work will consider the role of the temple in administering this system and its utilization in labor mobilization and monumentalization.

Byblos: Challenges and New Opportunities

The non-stratigraphic and otherwise problematic nature of the excavations at Byblos has been discussed by numerous authors, leading to the impression amongst scholars that the site has little new information to contribute to regional debates.[13] Attempts have been made over the years to sort through stratigraphy and documentation with varying degrees of success.[14] Jean Lauffray's 2008 publication greatly improved the availability of information on the Early Bronze Age levels of the site, and his architectural plans and thorough descriptions, together with previously unpublished notes by Dunand, offer a much more complete picture of the EBA settlement layout.[15] Crucially, his work gives much greater context to the originally published data, providing new interpretive options. Rather than dismissing the usefulness of Byblos because of what is lacking, the large body of material available and remarkably complete overview of Early Bronze Age town planning should encourage us to explore the data at levels that are viable, which will lead to important new insights.

Byblos remains one of the most extensively excavated archaeological settlements in the region, particularly for the Early Bronze Age, yielding temples, auxiliary buildings, streets, and alleys. Andrew Bevan's work on Egyptian stone objects and Marwan Kilani's study of the Late Bronze Age have shown that Dunand's recording system can be used to trace published objects to their find spots.[16] For objects not specifically mentioned as *in situ*, at least their location within a 10x10m square can be identified and used to trace patterns of artefact distribution (used consistently in the second Byblos excavation volume).[17] Vertical stratigraphic control is far more problematic because the site was dug in 20 cm spits; this, along with extensive rebuilding in the ancient past, has led to the mixing of archaeological material from various periods. Analysis of the material shows a tendency for earlier artifacts to 'migrate' vertically into later deposits, likely due to the extensive reuse of buildings (the same can be seen with typologically Early Bronze ceramics in later layers).[18] Crucially, however, objects generally remain within the approximate area of original deposition. Therefore, their horizontal distribution can still reveal interpretable patterns if considered carefully against the available stratigraphic information.

Considering the limitations of the methods and available documentation, we lack the details necessary to investigate most buildings on an individual level. Therefore, we apply a 'neighborhood' approach to better understand Byblos as a settlement during the EB III. Neighborhood studies have been utilized to argue for heterarchical models in the formation of urban landscapes.[19]

Early Bronze II–III: Monumentalizing Byblos and its Landscape

By the start of the EB III, Byblos and its sacred spring had already been a focus of ritual activity for millennia. Thousands of jar burials dating from the 5th and 4th millennium BCE were found at the site.[20] The first vestiges of monumental communal architecture are already visible during the 4th millennium BCE, with the creation of a stone 'footpath' that ran between elevated areas to the southern border of the sacred spring. The feature has close parallels to a contemporary structure, normally interpreted as a wall, at Sidon-Dakerman.[21] At the end of the EB I, a monumental wall with internal buttresses seems to have been built around the sacred spring, partly covering the older footpath, though its exact dating remains contested.[22]

Following these developments, a phase called the 'proto-Urban' phase by Lauffray features a building with several EB II vessels stored as a group, an element which finds very close parallels in the southern Levant[23] (Fig. 1), suggesting that the phase dates to either the very late EB I or very early EB II, around 3200–3000 cal BCE (ECL 1). The date suggested by the *in situ* ceramics places new building activity at Byblos in line with similar developments across the central and southern Levant.[24] The proto-urban plan is unclear due to incursions from later activity, but this initial building phase seems to have comprised clusters of buildings with courtyards encompassing a wide area without external walls.

The next phase at the site, labeled 'Sableux' by Lauffray because of the use of sandstone (called ramlah, locally), represents the first phase of large-scale building at Byblos and the establishment of the EB III settlement pattern.[25] The phase can be dated to the early EB III (ca. 2800 BC, ECL 3) based on comparative analyses of *in situ* ceramic assemblages found in building XXVII.[26] This assemblage of vessels includes combed cooking pots, platter bowls, radially burnished bowls and juglets, and can be placed during the early EB III phases as defined at Arqa and Fadous Kfarabida.[27]

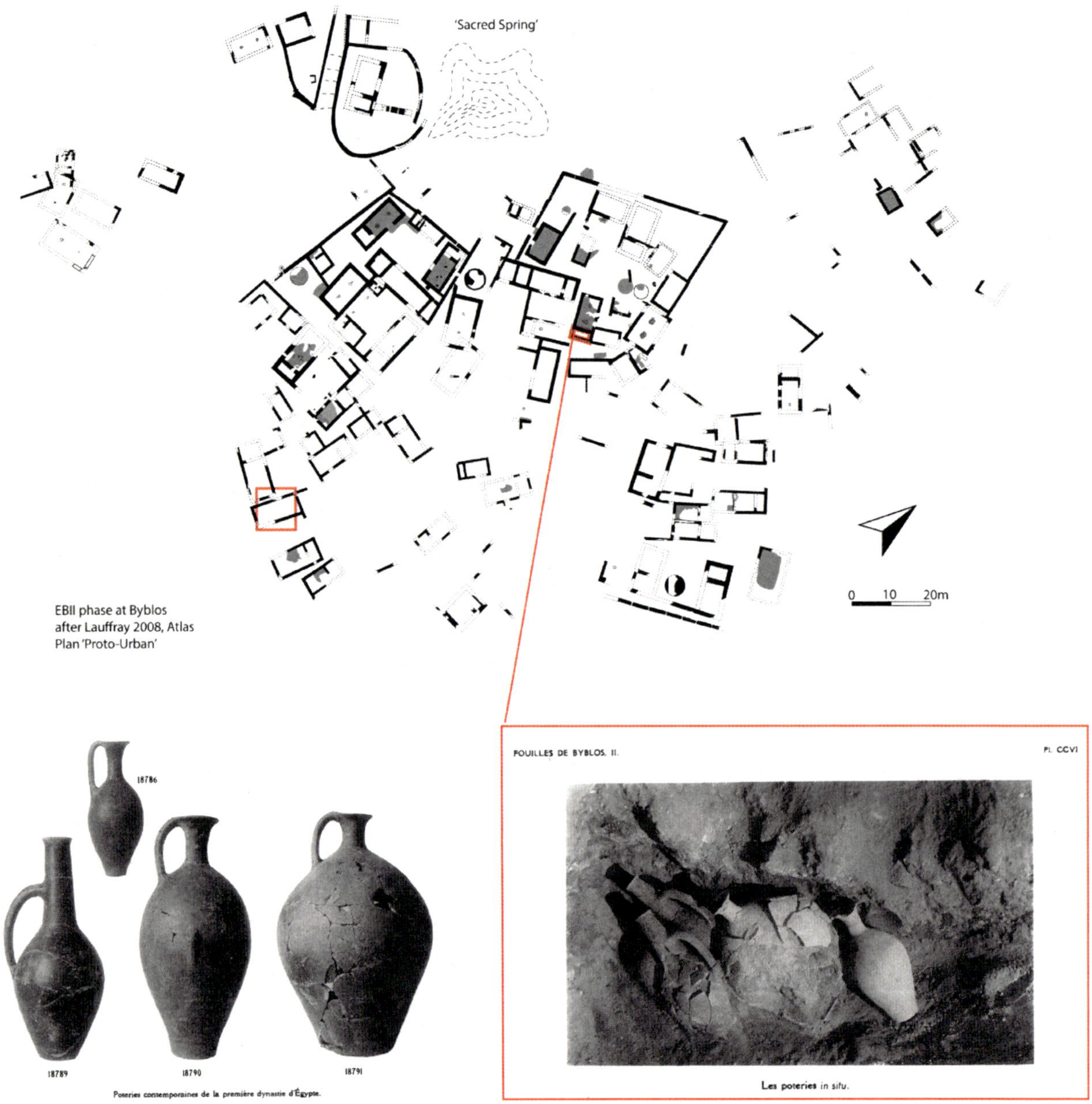

FIGURE 1: The late EB I–II (ECL 1) phase at Byblos with *in situ* Metallic Ware vessels stored in one of the buildings as published by Dunand (1958, PLCCVI).

Immediately following the 'Sableux' is the phase called 'Grosses Fondations,' marked by the presence of massive foundations and the use of ashlar blocks in larger buildings.[28] The architecture of this phase is mirrored at Fadous-Kfarabida, where it starts at roughly 2700 BCE.[29] During this phase, the 6-meter thick internally buttressed 'fortification' wall of Byblos is built.[30] Likewise, a new fortification wall at Fadous-Kfarabida can be attributed to this time, along with a large-buttressed enclosure wall at Tell Koubba.[31] Greenberg and Ashkenazi have recently pointed out the tactical weaknesses of these walls suggesting their construction was at least in part aimed at promoting social cohesion and the projection of power.[32] Notable at Byblos is that buttresses are otherwise used in association with sacred spaces and architecture, suggesting that the addition of an internally buttressed 'fortification wall' may have served to mark out the whole settlement as sacred. Although not conceived as a ritual space, the same might have applied to EB III Tell Yarmouth (Palace B1), which provides a striking parallel to internal buttresses marking the monumental enclosed space.[33] Many of the buildings at Byblos dating to this time contain stone bases adjacent to the walls and in corners of the rooms, presumably as supports for wood pillars that likely supported an upper story.[34] This feature is associated with settlements on the Lebanese coast and attested at least from Arqa to Byblos and as far as Tyre, for the remainder of the EBA.[35] Byblos, Fadous-Kfarabida, and Koubba constitute a region where buildings were primarily built of stone, in contrast to other parts of the Lebanese littoral (e.g., Arqa and Sidon) where mudbrick was preferred.

A final reorganizational phase of the late EB III, continuing into EB IV (ECL5–6; Old Kingdom Dynasties 4–6), was called by Lauffray *'Piqueté I–IV.'*[36] During this phase, existing temples were modified into even more monumental structures (L-shaped temple, Ba'alat Gebal temple; Western temple/sacred spring), and new temples were erected in the vicinity of older sacred structures (e.g., the Tower temple in the southwest).[37] Temples were often surrounded by larger free-standing structures, including many columned halls.[38] In general, buildings with larger rooms are created. A similar construction phase can be seen at Fadous-Kfarabida (phase IV), during which a major reorganization took place at the site, with earlier buildings infilled to accommodate new larger ones, including a columned hall (Building 3).[39] The material culture associated with these buildings at Fadous-Kfarabida suggests they had an administrative function.

As shown above, architectural forms, and to some extent, the phases of building activity at Byblos, are closely mirrored by those at Fadous-Kfarabida and Koubba, perhaps indicating they were planned and undertaken as broadly contemporaneous episodes of monumental building activity and did not reflect hundreds of years of organic growth. The C^{14} data, settlement plan, and sequence that emerged during excavation work at Fadous-Kfarabida further support this idea by showing that the settlement was carefully laid out in an initial EB III phase and reorganized later by infilling existing buildings.[40] The buildings of this initial phase are preserved to a height of up to 2 meters, suggesting that the infilling was fast. The evidence suggests that major building events in the region took place as defined episodes when the prevailing social conditions allowed for the organization and mobilization of large-scale cooperative labor parties.

Byblos: A Neighborhood Approach

Early Bronze III Byblos is distinguished from other contemporary central and southern Levantine sites by its large number of temples, suggesting ritual architecture played a key role in monumentality at the site. This large number of temples might be mirrored at other contemporary sites, but these were rarely excavated over such extensive areas. The main temples show evidence of continued reconstruction and investment, including the addition of ashlar masonry ('Grosses fondations' phase), the reorganizing of courtyards, and the addition of new buildings.[41] One can postulate that a large part of the site must have been given over to ritual activity. Likewise, a significant section of the 1.5-hectare site of Fadous-Kfarabida seems to have been given over to buildings of a public character, and this public building might, in fact, have been used to administer affairs as part of the Byblos hinterland.[42] Koubba has thus far not produced any clear evidence for domestic architecture.

The current evidence suggests that Byblos and known EB III sites in the surrounding region were dominated by ritual and or public/administrative contexts. Unlike Arqa or Sidon, clear evidence for domestic architecture remains elusive, save for one example from Fadous-Kfarabida. We cannot exclude a domestic role for some of the numerous buildings found at Byblos since the excavation methods employed there limit our understanding of their function in many cases. In the context of the EB III, categorization into ritual, public, or domestic spaces perhaps fails to fully capture the fluidity and dynamism of building use at the site. Looking at the plan of Byblos shows that most buildings were organized into several clusters and closely associated with a temple, suggesting linkage to the temple's activities.

Neighborhoods are integrative socio-spatial bodies lying somewhere between the household and the settlement.[43] As such, neighborhoods represent a useful unit of analysis for investigating social interactions, one not generally considered for the period and region. Byblos is often treated as a single entity when discussing its role in the region or as an intermediary in interregional exchange.[44]

The layout of the EB III site with its apparent clusters of buildings alternatively suggests the site was composed of several distinct socio-political or kinship groups with potentially varying regional and international interests.

From the Early EB III onward, the town plan of Byblos shows several densely built-up neighborhoods arranged around a central spring and lake (Fig. 2). The main neighborhoods can be visualized as islands within a network of streets and alleys, each dominated by a sacred building. We define a neighborhood as a cluster of buildings surrounding a temple and separated from each other by main streets running through the town of Byblos. The main streets lead to one of the gates in the town wall and/or are particularly wide. The neighborhoods are composed of house clusters spatially related to the temple, oriented towards it, or have their closest access to it. The temples are usually located directly on the street at important intersections, facilitating access and highlighting their prominence in the design of the site plan. Conceptualizing the site in this way yields at least seven major neighborhoods (Fig. 2), which we will number 1 to 7, moving clockwise from the center of the site.

Neighborhood 1 comprises the 'Western temple,' closely linked to the sacred spring (Fig. 2.1). This temple complex grew from its EB I–II antecedents and includes a courtyard and small temple edifice with associated buildings. House clusters surround this temple to the west and northwest.

Neighborhood 2 (Fig. 2.2) is found to the north and extends around the Ba'alat Gebal temple. Large residences from the Piqueté I–IV, including a building rich in Egyptian stone vessels, are associated with this temple.[45] The excavated segments of the site's monumental wall enclose this neighborhood on the north. The wall in this section contained a gate to a small sandy beach northwest of the site. The wall extended beyond this neighborhood, but whether it encircled the whole settlement remains unclear, as walls of the period are sometimes discontinuous.[46] The Ba'alat Gebal temple, and the household units surrounding it, saw several rearrangements during the Early Bronze Age, becoming incrementally monumental throughout the EB III ('Grosses Fondations'; Piqueté I–II).[47]

Neighborhood 3 (Fig. 2.3), located just east of Byblos' center, contains the L-shaped temple on its northwestern corner. Neighborhood 3 is further demarcated by a major street on the east and the sacred spring and lake on the northwest. Across a road, a small number of buildings to the north abut the city wall; we suggest these may have belonged to this cluster because they are oriented towards the L-shaped temple and further separated from Neighborhood 4 and its temple (see below) by a small alley. The L-shaped temple saw several reconstruction phases, and its architecture included a triple temple of Syrian 'in-antis' style in the early EB III period ('Grosses Fondations' phase), like those from Syria, and Megiddo and Khirbet ez-Zeraqon in the southern Levant.[48] Its extensive courtyard featured a monumental wall with internal buttresses.

Neighborhood 4 (Fig. 2.4) lies in the eastern part of the site. It contains the 'Oriental' Temple, so named because, like the L-shaped temple, it was built in a Syrian in-antis style with parallels in Syria and the southern Levant.[49] The neighborhood of this temple extends southeastwards up to the town wall.

Neighborhood 5 (Fig. 2.5), located just south of the site's center, contains the so-called 'sanctuaire meridional.'[50] This small temple, dating back at least to the late EB III, can be found in the cluster's southeastern corner. This temple developed into the well-known 'Champs des Offrandes' of the early MB period, again highlighting the continuity of sacred spaces into later periods.

Neighborhood 6 (Fig. 2.6), on the southeastern edge of the site, contained the 'Temple Sud' and another small temple with a row of obelisks.[51] This neighborhood is linked to the southeastern gate with direct access to Skhiny Beach, now thought to be Byblos's main port in the period.[52]

Lastly, Neighborhood 7 (Fig. 2.7) is located on the southwestern edge of the site. In an initial phase of the EB III ('Sableux'–'Grosses Fondations'), the area contained small cultic buildings, including the Southwest Temple.[53] The neighborhood extended from these temples to the south and southwest. The Southwest Temple fell out of use and was replaced with the more monumental 'Tower Temple' during the late EB III–IV (Piqueté) phase.[54] Monumental anchors in the Tower Temple's pavement point to the association of Neighborhood 7 with harbor activities taking place to its immediate south.

The Integrative Role of Byblos's Temples

Pongratz–Leisten has described temples in Mesopotamia as being at the heart of urban life.[55] The great

Figure 2: The seven EB III identified neighborhoods with their temples ('Grosses Fondations': Lauffray 2008, Plate III). The neighborhoods are distinguished by color and numbered 1–7, as discussed in the text.

scope of their remit saw them oversee administrative tasks, learning, healing, and economic activity. The evidence from Byblos and across the central and southern Levant shows that temples are, at least physically, at the very heart of early 'urban' communities.[56] Given their historically and archaeologically documented role in Mesopotamia and archaeological evidence from the Levant, it is plausible to conceptualize EB II–III Levantine temples as institutions spearheading socio-political and economic change. In rethinking the concept of 'temple economy' for the Bronze Age, Wengrow has also highlighted their multifaceted and integrative socio-economic role.[57] Byblos's temples were the monumental embodiment of communal identity and principles, but the evidence presented below also suggests they functioned as integrative hubs for redistribution (ceremonial or otherwise) and trade. In terms of monumentalizing the landscape, temples are ideal entities, as Greenberg and Ashkenazi have suggested, around which periodic and ritually sanctioned labor could be organized.[58] They further point out that the presence of temples is an important predictor of large-scale fortification work, further suggesting they play a key role in the economy and the organization of cooperative labor.[59]

The appearance of large (often combed) jars during the EB II–III represents a significant socio-economic development in which temples may have played a key role. The jars are the manifestation of an agriculture system thought to focus on olive, a system that intensified during the EB III and played an increasingly important role in local political economies.[60]

Large quantities of ceramics used for storing, transporting, and processing liquid products, like the huge *in situ* vats from Koubba, have been found at Byblos and nearby sites. At Koubba and Fadous-Kfarabida, these vessels have been found in association with a substantial proportion of charred olive, indicating that the EB III sites of the area functioned as nodes for mediating the storage and processing of these agricultural outputs. There is no direct evidence for the involvement of the temple in this activity, but Old Kingdom and later texts do stress the centrality of at least the Ba'alat Gebal temple in interregional interaction.[61] We can theorize that its resulting outputs represented a valuable resource base for provisioning ritual (and other) monumental building projects through associated communal feasting or other redistributive mechanisms.[62] The presence of these jars in Egypt also shows that they and their contents played a key role in interregional trade networks, and that these continued well into the second half of the 3rd millennium.[63]

The Distribution of Egyptian Objects: Commonalties and Competition

Byblos has yielded the largest EB III assemblage of Egyptian objects in the Levant. Sowada has usefully summarized and synthesized the rich evidence of the period, such as stone vessels, ivory furniture fittings (bovid hoofs), and bifacial flint knives.[64] Stone vessels, including numerous fragments of prestige types, and flint knives, form the main corpus of Egyptian objects recovered at the site. In Egypt, these objects are status markers, primarily restricted to elite contexts, such as cultic deposits, temple magazines, elite tombs, and installations.[65] These objects likely carried similar connotations and were used correspondingly in Levantine contexts.

Most of the stone vessels and some bifacial flint knives were associated with the Ba'alat Gebal temple and its environs, and to a lesser extent with the *Enceinte Sacrée*, suggesting their preeminence over other EB III temples at Byblos in terms of Egyptian interaction.[66]

At Byblos, at least 40 bifacial flint knives, or fragments of such knives, can be classified as Egyptian, constituting the largest assemblage of such knives outside of Egypt (see Table 1; Fig. 3).[67] In fact, outside of Byblos, bifacial flint knives are rare in the Levant and practically unknown after the EB I. From the Lebanese coast, only one example dating from the EB I is known from Sidon.[68] In the southern Levant, they sporadically occur at sites traditionally associated with Naqada II/III/late EB I Egyptian influence.[69] Bifacial knives date to the Early Dynastic–Old Kingdom period, with some examples possibly extending to the Middle Kingdom. Their production in Egypt was possibly managed by emerging elites as part of a prestige-goods economy.[70] The knives are strongly associated with the ritual slaughter of cattle.[71] Their presence at Byblos likely reflects the butchering and carving of bovine meat in ritual settings, suggesting that cattle were an important trade item and that feasting and sacrifice were significant features of Egyptian interactions at the site. Direct evidence for cattle trade between Egypt and the southern Levant is attested for this period.[72] The presence of these Egyptian bifacial knives suggests that Byblos might have been an important recipient of cattle and associated ritualized feasting.[73]

Bifacial Knives and their Distribution at Byblos

In contrast to stone vessels, which are mainly associated with the Ba'alat Gebal temple and its surroundings, and to a lesser degree with the *Enceinte Sacrée*, bifacial knives were found throughout the site, often associated with temples but also in other contexts (Table 1; Fig. 4). This distribution shows that the activities represented by these knives were practiced site-wide.

Thirteen knives can be attributed to EB III–IV levels (see Table 1), with the remaining 27 found in post-EBA levels or defined as surface finds. The distribution of most of these knives associates them with elements of the EB III or EB IV plan; this, along with their typology, suggests the knives were originally brought to the site during the EBA. As discussed above, the excavation methods at Byblos make the vertical position of objects difficult to reconstruct. Consequently, some have argued that typologically earlier stone vessels found in later contexts were brought to Byblos in post-EBA periods as heirlooms.[74] However, rather than applying this argument to typologically earlier bifacial knives

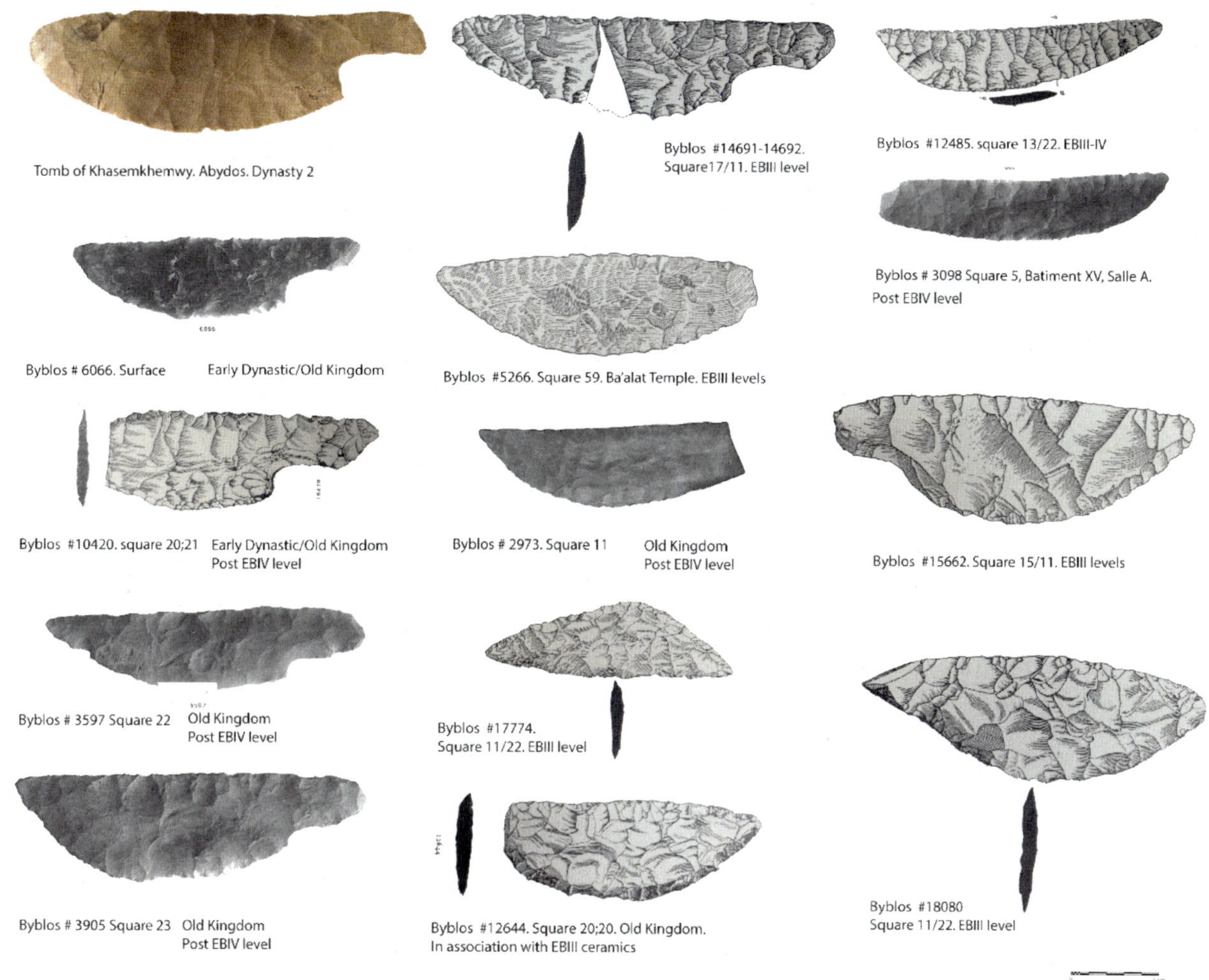

FIGURE 3: A selection of Egyptian bifacial knives from Byblos (after Dunand 1938; 1958). In the upper left corner is the knife from Khasekhemwy's tomb providing close comparison to the earliest types found at Byblos.

found in later contexts, we believe a more plausible explanation is that these and other Egyptian items of high socio-symbolic value found their way into later deposits through long-term use at Byblos or were carefully redeposited during later building activity.[75]

Five knives were found around the Ba'alat Gebal temple, and another seven were found in its associated neighborhood (FIG. 4). Most of these came from later contexts, but two fragmented knives were found together in the corner of one of the Ba'alat Gebal temples rooms (Table 1).[76] Dunand associated these with 'Salle C' dated to Lauffray's Piqueté phase (EB III–IV). However, the level where the knives were found, at a depth of 22.20–22.00 m, should rather correspond to the temple room underneath, dating from the preceding EB III phase ('Grosses Fondations').[77] Worth noting is that close to the knives were some other Egyptian objects such as ivory bovid hoofs probably belonging to a small table of a type known from Egypt and having parallels in Early Dynastic contexts.[78] These knives were thus probably used and stored in the EB III Ba'alat Gebal temple complex together with other Egyptian objects. The number of stone bowls, knives, and other Egyptian objects found associated with the Ba'alat Gebal temple clearly mark it out as a focal point for Egyptian-style cult activity.

In Neighborhood 1, three knives (14741–14743, see Table 1) were found within square 6/10, in the courtyard of the 'Western Temple' associated with the central well (7; 10) (FIG. 4). These knives were found in (secondary) Middle Bronze Age contexts but deposited just above the small EB

FIGURE 4: The distribution of Egyptian flint knives in the various neighborhoods. A correlation can be seen with several temple precincts. The spatial information, as available, derives from Dunand (1938; 1958) and is further summarized in Table 1.

III structure that Lauffray identifies as a chapel within the triangular courtyard.[79] Knives were also found in neighborhood 3.[80] A knife from a clear EB III–IV context was found in the L-shaped Temple courtyard, and two others were found in the vicinity. Several more were found in the L-shaped Temple's associated neighborhood. In Neighborhood 4, a knife (12855) was found in EB IV levels next to the Oriental Temple, with three other examples noted in its associated neighborhood.[81] Two knives were found in EB III–IV layers in a square belonging to Neighborhood 6 but close to the corner of the 'Temple Méridional' of Neighborhood 5.

Additional concentrations of knives were found in Neighborhood 6, one example near its associated temple (FIG. 4). One knife was found in Neighborhood 7, close to the southern 'Tower Temple,' though in a post-EB context.

The distribution of these flint knives is important in illustrating and reinforcing the association between various temples and their neighborhoods. The number of knives associated with a temple is a predictor of the number found in its postulated neighborhood. The varied designs among Byblos's temples, the plan of the site with its discrete building clusters, and the differential distribution of artifacts, such as the Egyptian stone vessels in the Ba'alat Gebal temple, support the idea of institutional differentiation and, therefore, of social heterogeneity among the site's inhabitants. At Byblos, various regional actors and a range of cultural affiliations were juxtaposed, creating an environment where competitive peer-polity interactions could develop. The knives, however, also serve to connect the various temples and neighborhoods to particular forms of feasting or ritual practice, probably involving cattle, linking the inhabitants by common threads despite varying regional and international interests.[82]

Constructing Social Identity at Byblos

In a recent work on Late Bronze sacred architecture in the Levant, Susnow estimates that the Middle Bronze Temple of the Obelisks at Byblos, with its large courtyard, could have welcomed a sizeable amount (47%) of the population living at the settlement for festivities and offering events.[83] The figure is significantly higher than other Middle Bronze Age settlements considered in his study. The courtyard of the preceding L-shaped Temple was equally impressive in scale, and these only represent one of the seven temple precincts known from EB III Byblos. This suggests that during the Early Bronze Age, Byblos and its temples had the capacity to accommodate a population far greater than that of the site itself, suggesting the temples were also intended to serve people from the surrounding area and, perhaps, illustrious international guests.

The construction of the temples and other monumental architecture would have required the pooling of aggregate labor from nearby communities, bolstering community identity and hierarchies. Communal activities at the constructed temple would have further magnified these impacts. Evidence for the production and movement of oil and wine at a regional level and the distribution of bifacial flint knives at Byblos already highlighted above suggest these events may also have involved redistribution and communal consumption of oil, wine, and cattle meat.

In his recent study, Susnow suggests that Canaanite cultic spaces played multiple integrative roles, as the houses and residencies of deities but also as venues for hosting feasts and commensal meals based around sacrifices.[84] Although Susnow's study focuses on Canaanite temples of the Middle and Late Bronze Ages, Byblos exhibits continuity in sacred architecture, suggesting the template for the monumentalization and utilization of sacred space originated in the EBA.

The evidence from Byblos presented above shows that seven distinct neighborhoods emerged during the EB III, each with its own developmental trajectories, motivations, and networks. Furthermore, the uneven distribution of Egyptian material culture, especially stone bowls, shows that some temples (e.g., Ba'alat Gebal) were preeminent in external interactions (in this case, with Egypt). We suggest that these temples and their associated neighborhoods embodied kin-groups or other units of socio-political organization that communally invested in sacred and other forms of monumental architecture. Key events for the community were linked to the temple, and it functioned as a depot for important objects.

The intensification, beginning in EB III, of monumental building and other communal events such as feasting and sacrifice underpinned the formation and maintenance of community identity and drove the development of the EBA landscape in this part of Lebanon. At Byblos itself, exchange networks with Egypt and Syria / Anatolia provided opportunities for interregional trade, which served to enhance the status of particular temples and the individuals and groups associated with them in an increasingly competitive environment.

The texts and archaeological evidence suggest that the Ba'alat Gebal Temple and its neighborhood were the focal points for Egyptian exchange from the EBA onward.[85] The development of interregional exchange networks enhanced the social status, influence, and power of associated individuals. Perhaps the representatives of other neighborhoods, like those associated with the Syrian-influenced 'L-Shaped' and 'Oriental' Temples looked north and east toward Syria to advance their own positions and access to resources, as evidence shows was the case by the Middle Bronze Age.

Monumental building, ritual activity, and communal feasting provided opportunities for competitive behavior. As an individual, a clear drawback to not participating in these events would be forgoing their associated social, material, and ideological rewards, including the expansion of social networks that ultimately improve access to resources and are important for mitigating risk in times of stress or duress.[86]

The plan of Byblos clearly shows that larger monumental 'residences,' monocellular buildings, and temples emerge toward the EB IV.[87] Lauffray argued for the dominance of several households over what we have here identified as distinct neighborhoods.[88] Signs of social inequality already emerge during the EBA III across the central and southern Levant.[89] This indicates that the establishment of elites and, eventually, MBA kingship at Byblos was gradual and perhaps rooted in competitive environments as described above.

Contemporary Regional Developments

Developments in the region of Byblos (including at Fadous-Kfarabida and Koubba) are mirrored in other parts of the Lebanese coast. Numerous similarities exist between the architecture of the Byblos region and EBA contexts at Tell Arqa, Sidon, and Tyre. For the EBA at Arqa, no clear architecturally distinctive sacred monumental buildings could be identified based on layout or associated artifacts.[90] The limited extent of the exposed area and position of the sounding in a more peripheral part of the site suggest that ritual building might still be uncovered as work progresses toward the center of the site.

According to Thalmann, two buildings of interest from phase 18A (ECL4) suggest a 'hierarchization' in space, though he ultimately argued for a domestic context.[91] Building 18.40 featured a large mudbrick bench that might have been used for communal activities, but it is not an uncommon feature in Levantine buildings. Notably, this room also contained a remarkably high-quality metallic-ware jar with radial pattern burnishing and net and figurative cylinder seal impressions decorating the body and base. Another room, thought to be for communal activity (18.05), contained a central pillar and a worked and coated floor opening onto the street.[92]

EBA Sidon shows no direct evidence of monumental architecture but large buildings and facilities for large-scale grain storage were uncovered, and the site attests to sacred architecture in later periods, starting from the Late Bronze onward, suggesting that earlier EBA temple-like buildings might have been present at the site, but not yet excavated.[93] A large structure was uncovered at Tyre, at the highest point on the island, which the excavator suggests may represent the first vestiges of sacred architecture at the site.[94]

As sites elsewhere on the Lebanese coast also provide architectural evidence for substantial storage structures, we suggest that monumental building projects and the associated management of agricultural commodities played a key role in shaping EB III political and economic landscapes throughout the area.

Conclusions and Future Prospects

A fresh look at the evidence from Byblos reshapes our understanding of the Early Bronze Age in this part of the Levant. Developments at Byblos during the EB II–III encapsulate region-wide phenomena simultaneously occurring across the landscape at several sites. Byblos was an exceptional place, recognized well beyond its surrounding region for its sacred character. Beginning in the EB III, the inhabitants of the site and region capitalized on its privileged location by extensively monumentalizing the site, creating new communal contexts for ritual activity and trade along with new opportunities for enhancing the status of communities and/or individuals. These themes offer a dynamic framework within which to comprehend the development of the EBA landscape and the changing regional and interregional interactions. In small-scale societies, which often lack coercive means of control, ritual serves as a functional alternative to political power, driving, through related monumental building projects, the regular establishment of cooperative labor parties, useful for developing and reinforcing community identity and hierarchical structures.[95]

The almost complete absence of Egyptian objects outside of Byblos during the EB III and the fact that the 'Combed Ware' jars found in Egypt during the Old Kingdom appear to have been produced in the Byblos region suggest that interregional contact took place mainly at Byblos, with the Ba'alat Gebal temple as a particular focus point.[96] At Byblos, the concentration of Egyptian durable prestige goods in this temple highlights its prominence in mediating the interactions with Egypt based on ritualized gift exchange.[97] Other temples, such as the L-shaped Temple (and the succeeding Temple of the Obelisks) and Oriental Temple, show Syrian-inspired designs that may likewise distinguish their communities as arbiters of contact with parts inland, like Syria and other Levantine sites, such as Megiddo Level J-7 and Khirbet ez-Zeraqon, where similar temples are present.[98]

Moving into the EB IV, emerging evidence, including from Ebla texts, places Byblos as a key intermediary in trade networks linking Egypt, the Levant, Anatolia, and Mesopotamia.[99] The EB IV at Byblos shows increased evidence of social differentiation in the form of larger buildings interpreted as elite residences, a process that begins to take shape during the Late EB III. In an increasingly competitive environment, winners emerged, in the form of communities, families, or individuals, buffered by the status gains made through developing interregional exchange contacts.[100] The increasingly outward-looking focus resulted in the gradual detachment of Byblos from the nearby landscape and the communities that inhabited them, as evidenced by the decline or abandonment of key sites. A further indication is the cessation or drastic decline in the production of Combed-Ware vessels on the Lebanese coast south of Arqa, which were an integral part of the system of communal agriculture underpinning activity in the EB II and III.[101]

The EB IV, often interpreted as a period of economic collapse, might be primarily characterized as a contraction of corporate will to engage with the ideological frameworks that encouraged monumental building activity. In the case of the region of Byblos, during the EB IV, this activity was left to a handful of individuals at the site focused on fostering interregional networks at the expense of relationships with regional communities and the monuments that once brought them together.[102]

Table 1: Egyptian bifacial knives as published from Byblos and associated stratigraphic information as aggregated from Dunand (1938; 1958) and Lauffray (2008).

Number	Object number	Short description	Period	Measurements (cm)	Location (Square and depth (Lévee))	Notes on location	Reference
1	2973	Bifacial knife. Handle broken	ED-Old Kingdom	Length 15 Width 5.4	Square 11; Levee 9	Post EB IV	Dunand 1938, 189-190; Plate CXII
2	3056	Bifacial knife	ED-Old Kingdom	11.2×3.9×0.6	Square 56 Levee IX	Post EB IV	Dunand 1938, 195, fig. 182: Plate CXI
3	3098	Bifacial knife	ED-Old Kingdom	Length 16.4 Width 3.4	Square 5 Levee IX	Bâtiment XV, salle A. Levée XI (de la côte 26.00 a la côte 25.80) Post EB IV	Dunand 1938, 228: Plate CXII
4	3349	Bifacial knife	ED-Old Kingdom		Square 10 Levee XVI (2500-24.80)	Post EB IV	Dunand 1938, 228: Plate CXII
5	3597	Bifacial knife. Short handle. Complete	ED-Old Kingdom	Length 18 Width 4.6 (max.) Thickness 2 (max.)	Square 22 Levee XVI (25.00-24.80)	Post EB IV	Dunand 1938, 246: Plate CXI
6	3883	Bifacial knife	ED-Old Kingdom	Length 9.3 Width 4.3 (max.) Thickness 0.9	Square 8 Levee XX (24.20-24.00)	Post EB IV	Dunand 1938, 269: Plate CXII
7	3905	Bifacial knife. Short handle. Complete	ED-Old Kingdom	Length 19.4 Width 5.7 Thickness 0.9	Square 23 Levee XX (24.20-24.00)	Post EB IV	Dunand 1938, 271: Plate CXI
8	5266	Bifacial knife	ED-Old Kingdom	Length 17.8 Width 5.7 Thickness 1.2	Square 59 Levee XXIX 22.40-22-20 Bâtiment XVIII (24-158) or predecessor.	EB III. Burnt phase Ba'alat Gebal temple. Corner Room C. Should be earlier phase (Piqueté I underneath Piqueté III final room 158 (Lauffray 2008, 369: Fig. 120; Plate XIII).	Dunand 1938, 355, 358, fig. 281
9	5267	Bifacial knife. Fragmentary	ED-Old Kingdom	Length 8.5 Width 6.2 Thickness 0.7 (max.)	Square 59 Levee XXIX 22.40-22-20. Bâtiment XVIII (24-158) or predecessor.	EB III. Burnt phase Ba'alat Gebal temple. Corner Room C. Should be earlier phase (Piqueté I underneath Piqueté III final room 158 (Lauffray 2008, 369: Fig. 120; Plate XIII).	Dunand 1938, 355
10	6062	Leaf shaped knife. Complete	Naqada II-III/EBI	Length 19 Width 3 Thickness 1.1 (max.)	Surface		Dunand 1938, 403: Plate CXI
11	6066	Bifacial knife. Short handle. Complete	ED	Length 15.2 Width 4.2 Thickness 0.75	Surface		Dunand 1938, 404: Plate CXII

Number	Object number	Short description	Period	Measurements (cm)	Location (Square and depth (Lévee))	Notes on location	Reference
12	6550	Bifacial knife	ED-Old Kingdom	Length 12 Width 4.3 Thickness 0.7	Surface		Dunand 1938, 424: Plate CXII
13	6948	Bifacial knife	ED-Old Kingdom	Length 20.2 Width 3.2 (max.)	8; 25 surface		Dunand 1958, 53: Plate CLXXXVI
14	7515	Bifacial knife. Fragmentary. Leaf shaped handle	ED-Old Kingdom	Length 10.2 Thickness 4.1 (max.)	u-wall		Dunand 1958, 108: Plate CLXXXVI
15	7475	Bifacial knife. Handle broken	ED-Old Kingdom	Length 13.1	7; 18 u-wall	Lake; later level.	Dunand 1958, 104; 136: fig. 128: Plate CLXXXVI
16	7694	Bifacial knife. Handle broken	ED-Old Kingdom	Length 11.2	8; 23 Levee 2	Post Early Bronze level	Dunand 1958, 136: Fig. 128
17	10420	Bifacial knife	ED	Length 15.5 Width 5.6 (max.)	20; 21 Levee 7	Post Early Bronze level	Dunand 1958, 493, fig. 398
18	11235	Bifacial knife. Broken in two	ED-Old Kingdom	Length 13	16; 23 Levee 9	Post Early Bronze level	Dunand 1958, 428, fig. 456
19	12485	Bifacial knife	ED-Old Kingdom	Length 16 Width 3.4 (max.) Thickness 0.6 (max.)	**13; 22** Levee 12 (25,80-25,60)	Temple oriental: Piqueté I–III (EB III–IV) Courtyard at level 25.90 (Lauffray 2008, 415)	Dunand 1958, 528, 527, fig. 600: Plate CLXXXVI
20	12644	Bifacial knife. Handle missing	ED-Old Kingdom	Length 14.3 Width 5.6 (max.) Thickness 0.85	**20: 20** Levee 12 (25,80-25,60)	Associated with EB II–III ceramics	Dunand 1958, 540, 566, fig. 639
21	12855	Bifacial knife. Point and handle missing.	ED-Old Kingdom	Length 13.2 Width 7 Thickness 1	**16; 13** Levee 13 (25,60-25,40)	Associated with Piqueté I level Temple meriodional. EB III (Lauffray 2008, 402–404)	Dunand 1958, 555, 556, fig. 639
22	12356	Bifacial knife. Convex handle	ED-Old Kingdom	Length 12.3	**16; 13** Levee 13 (25,60-25,40)	Associated with Piqueté I level Temple meridional. EB III (Lauffray 2008, 402-404)	Dunand 1958, 566, fig. 639
23	13093	Bifacial knife	ED-Old Kingdom	Length 14.4 Width 4 Thickness 0.9 (max.)	13; 18 Levee 14 (25,40-25,20)	Post EB IV/MBA level L-shape/Obelisks Temple (Lauffray 2008, Plate XI).	Dunand 1958, 574, 566, fig. 639
24	13241	Bifacial knife. Extremities missing	ED-Old Kingdom	Length 7.5	18; 15 Levee 14 (25,40-25,20)	Post EB IV level (Lauffray 2008, 411)	Dunand 1958, 585
25	14005	Bifacial knife. Handle missing	ED-Old Kingdom	Length 12.6	8; 11 Levee 16 (25,00-24,80)	MBA level (Lauffray 2008, 189-328).	Dunand 1958, 655, fig. 773

Number	Object number	Short description	Period	Measurements (cm)	Location (Square and depth (Lévee))	Notes on location	Reference
26	14061	Bifacial knife. Fragmentary	ED-Old Kingdom	Length 12.7 Width 4.2 (max.)	10; 23 Levee 16 (25,00-24,80)	Post EB IV level road (Lauffray 2008, 420: Fig. 232).	Dunand 1958, 660, 661; 730, fig. 869, Plate: CLXXXVI
27	14197	Bifacial knife	ED-Old Kingdom	Length 4.9 Thickness 0.7 (max.)	13; 19 Levee 16 (25,00-24,80)	Post EB IV/MBA level L-shape/Obelisks Temple (Lauffray 2008, Plate XI).	Dunand 1958, 672, fig. 799
28	14741	Bifacial knife. Short handle	ED-Old Kingdom	Length 15.5 Width 6 Thickness 1.7	6; 10 Levee 18 (24,60-24-40)	Post EB IV level (MB) courtyard West temple (Lauffray 2008, 325-330).	Dunand 1958, 723, 672, fig. 799
29	14691/ 14692	Bifacial knife. Two fragments	ED-Old Kingdom	Length 8.2 Width 4.9 Thickness 0.7/ Length 13.2 Width 5.6 (max.) Thickness 0.8	**17; 11** Levee 17 (24,80-24,60)	EB III level (Piqueté I) (Lauffray 2008, 402; fig. 219	Dunand 1958, 718, fig. 854
30	14742	Bifacial knife. Handle missing	ED-Old Kingdom	Length 17.7 Width 8.2 (max.) Thickness 0.8	6; 10 Levee 18 (24,60-24-40)	Post EB IV level (MBA). Courtyard West Temple (Lauffray 2008, 325–330).	Dunand 1958, 723, fig. 860
31	14743	Bifacial knife. Handle preserved	ED-Old Kingdom	Length 10.3 Width 7.3 (max.) Thickness 0.7	6; 10 Levee 18 (24,60-24-40)	Post EB IV level (MBA). Courtyard West Temple (Lauffray 2008, 325–330).	Dunand 1958, 723
32	14795	Bifacial knife. Handle is broken	ED-Old Kingdom	Length 12.2 Width 4.5 Thickness 1.2	**10; 28** Levee 18 (24,60-24-40)	NW gate. Below EB IV (Piqueté) (Lauffray 2008, 307; thus EB II–III.	Dunand 1958, 730, fig. 869
33	15662	Bifacial knife. Short handle	ED-Old Kingdom	Length 20.2 Width 7 Thickness 1.3	**15; 11** Levee 18 (24,60-24-40)	EB III level (Piqueté I) (Lauffray 2008, 402; fig. 219)	Dunand 1958, 790, fig. 897
34	15743	Bifacial knife. Fragmentary	ED-Old Kingdom	Length 13.3 Width 6.1 Thickness 0.8	7; 10 Levee 19 (24,60-24-40)	Post EB IV level (MBA). Courtyard West temple (Lauffray 2008, 325–330).	Dunand 1958, 792, fig. 900
35	15678	Bifacial knife. Tip and part handle missing	ED-Old Kingdom	Length 11.7 Width 6.1 (max.)	**16; 11** Levee 18 (24,60-24-40)	EB III level (Piqueté I) (Lauffray 2008, 402; fig. 219)	Dunand 1958, 792, fig. 900
36	16546	Bifacial knife. Short handle	ED-Old Kingdom	Length 12 Width 4.2	9; 22 Levee 20 (24,40-24,20)	Post EB IV level (Lauffray 2008, 421: Fig. 233)	Dunand 1958, 838, fig. 953, Plate: CLXXXVI

Number	Object number	Short description	Period	Measurements (cm)	Location (Square and depth (Lévee))	Notes on location	Reference
37	17774	Triangular knife	ED-Old Kingdom (see Angevin 2015, 9-11)	Length 13.7 Width 4.3 Thickness 0.8	**11; 22** Levee 22 (23,80-23,60)	EB III level. Floor of Sableux II–III at 23,25; levée XXIV (Lauffray 2008, 147)	Dunand 1958, 956, 955: fig. 1064
38	18080	Bifacial knife	ED-Old Kingdom	Length 19 Width 6.8 (max.)	**10; 21** Levee 23 (23,60-23,40)	Piqueté I. EB III level road (Lauffray 2008, 420: Fig. 232).	Dunand 1958, 981, fig. 1096
39	18278	Bifacial knife. Tip and large part handle missing	ED-Old Kingdom	Length 16 Width 8.8 (max.)	**11; 19** Levee 23 (23,60-23,40)	EB III–IV level Piqueté I–II (Lauffray 2008, section plate)	Dunand 1958, 981, fig. 1096
40	18667	Bifacial knife. Short handle	ED-Old Kingdom	Length 12.8 Width 3.3 Thickness 0.7	10; 6 Levee 24 (23,40-23,20)	Post EB III–IV level (Lauffray 2008, 183	Dunand 1958, 1022, fig. 1127

References

Adams, Matthew J., Israel Finkelstein, and David Ussishkin. 2014. "The Great Temple of Early Bronze I Megiddo." *American Journal of Archaeology* 118 (2): 285–305.

Angevin, Raphaël. 2015. "The hidden Egyptian workshop: the lithic grave goods of King Khasekhemwy." *Antiquity 89* (346): 818–837.

———. 2016. "Lithic Industries and Interregional Trade between Egypt and the Levant during the 4th Millennium BC: A Review of the Evidence." In Rolf A. Stucky, Oskar Kaelin, and Hans-Peter Mathys (eds.), *Proceedings of the 9th International Congress on the Archaeology of the Ancient Near East: June 9–13, 2014, University of Basel. Volume 2: Egypt and Ancient Near East – Perceptions of Alterity, Ancient Near Eastern Traditions Vs. Hellenization/Romanization, Reconstructing Ancient Eco-Systems, Islamic Session*, 11–22. Wiesbaden: Harrassowitz Verlag.

Artin, Gassia. 2009. *La "Nécropole Éneolithique" de Byblos: Nouvelles Interpretations*; BAR International Series 1993. Oxford: Archaeopress.

Arnold, Elizabeth R., Hartman, Gideon, Haskel Joseph, G., Shai, Iztaq, Babcock, Lindsay E., and Aren M. Maier. 2016. "Isotopic Evidence for Early Trade in Animals between Old Kingdom Egypt and Canaan." *PLoS ONE 11(6)*: https://doi.org/10.1371/journal.pone.0157650.

Ashkenazi, Hai. 2020. "Sometimes Defence is Just an Excuse: Fortification Walls of the Southern Levantine Early Bronze Age." *Cambridge Archaeological Journal* 30(1): 46–67.

Aubet, María Eugenia, 2020. "Tyre before Tyre: The Early Bronze Foundation." In Ayelet Gilboa and Assaf Yassur-Landau (eds.) *Nomads of the Mediterranean: Trade and Contact in the Bronze and Iron Ages. Studies in Honor of Michal Artzy*, 14–30. https://doi.org/10.1163/9789004430112_004.

Badreshany, Kamal, Graham Philip, and Melissa Kennedy. 2019. "The development of integrated regional economies in the Early Bronze Age Levant: new evidence from 'Combed Ware' jars." *Levant* 52: 160–190. https://doi.org/10.1080/00758914.2019.1641009.

Badreshany, Kamal, Karin Sowada, Mary Ownby, Mathilde Jean, Michel de Vreeze, Alice McClymont and Graham Philip. 2022. "The characterisation of ceramic production from the central Levant and Egyptian trade in the Pyramid Age." *Journal of Archaeological*

Science: Reports 41. https://doi.org/10.1016/j.jasrep.2021.103309.

Badreshany, Kamal., Michel de Vreeze, Melissa Kennedy, Stephanie Piper,, Hélène Sader, and Graham Philip. Forthcoming. "Report on Excavations at Tell Koubba, Northern Lebanon 2015–2017:" *BAAL: Bulletin d'archéologie et d'architecture libanaises.*

Ben-Tor, Amnon. 1975. *Two Burial Caves of the Proto-Urban Period at Azor, 1971*; Qedem 1, Jerusalem: Hebrew University of Jerusalem.

Bevan, Andrew. 2007. *Stone Vessels and Values in the Bronze Age Mediterranean.* Cambridge: Cambridge University Press.

———. 2010. "Making and marking relationships: Bronze Age brandings and Mediterranean commodities." In Andrew Bevan and David Wengrow (eds.), *Cultures of commodity branding*, 35–85. Walnut Creek: Left Coast Press.

Bietak, Manfred. 2019. "The Obelisk Temple in Byblos and its Predecessors. " In Agnieszka Pienkowska, Dariusz Szelag, and Iwona Zych (eds.), *Stories told around the fountain. Papers offered to Piotr Bieliński, on His 70th Bithday*, 165–186. Warsaw: Wydawnictwa Uniwersytetu Warszawskiego.

Biga, Maria Giovanna and Piotr Steinkeller. 2021. "In search of Dugurasu." *Journal of Cuneiform Studies* 73: 9–70.

Bikai, Patricia. M. 1978. *The Pottery of Tyre.* Warminster: Aris & Phillips.

D'Andrea, Marta. 2020. "The Religious Complexes of Megiddo and Khirbet ez-Zeraqon and the Early Bronze Age Interregional Connectivity." *Studia Eblaitica* 6: 1–39.

Chanteau, Julian. 2014. "L'Enceinte Sacrée et les origines de Byblos." *Syria* 91: 35–54.

Chesson, Meredith S. 2003. "Households, Houses, Neighborhoods and Corporate Villages: Modeling the Early Bronze Age as a House Society." *Journal of Mediterranean Archaeology* 16: 79–102.

Deckers, Katleen, Simone Riehl, Valentina Tumolo, Hermann Genz, and Dan Lawrence. 2021. "Intensive olive production at Levantine sites. New data from Fadous-Kfarabida and Khirbet-ez Zeraqon." *Journal of Archaeological Science: Reports* 36. https://doi.org/10.1016/j.jasrep.2021.102841.

Diego Espinel, Andres. 2002. "The Role of the Temple of Ba'alat Gebal as Intermediary between Egypt and Byblos during the Old Kingdom." *Studien zur Altägyptischen Kultur* 30: 103–119.

Dietrich, Oliver, Manfred Heun, Jens Notroff, Klaus Schmidt, and Martin Zarnkow,. 2012. "The role of cult and feasting in the emergence of Neolithic communities. New Evidence from Göbekli Tepe, Southeastern Turkey." *Antiquity* 86(333): 674–695. DOI: 10.1017/S0003598X00047840

Douglas, Khaled. 2011. "Beyond the City Walls: Life Activities outside the City Gates in the Early Bronze Age in Jordan: Evidence from Khirbet ez-Zeraqon." In Meredith. S. Chesson (ed.), *Daily Life, Materiality and Complexity in Early Urban Communities of the Southern Levant: Papers in Honor of Walter E. Rast and R. Thomas Schaub*, 3–22. Winona Lake: Eisenbrauns.

Doumet-Serhal, Claude. 2006, The Early Bronze in Sidon. "College Site" Excavations (1998–2000–2001). Amman–Beirut–Damascus: Institut Français du Proche-Orient.

———. 2013. *Sidon, 15 Years of Excavations: On the Occasion of the Exhibition Sidon "The best of 15 years" 3 September–3 November 2013, Sidon.* Beirut: The Lebanese British Friends of the National Museum.

Dunand, Maurice. 1938. *Fouilles de Byblos I.* Paris: Adrien Maisonneuve.

———. 1958. *Fouilles de Byblos II.* Paris: Adrien Maisonneuve.

Emberling, Geoff. 2015. "Structures of Authority: Feasting and Political Practice in the Earliest Mesopotamian States." In Geoff Emberling (ed.), *Social Theory in Archaeology and Ancient History: The Present and Future of Counternarratives*, 34–59. Cambridge: Cambridge University Press. DOI: 10.1017/CBO9781107282056.004.

Fargher, Lane F., Richard E. Blanton, and Ricardo R. Antorcha-Pedemonte. 2019. "The Archaeology of Intermediate-Scale Socio-Spatial Units in Urban Landscapes." In David Pacifico, and Lisa A. Truex (eds), *Excavating Neighborhoods: A Cross-Cultural Exploration*, 159–179; Archaeological Papers of the American Anthropological Association 30. Arlington, Virginia: American Anthropological Association.

Finkelstein, Israel 1995. "Two Notes on Early Bronze Age Urbanization and Urbanism." *Tel Aviv* 22: 47–69.

Francis-Allouche, Martine and Nicolas Grimal. 2016. "The Maritime Approaches to Ancient Byblos

(Lebanon)." *Journal of Eastern Mediterranean Archaeology and Heritage Studies* 4 (2–3): 242–277.

Friedman, Renée. *Nekhen News. Published for the Friends of Nekhen* 26: 1–36.

Frost, Honoré. 1998–1999. "Marine Prospection at Byblos." *BAAL: Bulletin d'archéologie et d'architecture libanaises* 3: 245–59.

Genz, Hermann. 2002. *Die frühbronzezeitliche Keramik von Hirbet ez-Zeraqon, Nordjordanien. Mit Studien zur Chronologie und funktionalen Deutung frühbronzezeitlicher Keramik der südlichen Levante (Deutsch-jordanische Ausgrabungen in Hirbet ez-Zeraqon 1984–1994. Endberichte Band V;* Abhandlungen des Deutschen Palästina-Vereins 27(2). Wiesbaden: Harrassowitz.

———. 2010. "Thoughts on the Function of 'Public Buildings' in the Early Bronze Age Southern Levant." In Diane Bolger, and Louise C. Maguire (ed), *The Development of Pre-State Communities in the Ancient Near East. Studies in Honour of Edgar Peltenburg*, 46–52: London: Oxbow Books.

———. 2011. "Restoring the balance: An Early Bronze Age scale beam from Tell Fadous-Kfarabida, Lebanon." *Antiquity* 85: 839–850.

———. 2014. "The northern Levant (Lebanon) during the Early Bronze Age." In Margreet L. Steiner and Anne E. Killebrew (eds.), *The Oxford Handbook of the Archaeology of the Levant. c. 8000–332 BCE*, 292–306. Oxford: Oxford University Press.

Genz, Hermann and Alexander Ahrens. 2021. "Recent Early Bronze Age Glyptic Finds from Lebanon: The Evidence from Tell Fadous Kfarabida" *BASOR* 386: 47–76. https://doi.org/10.1086/716612.

Genz, Hermann, Simone Riehl, Canan Çakırlar, Francesca Slim, and Alison Damick. 2016. "Economic and Political Organization of Early Bronze Age Coastal Communities: Tell Fadous-Kfarabida as a Case Study." *Berytus* 55: 79–119.

Greenberg, Raphael, 2020. *The Archaeology of the Bronze Age Levant: From Urban Origins to the Demise of City-States, 3700–1000 BCE*. Cambridge: Cambridge University Press.

Greenberg, Raphael and Hai Ashkenazi. 2019. "On the Collective Ethos of Fortification in the Levantine Bronze Age" In Hansen, Svend and Rüdiger Krause (eds.), *Bronze Age Fortresses in Europe. Proceedings of the Second International LOEWE Conference, 9-13 October 2017 in Albia Julia*, 17–28. Bonn: Verlag Dr. Rudolf Habelt.

Greenberg, Raphael and Mark Iserlis. 2014. "The Early Bronze Age Pottery Industries." In Raphael Greenberg (ed.), *Bet Yeraḥ—The Early Bronze Age Mound, Vol. II: Urban Structure and Material Culture, 1933–1986 Excavations*, 53–149; IAA Reports 54. Jerusalem: Israel Antiquities Authority.

Iserlis, Mark, Daniel Steiniger, and Raphael Greenberg. 2019. "Contact Between First Dynasty Egypt and Specific Sites in the Levant: New Evidence from Ceramic Analysis." *Journal of Archaeological Science: Reports* 24: 1023–1040.

Kempinski, Aharon 1978. *The Rise of an Urban Culture: the Urbanization of Palestine in the Early Bronze Age, 3000–2150 BC*. Jerusalem: Israel Ethnographic Society.

Kilani, Marwan. 2019. *Byblos in the Late Bronze Age. Interactions between the Levantine and Egyptian Worlds*. Leiden: Brill.

Klasens, Adolf. 1958. *The Excavations of the Leiden Museum of Antiquities at Abu-Roash. Report of the First Season: 1957, Part II*. Leiden: Rijksmuseum van Oudheden.

Kobusiewicz, Michal. 2015. *The Production, Use and Importance of Flint Tools in the Archaic Period and the Old Kingdom of Egypt*. Oxford: Archaeopress.

Lajs, Katarzyna. 2009. "Evolution of Ancient Egyptian Bifacial Flint Knives: A view from the Settlement in Tell el-Murra." *Studies in Ancient Art and Civilization*, 23: 7–27. https://doi.org/10.12797/SAAC.23.2019.23.01.

Lauffray, Jean. 1995. "La méthode de fouille de Maurice Dunand à Byblos. II. Introduction à la méthode M. Dunand." *Topoi Orient Occident* 15 (2): 453–468.

———. 2008. *Fouilles de Byblos, vol. VI: L'urbanisme et l'architecture de l'époque proto-urbaine à l'occupation amorite (de l'Énéolitique à l'âge du Bronze II*. Beirut: Institut Français du Proche-Orient.

Lehner, Mark. 2019. "Neighborhoods to National Network: Pyramid Settlement of Giza." In David Pacifico and Lisa A. Truex (eds), *Excavating Neighborhoods: A Cross-Cultural Exploration*, Archaeological Papers of the American Anthropological Association 30, 20-38.

Leriche, Pierre. 1995. "La méthode de fouille de Maurice Dunand à Byblos. I.M. Dunand et l'archéologie au Proche-Orient au début du XXe siècle." *Topoi Orient Occident* 5 (2): 439–452.

Liverani, Mario. 2006. *Uruk. The First city*. London: Equinox.

Lundt, Marquardt. 2015. "Egyptian depictions of flintknapping from the Old and Middle Kingdom, in the light of experiments and experience." In Carolyn Graves-Brown (ed.), *Egyptology in the Presence. Experiential and Experimental Methods in Archaeology*, 113–137. Swansea: Classical Press of Wales.

Marfoe, Leon. 1998. *Kamid El-Loz 14 Settlement History of the Biqa up to the Iron Age*. Bonn: Dr. Rudolf Habelt.

———. 1987. "Cedar Forest to Silver Mountain: Social Change and the Development of Long-Distance Trade in Early Near Eastern Societies." In Mogens Trolle Larsen, Michael J. Rowlands, and Kristian Kristiansen. *Centre and Periphery in the Ancient World*, 25–35. Cambridge: Cambridge University Press.

Margueron, Jean-Claude. 1994. "L'urbanisme de Byblos: certitudes et problems." In Enrico Acquero (ed.), *Biblo: una città e la sua cultura*, 13–35. Rome: Consiglio Nazionale delle Ricerche.

Mauss, Marcel. 2016 [1925]. *The Gift: Expanded Edition*. London: HAU.

Mazar, Amihay. 1990. *Archaeology of the Land of the Bible, 10,000–586 BCE*. New York: Doubleday.

Miroschedji, Pierre de. 2018. "The Urbanization of the Southern Levant in its Near Eastern Setting." *Origini: Prehistory and Protohistory of Ancient Civilizations* 2018 (2): 109–148.

———. 2019. "Early Bronze Age Palaces in the Southern Levant." In Manfred Bietak, Paolo Matthiae and Silvia Prell (eds.), *Ancient Egyptian and Ancient Near Eastern Palaces Volume II*, 159–179. Wiesbaden: Harrassowitz.

Miller, G. Logan. 2021. "Ritual, Labor Mobilization, and Monumental Construction in Small-Scale Societies. The Case of Adena and Hopewell in the Middle Ohio River Valley." *Current Anthropology* 62 (2): 164–197. 0011-3204/2021/6202-0005$10.00. DOI: 10.1086/713764.

Montet, Pierre. 1928–1929. *Byblos et L'Égypte: quatre campagnes de fouilles à Gebeil, 1921–1922–1923–1924*. Paris: P. Geuthner.

Müller, Miriam. (ed.) 2015. *Household Studies in Complex Societies: (Micro) Archaeological and Textual Approaches*; Oriental Institute Seminars 10. Chicago: The Oriental Institute.

Pacifico, David and Lisa A. Truex. 2019. "Chapter 1. Why Neighbourhoods? The Neighbourhood in Archaeological Theory and Practice." In David Pacifico and Lisa A. Truex (eds), *Excavating Neighbourhoods: A Cross-Cultural Exploration*, 5–19; Archaeological Papers of the American Anthropological Association 30. Arlington, Virginia: American Anthropological Association.

Padgett, John F. and Cristopher K. Ansell. 1993. "Robust Action and the Rise of the Medici, 1400-1434." *American Journal of Sociology* 98 (6): 1259–1319.

Paz, Sarit. 2012. "Changing Households at the Rise of Urbanism: The EB I–II transition at Tel Bet Yerah." In Bradley J. Parker and Catherine P. Foster (eds.), *New Perspectives on Household Archaeology*, 407–436. Eisenbrauns: Winona Lake.

Petrie, William Matthew Flinders. 1902. *Abydos. Part I*. London: The Egypt Exploration Fund.

Pongratz-Leisten, Beate. 2021. The Animated Temple and its Agency in the Urban Life of the City in Ancient Mesopotamia. *Religions* 12 (638). https://doi.org/10.3390/rel12080638.

Porter, Anne. 2012. *Mobile Pastoralism and the Formation of Near Eastern Civilizations: Weaving Together Society*. Cambridge: Cambridge University Press.

Prag, Kay. 1986. "Byblos and Egypt in the Fourth Millennium BC." *Levant* 18: 59–74.

Philip, Graham. 1988. "Hoards of the Early and Middle Bronze Ages in the Levant." *World Archaeology* 20 (2): 190–208.

———. 2002. "Contacts Between the 'Uruk' World and the Levant During the Fourth Millennium BC: Evidence and Interpretation." In J. Nicholas Postgate (ed.), *Artefacts of Complexity: Tracking the Uruk in the Near East*, 207–235; Archaeological Reports Volume 5. London: British School of Archaeology in Iraq.

———. 2008. "The Early Bronze Age I–III." In Russell B. Adams (ed.), *Jordan: An Archaeological Reader* 161–226. London: Equinox.

Phillip, Graham, and Meredith Chesson. 2003. "Tales of the City? 'Urbanism' in the Early Bronze Age Levant from Mediterranean and Levantine perspectives." *Journal of Mediterranean Archaeology* 16: 3–16.

Quibell, James Edward. 1900. *Hierakonpolis, Part* I. London: Bernard Quaritch.

Rainey, Anson Frank. 2015. *The El-Amarna Correspondence (2 vol. set). A New Edition of the*

Cuneiform Letters from the Site of El-Amarna Based on Collations of all Extant Tablets. Leiden: Brill.

Roaf, Michael. 1995. "Palaces and Temples in Ancient Mesopotamia." In Jack M. Sasson (ed.), *Civilizations of the Ancient Near East*, 423–441. New York: Scribner's.

Rotem, Yael, Mark Iserlis, F. Höflmayer, and Yorke M. Rowan. 2019. "Tel Yaqush—An Early Bronze Age Village in the Central Jordan Valley, Israel." *Bulletin of the American Schools of Oriental Research* 381.144–107-. DOI: 10.1086/703077.

Saïdah, Roger. 1979. "Fouilles de Sidon-Dakerman, L'agglomération Chalcolithique." *Berytus* 27: 29–56.

Saghieh, Muntaha 1983. *Byblos in the Third Millennium BC: A Reconstruction of the Stratigraphy and a Study of the Cultural Connections*. London: Warminster: Aris and Phillips.

Sala, Maura. 2007. "Early shrines at Byblos and Tell es-Sultan/ancient Jericho in the Early Bronze I (3300–3000 BC)." In Lorenzo Nigro (ed.), *Byblos and Jericho in the Early Bronze I. Social Dynamics and Cultural Interactions*, 47–68. Rome: La Sapienza Expedition to Palestine and Jordan.

———. 2008a. *L'architettura sacra della Palestina nell Eta del Bronzo Antico I–III. Contributi e Materiali di Archaeologica Orientale Rome*. Rome: University di Roma "La Sapienza."

———. 2008b. "Il Temple en L a Biblo." *Vicino & Medio Oriente* 14: 59–84.

———. 2015. "Early and Middle Bronze Age Temples at Byblos: Specifity and Levantine Interconnections." *BAAL: Bulletin d'archéologie et d'architecture libanaises* Hors Séries X: 31–58.

Seeden, Helga. 1980. *The Standing Armed Figurines in the Levant*; Prähistorische Bronzefunde, Abteilung I, Band I. Munich: C.H. Beck.

Sherratt, Andrew and Susan Sherratt 1991. "From luxuries to commodities: the nature of Mediterranean Bronze Age trading systems." In Noel H. Gale (ed.), *Bronze Age trade in the Mediterranean*, 351–386. Jonsered: Paul Åström Förlag.

Shimelmitz, Ron and Matthew J. Adams. 2014. "Flint Knapping and the Early Bronze Age I Temple of Megiddo, Israel: Some Aspects of the Organization of Late Prehistoric Cult." *Journal of Mediterranean Archaeology* 27(1): 51–78. https://doi.org/10.1558/jmea.v27i1.51.

Silver, Morris 1985. *Economic structures of the ancient Near East*. London: Croom Helm.

Sowada, Karin 2009. *Egypt in the Eastern Mediterranean during the Old Kingdom: An archaeological perspective, with a contribution by P. Grave*; Orbis Biblicus et Orientalis 237. Freiburg: Fribourg and Göttingen.

———. 2018. "Hidden exports: a likely Early Bronze Age exchange in Egyptian cattle to the Levant." *Bulletin of the Australian Centre for Egyptology* 26: 71–78.

Sowada, Karin, Mary Ownby, and Miroslav Bárta. 2021. "The Origin of Imported Jars from 6th Dynasty Abusir: New Light on Early Bronze Age Egyptian-Levantine Relations." *Bulletin of the American Schools of Oriental Research*: 221–236.

Sowada, Karin, Mary Ownby, and Anna Wodzińska 2020. "The petrography of imported Levantine Combed vessels from early Old Kingdom Giza." *Levant* 52 (1–2): 197–214.

Stein, Gill. J. 2001. "Indigenous Social Complexity at Hacınebi (Turkey) and the Organization of Uruk Colonial Contact." In Mitchell S. Rothman (ed.), *Uruk Mesopotamia & Its Neighbors. Cross-Cultural Interactions in the Era of State Formation*, 265–305. Santa Fe: School of American Research Press.

Susnow, Matthew. 2021. *The Practice of Canaanite Cult. The Middle and Late Bronze Ages*; Ägypten un Altes Testament, Band 106, Münster: Zaphon.

Thalmann, Jean-Paul. 2006a. *Tell Araq - I. Les niveaux de l'âge du Bronze. Volume I : Texte*. Beirut: Institut Français du Proche-Orient.

———. 2006b. "Nouvelles données sur l'architecture domestique du bronze ancien IV à Tell Arqa (Liban)." *Comptes rendus des séances de l'Académie des Inscriptions et Belles-Lettres* 150 (2): 841–73.

———. 2013. "Le lion, la chèvre et le poisson. À propos d'une jarre à empreintes de sceaux-cylindres de Tell Arqa (liban)." *Syria* 90: 255–312.

———. 2016. "Rapport préliminaire sur les campagnes de 2008 à 2012 à Tell Arqa." *BAAL: Bulletin d'archéologie et d'architecture libanaises* 16: 15–78.

———. 2019. "Un groupe de vases du Bronze Ancien au Musée de l'AUB." In Françoise Briquel Chatonnet, Emanuelle Capet, Eric Gubel and Carole Roche-Hawley (eds.), *Nuit de pleine lune sur Amurru. Mélanges offerts à Leila Badre*, 131–142. Paris: Geuthner.

Tristant, Yann. 2008. "Deux grands tombeaux du cimetière M d'Abou Rawach (Ire dynastie)." *Archéo-Nil* 18: 130–147.

Truex, Lisa. A. 2019. "Households and Institutions: A late 3rd Millennium BCE Neighbourhood at Tell Asma, Iraq (Ancient Eshnunna)." In David Pacifico and Lisa A. Truex (eds), *Excavating Neighbourhoods: A Cross-Cultural Exploration*, 39–61; Archaeological Papers of the American Anthropological Association 30. Arlington, Virginia: American Anthropological Association.

Tufnell, Olga and William Ayres Ward. 1966. "Relations Between Byblos, Egypt and Mesopotamia at the End of the Third Millenium BC. A Study of a Montet Jar." *Syria* 43 (3–4): 165–241.

Ussishkin, David. 2015. "The Sacred Area of Early Bronze Megiddo: History and Interpretation." *Bulletin of the American Schools of Oriental Research* 373: 69–104.

Wengrow, David. 2013. "Fleshpots of Egypt: rethinking temple economy in the ancient Near East." In Elizabeth Frood and Angela McDonald (eds.), *Decorum and experience: essays in ancient culture for John Baines*, 291–298. Oxford: University of Oxford.

Wilkinson, Toby A.H. 2002. "Uruk into Egypt: imports and imitations." In J. Nicholas Postgate (ed.), *Artefacts of Complexity: Tracking the Uruk in the Near East*, 237–248; Archaeological Reports Volume 5. London: British School of Archaeology in Iraq.

Notes

1 Genz 2016; Mazar 1990; Badreshany, Philip and Kennedy 2019; de Miroschedji 2018; Greenberg 2020; Marfoe 1998.

2 Mazar 1990; Marfoe 1998.

3 Finkelstein 1995; Kempinski 1987; Mazar 1990; Marfoe 1998.

4 Chesson 2003; Philip 2001; 2008; Paz 2012.

5 Greenberg 2019.

6 Miller 2021; Dietrich et al. 2012.

7 Miller 2021: 164.

8 Greenberg and Ashkenazi 2019; Ashkenazi 2020.

9 Greenberg and Askhenazi 2019.

10 Greenberg and Askhenazi 2019: 26.

11 Genz 2002; Douglas 2011; Adams, Finkelstein and Ussishkin 2015; Greenberg and Askhenazi 2019, 19.

12 Genz 2016; Badreshany forthcoming; Badreshany, Philip and Kennedy 2019; Deckers et al. 2021.

13 Genz 2014, 10; Kilani 2019; Lauffray 1995; 2008; Leriche 1995; Marqueron 1994.

14 Saghieh 1983.

15 Lauffray 2008. See also Margueron's 1994 observations on understanding 'urban' Byblos.

16 Bevan 2007, 77: Fig. 5.6. Kilani 2019; Dunand 1938; 1958.

17 Dunand 1958.

18 Sowada 2009; Bevan 2007. The same phenomenon can be argued for with chronologically earlier objects collected in the numerous EB IV–MB 'foundation' depots at Byblos. See also note 63 below.

19 Pacifico and Truex 2019; Stone 1987. See Lehner 2019 for an application of the neighborhood approach to the settlement at Giza.

20 Artin 2010. Overseas contacts, including but not solely with Egypt, are sporadically but well attested from these graves, including ivory or bone human figures well known from contemporary Hierakonpolis (Prag 1986; Quibell 1900).

21 Lauffray 2008, 22, Fig. 5 shows the same plan as the original by Saïdah 1972.

22 Lauffray 2008, 38: Fig. 11; Dunand 1973, fig. 143, 236-237: Fig. 143. See Chanteau 2014 on the debated chronology of this internally buttressed wall. A very similar internally buttressed monumental wall is associated with Hacinebi in Turkey, dating from the late Chalcolithic-EB I (Stein 2001), suggesting that Uruk-inspired monumental architecture, including internal buttresses (Roaf 1995), might have eventually influenced some of these local developments, as known from contemporary Egypt (Wilkinson 2002). The role of Uruk in Levantine developments remains a relevant theme (Philip 2002) that deserves more detailed consideration based on more recent archaeological developments.

23 Lauffray 2008, 30: Fig 1. The vessels show a clear resemblance to SLMW vessels associated with the (early) EB II but actually appear as early as the EB Ib-EB II transition at sites like Beth Yerah and Tel Yaqush (Greenberg and Iserlis 2014, 59; Regev, Paz, Greenberg and Boaretto 2020, 12; Rotem, Iserlis, Höflmayer, and Rowan 2019, 115).

24 Greenberg 2019.

25 Lauffray 2008. Interestingly, a shift away from burials as communal investment and ritual

display (during the Chalcolithic–EB I) might be noticed, where the onset of the EB II–III only attests to a single extra-mural burial so far with locally produced vessels as part of the funerary assemblage, currently on display at the AUB museum (Thalmann 2019).

26 Dunand 1938, 368–371, 369, fig. 288; Pl. CCVI: vessels 5390–5416.

27 For Arqa, see Thalmann 2016, Levels 18E-A; phase S3-2; phase S1. For Fadous-kfarabida (phase III) see Genz 2014, Table 21.2.

28 Lauffray 2008.

29 Genz 2016, 81; for the absolute dates associated with this phase at Fadous-Kfarabida, see Höflmayer et al. 2014.

30 Lauffray 2008, Planche III.

31 Badreshany et al. forthcoming.

32 Greenberg and Ashkenazi 2019; Ashkenazi 2020.

33 Miroschedji 2019, 168: Fig. 10.

34 Lauffray 2008, 70. Thalmann 2006b; 2016.

35 Thalmann 2006b, 2016, 74. For Tyre, see Aubet 2020. Future excavations may find this architectural style at EB sites in the interior (mountains) and Biq'a valley as well. It is attested at an MB site in the Biq'a (Hanan Charaf, personal communication).

36 Lauffray 2008, 279–446; Plan IV combines all of Lauffray's Piquete phases into a single plan. Lauffray calls the Piqueté phases the 'floruit' of urban life at Byblos (épanouissement de la vie urbaine).

37 On the so-called Tower temple and its location and possible function, see Frost 1998–1999, 255; Lauffray 2008, 391–395; Kilani 2019, 49

38 Lauffray 2008, 375–376.

39 Genz and Ahrens 2021, 50.

40 Genz et al. 2016.

41 Lauffray 2008.

42 Genz 2011; Genz et al. 2016; Genz and Ahrens 2021.

43 Pacifico and Truex 2019, 5; Fargher et al 2019; Truex 2019. This approach integrates the concept of neighborhoods with those of household archaeology to better understand settlement developments in the region, including Egypt: Müller 2015.

44 Biga and Steinkeller 2021; Greenberg 2020: 91; Marfoe 1987; Sowada 2009.

45 Lauffray 2008; Bevan 2007.

46 Ashkenazi 2020.

47 Lauffray 2008.

48 Genz 2002; Ussishkin 2015; D'Andrea 2020.

49 D'Andrea 2020; Genz 2002, 94–96; Genz 2010, 48: Fig. 6.2.

50 Lauffray 2008, 403–404.

51 Lauffray 2008, 132–133 Fig. 68; 243–244; Fig. 132.

52 See Francis-Allouche and Grimal 2016.

53 Lauffray 2008: 181.

54 Lauffray 2008, 391-395.

55 Pongratz-Leisten 2021, 1.

56 Miroschedji 2019 also argues for the development of competitive lineages with dominant lineages eventually reflected in more central public buildings (so-called 'palaces'), for instance, at Tell Yarmouth. Similarly, Greenberg (2019: 325) discusses this principle, referring to "tell factions" competing during the Late Bronze Age, for instance, at Lachish. Central to our argument at Byblos is that these processes started in a heterarchical way and predominantly reflected in monumental (temple) architecture but had the potential to spearhead one neighborhood faction or lineage group having foremost relevant external exchange contacts. The role of 'networking' in advancing one's social position has been argued convincingly for the Medici (Padgett and Ansell 1993). The roots of these social developments focused on temples can be traced at least to the Early Bronze Age in the Levant.

57 Wengrow 2013: 291; following Silver 1985; Sherratt and Sherratt 1991; Bevan 2010.

58 Greenberg and Askhenazi 2019.

59 Greenberg and Askhenazi 2019, 26.

60 Badreshany, Philip and Kennedy 2019; Deckers et al. 2021, see also Badreshany et al. 2022.

61 Diego Espinel 2002; see Rainey 2015 for the central role of the Ba'alat Gebal temple in the Amarna correspondence related to Byblos. The central role of the Ba'alat Gebal temple in interregional affairs, as we currently understand, is a particular textual artifact supported by material cultural finds. Most stressed in these texts is the strong link that the Ba'alat Gebal temple, and, as we suggest, its neighborhood, had primarily with Egypt. Ongoing research on the Ebla texts, where Byblos is now most certainly identified as DU/GUBlu (Biga and Steinkeller 2021), might give further evidence of particularly strong links

with certain other temples in Byblos, perhaps foremost with the L-shaped later temple of the Obelisks, sometimes identified with Reshef but awaiting further confirmation.

62 Emberling 2015 describes a similar scenario for the role of feasting and forms of social authority in Mesopotamia.

63 Badreshany et al. 2022; Sowada et al. 2020; Sowada et al. 2021; Sowada Ownby and Wodzińska 2020; Sowada Ownby Bárta 2021; Iserlis Steiniger and Greenberg 2019. Significantly, not only combed jar jars for transport seem to have been exported to Egypt. A rim sherd of a combed vat, of Lebanese origin, was found at Heit el-Ghurab (Giza): Sowada Ownby and Wodzińska 2020, Fig. 4a. These have exact parallels at sites such as Fadous and Koubba and suggest that beyond transport, combed ware vessels and their associated economic activity found a place in Old Kingdom Egypt.

64 Sowada 2009.

65 For the presence and social role of Egyptian stone vessels at Byblos, see Bevan 2007: 63–75. Some of these Early Bronze II–III objects found their eventual way into later EB IV–MB depots at Byblos (Tufnell and Ward 1960; Philip 1988; Seeden 1980). The foundation depots might be seen as final attestations of these ritually exchanged goods deposited within respective temples at Byblos.

66 Sowada 2009, Bevan 2007; Montet 1928–1929; Dunand 1938 and 1958

67 Dunand 1938; 1958.

68 The Egyptian knife was found in the earliest phase, dated to the EB I (Doumet-Serhal 2006, 293; Fig 2.d; phase I).

69 Kobusiewicz 2015, 64–65. Angevin 2016. Most of these knives seem Early Dynastic in date. As judged by published drawings and photographs, all the knives seem cruder, in execution, than the finer ripple-flaked Naqada II–III examples. So far, the only example of this earlier ripple-flaked knife type found outside of Egypt originates from the EB Ib tombs of Azor, possibly intentionally fragmented (broken in half) and associated with other Egyptian objects (Ben-Tor 1975, 24: plate 21).

70 Angevin 2015: detailed analysis of flint working associated with Khasekhemwy's tomb suggests bifacial knives were part of elite-controlled prestige goods. Perhaps not coincidentally, two of the flint knives ((#6066; 10420) from Byblos (although from a surface context) show particularly good comparison with those from Khasekhemwy's tomb (Petrie 1902, 8, Pl. XV, group marked V. EA 68775; Angevin 2015: 823: Fig. 5, see Figure 3 this article). Khasekhemwy's inscription on a stone vessel (again from a surface context: Montet 1928–1929, Diego Espinel 2002 105; Sowada 2009: 10) suggests that these flint knives could have been part of the exchange with Byblos from at least his reign onwards. Considering the prolonged use of Egyptian objects at Byblos as heirlooms, it strongly suggests that these types of knives and associated practices started arriving as early as the stone vessels, brought as gifts in exchange with Early Dynastic Egypt, in any case, as early as the Early Bronze III period (ECL 3; late Dynasty II), c. 2700 BCE, if not earlier.

71 Lajs 2019; Lund 2015; contribution this volume

72 Arnold et al. 2016; Sowada 2018.

73 It would be useful to conduct isotopic studies on the preserved faunal remains from the Dunand excavations in reliable contexts at Byblos to find direct evidence of (imported) cattle from Egypt. Similar studies are planned for the assemblages from Fadous-Kfarabida (Hermann Genz and Canan Cakirlar, personal communication) and Koubba.

74 Bevan 2007.

75 Foundation depots must most likely be seen as part of these redepositing events in association with the respective temples. Although most offering depots date to the EB IV and MB I, Lauffray (2008: 182–184) makes significant note of two slightly earlier (EB III-early EB IV) offering depots associated with the Southwest Temple, placed under an altar and in a small room. Unfortunately, the finds associated with these depots are neither further mentioned nor illustrated, but these two depots do show that the principle of burying valuable commodities obtained through exchange and collected at the temples took place from the EBA onward. Thus, the well-known EB IV–MB I depots, which indeed include some earlier EBA objects, must be seen as the culmination of these practices (see note 64).

76 Dunand 1938, 355–356: find numbers 5266; 6267.

77 For a review of the stratigraphy, see Lauffray 2008, 228, room 24-96; 'Grosses Fondations' phase.

78 Sowada 2009, Fig. 30; Dunand 1938, 356; 5269; Pl. CXLVI; contemporary ivory hoofs are known from 2nd Dynasty Abu Rawash: Klasens 1959, Pl. 59 C1, fig. 10.1–2; Pl. XXVII. See also Tristant (2008) for more recent results from Abu Rawash, including further evidence of boat burials that might reflect elite concerns with overseas trade.

79 Lauffray 2008: 203

80 Dunand 1958, 981, fig. 1096: 18278: EB III–IV; post EB IV: Dunand 1958, 574, 566, fig. 639: 13093; Dunand 1958, 672, fig. 799: 14197.

81 Dunand 1958, 555, 556, fig. 639: 12855.

82 The association of lithics with temple precincts is also noted for late EB I Megiddo: Shimelmitz Adams 2014. Both lithic manufacture and use are strongly associated with sacrificial animal remains and suggest the strong association of temples with communal processes of food preparation and consumption. At Megiddo, the lithic traditions are of a distinctly local Levantine nature.

83 2021: 266, Table I.

84 Susnow 2021, 222.

85 Diego Espinel 2002.

86 Miller 2021, 167.

87 'Piqueté' III phase: Lauffray 2008, 286, plan IV.

88 Lauffray 2008, 445–446.

89 Greenberg 2019 and Greenberg and Ashkenazi 2019.

90 Thalmann 2006a, 2016.

91 Thalmann 2016, 27. Thalmann 2013, 259: here, Thalmann argues for a domestic context.

92 Thalmann 2016, 27.

93 Doument-Serhal 2006. The multi-room building is described in more detail in Doumet Serhal 2013 (no page numbers).

94 Aubet 2020. Bikai 1978.

95 See Rappaport 1971 for the role of ritual in small-scale societies.

96 See Genz and Ahrens 2021, 65–66 for the general absence of Egyptian objects outside of Byblos. See Badreshany et al. 2022 for evidence suggesting that interregional contact, as evidenced by combed ware exported to Egypt, took place mainly at Byblos (Badreshany et al. 2022). For the Ba'alat Gebal temple as a particular focus point, see Diego Espinel 2002.

97 Diego Espinel 2002. Mauss 2016 [1925].

98 See D'Andrea 2020; Genz 2002 and 2010 for Khirbet ez-Zeraqon; Usshishkin 2015, 94: Fig. 27 for the Megiddo temple.

99 Biga and Steinkeller 2021; Greenberg 2020: 91; Marfoe 1987; Sowada 2009. Beyond maritime contact, overland routes and the role of non-sedentary (pastoral) segments of society in these exchange networks, particularly with Syria (for instance, Ebla) and the inland southern Levant should not be neglected, see also Porter 2012 on their significance.

100 See also Miroschedji 2019 for a similar argument relating to the southern Levant. See also note 54.

101 Badreshany, Philip and Kennedy 2019, Badreshany et al. 2022.

102 Greenberg (2019, 272) describes a similar situation for the Late Bronze Age in the southern Levant, indicating that these patterns may be cyclical.

Journal of Ancient Egyptian Interconnections

In the Shadow of Byblos: The Early Bronze Age Aegyptiaca from Tell Fadous-Kfarabida

Hermann Genz
American University of Beirut

Alexander Ahrens
German Archaeological Institute

Abstract
During the Old Kingdom, Byblos emerged as one of the main ports of trade between Egypt and the Levant. This is not only suggested by Egyptian textual references but also by a surprisingly large number of Egyptian objects dating to the Old Kingdom from Byblos. However, various chronological and contextual problems hugely diminish the value of the Aegyptiaca from Byblos for the reconstruction of the relations between Egypt and the Levantine coast. Excavations at Tell Fadous-Kfarabida undertaken between 2004 and 2016 helped establish a more secure chronology for the Early Bronze Age in Byblos. As the site is only 12 km north of Byblos, it certainly must have been in the economic and political orbit of Byblos. This paper presents the few Aegyptiaca from Tell Fadous-Kfarabida and discusses Tell Fadous-Kfarabida's relationship to Byblos. As Fadous-Kfarabida lacks a good natural harbor, it is very likely that the Aegyptiaca retrieved reached the site via Byblos.

Keywords
Central Levant; Byblos; Tell Fadous-Kfarabida; Old Kingdom; Early Bronze Age

Introduction

Connections between Egypt and the Levant during the 4th and 3rd millennia BCE have frequently been discussed. It is generally believed that contacts between Egypt and Byblos intensified with the beginning of the Old Kingdom in Egypt (Helck 1971, 21–28; Saghieh 1983, 104–106; Wright 1988, 146–152; de Miroschedji 2002, 45–46; Sowada 2009, 7–10; Genz 2014a, 303–304). The notion that Byblos already played a crucial role for trade with Egypt during the 4th millennium (Prag 1986) is based on stylistic comparisons rather than the identification of actual imports (Genz 2014a, 296–297); however, there is growing evidence for contacts between Egypt and the coast of Northern Lebanon already during the 1st and 2nd Dynasties (Köhler and Ownby 2011; Köhler and Thalmann 2014; Hartung et al. 2015; Iserlis et al. 2019; Sowada et al. 2021).

Egypt was primarily interested in obtaining high-quality timber, notably cedar and other coniferous wood, from Mount Lebanon (Gale et al. 2000, 348–352; Sowada 2009, 194–196), but other tree products such as various resins and oils were of interest as well (Sowada 2009, 198–200). The latter products were transported to Egypt in the so-called combed-ware jars, which are reported in growing frequency from many Old Kingdom sites (Helck 1971, 30–35; Mazzoni 1985; Forstner-Müller and Raue 2008;

Sowada 2009, 155–158; Knoblauch 2010; Forstner-Müller and Raue 2014; Thalmann and Sowada 2014; Sowada et al. 2019).

Egypt, on the other hand, seems to have largely exported luxury objects like stone vessels, a large number of which were found in Byblos (Saghieh 1983, 104–106; Wright 1988, 146–152; Sowada 2009, 130–137). Other objects of Egyptian origin are attested at the site, such as copper axes (Gernez 2011, 239 and Fig. 2) and flint tools (Montet 1928, Pl. LVII, 313; Sowada 2009, 138), which so far have rarely featured in the discussion of relations between Egypt and Byblos.

However, the incomplete publication and the stratigraphic problems associated with most of the Aegyptiaca from Byblos hugely diminish their value for reconstructing the relations between Egypt and the Levant (Saghieh 1983; Wright 1988; Sowada 2009, 139–141).

Another important issue is whether Byblos monopolized the contacts with Egypt during the Old Kingdom or whether other coastal sites in the Central and possibly even Northern Levant also participated in these interactions. Except for Byblos, Old Kingdom imports are rarely attested along the Lebanese coast. Tyre has produced an Egyptian cylinder seal (Ward 1978), and flint tools of Egyptian origin are attested from Sidon (Yazbeck 2006, 293 and Fig. 2d).

In this contribution, the Aegyptiaca from Tell Fadous-Kfarabida, located only 12 km north of Byblos on the Lebanese coast (Fig. 1), will be presented to investigate the extent of Egyptian influence at a site most likely belonging to the political and economic sphere of Byblos.

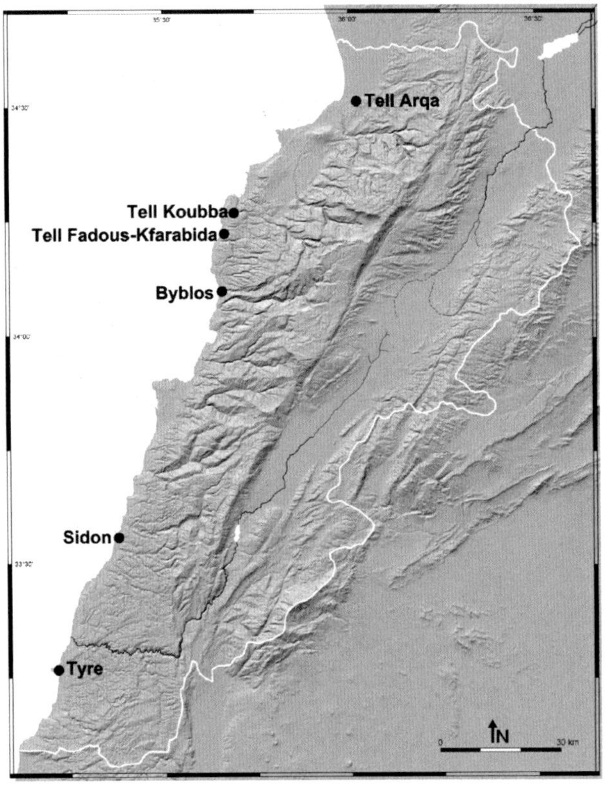

Figure 1: Map showing the location of Tell Fadous-Kfarabida and other Early Bronze Age III sites along the Lebanese coast (Tell Fadous-Kfarabida Project).

Tell Fadous-Kfarabida

Tell Fadous-Kfarabida is, for the time being, the most intensively excavated Early Bronze Age site in the vicinity of Byblos.

The site was investigated between 2004 and 2016 by a team from the Department of History and Archaeology at the American University of Beirut (Badreshany et al. 2005; Genz 2010; Genz 2014a; Genz and Sader 2007; Genz and Sader 2008; Genz et al. 2009; Genz et al. 2010; Genz et al. 2011; Genz et al. 2018; Genz et al., submitted).

It was settled from the Chalcolithic Period to the Middle Bronze Age, albeit with a few interruptions (Tab. 1). Since the Early Bronze Age III— our local phases III and IV—produced the most substantial remains, this contribution will focus on these phases.

With a size of only 1.5 hectares, the site at first was thought to represent a third-order settlement, that is, a village according to the criteria suggested by Marfoe for the Bekaa (Marfoe 1998) and Thalmann for the Akkar Plain (Thalmann 2007).

However, according to the results obtained from the five different areas opened in various parts of the hill, the site was densely built-up with multi-roomed houses separated by small streets (Fig. 2). Areas I and IV provided evidence for a massive fortification wall, which surrounded the site from at least Phase III onward and very likely continued in use during Phase IV.

Area II, located in the western central part of the mound, provided the most substantial results (Fig. 3). In Phase III (2800-2600 BCE), the area was dominated by an extremely large building (Building 4). Although large parts of it fell victim to bulldozing operations prior to the discovery of the site, its preserved north-south extension of at least 25 m makes it the largest building on the site. Large built-in bins in Rooms 4 and 5 suggest that these

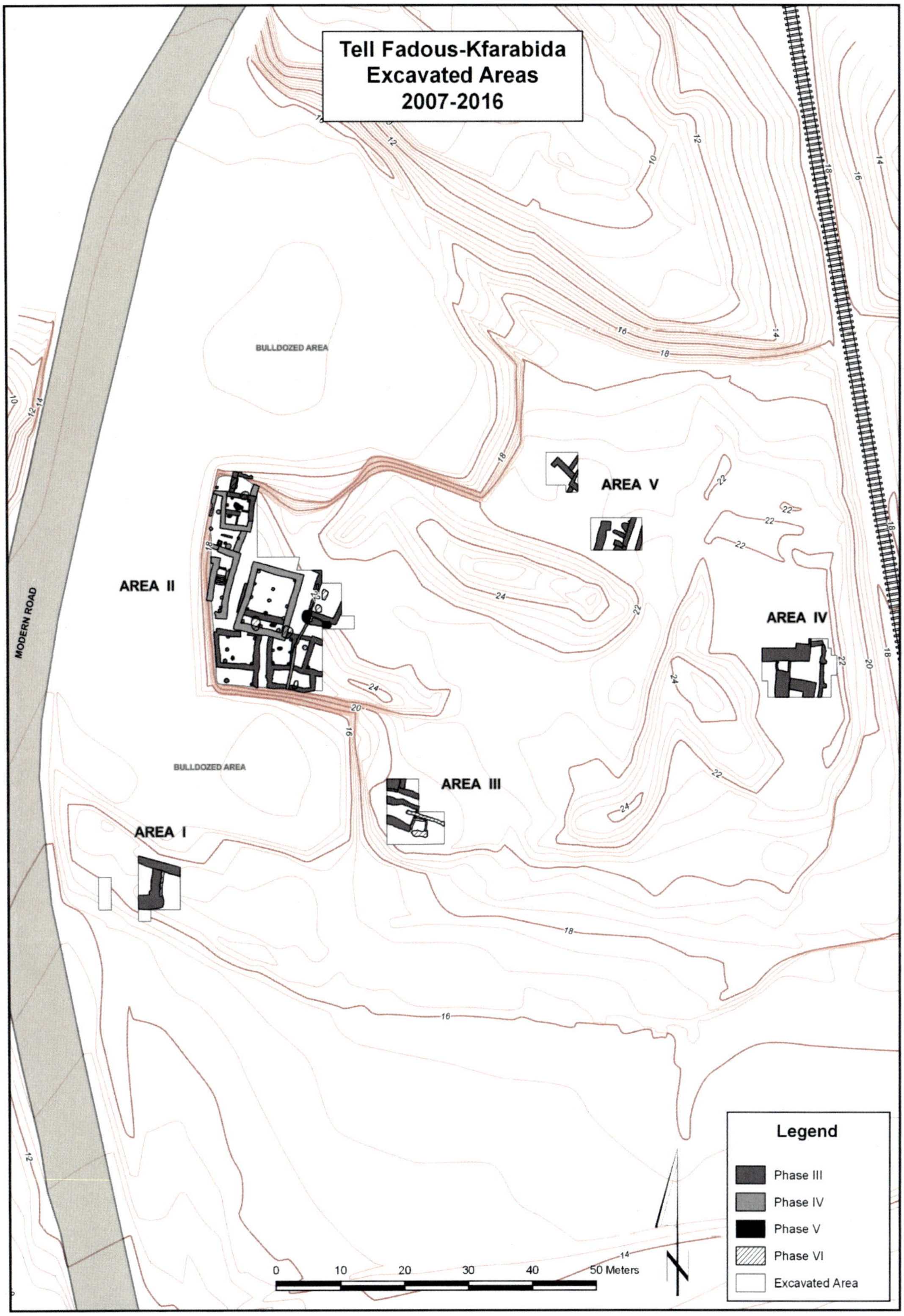

FIGURE 2: Plan of Tell Fadous-Kfarabida showing the location of the excavated areas (Tell Fadous-Kfarabida Project).

Table 1: Periods of occupation at Tell Fadous-Kfarabida.

Phase	Archaeological Period	ARCANE Periodization	Type of Occupation
Phase VI	Middle Bronze Age I/II	–	Pits, burials
Hiatus	Middle Bronze Age I	–	–
Phase V	Early Bronze Age IVB	ECL 6	Pits
Hiatus	Early Bronze Age IVA	ECL 5	–
Phase IV	Early Bronze Age III	ECL 4	Public buildings
Phase III	Early Bronze Age III	ECL 4	Domestic and public buildings, fortification
Phase II	Early Bronze Age II	ECL 3	Domestic buildings
Hiatus	Early Bronze Age I	ECL 1–2	–
Phase I	Chalcolithic	–	Child burials and stray finds

rooms were used for storing substantial amounts of presumably agricultural products. East and south of this building, some large domestic dwellings were partially excavated (Buildings 1, 2, and 5). Room 3 of Building 2 contained a small-scale beam made of bone, suggesting that complex exchange transactions may have been conducted there (Fig. 4) (Genz 2011).

In Phase IV (2600-2500 BCE), Building 4 continued to be used with a few minor modifications. The discovery of a stairwell in Room 2 clearly suggests that the Building had at least one upper story during this Phase (but possibly already earlier). East and south of Building 4, the earlier domestic structures 1, 2, and 5 were abandoned, and partly above them, the columned-hall Building 3 was erected, which only consists of one large rectangular room with inner dimensions of 6.4 x 8.3 m. Thirteen of its original 15 column bases were still found in situ, revealing a regular arrangement of three rows, each containing five column bases (Fig. 5). With a width of approximately 1 m, its walls are rather massive, and the corners are constructed of dressed ashlars. The layout of the building, as well as its impressive dimensions, and, above all, the lack of any indications of domestic activities, suggest that it served administrative or representational purposes.

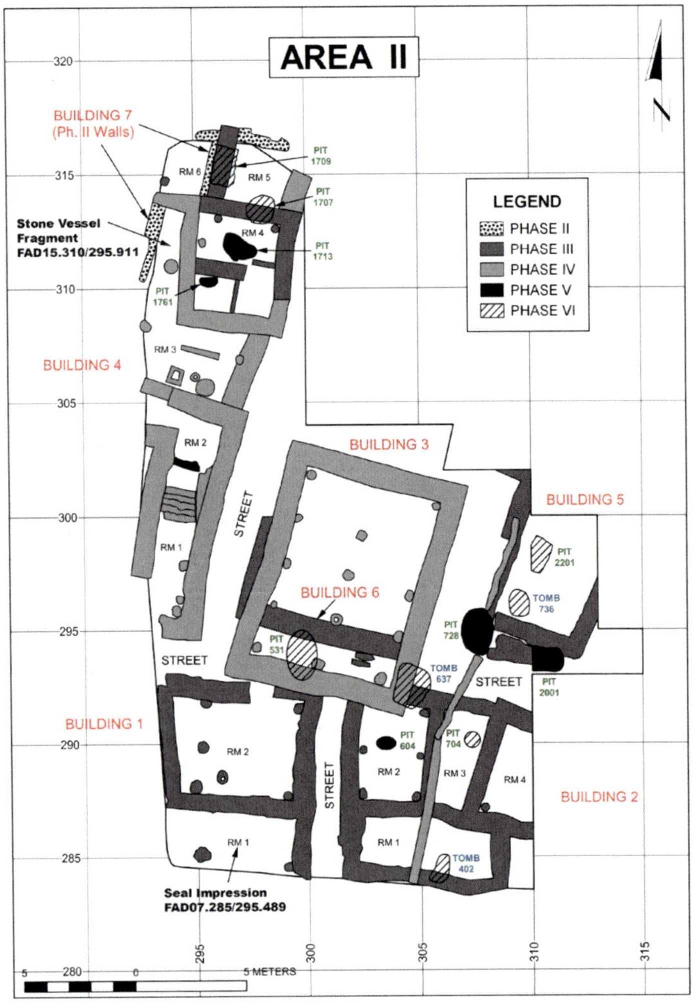

Figure 3: Schematic plan of Area II at Tell Fadous-Kfarabida (Tell Fadous-Kfarabida Project) with the indication of the find locations of the two objects presented in this article.

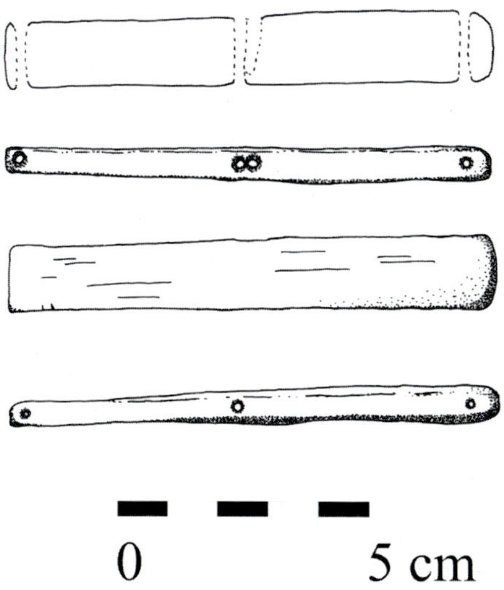

Figure 4: Scale beam FAD09.290/305.124 (Phase III) (Tell Fadous-Kfarabida Project).

The results obtained clearly show that despite its rather small size of 1.5 hectares, Fadous-Kfarabida does not exhibit any features usually associated with villages during the Early Bronze Age. The site was surrounded by a rather massive fortification, and the densely built-up interior with at least partly multi-story houses are features normally associated with urban settlements. Furthermore, Buildings 3 and 4 in Area II and possibly also the partially excavated buildings in Area V fall into the category of 'public' or 'special' buildings due to their size and layout. This idea is also supported by their central position on the site and the finds associated with them.

Tell Fadous-Kfarabida has produced a surprisingly large number of cylinder seal impressions and nine actual cylinder seals (Fig. 6) (Genz and Ahrens 2021). Both the seals and the impressions show a

Figure 5: Aerial view of the columned-hall Building 3 (Phase IV) (Tell Fadous-Kfarabida Project).

close connection between Byblos and Tell Fadous-Kfarabida. In one case, we are virtually certain that the same seal was used for an impression at Byblos and at Tell Fadous-Kfarabida (Genz and Ahrens 2021, 62 and Fig. 13 [FAD07.285/295.89]).

All of the nine cylinder seals found so far at the site come from Buildings 3 and 4 or their immediate vicinity, suggesting that their use was restricted to elite contexts. Three of these seals were manufactured out of hippopotamus ivory, clearly placing them in the category of prestige items (Genz and Ahrens 2021). Additional prestige items, such as a fragment of an Egyptian stone bowl (see below), imported steatite beads (Damick and Woodworth 2015), and extremely finely made ceramic drinking bowls, provide additional evidence for the importance of Building 4 and its association with elites.

According to the radiocarbon evidence, Phase IV came to an end around the middle of the 3rd millennium BCE, which supports the evidence from the Southern Levant for a considerably earlier date for the Early Bronze Age III-IV transition around the middle of the 3rd millennium BCE (Höflmayer et al. 2014). Unfortunately, the Early Bronze Age IVA, that is, the period between approximately 2500 to 2200 BCE at Tell Fadous-Kfarabida, is represented by a hiatus. Ephemeral activities, represented mainly by pits, are only attested again for the Early Bronze Age IVB (Phase V).

Figure 6: Selection of Early Bronze Age cylinder seals from Tell Fadous-Kfarabida (Tell Fadous-Kfarabida Project)

The Aegyptiaca from Tell Fadous-Kfarabida

1. A Fragment of an Egyptian Stone Vessel

One fragment of an Egyptian stone vessel (FAD15.310/295.911; from Context 2313) was found during the excavation campaign of 2015 at Tell Fadous-Kfarabida in Area II in a Phase IV context (Early Bronze Age III) (Fig. 7) (Genz et al. 2018, 61-62, fig. 29, pl. 5). The raw material was identified as porphyritic rhyolite, which belongs to the Dokhan Volcanic Formation from the Red Sea or Eastern Desert of Egypt.[1]

Although only a small fragment of this vessel was preserved, it can typologically be assigned to an open straight-sided bowl with a plain rim, typically found during the Egyptian Early Dynastic Period (1st–3rd Dynasty) but also continuing into the Old Kingdom (4th–6th Dynasty), with an early Old kingdom date to be preferred here. Parallels in Egypt are numerous (see Aston 1994, 108–113, types 44–52, with parallels). In the central and northern Levant, open bowls of similar type are largely confined to the coastal site of Byblos (Sowada 2009, 128–136, no. 164; Dunand 1958, 934, fig. 1047). A few similar fragments from Tell Mardikh/Ebla in inland western Syria (Sowada 2009, 150–153, pls. 28, 31.179) may originally also have reached the site via Byblos.

Based on its shape and the material used, the vessel fragment most probably dates to the Egyptian Early Dynastic Period or the Old Kingdom, roughly c. 3000–2200 BCE. Due to the fragmented state of the object, it is not possible to further refine its date of production. However, its find context at Tell Fadous-Kfarabida may seem to additionally give a good *terminus ante quem* for its production and deposition in the northern Levant.

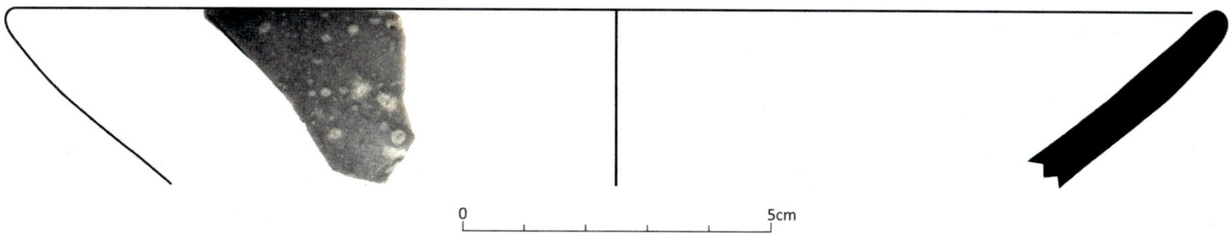

FIGURE 7: Stone vessel fragment FAD15.310/295.911 (Phase IV) (Tell Fadous-Kfarabida Project).

FIGURE 8: Cylinder seal impression on Jar Handle FAD07.285/295.489 (Phase III) (Tell Fadous-Kfarabida Project).

2. A Cylinder Seal Impression on a Jar Handle

Among the seals and impressions found at Tell Fadous-Kfarabida, Impression FAD07.285/295.489, executed on a handle of a storage jar made of local clay (Fig. 8), is markedly different and therefore, particularly striking. The find context of this fragment dates to Phase III (from Context 208), the Early Bronze Age III. Unfortunately, the impression was only partially preserved on the handle fragment and was apparently very carelessly impressed prior to firing.[2] For these reasons, attempting to ascertain precisely which features belong to the actual seal impression and which result from the hasty execution of the impression becomes challenging, making it impossible to cite exact parallels. Therefore, a complete and secure reconstruction of the original seal used seems to be unattainable at the moment. Few signs on the impression can tentatively be identified, possibly depicting, at least in part, Egyptian hieroglyphs or local Levantine emulations of such. The engraved image or inscription appears to be aligned and "read" horizontally. Intriguing is at least one vertical line that seems to divide two separate parts of the inscription or two separate motifs, a particular feature which is also commonly found on Egyptian cylinder seals of the Early Dynastic Period and the Old Kingdom (Kaplony 1963, pls. 96–116; 1981a, 543–145; 1981b, pls. 151–183).[3] The seal's engraving seems to consist of hieroglyphic signs. A large number of Egyptian cylinder seals dating from the Early Dynastic Period and the Old Kingdom feature multiple variations of hieroglyphs—ranging from highly structured, finely crafted down to extremely idiosyncratic, crude examples—showing predominantly graphical arrangements of hieroglyphs or other kinds of figures that are difficult or impossible to actually "read."[4] This also holds true for most of the few locally produced Levantine cylinder seals dating from the Early Bronze Age depicting "hieroglyphs" or featuring Egyptian iconography and motifs. One could tentatively try to identify specific hieroglyphs depicted here: at the right side of the preserved part of the seal impression, one could identify a cane/rush with shoots sign (i.e., sign M 22 in Gardiner's sign list (1957), phonetic value *nḫb*) or a *św̓t* plant (M 23, thus part of a word with the component *njśwt*?), and—just left of it—perhaps a single reed sign (M 17, phonetic value *j*). These signs, therefore, are possibly either fragmentary remnants of the toponym Nekheb (el-Kab in Upper Egypt) or even the name of the goddess Nekhbet (i.e., "She of Nekheb"), or a word involving the lexeme "king" or "royal"(?). However, during the Early Dynastic Period—and probably continuing into the Old Kingdom—the sign M 22 (i.e., cane/rush with shoots) can also be read as "*rnw*," the sign often being part of the designation of a function, social status, or even title referred to as "*rnw/rnwtj*" ("*jrj-nw.tj*") in a specific group of seals called "*Zivilsiegel*" (Pätznick 2005, 124–137; Nolan 2010, 70; Kaplony had identified this term as a personal name, see Kaplony 1963, 389–390, 556–57, 764–65, and, for example, pls. 93 [no. 358], 97 [no. 396], 115; see also Kahl et al. 1995, 23–27 [seals Ne/Be/17 and Ne/Be/23]; Engel 2021, 25). The title seems to be related to provincial levels of administration in Egypt ("*Lokalbeamter*," Pätznick 2005, 135–137), though it is unclear whether or not such a function could also be applied to a Levantine context. Interestingly to note, however, is that the term is also attested on a cylinder seal dating from the 3rd–4th Dynasties from Tyre (Fig. 9; see Ward 1978).

Left of the vertical line, the outline of a single individual (or perhaps god/goddess?) standing or sitting on or in an unknown device or furniture (maybe a shrine or a chair?) can be tentatively discerned, a motif that is also often found on cylinder seals of the Early Dynastic Period and continuing into the Old Kingdom (referred to as "*Figur am Speisetisch*," see Kaplony 1963, 37–45, pls. 105–17; 1964, pls. 6–17; 1977, 16–19, possibly to be read as *Sps*, lit. meaning "august," "noble," or "honored;" Pätznick 2005, 526, no. 497; Nolan 2010, 68; Wegner 2018, 234, fig. 13.1; Engel 2021, 17–20).[5] A depiction of such an individual is also attested in the Southern Levant on a cylinder seal from Bab edh-Dhra' (Lapp 2003, 547–50, fig. 18.21 [no. 2823]).

Admittedly, the identification of these signs is to be understood as highly speculative and far from secure. However, all in all, the combination of these features would seem to argue for an Old Kingdom date for the cylinder seal's production. As it is extremely difficult to securely "read" the seal impression and identify individual signs, it remains a moot point to decide whether the seal used for the impression was a genuine Egyptian or a locally produced Egyptianizing Levantine seal.[6] Since the vessel is made of local clay, and thus clearly not an Egyptian import, this could additionally argue for a local Levantine Egyptianizing seal. Further supporting this identification is the fact that Egyptian ceramic containers in the Early Bronze Age only rarely feature seal impressions executed on the vessel prior to firing, while, in the Levant, this practice is frequently attested (Ben-Tor 1978; Mazzoni 1992; Flender 2000; Thalmann 2013), although cylinder seal impressions executed specifically on handles of storage containers are equally rare. Still, also an Egyptian seal could have been used for such a procedure in the Levant and could lead us to speculate about the presence of Egyptians at Tell Fadous-Kfarabida, or the presence of an ill-defined Egyptian administrative system, perhaps centered at nearby Byblos.

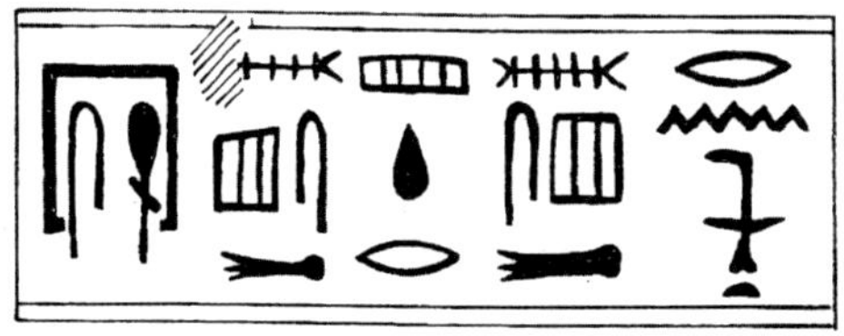

Figure 9: Old Kingdom cylinder seal from Tyre, 3rd–4th Dynasty (from Ward 1978, 84, pl. LIV:6).

This seal impression would thus be the first featuring an Egyptian cylinder seal coming from a secure Early Bronze Age III context in the Central Levant.

Egyptian and Egyptianizing Cylinder Seals in the Early Bronze Age Levant

While cylinder seals and cylinder seal impressions with local Levantine motifs and iconography are attested at various sites in almost all regions of the Early Bronze Age Levant (Mazzoni 1992; Flender 2000; Genz and Ahrens 2021), evidence for the actual employment of Egyptian hieroglyphs or the use of Egyptian or Egyptianizing motifs (here understood as local Levantine executions and interpretations of Egyptian hieroglyphic signs or motifs) on cylinder seals are only rarely attested thus far.

The few cylinder seals featuring Egyptian or Egyptianizing iconography and motifs from the Southern Levant—apart from the Egyptian seal impressions from the 1st Dynasty way-station of 'En Besor (Schulman 1976, 1980, 1995)—include one imported Egyptian cylinder seal from Bab edh-Dhra' dating from the Early Bronze Age II Period/late 1st Dynasty, but coming from an Early Bronze Age III context (Lapp 2003, 547–50, fig. 18.21 [no.

2823]), and a possible second cylinder seal made of pink calcite-alabaster that might exhibit some Egyptian influence, although this is much less clear due to its unfinished state of production (Lapp 2003, 541–43, fig. 18.16 [no. 2860]; Sala 2014, 69–72, tab. 1; 80, fig. 2). One unperforated clay cylinder seal from Gezer seems to feature Egyptian iconography, and—although without a secure find context—probably dates to the late Early Bronze Age I to earlier Early Bronze Age II period (Macalister 1912, 346 [35], pl. CCXIV.27; Ben-Tor 1978, 30, fig. 58 [no. IIIA–1], 83–87; 1985, 8–9, fig. 14). A second cylinder seal from Gezer probably also is to be identified as Egyptian (Macalister 1912, 346 [31], pl. CCXIV.12; Lapp 2003, 549). Another cylinder seal dating from the Early Bronze Age II period from the Sharon Plain is clearly Egyptian in origin but has no secure find context (Rowe 1936, 233, pl. XXVI, S.1; Ben-Tor 1985, 9, fig. 15; see Kaplony 1963, 37–40, pls. 101–15; 1964, pl. 16). Unfortunately, additional and more detailed information on the actual use of these seals cannot be given based on their find contexts.

In the central Levant, an enigmatic cylinder seal of possibly Old Kingdom date—the so-called "Byblos Cylinder Seal"—displays a much-discussed inscription in Egyptian hieroglyphs but seems to be a Levantine production (Sowada 2009, 137, fig. 30b, pl. 17b). A cylinder seal featuring the name of Khafre (4th Dynasty) from Byblos stems from a later context and, therefore, cannot be used for evidence of interregional contacts (Sowada 2009, 137). Finally, the already mentioned cylinder seal from Tyre (see above, Fig. 9), clearly an Egyptian import apparently made of quartz, dates to the first half of the Old Kingdom (3rd–4th Dynasties) but is unfortunately associated with a find context of the late 3rd millennium BCE (Ward 1978, 84–87, pl. LIV.6 [no. 74/11/583]).

Thus, the corpus consists of both Egyptian imports and local Levantine cylinder seals with emulations of Egyptian motifs. It is also interesting to note here that the relative dearth of cylinder seal impressions seems to reflect the meager number of cylinder seals that feature Egyptian or Egyptianizing motifs or hieroglyphs. The brief chronological and geographical survey of the distribution of the admittedly scant evidence for Egyptian and Egyptianizing cylinder seals and seal impressions might be seen in the light of the major shift in Egypt's relations with the Levant from the Early Bronze Age II onward and especially in the Early Bronze Age III (Old Kingdom), when it primarily started focusing on the central and northern Levant with their important ports, along with a contemporaneous contraction or diminution, but not necessarily a cessation, of activities in the southern Levant (Arnold et al. 2016). This change is also in general concordance with other groups of *Aegyptiaca* and Egyptian or Levantine pottery found in stratified contexts of the Early Bronze Age Levant and Early Dynastic and Old Kingdom Egypt (Sowada 2009; Sala 2012, 2014, 2016).

Chronological and Historical Considerations: Contextualizing the Seal Impression

Contacts between Egypt and the central and northern Levant are well attested in the archaeological record of both regions since the 4th millennium BCE, as exemplified by the hundreds of pottery vessels from the Levant found in Tomb U-j in Abydos (Hartung 2001). Pottery originating in the central and northern Levantine coastal regions, among other goods, is also found in Egypt at the beginning of the 3rd millennium BCE (Köhler and Ownby 2011; Köhler and Thalmann 2014), continuing until the end of the Old Kingdom (Sowada 2009, 2014; Forstner-Müller and Raue 2008; 2014; Müller 2014; Wodzińska and Ownby 2011; Thalmann and Sowada 2014).

The southern Levant is primarily within Egypt's focus in the Early Dynastic Period (1st–2nd Dynasties), with several trading posts and the installation of an Egyptian administrative system, as evidenced at the site of 'En Besor and other sites west and possibly even east of the Jordan River (Miroschedji 2002; Adams 2017; cf. however Ussishkin 2018; Finkelstein and Ussishkin 2003; Ilan and Goren 2003; Greenberg and Eisenberg 2002; Greenberg 2014; Sala 2012, 2014, 2016; Arnold et al. 2016; Cohen 2016, 22–38; Nigro et al. 2018; Iserlis et al. 2019). These activities are perhaps also reflected in the glyptic evidence from this period.

During the end of the 2nd Dynasty (late Early Dynastic Period) and the start of the 3rd Dynasty (early Old Kingdom), a shift in Egypt's relations with the central and northern Levant, especially at Byblos, is apparent in both the archaeological and the textual record. This change may have been triggered by the establishment of new seafaring techniques but certainly also concerns the merging of important trade routes and, thus, the acquisition of precious resources in the region of both the central and northern Levant (Wilkinson 1999, 136–137;

Marcus 2002). It is perhaps not a coincidence that a fragment of a stone vessel with the name of King Khasekhemwy of the late 2nd Dynasty is attested at Byblos—however, without a secure find context—while some of the boats buried adjacent to this king's funerary enclosure in Egypt were apparently made of Lebanese cedar wood (Sowada 2009; Wilkinson 1999, 136; Dreyer et al. 2003, 112–114).

The emergence—or availability—of more detailed written and also pictorial sources in Egypt in the course of the 3rd millennium BCE has enabled reconstructing these contacts more precisely, which need not be repeated in detail here (see Helck 1971, 12–37; Redford 1992, 11–64; Sowada 2009, 2014, 2018; Ahrens 2015).[7] The central Levantine city of Byblos seems to have been the focal point of interest for the Egyptians throughout the Old Kingdom; the reliefs from the causeway of Sahure (5th Dynasty) showing goods and people coming to Egypt from the Levant amply corroborate the contacts between the two regions. These strong relations do not seem to break off until the collapse of the Old Kingdom after the 6th Dynasty. New evidence from Egypt and the Central and Northern Levant may indeed argue for an intensification of contacts during the late Old Kingdom, albeit this may be due to the fragmentary nature of the archaeological and historical records for earlier periods of the Old Kingdom (Marcolin and Espinel 2011; see Ahrens 2015 with a compilation of the sources; Schneider 2015; see also Biga and Steinkeller 2021).

With regard to the presence of the stone vessel mentioned above—clearly, to be considered a prestige item—as well as the seal impression at Tell Fadous-Kfarabida—one is tempted to think of an Egyptian presence at the site during the Early Bronze Age III. While the Egyptian administration of the Old Kingdom seems to have focused on Byblos as the main trading partner in the Levant, a presence of administrative elements at other sites may also seem likely.[8]

Since the site of Tell Fadous-Kfarabida must have belonged to the sphere of political influence, if not dominance, exercised by Byblos during the Early Bronze Age, it would not be surprising to find Egyptian personnel present at the site. The site may then have served, at least partly, as a collecting point or redistribution center for goods (presumably olive oil) coming from its hinterland, perhaps channeled to Egypt via Byblos (for the economic and political status of the site during the Early Bronze Age, see already Genz et al. 2016). Supporting the contacts with the site, along with several other sites along the central Levantine coast, several examples of ram's head applications on pottery are attested in Phases III and IV (Genz 2014a, 72, fig. 12; see also Peršin, this volume), an example of which is also found on a Lebanese import from 4th Dynasty Giza (i.e., Tomb G 7330 A, see Mazzoni 1985; Sowada 2009; Sowada et al. 2020; see also Sowada et al. 2021; Badreshany et al. 2022). Such collecting points or redistribution centers with an Egyptian presence would, along with Byblos as the main hub, perhaps also help explain the Egyptian finds dating to the Old Kingdom farther north, among these the Egyptian stone vessels found at Tell Mardikh/Ebla (Scandone Matthiae 1981; Sowada 2009, 2018).

When trying to contextualize the seal impression, the intensified contacts between Egypt and the central and northern Levantine rulers since at least the beginning of the Early Bronze Age III would seem to provide the basis for an increased presence of Egyptian emissaries and objects, and thus also an increase of Egyptian iconography and motifs used in the Early Bronze Age central and northern Levant. However, it could also well be that Levantine individuals, and not Egyptians, transported the objects to the site.

Further Possible Connections with Egypt

Further tentative connections with Egypt at Tell Fadous-Kfarabida may be attested by the presence of date palm phytoliths at the site (Damick 2019). The date palm (Phoenix dactylifera) is not endemic to the coastal Levant (Zohary and Hopf 2000, 165–170), while its use in Egypt during the Old Kingdom is amply attested in the archaeobotanical record (Gale et al. 2000, 347–348). As the date palm phytoliths from Fadous-Kfarabida are restricted to storage compartments in the Early Bronze Age III buildings, it suggests the use of mats, bags, or baskets made out of palm fibers rather than the consumption of the actual fruits. This could be another hint that Fadous-Kfarabida contributed to supplying Egypt with valuable agricultural products, but probably indirectly via Byblos.[9]

A number of fired steatite beads were retrieved from Tell Fadous-Kfarabida Phase III and IV contexts (Damick and Woodworth 2015). Steatite is not attested in Lebanon, so these beads definitely represent imports. While Egypt, with its long tradition of fired steatite products, remains a very probable source of these beads, an origin in Mesopotamia or even the Indus Valley cannot be ruled out (Damick and Woodworth 2015, 613–614).

The presence of jars with combed decoration in Old Kingdom contexts throughout Egypt has long been recognized as evidence of the import of various organic commodities from the Levant (Helck 1971, 30–35; Mazzoni 1985; Forstner-Müller and Raue 2008; Sowada 2009, 155–158; Knoblauch 2010; Forstner-Müller and Raue 2014; Thalmann and Sowada 2014, 369–373; Sowada et al. 2019), including—but not restricted to—various oils and tree resins. Petrographic and chemical evidence (Sowada 2009, 167–179; Badreshany et al. 2020; Sowada et al. 2019), as well as the presence of ram's head applications (Mazzoni 1985), which show a marked concentration on the Central Levantine coast north of the Carmel Ridge, clearly demonstrate the importance of the central Levantine coast in this trade. As with Byblos (Mazzoni 1985) and Sidon (Doumet-Serhal 2006, 27 and Pl. 174, 5–7), ram's head applications on combed jars are well attested at Fadous-Kfarabida (Genz 2014b, 72 and Fig. 12), again suggesting that the site may have contributed in supplying various organic commodities to Egypt.

Conclusions

Far from just being a small village site, the combined artefactual and archaeobiological evidence from Tell Fadous-Kfarabida suggests that the site should be interpreted as an Early Bronze Age III administrative subcenter connected to the more important site of Byblos. If this interpretation is accepted, it suggests a more complex economic and political organization during the Early Bronze Age III in coastal Lebanon than hitherto envisaged (Genz et al. 2016). Byblos seems to be the only large Early Bronze Age site on the central coast of Lebanon, controlling all or at least large parts of this region. Tell Fadous-Kfarabida, within such a picture, would have most likely served as an administrative outpost for Byblos, presumably for collecting valuable crops like wheat and olives to sustain Byblos and its trade networks. The macrobotanical evidence from Tell Fadous-Kfarabida with a clear focus on wheat and olive suggests that production was less geared towards local consumption, but the site most likely funneled these products into a larger trade network, certainly involving Byblos (Deckers et al. 2021; Genz et al. 2016).

The limited number of Egyptian finds from Tell Fadous-Kfarabida fits quite well into such a picture. It is highly unlikely that the *Aegyptiaca* reached the site directly due to the absence of a natural harbor (Pedersen 2007; Pedersen 2012, 6–7). Thus, the more likely scenario is that these few Egyptian or Egyptianizing objects reached the site via Byblos.

At present, Fadous-Kfarabida's connections with Egypt seem to be restricted to the Early Bronze Age III (our Phases III and IV), corresponding to the early Old Kingdom in Egypt. At Byblos, on the other hand, contacts with Egypt seem to have intensified during the later Old Kingdom, now to be equated with the Early Bronze Age IVA in the Levant (Ahrens 2015). Unfortunately, this period at Tell Fadous-Kfarabida is represented by a hiatus. Only in the Early Bronze Age IVB activities are attested again at Tell Fadous-Kfarabida (Phase V), but no connections with Egypt are attested anymore, probably because trade relations with the Levant ceased due to the instability associated with the First Intermediate Period in Egypt.

Acknowledgments

The Tell Fadous-Kfarabida project is financed by University Research Board grants of the American University of Beirut. Since 2008, the Gerda Henkel Foundation, Germany, has provided additional funds. In 2010 and 2015, the German Society for the Exploration of Palestine (Deutscher Verein zur Erforschung Palästinas) supported the project. From 2014 to 2016, additional funds were provided by Columbia University. We would like to thank the codirectors, Dr. Hélène Sader (AUB, 2004–2008) and Dr. Alison Damick (Columbia University, 2014–2016) for an extremely fruitful cooperation, and the Direction Générale des Antiquités, especially its director Sarkis el-Khouri and Ms. Samar Karam, for their constant support.

References

Adams, Matthew J. 2017. "The Egyptianized Pottery Cache from Megiddo's Area J: A Foundation Deposit for Temple 4040." *Tel Aviv* 44 (2): 141–164.

Ahrens, Alexander. 2015. "Objects from Afar – The Distribution of Egyptian Imports in the Northern Levant: Parameters for Ascertaining the Character of Diplomatic Contacts between Egypt and the Levant during the Bronze Age?". In Brigitta Eder and Regine Pruzsinszky (eds.), *Policies of Exchange: Political Systems and Modes of Interaction in the Aegean and the Near East in the 2nd Millennium B.C.E. Proceedings of the International Symposium at the University of Freiburg, Institute for Archaeological Studies, 30th May–2nd June 2012*, 141–156. Oriental and European Archaeology 2. Vienna: Austrian Academy of Sciences Press.

Andrássy, Petra. 2008. *Untersuchungen zum ägyptischen Staat des Alten Reiches und seinen Institutionen*. Internet-Beiträge zur Ägyptologie und Sudanarchäologie 11. London: Golden House Publications.

Arnold, Elizabeth R., Gideon Hartman, Greenfield, Haskel J., Izchaq Shai, Louise E. Babcock, and Aren M. Maeir. 2016. "Isotopic Evidence for Early Trade in Animals between Old Kingdom Egypt and Canaan." *PLoS ONE* 11(6): e0157650. DOI: https://doi.org/10.1371/journal.pone.0157650.

Badreshany, Kamal, Hermann Genz, and Hélène Sader, with contributions by Peter Breuer, Canan Çakırlar, Katleen Deckers, Barbara Jungklaus, Fadi Nader, Simone Riehl, Dörte Rokitta and Sandra Yanni. 2005. "An Early Bronze Age Site on the Lebanese Coast. Tell Fadous-Kfarabida 2004 and 2005: Final Report." *Bulletin d'Archéologie et d'Architecture Libanaises* 9: 5–115.

Badreshany, Kamal, Graham Philip and Melissa Kennedy. 2020. "The Development of Integrated Regional Economies in the Early Bronze Age Levant: New Evidence from 'Combed Ware' Jars." *Levant* 52. DOI: 10.1080/00758914.2019.1641009.

Badreshany, Kamal, Karin Sowada, Mary Ownby, Mathilde Jean, Michel de Vreeze, Alice McClymont and Graham Philip. 2022. "The characterisation of ceramic production from the central Levant and Egyptian trade in the Pyramid Age." *Journal of Archaeological Science: Reports* 41. 103309. https://www.sciencedirect.com/science/article/abs/pii/S2352409X21005216?via%3Dihub

Bárta, Miroslav. 2013. "Kings, Viziers, and Courtiers: Executive Power in the Third Millennium B.C." In Juan C. Moreno García (ed.), *Ancient Egyptian Administration*, 153–176. Handbook of Oriental Studies, Section 1, Ancient Near East, Volume 104. Brill: Leiden. https://doi.org/10.1163/9789004250086_006.

Ben-Tor, Amnon. 1978. *Cylinder Seals of Third-Millennium Palestine*. Bulletin of the American Schools of Oriental Research Supplement Series No. 22. Cambridge: American Schools of Oriental Research.

———. 1985. "Glyptic Art of Early Bronze Age Palestine and its Foreign Relations." In Eduard Lipiński (ed.), *The Land of Israel: Crossroads of Civilizations*, 1–25. Orientalia Lovaniensia Analecta 19. Leuven: Peeters.

———. 1994. "Early Bronze Age Cylinder Seal Impressions and a Stamp Seal from Tel Qashish." *Bulletin of the American Schools of Oriental Research* 295: 15–29. https://doi.org/10.2307/1357102.

———. 2017. "Early Bronze Age Cylinder-Seal Impressions." In Amnon Ben-Tor, Sharon Zuckerman, Shlomit Bechar, and Debora Sandhaus (eds.), *Hazor VII: The 1990–2012 Excavations. The Bronze Age*, 471–474. Jerusalem: Israel Exploration Society, Institute of Archaeology, The Hebrew University of Jerusalem.

Biga, Maria Giovanna and Piotr Steinkeller. 2021. "In Search of Dugurasu." *Journal of Cuneiform Studies* 73: 9–70.

Cohen, Susan L. 2016. *Peripheral Concerns: Urban Development in the Bronze Age Southern Levant. New Directions in Anthropological Archaeology*. Sheffield: Equinox.

Damick, Alison. 2019. "The First Identification of Phoenix dactylifera (Date Palm) from Early Bronze Age Lebanon." *Vegetation History and Archaeobotany*. https://doi.org/10.1007/s00334-019-00723-8.

Damick, Alison and Marshall Woodworth. 2015. "Steatite Beads from Tell Fadous-Kfarabida: A Case Study in Early Bronze Age Technology in Northern Coastal Lebanon." *Journal of Archaeological Science Reports* 3: 603–614.

Deckers, Katleen, Simone Riehl, Valentina Tumolo, Hermann Genz and Dan Lawrence. 2021. "Intensive Olive Production at Two Early Bronze Age Levantine Sites." *Journal of Archaeological Science: Reports* 36. https://doi.org/10.1016/j.jasrep.2021.102841.

Doumet-Serhal, Claude. 2006. *The Early Bronze Age in Sidon. "College Site" Excavations (1998-2000-2001)*. Bibliothèque Archéologique et Historique 178. Beirut: Institut Français du Proche-Orient.

Dreyer, Günter, Rita Hartmann, Ulrich Hartung, Thomas Hikade, Heid Köpp, Claudia Lacher, Vera Müller, Andreas Nerlich and Albert Zink. 2003. "Umm el-Qaab. Nachuntersuchungen im frühzeitlichen Königsfriedhof. 13./14./15. Vorbericht." *Mitteilungen des Deutschen Archäologischen Instituts Kairo* (MDAIK) 59: 67–138.

Dunand, Maurice. 1958. *Fouilles de Byblos II, 1933-1938*. Texte. Paris: Adrien Maisonneuve.

Engel, Eva-Maria. 2013. "The Organisation of a Nascent State: Egypt until the Beginning of the 4th Dynasty." In Juan C. Moreno García (ed.), *Ancient Egyptian Administration*, 19–39. Handbook of Oriental Studies, Section 1, Ancient Near East, Volume 104. Brill: Leiden. https://doi.org/10.1163/9789004250086_003.

———. 2021. *Private Rollsiegel der Frühzeit und des frühen Alten Reiches. Versuch einer Einordnung*. Menes: Studien zur Kultur und Sprache der ägyptischen Frühzeit und des Alten Reiches 8. Wiesbaden: Harrassowitz.

Finkelstein, Israel, and David Ussishkin. 2003. "The Cache of Egyptianized Vessels from Megiddo: A Stratigraphical Update." *Tel Aviv* 30: 27–41. https://doi.org/10.1179/tav.2003.2003.1.27.

Flender, Matthias. 2000. "Cylinder Seal Impressed Vessels of the Early Bronze Age III in Northern Palestine." In Graham Philip and Douglas Baird (eds.), *Ceramics and Change in the Early Bronze Age of the Southern Levant*, 295–313. Levantine Archaeology 2. Sheffield: Sheffield Academic.

Forstner-Müller, Irene and Dietrich Raue. 2008. "Elephantine and the Levant." In Eva-Maria Engel, Vera Müller and Ulrich Hartung (eds.), *Zeichen aus dem Sand. Streiflichter aus Ägyptens Geschichte zu Ehren von Günter Dreyer*, 127–148. Wiesbaden: Harrassowitz.

———. 2014. "Contacts between Egypt and the Levant in the 3rd Millennium BC." In Felix Höflmayer and Ricardo Eichmann (eds.), *Egypt and the Southern Levant in the Early Bronze Age*. Orient-Archäologie 31, 57–67. Rahden: Marie Leidorf.

Gale, Rowena, Peter Gasson, Nigel Hepper, and Geoffrey Killen. 2000. "Wood." In Paul T. Nicholson and Ian Shaw (eds.), *Ancient Egyptian Materials and Technology*, 334–371. Cambridge: Cambridge University Press.

Gardiner, Allan. 1957. *Egyptian Grammar. Being an Introduction to the Study of Hieroglyphs* (Third Edition, Revised). Oxford: Griffith Institute.

Genz, Hermann. 2010. "Recent Excavations at Tell Fadous-Kfarabida." *Near Eastern Archaeology* 73.2/3: 102–113.

———. 2011. "Restoring the Balance: An Early Bronze Age Scale Beam from Tell Fadous-Kfarabida, Lebanon." *Antiquity* 85/329: 839–850.

———. 2014a. "Excavations at Tell Fadous-Kfarabida 2004–2011: An Early and Middle Bronze Age Site on the Lebanese Coast." In Felix Höflmayer and Ricardo Eichmann (eds.), *Egypt and the Southern Levant in the Early Bronze Age*, 69–91. Orient-Archäologie 31. Rahden/Westf.: Marie Leidorf.

———. 2014b. "The Northern Levant (Lebanon) during the Early Bronze Age." In Margreet Steiner and Ann E. Killebrew (eds.), *The Oxford Handbook of The Archaeology of the Levant, c. 8000–332 BCE*, 292–306. Oxford: Oxford University. https://doi.org/10.1093/oxfordhb/9780199212972.013.021.

Genz, Hermann and Hélène Sader. 2007. "Excavations at the Early Bronze Age Site of Tell Fadous-Kfarabida: Preliminary Report on the 2007 Season of Excavations." *Bulletin d'archéologie et d'architecture libanaises* 11: 7–16.

———. 2008. "Excavations at Tell Fadous-Kfarabida: Preliminary Report on the 2008 Season of Excavations." *Bulletin d'archéologie et d'architecture libanaises* 12: 149–59.

Genz, Hermann, Canan Çakırlar, Alison Damick, Emilia Jastrzębska, Simone Riehl, Katleen Deckers, and Ann Donkin. 2009. "Excavations at Tell Fadous-Kfarabida: Preliminary Report on the 2009 Season of Excavations." *Bulletin d'archéologie et d'architecture libanaises* 13: 71–123.

Genz, Hermann, Riva Daniel, Alison Damick, Alexander Ahrens, Sireen El-Zaatari, Felix Höflmayer, Walter Kutschera, and Eva Maria Wild. 2010. "Excavations at Tell Fadous-Kfarabida: Preliminary Report on the 2010 Season of Excavations." *Bulletin d'archéologie et d'architecture libanaises* 14: 241–73.

Genz, Hermann, Riva Daniel, Konstantin Pustovoytov, and Marshall Woodworth. 2011. "Excavations at Tell Fadous-Kfarabida: Preliminary Report on the 2011 Season of Excavations." *Bulletin d'archéologie et d'architecture libanaises* 15: 151–74.

Genz, Hermann, Simone Riehl, Canan Çakırlar, Francesca Slim, and Alison Damick. 2016.

"Economic and Political Organization of Early Bronze Age Coastal Communities: Tell Fadous-Kfarabida as a Case Study." *Berytus* 55: 79–119.

Genz, Hermann, Alison Damick, Stephen Berquist, Martin Makinson, Zuzanna Wygnanska, Mahmoud Mardini, Metoda Peršin, Naseem Raad, Jana Alameh, Alexander Ahrens, Nathalie El-Dana, Jean Edwards, and Sireen El-Zaatari. 2018. "Excavations at Tell Fadous-Kfarabida: Preliminary Report on the 2014 and 2015 Seasons of Excavations." *Bulletin d'Archéologie et d'Architecture Libanaises* 18: 37–78.

Genz, Hermann and Alexander Ahrens. 2021. "Recent Early Bronze Age Glyptic Finds from Lebanon: The Evidence from Tell Fadous-Kfarabida." *Bulletin of the American Schools of Oriental Research* 386: 47–76.

Genz, Hermann, Alison Damick, Zuzanna Wygnańska, Martin Makinson, Marshall Woodworth, Mahmoud Mardini, Naseem Raad, Anja Rutter, Jana Alameh, Berj Wanessian, Sidney Rempel, Johnny Baldi, Marta D'Andrea, Metoda Peršin, Karin Kopetzky, Ziad El Morr, Canan Çakırlar, Francesca Slim, Yuri van den Hurk, Francis Koolstra, Max Price, Cheryl Makarewicz, Michiel Vanhecke, Rachel Winter, Willemien de Kock, Chris Stantis, Nina Maaranen, Joanne Peterkin, Geoff M. Nowell, Colin MacPherson, and Holger Schutkowski. "Excavations at Tell Fadous-Kfarabida: Preliminary Report on the 2016 Season of Excavations." Submitted to the *Bulletin d'Archéologie et d'Architecture Libanaises.*

Gernez, Guillaume. 2011. "The Exchange of Products and Concepts between the Near East and the Mediterranean: the Example of Weapons during the Early and Middle Bronze Ages." In Kim Duistermaat and Ilona Regulski (eds.), *Intercultural Contacts in the Ancient Mediterranean. Proceedings of the International Conference at the Netherlands-Flemish Institute in Cairo, 25th to 29th October 2008*, 327–341. Orientalia Lovaniensa Analecta 202. Leuven–Paris–Walpole: Peeters.

Greenberg, Raphael. 2014. "Tel Beth Yerah: Synchronising Egyptian and South Caucasian Connections." In Felix Höflmayer and Ricardo Eichmann (eds.), *Egypt and the Southern Levant in the Early Bronze Age*, 91–105. Orient-Archäologie 31. Rahden/Westf.: Marie Leidorf.

Greenberg, Raphael, and Emanuel Eisenberg. 2002. "Egypt, Bet Yerah and Early Canaanite Urbanization." In Edwin C. M. van den Brink and Thomas E. Levy (eds.), *Egypt and the Levant: Interrelations from the 4th through the Early 3rd Millennium B.C.E.*, 213–222. New Approaches to Anthropological Archaeology. London/New York: Leicester University.

Hartung, Ulrich. 2001. *Umm el-Qaab II: Importkeramik aus dem Friedhof U in Abydos (Umm el-Qaab) und die Beziehungen Ägyptens zu Vorderasien im 4. Jahrtausend vor Chr.* Archäologische Veröffentlichungen 92. Mainz: Verlag Philipp von Zabern.

Hartung, Ulrich, E. Christiana Köhler, Vera Müller, and Mary F. Ownby. 2015. "Imported Pottery from Abydos: A new Petrographic Perspective." Ägypten und Levante 25: 295–333.

Helck, Wolfgang. 1971. *Die Beziehungen Ägyptens zu Vorderasien* (2nd ed.). Wiesbaden: Harrassowitz.

Höflmayer, Felix, Michael Dee, Hermann Genz, and Simone Riehl. 2014. "Radiocarbon Evidence for the Early Bronze Age Levant: The Site of Tell Fadous-Kfarabida (Lebanon) and the End of the Early Bronze III Period." *Radiocarbon* 56/2: 529–542.

Ilan, Oren, and Yuval Goren. 2003. "The Egyptianized Pottery Vessels of Early Bronze Age Megiddo." *Tel Aviv* 30 (1): 42–53. https://doi.org/10.1179/tav.2003.2003.1.42.

Iserlis, Mark, Daniel Steiniger, and Raphael Greenberg. 2019. "Contact Between First Dynasty Egypt and Specific Sites in the Levant: New Evidence from Ceramic Analysis." *Journal of Archaeological Science: Reports* 24: 1023–1040. https://doi.org/10.1016/j.jasrep.2019.03.021.

Kahl, Jochem, Nicole Kloth, and Ursula Zimmermann. 1995. *Die Inschriften der 3. Dynastie. Eine Bestandsaufnahme.* Ägyptologische Abhandlungen 56. Wiesbaden: Harrassowitz.

Kaplony, Peter. 1963. *Die Inschriften der ägyptischen Frühzeit, I.–III. Band.* Ägyptologische Abhandlungen 8. Wiesbaden: Harrassowitz.

———. 1964. *Die Inschriften der ägyptischen Frühzeit, Supplement*. Ägyptologische Abhandlungen 9. Wiesbaden: Harrassowitz.

———. 1977. *Die Rollsiegel des Alten Reiches I: Allgemeiner Teil mit Studien zum Königtum des Alten Reiches.* Monumenta Aegyptiaca 2. Brussels: Fondation Égyptologique Reine Élisabeth.

———. 1981a. *Die Rollsiegel des Alten Reiches II: Katalog der Rollsiegel, A. Text*. Monumenta Aegyptiaca 3a. Brussels: Fondation Égyptologique Reine Élisabeth.

———. 1981b. *Die Rollsiegel des Alten Reiches II: Katalog der Rollsiegel, B. Tafeln*. Monumenta Aegyptiaca 3b. Brussels: Fondation Égyptologique Reine Élisabeth.

Köhler, E. Christina and Mary Ownby. 2011. "Levantine Imports and their Imitations from Helwan." Ägypten und Levante 21: 31–46.

Köhler, E. Christina and Jean-Paul Thalmann. 2014. "Synchronising Early Egyptian Chronologies and the Northern Levant." In Felix Höflmayer and Ricardo Eichmann (eds.), *Egypt and the Southern Levant in the Early Bronze Age*, 181–206. Orient-Archäologie 31. Rahden: Marie Leidorf.

Knoblauch, Christian. 2010. "Preliminary Report on the Early Bronze Age III Pottery from Contexts of the 6th Dynasty in the Abydos Middle Cemetery." Ägypten *und Levante* 20: 243–261.

Lapp, Nancy. 2003. "Cylinder Seals, Impressions, and Incised Sherds." In Walter E. Rast and R. Thomas Schaub (eds.), Bâb edh-Dhrâʿ: Excavations at the Town Site (1975–1981), Part 1: Text, 522–565. Reports of the Expedition to the Dead Sea Plain, Jordan 2. Winona Lake, IN: Eisenbrauns.

Macalister, Robert Alexander Stewart. 1912. *The Excavation of Gezer, 1902–1905 and 1907–1909, Volumes I–III*. London: John Murray.

Marcolin, Michele and Andrés Diego Espinel. 2011. "The Sixth Dynasty Inscription of Iny: More Pieces to the Puzzle." In Miroslav Bárta, Filip Coppens and Jaromír Krejčí (eds.), *Abusir and Saqqara in the Year 2010*, 570–615. Prague: Czech Institute of Egyptology.

Marfoe, Leon. 1998. *Kamid el-Loz 14. Settlement History of the Biqāʿ up to the Iron Age*. Saarbrücker Beiträge zur Altertumskunde 53. Bonn: Rudolf Habelt.

Marcus, Ezra. 2002. "Early Seafaring and Maritime Activity in the Southern Levant from Prehistory through the Third Millennium bce." In Edwin C. M. van den Brink and Thomas E. Levy (eds.), *Egypt and the Levant: Interrelations from the 4th through the Early 3rd Millennium B.C.E.*, 403–417. London and New York: Leicester University.

Mazzoni, Stefania. 1985. "Giza ed una produzione vascolare di Biblo." In Sandro Filippo Bondi, Sergio Pernigotti, Francesca Serra, and Angelo Vivian (eds.), *Studi in onore di Edda Bresciani*, 317–338. Pisa: Giardini.

———. 1992. *Le impronte su giara eblaite e siriane nel Bronzo Antico*. Materiali e Studi Archeologici di Ebla I. Rome: Missione Archaeologica Italiana in Siria.

Miroschedji, Pierre de. 2002. "The Socio-political Dynamics of Egyptian-Canaanite Interaction in the Early Bronze Age." In Edwin C. M. van den Brink and Thomas E. Levy (eds.), *Egypt and the Levant. Interrelations from the 4th through the Early 3rd Millennium B.C.E.*, 39–57. London–New York: Leicester University Press.

Montet, Pierre. 1928. *Byblos et l'Égypte, quatre campagnes de fouilles à Gebeil, 1921–1922–1923–1924*. Bibliothèque Archéologique et Historique 11. Paris: Paul Geuthner.

Moreno García, Juan C. 2013. "The Territorial Administration of the Kingdom in the 3rd Millennium." In Juan C. Moreno García (ed.), *Ancient Egyptian Administration*, 85–152. Handbook of Oriental Studies, Section 1, Ancient Near East 104. Brill: Leiden. https://doi.org/10.1163/9789004250086_005.

Müller, Vera. 2014. "Relations Between Egypt and the Near East During the 1st Egyptian Dynasty as Represented by the Royal Tomb of Den at Umm el-Qaab/Abydos." In Felix Höflmayer and Ricardo Eichmann (eds.), *Egypt and the Southern Levant in the Early Bronze Age*, 241–258. Orient-Archäologie 31. Rahden/Westf.: Marie Leidorf.

Nigro, Lorenzo, Daria Montanari, Francesco Mura, Jehad Yasine, and Teresa Rinaldi. 2018. "A Hoard of Nilotic Nacreous Shells from Egypt to Jericho (Early Bronze II, 3000–2800 bce): Their Finding, Content and Historical Archaeological Implications." *Palestine Exploration Quarterly* 150 (2): 110–125. https://doi.org/10.1080/00310328.2018.1425957.

Nolan, John S. 2010. *Mud Sealings and Fourth Dynasty Administration at Giza*, Ph.D. dissertation, University of Chicago. DOI: https://oi.uchicago.edu/research/research-archives-library/dissertations/mud-sealings-and-fourth-dynasty-administration-giza.

———. 2018. Sealings and Seals from Pyramid Age Egypt. In Marta Ameri, Sarah Kielt Costello, Gregg Jamieson, and Sarah Jarmer Scott (eds.), *Seals and Sealing in the Ancient World: Case Studies from the Near East, Egypt, the Aegean, and*

South Asia, 271–288. Cambridge and New York: Cambridge University.

Pätznick, Jean-Pierre. 2005. *Die Siegelabrollungen und Rollsiegel der Stadt Elephantine im 3. Jahrtausend v. Chr.: Spurensicherung eines archäologischen Artefaktes*. British Archaeology Reports, International Series 1339. Oxford: Archaeopress.

Papazian, Hratch. 2012. *Domain of Pharaoh: The Structure and Components of the Economy of Old Kingdom Egypt*. Hildesheimer Ägyptologische Beiträge 52. Hildesheim: Gerstenberg.

———. 2013. "The Central Administration of the Resources in the Old Kingdom: Departments, Treasuries, Granaries and Work Centers." In Juan C. Moreno García (ed.), *Ancient Egyptian Administration*, 41–83. Handbook of Oriental Studies, Section 1, Ancient Near East 104. Brill: Leiden. https://doi.org/10.1163/9789004250086_004.

Pedersen, Ralph K. 2007. "The Underwater Survey at Tell Fadous-Kfarabida." *Bulletin d'Archéologie et d'Architecture Libanaises* 11: 17–23.

———. 2012. "Emerging Maritime Paradigms for the Bronze Age in Lebanon." *Skyllis* 12: 5–10.

Prag, Kay. 1986. "Byblos and Egypt in the Fourth Millennium B.C." *Levant* 18: 59–74.

Redford, Donald B. 1992. *Egypt, Canaan, and Israel in Ancient Times*. Princeton: Princeton University Press.

Rowe, Alan. 1936. *A Catalogue of Egyptian Scarabs, Scaraboids, Seals and Amulets in the Palestine Archaeological Museum*. Cairo: Institut français d'archéologie orientale.

Saghieh, Muntaha. 1983. *Byblos in the Third Millennium B.C. A Reconstruction of the Stratigraphy and a Study of the Cultural Connections*. Warminster: Aris & Phillips.

Sala, Maura. 2012. "Egyptian and Egyptianizing Objects from EB I–III Tell es-Sultan/Jericho." *Vicino Oriente* 16: 277–303.

———. 2014. "EB II–III *Aegyptiaca* East of the Jordan: A Reevaluation of Trade and Cultural Interactions between Egypt and the Transjordanian Urban Centres." *Vicino Oriente* 18: 65–81.

———. 2016. "The Ceramic Ensemble from the EB IIIB Palace B at Khirbat al-Batrāwi (North-Central Jordan): A Preliminary Report in the Context of EBA Palestine and Transjordan." In Department of Antiquities of Jordan (ed.), *Studies in the History and Archaeology of Jordan 12*, 117–134. Amman: The Department of Antiquities.

Scandone Matthiae, Gabriela. 1981. "I vasi egiziani in pietra del Palazzo Reale G." *Studi Eblaiti* 4: 99–127.

Schneider, Thomas. 2015. "The Old Kingdom Abroad: An Epistemological Perspective, with Remarks on the Biography of Iny and the Kingdom of Dugurasu." In Peter Der Manuelian and Thomas Schneider (eds.), *Towards a New History for the Egyptian Old Kingdom: Perspectives on the Pyramid Age*, 429–454. Harvard Egyptological Studies 1. Leiden: Brill. https://doi.org/10.1163/9789004301894_012.

Schulman, Alan R. 1976. "The Egyptian Seal Impression from 'En Besor." *'Atiqot* 11: 16–26.

———. 1980. "More Egyptian Seal Impressions from 'En Besor." *'Atiqot* 14: 17–32.

———. 1995. "Still More Egyptian Seal Impressions from 'En Besor. In Edwin C. M. van den Brink (ed.), *The Delta in Transition: 4th and 3rd Millennium b.c., Proceedings of the Seminar held in Cairo, 21st–24th October 1990, at the Netherlands Institute of Archaeology and Arabic Studies*, 395–417. Tel Aviv: Tel Aviv University.

Sowada, Karin N. 2009. *Egypt and the Eastern Mediterranean During the Old Kingdom: An Archaeological Perspective*. Orbis Biblicus et Orientalis 237. Fribourg: Academic Press; Göttingen: Vandenhoeck & Ruprecht.

———. 2014. "Never the Twain Shall Meet? Synchronising Egyptian and Levantine Chronologies in the 3rd Millennium BC." In Felix Höflmayer and Ricardo Eichmann (eds.), *Egypt and the Southern Levant in the Early Bronze Age*, 293–313. Orient-Archäologie 31. Rahden/Westf.: Marie Leidorf.

———. 2018. "Stone Vessels." In M. Lebeau (ed.), *Associated Regional Chronologies for the Ancient Near East and the Eastern Mediterranean: Interregional, Vol. II: Artefacts*, 245–276. Turnhout: Brepols.

Sowada, Karin, Mary F. Ownby, and Anna Wodzińska. 2020. "The Petrography of Imported Levantine Combed Vessels from Early Old Kingdom Giza." *Levant* 52: 1–2, 197–214.

Sowada, Karin, Mary F. Ownby, and Miroslav Bárta. 2021. "The Origin of Imported Jars from 6th Dynasty Abusir: New Light on Early Bronze Age Egyptian-Levantine Relations." *Bulletin of the American Schools of Oriental Research* 386: 221–236. https://doi.org/10.1086/715651.

Sowada Karin, Mary F. Ownby, Jane Smythe, Sylvie Marchand, and Yann Tristant. 2021. "Early Bronze Age Exchange Patterns between Egypt and the Levant: a View from First Dynasty Abu Rawash." Ägypten und Levante 31: 425–450 https://doi.org/10.1553/AEundL31s425.

Thalmann, Jean-Paul. 2007. "Settlement Patterns and Agriculture in the Akkar Plain during the Late Early and Early Middle Bronze Ages." In Daniele Morandi Bonacossi (ed.), *Urban and Natural Landscapes of an Ancient Syrian Capital, Settlement and Environment at Tell Mishrifeh/Qatna and in Central Western Syria*, 219–232. Udine: Forum.

———. 2013. "Le lion, la chèvre et le poisson. À propos d'une jarre à empreintes de sceaux-cylindres de Tell Arqa (Liban)." *Syria* 90: 255–312. https://doi.org/10.4000/syria.1848.

Thalmann, Jean-Paul and Karin Sowada. 2014. "Levantine "Combed Ware"." In Marc Lebeau (ed.), *Associated Regional Chronologies for the Ancient Near East and the Eastern Mediterranean. Interregional Volume I: Ceramics*, 355–378. Turnhout: Brepols.

Ussishkin, David. 2018. "Was the Egyptianized Pottery Cache from Megiddo a Foundation Deposit of Megaron Temple 4040? Response to Matthew J. Adams." *Tel Aviv* 45 (2): 216–223. https://doi.org/10.1080/03344355.2018.1494790.

Ward, William A. 1978. "The Egyptian Objects (Appendix B)." In Patricia M. Bikai, *The Pottery of Tyre*, 83–87. Warminster: Aris and Phillips.

Wegner, Josef M. 2018. "The Evolution of Ancient Egyptian Seals and Sealing Systems." In Marta Ameri, Sarah Kielt Costello, Gregg Jamieson, and Sarah Jarmer Scott (eds.), *Seals and Sealing in the Ancient World: Case Studies from the Near East, Egypt, the Aegean, and South Asia*, 229–257. Cambridge and New York: Cambridge University.

Wilkinson, Toby A. H. 1999. *Early Dynastic Egypt*. London: Routledge.

Willems, Harco. 2018. "Cylinder Seals for the Lower Classes: Ein Merkmal der Provinzkultur des ausgehenden Alten Reiches?" *Zeitschrift für ägyptische Sprache und Altertumskunde* 145 (2): 187–204. https://doi.org/10.1515/zaes-2018-0017.

Wodzińska, Anna, and Mary F. Ownby. 2011. "Tentative Remarks on Levantine Combed Ware from Heit el-Ghurab, Giza." In Jana Mynářová (ed.), *Egypt and the Near East – The Crossroads. Proceedings of an International Conference on the Relations of Egypt and the Near East in the Bronze Age, Prague, September 1–3, 2010*, 285–295. Prague: Institute of Egyptology.

Wright, Mary. 1988. "Contacts between Egypt and Syro-Palestine during the Old Kingdom." *Biblical Archaeologist* 51: 143–162.

Yazbeck, Corine. 2006. "The Early Bronze Age Industries of Sidon ("College Site" Excavations)." In Claude Doumet Serhal, *The Early Bronze Age in Sidon. "College Site" Excavations (1998-2000-2001)*, 291–300. Bibliothèque Archéologique et Historique 178. Beirut: Institut Français du Proche-Orient).

Zohary, Daniel and Maria Hopf. 2000. *Domestication of Plants in the Old World*. Oxford: Oxford University Press.

Notes

1 We would like to thank Prof. A. Abdel Rahman (Geology Department, American University of Beirut) for the geological examination.

2 The reconstructed height of the seal is approximately 15–20 mm, the diameter is unknown. The actual seal was presumably made of stone or even wood, which is amply attested in Egypt for the periods of the Early Dynastic Period and the Old Kingdom, see Kaplony 1963; Wegner 2018: 227–324.

3 Among the motifs of Levantine Early Bronze Age seal impressions, vertical lines are also attested, albeit almost exclusively in connection with geometric patterns (i.e., net or herring-bone patterns, concentric circles, spirals, or rhomboids), either as a sole motif or as a combination of these (see Ben-Tor 1978; 1985). This, however, clearly is not the case with the seal impression under discussion here.

4 See Nolan 2018, 272–75; Wegner 2018, 233–36; Willems 2018; Engel 2021). Peter Kaplony (1981a, 543) also refers to some of these seals as "*Figurensiegel/-zylinder*" ("Figurative Seals"). In this respect, it must be noted here that most of Kaplony's seals belonging to this category come from unprovenanced contexts and collections, so there is the probability that some

of these seals actually originate from the Levant (Kaplony 1981a, 543–45).

5 In the Old Kingdom, belonging to a specific group of administrative seals ("*Verwaltungssiegel*") referred to by Kaplony as "*Totensiegel*" ("Seals of the Dead"), see Kaplony 1977: 16–19; Engel 2021.

6 The lack of such seals or seal impressions may simply be a reflection of the scant archaeological evidence and the scarcity of comparable excavated settlements in the region for this period.

7 This is not to say that all contacts between Egypt and the southern Levant come to a halt during this period; see Greenberg and Eisenberg 2002; Sala 2012, 2014, 2016.

8 For the organization of the Egyptian administrative system during the Early Dynastic Period and the Old Kingdom, see Andrássy 2008; Bárta 2013; Engel 2013; Moreno García 2013; Papazian 2012, 2013.

9 It remains unknown if, prior to their use in the storage compartments in Fadous-Kfarabida, the palm fiber containers had been used to transport Egyptian commodities to the Levant.

Journal of Ancient Egyptian Interconnections

Metal as a Mechanism for Understanding Social Complexity during the Third millennium BCE: A Comparative Zooarchaeological Perspective on Egypt and the Southern Levant

Eleutério Abreu De Sousa
Macquarie University

Haskel J. Greenfield
University of Manitoba

Abstract

Most studies of the spread of copper and bronze metallurgy across the Near East rely upon the relatively few surviving metal artifacts, most of which originate in mortuary contexts and thus indicate little about daily life activities. In recent years, a new method that circumvents the biased metallurgical record has been developed using microscopic groove analysis of animal butchering on zooarchaeological remains. In this paper, we present and compare our data from the southern Levant and Egypt to assess the spreading of copper and bronze metallurgy in the two regions. Our analysis allows for an initial assessment of the relative importance of metal versus stone tools for quotidian activities during the third millennium BCE in different parts of the eastern Mediterranean. Furthermore, the results have demonstrated that access to copper and metal tools for even such quotidian activities as meat processing in the eastern Mediterranean was differentiated by social status.

Introduction

Little is known about the rate of change from lithic- to metal-based (copper and bronze) technologies and how this has affected our interpretations of ancient societies. The role of metallurgy in the development of early complex societies has long been studied from an artifactual perspective. The presence of copper and bronze objects in archaeological contexts, such as needles, daggers, axes, and mirrors, in sites dating from the period of early-state formation societies across the Near East, has long been used to point to the intensification of resources, craft specialization, and social differentiation, all characteristics of a complex society (Childe 1930, 1934, 1950; Johnson 1977; Philip 1988, 1989, 2003; Philip, Clogg, and Dungworth 2003; Sanders, Wright, and McCormick Adams 1984; Wenke 1989; Wright, Neely, and Johnson 1975; Wright 1986). The focus on metal objects is, in fact, part of the bias that archaeologists working in the region have toward elite and public contexts and associated artifacts. Given that non-elite (lower) strata of early state societies in the eastern Mediterranean had limited access to goods signaling higher status affiliation (e.g., metals), only part of the picture is archaeologically visible.

There is a growing number of studies across the Near East, Europe, and elsewhere in the eastern Mediterranean, which demonstrate that stone tools continue to be of great importance during the Bronze Age and later periods, particularly in non-elite quotidian activities (e.g., Blitzer 1995; Carter 2004a, b; Dierckx 2008; Eriksen 2010; Greenfield 2017;

Khalaily 2008; Rosen 1997). This begs the question: what types of raw materials used for making tools commonly served utilitarian purposes during this critical time in the evolution of complex societies in the eastern Mediterranean region?

The quantity and range of ancient metal goods having survived degradation processes are likely a low fraction of the original deposited amount (Greenfield 1999, 2013; Olsen 1988a). This is concerning since most studies of the origins and spread of metallurgy rely upon the few metal artifacts recovered from archaeological context (Chernykh 1992; Levy and Shalev 1989; Moorey 1988, 1994a; Shephard 1980; Tylecote 1986, 1987, 1992). In fact, metal finds are recovered within a very restricted range of depositional contexts, such as hoards and burials. (Harding 2000; Philip 1988; Tadmor et al. 1995). Moreover, very few metal objects come from living floors in settlements where they were used in daily life (Philip 1989, 2008; Taylor 1993). It is thus difficult to document social changes (i.e., complex society) based only on evidence from copper objects (Eriksen 2010) when stone tool use evidence suggests continued use by the majority of the population (Greenfield 2013).

The frequency of metal objects in domestic contexts, particularly from the Early Bronze Age, is exceptionally lower than that of stone tools. For example, the excavations at Tell eṣ-Ṣâfi/Gath recovered only two pieces of copper objects among hundreds of chipped stone tools from the same Early Bronze Age levels at the site (Manclossi and Rosen in press; Manclossi and Rosen 2017; Eliyahu-Behar and Yahalom-Mack in press). In Egypt, only 5% of copper objects from the Old Kingdom derive from settlement contexts, while 95% were recovered from tomb contexts (Abreu de Sousa 2020, 86–87; Odler 2016).

An alternative approach has been pioneered over the past two decades to explore the impact of the development or adoption of metal tools for use in quotidian activities in emerging complex societies in the Near East. This twofold approach includes evaluating and combining the archaeological evidence (including objects, text, and iconography) with zooarchaeology (analysis of animal remains from archaeological contexts). In this approach, the ancient evidence of tool use for animal butchery is reconstructed through microscopic examination of butchering marks on animal bones. These are utilized as a proxy measure for the frequency of stone versus metal butchering implements (Greenfield 1999, 2006, 2013). The advantage of this method is that it allows for investigating whether metal or stone butchering tools were used to service all or only some elements of society. By investigating such a quotidian activity as animal carcass processing (i.e., slaughtering, skinning, dismemberment, disarticulation, and filleting), it is possible to investigate whether stone or metal was widely used even among the lower strata of society in Egypt and the Levant. The results allow for contemplating the effect (or lack) of the introduction of metallurgy into local societies, as well as for an increased understanding of the role that bronze metallurgy played in the development of complex societies.

In this paper, we use a microscopic zooarchaeological approach to document the continued use of stone and/or its replacements by metal tools for quotidian activities in Old Kingdom Egypt and Early Bronze (EB) southern Levant. Slice marks on animal bones are employed as a proxy measure for the use of either chipped stone or metal (copper-based) blades for animal butchery. Previously collected data from the EB of the southern Levant are compared with newly collected data from the Old Kingdom in Egypt to assess the use of copper-based tools for animal butchery during the Egyptian Old Kingdom. This is the first time such analyses have been conducted on Egyptian material. Data from the Fourth Dynasty pyramid builders' complexes (i.e., the Kromer Dump) are compared with the data from contemporary assemblages in the southern Levant. The Kromer Dump is used as a case study to evaluate the adoption of metallurgy at a state level as it is a "company town" designed for support of elite state-level activities (i.e., to build the pyramid complexes of the Fourth Dynasty).

Zooarchaeology and Slice Mark Analysis: A Method for Monitoring the Use of Metal and Retention of Stone Tools

Slice Mark Morphology

One available way to examine the development of metallurgy is through the faunal remains. Slice marks on animal bones can be identified as a butchering-related slicing activity made with a sharp tool, and their criteria have long been defined and tested by various analysts (Fig. 1) (Greenfield 1999; Olsen 1988b; Potts and Shipman 1981; Shipman 1981; Walker 1978; Walker and Long 1977).

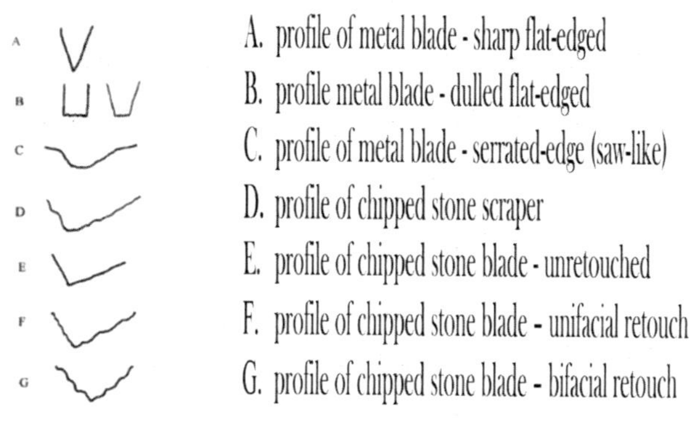

Figure 1: Greenfield's protocols for stone and metal slice mark morphology (cf. Greenfield 2013).

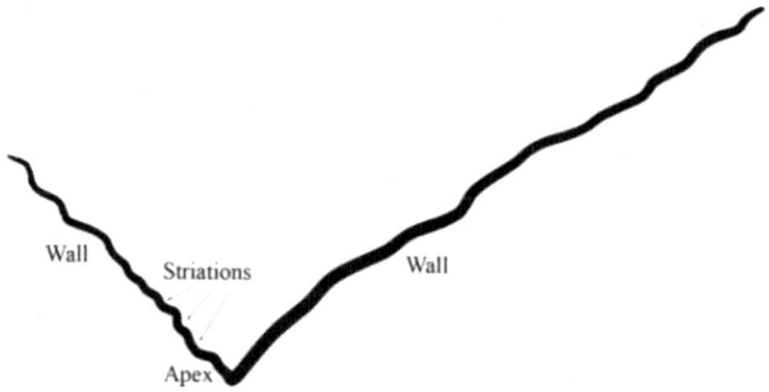

Figure 2: Example of a slice mark profile with the walls, apex, and striations.

Also, the criteria for identifying tool types, based upon the microscopic morphology of butchering slice marks, are fairly straightforward and are now being replicated with AI and other quantitative studies (Abe et al. 2002; Bello, Parfitt, and Stringer 2009; Cifuentes-Alcobendas and Domínguez-Rodrigo 2019; Courtenay et al. 2018; Domínguez-Rodrigo et al. 2021; Domínguez-Rodrigo et al. 2020; Kooi and Fairgrieve 2013; Maté-González et al. 2018). Simply put, there are clear morphological differences between slice marks caused by chipped stone or metal tools. The impression created by a metal or stone knife blade (or flake) on the bone can be distinguished by differences in several characteristics: apex, wall, and lateral striations (Fig. 2).

Metal-based tool implements leave a clear, straight, deep, V-shaped or |_|-shaped (if dull) impression on the bone (Fig. 1A–B). The apex is usually straight, and there are few (if any) lateral striations. In contrast, chipped stone tools create a greater variety of shapes since they are more complex (Fig. 1E–G). Thus, they display a variety of characteristics depending on the type of tool used in the butchering process. Generally, chipped stone tools have shallow apexes with rough, wavy, and irregular walls. There are invariably one or more lateral striations on one or both walls, depending on whether it is unifacially or bifacially produced and retouched. The variety of shapes among chipped stone implements that can be used for animal butchery leaves an equal variety of impressions on the bone. Stone tool production methods (i.e., unifacial, bifacial, unretouched, and retouched) will result in different morphological characteristics in the groove as they slice into bones.

Microscopic Approach to Zooarchaeology

All bones discussed in the present analysis were visually examined through an optical microscope for any evidence of slice marks. Samples with slice marks were further subject to microscopic and SEM analysis to identify the morphology of these marks. Following the protocols set by Greenfield (1999), the method was applied to bones from the Levant and Egypt to determine if stone or metal-based tools were adopted in animal butchery during the Early Bronze Age.

Two forms of microscopic analyses were adopted to achieve accurate results. First, a light optical microscope was used to initially identify the morphology of the slice mark following established guidelines (Walker and Long 1977; Walker 1978). Next, another level of microscopic analysis was conducted using a Scanning Electron Microscope (SEM). The SEM provides a depth of field and resolution that allows for a much more accurate identification of tool type (Olsen 1988b, 358; Potts and Shipman 1981; Shipman 1981; Shipman and Rose 1988).

Without microscopy, identifying tool type in slice marks is mostly guesswork; this is particularly true when fine-grained chipped stone tools (e.g., those made from obsidian) are used (Greenfield and Marciniak 2019). Greenfield's (1999) results not only refined earlier research but also demonstrated that this analysis method can be applied to answer broad questions, such as the transition from stone to metal tools in butchering across sites within a region (e.g., Greenfield 2013) and also between regions and continents (e.g., Greenfield 2018). Thus, this method is useful for investigating the development of metallurgy for quotidian purposes on a regional scale.

Based on a series of previous research, it is now understood that the transition from stone to metal tools for butchering began to occur on a large scale only during the Middle Bronze Age in the Levant and central Balkans (Greenfield 1999, 2002, 2008, 2013, 2017, 2021; Greenfield and Brown 2016; Greenfield, Brown, and Miroschedji 2021; Greenfield and Marciniak 2019), and in the Late Bronze Age in central Poland (Greenfield 2018; Marciniak and Greenfield 2013). However, certain areas of the Near East (i.e., Anatolia) lagged in the transition to metal tools for butchering since obsidian was easily available and sharper than metal (Greenfield and Chaput 2021; Greenfield and Marciniak 2019). Thus, it is clear that the transition did not occur uniformly throughout the Early Bronze Age but that each region must be investigated separately.

Previous Studies on Utilitarian Metallurgy in the Southern Levant

Early copper-based metallurgy in the Near East has its origins in the shaping of metal objects, such as beads, during the Pre-pottery Neolithic. Such early metal items were largely used for display purposes and quickly spread throughout the Near East (Greenfield 2008; Muhly 1980, 1988, 2011; North 1955; Tylecote 1992). During the Chalcolithic, a local copper mining and smelting industry developed in the southern Levant, allowing for new shapes (Garfinkel et al. 2014; Hauptmann 2007; Levy and Shalev 1989; Shalev 1994; Shugar and Gohm 2011). It has been suggested that the development of the early copper industry in Egypt had its roots in the Levant and neighboring areas of Sinai, where large copper mines are located (Adams 1997, 2002; Adams and Genz 1995; Ben-Yosef et al. 2016; Golden 2002, 2010; Hauptmann et al. 2015; Levy et al. 2002; Philip, Clogg, and Dungworth 2003; Rosenberg et al. 2020). However, early copper objects have been found in Egypt dating to the Chalcolithic, suggesting that a local industry had already developed concurrently with the Early Bronze Age (Odler 2015).

While the alloying of copper with other metals is an innovation of the Early Bronze Age, most copper objects from this period are not yet alloyed with tin or arsenic (Hauptmann and Pernicka 2004; Moorey 1988, 1994b). Alloying strengthens the material and makes it more widely usable for daily quotidian tasks. Consequently, it was during the Early Bronze Age in the Levant that the presence of metal for quotidian tasks began to increase and displace chipped stone tools. However, it was not until the Middle Bronze Age that metallurgy began to be truly quotidian in the southern Levant, across the Near East, and beyond (Greenfield 2008, 2013; Greenfield 2017; Greenfield and Greenfield 2018; Greenfield and Marciniak 2019; Manclossi, Rosen, and Lehmann 2018; Rosen 1984, 1997;).

The transition from stone-based to metal-based quotidian technology can be a slow or rapid process that differs between cultures. The adoption of bronze metallurgy in the Levant has proven to have occurred much later than previously expected; it took over a millennium from the earliest bronze objects for chipped stone tools to be replaced. Other types of stone tools for quotidian purposes continued in use throughout the Bronze Age (Greenfield 2013, 2017; Manclossi, Rosen, and Böeda 2019; Rosen 1997; Rosenfeld, Ilani, and Dvorachek 1997). While traditional methods of tool use (i.e., chipped stone, such as flint) continued well into the latter parts of the Bronze Age across the Near East, the ratio between stone and metal objects changed over time. In some domains, stone tools were rapidly replaced (e.g., prestige or display items), while in others, there was a slow replacement over time (e.g., food processing) (Greenfield 2013, 2017; Manclossi, Rosen, and Böeda 2019; Rosen 1997).

Studies of stone versus metal use focusing on the Levant involved well-curated and temporally controlled samples (Greenfield 2013, 2017). Over 20000 bones from various settlement contexts were examined. Initially, the data were not well separated within the Early Bronze Age. Reanalysis of the stratigraphic associations of remains from older excavations (e.g., from Tell es-Sultan/Jericho) and addition of new data from more modern scientific and systematic excavations (Tall Zirā'a, Tell eṣ-Ṣâfi/Gath) suggest that while a few metal slice marks appear early in the EBA, it is only toward its end (during the latter half of the EB IV) that metal slice marks begin to appear consistently, but in very small quantities (Table 1) (Eliyahu-Behar and Yahalom-Mack 2018; Greenfield et al. 2022). Metal chop marks are consistently found only for the MB, and in small frequencies until the Iron Age (e.g. Tall Zirā'a, Jordan, Greenfield et al. 2022). While daggers and axes appear prior to this EBA phase, they are clearly not used for animal butchery since they are made of copper. Tin-bronze daggers begin to appear in the Intermediate Bronze (Nigro et al. 2018). Metal knife marks become more common

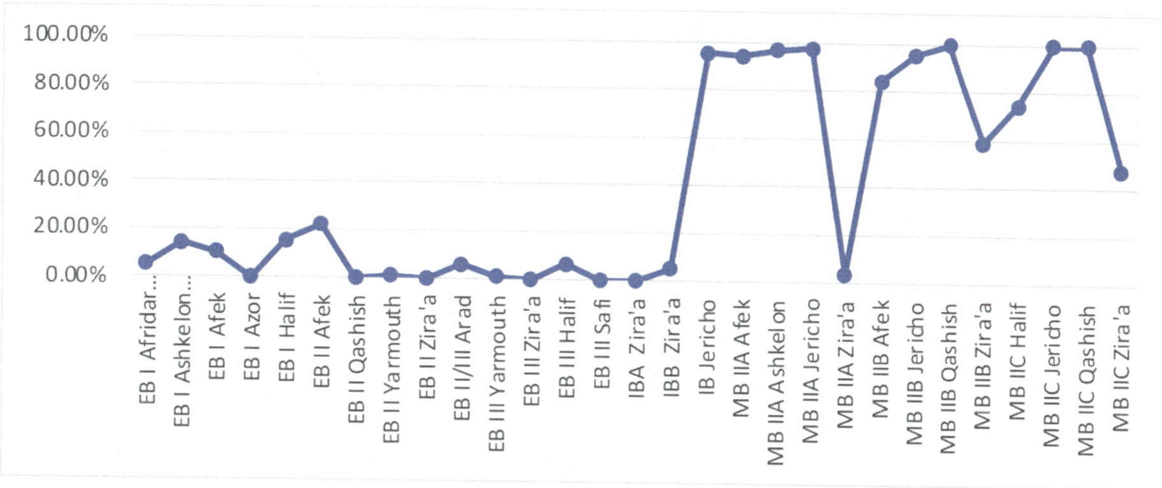

FIGURE 3: Histogram showing the quantitative distribution of metal butchering marks from southern Levantine sites during the Early and Middle Bronze Ages. Current reanalysis of the Jericho material suggests that the high frequency of metal in the IB is not supported.

during the Middle Bronze (MB), where there is a c. 50% average distribution between metal and stone marks (Greenfield, Beller, and Gaastra 2021; Greenfield et al. 2016). This pattern coincides with the development of bronze knives late in the EB (Moorey 1994b). This temporal pattern makes sense, given that a bronze knife is much harder and more durable than a copper one (Greenfield 1999).

The Development of Metallurgy in Pre-Dynastic to Old Kingdom Egypt (2592–2153 BCE)

The Old Kingdom (OK) marks a period of major advancement for Egypt, when massive monumental architecture requiring plentiful resources and a large labor force is commissioned by the kings. Also, foreign missions expand borders and supply luxury items and resources (e.g., copper ingots) through trade resources (Baud 2010, 70; Muhs 2016, 8; Odler 2015; Rosińska-Balik et al. 2015; Wengrow 2005, 14, 138). These projects are associated with innovative technologies, such as the development of a local copper industry to make fine objects for the elites to display, both in life and death (Cowell 1986; Garland and Bannister 1927, 33; Lucas 1927; for a corpus of objects see Odler 2016; Ogden 2000; Richards 2005; Scheel 1989, 34–46).

Unlike in the southern Levant, visual and textual evidence of copper production in Egypt abound and suggest that production of copper in Egypt was multi-layered. It involved individuals at various levels of society, including miners, metalsmiths, overseers, administrators, and transporters (Abreu

EB I Afridar combined	5.26%
EB I Ashkelon marina	14.29%
EB I Afek	10.53
EB I Azor	0
EB I Halif	15.38
EB II Afek	22.22
EB II Qashish	0
EB II Yarmouth	1.15
EB II Zira'a	0
EB II/III Arad	6.08
EB III Yarmouth	1.15
EB III Zira'a	0
EB III Halif	6.64
EB III Safi	0
IBA Zira'a	0
IBB Zira'a	5.26
IB Jericho	95.45
MB IIA Afek	94.29
MB IIA Ashkelon	97.06
MB IIA Jericho	97.87
MB IIA Zira'a	3.81
MB IIB Afek	84.62
MB IIB Jericho	95.45
MB IIB Qashish	100
MB IIB Zira'a	59.09
MB IIC Halif	74.7
MB IIC Jericho	100
MB IIC Qashish	100
MB IIC Zira'a	48.05

TABLE 1: Frequency distribution of metal slice marks on animal bones from southern Levantine sites. Data are derived from each of Greenfield's many studies (summarized in Greenfield 2013; Greenfield and Brown 2016; Greenfield, Beller, and Gaastra 2021). Data from Jericho are currently being reanalyzed with finer chronological control than previously published (Greenfield 2005). Hence, the Jericho data reported here are preliminary and not reliable.

de Sousa 2020, 72–87). Recent studies on the smelting practices of the later Middle Kingdom suggest that a variety of fuel types were used in copper manufacturing (Verly et al. 2021), which would have required several individuals at different social strata to manage logistically. On top of these activities (Delage 2017; Hauptmann 2007, 8), the King's administration oversaw the production of precious resources, including copper, and heavily guarded its copper stores (likely in a centralized treasury), at least in the later periods of Egyptian history (Cour-Marty 1997; Desplancques 2006, 157, 396).

The *Chaîne Opératoire* of copper development in Egypt during the Pre-Dynastic and until the Old Kingdom demonstrates that mining, production, and distribution efforts were administered by the crown and its officials, who oversaw the entire operation (Klemm and Klemm 2013; Odler and Kmošek 2020, 152). The earliest mining expedition recorded for the Eastern Desert and Sinai regions is from the late Pre-Dynastic period (Abdel-Motelib et al., 2012; Tallet, 2018; Tallet and Laisney, 2012). Another early mining expedition occurred in the First Dynasty (likely by Semerkhet) in the Sinai region (Lucas 1927, 167; Tallet 2010). Inscriptions from mining or production sites suggest extensive mining operations occurred through Dynasties 1–6 (Emery 1963; Klemm and Klemm 2008, 1685; Lucas 1927). Copper became a highly desired commodity by the First Dynasty, and by the Third Dynasty the Egyptian court secured *"control over the copper mines of south-western Sinai"* (Wengrow 2005: 147; see also Stager 1992, 35). A large number of sites in the Sinai and Eastern Desert yielded archaeological evidence of early copper working (Odler and Kmošek 2020, 196). The evidence for smelting and copper production in the Nubian site of Buhen, suggests that areas to the south were also controlled by the Egyptian state, where a copper smelting production area comprising three furnaces was found (Lucas 1927, 163–165; Muhly 1999, 630). However, despite the location of mining in Egypt, the royal agenda during the Old Kingdom included the control of copper mining, production, storage, and circulation (Cour-Marty 1997; Desplancques 2006; Wengrow 2005, 146–147). Rare resources, including copper, were purposefully reserved for royal officials and individuals from the higher strata of society (Baud 2010, 72; Tillmann 1999, 314).

The consumption of copper during the Early Dynastic and Old Kingdom is materially evident from artifacts in both household and funerary contexts. The first uses of copper in Egypt were cosmetic (Lucas 1959, 245–249). Slowly, the range of uses expanded also to include more functional quotidian tasks (e.g., copper chisels for stone working). The earliest metal objects appear among grave goods during the Neolithic Badarian period (c.4500–3500 BCE) (i.e., copper beads recovered from Grave 596 at el-Mustagidda; Muhly 1999, 629; Scheel 1989, 8), Chalcolithic Naqada I–II cultures (c. 4000–3200 BCE) (i.e., axes, adzes, chisels, razors, knives) (Needler 1984, 280–282, cat. 180–183), and Early Dynastic, Old Kingdom, and later periods (for a corpus of Old Kingdom copper objects see Kobusiewicz 2015, 1–2; Odler 2016). Copper knives resembling those used in animal butchery iconography are found in tombs dating from the Early Dynastic and Old Kingdom periods (Maddin et al. 1984; Muhly 1999; Odler 2016, 66–69; Petrie 1913). The question is whether they were used only to service the elite (particularly in mortuary contexts) or for more quotidian tasks among the general population. It is even questionable whether objects, such as knives, were used in the same manner that their name suggests, considering that unalloyed copper knives would have been relatively soft and easily damaged.

The adoption of metal-based tools for quotidian tasks in Egypt is similar to that in neighboring regions in that it was a slow transition over time (Graves-Brown 2010, 97). In Egypt, alloyed copper (bronze) metallurgy is thought to have been adopted for quotidian purposes during the Middle and New Kingdoms (Graves-Brown 2010, 83; Ikram 1995, 65–69; Kobusiewicz 2015, 13). However, chipped stone (flint) tools continued being used alongside copper tools throughout the Old and Middle Kingdoms. It is only in the New Kingdom that bronze technology is widely adopted for quotidian tasks (Graves-Brown 2010, 97). This study is the first of its kind conducted on Egyptian faunal remains and is only representative of a non-elite context organized for and supplied by the Egyptian state (i.e., a company town). Despite an increase of copper objects from the Old Kingdom, compared to earlier periods, it cannot be assumed that the increased use of copper reflects the replacement of stone tools, particularly in quotidian activities such as animal butchery.

The disparity in copper finds between elite and lower stratum contexts is a gap that must be studied to understand the impact of metallurgical

Element	Bovines	%	Caprines	%
Calcaneus	0	0.00%	1	0.61%
Cranial	2	3.39%	0	0.00%
Femur	0	0.00%	3	1.82%
Fibula	0	0.00%	0	0.00%
Humerus	0	0.00%	14	8.48%
Innominate	1	1.69%	9	5.45%
Long bone fragment	19	32.20%	1	0.61%
Mandible	4	6.78%	11	6.67%
Metacarpal	2	3.39%	6	3.64%
Metatarsal	0	0.00%	11	6.67%
Phalanx	0	0.00%	1	0.61%
Radius	0	0.00%	23	13.94%
Rib	19	32.20%	44	26.67%
Scapula	6	10.17%	8	4.85%
Tibia	0	0.00%	18	10.91%
Ulna	0	0.00%	4	2.42%
Vertebra	6	10.17%	11	6.67%
Total limbs (bNISP)	**59**	100.00%	**165**	100.00%

Table 2: Frequency distribution of osteological elements for each taxon (bNISP).

development and consumption upon the development of Old Kingdom society. Most copper objects from the Early Dynastic and Old Kingdom periods derive from funerary contexts in tombs (Maddin et al. 1984; Muhly 1999; Odler 2016, 66–69; Petrie 1913), while evidence for household consumption of copper is limited to a few isolated finds from the Pre-Dynastic to the Old Kingdom (Odler 2016, 66–69). While it can be argued that the absence of copper objects in settlement contexts may be due to melting, reuse, or degrading over time, its absence or minimal presence in household contexts raises the question of what the lower strata of society used for quotidian purposes, such as food processing. This question is discussed below from the perspective of the workers' settlement at Giza.

Case Study: Giza and the Kromer Dump in Context

The zooarchaeological assemblage from the Kromer Dump (KRO) found during excavations at Giza, Egypt, is used as a case study to investigate the above questions. Austrian prehistorian Karl Kromer excavated the site between 1971 and 1975 and cleared 1550 cubic meters (up to a depth of 6.5 meters) of a settlement that contained a 4500-year-old trash dump (midden) on the high western slope of the Gebel el-Qibli (Southern Mound), south of the Heit el-Ghurab (HeG) (Kromer 1978). The mound is composed of trash dumped by the workers who built the Fourth Dynasty pyramids on the Giza Plateau. It includes pottery, flint blades, mud bricks, faunal remains, bone implements, mud sealings, and copper implements (Kromer 1978).

In 2018, AERA re-excavated Kromer's Dump (Sondage 185=Kromer Dump=KRO) and determined that it contained the rubbish from the nearby seasonal camp of the workers who built the pyramids of Pharaoh Khafre, and possibly Menkaure, of the Fourth Dynasty, representing over a 60-year time span (Lehner 2018).

Data and Sample Size

The faunal remains from KRO provide a rich source of information on animal consumption and butchery practices (Redding 2020, 51–54). A vast number of mammal bones (35512 fragments) were unearthed (Redding 2020, 51). A large share of these included proximal and distal limb shaft fragments (femur, humerus, tibia, radius, metapodia).

Sample #	Taxa	Element	SEM raw material identification	Stone Tool production type	Stone tool retouch type	Blade type	bNISP	Type of butchering mark	Type of slicing instrument
16a	Caprine	Femur	Stone	Unifacial	Not = |/	Unifacial	1	Slice	Blade
16b	Caprine	Femur	Stone	Unifacial	Not = |/	Unifacial		Slice	Blade
144	Caprine	Vertebrae	Stone	Unifacial	Not = |/	Unifacial	1	Slice	Blade
145	Caprine	Vertebrae	Stone	Unifacial	Not = |/	Unifacial	1	Slice	Blade
148	Caprine	Vertebrae	Stone	Unifacial	Not = |/	Unifacial	1	Slice	Blade
172a	Bovine	Vertebrae	Stone	Unifacial	Not = |/	Unifacial	1	Slice	Blade
172b	Bovine	Vertebrae	Stone	Unifacial	Not = |/	Unifacial		Slice	Blade
172c	Bovine	Vertebrae	Stone	Unifacial	Not = |/	Unifacial		Slice	Blade
174	Bovine	Vertebrae	Stone	Unifacial	Not = |/	Unifacial	1	Slice	Blade
192	Bovine	Rib	Stone	Unifacial	Unidentifiable	Unifacial	1	Slice	Blade
193	Bovine	Rib	Stone	Unifacial	Not = |/	Unifacial	1	Slice	Blade
199	Bovine	Rib	Stone	Unifacial	Not = |/	Unifacial	1	Slice	Blade
204a	Bovine	Rib	Stone	Unifacial	Bifacial - V	Bifacial	1	Slice	Blade
204b	Bovine	Rib	Stone	Unifacial	Bifacial - V	Bifacial		Slice	Blade
204c	Bovine	Rib	Stone	Unifacial	Bifacial - V	Bifacial		Slice	Blade
205	Bovine	Long bone	Stone	Unifacial	Bifacial - V	Bifacial	1	Slice	Blade
208	Bovine	Long bone	Stone	Unifacial	Bifacial - V	Bifacial	1	Slice	Blade
220a	Bovine	Long bone	Stone	Unifacial	Bifacial - V	Bifacial	1	Slice	Blade
220b	Bovine	Long bone	Stone	Unifacial	Bifacial - V	Bifacial		Slice	Blade
220c	Bovine	Long bone	Stone	Unifacial	Bifacial - V	Bifacial		Slice	Blade
220d	Bovine	Long bone	Stone	Unifacial	Bifacial - V	Bifacial		Slice	Blade
220e	Bovine	Long bone	Stone	Unifacial	Bifacial - V	Bifacial		Slice	Blade

TABLE 3: Detailed information on each of the butchering incidences examined in the SEM (BI). Note the difference between the initial identification under Dino-Lite and the confirmed SEM identification.

Many of the faunal specimens displayed some evidence of butchery, such as slices, chops, and/ or skinning (butchered individuals=bNISP). Over 5000 specimens were examined (50% of the total faunal mammalian assemblage), of which only 224 specimens had slice marks (Table 2). The 224 specimens (bNISP) were examined under an optical binocular microscope, and those thought to bear metal slice marks (a total of 13 specimens) were selected for further examination under SEM.

Such butchery extent makes the Kromer Dump a valuable assemblage for the study of slice marks to determine the nature of tool types utilized in the animal butchery process at Giza. In fact, it has been suggested that the workers from the quarries consumed the proximal and distal parts of the animal in a highly nutritious stew similar to *the "Kaware*h" consumed in Egypt today (Ahmed and Redding 2021; Redding 2011). The study of the vast number of butchered animal bones from KRO has provided valuable information on animal consumption at Giza during the Fourth Dynasty, particularly by those individuals who worked in the quarry and may have resided in a settlement within the Tafla Bowl.

RESULTS

Based on the light optical microscopic and SEM levels of analysis, only chipped stone tools, such as blades and flakes, accounted for each of the slice marks on the specimens. No metal slice marks were present on the specimens identified. Furthermore, a variety of stone blade types appeared: the butchery of sheep and goats was conducted with unifacially produced chipped stone blades, while cattle were butchered using larger bifacially produced chipped stone blades (Table 3).

The samples studied under SEM demonstrated clear characteristics of chipped stone-tool-based slice marks. These included the presence of lateral striations (either on one or both sides), uneven apex, and asymmetrical profiles characteristic of unifacially or bifacially produced chipped stone blades (Greenfield 2006; Greenfield and Brown 2016; Shipman 1981). Lateral striations were present on one or both sides of the slice marks in all the samples examined under SEM. Their presence suggests that most of the chipped stone tool flakes or blades employed in animal butchery were made by unifacial production, without retouch (FIG. 4). A small number of marks also exhibited bifacial retouch, but these were for butchering of larger animals (i.e., cattle).

Two interesting conclusions can be drawn from the current study of slice marks. First, the absence of metal-based slice marks on the faunal remains suggests an exclusive use of a stone-based tool technology in animal butchery by the pyramid workers at the quarry settlement at Giza during the Old Kingdom. Second, a variety of stone-based tool types were adopted in animal butchery. These two observations shed light on the tool types and their raw material adopted in the animal butchering process during the Old Kingdom.

The raw material of the blades depicted in two-dimensional animal butchery scenes from the Egyptian Old and Middle Kingdoms has previously been suggested to be flint (Ikram 1995, 63–69). The

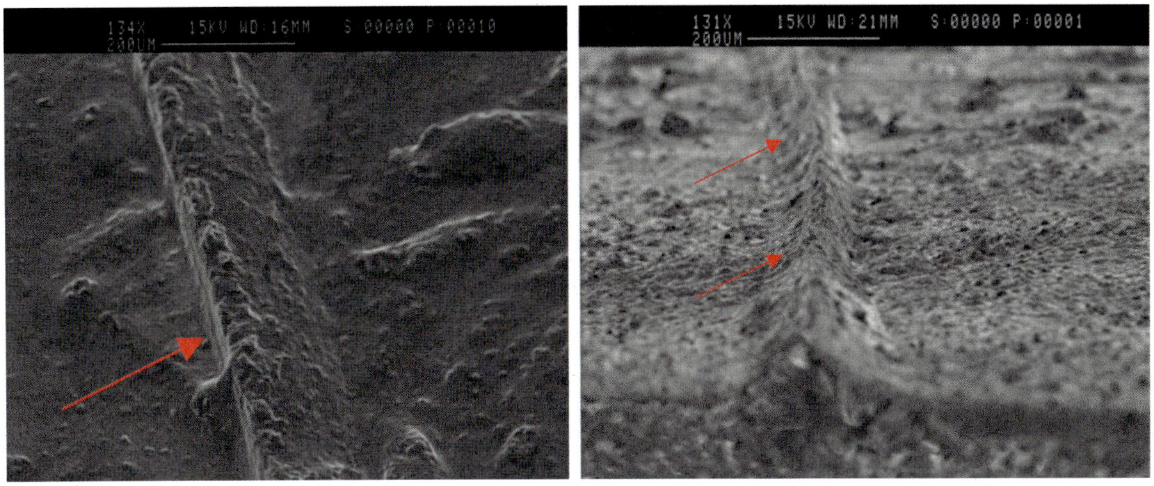

FIGURE 4: SEM Micrography of a unifacially produced slice mark. LEFT: KRO sample 174, Bos taurus, slice mark found on the spinous process fragment, thoracic vertebra. 200μ side angle. Note the clear steep slope on one side (red arrow). RIGHT: SEM Micrography of a unifacially produced slice mark. KRO sample 144, Ovis/Capra, slice mark found on the spinous process fragment, thoracic vertebra. 200μ side angle. The striations (denoted by the arrows) are present in these images and are reflective of a stone unifacial retouched knife.

knife blade in the Old Kingdom scenes that depict the slaughter of cattle with a knife is believed to be a chipped stone knife (e.g., Tomb of Nianchenesut, Saqqara. Old Kingdom, AS5967, Tomb 67, PM III. II: 696). The KRO case study data corroborates the ancient evidence and overwhelmingly demonstrates that butchering was also conducted using chipped stone tool blades in non-religious contexts.

Conclusions and Discussion

In the southern Levant, the distribution of metal objects vastly differs from that in neighboring Egypt during the third millennium BCE. In the latter, metal objects are largely recovered in mortuary contexts (Odler 2016, 66–69). During this time, copper use was limited to elite activities (which is why it shows up mainly in funerary deposits) or by the state for the construction of Pharaonic projects. However, whether the consumption of copper objects was restricted to these parameters is unknown.

In the southern Levant, by contrast, mortuary contexts are few and far between (Greenberg 2019, 336–338; Richard 2003, 175; Steiner and Killebrew 2014, 270), and most metal objects are recovered from settlements (Montanari 2015). While the aggregate data from the southern Levant allows us to infer the behavior of the lower strata, the data from Egypt also allows inference of elite behavior. Hence, the data from the two regions complement each other.

Metal as a Mechanism for Change

> "Technological change…is not always a progressive sequence of innovations but can also be characterised by continued use of traditional methods or artefacts, and even the surprisingly frequent re-introduction of techniques that might be assumed to become outmodeled" (Shaw 2012:1).

This statement by Ian Shaw stresses how technological advancements can be heavily influenced by traditional *and* progressive viewpoints. Indeed, in Egypt and the Levant, chipped stone tools continue to be extensively used through the development and rare consumption of copper tools. This pattern concurs with what is known about the relationship between technological innovations that ultimately replace older technologies (Edgerton 2008, 212). In fact, according to the evidence, the adoption of newer technologies (in this case, copper tools) in the Early Bronze Age was limited to high-status individuals or their administrators.

The Implications of Restricted Access to Metal in the Development of Early Complex Societies

Individuals who reside in a complex society typically have "differential access to and/or control of economic, productive, or symbolic resources and the mechanisms of enhancing socioeconomic status and the methods of displaying it …" (Richards

2005, 13). The shift from a socially egalitarian to a stratified, complex society is driven by several factors or mechanisms that serve as agents for change. Differential access to metal goods reinforces changes happening in the larger society. Metal enhances socioeconomic status through differential access to resources. Moreover, the distribution of copper objects in burials differs among the ranks of Egyptian officials (Kmošek et al. 2018, 205). The development of metallurgy and the adoption of metal-based tools enhances the social changes occurring in Egypt and the Levant—it supports and enhances the status quo among the higher-status individuals and differentiates them from the lower strata of society.

Social Differentiation in the Southern Levant

Evidence for social differentiation in the EB of southern Levant and metal consumption appears to play a role in the development of early complex society. In his description of EB II–III Jericho, for instance, Nigro stated that

> "The emergence of a distinguished ruling class, basically evidenced by funerary customs in tombs, as well as the functional differentiation of public areas within the city … point to an increased social complexity within, however, the framework of a strong concentration of wealth, power and ideology in the hands of the emerging elite" (Nigro 2014a, 71).

This may explain why the IB Jericho butchering data is so out of sync with that of most of the region. Differential access to goods, such as tin-bronze (Nigro et al. 2018), seems to occur much earlier at Jericho than in nearby settlements in the Jordan Valley drainage (e.g., Tall Zirā'a) (Greenfield, Beller, and Gaastra 2021). Others discussing changes in the Levant from a social perspective also recognize that society became more complex socially during the EB II and III, particularly in larger cities (Chesson 2019). However, given the dearth of EB tombs across most of the southern Levant beyond the Jordan Valley, it is difficult to make pan-regional comparisons with Jericho. Each major settlement has yielded various copper artifacts, but they are found in both elite (Nigro et al. 2018; Greenberg 2019) and non-elite residential contexts, such as at Tell eṣ-Ṣâfi/Gath (Eliyahu-Behar and Yahalom-Mack, in press; Greenfield 2021). The absence of a pan-regional study of EB copper and bronze metal tools across the southern Levant impedes any definitive comparison with Egypt. The lack of EB I–III iconography or tomb contexts in the southern Levant does not allow for an in-depth understanding of how the use of early metal objects coincided with the development of early state-level societies. Contrary to Egypt, with its rich mortuary archaeological record, it is difficult to distinguish between elite and non-elite use of metal in the southern Levant. It is not yet clear if Jericho is an exception or the rule. If Jericho is the rule, the use of copper by elite members of society, as exemplified in Old Kingdom society, also becomes apparent in the Levant (Nigro 2019, 93).[1]

Interconnections and Metallurgy

The presence of exchange, particularly of prestige items to and from the Levant and Egypt, suggests an interregional trade network that included copper (Nigro 2014b). Nigro stated that at Jericho,

> "Increasing wealth, reflected into technological progress, material culture standardization and functional specialization supported the city interaction on an extra-regional scenario, enhancing exchange of typical Jericho products with prestigious items both from Egypt (on a route active since EB I), and Northern Levant (Syria and the Lebanese coast)" (Nigro 2014a).

From this perspective, Nigro suggests a world-systems view of copper distribution routes (Nigro 2014b), similar to what Algaze (1993) proposed for Chalcolithic Mesopotamia. The Levant served as the periphery of the copper world (supplier). In fact, the recent metallurgical studies of copper objects from Early Dynastic and Old Kingdom Egypt (Martin Odler, this volume, and previous work) suggest that some early copper objects came from as far as Anatolia (Kmošek et al. 2018; Odler and Kmošek 2020, 69). While the use of archaeometallurgy to understand the interconnections between Egypt, the Levant, Anatolia, and elsewhere in the Eastern Mediterranean has proven useful for tracing exchange routes, the adoption of a zooarchaeological perspective (as presented here) complements this perspective—it furthers our understanding by being more socially inclusive, being able to see that access to non-local goods was socially differentiated. Thus, in conclusion, we suggest that such resources were more likely to be available to the "state," elite individuals, and/or officials or individuals with the capabilities of procuring them in early complex societies (e.g., merchants acting on behalf of the state). As can be seen in our discussion above, the spread of new technologies (e.g., metallurgy) is a more complex process than previously conceptualized. It requires rethinking basic concepts within archaeology about the transmission of new knowledge across time and space (Straub 2009).

Based on the results of this analysis from Egypt and previous research in other regions, the transition from stone to metal tools for butchering began, on a large scale, only during the Middle Bronze Age, in the Levant and the central Balkans (Greenfield 1999, 2002, 2008, 2013, 2017, 2021; Greenfield and Brown 2016; Greenfield, Brown, and Miroschedji 2021; Greenfield and Marciniak 2019), and, in the Late Bronze Age, in central Poland (Greenfield 2017; Greenfield and Marciniak 2021; Marciniak and Greenfield 2013). Certain areas of the Near East (i.e., Anatolia) lagged in the transition to metal tools for butchering since obsidian was easily available and sharper than metal (Greenfield and Chaput 2021; Greenfield and Marciniak 2019). It is clear, thus, that one cannot assume the transition occurred broadly in the Early Bronze Age and that each region must be investigated separately.

Acknowledgments

The authors gratefully acknowledge the multitude of archaeologists and zooarchaeologists working in or from the southern Levant who opened their laboratories and collections for analysis here. We also gratefully acknowledge the AERA project for permission to analyze and report our analysis of the butchered faunal remains from the Kromer Dump. In particular, we would like to thank Mark Lehner and Richard Redding for making this research possible. Funds for this research were granted by the Social Science and Humanities Research Council of Canada to Haskel J. Greenfield. We also gratefully acknowledge the support provided by the University of Manitoba and St. Paul's College for making it possible to analyze the data in the Near Eastern and Biblical Archaeology Laboratory. Any errors in this paper are the responsibility of the authors.

References

Abe, Yoshiko, Curtis W. Marean, Peter John Nilssen, Zelalem Assefa, and Elizabeth C. Stone. 2002. "The Analysis of Cutmarks on Archaeofauna: A Review and Critique of Quantification Procedures, and a New Image-Analysis GIS Approach." *American Antiquity* 67(4): 643–663.

Abreu de Sousa, Eleutério. 2020. "On the Chopping Block: Animal Butchery Technologies in Old Kingdom Egypt." MA Thesis, Anthropology Department, University of Manitoba, Winnipeg (35088).

Adams, Russell B. 1997. "On Early Copper Metallurgy in the Levant: A Response to Claims of Neolithic Metallurgy." In Hans Georg K. Gebel, Zeidan Kafafi, Gary O. Rollefson (eds.), *The Prehistory of Jordan II: The Perspectives from 1997*, 651–655. Berlin: ex Oriente.

———. 2002. "From Farms to Factories: The Development of Copper Production at Faynan, Southern Jordan, during the Early Bronze Age." In Barbara S. Ottaway and Emma C. Wager (eds.), *Metals and Society: Papers from a Session Held at the European Association of Archaeologists Sixth Annual Meeting in Lisbon 2000*, 21–32. Oxford: Archaeopress.

Adams, Russell B., and Hermann Genz. 1995. "Excavations at Wadi Fidan 4: A Chalcolithic Village Complex in the Copper Ore District of Feinan, Southern Jordan." *Palestine Exploration Quarterly* 127: 8–20.

Ahmed, Mohamed Hussein, and Richard Redding. 2021. "Faunal Remains from Excavations at the Menkaure Valley Temple (MVT-W), 2019." *Journal of the American Research Center in Egypt* 56: 17–34. DOI: https://doi.org/10.5913/jarce.56.2020.a002.

Algaze, Guillermo. 1993. *The Uruk World System: The Dynamics of Expansion of Early Mesopotamian Civilization.* Chicago: University of Chicago Press.

Baud, Michel. 2010. "The Old Kingdom." In Alan B. Lloyd (ed.), *A Companion to Ancient Egypt*, 63–80. Chichester West Sussex: Wiley–Blackwell.

Bello, Silvia M., Simon A. Parfitt, and Chris Stringer. 2009. "Quantitative Micromorphological Analyses of Cut Marks Produced by Ancient and Modern Handaxes." *Journal of Archaeological Science* 36:1869–1880.

Ben-Yosef, Erez, Aaron D. Gidding, L. Tauxe, Uri Davidovich, Mohammed Najjar, and Thomas

E. Levy. 2016. "Early Bronze Age Copper Production Systems in the Northern Arabah Valley: New Insights from Archaeomagnetic Study of Slag Deposits in Jordan and Israel." *Journal of Archaeological Science* 72: 71–84.

Blitzer, Harriet. 1995. "The Chipped Stone Industry (CS 1-96)." In Joseph W. Shaw and Maria C. Shaw (eds.), *Kommos I: The Kommos Region and Houses of the Minoan Town, Part 1: The Kommos Region, Ecology, and the Minoan Industries*, 488–496. Princeton: Princeton University Press.

Carter, Tristan. 2004a. "The Chipped Stone." In Jeffrey S. Soles (ed.), *Mochlos IC: Period III. Neopalatial Settlement on the Coast: The Artisans' Quarter and the Farmhouse at Chalinomouri*, 91–107. Philadelphia: INSTAP Academic Press.

———. 2004b. "Transformative Processes in Liminal Spaces: Craft as Ritual Action in the Throne Room Area." *British School at Athens Studies* 12: 273–282.

Chernykh, Evgeniĭ Nikolaevich. 1992. *Ancient Metallurgy in the USSR: The Early Metal Age.* Cambridge: Cambridge University Press.

Chesson, Meredith S. 2019. "The Southern Levant during the Early Bronze Age I–III." In Assaf Yasur-Landau, Eric H. Cline and Yorke Rowan (eds.), *The Social Archaeology of the Levant: From Prehistory to the Present*, 163–182. Cambridge: Cambridge University Press.

Childe, V. Gordon. 1930. *The Bronze Age.* Cambridge: Cambridge University Press.

———. 1934. *New Light on the Most Ancient Near East.* London: Routledge & Kegan Paul.

———. 1950. "The Urban Revolution." *The Town Planning Review* 21(1): 3–17.

Cifuentes-Alcobendas, Gabriel, and Manuel Domínguez-Rodrigo. 2019. "Deep Learning and Taphonomy: High Accuracy in the Classification of Cut Marks Made on Fleshed and Defleshed Bones Using Convolutional Neural Networks." *Scientific Reports* 9(1): 1–12.

Cour-Marty, M.A. 1997. "Les poids inscrits de l'Ancien Empire." In Jean-Philippe Lauer, Catherine Berger and Bernard Mathieu (eds.), *Etudes sur l'Ancien Empire et la nécropole de Saqqâra dédiées à Jean-Philippe Lauer*, 129–145. Montpellier: Université Paul Valéry-Montpellier III.

Courtenay, Lloyd A., Miguel Ángel Maté-González, Julia Aramendi, José Yravedra, González-Aguilera Diego, and Manuel Domínguez-Rodrigo. 2018. "Testing Accuracy in 2D and 3D Geometric Morphometric Methods for Cut Mark Identification and Classification." *PeerJ* 6: e5133. DOI: 10.7717/peerj.5133.

Cowell, Michael. 1986. "The Composition of Egyptian Copper-Based Metalwork." In Science in Egyptology, edited by R.A. David, 463–468. Manchester: Manchester University Press.

Delage, Christophe. 2017. "Once Upon a Time…the (hi)story of the Concept of the Chaîne Opératoire in French Prehistory." *World Archaeology* 49(2): 158–173. DOI: 10.1080/00438243.2017.1300104.

Desplancques, Sophie. 2006. *Institution du trésor des origines à la fin du moyen empire*. Paris: Presses de l'Université de Paris-Sorbonne.

Dierckx, Heidi M. C. 2008. "The Chipped Stone from Hagios Charalambos," in Excavations in the Hagios Charalambos Cave: A Preliminary Report by Philip P. Betancourt, Costis Davaras, Heidi M. C. Dierckx, Susan C. Ferrence, Jane Hickman, Panagiotis Karkanas, et al. *Hesperia* 77: 562–566.

Domínguez-Rodrigo, Manuel, Enrique Baquedano, Luciano Varela, P. Sebastián Tambusso, María Julia Melián, and Richard A. Fariña. 2021. "Deep Classification of Cut-Marks on Bones from Arroyo del Vizcaíno (Uruguay)." Proceedings of the Royal Society B 288, 1954. DOI: https://doi.org/10.1098/rspb.2021.0711.

Domínguez-Rodrigo, Manuel, Gabriel Cifuentes-Alcobendas, Blanca Jiménez-García, Natalia Abellán, Marcos Pizarro-Monzo, Elia Organista, and Enrique Baquedano. 2020. "Artificial Intelligence Provides Greater Accuracy in the Classification of Modern and Ancient Bone Surface Modifications." *Scientific Reports* 10, 18862. DOI: https://doi.org/10.1038/s41598-020-75994-7.

Edgerton, David. 2008. *The Shock of the Old: Technology and Global History Since 1900.* London: Profile Books.

Eliyahu-Behar, Adi, and Naama Yahalom-Mack. 2018. "Metallurgical Investigations at Tell eṣ-Ṣâfi/Gath." In Itzhaq Shai, Jeffrey R. Chadwick, Louise Hitchcock, Amit Dagan, Chris McKinny and Joe Uziel (eds.), *Tell it in Gath: Studies in the History and Archaeology of Israel: Essays in honor of Aren M. Maeir on the Occasion of the Sixtieth Birthday*, 811–815. Münster: Zaphon.

Eliyahu-Behar, Adi, and Naama Yahalom-Mack. In press. "Copper Objects and their Provenance." In Itzhaq Shai, Haskel J. Greenfield and Aren M.

Maeir (Eds.), *Tell eṣ-Ṣâfi/Gath III: the Early Bronze Age III*. Wiesbaden: Harrassowitz.

Emery, Walter B. 1963. "Egypt Exploration Society: Preliminary Report on the Excavations at Buhen, 1962." *Kush: Journal of the Sudan Antiquities Service*. 11: 116–120.

Eriksen, Berit V., ed. 2010. *Lithic Technology in Metal Using Societies (Proceedings of a UISPP Workshop, Lisbon, September 2006, Moesgaard)*. Jutland Archaeological Society Vol. 67. Hojbjerg: Jutland Archaeological Society.

Garfinkel, Yosef, Florian Klimscha, Sariel Shalev, and Danny Rosenberg. 2014. "The Beginning of Metallurgy in the Southern Levant: A Late 6th Millennium Calbc Copper Awl from Tel Tsaf, Israel." *PLoS One* 9(3), e92591. https://doi.org/10.1371/journal.pone.0092591.

Garland, H., and Charles Olden Bannister. 1927. *Ancient Egyptian Metallurgy*. London: Griffin.

Golden, Jonathan. 2002. "The Origins of the Metals Trade in the Eastern Mediterranean: Social Organization of Production in the Early Copper Industries." In Edwin CM Van Den Brink and Thomas Levy (eds.), *Egypt and the Levant: Interrelations from the 4th through the Early 3rd Millenium BCE*, 225–238. New York: Bloomsbury Academic.

———. 2010. *Dawn of the Metal Age: Technology and Society during the Levantine Chalcolithic* (Approaches to Anthropological Archaeology Series). Edited by Thomas E. Levy. London: Equinox Publishing Ltd.

Graves-Brown, Carolyn A. 2010. *The Ideological Significance of Flint in Dynastic Egypt*. Unpublished Ph.D. Dissertation. London: Institute of Archaeology, University College London.

Greenberg, Raphael. 2019. *The Archaeology of the Bronze Age Levant: From Urban Origins to the Demise of City-States, 3700–1000 BCE*. Cambridge World Archaeology. Cambridge: Cambridge University Press.

Greenfield, Haskel J. 1999. "The Origins of Metallurgy: Distinguishing Stone from Metal Cut Marks on Bones from Archaeological Sites." *Journal of Archaeological Science* 26(7): 797–808.

———. 2002. "Distinguishing Metal (Steel and Low-Tin Bronze) from Stone (Flint and Obsidian) Tool Cut Marks on Bone: An Experimental Approach." In James R. Mathieu (ed.), *Experimental Archaeology: Replicating Past Objects, Behaviors, and Processes*. British Archaeological Reports, International Series 1035, 35–54. Oxford: Archaeopress.

———. 2005. The Origins of Metallurgy at Jericho (Tel es-Sultan): A Preliminary Report on Distinguishing Stone from Metal Cut Marks on Mammalian Remains. In H. Buitenhuis, A. Choyke, L. Martin, L. Bartosiewicz and M. Mashkour, *Archaeozoology of the Near East VI: Proceedings of the 6th Sixth International Symposium on the Archaeozoology of Southwestern Asia and Adjacent Areas*, 178–186. ARC/Archeological Research and Consultancy Publications: Groningen.

———. 2006. "Slicing Cut Marks on Animal Bones: Diagnostics for Identifying Stone Tool Type and Raw Material." *Journal of Field Archaeology* 31: 147–163.

———. 2008. "Metallurgy in the Near East. A Zooarchaeological Perspective on the Origins of Metallurgy in the Near East: Analysis of Stone and Metal Cut Marks on Bone from Israel." In Helaine Selin (ed.), *Encyclopedia of the History of Science, Technology, and Medicine in Non–Western Cultures*, 1639–1647. Dordrecht: Springer Academic Publishers.

———. 2013. "'The Fall of the House of Flint': A Zooarchaeological Perspective on the Decline of Chipped Stone Tools for Butchering Animals in the Bronze and Iron Ages of the Southern Levant." *Lithic Technology* 38(3): 161–178.

———. 2017. "The Spread of Productive and Technological Innovations in Europe and Near East: An Integrated Zooarchaeological Perspective on Secondary Animal Products and Bronze Utilitarian Metallurgy." In Philipp W. Stockhammer and Joseph Moran (eds.), *Appropriating Innovations (Proceedings of the Entangled Knowledge in Late Neolithic and Early Bronze Age Eurasia Conference, Heidelberg, 15th–17th January 2015)*, 50–68. Oxford: Oxbow Books.

———. 2021. "Insufficient Evidence for Metal Butchering Marks at Tell El-Hesi during the Early Bronze Age: Critique of the Analysis of Microscopic Grooves in 'Cultural Modification Analyses on Faunal Remains in Relation to Space Use and Direct Provisioning from Field VI EBIIIA Tell el-Hesi' by Kara Larson, James W. Hardin, and Sara Cody." *Palestine Exploration Quarterly* 160(2): 144–155. DOI: 10.1080/00310328.2021.1921436.

Greenfield, Haskel J., Jeremy A. Beller, and Jane Gaastra. 2021. "Changes in Butchering Technology and Efficiency Patterns between the Early and Middle Bronze Ages from Tell Zirā´A, Jordan." In Dieter Vieweger and Jütta Häser (eds.), *Tall Zirā'a, The Gadara Region Project (2001–2011) Final Report Volume 3: Early and Middle Bronze Age (Strata 25–17)*. Wuppertal: Deutsches Evangelisches Institut.

Greenfield, Haskel J., Jeremy A. Beller, Jane S. Gaastra, and Dieter Vieweger. 2022. "Filling the Gap: A Microscopic Zooarchaeological Approach to Changes in Butchering Technology During the Early and Middle Bronze Periods at Tall Zirā´A, Jordan." *Palestine Exploration Quarterly*: 1–37. DOI: https://doi.org/10.1080/00310328.2022.2050094.

Greenfield, Haskel J., and Annie Brown. 2016. "'Making the cut': Changes in Butchering Technology and Efficiency Patterns from the Chalcolithic to modern Arab Occupations at Tell Halif, Israel." In Nimrod Marom, Reuven Yeshurun, Lior Weissbrod and Guy Bar-Oz (eds.), *Bones and Identity: Zooarchaeological Approaches to Reconstructing Social and Cultural Landscapes in Southwest Asia (Proceedings of the ICAZ-SW Asia Conference, Haifa, June 23–28, 2013)*, 273–291. Oxford: Oxbow Press.

Greenfield, Haskel J., Annie Brown, and Pierre de Miroschedji. 2021. "Origins of Metallurgy in the Southern Levant: Microscopic Examination of Butchering Marks on Animal Bones at Tel Yarmuth, Israel." In Umberto Albarella, Cleia Detry, Sónia Gabriel, Catarina Ginja, Ana Elisabete Pires and João Pedro Tereso (eds.), *Themes in Old World Zooarchaeology: from the Mediterranean to the Atlantic*, 95–107. Oxford, United Kingdom: Oxbow Books.

Greenfield, Haskel J., Annie Brown, Itzhaq Shai, and Aren M. Maeir. 2016. "Preliminary Analysis of the Fauna from the Early Bronze Age III Neighbourhood at Tell Eṣ-Ṣâfi/Gath, Israel." In Nimrod Marom, Reuven Yeshurun, Lior Weissbrod and Guy Bar-Oz (eds.), *Bones and Identity: Zooarchaeological Approaches to Reconstructing Social and Cultural Landscapes in Southwest Asia (Proceedings of the ICAZ-SW Asia Conference, Haifa, June 23–28, 2013)*, 170–192. Oxford: Oxbow Press.

Greenfield, Haskel J., and Talisha Chaput. 2021. "Butchering Technology at the Early Tin Metal Producing Site of Göltepe." In K. Aslihan Yener (ed.), *Tin Production at Göltepe: Excavations at an Early Bronze Age Mining Town in the Central Taurus Mountains, Turkey*, 160–176. Philadelphia: Institute for Aegean Academic Press.

Greenfield, Haskel J., and Tina L. Greenfield. 2018. "Butchering Technology in Middle Bronze Age Ashkelon." In Lawrence E. Stager, Daniel M. Master, and J. David Schloen (eds.), *Final Reports of the Leon Levy Expedition to Ashkelon: Ashkelon 6: The Middle Bronze Age Ramparts and Gates of the North Slope and Later Fortifications*, 509–520. University Park, PA: Harvard Semitic Museum Publications and Eisenbrauns.

Greenfield, Haskel J., and Arkadiusz Marciniak. 2019. "Retention of Old Technologies Following the End of the Neolithic: Microscopic Analysis of the Butchering Marks on Animal Bones from Çatalhöyük East." *World Archaeology* 51(1): 76–103. DOI: https://doi.org/10.1080/00438243.2018.1525310.

———. 2021. "The Emergence and Transmission of Metallurgical Technology for Subsistence Activities in Daily Life in Northern Europe: A Microscopic Zooarchaeological Perspective." *Journal of Field Archaeology* 46: 275–288. DOI: https://doi.org/10.1080/00934690.2021.1909279.

Harding, Anthony F. 2000. "Hoards and Hoarding." In Anthony F. Harding (ed.), *European Societies in the Bronze Age*, 352–368. Cambridge University Press.

Hauptmann, Andreas. 2007. *The Archaeometallurgy of Copper: Evidence from Faynan, Jordan*. New York: Springer.

Hauptmann, Andreas, Sigrid Schmitt-Strecker, Thomas E. Levy, and Friedrich Begemann. 2015. "On Early Bronze Age Copper Bar Ingots from the Southern Levant." *Bulletin of the American Schools of Oriental Research* 373: 1–24.

Hauptmann, Harald, and Ernst Pernicka, eds. 2004. *Die Metallindustrie Mesopotamiens von den Anfängen bis zum 2*. Jahrtausend v. Chr., Orient-Archäologie. Rahden, Germany: Verlag Marie Leidorf.

Ikram, Salima. 1995. *Choice Cuts: Meat Products in Ancient Egypt*. Leuven: Peeters Press.

Johnson, Gregory A. 1977. "Aspects of Regional Analysis in Archaeology." *Annual Review of Anthropology* 6: 479–508.

Khalaily, Hamoudi. 2008. "The Flint Assemblage," in The Early Bronze Age Site of Ashqelon, Afridar – Area M by Amir Golani. *'Atiqot* 60: 36–40.

Klemm, Dietrich, and Rosemarie Klemm. 2008. "Mining in Ancient Egypt and Nubia." In Helaine Selin (ed.), *Encyclopaedia of the History of Science, Technology, and Medicine in Non-Western Cultures*, 1685–1698. New York: Springer.

———. 2013. *Gold and Gold Mining in Ancient Egypt and Nubia: Geoarchaeology of the Ancient Gold Mining Sites in the Egyptian and Sudanese Eastern Deserts*. Heidelberg: Springer.

Kmošek, Jiří, Martin Odler, Marek Fikrle, and Yulia V. Kochergina. 2018. "Invisible Connections. Early Dynastic and Old Kingdom Egyptian Metalwork in the Egyptian Museum of Leipzig University." *Journal of Archaeological Science* 96: 191–207. DOI: 10.1016/j.jas.2018.04.004.

Kobusiewicz, Michal. 2015. *The Production, Use and Importance of Flint Tools in the Archaic Period and the Old Kingdom in Egypt*. Archaeopress Egyptology 12. Oxford: Archaeopress.

Kooi, Rebecca J., and Scott I. Fairgrieve. 2013. "SEM and Stereomicroscopic Analysis of Cut Marks in Fresh and Burned Bone." *Journal of Forensic Sciences* 58(2): 452–458. DOI: https://doi.org/10.1111/1556-4029.12050.

Kromer, Karl. 1978. *Siedlungsfunde aus dem frühen alten Reich in Giseh: Österreichische Ausgrabungen 1971–1975, Denkschriften der Philosophisch–Historischen Klasse*. Wien: Österreichische Akademie der Wissenschaften.

Lehner, Mark. 2018. "Kromer in Context: Biography of an Ancient Dump." *AERAGRAM* (Ancient Egypt Research Associates), 19(2): 2–13. https://www.aeraweb.org/wp-content/uploads/2020/04/AG19_2.pdf.

Levy, Thomas E., Russell B. Adams, Andreas Hauptmann, Michael Prange, Sigrid Schmitt-Strecker, and Mohammad Najjar. 2002. "Early Bronze Age Metallurgy: A Newly Discovered Copper Manufactory in Southern Jordan." *Antiquity* 76: 425–437.

Levy, Thomas E., and Sariel Shalev. 1989. "Prehistoric Metalworking in the Southern Levant: Archaeometallurgical and Social Perspectives." *World Archaeology* 20(3): 353–372.

Lucas, A. 1927. *Copper in Ancient Egypt*. London: Egypt Exploration Society.

———. 1959. *Ancient Egyptian Materials and Industries*. Third edition. London: Edward Arnold Publishers Ltd.

Maddin, R., Tamara Stech, James D. Muhly, and E. Brovarski. 1984. "Old Kingdom Models from the Tomb of Impy: Metallurgical Studies." *The Journal of Egyptian Archaeology* 70(1): 33–41.

Manclossi, Francesca, and Steve A. Rosen. 2017. "What We Can Learn from the Flint Industries from Tell eṣ-Ṣâfi/Gath." *Near East Archaeology* 81: 84.

Manclossi, Francesca, Steve A. Rosen, and Eric Böeda. 2019. "From Stone to Metal: The Dynamics of Technological Change in the Decline of Chipped Stone Tool Production: A Case Study from the Southern Levant (5th–1st Millennia BCE)." *Journal of Archaeological Method and Theory* 26: 1276–1326. DOI: 10.1007/s10816-019-09412-2.

Manclossi, Francesca, and Steven A. Rosen. In press. "The Early Bronze Age Lithic Assemblage from Tell eṣ-Ṣâfi/Gath." In Itzhaq Shai, Haskel J. Greenfield, and Aren M. Maeir eds.), *Tell eṣ-Ṣâfi/Gath III: The Early Bronze Age*. Wiesbaden: Harrasowitz.

Manclossi, Francesca, Steven A. Rosen, and Gunnar Lehmann. 2018. "The Decline and Disappearance of Chipped-Stone Tools: New Insights from Qubur El-Walaydah, a Late Bronze/Iron Age Site in Israel." *Lithic Technology* 42(2): 93–124. DOI: https://doi.org/10.1080/01977261.2018.1438336.

Marciniak, Arkadiusz, and Haskel J. Greenfield. 2013. "A Zooarchaeological Perspective on the Origins of Metallurgy in the North European Plain: Butchering Marks on Bones from Central Poland." In Sophie Bergerbrant and Serena Sabatini (eds.), *Counterpoint: Essays in Archaeology and Heritage Studies in Honour of Professor Kristian Kristiansen*. British Archaeological Reports, International Series 2508, 457–468. Oxford: Archaeopress.

Maté-González, Miguel Ángel, Juan Francisco Palomeque-González, José Yravedra, Diego González-Aguilera, and Manuel Domínguez-Rodrigo. 2018. "Micro-Photogrammetric and Morphometric Differentiation of Cut Marks on Bones Using Metal Knives, Quartzite, and Flint Flakes." *Archaeological and Anthropological Sciences* 10(4): 805–816.

Montanari, Daria. 2015. "Metal Weapons in the Southern Levant during the Early Bronze Age: An Overview." In Karolina Rosińska-Balik, Agnieszka Ochał-Czarnowicz, Marcin Czarnowicz and Joanna Dębowska-Judwin (eds.), *Copper and Trade in the South-Eastern Mediterranean: Trade Routes of the Near East in Antiquity*. British Archaeological Reports, International Series 2753, 67–76. England: BAR Publishing.

Moorey, P.R.S. 1988. "Early Metallurgy in Mesopotamia." In Robert Maddin (ed.), *The Beginning of the Use of Metals and Alloys: Papers from the Second International Conference on the Beginning of the Use of Metals and Alloys Zhengzhou China 21-26 October 1986*, 28–33. Cambridge Mass.: MIT Press.

———. 1994a. *Ancient Mesopotamian Materials and Industries*. Oxford: Oxford University Press.

———. 1994b. *Ancient Mesopotamian Materials and Industries: The Archaeological Evidence*. Oxford: Oxford University Press.

Muhly, James D. 1980. "The Bronze Age Setting." In Theodore A. Wertime and James D. Muhly (eds.), *The Coming of the Age of Iron*, 25–68. New Haven: Yale University Press.

———. 1988. "The Beginning of Metallurgy in the Old World." In Robert Maddin (ed.), *The Beginning of the Use of Metals and Alloys: Papers from the Second International Conference on the Beginning of the Use of Metals and Alloys Zhengzhou China 21-26 October 1986*, 2–20. Cambridge Mass.: The MIT Press.

———. 1999. "Metallurgy." In Kathryn A. Bard (ed.), *Encyclopedia of the Archaeology of Ancient Egypt*, 628–634. London: Routledge.

———. 2011. "Metals and Metallurgy." In Sharon R. Steadman and G. McMahon (eds.), *The Oxford Handbook of Ancient Anatolia (10000–323 BCE)*, 858–876. Oxford: Oxford University Press.

Muhs, Brian. 2016. *The Ancient Egyptian Economy: 3000–30 BCE*. Cambridge, United Kingdom: Cambridge University Press.

Needler, Winifred. 1984. *Pre-dynastic and Archaic Egypt in the Brooklyn Museum*. Brooklyn, N.Y.: Brooklyn Museum.

Nigro, Lorenzo. 2014a. "The Archaeology of Collapse and Resilience: Tell es-Sultan/Ancient Jericho as a Case Study." In Lorenzo Nigro (ed.), *Overcoming Catastrophes: Essays on Disastrous Agents Characterization and Resilience Strategies in Pre-Classical Southern Levant*, 55–85. Rome: "La Sapienza" Expedition to Palestine & Jordan.

———. 2014b. "The Copper Route and the Egyptian Connection in 3rd Millennium BC Jordan seen from the Caravan City of Khirbet al-Batrawy." *Vicino Oriente* 18: 39–64.

———. 2019. "Tell es-Sultan/ancient Jericho in the Early Bronze Age II–III." In Elisabetta Gallo (ed.), *Conceptualizing Urban Experiences: Tell es-Sultan and Tall al-Ḥammām Early Bronze Cities across the Jordan. Proceedings of a Workshop held in Palermo, G. Whitaker Foundation, June 19th, 2017, Rome "La Sapienza" Studies on the Archaeology of Palestine & Transjordan, vol. 13*, 79–108. Rome: La Sapienza.

Nigro, Lorenzo, Daria Montanari, Francesco Mura, and Ruggero Caminiti. 2018. "Not Invasive Analyses on a Tin-Bronze Dagger from Jericho: A Case Study." *Mediterranean Archaeology and Archaeometry* 18(1): 199–207. DOI: 10.5281/zenodo.1161359.

North, Robert. 1955. "Metallurgy in the Ancient Near East." *Orientalia Nova Series* 24(1): 78–88.

Odler, Martin. 2015. "Adzes in the Early Dynastic Period and the Old Kingdom." In Karolina Rosińska-Balik, Agnieszka Ochał-Czarnowicz, Marcin Czarnowicz and Joanna Dębowska-Ludwin (eds.), *Copper and Trade in the South–Eastern Mediterranean: Trade routes of the Near East in Antiquity*, 85–153. Oxford: Archaeopress.

———. 2016. *Old Kingdom Copper Tools and Model Tools*. Archaeopress Egyptology 14. Oxford: Archaeopress.

Odler, Martin, and Jiří Kmošek. 2020. *Invisible Connections: An Archaeometallurgical Analysis of the Bronze Age Metalwork from the Egyptian Museum of the University of Leipzig*. Oxford: Archaeopress.

Ogden, Jack. 2000. "Metals." In Paul Nicholson and Ian Shaw (eds.), *Ancient Egyptian Materials and Technology*, 148–176. Cambridge, UK: Cambridge University Press.

Olsen, Sandra L. 1988a. "The Identification of Stone and Metal Tool Marks on Bone Artifacts." In Sandra L. Olsen (ed.), *Scanning Electron Microscopy in Archaeology*, 337–360. Oxford: BAR.

———. 1988b. "The identification of stone and metal tool marks on bone artifacts." In Sandra L. Olsen (ed.), *Scanning Electron Microscopy in Archaeology*, 337–360. Oxford: BAR.

Petrie, William Matthew Flinders. 1913. *Tarkhan I and Memphis V*. London: School of Archaeology in Egypt, Univ. College.

Philip, Graham. 1988. "Hoards of the Early and Middle Bronze Ages in the Levant." *World Archaeology* 20(2): 109–208.

———.1989. *Metal Weapons of the Early and Middle Bronze Ages in Syria-Palestine*. British Archaeological Reports, International Series 526. Oxford: BAR.

———. 2003. "The Early Bronze Age of the Southern Levant: A Landscape Approach." *Journal of Mediterranean Archaeology* 16: 103–132.

———. 2008. "The Early Bronze Age I–III." In Russell B. Adams (ed.), *Jordan: An Archaeological Reader*, 2nd edition, 161–226. London: Equinox.

Philip, Graham, Philip W. Clogg, and David Dungworth. 2003. "Copper Metallurgy in the Jordan Valley from the Third to the First millennia BC: Chemical, Metallographic and Lead Isotope Analyses of Artefacts from Pella." *Levant* 35: 71–100.

Potts, Richard, and Pat Shipman. 1981. "Cutmarks Made by Stone Tools on Bones from Olduvai Gorge, Tanzania." *Nature* 291(5816): 577–580.

Redding, Richard. 2011. "Stews, Meat, and Marrow: Extracting Protein and Fat for the Lost City." *AERAGRAM* 12(2): 13.

———. Fortchoming. Cattle in Egypt.

Richard, Suzanne. 2003. "The Early Bronze Age of the Southern Levant." In Suzanne Richard (ed.), *Near Eastern Archaeology: A Reader*, 280–296. Winona Lake, IN: Eisenbrauns.

Richards, Janet. 2005. *Society and Death in Ancient Egypt: Mortuary Landscapes of the Middle Kingdom*. Cambridge: Cambridge University Press.

Rosen, Steven A. 1984. "The Adoption of Metallurgy in the Levant: A Lithic Perspective." *Current Anthropology* 25: 504–505.

Rosen, Steven A. 1997. *Lithics after the Stone Age: A Handbook of Stone Tools from the Levant*. Walnut Creek, CA: Altamira Press.

Rosenberg, Danny, Eli Buchman, Sariel Shalev, and Shay Bar. 2020. "A Large Copper Artefacts Assemblage of Fazael, Jordan Valley: New Evidence of Late Chalcolithic Copper Metallurgy in the Southern Levant." *Documenta Praehistorica* 47: 246–261. DOI: 10.4312\dp.47.14.

Rosenfeld, Amnon, Shimon Ilani, and Michael Dvorachek. 1997. "Bronze Alloys from Canaan during the Middle Bronze Age." *Journal of Archaeological Science* 24(9): 857–864.

Rosińska-Balik, Karolina, Agnieszka Ochał-Czarnowicz, Marcin Czarnowicz, and Joanna Dębowska-Judwin, eds. 2015. *Copper and Trade in the South-Eastern Mediterranean: Trade Routes of the Near East in Antiquity*. England: BAR Publishing.

Sanders, William, Henry T. Wright, and Robert McCormick Adams. 1984. *On the Evolution of Complex Societies; Essays in Honor of Harry Hoiger 1982*. Malibu: Published for the UCLA Dept. of Anthropology by Undena Publications.

Scheel, Bernd. 1989. *Egyptian Metalworking and Tools*. Aylesbury: Shire Publishers.

Shalev, Sariel. 1994. "The Change in Metal Production from the Chalcolithic Period to the Early Bronze Age in Israel and Jordan." *Antiquity* 68: 630–637.

Shephard, R. 1980. *Prehistoric Mining and Allied Industries*. London: Academic Press.

Shipman, Pat. 1981. "Application of Scanning Electron Microscopy to Taphonomic Problems." *Annals of the New York Academy of Sciences* 375: 357–385.

Shipman, Pat, and Jennie Rose. 1988. "Bone Tools: An Experimental Approach." In Sandra J. Olsen (ed.), *Scanning Electron Microscopy in Archaeology*, British Archaeological Reports, International Series 452, 303–336. Oxford: BAR.

Shugar, Aaron N., and Christopher J. Gohm. 2011. "Developmental Trends in Chalcolithic Copper Metallurgy: A Radiometric Perspective Changed the World." In Jaimie Lovell and Yorke M. Rowan (eds.), *Culture, Chronology and the Chalcolithic: Theory and Transition*. Levant Supplementary vol. 9. Oxford: Council for British Research in the Levant and Oxbow Books.

Steiner, Margreet L., and Ann E. Killebrew, eds. 2014. *The Oxford Handbook of the Archaeology of the Levant c. 8000–332 BCE*. Oxford Handbooks in Archaeology. Oxford: Oxford University Press.

Straub, Evan T. 2009. "Understanding Technology Adoption: Theory and Future Directions for Informal Learning." *Review of Educational Research* 79(2): 625–649.

Tadmor, M., D. Kedem, F. Begemann, A. Hauptmann, E. Pernicka, and S. Schmitt-Strecker. 1995. "The Naḥal Mishmar Hoard from the Judean Desert:

Technology, Composition, Provenance." *'Atiqot* 27: 93–146.

Tallet, Pierre. 2010. "Le roi Den et les Iountiou. Les Égyptiens au Sud-Sinaï sous la 1re dynastie." *Archéo-Nil* 20: 97–105.

Taylor, Robin J. 1993. *Hoards of the Bronze Age in Southern Britain: Analysis and Interpretation.* Oxford: BAR.

Tillmann, Andreas. 1999. "Dynastic Stone Tools." In Kathryn A. Bard (ed.), *Encyclopedia of the Archaeology of Ancient Egypt*, 310–314. London: Routledge.

Tylecote, R. F. 1986. *The Prehistory of Metallurgy in the British Isles*. London: The Institute of Metals.

———. 1987. *The Early History of Metallurgy in Europe*. London: Longman.

———. 1992. *A History of Metallurgy*. 2nd ed. London: The Institute of Metals.

Verly, Georges, Frederik W. Rademakers, Claire Somaglino, Pierre Tallet, Luc Delvaux, and Patrick Degryse. 2021. "The Chaîne Opératoire of Middle Kingdom Smelting Batteries and the Problem of Fuel: Excavation, Experimental and Analytical Studies on Ancient Egyptian Metallurgy." *Journal of Archaeological Science: Reports 37*: 102708. DOI: https://doi.org/10.1016/j.jasrep.2020.102708.

Walker, Phillip L. 1978. "Butchering and Stone Tool Function." *American Antiquity* 43(4): 710–715.

Walker, Phillip L., and Jeffrey C. Long. 1977. "An Experimental Study of the Morphological Characteristics of Tool Marks." *American Antiquity* 42(4): 605–616.

Wengrow, David. 2005. *The Archaeology of Early Egypt. Social Transformations in North East-Africa 10000 to 2650 BC.* Cambridge: Cambridge University Press.

Wenke, Robert J. 1989. "Egypt: Origins of Complex Societies." *Annual Review of Anthropology* 18: 129–155.

Wright, Henry T. 1986. "The Evolution of Civilizations." In David. J. Meltzer, Don D. Fowler, Jeremy A. Sabloff and Society for American Archaeology (eds.), *American Archaeology Past and Future: A Celebration of the Society for American Archaeology 1935–1985*, edited by, 323–365. Washington, D.C.: Smithsonian Institution Press.

Wright, Henry T., James A. Neely, and Gregory A. Johnson. 1975. "Early Fourth Millennium Developments in Southwestern Iran." *Iran* 13: 129–147.

Notes

1 Recent reanalysis of the IB Jericho material is now pointing to the absence of metal butchering marks in the faunal assemblage, and lower frequencies in the MB IIA material than previously reported elsewhere (Greenfield 2005). Hence, for now, the Jericho material must be discounted.

Journal of Ancient Egyptian Interconnections

Egyptian Trade on the Central Levantine Coast During the Early Dynastic Period: A Ceramic-Material Perspective

Mathilde Jean
Sorbonne University

Kamal Badreshany
Durham University

Abstract

This paper compares pottery finds from the Central Levant (Lebanon) and imported vessels found in Egyptian Early Dynastic contexts to help unravel the dynamics of trade activities between the two regions at the beginning of the third millennium BCE. New typological, technological, petrographic, and geochemical datasets from Lebanese sites such as Tell Arqa, Byblos, Tell Koubba, Tell Fadous, and the Beqaa Valley are compared with published data from funerary contexts at Abydos (Umm el-Qaab, tomb of king Den) and Helwan (Operation 4). By consolidating recent evidence, this study aims to provide a framework aiding in provenancing imported vessels of likely central Levantine origin found in Egyptian Early Dynastic contexts. The evidence suggests a gradual shift in trade links between Egypt and the Levant, with land routes through the Sinai being abandoned in favor of maritime ones. Likewise, Egyptian contacts are refocused from the Southern to the Central Levant. Recent evidence from the Central Levant provides finer-grained provenance analysis, shown to be the key to further defining and understanding these subtle and gradual shifts. Moreover, our study highlights chronological discrepancies pointing to practices of saving imported goods as heirlooms for more than a century to repurpose them for funerary contexts.

Keywords

Egypt; Central Levant; Lebanon; Early Dynastic; Early Bronze Age; Ceramic analysis; Petrography; Trade

Introduction

Clear evidence exists for significant interaction between Egypt and the Levant from the fourth millennium BCE during the Predynastic period. The available evidence shows that Egypt initially maintained contact primarily with the southern Levant along land routes through the Sinai. Egypt established a colonial network of sites in the region, such as Tell es-Sakan (Miroschedji 2015; Greenberg 2019). Later, during the Old Kingdom, archaeological and historical data show the reorientation of interactions northwards, toward the central Levantine coast (Badreshany et al. 2020; Greenberg and Iserlis 2020; Sowada et al. 2020).

From 2700 BCE, Byblos emerged as a leading harbor and became the primary favored Egyptian partner during the third millennium. Old Kingdom Egyptian objects found at Byblos are, in the main, of sacred character and found in sacred contexts (Espinel 2002; Badreshany et al. 2022; de Vreeze and Badreshany, this volume), illustrating long-standing, deeply embedded connections between the two regions well beyond transactional economics. The nature of Egyptian contacts with the central Levantine coast during the early third millennium (Early Dynastic period) remains poorly understood. Some Early Dynastic stone vessels found at Byblos could indicate early trade between the central Levant and the Egyptian royal court, especially for the acquisition of cedar timbers (Sowada 2009, 50). In contrast, considerable evidence shows intensive interactions between Egypt and the northern part of the southern Levant during the Early Dynastic period (Miroschedji 2018; Iserlis et al. 2019; Greenberg and Iserlis 2020).

The ascription by scholars of the existence of intensive trade links between the central Levantine coast and Egypt during the early third millennium is predicated on outdated chronological information and assumptions based on later evidence. A number of studies of material from Egypt, for example, have used petrography to ascribe the origin of some vessels found in Early Dynastic tombs to the Lebanese coast based on geological information, but high-quality comparative Levantine data from the period was until very recently lacking (Köhler and Ownby 2011; Hartung et al. 2015; Sowada et al. 2020).

With the emergence of new early third-millennium ceramic datasets from central and northern Lebanon showing shale-derived fabrics were used almost exclusively at the time, we can say, with some certainty, that non-shale tempered vessels from that period found in Egypt probably originated somewhere else. Recent archaeological data, covering much of the central Levantine coast, has made clear the typological and petrographic development for the early to the mid-third millennium (Doumet-Serhal 2006; Badreshany and Genz 2009; Thalmann 2016; Badreshany et al. 2020; Jean 2020a), providing us an important tool for exploring the intensity, development, and orientation of Egyptian trade with this area, and further illuminating this hitherto obscure relationship. With this information, we hope to eventually explore the mechanisms behind the shift in Egyptian interaction from the southern to the central Levant during the Old Kingdom. As discussed below, repeated contacts occurred during the First Dynasty but seem to have declined through the Second Dynasty (Sowada et al. 2021), corresponding to the Levantine Early Bronze Age II–III. The absence of imported vessels in the tomb of Ninetjer, the third king of the Second Dynasty, at Saqqara, supports this point (Lacher-Raschdorff 2014, 87–89). Contacts with the Levant would develop again during the Old Kingdom.

This paper compares Levantine imports from selected Egyptian contexts with contemporary central Levantine assemblages (Fig. 1) in terms of typology, technology, petrography, and geochemistry to gain a better understanding of the nature and intensity of ED interactions with the central Levantine coast. The results will provide a better qualitative understanding of trade between Egypt and the central Levant during the key Early Dynastic period and establish building blocks for future research.

Third Millennium Egypt and Central Levant: The Contribution of Ceramic Studies

Early Exchange between Egypt and the Levant during the Predynastic Period

Beginning in the Predynastic period, Abydos became a center of power where elite members of society were buried. At Abydos-Umm el-Qaab, imported vessels were found in several tombs. In tomb U-j, in cemetery U, three-hundred and sixty imported vessels from the Levant were unearthed in a Naqada IIIA context (Hartung 2002). The tomb's inhabitant was probably an early ruler of Egypt during the late Predynastic period, around 3320 BCE, as indicated by ^{14}C analyses of wood samples from this tomb (Hartung et al. 2015, 298). Some scholars suggested he could have reigned over much of the Nile Valley, being one of the pioneers of Egyptian unity (Wilkinson 1999, 41; Köhler and Thalmann 2014, 182). Among the imported pottery found in his tomb were Levantine types. These were presumably marks of prestige linked to wine consumption in the ancient Egyptian court.

The imported Levantine vessels were investigated via petrography, but their provenance was difficult to assess because a great variety of ceramic raw materials were used in their production. Initial assessments by some scholars proposed that the vessels were made in Upper Egypt using southern Levantine know-how (Porat and Goren 2002). However, more recent work proposed several production locations covering the whole Levantine coastline (Hartung 2002; Hartung et al. 2015). Given the potential geographic scope, the provenancing of imported materials necessitates extended comparison with contemporary Levantine

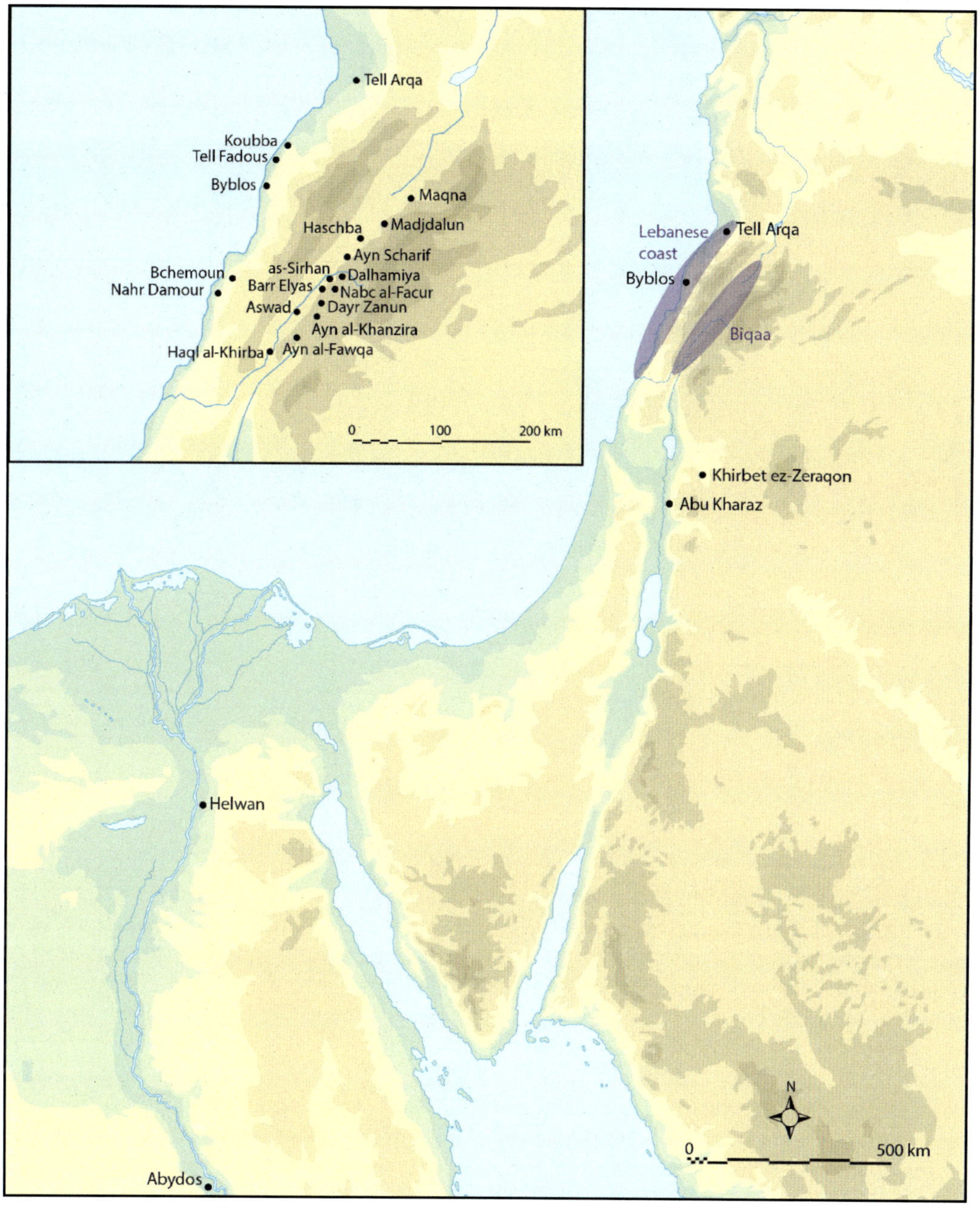

FIGURE 1: Map of the sites and regions mentioned in the paper (background maps: Martin Sauvage).

assemblages. In this sense, recent ceramic evidence and good chronological comparisons from the Central Levant (Doumet-Serhal 2006; Badreshany and Genz 2009; Thalmann 2016; Badreshany et al. 2020) provide a new basis for the provenancing of Egyptian ceramic finds of Levantine origin dating to the late Predynastic and Early Dynastic period.

Early Dynastic Egypt, Early Bronze Age Central Levant: Chronological Issues

The Early Dynastic period corresponds to the establishment of the Egyptian state, unifying Upper and Lower Egypt under the authority of the king. This period includes the First and Second Dynasties (Naqada IIIC and Naqada IIID, respectively). During the First Dynasty, Memphis appears as the

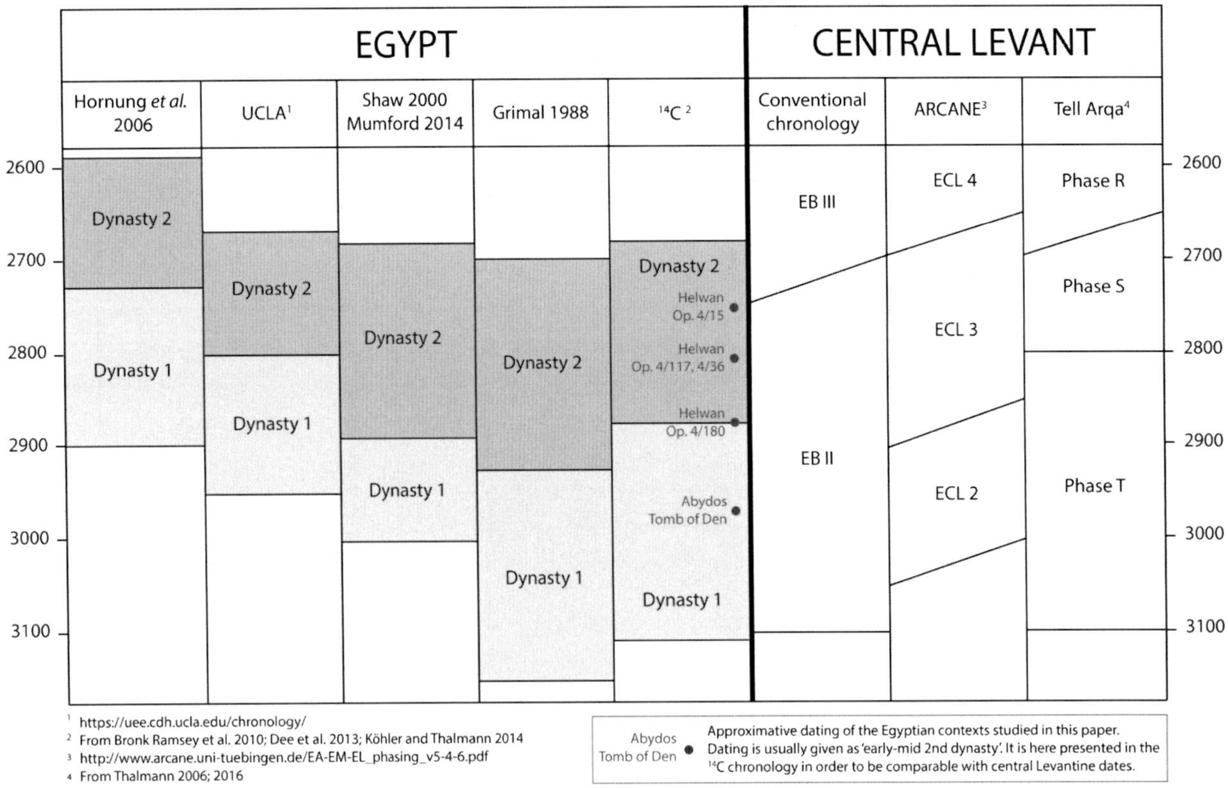

Figure 2: Chronological table of Early Dynastic Egypt and contemporary central Levant.

new royal capital, and some official elite tombs are installed in Helwan, in the vicinity of the Memphite court in Lower Egypt. However, Abydos is still an important symbolic site in Upper Egypt, where kingship originated, and sovereigns continue being buried in the royal cemetery.

To understand the relationships between Egypt and the central Levant during this period, good chronological synchronism is essential for comparing contemporary ceramic assemblages. In Egypt, the royal chronology is established from textual records such as the list of kings from the temple of Seti I at Abydos and the Turin Canon. However, the absolute date ranges for reigns and dynasties vary and rarely fit with ^{14}C dating. Moreover, chronological schemes may differ by upwards of a hundred years, depending on the sources. Comparisons with the central Levant are complicated further due to the existence of several chronological schemes.

A synchronism of chronologies based on previous work (especially Köhler and Thalmann 2014) is given in Fig. 2. The central Levantine chronology includes the so-called traditional subdivision (Early Bronze Age, EBA), the ARCANE chronology (Early Central Levant, ECL), and the archaeological sequence from Tell Arqa, which represents the best stratigraphic and ^{14}C sequence in the region (Thalmann 2006, 2016). In this paper, we use the Levantine chronologies as well as the ^{14}C dates (as mentioned in Ramsey et al. 2010; Dee et al. 2013; Köhler and Thalmann 2014) and Mumford's Egyptian chronology (Mumford 2014; also corresponding to Sowada's chronology in Badreshany et al. 2022). Figure 2 shows that the Early Dynastic period maps onto the central Levantine EB II and II/III transition. More precisely, the First Dynasty roughly corresponds to ECL2 and Arqa phase T, while the second Dynasty corresponds to ECL3 and Arqa phase S, making it possible to compare the development of the pottery assemblages directly.

Recent Work on Levantine Ceramics in Egypt

In part, Egyptian interaction with the Levant aimed at procuring resources unavailable in the Nile Valley, mostly wine, olive oil, and cedar (Thalmann and

Sowada 2014, 326; Sowada 2014, 294). The content of imported vessels is yet to be defined, though work is progressing in this area for Old Kingdom vessels from Egypt (Karin Sowada personal communication). The shift from northward, from the southern to the central Levant, of interaction networks has been proposed by scholars as linked to an increasing need for timber from Lebanon for use in Egyptian royal building projects. Generally, scholars also believe that trade developed along maritime routes, causing the abandonment of the land routes through the northern Sinai (Marcus 2002; Müller 2014; Greenberg and Iserlis 2020).

Recent ceramic studies offer new insights for understanding this important change in Egyptian relations with the Levant. Petrographic and geochemical analyses on imported materials found in Egypt provide new data on the possible provenance of these vessels (Köhler and Ownby 2011; Hartung et al. 2015; Iserlis et al. 2019; Sowada, Ownby and Wodzińska 2020; Sowada et al. 2021; Badreshany et al. 2022). These studies also show the complexity of these interactions and that archaeological context must be considered in concert with the petrographic and geochemical data to determine provenance when identified ceramic raw materials provide a good fit with local geology but archaeological evidence for production is completely lacking.

Here, we apply our new understanding of local coastal central Levantine pottery production and *Chaînes Operatoires* together with the geological evidence to provide more robust provenancing information of imported central Levantine vessels found in Egypt. The disputed provenance of imported vessels from the Predynastic Tomb U-j mentioned earlier is a good example of why such an approach is needed to prevent ambiguity (Hartung 2002; Porat and Goren 2002). Based on typological and geological data, some Early Dynastic vessels of suspected Levantine origin uncovered in Egypt have been ascribed to production on the central Levantine coast (Köhler and Ownby 2011; Köhler and Thalmann 2014; Hartung et al. 2015). To provide greater clarity on the origin of these vessels, the information is reassessed in light of recently published data from contemporary central Levantine assemblages.

Materials and Methods: The View from the Central Levant

Egyptian Sites: Abydos and Helwan

This paper investigates Early Dynastic contexts in Egypt, at Abydos and Helwan, which yielded imported pottery from the Levant dating to First and Second Dynasty contexts and where the publication included petrographic data. Contexts from Abydos are dated to the First Dynasty (ECL2), while Helwan tombs date to the Second Dynasty (ECL3); the comparative material from those sites is based on 14 published examples (Table 1). At Abydos-Umm el-Qaab, in Upper Egypt, the tomb of king Den dates from the middle of the First Dynasty, corresponding to Naqada IIIC. The grave is located in the southern part of the necropolis, dedicated to First Dynasty kings. The tomb of king Den is one of the largest tombs on the site, consisting of a large burial chamber associated with storerooms. Within the tomb, a large number of imported vessels were uncovered, among which nine samples with petrographic data were published (Hartung et al. 2015).

At Helwan, close to the royal Memphite court, imported vessels were found during Operation 4 (Köhler and Ownby 2011) in several tombs from the Second Dynasty (Naqada IIID). Operation 4 revealed more than 200 tombs spanning from the First to the Fourth Dynasty. Their diversity illustrates the long chronological range attested and the diversity in social status of the deceased buried in the necropolis. The five tombs from the Second Dynasty considered in this paper are non-elite tombs, probably belonging to urban middle-class individuals, providing an interesting, more modest contrast to the royal tomb of king Den (Köhler and Thalmann 2014). One sample from each tomb has been published with petrographic data (Köhler and Ownby 2011).

The pottery from the tomb of king Den, in Abydos, dated to the mid-first Dynasty, should be directly compared to materials from ECL2 and Arqa Phase T. On the other hand, materials from the Helwan necropolis, dating to the early- to mid-second Dynasty, should be compared to ECL3 pottery and the Arqa Phase S assemblage (Fig. 2).

Vessel Type	Site	Tomb	Date (Egypt)	Date (Central Levant)	Sample Number	Vessel Number
Jug	Abydos	Den	Dynasty 1	ECL2	#17	T-aB/251
Jug	Abydos	Den	Dynasty 1	ECL2	#11	T-KK/75
Jug	Abydos	Den	Dynasty 1	ECL2	#18	T-aB/271
Jug	Abydos	Den	Dynasty 1	ECL2	#12	T-W/71
Jug	Abydos	Den	Dynasty 1	ECL2	#13	T-aB/288
Jar	Abydos	Den	Dynasty 1	ECL2	#14	T-aB/257
Squat jar	Abydos	Den	Dynasty 1	ECL2	#19	T-aB/283
Squat jar	Abydos	Den	Dynasty 1	ECL2	#20	T-aB/290
Jug	Abydos	Den	Dynasty 1	ECL2	#16	T-aB/253
Jug	Helwan	Op. 1/1	?	?		
Jug	Helwan	Op. 4/180	Dynasty 1/2	ECL2/3		
Jug	Helwan	Op. 4/36	Dynasty 2	ECL3		
Jug	Helwan	Op. 4/117	Dynasty 2	ECL3		P06-26
Jar	Helwan	Op. 4/15	Dynasty 2	ECL3		P01-10

Table 1: List of the 14 imported vessels found in Egypt presumably from Levantine origin (from Köhler and Ownby 2011; Hartung et al. 2015).

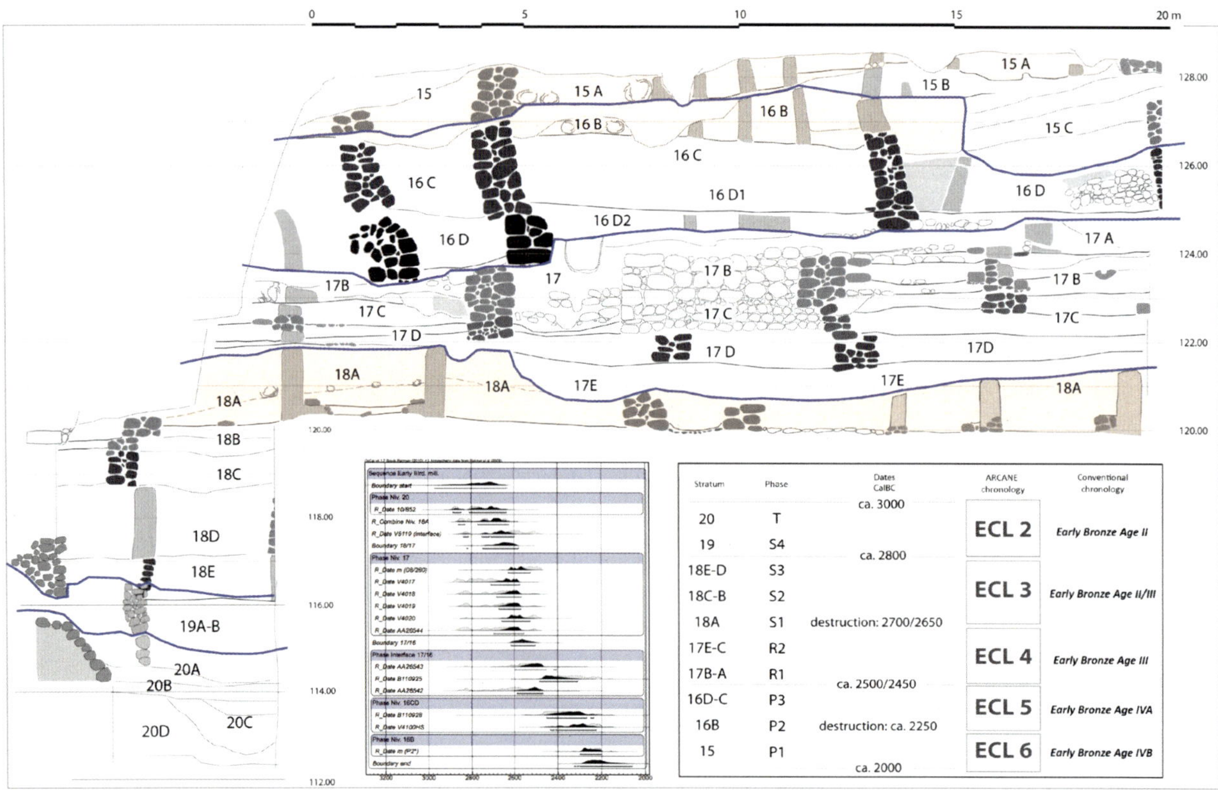

Figure 3: Stratigraphic sequence and dating of the Early Bronze Age occupation at Tell Arqa (from Thalmann 2013, Fig. 1).

The Central Levant: Tell Arqa, the Region of Byblos, and the Beqaa

In the central Levant, several ECL 2 and 3 contexts, broadly contemporary with the Early Dynastic tombs listed above, were selected for comparison: from Tell Arqa, the Byblos region, and the Beqaa Valley.

Tell Arqa, located on the southern edge of the Akkar plain in northern Lebanon, offers, until today, the best Early Bronze Age sequence among all the sites of the central Levant. The excavation led by Thalmann focused on the edge of the tell and revealed some domestic structures. Burned destruction layers punctuate the 16 m high EBA stratigraphic sequence (Layer 18A, Phase S; Layers 16A–B and 15A, Phase P) and are well-associated with radiocarbon dates (Fig. 3; Thalmann 2006, 2016). Phases T and S are contemporary with the Egyptian Early Dynastic period. Phase T (Layers 20 and 19; ECL2), the earliest EB phase excavated at Tell Arqa, was reached in a 40 sq m sounding. At the bottom of the sequence, layer 20 consists of several earthen floors and a peripheral wall probably delimiting the settlement. Layer 19 revealed the first dense settlement in the area, built of mudbricks. Phase S (Layer 18; ECL3) also comprised dense dwellings, made of stone and mudbrick walls. Stratum 18A corresponds to the first instance of destruction by fire, dated c. 2700–2650 cal BCE and excavated in a 250 sq m area. The dwellings are organized along a street, and the occupation is sealed by the destruction, which preserved a large number of complete vessels *in situ*. Pottery assemblages are well-defined for each occupation phase, including typology (Thalmann 2006, 2016), technology (Roux and Thalmann 2016), and petrography (Jean 2019, 2020), making Tell Arqa a reference for the ceramics of the EBA central Levant.

Ceramics from Byblos were obtained through surface collection, while well-stratified assemblages were investigated from the surrounding region at the sites of Tell Fadous-Kfarabida and Tell Koubba. Ceramics from these sites were unearthed in administrative, sacred, communal production, and storage contexts (see de Vreeze and Badreshany this volume, and Badreshany et al. 2020 and 2022 for a full analysis). The materials from the Beqaa originate entirely in survey materials and are chronologically much less secure than the coastal materials (Badreshany 2013; Badreshany et al. 2020).

Analytical Methods: Multiproxy Analysis

The methodology applied to this study is based on a comparative multiproxy analysis of the pottery assemblages, including chronology, typology, technology, petrography, and geochemistry. The contemporaneity of the contexts is assessed as precisely as possible based on the archaeological data. Data for Egyptian materials are taken from published sources, while the central Levantine assemblages were studied by the authors in person.

First, imports found in Egypt will be compared with local central Levantine pottery to establish degrees of chronological correlation. Next, typological characteristics will be examined, including shape, dimensions, and decoration. Technological aspects will also be considered regarding the manufacturing processes and surface treatment techniques. Finally, the utilization of raw materials to produce Levantine ceramics found in Egyptian tombs will be assessed and compared with data from the central Levant in an attempt to further narrow the provenance of the former. This last step will be undertaken at complementary scales of observation, from macroscopy to geochemistry. Macroscopic observation of central Levantine pottery has been carried out using both the naked eye and stereomicroscope. Microscopic observation in thin section was performed under a polarising microscope on a Lietz petrographic microscope at the Durham Archaeomaterials Research Centre (DARC, Durham University, UK) and a Nikon Eclipse E600 POL microscope at the MSH Mondes (Nanterre, France).

The geochemical analysis was undertaken by obtaining 100 mg of powder across the profile of each sherd using a 12-volt dental drill fitted with a 2-mm diameter solid tungsten carbide bit. The samples were prepared at the Durham Archaeomaterials Research Centre (DARC). The powders were acid digested using hydrofluoric acid and analyzed by ICP-AES and ICP-MS at the Department of Earth Sciences, Durham University, using protocols established by Ottley et al. (2003). 0.100 +/- 0.001g of powder was digested in a 4ml 40% HF e 1ml 69% HNO3 solution for 48h before evaporating to dryness and redissolving in HNO3 acid, the resulting solution being 3.5% HNO3. Next, a Re and Rh internal standard was added to this solution to compensate for possible calibration drift, matrix suppression, and dilution errors. The analysis measured 43 elements. The major elements,

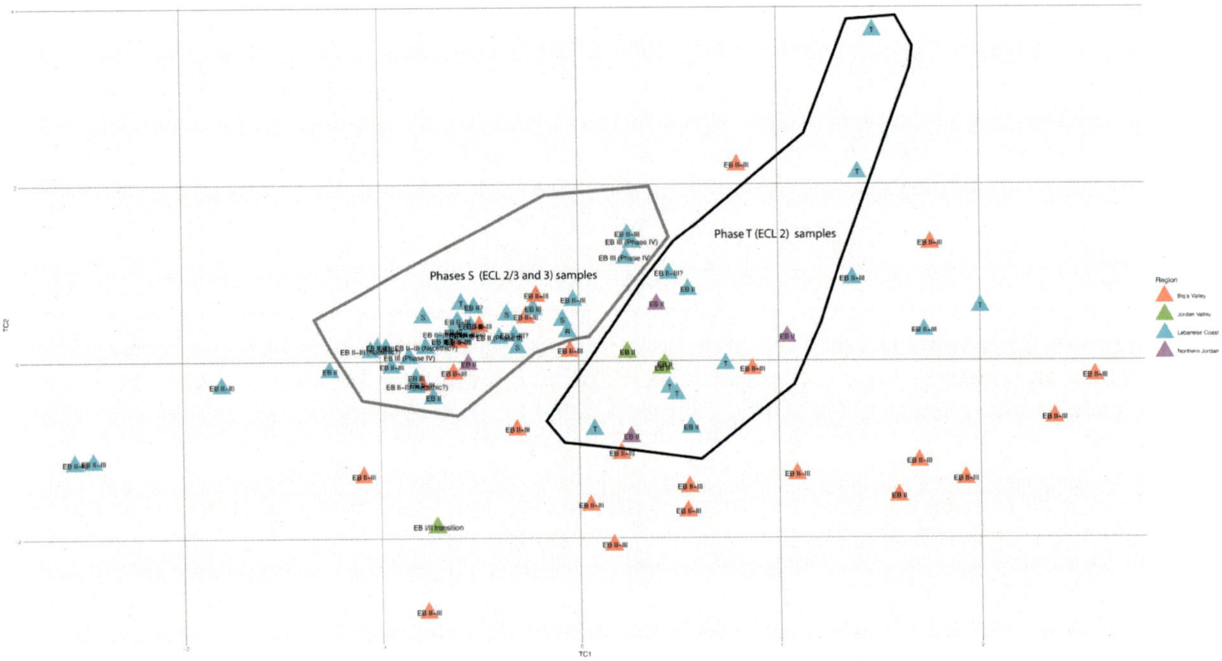

Figure 4: Plot of the factor scores generated from the Principal Components Analysis of the chemical data generated by ICP-AES and -MS for shale fabrics sorted by petrofabric and region. Factor 1 explains 62.6% of the variation and factor 2 explains 16.9%. The graph shows the existence of two groups of shale vessels produced in the northern Central Levant. One slightly coarser group dates to ECL2/phase T Arqa/first dynasty and the second dates mostly to the ECL 2/3 and 3/phase S Arqa/second dynasty).

analyzed by ICP-AES as weight percentage oxide, include Al_2O_3, Fe_2O_3, MgO, CaO, Na_2O, K_2O, TiO_2, P_2O_5, and MnO. The minor and trace elements analyzed by ICP-MS as parts per million (ppm) include Co, Cr, Cu, Ni, Sc, Sr, V, Zn, Rb, Y, Zr, Nb, Cs, Ba, Pb, La, Ce, Pr, Nd, Sm, Eu, Gd, Tb, Dy, Ho, Er, Tm, Yb, Lu, Hf, Ta, Pb, Th, and U. Calibration was achieved via the use of in-house standards and international reference materials (W-2, BHVO-1 and AGV-1 standards) as well as a blank and standard sample being run every 10 samples to ascertain instrument calibration stability.

A Principal Components Analysis (PCA) (Orton and Hughes 2013, 176–180) was conducted to plot the similarity of the chemical composition of each sample (Fig. 4). The R software package, version 3.5.0 (R Core Team) was used for the analysis and the figures were produced using the package ggplot2 (Wickham 2009). A Log-ratio transform (base 10) was applied to the raw data (Buxeda i Garrigós 1999; Papageorgiou 2020) before processing.

Some Characteristics of ECL2-3 Pottery from the Central Levant

Based on the evidence, we list some basic criteria useful for excluding the possibility of a central Levantine provenance for ceramics found in Early Dynastic Egypt. For instance, the abundant ceramic data from Tell Arqa highlighted the systematic presence of burnishing and/or combing in non-cooking vessels (no smoothed surfaces) and the absence of slipping on local wares (contrary to vessels produced in the southern Levant; Thalmann 2016). The same can be said for other assemblages from the Lebanese coast, such as Beirut (Badre 1997), Byblos, Fadous, Koubba, and Enfeh (the authors' personal observations; Jean 2019). For all of these assemblages, slip is either non-existent or very rare.

In Lebanon, the Beqaa and the southern coast are possible exceptions to this rule (Doumet-Serhal 2006; Badreshany 2013). At Sidon, slipped vessels and vessels comparable to examples known from the southern Levant occur in limited amounts. That they are less common than non-slipped vessels suggests they are imports to Sidon rather than having been produced there. For the Beqaa, the literature suggests that, like the rest of Lebanon, slipping is rare during the ECL2-4. However, as the material is drawn from surveys, the chronological resolution is too poor to be certain. The identification of smoothed or slipped surfaces on imported vessels found in Early Dynastic Egypt may thus be

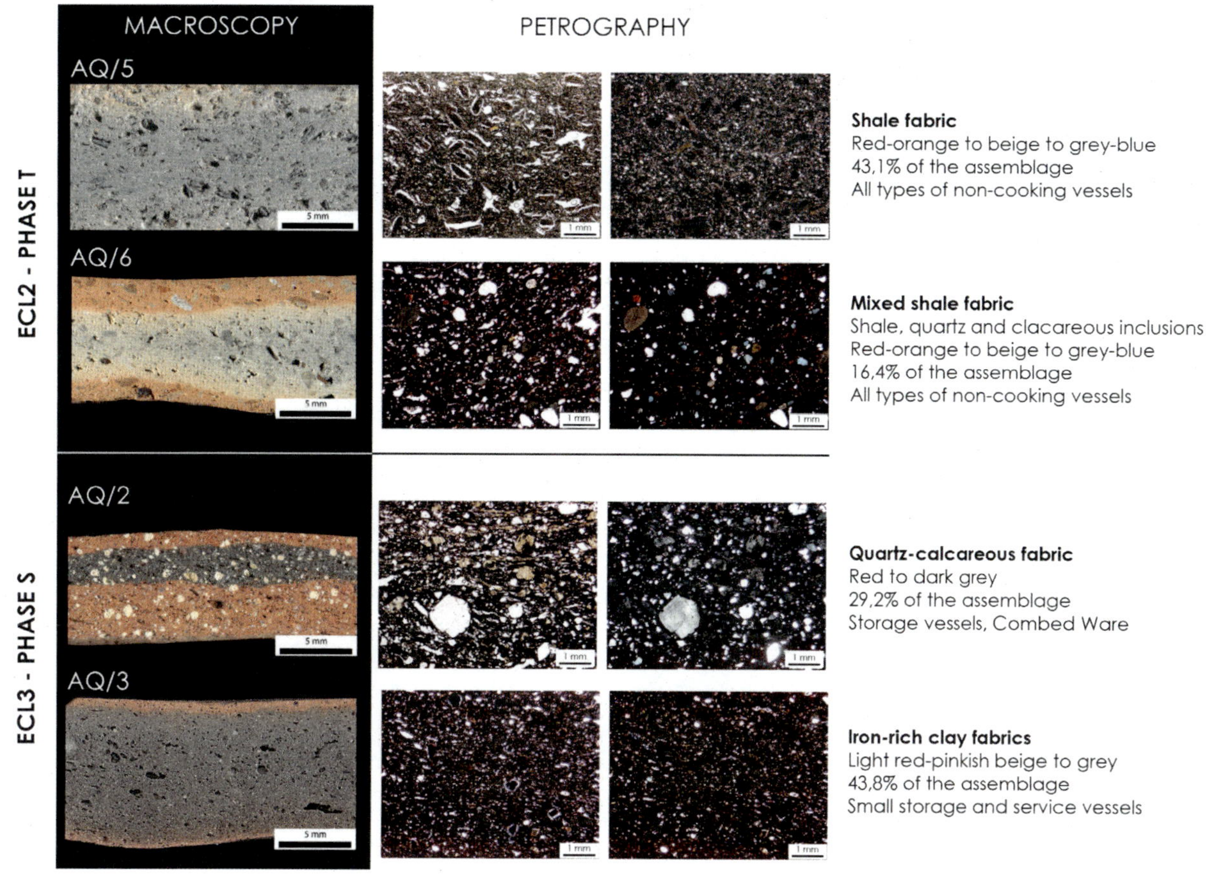

Figure 5: Main fabrics from Tell Arqa during ECL2 (Phase T) and ECL3 (Phase S), showing the shift from shale fabrics to quartz-calcareous and iron-rich fabrics (after Jean 2019).

considered an excluding criterion: they are almost certainly not from the region of Arqa, and very likely not produced on the Lebanese coast or in the central Levant. Based on those statements, we may already exclude four Egyptian samples originating in the central Levant due to the presence of a slip (Helwan, Op. 1/1 and Op. 4/36) and the absence of burnishing and/or combing (Abydos, Samples #11 and #17). Out of 14 Egyptian samples from Helwan and Abydos, nine could still fit well with central Levantine materials and need further comparison.

The macroscopic observation of fabrics is another relevant element for determining central Levantine provenance. At Tell Arqa, fabrics show clear evolution between ECL2 (Phase T) and ECL3 (Phase S) (Jean 2019, 2020). During Phase T, shale fabrics are the most common and make up 60% of the total assemblage: contemporaneous exports to Egypt should primarily be made of these fabrics (Fig. 5). An important change in pottery production is observed during Phase S when new fabrics developed. Quartz-calcareous fabrics are predominant for storage vessels and Combed Ware, while iron-rich fabrics are preferred for producing small storage and service vessels. At that time, shale fabrics became restricted to two specific pottery types: slender pattern-burnished red jugs and a unique seal-impressed jar (Thalmann 2013). This pattern is also observed on other Lebanese sites and probably reveals a region-level restructuring of pottery production systems (Badreshany et al. 2020). Identification of Levantine imports in Egypt should emphasize this technological aspect which could help clarify issues of provenance and chronology.

Abydos and the Central Levant: First Dynasty and ECL2 (Arqa Phase T)

Two types of imported vessels were identified among the samples from the tomb of king Den: jugs and jars. However, the vessels vary in shape, surface treatments, and fabrics, suggesting the coexistence of several productions and disparate provenances.

	Abydos	Tell Arqa
Sample Number	#20	1187
Vessel Number	T-aB/290	09/760.006
Context	Tomb of Den	Layer 19A
Date	Dynasty 1	Phase T, ECL2, EB II
Vessel Type	Squat jar	Small jar
Surface Treatment	Horizontal combing under lose vertical burnishing	Light combing under vertical burnishing
Technology	Coil-built	Coil-built
Base Diameter	c. 15 cm	c. 25 cm
Colour	Reddish brown surface, gray core	Orange-brown surface, gray-blue core
Fabric	Silty shale group	AQ/6.a: mixed shale fabric

TABLE 2: Comparison of the characteristics of squat jars from Abydos and Tell Arqa (from Hartung et al. 2015 and Jean 2019).

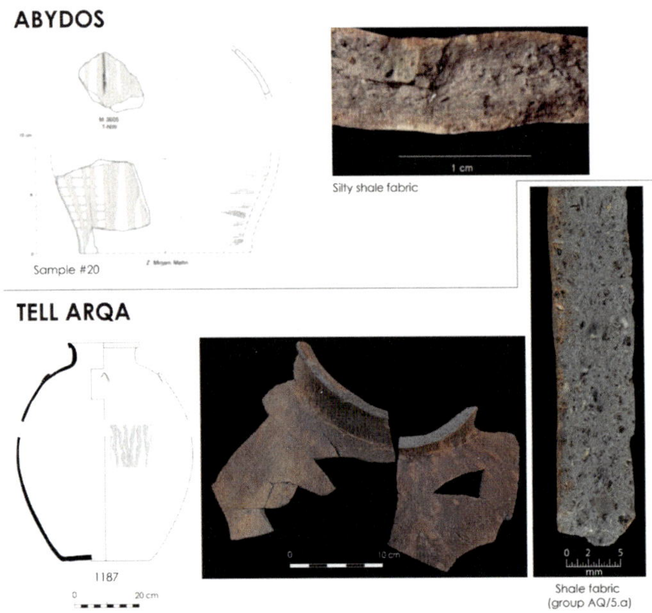

FIGURE 6: Comparison of the typology, technology, and fabrics of squat jars from Abydos and Tell Arqa (after Hartung et al. 2015: Figs. 16, 17:9; Jean 2019).

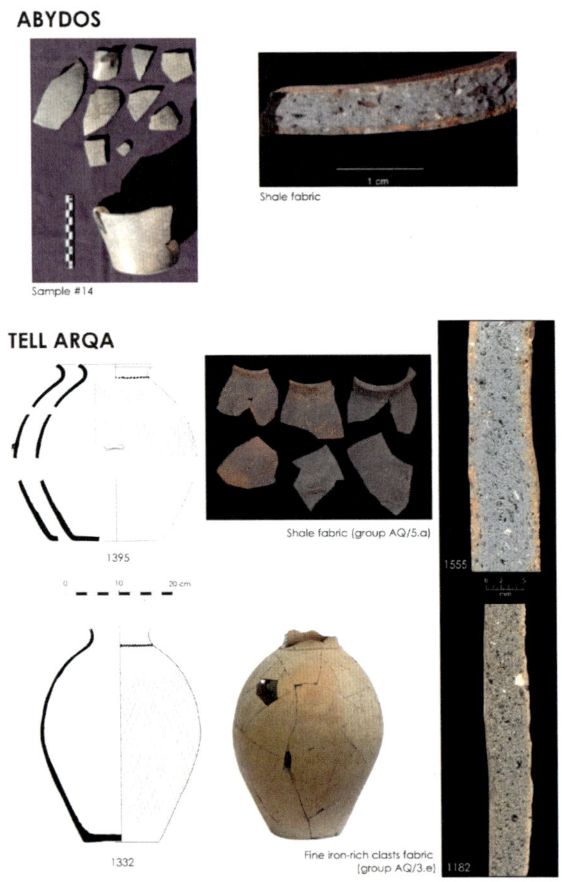

FIGURE 7: Comparison of the typology, technology, and fabrics of pattern-burnished jars from Abydos and Tell Arqa (from Hartung et al. 2015: Figs. 14, 17:7; Jean 2019).

Squat Vertically Burnished Jars

Two squat jars from Abydos were analyzed and published (Hartung et al. 2015). Sample #20 (Vessel T-aB/290; Hartung et al. 2015: Figs. 16, 17:9) finds a good match in the assemblage from Tell Arqa: both the shape and the surface treatments are similar, though the jar from Arqa is larger than the one from Abydos (Table 2, Fig. 6). On the other hand, sample #19 (Hartung et al. 2015, Figs. 13, 17:6), another squat jar, has no parallel

	Abydos	Tell Arqa	
Sample Number	#14	1395	1332
Vessel Number	T-aB/257	10/826.013	10/819.008
Context	Tomb of Den	Layer 19	Layer 19
Date	Dynasty 1	Phase T, ECL2, EB II	Phase T, ECL2, EB II
Vessel Type	Jar with loop handle	Medium squat jar with small horizontal lugs on the middle of the body	Medium elongated jar
Surface Treatment	Red wash, pattern burnishing on the body, between vertically burnished stripes; vertical burnishing on the neck	Pattern burnishing on the body; row of impressions at the bottom of the neck	Pattern burnishing on the body; row of impressions at the bottom of the neck
Technology	Coil-built with rotation	Coil-built	Coil-built
Measurements	c. 35 cm high; rim diameter 9.8 cm	c. 35 cm high; rim diameter c. 13–14 cm	c. 40 cm high; rim diameter c. 13–14 cm
Colour	Light red surface, gray core	Orange-brown	Beige-brown to brown purplish
Fabric	Shale group	AQ/5.a: shale fabric	AQ/3.e: fine iron-rich clasts fabric

Table 3: Comparison of the characteristics of pattern-burnished jars from Abydos and Arqa (from Hartung et al. 2015 and Jean 2019).

amongst materials from the northern Lebanese coast; it exhibits red wash and an irregularly burnished surface, suggesting it was produced in another region.

The Pattern-burnished Jars

One imported jar with a loop handle (sample #14), from Abydos, is decorated with pattern-burnishing (Hartung et al. 2015, Figs. 14, 17:7). Although the shape is not entirely preserved, satisfying parallels may be found at Arqa in jars from Phase T (Table 3, Fig. 7) with similar shapes, dimensions, and surface treatments. Some differences are nevertheless observed between the jars from Abydos and Arqa as the organization of the pattern-burnished areas in the former is delimited by large vertically burnished stripes that are not attested at Arqa. In addition, the vessels from Arqa are small jars often decorated with a row of impressions at the bottom of the neck and have either lug handles or no handles. However, loop handles are common on larger jars at Arqa and contemporary forms along the Lebanese coast; thus, their appearance on jars in Egypt should not be considered an excluding criterion for a coastal central Levantine provenance. Though this vessel is not a perfect match to central Levantine examples, the typological and decorative elements are common in the region, suggesting the vessel could have originated in the central Levant.

Recent analyses of Old Kingdom ceramics of Levantine origin suggest disparities in size and in some morphology aspects with those intended for circulation in the Levant (Thalmann and Sowada 2014; Badreshany et al. 2022); thus, it might be expected for ED vessels from the Levant to have varied from their locally distributed counterparts as well. Moreover, at Arqa, the jars might be separated into two slightly different types according to typology and petrography. The shale fabric squat jar (Fig. 7: 1395) compares well to the sample from Egypt, as well as a more elongated jar made of the fine iron-rich fabric (Fig. 7: 1332) that becomes much more common during ECL3. Further petrographic and typological analyses of the Abydos jars could help clarify the occurrence patterns of these distinct fabrics.

Jugs

The jugs from the tomb of king Den at Abydos are ovoid with flat bases. The upper part of the body is not preserved, and the shapes of the neck, rims, and whether handles occurred remain unclear.

The jugs are burnished in different ways, including short vertical strokes, fine vertical stripes, and pattern and horizontal burnishing. The fabrics are quite diverse as well, suggesting the coexistence of several regional productions in this tomb.

At Tell Arqa, pottery studies demonstrated that surface treatment and fabric are key characteristics to identifying and dating local productions (Thalmann 2016; Jean 2020b). Only vertical and pattern burnishing are documented in the assemblage from Phase T, and the production is primarily made of shale fabrics. A similar picture has emerged along the northern central Levantine coast (see below). These criteria are sufficiently well-defined to enable a reassessment of the provenance of some of the imported jugs at Abydos.

Beginning with Sample #13 (Hartung et al. 2015: Figs. 15, 17:8), strong typological parallels with material from the central Levantine coast could not be found, though the elements can be compared to the material at Arqa. As such, a possible origin for sample #13 in the central Levant can be suggested, though more data is needed to be certain because examples of jugs from Phase T are limited at Arqa (Table 4, Fig. 8). The other jugs are excluded for several reasons. Sample #12 (Hartung et al. 2015,

Figure 8: Comparison of the typology, technology, and fabrics of jugs from Abydos and Tell Arqa (from Hartung et al. 2015: fig. 15, 17:8; Thalmann 2016: Pl. 4; Jean 2019).

	Abydos	Arqa
Sample	#13	1493
Vessel	T-aB/288	10/851.003(A)
Context	Tomb of Den	Layer 20B
Date	Dynasty 1	Phase T, ECL2, EB II
Shape	Elongated jug	Large ovoid jug with a ridge at the bottom of the neck
Surface treatment	Vertical burnishing on the neck, pattern burnishing on the body	Neat vertical burnishing
Technology	Coil-built on a turning device	Coil-built
Measurement	ca. 35 cm (reconstructed)	ca. 52 cm
Colour	Pink surface, grey core	Orange-yellowish surface, grey core
Fabric	Shale fabric with quartz, few limestone	AQ/5.a: shale fabric

Table 4: Comparison of the characteristics of jugs from Abydos and Tell Arqa (from Hartung et al. 2015, Thalmann 2016 and Jean 2019).

Figs. 8, 17:1) because of its calcareous-igneous fabric which is not known at Arqa or in the central Levant during the period. Samples #16 (Hartung et al. 2015, Figs. 9, 17:2) and #18 (Hartung et al. 2015, Figs. 10, 17:3, 18:e) exhibit burnishing patterns not attested at Arqa or the wider region during the period (respectively, vertical/horizontal and short vertical strokes).

At present, the evidence from the central Levant does not support an origin from that region for three out of four imported jugs from Abydos. Only one example, #13, represents a potential match with the assemblage from Arqa and the wider region.

Abydos, Tomb of King Den: Discussion

The outcomes of the typological, technological, and macroscopic comparison show that only some of the imported vessels from Abydos may actually be attributed to the central Levant. We have shown a comprehensive approach to ceramics combining typology and petrography, but also considering local knowledge networks, technical choices, and savoir-faire, all crucial for provenancing artifacts. A reassessment of the provenance of Levantine imports from the First Dynasty at Abydos, in the tomb of king Den, shows that from the nine samples previously attributed to the central Levant and northern Lebanese coast, only three can be considered good matches with contemporary central Levantine assemblages. This conclusion is most valid for northern Lebanon and the region of Byblos, where a large amount of well-stratified data is available. The situation is less clear for the very beginning of the third millennium in the rest of the central Levant, like southern Lebanon, the Lebanese mountains, and the Beqaa, so future research might support an origin of these vessels from those areas.

Helwan and the Central Levant: Second Dynasty and ECL3 (Arqa Phase S)

At Helwan, the imported materials are represented by four jugs and one jar (Köhler and Ownby 2011). Typological description of the vessels is given for comparison with central Levantine types from Arqa and Byblos.

Pattern-burnished Slender Jugs: An ECL3 Characteristic Central Levantine Production

The Helwan imported jugs have a small flat base (base diameter c. 5 cm), elongated body, long neck, simple everted rim, and vertical handle on the rim and shoulder. One example (Op. 4/180) has a ridge below the neck and small vertical lugs on the upper body. The vessels are handmade and decorated by burnishing: pattern burnishing on the body and vertical burnishing on the neck; light combing can be observed under the burnishing on Op. 4/180 (Köhler and Ownby 2011) (Table 5, Fig. 9).

The dating of the jugs corresponds, in the central Levant, to the ECL3 and Arqa Phase S. At Tell Arqa, one group of jugs has strong typological parallels with the examples found at Helwan; these are red jugs with similar shapes and surface treatments, coil-built and made of a specific very oxidized shale fabric. These examples constitute one of the only types of shale vessels during Phase S/ECL3 (Fig. 10) in the Arqa or Byblos regions. At Arqa, the idiosyncratic nature of the shale-made jugs in the assemblage suggests that they are non-local. Based on typological, technological, and macroscopic comparisons, these jugs could originate in the Byblos region, where the red shale fabrics seem more common during the ECL3/4 despite the uncertain dating of the pottery sequence (author's personal observation).

At Byblos, similar jug types were discovered in a rock grave north of the tell, which could be dated to ECL3 (Table 5, Fig. 11; Thalmann 2019). The pottery assemblage from this tomb at Byblos also includes typical central Levantine double jugs with ram decoration (Fig. 11), which are also known at Tell Fadous (Genz et al. 2010, Pl. 6) and Sidon (Doumet-Serhal 2006, Pl. 117). Unfortunately, Thalmann's publication does not provide macroscopic or petrographic descriptions of the vessels from Byblos. However, the typological and technological match and the presence of shale fabrics in other assemblages from Byblos lend support to the notion that the red-shale pattern-burnished slender jugs originate in the Byblos region. Furthermore, based on the published evidence, they are more frequent there than in any other area, including Sidon. Similar observations have been made by the authors at Koubba, where a number of these jugs were found, belonging to the same type and made of the same fabric (Fig. 11). This type seems characteristic of the ECL3 in the region of Byblos and is probably distributed throughout the central Levant. Coastal examples are known at Bechemoun (Badreshany *et al.* 2020) and Sidon strata 4–5 (Doumet-Serhal 2006, Photos 9–10, Pls. 28:18, 58:19). Some examples are known from the Beqaa (a sherd from Tell Aswad, Fig. 11; Badreshany 2013).

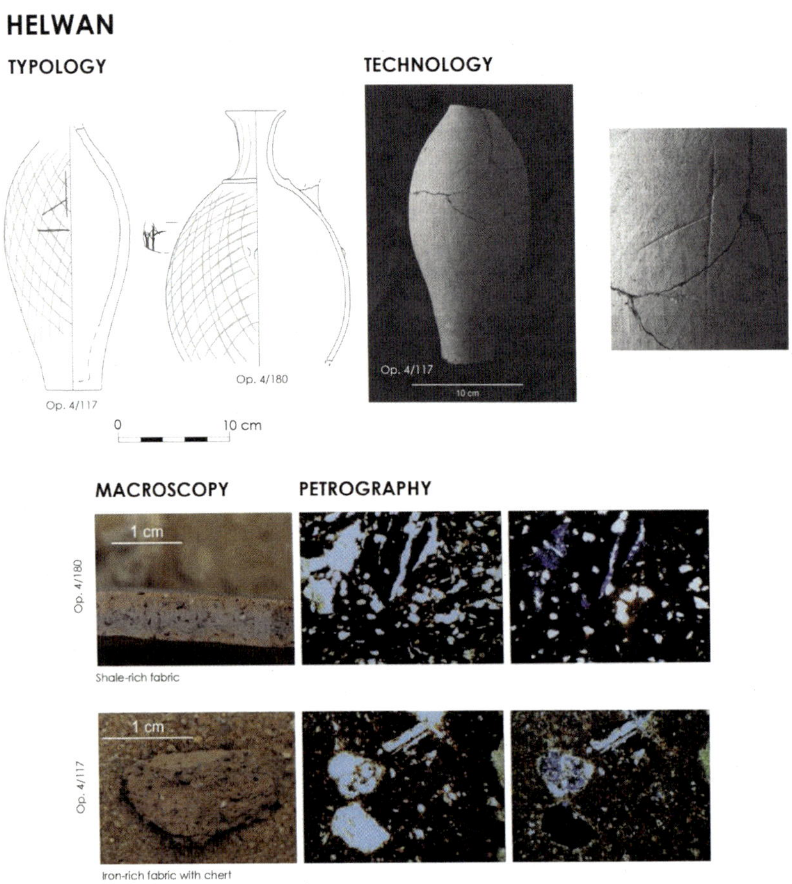

FIGURE 9: Typology, technology, and fabrics of slender jugs from Helwan (from Köhler and Ownby 2011: Figs. 2, 3:1, 2, 10, 11).

	Helwan		Arqa
Sample	Op. 4/180	Op. 4/117	951
Vessel		P06-26	09/720.154
Context	Op. 4/180	Op. 4/180	Layer 18C
Date	Late 1st/early 2nd dynasty	Early 2nd dynasty	Phase S, ECL3, EB II/III
Shape	Slender jug	Slender jug	Slender jug
Surface treatment	Pattern burnishing on the body and verticak burnishing on the neck. Light horizontal combing under the burnishing	Pattern burnishing	Pattern burnishing on the body and vertical burnishing on the neck, ridge below the neck
Technology	Handmade	Handmade	Coil-built
Maximal diameter	16.5 cm	11 cm	ca. 12 cm
Colour	Grey buff	Red buff	Red buff
Fabric	Shale-rich fabric	Iron-rich fabric with chert	AQ/5.b: oxydised shale fabric

TABLE 5: Comparison of the characteristics of slender jugs from Helwan and Tell Arqa (from Köhler and Ownby 2011 and Jean 2019).

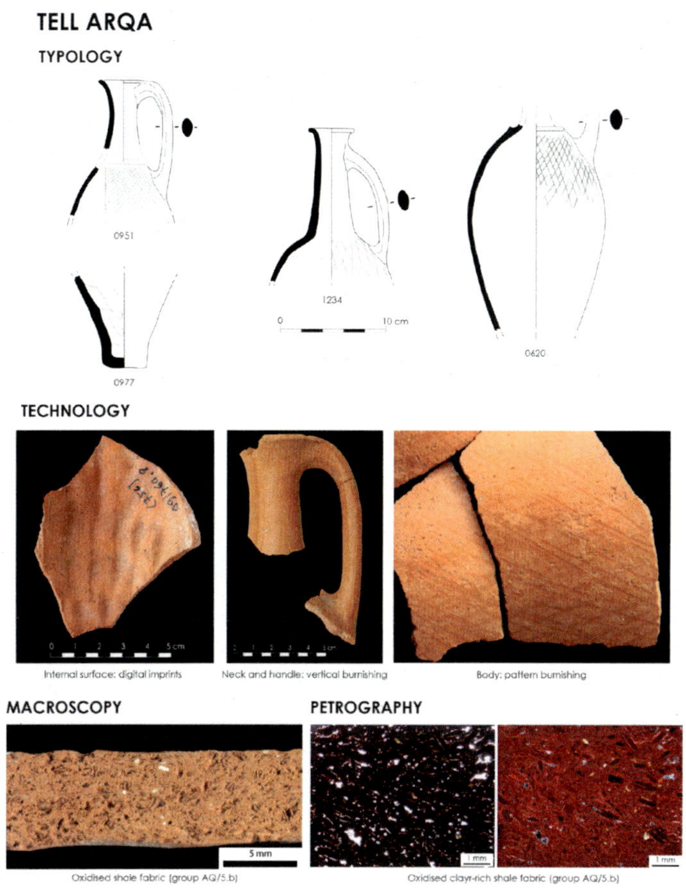

Figure 10: Typology, technology, and fabrics of slender jugs from Tell Arqa (from Thalmann 2016: Pls. 9, 13; Jean 2019).

The Globular Jar: An Heirloom Vessel?

The imported jar found in Tomb Op. 4/15 at Helwan is a large vessel with a globular upper body, short neck, and rounded rim. It is handmade, and the surface shows irregular, wavy vertical burnishing and a gritty quartz-calcareous fabric (Köhler and Ownby 2011). Jars with irregular burnishing are only known at Tell Arqa during ECL2/Phase T (Table 6, Fig. 12; Thalmann 2016, Pl. 5), earlier than Tomb Op.4/15 at Helwan, which dates to the mid-second Dynasty. At Arqa, Phase T jars are almost always made of shale fabrics, while quartz-calcareous fabrics mostly appear during ECL3/Phase S for the production of Combed Ware (Badreshany et al. 2020; Jean 2020a). This discrepancy between an older type and a new fabric indicates the presence of transitional production stage in the central Levant at the ECL2–ECL3 interface. Two examples of this type/fabric combination are known at Arqa at the end of Phase T/ECL2 (Table 6).

The jar found at Helwan cannot be identified among contemporary assemblages from Tell Arqa or the central Levant from the mid-late ECL3 but is a good match in both form and fabric with earlier vessels dating to the ECL2/3 transition. Given our current understanding of the data, the most likely explanation is that the jar is of central Levantine origin but was kept as an heirloom for c. 100 years after its production and deposited in a later grave. Typologically early jars (along with other materials) have been recognized in later tombs in Egypt (Sparks 2003; Sowada 2009, 18; Sowada, Ownby, and Bárta 2021). Likewise, there is a growing awareness that typologically earlier objects are being found in later deposits at Byblos (de Vreeze and Badreshany, this volume), indicating some commonalities between the two contexts.

Petrographic and Geochemical Comparison: The Issue of Shale Wares

Studies have confirmed that most ECL2 (EB II) pottery from central Levant was produced utilizing distinctive shale wares (Griffiths 2006; Badreshany 2013; Badreshany et al. 2020; Jean 2020a). Calcareous wares are used for cooking pots of the ECL2 and then gradually become dominant, starting with the ECL2–3 (EB II–III) transition and into the ECL3. In Sidon (and the south) and the Beqaa, the situation is difficult to assess with certainty due to fewer chronologically secure contexts, but shale fabrics are very common in both places. Little is known about the EB ceramic traditions of the Lebanese mountains at present; still, given the evidence, we expect that most vessels imported to Egypt from the central Levant during the First and Second Dynasties would have been made of shale fabrics. Jean argues that shale vessels from Phase T at Arqa are more diverse, generally coarser, and/or mixed with other inclusions, such as limestone, to a greater degree than those from Phase S, less common in the local assemblage (Jean 2020a). A preliminary study, by the authors, of the ECL2 material from Koubba I, contemporary with Phase T at Arqa, seems to validate these assessments.

We present some preliminary geochemical results comparing the shale fabrics from Arqa with regional datasets published by Badreshany *et al.* 2020. The PCA (Fig. 4)

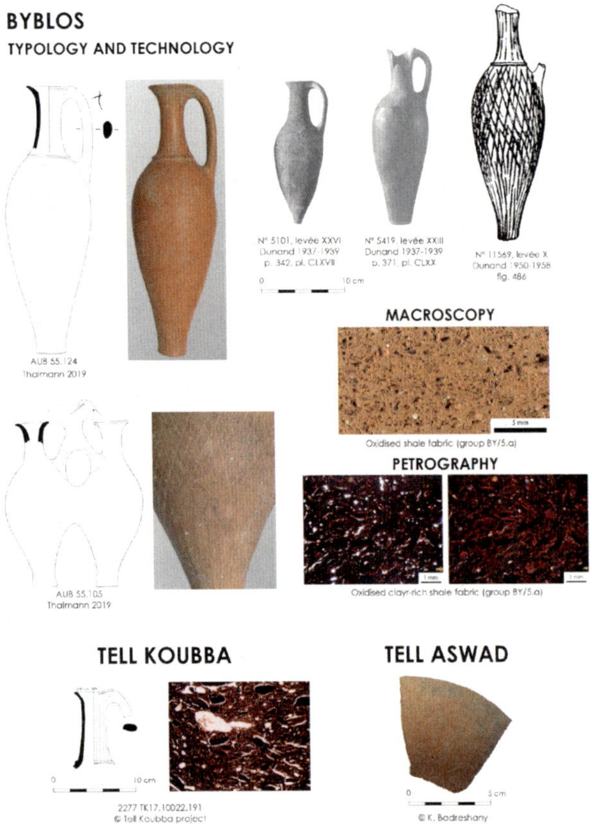

FIGURE 11: Typology, technology, and fabrics of slender jugs from Byblos (from Dunand 1937–1939, 1950–1958; Thalmann 2019; Jean 2019).

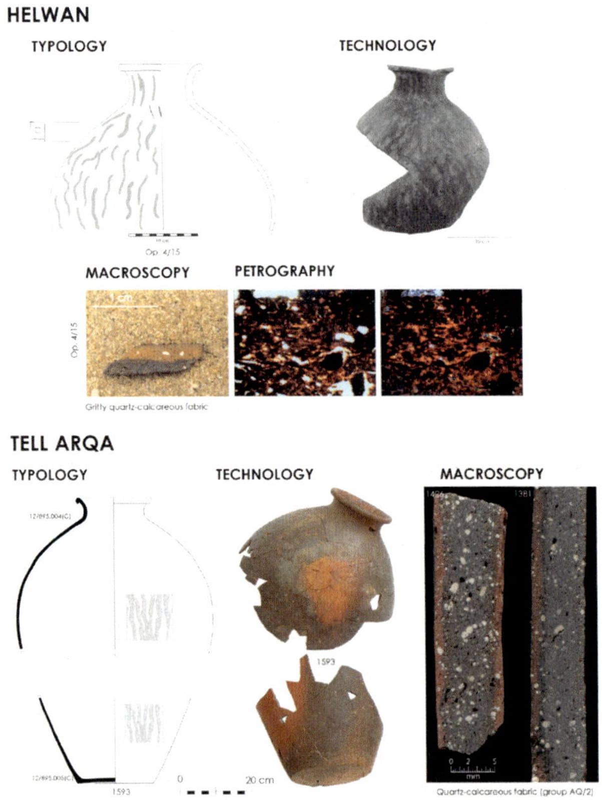

FIGURE 12: Typology, technology and fabrics of jars from Helwan and Tell Arqa (from Köhler and Ownby 2011: Figs. 3:5, 6:a, 8; Thalmann 2016; Jean 2019).

shows that, with a small number of exceptions, the majority of the Phase T vessels group with wares of confirmed ECL2 date to the right of the graph, while the main grouping in the center of the graph contains vessels from the ECL2–3 transition and early ECL3 (Phase S). Furthermore, the ECL2 (Phase T) vessels from Arqa tend to be somewhat higher in Calcium and lower in Rare Earth Elements than those from ECL3 (Phase S). This data will be discussed in more detail, along with the petrographic analysis of the ECL2 materials from Koubba, in a forthcoming publication.

This graph and the evidence presented above provide a basis for petrographically and geochemically distinguishing vessels of central Levantine origin produced during the First and Second Dynasties (ECL2 and ECL3). This information will hopefully be of great use in future studies for clarifying issues of chronology and provenance of ceramic vessels of central Levantine origin found in Egyptian contexts.

Conclusion

Our re-analysis of the ceramic evidence reinforces earlier notions of broad connections between Egypt and the Levant during the Early Dynastic period. Fourteen imported vessels found in Egyptian tombs were compared to contemporary central Levantine productions to refine and reassess their postulated provenance (Table 1) in light of newly available data. At Abydos, the royal tomb of Den provided a case study for First Dynasty/ECL2 contexts (Hartung et al. 2015), and the results confirmed a central Levantine provenance of three samples out of nine: two different types of jars and one jug. At Helwan Operation 4, several non-elite tombs from the Second Dynasty/ECL3 were investigated (Köhler and Ownby 2011). Out of five samples, three are highly comparable to central Levantine productions. This approach should now be extended to additional imported vessels to test their Levantine provenance by comparing them to Levantine assemblages. Based on the typological

	Helwan	Tell Arqa		
Sample Number	Op. 4/15	1381	1426	1593
Vessel Number	P01-10	10/824.e	10/829.b	12/895.004-005C
Context	Op. 4/15	Layer 19	Layer 20A	Layer 20
Date	Mid-2nd Dynasty/ Naqada IIID2	Phase T/S4, ECL2, EB II	Phase T, ECL2, EB II	Phase T, ECL2, EB II
Vessel Type	Jar with globular upper body, short cylindrical nexk and rounded rim	Jar (body sherd)	Jar (body sherd)	Jar with ovoid body, short cylindrical neck and rounded rim
Surface Treatment	Irregular wavy vertical burnishing	Irregular wavy vertical burnishing	Irregular wavy vertical burnishing	Irregular wavy vertical burnishing
Technology	Handmade	Coil-built	Coil-built	Coil-built
Measurements	Rim diameter: 12 cm; Maximal diameter: 33 cm			Rim diameter: 20 cm; Maximal diameter: 47 cm; Reconstructed height: c. 80 cm
Colour	Buff surface; orange-buff to gray-buff core	Buff surface; red-buff to gray core	Red surfaces and gray-buff core	Orange surfaces; gray-blue core
Fabric	Quartz-calcareous fabric	AQ/2: quartz-calcareous fabric	AQ/2: quartz-calcareous fabric	AQ/5.a: shale fabric

Table 6: Comparison of the characteristics of jars from Helwan and Tell Arqa (from Köhler and Ownby 2011; Thalmann 2016; and Jean 2019).

studies, it already seems that more vessels from Egypt can be attributed to the central Levant, reinforcing the conclusions of this paper.

Though based on a few samples, our study suggests that relations between Egypt and the central Levant changed in the early third millennium, from periodic to more focused and regular activity. From the earliest ECL2, the central coastal Levant is a focal point of Egyptian activity, but one of many across the central and southern Levant. Central Levantine vessels are found in similar proportions to a wide range of southern Levantine productions imported to the Egyptian court (Iserlis et al. 2019).

It is during the ECL 2–3 transition that changes are perceptible and contact with the central Levant progressively increases. During the ECL3/Second Dynasty, imported materials were less common in Egypt, and vessels from the central Levant were comparatively more frequent among them, especially typical vessels such as the red pattern-burnished jugs likely produced in the Byblos region. This leads to two distinct statements, partly contradictory, which could contribute to the complexity of understanding Levant–Egypt relations during the Second Dynasty.

First, a new practice seems to emerge, repurposing imported vessels as heirlooms for deposit in later graves. These actions may attest to an increasing status afforded to these vessels and their contents, possibly related to the relative scarcity of Levantine goods in Egypt during the Second Dynasty when compared to the first one. This practice becomes even more apparent in Old Kingdom contexts (Sparks 2003; Sowada 2009; Sowada et al. 2021). Second, Egyptian Early Dynastic contexts suggest that Levantine imports are becoming more widespread among differing social classes, from the royal tombs of the First Dynasty to non-elite tombs of the Second Dynasty attributed to the urban middle-class (though notably absent from the tomb of king Ninetjer; Lacher-Raschdorff 2014, 85–87). Both statements are supported by archaeological evidence and could have resulted from the weakening of the Second Dynasty central economy benefitting other social classes, thus making it harder to reconstruct Second Dynasty trade networks.

The evidence indicates that the central Levant progressively becomes a focus for Early Dynastic Egypt, underpinning the region's development as its primary trade partner during the Old Kingdom. These changes, beginning during the ECL2/3 transition, are coincident with an increase in the number of settlements and building activity at many sites on the northern Lebanese coast and continue through the ECL 3/4, providing new settings for interactions between the region and the Egyptian state during the Old Kingdom (see de Vreeze and Badreshany, this volume).

Finally, this paper highlights new and existing criteria aiding in the provenance determinations of Levantine imports to Egypt based on the recent examination of several contemporaneous and stratified assemblages from Lebanon. These new datasets will help further develop the research on Egyptian–Levantine trade to better understand the role of the Levantine regions in networks and the evolution of sociopolitical and economic relationships between Egypt and the Levant during the third millennium.

Acknowledgments

Research for this paper was funded by Hesam Université, Université Paris 1 Panthéon-Sorbonne, UMR 7041 Arscan/VEPMO, and the Computational Research on the Ancient Near East (CRANE) project supported by the Social Sciences and Humanities Research Council of Canada. We would like to especially recognize Dr. Mary Ownby, Dr. Christiana Köhler, and Dr. Ulrich Hartung for their many years of work on Levantine imports in Egypt and thank them for shared insights and fruitful discussions on the topic that served as the inspiration for this paper. Of course, the responsibility for the conclusions presented here lies with the authors. We are especially grateful to the Directorate General of Antiquities of Lebanon for authorizing the authors' missions in the field and the export of pottery samples for analysis. We are indebted to the late Dr. Jean-Paul Thalmann for initiating direct comparisons between materials from Egypt and Tell Arqa and supporting the petrographic analysis of EBA pottery. Thanks are due to Attila Kreiter at the Hungarian National Museum for preparing the thin sections, and to Chris Ottley, at the Department of Earth Sciences at Durham University for undertaking the geochemical analyses by ICP-AES and -MS. Finally, we are grateful to the reviewers of this paper for their helpful comments.

References

Badreshany, Kamal. 2013. *Urbanization in the Levant: an archaeometric approach to understanding the social ad economic impact of settlement nucleation in the Biqa' valley*, Unpublished PhD dissertation, University of Chicago.

Badreshany, Kamal and Hermann Genz. 2009. "Pottery production on the northern Lebanese coast during the Early Bronze Age II–III: The petrographic analysis of the ceramics from Tell Fadous-Kfarabida." *Bulletin of the American School of Oriental Research* 355: 51–83.

Badreshany, Kamal, Graham Philip, and Melissa Kennedy. 2020. "The development of integrated regional economies in the Early Bronze Age Levant: new evidence from 'Combed Ware' jars." *Levant* 52(1–2): 160–196.

Badreshany, Kamal, Karin Sowada, Mary Ownby, Mathilde Jean, Michel De Vreeze, Alice McClymont, and Graham Philip. 2022. "The characterisation of Levantine ceramic production and Egyptian trade in the Pyramid Age." *Journal of Archaeological Science: Reports, Volume* 41. https://doi.org/10.1016/j.jasrep.2021.103309.

Bronk Ramsey, Christopher, Michael W. Dee, Joanne M. Rowland, Thomas F.G. Higham, Stehpen A. Harris, Fiona Brock, Anita Quiles, Eva M. Wild, Ezra S. Marcus, and Andrew J. Shortland. 2010. "Radiocarbon-Based Chronology for Dynastic Egypt." *Science* 328: 1554–1557.

Buxeda i Garrigós, Jaume. 1999. "Alteration and contamination of archaeological ceramics: the perturbation problem." *Journal of Archaeological Science* 26(3): 295–313.

Dee, Michael, David Wengrow, Andrew Shortland, Alice Stevenson, Fiona Brock, Linus Girdland Flink, and Christopher Bronk Ramsey. 2013. "An absolute chronology for early Egypt using radiocarbon dating and Bayesian statistical modelling." *Proceedings of the Royal Society.* https://doi.org/10.1098/rspa.2013.0395.

Doumet-Serhal, Claude. 2006. *The Early Bronze Age in Sidon: "College site" Excavations (1998–2000–2001).* Bibliothèque Archéologique et Historique 178. Beyrouth: Institut Français du Proche-Orient.

Dunand Maurice. 1937–1939. *Fouilles de Byblos I, 1926–1932* : Atlas. Paris: Geuthner.

———. 1950–1958. *Fouilles de Byblos II, 1933–1938.* Paris: Geuthner.

Espinel, Andrés Diego. 2002. "The Role of the Temple of Ba'alat Gebal as Intermediary Between Egypt and Byblos During the Old Kingdom." *Studien zur Altägyptischen Kultur* 30: 103–119.

Genz, Hermann, Riva Daniel, Alison Damick, Alexander Ahrens, Sireen el-Zaatari, Felix Höflmayer, Walter Kutschera, and Eva M. Wild. 2010. "Excavations at Tell Fadous-Kfarabida. Preliminary Report on the 2010 Season of Excavations." *Bulletin d'Archéologie et d'Architecture Libanaises* 14: 241–274.

Greenberg, Raphael. 2019. *The Archaeology of the Bronze Age Levant. From Urban Origins to the Demise of City-States, 3700–1000 BCE.* Cambridge: Cambridge University Press.

Greenberg, Raphael and M. Iserlis. 2020. "A Note on First Dynasty Egypt, Tel Bet Yerah and the Origins of Commodity Exchange on the Levantine Seaboard." *Journal of Ancient Egyptian Interconnections* 27: 38–50.

Grimal, Nicolas. 1988. *Histoire de l'Egypte ancienne.* Paris: Fayard.

Hartung, Ulrich. 2002. "Imported jars from cemetery U at Abydos and the Relations between Egypt and Canaan in Predynastic Times." In Edwin C.M. van den Brink and T.E. Levy (eds.), *Egypt and the Levant. Interrelations from the 4th through the Early 3rd Millennium B.C.E.*, 437–449. London—New York: Leicester University Press.

Hartung, Ulrich, E. Christiana Köhler, Vera Müller, and Mary F. Ownby. 2015. "Imported Pottery from Abydos: A New Petrographic Perspective." Ägypten *und Levante* 25: 295–333.

Hornung, Erik, Rolf Krauss, and David A. Warburton (eds.). 2006. *Ancient Egyptian Chronology*. Leiden, Boston: Brill.

Iserlis, Mark, Daniel Steiniger, and Raphael Greenberg. 2019. "Contact between first dynasty Egypt and specific sites in the Levant: new evidence from ceramic analysis." *Journal of Archaeological Science: Reports* 24: 1023–1040.

Jean, Mathilde. 2019. *Mémoires de terres. L'urbanisation du Levant nord au IIIe millénaire par la pétrographie céramique.* Unpublished PhD dissertation, Université Paris 1, Panthéon-Sorbonne.

———. 2020a. "Pottery Production at Tell Arqa (Lebanon) during the 3rd millennium BC: Preliminary Results of Petrographic Analysis." *Levant* 52(1–2): 136–159.

———. 2020b. "Evolutions of pottery production over a millennium: petrographic analysis of the EB ceramic assemblage from Tell Arqa." In Melissa A. Kennedy (ed.), *A Land in Between. The Orontes Valley in the Early Urban Age*, 173–193. Sydney: Sydney University Press.

Köhler, E. Christiana. and Jean-Paul Thalmann. 2014. "Synchronising Early Egyptian Chronologies and the Northern Levant." In Felix Höflmayer and Ricardo Eichmann (eds.), *Egypt and the Southern Levant in the Early Bronze Age*, 181–206. Rahden: Verlag Marie Leidorf.

Köhler, E. Christiana, and Mary F. Ownby. 2011. "Levantine Imports and their Imitations from Helwan." Ägypten *und Levante* 21: 31-46.

Lacher-Raschdorff, Claudia M. 2014. *Das Grab des Königs Ninetjer in Saqqara. Architektonische Entwicklug frühzeitlicher Grabanlagen in* Ägypten. Deutsches Archäologisches Institut Kairo. Wiesbaden: Harrassowitz Verlag.

Marcus, Ezra. 2002. "Early seafaring and maritime activity in the southern Levant from Prehistory through the third millennium BCE." In Edwin C.M. van den Brink and Thomas E. Levy (eds.), *Egypt and the Levant. Interrelations from the 4th through the Early 3rd Millennium B.C.E.*, 403–417. London, New York: Leicester University Press.

Miroschedji, Pierre de. 2015. "Les relations entre l'Egypte et le Levant aux IVe et IIIe millénaires à la lumière des fouilles de Tell as-Sakan. " In *Comptes-rendus des séances de l'Académie des Inscriptions et Belles Lettres*, Avril-Juin 2015 : 1003–1038. Paris: Diffusion de Boccard.

———. 2018. "The urbanization of the Southern Levant in its Near Eastern Setting." In Marcella Frangipane and Linda R. Manzanilla (eds.), *Rethinking Urbanization and Its Living Landscapes from the Inspiring Perspective of a Great "Maestro"* in Memory of Robert McC. Adams: 109–148. Origini, Prehistory and Protohistory of Ancient Civilizations 42. Roma: Gangemi.

Müller, Vera. 2014. "Relations between Egypt and the Near-East during the 1st Egyptian Dynasty as represented by the royal tomb of Den at Umm el-Qaab/Abydos." In Felix Höflmayer and Ricardo Eichmann (eds.), *Egypt and the Southern Levant in the Early Bronze Age*, 241–258. Rahden: Verlag Marie Leidorf.

Mumford, Gregory D. 2014. "Egypt and the Levant." In Margreet L. Steiner and Ann E. Killebrew (eds.), *The Oxford Handbook of the Archaeology of the Levant c. 8000-332 BCE*, 69–89. Oxford: Oxford University Press.

Orton, Clive and Michael Hughes. 2013. *Pottery in Archaeology*. Cambridge Manuals in Archaeology. Cambridge: Cambridge University Press.

Ottley, Chris J., D. Graham Pearson, and Gordon J. Irvine. 2003. "A Routine Method for the Dissolution of Geological Samples for the Analysis of REE and Trace Elements via ICP-MS." In J. Grenville Holland and Scott D. Tanner (eds.), *Plasma Source Mass Spectrometry: Applications and Emerging Technologies*, 221–230. Cambridge: Royal Society of Chemistry.

Papageorgiou, Ioulia. 2020. "Ceramic investigation. How to perform statistical analyses." *Archaeological and Anthropological Sciences* 12: 210.

Porat, Naomi, and Yuval Goren. 2002. "Petrography of the Naqada IIIa Canaanite pottery from tomb U-j in Abydos." In Edwin C.M. van den Brink and Thomas E. Levy (eds.), *Egypt and the Levant. Interrelations from the 4th through the early 3rd millennium B.C.E.*, 252–270. London: Leicester University Press.

Roux, Valentine and Jean-Paul Thalmann. 2016. "Évolution technologique et morpho-stylistique des assemblages céramiques de Tell Arqa (Liban, 3e millénaire av. J.-C.) : stabilité sociologique et changements culturels." *Paléorient* 42/1: 101–127.

Shaw, Ian (ed.). 2000. *The Oxford History of Ancient Egypt*. Oxford: Oxford University Press.

Sowada, Karin N. 2009. *Egypt in the Eastern Mediterranean during the Old Kingdom: An Archaeological Perspective*. Orbis Biblicus et Orientalis 237. Fribourg, Göttingen: Academic Press, Vandenhoeck & Ruprecht.

———. 2014. "Never the Twain Shall Meet? Synchronising Egyptian and Levantine Chronologies in the 3rd Millennium BC." In Felix Höflmayer and Ricardo Eichmann (eds.), *Egypt and the Southern Levant in the Early Bronze Age*, 293–313. Rahden: Verlag Marie Leidorf.

Sowada, Karin, Mary Ownby, and Anna Wodzińska. 2020. "The Petrography of Imported Levantine Combed Vessels from Early Old Kingdom Giza." *Levant* 52(1–2):197–214.

Sowada, Karin, Mary Ownby, and Miroslav Bárta. 2021. "The Origin of Imported Jars from 6th Dynasty Abusir: New Light on Early Bronze Age Egyptian-Levantine Relations." *Bulletin of the American Schools of Oriental Research* 386: 221–236.

Sowada, Karin, Mary Ownby, Jane Smythe, Sylvie Marchand, and Yann Tristant. 2021. "Early Bronze Age Exchange Patterns between Egypt and the Levant: A View from First Dynasty Abu Rawash." *Egypt and the Levant* 31: 425–449.

Sparks, Rachael "Egyptian Stone Vessels and the Politics of Exchange (2617–1070 BC)." In Roger J. Matthews and Cornelia Roemer (eds.), *Ancient Perspectives on Egypt*, 39–56. London: UCL Press.

Thalmann, Jean-Paul. 2006. *Tell Arqa - I: Les niveaux de l'âge du Bronze*. Bibliothèque Archéologique et Historique 177. Beyrouth: Institut Français du Proche-Orient.

———. 2016. "Rapport préliminaire sur les campagnes de 2008 à 2012 à Tell Arqa." *Bulletin d'Archéologie et d'Architecture Libanaises* 16: 15–78.

———. 2019. "Un groupe de vases du Bronze Ancien au musée de l'AUB." In Françoise Briquel-Chatonnet, Emmanuelle Capet, Eric Gubel and Carol Roche-Hawley, *Nuit de pleine lune sur Amurru* : Mélanges offerts à Leila Badrę, 383–400. Paris: Geuthner.

Thalmann, Jean-Paul and Karin Sowada. 2014. "Levantine 'Combed Ware'." In Marc Lebeau (ed.), *Associated Regional Chronologies for the Ancient Near-East and the Eastern Mediterranean, ARCANE Interregional Vol. I: Ceramics*, 355–378. Turnhout: Brepols.

Wickham, Hadley. (ed.) 2009. *ggplot2: Elegant Graphics for Data Analysis*. New York: Springer.

Wilkinson, Toby A.H. 1999. *Early Dynastic Egypt*. London: Routledge.

Journal of Ancient Egyptian Interconnections

Early Dynastic/Old Kingdom Egypt and the Early Bronze Age Levant: The History of the 3rd and 4th Dynasties and New Radiocarbon Dates in Dialogue

Johannes Jüngling
Austrian Academy of Sciences

Felix Höflmayer
Austrian Academy of Sciences

Abstract[1]
This paper aims to give an overview of the current state of research on (contemporaneous) inscriptional evidence for a historical chronology of the 3rd and 4th dynasties, to explore the impact of different modes of interpreting this evidence on radiocarbon dates from Egypt, and to consider possible synchronizations between Egyptian history and the transitions from Early Bronze Age III to IV in the Southern Levant. Therefore, the currently available data are re-evaluated, and a model for a biennial cattle count in the early Old Kingdom is proposed. In order to specify the EB III–IV transition, recent radiocarbon sequences from nine different sites in the Southern Levant are surveyed.

Keywords
Chronology, 3rd Millennium BCE, Old Kingdom, Early Bronze Age, Southern Levant, 3rd Dynasty, 4th Dynasty, Sneferu, Khufu, Palermo Stone, Turin Canon

1. Introduction

Reconstructing absolute (calendrical) dates for historical events and archaeological contexts of ancient Egypt and the ancient Near East can, at times, be a challenging task. While one should suspect that the application of radiocarbon dating, especially when coupled with Bayesian analysis, might be used as a powerful tool for unravelling still persistent chronological questions and uncertainties, observation of academic manners and customs in Egyptology and Biblical Archaeology in fact shows that more often than not scientific facts do not supersede academic fiction. Lengthy discussions around absolute dates for the Iron Age and Biblical Archaeology in the southern Levant,[2] the absolute date of the Santorini (ancient Thera) volcanic eruption,[3] and questions of absolute Middle Bronze Age chronology[4] are but few examples where scientific application of radiocarbon dating and Bayesian analysis is either outright rejected, ridiculed or simply ignored.

With this background in mind, it comes as a surprise that new absolute dating evidence for the Early Bronze Age that suggested major shifts of more than 100 years for relative chronological periods did not face major resistance in our academic disciplines. Since the initial publication by Johanna Regev and colleagues in 2012 that for the first time suggested a short (<100 years) Early Bronze II period and that the end of Early Bronze III should be dated to around 2500 BCE instead of ca. 2300/2200 BCE, as previously suggested,[5] several other radiocarbon sequences were published that basically came to the same result.[6] Only a few years later, this new chronology was actually applied to our archaeological data at hand, and the impact on our understanding of Egyptian-Levantine relations in the Early Bronze Age explored.[7] Nowadays, the high Early Bronze Age chronology has become the standard chronology of modern textbooks.[8]

The application of radiocarbon dating in the field of Egyptology was also not easy from the beginning. After several early attempts in checking the historical dates with radiocarbon data,[9] it was only in 2010, when Christopher Bronk Ramsey, Michael Dee and others published their assessment based on over 200 new high-precision radiocarbon determinations. They found that Bayesian modelling based on (historically) reconstructed reign lengths actually provided a close fit between modelled radiocarbon determinations and historical assessments for the Old, Middle, and New Kingdoms.[10] Only modelled dates for the 5th and 6th dynasties seemed to be slightly older than historical assessments.

Since conclusive radiocarbon sequences for the Early Bronze Age southern Levant and for Old Kingdom Egypt were available, for the first time it was possible to provide a synchronized chronology based on independent radiocarbon dating. It was found that the now shortened Early Bronze II would be contemporary with the Egyptian 1st dynasty and that the end of Early Bronze III would fall approximately to the late 4th or early 5th dynasty.[11]

But how robust are these (modelled) dates and the Egyptian-Levantine chronological synchronization in light of recent research in the relative chronology of Old Kingdom reign lengths and can we still support a ca. 2500 BCE date for the end of Early Bronze III a decade after the initial publication? The following paper aims to explore some chronological issues of the Early Dynastic Period and the Old Kingdom in the light of re-evaluated and newly discovered material, including two case studies (cf. below, sections 4.2–3) and several chronological models (cf. below, section 5) that demonstrate how uncertain and open to re-consideration and re-interpretation Early Dynastic and Old Kingdom chronology still is today. Further, we will review existent radiocarbon sequences for Early Bronze III and will try to explore potential shifts in the synchronization with Old Kingdom Egypt.

2. The Egyptian Chronology

Ancient Egyptian chronography, like many pre-modern chronographic systems, is essentially a royal one—i. e., time is measured and periodized according to royal personage and royal activities.[12] Chronological research has had to adapt to these factors, especially in the case of two of the earliest epochs accessible by means of Egyptian philology, the so-called 'Early Dynastic Period'[13] and the 'Old Kingdom.'[14] Yet, given the relative paucity of textual sources, many aspects of those periods still remain obscure—among them chronological issues like the exact length of individual reigns, but also the very number of reigning kings or their names.[15] The results of this philological approach to Egyptian chronology may illustrate how great an impact seemingly small variations within the interpretation of textual material can have, even more so when connected to recent radiocarbon data used as a base of Bayesian modelling (on this, cf. below, section 7).

The two epochs in question cover a timespan of roughly 1,000 years, and comprise—at least—dynasties 0 to 6. [16] For a long time, Egyptology's internal periodization considered dynasties 0/1–2 as 'Archaic' or 'Early Dynastic Period', the Old Kingdom starting with the onset of the 3rd dynasty. This view began to shift markedly in the 1990s, most notably with the seminal work of Toby Wilkinson, *Early Dynastic Egypt*.[17] Throughout the present paper, this view will be adopted, although a clear-cut separation of the Early Dynastic Period and the subsequent Old Kingdom would be somewhat artificial, anyway.[18]

This paper will focus on the kings of the 3rd and 4th dynasties as an up-to-date starting point for further investigations. The kings of these dynasties have recently been subject to studies on onomastics[19] and later traditions regarding chronological questions[20] by Roman Gundacker, and the investigation can therefore rest on a sound philological fundament. Following the results of the aforementioned studies, the order of the kings of the 3rd and 4th dynasties according to their contemporaneously attested names[21] is to be reconstructed as shown in Table 1.

At the end of the 4th dynasty, the Turin Canon (x+III,16; name lost in a lacuna—column- and line count after Gardiner 1959) as well as the Manethonian tradition[22] (Θαμφθίς[23] 'Thamphthis') mention another king after Shepseskaf. So far, however, no contemporaneous evidence for this king has surfaced, so his historicity is questionable

Horus Name	*Nomen*[24]	Two-Ladies Name	Gold Name
3rd Dynasty[25]			
Horus Netjerykhet (*Ḥrw Nṯr.j-ḫ.t*)	(*Djoser **Ḏsr*)[26]	*Nṯr.j-ḫ.t-Nb.tj*	*Reading uncertain*[27]
Horus Sekhemkhet (*Ḥrw Sḫm-ḫ.t*)	Djosertety (*Ḏsr-ttj*)	*Ḏsr.tj-Nb.tj*[28]	*Unknown*
Horus Khaba (*Ḥrw Ḫꜥi-bꜣ*)	*Unknown*[29]	*Unknown*	*Nṯr-nbw* (?)[30]
Horus Sanakht (*Ḥrw Zꜣ-nḫt*)	Nebka (*Nb-kꜣ*)	*Unknown*[31]	*Unknown*
Horus Qahedjet (*Ḥrw Qꜣi-ḥḏ.t*)[32]	Huni (*Njswt-ḥwi(.w)*)	*Unknown*	*Unknown*
4th Dynasty[33]			
Horus Neb-Maat (*Ḥrw Nb-mꜣꜥ.t*)	Sneferu (*Snfr.w*)	*Nb-mꜣꜥ.t-Nb.tj*	*Bjk-nbw*
Horus Medjedu (*Ḥrw Mḏd.w*)	(Khnum-)Khufu ((*Ḫnmw-)Ḫwi=f-w(j)*))	*Mḏd-r-Nb.tj*	*Bjk.wj-nbw*
Horus Kheper (*Ḥrw Ḫpr*)	Radjedef (*Rꜥw-ḏdi=f*)	*Ḫpr-m-Nb.tj*	*Nṯr.w-nbw*[34]
Horus User-Ib (*Ḥrw Wsr-jb*)	Khafre (*Ḫꜥi=f-Rꜥw*)	*Wsr-m-Nb.tj*	*Sḫm-nṯr-nbw*
Unknown	Baka (*Bꜣ-kꜣ(=j)*)[35]	*Unknown*	*Unknown*
Horus Ka-Khet (*Ḥrw Kꜣ-ḫ.t*)	Menkaura (*Mn-kꜣ.w-Rꜥw*)	*Kꜣ-ḫ.t-Nb.tj*	*Nṯr.j-nṯr-nbw*
Horus Shepes-Khet (*Ḥrw Šps-ḫ.t*)	Shepseskaf (*Špss-kꜣ=f*)	*Šps-Nb.tj*	*Unknown*

Table 1: The names of the kings of the 3rd and 4th dynasties.

in the least.[36] He is therefore disregarded in the following.

The following discussion is, as far as possible, based on contemporaneous evidence, yet, in some cases, non-contemporaneous sources need to be considered, too.

3. The 3rd Dynasty

Although scarce, there are several groups of sources of inscriptional evidence for the chronology of the 3rd dynasty. As different texts serve different purposes, it is necessary to differentiate inscriptional evidence for the period with regard not only to their chronological (contemporaneous vs. non-contemporaneous), but also to their typological (~genre) features.

Non-contemporaneous source groups for the chronology of the 3rd dynasty include:

- King lists of the Greek, Latin, and Armenian literary traditions, above all Manetho;[37]
- Egyptian (historiographical-)annalistic records:[38]
  - The 'Turin Canon'[39]
  - The annals of the 5th dynasty[40] i.e., the 'Palermo Stone' and its associated fragments[41]

The Turin Canon (pTurin Cat. 1874 *vso.*) is a copy of an older systematic list of Egyptian kings[42] updated in the New Kingdom, covering the time from a supposed reign of gods and demigods down to (at least) the 17th dynasty. Nowadays largely fragmentary, the papyrus in its original state would have provided an extensive record of the names and reign lengths of Egyptian rulers of the respective periods. The kings of the 3rd dynasty—as well as their successors of the 4th dynasty—are listed in column x+III, lines 4–16 (column x+III being only badly preserved), but not all of the recorded names conform to the ones attested in the contemporaneous material, i. e., they probably went through at least one stage of re-analysis and re-interpretation.[43] Furthermore, the figures given for the individual reigns of the 3rd and 4th dynasties very probably influenced one another, resulting in pairs of equals.[44] Despite the Turin Canon thus being riddled with problems, it is still an indispensable source especially for epochs lacking contemporaneous inscriptional evidence—if treated with due (that is: enormous) caution and criticism. Nevertheless, the only two things that possibly could be worse than using the Turin Canon for reconstructing the historical chronology of the 3rd and 4th dynasties would be (a) using it uncritically, or (b) not using it at all.

The term 'Palermo Stone' refers to a *corpus* of seven greyish-black fragments (only one of which is actually stored in Palermo) of a basalt stela. While the pertinence and date of the single fragments are debated, all of them contain information on individual regnal years of the kings of the 1st to the 5th dynasties in order of succession. The names of the kings and their mothers are listed in horizontal bands; below each band, the regnal years of the respective king are presented in individual rectangular compartments detailing royal activities and other major events of that specific year. Giving even more information in its surviving parts than does the Turin Canon, the list of the Palermo Stone in its original state would arguably have been the most detailed account of Egypt's first five dynasties. However, due to its poor state of conservation, only small scraps of evidence regarding the 3rd and 4th dynasties survive.

Of the 3rd dynasty, the beginning of only one reign is preserved (PS r.V.8–12,[45] most likely that of Netjerykhet ~ Djoser), and according to the drawing in Wilkinson 2000, fig. 4, only isolated signs survive from two further reigns that *per definitionem* must belong to the 3rd dynasty (CF 1, r.V).[46] From the 4th dynasty, only a few regnal years from four distinct reigns (PS r.VI.1–5[47] (Sneferu); v.I.1–3[48] (Menkaura – Shepseskaf); CF 2 r.I.1[49] (Khufu), CF 4 r.I.1–2[50] (Sneferu)) can be discerned. Being the product of a process of compilation and redaction that most likely took place in the 5th dynasty,[51] the inscriptions of the Palermo Stone and its associated fragments could draw from an unbroken stream of 'annalistic-historiographic' tradition,[52] at least as regards the 3rd and 4th dynasties, so, although no contemporaneous source *sensu stricto*, the annals of the 5th dynasty may nevertheless claim a higher degree of credibility than any other non-contemporaneous source for the chronology of the 3rd and 4th dynasties.

Direct contemporaneous evidence is still rather meagre in comparison. Out of an undoubtedly larger original corpus, only three hieratic jar inscriptions mentioning regnal years are known to date (*rnp.t šms.w-Ḥrw zp 11 ḥsb Jwnw pr-zr*, 'Year of the following of Horus; 11th occurrence of the "calculation" of Heliopolis, (namely) the House of the Ram'; (*rnp.t*) *šms.w-Ḥrw ḳd* (*m*) *jnr*, '(Year of the) following of Horus; building (in) stone'; *rnp.t ḫꜥ(.w) njswt ḫꜥ(.w) bj.tj zp 3 ꜥḥꜣ ḫ(n)p.tjw*, 'Year of the appearance of the *njswt*-king and the appearance of the *bj.tj*-king; 3rd time of fighting the raiders').[53] However, as none of these inscriptions is to be attributed directly to any specific king, their immediate chronological value seems to be limited.

With so little information surviving from the pre-eminent sources of Egyptian chronology, and even the very number and order of rulers being (partially) uncertain, reconstructing the number of regnal years of the kings of the 3rd dynasty is little more than educated guesswork. Hence, the size and state of completion of the (funerary) monuments of that period[54] may serve as invaluable 'circumstantial evidence' for the regnal length of the respective king.[55] If necessary (see esp. below, section 5), the much later and more complicated Manethonian tradition will be drawn upon.

One specific feature of the 3rd dynasty—and the Early Dynastic Period in general—is the mode of counting regnal years. In contrast to the system used in the 4th dynasty (cf. below), regnal years were not *counted* in the strict sense, but rather *named* after a set of (perhaps pre-defined) eponymous events.[56] Out of these, the biennial 'Following of Horus' (*šms.w-Ḥrw*), still visible in the Netjerykhet compartments of the Palermo Stone, is probably the one most important for reconstructing the chronology of the 3rd dynasty. Whether this action is connected to the various counting events recorded in the Palermo Stone compartments of the 2nd, 4th, and 5th dynasties[57] is still a matter of debate.[58]

Model from	Mode of extrapolation	Length of the 4th dynasty	Absolute dates of the 4th dynasty[59]
Beckerath 1997	Biennial/irregular[60]	135 years	2639/2589–2504/2454 BCE
Nolan 2003	Regular[61]	*≈ 112 years[62]	-
Hornung et al. 2006a	Biennial/irregular[63]	107 years	2543–2436^{+25} BCE
Gundacker 2006	Biennial	152 years	2658–2506 BCE

Table 2: Chronological models for the 4th dynasty according to their mode of extrapolation.

4. The 4th Dynasty

4.1. Fourth dynasty sources

The non-contemporaneous sources for the chronology of the 4th dynasty are the same as those for the 3rd dynasty (cf. above, section 3), whereas direct contemporaneous evidence is to be found in a broader variety of further source groups,[64] viz.:

- Construction *dipinti*[65] (hieratic)
- Administrative documents[66] (hieratic; cursive hieroglyphs)
- Expedition *graffiti* ([cursive] hieroglyphs)
- Inscriptions in private tombs (hieroglyphs)

With their different backgrounds, contexts, layouts, and addressees—reflecting different scribal traditions, practices, and intentions—, all of these source groups have one feature in common: in contrast to the year designations of the 3rd dynasty, dates from the 4th dynasty until the end of the Old Kingdom strictly adhere to a counting system that is centred around the ruling king and allows for only one out of three year designations:

(a) *rnp.t*[67] *zmꜣ tꜣ.wj* — 'year of Joining the Two Lands'[68]
(b) *rnp.t zp N ṯnw.t* — 'year of the Nth occasion of the count'
(c) *rnp.t m-ḫt zp N ṯnw.t* — 'year after the Nth occasion of the count'

This 'count' certainly refers to an actual activity, the 'Counting of All Cattle and Livestock of Upper and Lower Egypt' (*ṯnw.t (var.: *jp.t*) *jḥ.w ꜥw.t nb(.t) Šmꜥ.w Tꜣ-Mḥ.w*).[69] This event has been a matter of constant debate, the major questions being the count's character (cultic vs. administrative),[70] its regularity, and its abolition and replacement by a system based on continuously counting a king's regnal years (in the style of *rnp.t-zp* N, N+1, N+2, …) towards the end of the Old Kingdom.[71]

The count's regularity is of particular interest in this context as several studies have noted a certain imbalance between the numbers of attestations of years of the count and years after the count.[72] Additionally, the occurrence of a 7th and an 8th count in two successive years as displayed by the Palermo Stone (PS r.VI.3–4)[73] for Sneferu has given rise to certain suspicions regarding at least the reign of this king.[74] Hence, in the course of the last 150 years, very different theories have been put forward, ranging from a proposed stable biennial census cycle[75] to a system with regular (yet neither annual nor biennial)[76] or (partly) irregular[77] omissions of years after the count. Since the exact date of neither death nor accession of any individual ruler of the 4th dynasty is known, extrapolating regnal lengths based on inscriptional data remains the most important means of establishing the historical chronology of that period if sources like the Palermo Stone or the Turin Canon are excluded due to their anachronistic character. Different modes of extrapolation result in differing absolute dates and totals for regnal lengths, as can be shown in an overview of some of the extant (recent)[78] models Table 2).

Given the impact of extrapolation modes on reign-length calculations, a sound basis for a prospective reconciliation of written evidence and radiocarbon dates has to provide a plausible solution for the problem of census regularity. Arguably the best method for this is to return *ad fontes*, i.e., a) to integrate newly available material into the extant models, and b) to re-evaluate the known data—primarily with respect to their direct chronological value (~ dates and numbers), but also to their philological features (~ script, palaeography, lexicology, grammar, co(n) text, etc.). A first attempt for the latter has been made by Roman Gundacker,[79] who put the then-known inscriptional data from the time of Sneferu under severe scrutiny and especially questioned some of the readings of dated construction *dipinti* by Petrie

1910 and Posener-Kriéger 1991—however, single readings in that study must remain questionable due to limited access to the original material,[80] and are therefore precluded from the following case study I (cf. below, section 4.2). The actual potential of approach a) will be shown in case study II (cf. below, section 4.3).

4.2 The reign of Sneferu: Case Study I

For the reign of Sneferu, Gundacker 2006 as the most extensive study has compiled 76 different inscriptional dates; he is certainly right in correcting the reading of some crucial dates,[81] whereas others still remain doubtful. In 2017, Felix Arnold published 7 newly discovered dated construction *dipinti* from the 'valley' temple at the Bent Pyramid (Dahshur) with exact *facsimile* drawings;[82] doubtless, more are yet to be excavated at the various sites that are linked to Sneferu's reign. Until the definitive publication of the Meidum material (cf. below, endnote 80), the regnal years of Sneferu's reign as securely attested by inscriptions may be presented as seen in Table 3.[83]

Although frequently cited as a secure attestation,[84] the Dahshur *dipinto* supposedly mentioning Sneferu's 24th count[85] does not technically belong to this list, as it is damaged in the upper as well as in the lower part—only the cardinal number *2⸢4⸣* is still recognizable. Because the upper part of the *dipinto* is lost, it cannot securely be attributed to a *rnp.t zp* or a *rnp.t m-ḫt zp*; the damage in the lower part, however, prevents us from ascertaining the exact number of single strokes indicating the ones digit. The hieratic standard configuration of ones within year specifications being applied here, only a second row with 3 or 4 additional strokes below the surviving row, hence a figure **27*/**28*, might be reconstructed here, **29* at the most if a further stroke is lost to the right of the 4 surviving strokes. Thus, the *dipinto* in question may serve a) as a proof of Sneferu's 24th census, and b) as a general warning not to stumble into the epistemological pitfall of confusing attested *counts* with attested *years of the count*.

Excluding, for the moment, a number of very doubtful *dipinti* for the moment, 16 distinct regnal years of Sneferu are attested directly from 25 single inscriptional sources (the Palermo Stone as well as construction *dipinti* from several pyramid construction sites).[86] Of those distinct regnal years, 9 belong to a specific year of the count, whereas 5 securely belong to distinct years after the count, the pertinence of another 3 remaining unclear. The appearance of years of the count and years after the count displays no obvious regularity. While this 9:5 (17:5:3) ratio is still (heavily) imbalanced, it nevertheless differs considerably from the 12:3 ratio given by Miroslav Verner.[87] With 25 single attestations, however, this is not surprising: the number of surviving clear attestations from Sneferu's reign is not even close to any kind of statistical significance. Keeping this in mind is all the more important as it shows the necessity of a careful philological treatment of the sources.

4.3. The Reign of Khufu: Case Study II

The reign of Khufu has so far not been subject to an individual study, although especially in its last phase, it may yield even better source material than that of his predecessor. A systematic overview of Khufu's inscriptionally attested regnal years therefore has to draw mainly from the compilations of Anthony Spalinger[88] and Miroslav Verner,[89] which need to be augmented and corrected in some instances, though (cf. Table 4). Those necessary improvements, on the other hand, are mainly due to the integration of new material recovered after 2008, viz. the Wadi el-Jarf papyri,[90] and the *dipinti* of the second boat pit[91] at the Great Pyramid published by Akiko Nishisaka and Kazumitsu Takahashi in their preliminary, yet ground-breaking 2016 report.[92] According to these sources, the regnal years of Khufu's reign seen in Table 4 are attested directly.

With *15 separate inscriptional attestations accounting for 10 distinct regnal years, Khufu's reign is among the best documented of the 4th dynasty, especially regarding the later years of his reign, the final six years of which are attested by at least one inscription each (if *zp 14* indeed *is* Khufu's last regnal year).[93] These last six—with the unattested year of the 11th count, nine—regnal years display a constant succession of years of the count and years after the count, suggesting a regular biennial census rhythm at least in the later phase of Khufu's reign.[94] In total, there are 6 securely attested years of the count versus 4 securely attested years after the count.

It is mainly the influx of new material that has made it possible to extend Khufu's known regnal length by a whole year, to reassess the extant material and hence to solve the debated matter of the date *dipinto* in the first boat pit.[95] Miroslav Verner[96] attributed this inscription to Radjedef,

Regnal year	Number of attestations + source(s)
zp 2	1 (CF 4 r.I.1)[97]
Year after *zp 2*[98]	1 (CF 4 r.I.2)
Year after year after *zp 2*	1 (PS r.VI.1)[99]
**m-ḫt zp 6*[100]	1 (PS r.VI.2)
zp 7	1 (PS r.VI.3)
zp 8	1 (PS r.VI.4)
year after *zp 8*	1 (PS r.VI.5)
zp 13[101]	1 (Meidum) = Posener-Kriéger 1991, pl. 7, A.9
zp 14	2 (Meidum) = Posener-Kriéger 1991, pl. 8, A.23-24
zp 15	2 (Dahshur) = Stadelmann 1987, 234, fig. 1; Stadelmann 2004, 17
m-ḫt zp 15	1 (Meidum) = Petrie 1910, pl. 5, no. 6
zp 16	2 (Dahshur) = Lepsius 1859, II.3, 1, g; Stadelmann 1993, 11
m-ḫt zp 16	1 (Meidum) = Posener-Kriéger 1991, pl. 7, no. A.3
zp 17	7 (Meidum) = Posener-Kriéger 1991, pl. 7, A.12-16; Petrie 1910, pl. 5, no. 3-4
zp 18	1 (Meidum) = Posener-Kriéger 1991, pl. 8, A.29
m-ḫt zp 18	1 (Meidum) = Posener-Kriéger 1991, pl. 8, A.28

Table 3: Attested regnal years (Sneferu).

Regnal year	Number of attestations + source(s)
zp 5	1 (Giza) = Boston MFA 38-2-5; Smith 1952, 118, fig. 6, top left side
zp 8	2 (Giza) = Junker 1929, 159, fig. 24, no. 10; Smith 1952, 119, fig. 7, bottom left side = HUMFA_C10906_NS
zp 10	3 (Giza) = Junker 1929, 159, fig. 24, no. 1–2. 161
m-ḫt zp 10	1 (Giza) = Steindorff 1906, 32
m-ḫt zp 11[102]	1 (Giza, first boat pit) = Abubakr and Mustafa 1971, 11, fig. 6, bottom left side
zp 12	3 (Giza) = Smith 1952, 118, fig. 6, bottom left side. 119, fig. 7, 3rd row, left side.[103] 119, fig. 7, bottom right side
m-ḫt zp 12	1 (Dakhla Oasis) = Kuhlmann 2005, 144, fig. 1
zp 13	2 (Giza; Wadi el-Jarf) = Smith 1952, 119, fig. 7, 2nd row, left side; Tallet 2017, 101, pl. 1, Fragment T - éch. 1/2[104]
m-ḫt zp 13	1 (Dakhla Oasis) = Kuhlmann 2005, 248, fig. 5
zp 14	1 (Giza, second boat pit) = Nishisaka – Takahashi 2016, 9, fig. 9

Table 4: Attested regnal years (Khufu).

chiefly because of the occurrence of basilophoric crew names construed on the basis of Radjedef's names on the roofing blocks, and the difficulty of discerning different working stages. However, this reason does not apply anymore. First, it is highly improbable to assume that Radjedef sealed both boat pits separately in the year after his 11th count and the year of his 14th count, respectively.[105] Second, as several observations from the second boat pit confirm, one has to assume at least two different stages within a complex working process,[106] the earlier one of which dates to the reign of Khufu—hence the *dipinti* containing crew names based on Khufu's name.[107] Third, the *dipinti* containing dates certainly belong to this earlier stage, that is, they were painted on the cover stones when still in the quarries.[108]

5. Synthesis and Chronological Models for Dynasties 3–4

While all of the above, of course, needs further exhaustive treatment—which is beyond the scope of the present paper—the implications of these two case studies are clear. First, we need to keep in mind that the direct chronological information of the 4th and in particular of the 3rd dynasties is disparate and incomplete; all the more care must be taken in evaluating single attestations in order not to draw erroneous conclusions. Second, while the rest of the 4th dynasty still suffers from a lack of contemporaneous written data, the evidence from the later years of Khufu's reign suggests a regular biennial rhythm of cattle counts, which may with all due caution be extended to the early, possibly the entire 4th dynasty. Third, the chronology of the 3rd dynasty is even more dependent on 'circumstantial evidence', reconstructions, and interpolations; due to a lack of source material, these problems are probably not going to dissolve in the foreseeable future. Fourth, as single inscriptions may still rapidly change our understanding of Old Kingdom and Early Dynastic chronology, the results of those necessary extrapolations can hardly be regarded as anything other than preliminary.

Considering all of these factors, it becomes clear that contemporaneous evidence alone does not, as of yet, suffice to establish a comprehensive historical chronology of the 3rd and 4th dynasties. Non-contemporaneous evidence, like the Turin Canon or the Manetho epitomes, may come to our aid, but is often lacunous and notoriously prone to errors, conflations, and re-interpretations. Based on these premises, three relevant models for use in combination with radiocarbon dates may be derived from the available numbers: a minimal (A), a maximal (B), and a critically assessed (C) model, each of which shall be detailed in the following. The main goal of these models is *not*, as already emphasized, to propose a steadfast chronology of the 3rd and 4th dynasties, but rather to illustrate the range of chronological possibilities that the available data allow. The actual impact of the different variants on radiocarbon models for the periods under consideration will be demonstrated in section 7.

For the sake of simplicity, the question of whether a king's accession year (*rnp.t zmꜣ tꜣ.wj*) was identical with the first census year (*rnp.t zp 1 / tp.j*) shall remain untouched here as it can not *de facto* be answered with the available sources. Instead, this possible identity is presumed for model (A), whereas models (B) and (C) presuppose the two to have been different regnal years. However, reality surely was a bit more complex.[109] Except at the beginning of the 3rd and the end of the 4th dynasty, the proposed last regnal year of a king and the accession year of his successor are treated as *one single* calendar year.[110]

Model A: minimal regnal lengths

With few exceptions, the minimal model operates on the premises defined by Miroslav Verner (cf. above, endnote 62). While a consequent 'minimal' model in the strictest sense excludes all non-contemporaneous data, thus resulting in a series of reign-length estimations of 0/1 year(s) for the kings of the middle of the 3rd dynasty, this does seem rather unlikely for statistical reasons. Therefore, in order to account for incompletely documented reigns, in some cases—i. e., mainly Sekhemkhet, Khaba, and Sanakht, for whom virtually no securely attributable (semi-)contemporaneous data, either from the annals of the Palermo Stone or from other sources, exist—the figure of the Turin Canon (or a derivate thereof) has been chosen as minimal regnal length (cf. the respective endnote). However, in order to display the *utter* minimum, it would be possible to leave out the respective regnal years added to the reigns of Sekhemkhet (5), Khaba (5), Sanakht (8), Radjedef (7), Menkaura (3), and Shepseskaf (2) using the TC data. The length of the 3rd dynasty would thus be reduced to ≈ 33 years, that of the 4th, to ≈ 74 (Table 5).

King	Regnal years
Horus Netjerykhet ~ Djoser	19[111]
Horus Sekhemkhet ~ Djosertety	6[112]
Horus Khaba ~ ?	6[113]
Horus Sanakht ~ Nebka	9[114]
Horus Qahedjet ~ Huni	> 11[115]
∑dyn. 3	**≈ 47**
Horus Neb-Maat ~ Sneferu	30
Horus Medjedu ~ Khufu	18
Horus Kheper ~ Radjedef	8[116]
Horus User-Ib ~ Khafre	13[117]
Horus ? ~ Baka	< 1[118]
Horus Ka-Khet ~ Menkaura	18[119]
Horus Shepes-Khet ~ Shepseskaf	4[120]
∑dyn. 4	**86**

Table 5: The kings of the 3rd and 4th dynasties and their minimal regnal lengths.

King	Regnal years
Horus Netjerykhet ~ Djoser	29[121]
Horus Sekhemkhet ~ Djosertety	19[122]
Horus Khaba ~ ?	17[123]
Horus Sanakht ~ Nebka	28[124]
Horus Qahedjet ~ Huni	24[125]
∑dyn. 3	**113**
Horus Neb-Maat ~ Sneferu	49[126]
Horus Medjedu ~ Khufu	29[127]
Horus Kheper ~ Radjedef	17[128]
Horus User-Ib ~ Khafre	26[129]
Horus ? ~ Baka	2[130]
Horus Ka-Khet ~ Menkaura	28[131]
Horus Shepes-Khet ~ Shepseskaf	9[132]
∑dyn. 4	**154**

Table 6: The kings of the 3rd and 4th dynasties and their maximal regnal lengths.

King	Regnal years
Horus Netjerykhet ~ Djoser	29
Horus Sekhemkhet ~ Djosertety	7[133]
Horus Khaba ~ ?	7[134]
Horus Sanakht ~ Nebka	9[135]
Horus Qahedjet ~ Huni	14[136]
∑dyn. 3	**62**
Horus Neb-Maat ~ Sneferu	47[137]
Horus Medjedu ~ Khufu	29
Horus Kheper ~ Radjedef	16
Horus User-Ib ~ Khafre	21[138]
Horus ? ~ Baka	2
Horus Ka-Khet ~ Menkaura	28
Horus Shepes-Khet ~ Shepseskaf	8
∑dyn. 4	**145**

Table 7: The kings of the 3rd and 4th dynasties and their critically assessed regnal lengths.

Model B: maximal regnal lengths

The maximal model is based on the assumptions that throughout the 3rd and 4th dynasties, a consequent biennial census system was used, that the first count actually took place in the year after the respective king's accession, and that there was a year after the last count (**rnp.t m-ḫt zp* N*max*) in any individual reign. The single counts would then have been misinterpreted as regnal years in later annalistic records (most notably, the Turin Canon) (Table 6). For exceptions and further information, see the respective endnote.

Model C: critically assessed regnal lengths

The critically assessed model, operating on a regular biennial census rhythm (as is suggested by the data from the early 4th dynasty), is basically a slight modification of the 'maximal' model, but assumes a less extreme position towards unattested years after the count at the end of each individual reign. While being based principally on the contemporaneous record, substantiated reconstructions (like the 29 regnal years for Netjerykhet) and limitations (like the immediate succession of Sneferu's 7th and 8th counts) are accepted. In some cases, 'circumstantial evidence' like the respective funerary monument's state of completeness is used to rule out implausibly short reigns (Table 7).

While the 'minimal' model with its 132 years proposes a lower chronology for the 3rd and 4th dynasties than does the lowest recent model (155 years) according to Hornung et al. (2006a, 490), the 'maximal' model (266 years) exceeds even the 215 years assigned to these two dynasties by Gundacker 2006, 379. The former mainly derives from a considerably lower number for the length of the 4th dynasty (86 vs. 107 years), the latter, from a significantly higher number for the length of the 3rd dynasty (113 vs. 63 years). The 'critically assessed' model with 206 years for both dynasties differs by only 3 years from the 203 years given by Beckerath 1997, 187 (yet with a different internal distribution), and by 9 years from Roman Gundacker's assumption of 215 years, but, again, yields a considerable difference from the 155 years suggested by Erik Hornung, Rolf Krauss, and David Warburton.[139] The figure of *≈ 112 years for the length of the 4th dynasty construed according to the model of John Nolan (cf. above, section 4.1, Table 2), differing from the 145 years of the 'critically assessed' model by multiple decades, is based on data and assumptions which are now largely obsolete, as has been demonstrated above in sections 4.1–2.

While both the 'minimal' and the 'maximal' models operate on debatable premises, (sometimes) not adequately applying methods of textual criticism, that is, either totally dismissing or blindly trusting the Turin Canon and its sources, and are therefore 'improbable', the 'critically assessed' model, in contrast, may claim a certain degree of legitimacy—at least according to the data currently available. Needless to say, this model will have to be re-considered, re-evaluated, and adjusted in the course of further research, especially since substantial parts of it still do not rest on (securely attributable) contemporaneous evidence and many chronologically valuable inscriptions still remain unedited.[140]

6. Outlook

Section 5 has shown the arithmetical impact that different modes of extrapolating the currently available data and different attributions of single attestations have on chronological models. While the comparison of these different models may serve as a means of illustrating the dynamics and the volatility of research on Early Dynastic and Old Kingdom chronology, it is also a mandate for future researchers to develop strategies and to define criteria to advance beyond chronologies based on the 'bare' face value of textual sources.

First and foremost, the internal features of textual sources need to be taken into consideration in their entirety. Criteria like palaeography, lexicology, grammar, or co(n)text (cf. above) have only occasionally been examined (or even described) when dealing with written sources for Egyptian chronology, especially as regards the Early Dynastic Period and the Old Kingdom. Second, non-royal chronological lines, like genealogies or succession and terms of office of high-ranking officials, have long since been recognized as means of chronological research,[141] but have not so far been collected and examined in a systematic way.[142] Reconstructing genealogies and lists of office holders may provide a(n independent) way to put established regnal lengths to the test and thus to corroborate chronological models.

While these different approaches to the inscriptional material of the Early Dynastic Period and the Old Kingdom and the chronological questions arising thence, even when combined, will not yet suffice in establishing a 'waterproof' historical chronology of the said epochs, it is nevertheless to be hoped that integrating newly discovered material, re-evaluating extant data, and, finally, piecing together the available scraps of evidence will continuously expand our secure chronological knowledge. Meanwhile, the results of natural-scientific methods, above all Bayesian radiocarbon dating, may further help to interpret inscriptional evidence and lend plausibility to extant chronological models.

7. Radiocarbon dates for Old Kingdom Egypt

For this contribution, we used Old Kingdom radiocarbon data as published by Bronk Ramsey, Dee and colleagues.[143] Our models follow essentially the Old Kingdom model as published in 2010, but are adapted to meet the requirements of the maximal, minimal, and critically assessed reign lengths for the 3rd and 4th dynasties as outlined above. No historical constrains were employed for the 5th and 6th dynasties as current research does not (yet) permit robust reign length estimates that

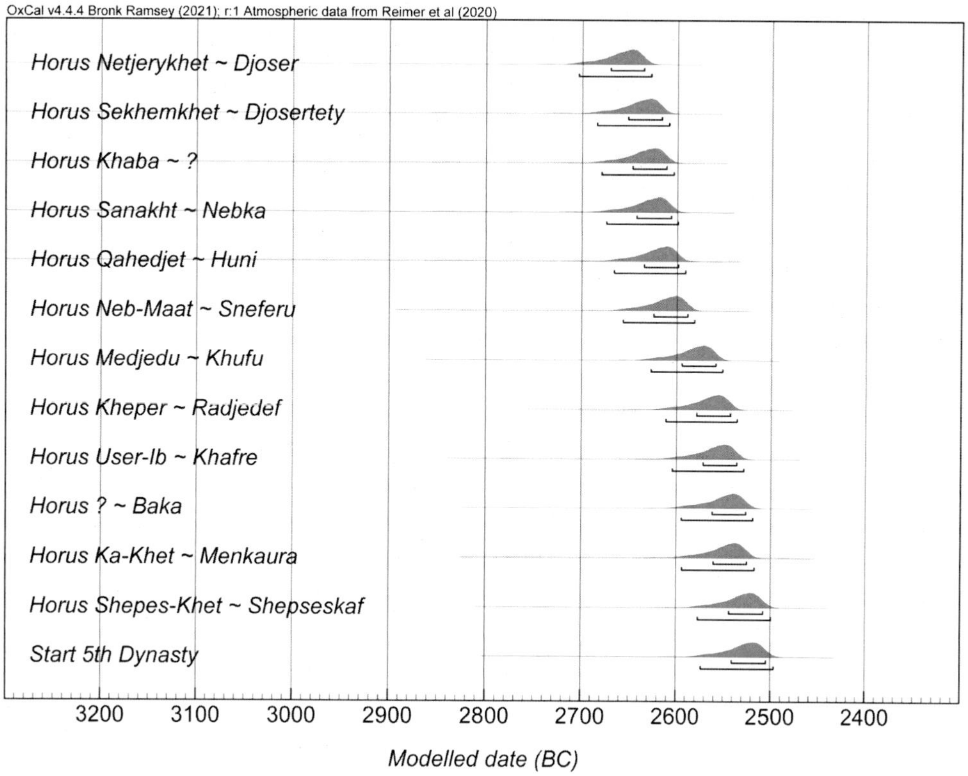

Figure 1: Modelled accession dates of 3rd and 4th dynasty kings based on the minimal model.

are actually based on published data. Instead, the only prior information used was the succession of kings. Further, we used a Student's t-distribution with five degrees of freedom (T(5)) as in the original model, except for the fact that we did not employ the factor of 5 to increase the degree of flexibility. Calibration and modelling were done using OxCal 4.4 and the current IntCal20 radiocarbon calibration curve.[144] Additionally a small regional offset of 19±5 radiocarbon years (Delta_R) was employed to account for different growing seasons for samples from Egypt and samples from European/North American trees upon which the IntCal curve is based.[145]

Figure 1 shows the modeled accession dates of the kings of the 3rd and 4th dynasties according to the minimal model outlined above. The start of the 3rd dynasty (accession of Horus Netjerykhet ~ Djoser) would fall in the mid-27th century BCE and would be very much in line with what the original study proposed. The start of the 4th dynasty (accession of Horus Neb-Maat ~ Sneferu) would fall to around 2600 BCE, also in line with what Bronk Ramsey and colleagues proposed in 2010. And also the beginning of the 5th dynasty falls to more or less the same period as in the original study, around, or just before, 2500 BCE.

Figure 2 shows the modelled accession dates according to the maximal model outlined above. Here, the modelled date for the start of the 3rd dynasty (accession of Horus Netjerykhet ~ Djoser) would be approximately a century earlier, in the mid-28th century BCE. The accession date of Horus Neb-Maat ~ Sneferu and the beginning of the 4th Dynasty would fall to the mid-27th century BCE, and the start of the 5th dynasty would fall to just after 2500 BCE. At first glance a later beginning of the 5th dynasty in the maximal model seems to be counter-intuitive, but since the prior information for this model is based on longer reign-lengths, the model has to allow for more calendar years between the beginning of the 3rd and the end of the 4th dynasty, which 'stretches' the overall model over time, resulting in older dates for the beginning and younger dates for the end.

Figure 3 shows the modelled accession dates based on the critically assessed model outlined above. In this model the beginning of the 3rd dynasty falls to

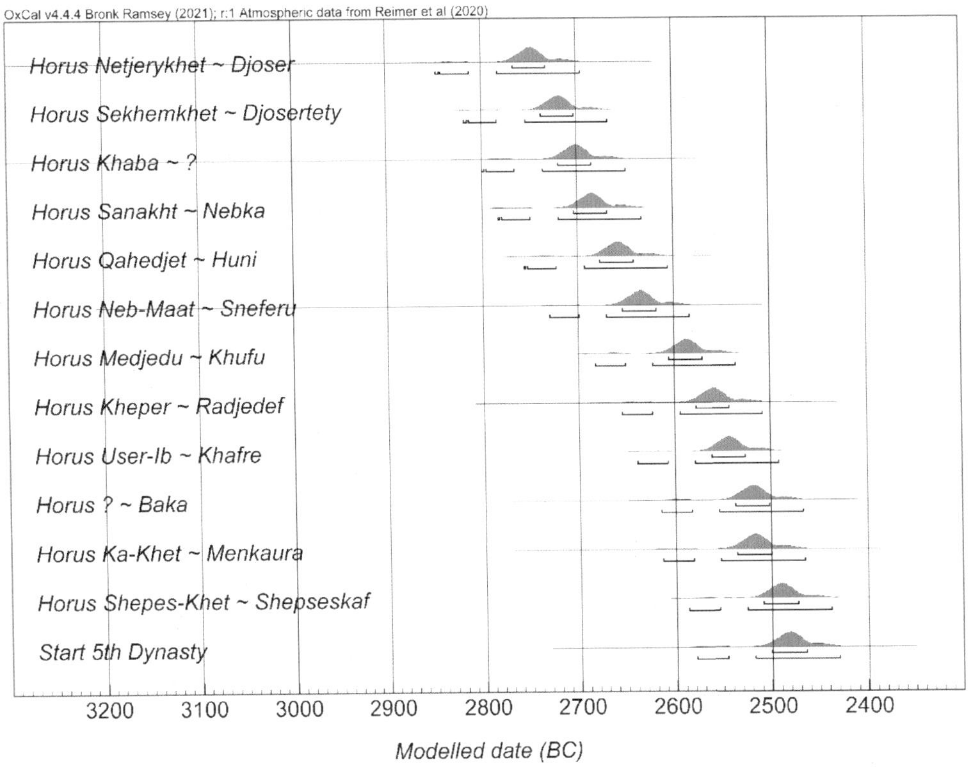

Figure 2: Modelled accession dates of 3rd and 4th dynasty kings based on the maximal model.

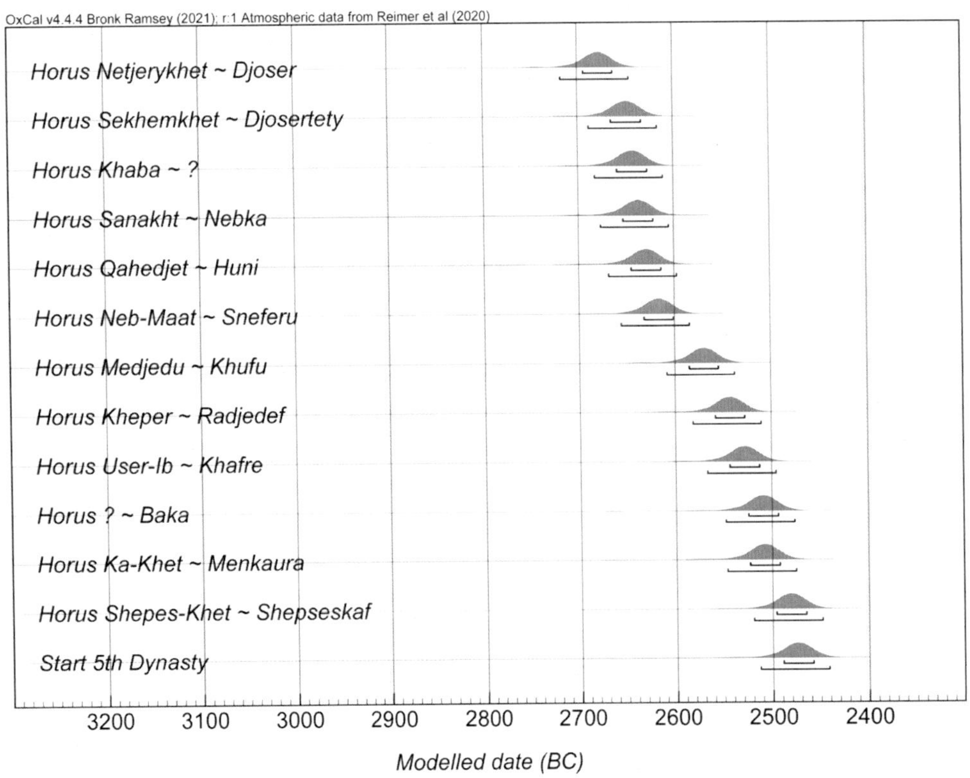

Figure 3: Modelled accession dates of 3rd and 4th dynasty kings based on the critically assessed model.

Site	EB I		EB II		EB III		EB IV	
	SL	*IBA*	SL	*IBA*	SL	*IBA*	SL	*IBA*
Tel Yarmuth	2	*1*	7	*8*	7	*11*		
Tel Yaqush	9.5		1.5	*4*	1			
Khirbet ez-Zeraqon			7	*8.5*	6	*6.5*		
Jericho	4	*6*	4	*9*		*12*		*2*
Megiddo	5	*1*			9			
Arad			23					
Tel Beth Yerah	3	*2*	9		2	*3*		
Tell Fadous Kfarabida			3		20		6	
Tell Abu en-Niʿaj							25	

TABLE 8: Levantine sites and their radiocarbon samples from EB I–IV (SL: short-lived samples; IBA: samples with in-built age, mostly charcoal).

just after 2700 BCE, the start of the 4th dynasty to just before 2600 BCE and again suggests a somewhat younger date for the beginning of the 5th dynasty, just after 2500 BCE.

These models show a distinct flexibility in the radiocarbon dates and suggest caution in arguing that the historical chronology as outlined by standard textbooks can be proven with radiocarbon dating. Using different reign lengths show that the modelled date for the beginning of the 3rd dynasty can shift by as much as a century and also the dates for the beginning of the 4th and 5th dynasties are far from fixed and can vary by several decades. Another issue is the fact that the Old Kingdom model is only based on few radiocarbon determinations: only 17 radiocarbon measurements were available for the Old Kingdom.[146] It also has to be stressed that precise data for the reign lengths of the 5th and 6th dynasties are still missing and/or disputed.

8. Radiocarbon Data for the Southern Levant

Where does this leave the chronology of the southern Levant and the chronological synchronization with the Egyptian Old Kingdom? Since the initial publication of Regev, de Miroschedji, and Boaretto,[147] a radiocarbon-derived ca. 2500 BCE date for the end of the Early Bronze III period has been widely accepted.[148] However, dating the transition from Early Bronze III to Early Bronze IV in the southern Levant is not easy: For most sequences (Tel Yarmuth,[149] Tel Yaqush,[150] Khirbet ez-Zeraqon,[151] Megiddo,[152] and Tel Beth Yerah)[153] no radiocarbon determinations for Early Bronze IV contexts are available and hence a modelled date for the transition from Early Bronze III to Early Bronze IV cannot be calculated. Only Tell Fadous-Kfarabida in the central Levant[154] and a recently published sequence from Jericho[155] provide data for both Early Bronze III and Early Bronze IV. Additional information can be gleaned from a substantial sequence of the Early Bronze IV site of Tell Abu en-Niʿaj in the Jordan Valley.[156]

Another limitation is the lack of short-lived samples that were used for radiocarbon dating. Table 8 shows that only the transition from Early Bronze III to Early Bronze IV at Tell Fadous-Kfarabida in Lebanon is based on short-lived data. Radiocarbon determinations from Jericho are exceptionally problematic as only samples with in-built age have been used for Early Bronze III and Early Bronze IV (Table 8).

Nevertheless, in the following we will make a short survey of Early Bronze III and IV dates of the available sequences.

Tell Abu en-Niʿaj in the Jordan Valley is a rural Early Bronze IV site with a substantial radiocarbon sequence.[157] Based on the available radiocarbon data, settlement at the site started around 2500 BCE (FIG. 4), thus a mid-third millennium BCE date for the end of Early Bronze III as proposed by Regev et al. in 2012 would be in agreement with this sequence.

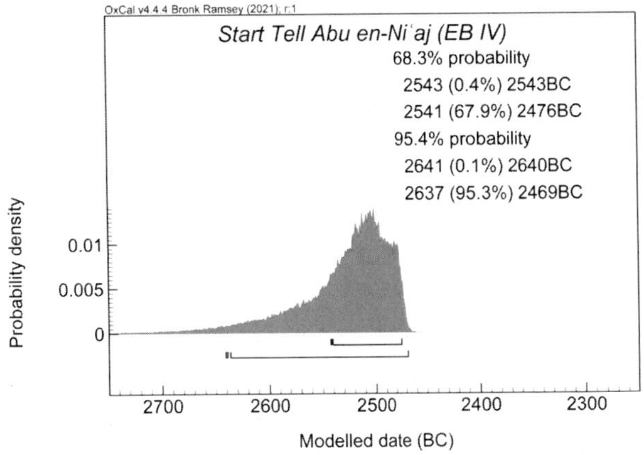

FIGURE 4: Modelled date for the start of the Early Bronze Age IV settlement at Tell Abu en-Ni ʿaj.

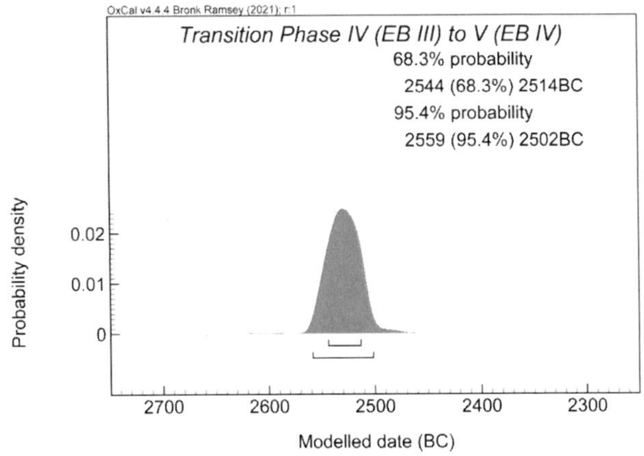

FIGURE 5: Modelled date for the transition from Phase IV (Early Bronze III) to Phase V (Early Bronze IV) at Tell Fadous-Kfarabida.

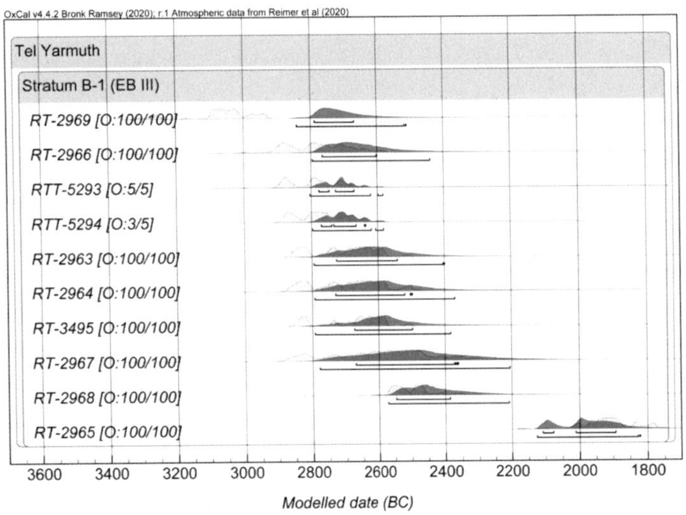

FIGURE 6: Modelled radiocarbon determinations for Stratum B-1 (Early Bronze III) at Tel Yarmuth.

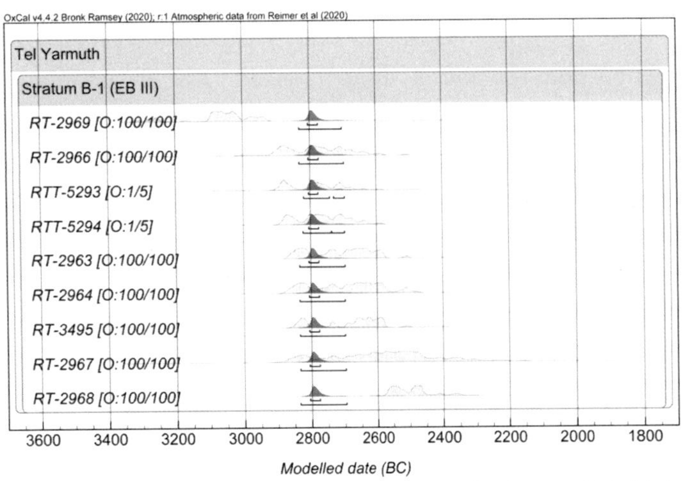

FIGURE 7: Modelled radiocarbon determinations for Stratum B-1 (Early Bronze III) at Tel Yarmuth (after exclusion of RT-2965).

Also, the transition from Phase IV (dated to Early Bronze III) to Phase V (Early Bronze IV) at the small site of Tell Fadous-Kfarabida in modern-day Lebanon would be in agreement with a general ca. 2500 BCE date for the end of Early Bronze III (FIG. 5).[158] Here, the modelled date for the transition to Early Bronze IV falls to just before 2500 BCE.

However, as mentioned above, finding suitable sequences for dating the transition in question in the southern Levant proper, is problematic. The sequence from Tel Yarmuth that served as a cornerstone for the high chronology of the Early Bronze Age is not as straightforward as it initially seemed. Figure 6 shows the modelled radiocarbon dates for Stratum B-1, dated to the late Early Bronze III period. The youngest date (RT-2965) was qualified as an outlier by the authors and thus they argued that the 'real' end date for Stratum B-1 should be around 2500 BCE, apparently represented by radiocarbon determination RT-2968. However, if the youngest sample is excluded from the OxCal model, also RT-2968 is qualified as an outlier (FIG. 7) and the model calculates the end-date of Stratum B-1 much earlier, at ca. 2800 BCE (FIG. 8).

But is such a shift of about 300 years for the end of Stratum B-1 at Tel Yarmuth feasible? Of course, this can only be checked through careful stratigraphic analysis, but the published model does indeed give an

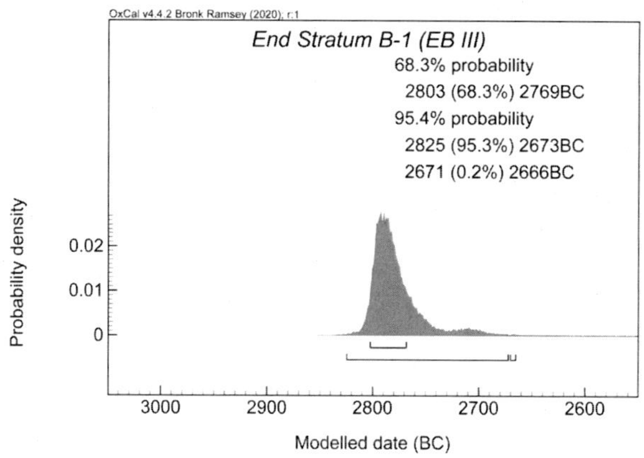

FIGURE 8: Modelled date for the end of Stratum B-1 (Early Bronze III) at Tel Yarmuth.

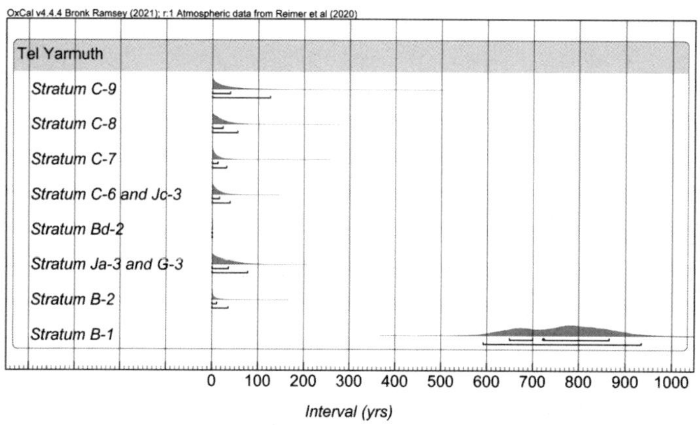

FIGURE 9: Calculated length of stratigraphic phases at Tel Yarmuth.

indication that some adjustment of the ca. 2500 BCE date might be in order. While the radiocarbon model calculates the duration of previous stratigraphic phases less than 50 years, the last Stratum B-1 would have been exceedingly long and would have lasted for 300 years if an end-date of 2500 BCE would be maintained and up to ca. 800 years if the youngest date (which is most likely an outlier) would not be eliminated (FIG. 9). Clearly, such a long-lived settlement phase would require an explanation and thus one should at least consider the possibility that the Early Bronze III phase at Tel Yarmuth ended significantly earlier than previously estimated.

Additionally, this would bring data for Early Bronze III Tel Yarmuth in the general date range of other modelled Early Bronze III dates from other site sequences. Early Bronze III dates at Tel Beth Yerah fall to the 29th and 28th centuries BCE,[159] at Megiddo Early Bronze III dates also fall from the 29th to the first half of the 27th centuries BCE,[160] and at Khirbet ez-Zeraqon, Early Bronze III is already attested around 2900 BCE.[161] It is only at Jericho, that a few questionable long-lived samples suggest a late date in the 24th century BCE for the end of Early Bronze III.[162] The end of the Early Bronze III period is thus still an open question – from the region of the southern Levant proper, there is currently no convincing evidence that a ca. 2500 BCE date is in order.

9. CONCLUSIONS

Where does this leave the synchronization between the southern Levant and the Egyptian Old Kingdom? If a ca. 2500 BCE date for the end of the Early Bronze III period is maintained, the onset of the de-urbanized Early Bronze IV period would fall to the late 4th dynasty based on the critically assessed and the maximal model. If the minimal model is employed, then the transition from Early Bronze III to Early Bronze IV would fall to the early 5th dynasty.

An earlier date for the end of Early Bronze III, maybe around 2700/2650 BCE (end of the Early Bronze Age III Stratum D at Tel Beth Yerah or Stratum J-6a at Megiddo) would coincide with the beginning of the 3rd dynasty if the critically assessed or the minimal model is employed. Employing the maximal model, such an end-date for Early Bronze III would coincide with the late 3rd dynasty.

As we can see, even with much more radiocarbon data at hand, there are still several open questions that need to be answered. One should also keep in mind that the relative chronological framework of the southern Levant is based on the axiomatic assumption that similarity in material culture (e.g., in the shape and decoration of pottery) equals similarity in (relative) date.[163] It is assumed that two archaeological contexts at two different sites showing the same or a similar set of material culture should be regarded as approximately contemporary. It has been shown in the past that this assumption cannot be upheld for the Early Bronze Age sequence.[164]

While this contribution necessarily leaves many questions open by exposing the weaknesses of our current chronological frameworks, we hope that this contribution stimulates renewed research in both the historical basis for reign lengths for the Egyptian Old Kingdom, as well as the radiocarbon chronology of the Early Bronze Age in the southern Levant. Every new dataset, every new radiocarbon sequence and every new philological conclusion will refine our current understanding and ultimately may lead to a robust synchronized chronology of the 3rd millennium BCE in the ancient Near East.

Abbreviations

Wb 1–5 Erman, Adolf and Hermann Grapow (eds). 1926–1931. *Wörterbuch der ägyptischen Sprache 1–5*. Leipzig: Hinrichs.

References

Abubakr, Moneim and Ahmed Y. Moustafa. 1971. "The Funerary Boat of Khufu." In G. Haeny (ed.), *Aufsätze zum 70. Geburtstag von Herbert Ricke, Beiträge zur ägyptischen Bauforschung und Altertumskunde 12*, 1–16. Wiesbaden: Franz Steiner.

Arnold, Dieter. 1981. "Überlegungen zum Problem des Pyramidenbaues." *Mitteilungen des Deutschen Archäologischen Instituts, Abteilung Kairo* 37: 15–28.

Arnold, Felix. 1990. *The South Cemeteries of Lisht, Volume II: The Control Notes and Team Marks*. New York: The Metropolitan Museum of Art.

———. 2017. "Logistik einer Pyramidenbaustelle: Markierungen am Baumaterial der Pyramidenanlagen des Königs Snofru in Dahschur." In Dietmar Kurapkat and Ulrike Wulf-Rheidt (eds), *Werkspuren. Materialverarbeitung und handwerkliches Wissen im antiken Bauwesen: Internationales Kolloquium in Berlin vom 13.-16. Mai 2015, veranstaltet vom Architekturreferat des DAI im Henry-Ford-Bau der Freien Universität Berlin*, 389–398 . Regensburg: Schnell & Steiner.

———. 2021. *Tempelanlagen im Tal der Knickpyramide*. Archäologische Veröffentlichungen 133. Wiesbaden: Harrassowitz.

Asscher, Yotam and Elisabetta Boaretto. 2019. "Absolute Time Ranges in the Plateau of the Late Bronze to Iron Age Transition and the Appearance of Bichrome Pottery in Canaan, Southern Levant." *Radiocarbon* 61: 13–37.

Baer, Klaus. 1960. *Rank and Title in the Old Kingdom: The Structure of the Egyptian Administration in the Fifth and Sixth Dynasties*. Chicago: The University of Chicago Press.

Barsanti, Alexandre. 1907. "Fouilles de Zaouiét el-Aryân (1904-1905.)." *Annales du Service des Antiquités de l'Égypte* 7: 257–286.

Bárta, Miroslav. 2017. "Radjedef to the Eighth Dynasty." In Wolfram Grajetzki and Willeke Wendrich (eds), *UCLA Encyclopedia of Egyptology*. Los Angeles. https://escholarship.org/uc/item/67n4m4c4, accessed 27 October 2021.

Barta, Winfried. 1981. "Die Chronologie der 1. bis 5. Dynastie nach den Angaben des rekonstruierten Annalensteins." *Zeitschrift für ägyptische Sprache und Altertumskunde* 108: 11–23.

Baud, Michel. 2000. "Les frontières des quatre premières dynasties: annales royales et historiographie égyptienne." *Bulletin de la Société Française d'Égyptologie* 149: 32–46.

———. 2002. *Djéser et la IIIe dynastie: Les grands pharaons*. Paris: Pygmalion - Gérard Watelet.

Beckerath, Jürgen von. 1997. *Chronologie des pharaonischen Ägypten: die Zeitbestimmung der ägyptischen Geschichte von der Vorzeit bis 332 v. Chr*. Münchener Ägyptologische Studien 46. Mainz: Philipp von Zabern.

———. 1999. *Handbuch der ägyptischen Königsnamen*. Münchener Ägyptologische Studien 49. Mainz: Philipp von Zabern.

Ben-Tor, Daphna. 2016. "Evidence for Middle Bronze Age Chronology and Synchronisms in the Levant: A Response to Höflmayer et al. 2016." *Bulletin of the American Schools of Oriental Research* 379: 43–54.

Bierbrier, Morris L. 2006. "Genealogy and Chronology." In Erik Hornung, Rolf Krauss, and David A. Warburton (eds), *Ancient Egyptian Chronology*. Handbuch der Orientalistik 83, 37–44. Leiden, Boston: Brill.

Bietak, Manfred. 2013. "Antagonisms in Historical and Radiocarbon Chronology." In Andrew J. Shortland and Christopher Bronk Ramsey (eds), *Radiocarbon and the Chronologies of Ancient Egypt*, 76–109. Oxford: Oxbow Books.

———. 2021. "The End of High Chronology in the Aegean and the Levant?: Recent Discussions about the Chronology of the Middle and the Late Bronze Ages in the Eastern Mediterranean: Part II." *Bibliotheca Orientalis* 78: 20–56.

Blumenthal, Vera. 2019. *Das ägyptische Alte Reich: Diskussionen zur „Ereignisgeschichte" der 3. bis 6. Dynastie*. Göttinger Orientforschungen, 4. Reihe: Ägypten 66. Wiesbaden: Harrassowitz.

Boaretto, Elisabetta, Yotam Asscher, Louise A. Hitchcock, Gunnar Lehmann, Aren M. Maeir, and Stephen Weiner. 2019. "The Chronology of the Late Bronze (LB)-Iron Age (IA) Transition in the Southern Levant: A Response to Finkelstein's Critique." *Radiocarbon* 61: 1–11.

Bonani, Georges, H. Haas, Zahi A. Hawass, Mark Lehner, S. Nakhla, J. Nolan, Robert J. Wenke, and W. Wölfli. 2001. "Radiocarbon Dates of Old and Middle Kingdom Monuments in Egypt." *Radiocarbon* 43: 1297–1320.

Bronk Ramsey, Christopher. 1995. "Radiocarbon Calibration and Analysis of Stratigraphy: The OxCal Program." *Radiocarbon* 37: 425–430.

———. 2001. "Development of the Radiocarbon Calibration Program OxCal." *Radiocarbon* 43: 355–363.

———. 2009a. "Bayesian Analysis of Radiocarbon Dates." *Radiocarbon* 51: 337–360.

———. 2009b. "Dealing with Outliers and Offsets in Radiocarbon Dating." *Radiocarbon* 51: 1023–1045.

Bronk Ramsey, Christopher, Michael W. Dee, Joanne M. Rowland, Thomas F. G. Higham, Stephen A. Harris, Fiona Brock, Anita Quiles, Eva M. Wild, Ezra S. Marcus, and Andrew J. Shortland. 2010. "Radiocarbon-Based Chronology for Dynastic Egypt." *Science* 328: 1554–1557.

Brovarski, Edward. 2016. "Old Kingdom Marginalia." *Göttinger Miszellen* 250: 75–80.

Bruins, Hendrik J. and Johannes van der Plicht. 2019. "Radiocarbon Dating Comparée of Hyksos-Related Phases at Ashkelon and Tell el-Dabʿa." In Manfred Bietak and Silvia Prell (eds): *ASOR Conference Boston 2017 – ICAANE Conference Munich 2018 – Collected Papers, The Enigma of the Hyksos Volume I*, 353–367. Wiesbaden: Harrassowitz.

Castle, Edward W. 1994. "Further Observations on the Dedication Formula *ir.n.f m mnw.f.*" *Journal of Egyptian Archaeology* 80: 187–191.

Cenival, Jean-Louis de. 1965. "Un nouveau fragment de la Pierre de Palerme." *Bulletin de la Société Française d'Égyptologie* 44: 13–17.

Chassinat, Émile. 1921. "À propos d'une tête en grès rouge du roi Didoufrî (IVe dynastie) conservée au Musée du Louvre." *Monuments et mémoires de la fondation Eugène Piot* 25: 53–75.

Ciavatti, Aurore. 2019. "L'octaétéride et la chronologie de l'Ancien Empire: prolégomènes." *Bulletin de la Société Française d'Égyptologie* 202: 8–18.

———. 2022. "Le règne de Snéfrou: nouvel examen des sources chronologiques." *BIFAO* 122: 107–153

Clagett, Marshall. 1989. *Ancient Egyptian Science: A Source Book: Volume One: Knowledge and Order*. Memoirs of the American Philosophical Society 184. Philadelphia: American Philosophical Society.

Ćwiek, Andrzej. 2008. "History of the Third Dynasty, Another Update on the Kings and Monuments." In Miroslav Bárta and Hana Vymazalová (eds), *Chronology and Archaeology in Ancient Egypt (the Third Millennium B.C.)*, 87–103. Prague: Czech Institute of Egyptology, Faculty of Arts, Charles University in Prague.

Dee, Michael W. 2013. "A Radiocarbon-based Chronology for the Old Kingdom." In Andrew J. Shortland and Christopher Bronk Ramsey (eds), *Radiocarbon and the Chronologies of Ancient Egypt*, 209–217. Oxford: Oxbow Books.

Dorman, Peter F. 2002. "The Biographical Inscription of Ptahshepses from Saqqara: A Newly Identified Fragment." *Journal of Egyptian Archaeology* 88: 95–110.

Dreyer, Günter. 1987. "Drei archaisch-hieratische Gefässaufschriften mit Jahresnamen aus Elephantine." In Günter Dreyer and Jürgen Osing (eds), *Form und Mass: Beiträge zur Literatur, Sprache und Kunst des alten Ägypten. Festschrift für Gerhard Fecht zum 65. Geburtstag am 6. Februar 1987*, 98–109. Wiesbaden: Harrassowitz.

———. 1998. "Der erste König der 3. Dynastie." In Heike Guksch and Daniel Polz (eds), *Stationen: Beiträge zur Kulturgeschichte Ägyptens, Rainer Stadelmann gewidmet*, 31–34. Mainz: Philipp von Zabern.

Erbkam, Gustav G. Unpublished. *Skizzenbuch* 1.

Fakhry, Ahmed. 1959. *The Bent Pyramid: The monuments of Sneferu at Dahshur 1*. Cairo: General Organization for Government Printing Offices.

Falconer, Steven E. and Patricia L. Fall. 2016. "A Radiocarbon Sequence from Tell Abu en-Niʿaj, Jordan and its Implications for Early Bronze IV Chronology in the Southern Levant." *Radiocarbon* 58: 615–647.

———. 2017. "Radiocarbon Evidence from Tell Abu en-Niʿaj and Tell el-Hayyat, Jordan, and Its Implications for Bronze Age Levantine and

Egyptian Chronologies." *Journal of Ancient Egyptian Interconnections* 13: 7–19.

Fall, Patricia L., Steven E. Falconer, and Felix Höflmayer. 2021. "New Bayesian Radiocarbon Models for Early Bronze IV Tell Abu en-Niʿaj and Middle Bronze Age Tell el-Hayyat, Jordan." *Radiocarbon* 63: 41–76.

Farina, Giulio. 1938. *Il papiro dei re restaurato.* Roma: Bardi.

Fecht, Gerhard. 1985. "Die Lesung von  „Regierungsjahr" als *rnpt-zp*." In Anonymous (ed.), *Ägypten: Dauer und Wandel: Symposium anlässlich des 75jährigen Bestehens des DAI Kairo am 10. und 11. Oktober 1982,* 85–96. Mainz: Philipp von Zabern.

Finkelstein, Israel. 2020. "Iron Age Chronology and Biblical History Rejoinders: The Late Bronze/Iron Age Transition, Tel ʿEton and Lachish." *Palestine Exploration Quarterly* 152: 82–93.

Fischer, Henry G. 1960. "The Butcher *Pḥ-r-nfr*." *Orientalia* 29,2: 168–190.

———. 1976. "Archaeological Aspects of Epigraphy and Palaeography." In The Metropolitan Museum of Art (ed.), *Ancient Egyptian Epigraphy and Palaeography,* 27–50. New York: The Metropolitan Museum of Art.

Flentye, Laurel. 2007. "The Mastabas of Ankh-haf (G7510) and Akhethetep and Meretites (G7650) in the Eastern Cemetery at Giza: A Reassessment." In Zahi A. Hawass and Janet E. Richards (eds), *The Archaeology and Art of Ancient Egypt: Essays in Honor of David B. O'Connor* vol. 1, 291–308. Le Caire: Conseil Suprême des Antiquités de l'Egypte.

Gardiner, Alan H. 1945. "Regnal Years and Civil Calendar in Pharaonic Egypt." *Journal of Egyptian Archaeology* 31: 11–28.

———. 1959. *The Royal Canon of Turin.* Oxford: Oxford University Press.

Garfinkel, Yosef, Michael G. Hasel, Martin G. Klingbeil, Hoo-Goo Kang, Gwanghyun Choi, Sang-Yeup Chang, Soonhwa Hong, Saar Ganor, Igor Kreimerman, and Christopher Bronk Ramsey. 2019. "Lachish Fortifications and State Formation in the Biblical Kingdom of Judah in Light of Radiometric Datings." *Radiocarbon* 61: 695–712.

Gauthier, Henri. 1907. *Le livre des rois d'Égypte: recueil de titres et protocoles royaux, noms propres de rois, reines, princes et princesses, noms de pyramides et de temples solaires, suivi d'un index alphabétique.* Mémoires publiés par les membres de l'Institut Français d'Archéologie Orientale 17. Cairo: Imprimerie de l'IFAO.

———. 1915. "Quatre nouveaux fragments de la pierre de Palerme." In Eugène Grébaut and Gaston Maspero (eds), *Le Musée Égyptien: recueil de monuments et de notices sur les fouilles d'Égypte* vol. 3, 29–53. Le Caire: Institut Français d'Archéologie Orientale.

Goedicke, Hans. 1967. *Königliche Dokumente aus dem alten Reich.* Ägyptologische Abhandlungen 14. Wiesbaden: Harrassowitz.

———. 1968. "Four Hieratic Ostraca of the Old Kingdom." *Journal of Egyptian Archaeology* 54: 23–30.

———. 1970. *Die privaten Rechtsinschriften aus dem Alten Reich.* Beihefte zur Wiener Zeitschrift für die Kunde des Morgenlandes 5. Wien: Notring.

Gozzoli, Roberto B. 2006. *The Writing of History in Ancient Egypt During the First Millennium BC (ca. 1070–180 BC): Trends and Perspectives.* Egyptology (Golden House) 5. London: Golden House Publications.

Greenberg, Raphael. 2019. *The Archaeology of the Bronze Age Levant: From Urban Origins to the Demise of City-States, 3700–1000 BCE.* Cambridge: Cambridge University Press.

Gundacker, Roman. 2006. *Untersuchungen zur Chronologie der Herrschaft Snofrus.* Beiträge zur Ägyptologie 22. Wien: Afro-Pub.

———. 2010. "Materialien zur Länge der Regierung des Mykerinos." *Sokar* 21: 30–43.

———. 2013. "Die Eigennamen der Könige der IV. Dynastie: ihre Struktur und Bedeutung gemäß ägyptischen und griechischen Graphien." *Lingua Aegyptia* 21: 35–130.

———. 2015. "The Chronology of the Third and Fourth Dynasties According to Manetho's Aegyptiaca." In Peter Der Manuelian and Thomas Schneider (eds), *Towards a New History for the Egyptian Old Kingdom: Perspectives on the Pyramid Age,* 76–199. Leiden, Boston: Brill.

———. 2018. "Manetho." In Michaela Bauks, Klaus Koenen, and Michael Pietsch (eds), *Wissenschaftliches Bibellexikon im Internet.* Stuttgart: Deutsche Bibel-Gesellschaft. https://www.bibelwissenschaft.de/stichwort/25466/, accessed 27 October 2021.

Haring, Ben J. J. 2020. "The Survival of Pharaonic Ostraca: Coincidence or Meaningful Patterns?" In Clementina Caputo and Julia Lougovaya (eds), *Using Ostraca in the Ancient World: New Discoveries and Methodologies*, 89–108. Berlin: De Gruyter.

Hassan, Fekri A. and S. W. Robinson. 1987. "High-precision Radiocarbon Chronometry of Ancient Egypt, and Comparisons with Nubia, Palestine and Mesopotamia." *Antiquity* 61: 119–135.

Helck, Wolfgang. 1956. *Untersuchungen zu Manetho und den ägyptischen Königslisten*. Untersuchungen zur Geschichte und Altertumskunde Aegyptens 18. Berlin: Akademie-Verlag.

———. 1970. "Zwei Einzelprobleme der thinitischen Chronologie." *Mitteilungen des Deutschen Archäologischen Instituts, Abteilung Kairo* 26: 83–85.

Henige, David. 1981. "Generation-Counting and Late New Kingdom Chronology." *Journal of Egyptian Archaeology* 67: 182–184.

Höflmayer, Felix. 2016. "Radiocarbon Dating and Egyptian Chronology – From the 'Curve of Knowns' to Bayesian Modeling." In Oxford Handbooks (ed.), *Archaeology, Oxford Handbooks Online*. Oxford: Oxford University Press. https://doi.org/10.1093/oxfordhb/9780199935413.013.64, accessed: 27 October 2021.

———. 2017a. "A Radiocarbon Chronology for the Middle Bronze Age Southern Levant." *Journal of Ancient Egyptian Interconnections* 13: 20–33.

———. 2017b. "Introduction: The Late Third Millennium BC in the Ancient Near East and Eastern Mediterranean - A Time of Collapse and Transformation." In Felix Höflmayer (ed.), *The Late Third Millennium in the Ancient Near East: Chronology, C14 and Climate Change: Papers from the Oriental Institute Seminar Held at the Oriental Institute of the University of Chicago 7-8 March 2014*, 1–29. Chicago: The Oriental Institute of the University of Chicago.

———. (ed.). 2017c. *The Late Third Millennium in the Ancient Near East: Chronology, C14 and Climate Change: Papers from the Oriental Institute Seminar Held at the Oriental Institute of the University of Chicago 7-8 March 2014*. Chicago: The Oriental Institute of the University of Chicago.

———. 2022a. "Tel Nami, Cyprus, and Egypt: Radiocarbon Dates and Early Middle Bronze Age Chronology." *Palestine Exploration Quarterly* 54,1: 52–69.

———. 2022b. "Establishing an Absolute Chronology of the Middle Bronze Age." In Nadine Moeller, D. T. Potts and Karen Radner (eds), *Oxford History of the Ancient Near East. Volume II: From the End of the Third Millennium BC to the Fall of Babylon*, 1–46. New York: Oxford University Press.

Höflmayer, Felix and Sturt W. Manning. 2022. "A Synchronized Early Middle Bronze Age Chronology for Egypt, the Levant, and Mesopotamia." *Journal of Near Eastern Studies* 81,1: 1–2.

Höflmayer, Felix and Katharina Streit. 2019. "The Impact of Radiocarbon Dating and Absolute Chronology in the Holy Land: A Social Archaeological Perspective." In Assaf Yasur-Landau, Eric H. Cline, and Yorke M. Rowan (eds), *From Prehistory to the Present, The Social Archaeology of the Levant*, 573–593. Cambridge: Cambridge University Press.

Höflmayer, Felix, Michael W. Dee, Hermann Genz, and Simone Riehl. 2014. "Radiocarbon Evidence for the Early Bronze Age Levant: Tell Fadous-Kfarabida (Lebanon) and the End of the Early Bronze III Period." *Radiocarbon* 56: 529–542.

Hornung, Erik. 2005. *Der Eine und die Vielen: altägyptische Götterwelt*. Darmstadt: Primus.

Hornung, Erik, Rolf Krauss, and David A. Warburton. 2006a. "Methods of Dating and the Egyptian Calendar." In Erik Hornung, Rolf Krauss, and David A. Warburton (eds), *Ancient Egyptian Chronology*. Handbuch der Orientalistik 83, 45–51. Leiden, Boston: Brill.

———. 2006b. "Royal Annals." In Erik Hornung, Rolf Krauss, and David A. Warburton (eds), *Ancient Egyptian Chronology*. Handbuch der Orientalistik 83, 19–25. Leiden, Boston: Brill.

Incordino, Ilaria. 2007. "The Third Dynasty: A Chronological Hypothesis." In Jean-Claude Goyon and Christine Cardin (eds), *Proceedings of the Ninth International Congress of Egyptologists: Grenoble, 6-12 septembre 2004* vol. 1, 961–968. Leuven: Peeters.

———. 2008. *Chronological Problems of the IIIrd Egyptian Dynasty: A Re-Examination of the Archaeological Documents*. British Archaeological Reports International Series 1882. Oxford: Archaeopress.

———. 2010. "Reign of Horus Sanakht: Possible Founder of the Third Dynasty." In Francesco

Raffaele, Massimiliano Nuzzolo, and Ilaria Incordino (eds), *Recent Discoveries and Latest Researches in Egyptology: Proceedings of the First Neapolitan Congress of Egyptology, June 18th-20th 2008*, 145–155. Wiesbaden: Harrassowitz.

Jacoby, Felix. 1958. *Die Fragmente der griechischen Historiker (F Gr Hist): Dritter Teil. Geschichte von Staedten und Voelkern (Horographie und Ethnographie). C. Autoren ueber einzelne Laender. Nr. 608 a - 856 (Erster Band: Aegypten-Geten Nr. 608 a - 708).* Leiden: Brill.

Jánosi, Peter. 2005. *Giza in der 4. Dynastie: die Baugeschichte und Belegung einer Nekropole des Alten Reiches. Band. 1: die Mastabas der Kernfriedhöfe und die Felsgräber.* Denkschriften der Gesamtakademie 30; Untersuchungen der Zweigstelle Kairo des Österreichischen Archäologischen Institutes 24. Wien: Verlag der Österreichischen Akademie der Wissenschaften.

Junker, Hermann. 1929. *Gîza I: Bericht über die von der Akademie der Wissenschaften in Wien auf gemeinsame Kosten mit Dr. Wilhelm Pelizaeus unternommenen Grabungen auf dem Friedhof des Alten Reiches bei den Pyramiden von Gîza: Die Maṣṭabas der IV. Dynastie auf dem Westfriedhof.* Österreichische Akademie der Wissenschaften, Denkschriften der Philosophisch-Historischen Klasse 69. Wien, Leipzig: Hölder-Pichler-Tempsky.

Kahl, Jochem, Nicole Kloth, and Ursula Zimmermann. 1995. *Die Inschriften der 3. Dynastie: eine Bestandsaufnahme.* Ägyptologische Abhandlungen 56. Wiesbaden: Harrassowitz.

Kaplony, Peter. 1963. *Die Inschriften der ägyptischen Frühzeit.* Ägyptologische Abhandlungen 8. Wiesbaden: Harrassowitz.

Kitchen, Kenneth A. 1999. "Review: Beckerath, Jürgen von 1997. Chronologie des pharaonischen Ägypten: die Zeitbestimmung der ägyptischen Geschichte von der Vorzeit bis 332 v. Chr. Münchner Ägyptologische Studien 46; Münchener Universitätsschriften, Philosophische Fakultät. Mainz: von Zabern." *Journal of Egyptian Archaeology* 85: 245–248.

Krauss, Rolf. 1996. "The Length of Sneferu's Reign and How Long It Took to Build the 'Red Pyramid'." *Journal of Egyptian Archaeology* 82: 43–50.

———. 1997. "Chronologie und Pyramidenbau in der 4. Dynastie." *Orientalia* 66,1: 1–14.

———. 1998. "Zur Berechnung der Bauzeit an Snofrus Roter Pyramide." *Zeitschrift für ägyptische Sprache und Altertumskunde* 125: 29–37.

Kuhlmann, Klaus P. 2005. "Der ‚Wasserberg des Djedefre' (Chufu 01/1). Ein Lagerplatz mit Expeditionsinschriften der 4. Dynastie im Raum der Oase Dachla." *Mitteilungen des Deutschen Archäologischen Instituts, Abteilung Kairo* 61: 243–289.

Kurokochi, Hiromasa and Sakuji Yoshimura. 2013. "2012年太陽の船プロジェクト活動報告 / Report of the Activity in 2012, Project of the Solar Boat." *The Journal of Egyptian Studies* 19: 5–13.

Leprohon, Ronald J. 2013. *The Great Name: Ancient Egyptian Royal Titulary.* Writings from the Ancient World 33. Atlanta, GA: Society of Biblical Literature.

Lepsius, Carl R. 1859. *Denkmaeler aus Aegypten und Aethiopien.* Berlin: Nicolaische Buchhandlung.

Manning, Sturt W. 2014. *A Test of Time and A Test of Time Revisited: The Volcano of Thera and the Chronology and History of the Aegean and East Mediterranean in the Mid-second Millennium BC.* Oxford, Philadelphia: Oxbow Books.

Manning, Sturt W., Felix Höflmayer, Nadine Moeller, Michael W. Dee, Christopher Bronk Ramsey, Dominik Fleitmann, Thomas F. G. Higham, Walter Kutschera, and Eva M. Wild. 2014. "Dating the Thera (Santorini) Eruption: Coherent Archaeological and Scientific Evidence Supporting a High Chronology." *Antiquity* 88: 1164–1179.

Manning, Sturt W., Lukas Wacker, Ulf Büntgen, Christopher Bronk Ramsey, Michael W. Dee, Bernd Kromer, Brita Lorentzen, and Willy Tegel. 2020. "Radiocarbon Offsets and Old World Chronology as Relevant to Mesopotamia, Egypt, Anatolia and Thera (Santorini)." *Scientific Reports* 10: 13785.

Manning, Sturt W., Bernd Kromer, Mauro Cremaschi, Michael W. Dee, Ronny Friedrich, Carol B. Griggs, and Carla S. Hadden. 2020. "Mediterranean Radiocarbon Offsets and Calendar Dates for Prehistory." *Science Advances* 6, https://doi.org/10.1126/sciadv.aaz1096, accessed 27 October 2021.

Maystre, Charles. 1935. "Les dates des pyramides de Snefrou." *Bulletin de l'Institut Français d'Archéologie Orientale* 35: 89–98.

Mazar, Amihai and Katharina Streit. 2020. "Radiometric Dates from Tel Reḥov." In Amihai

Mazar and Nava Panitz-Cohen (eds): *Volume V. Various Objects and Natural-Science Studies: Tel Reḥov. A Bronze and Iron Age City in the Beth-Shean Valley*, 455–494. Jerusalem: The Institute of Archaeology. The Hebrew University of Jerusalem.

Möller, Georg. 1909. *Hieratische Paläographie. Die aegyptische Buchschrift in ihrer Entwicklung von der fünften Dynastie bis zur römischen Kaiserzeit. Zweiter Band. Von der Zeit Thutmosis' III. bis zum Ende der einundzwanzigsten Dynastie*. Leipzig: Hinrichs.

Mosshammer, Alden A. 1984. *Georgii Syncelli Ecloga Chronographica*. Leipzig: Teubner.

Nigro, Lorenzo, Lucio Calcagnile, Jehad Yasine, Elisabetta Gallo, and Gianluca Quarta. 2019. "Jericho and the Chronology of Palestine in the Early Bronze Age: A Radiometric Re-assessment." *Radiocarbon* 61: 211–241.

Nishisaka, Akiko, Kazumitsu Takahashi, Hiromasa Kurokochi, and Sakuji Yoshimura. 2011. "ギザ、クフ王第2の船の船坑上の壁体発掘調査概報." *The Journal of Egyptian Studies* 17: 5–44.

Nishisaka, Akiko and Kazumitsu Takahashi. 2016. "Some Notes on the Graffiti Written on the Cover Stones from the Second Boat Pit of Khufu." *Bulletin of the Society for Near Eastern Studies in Japan* 59,1: 2–13.

Nolan, John S. 2003. "The Original Lunar Calendar and Cattle Counts in Old Kingdom Egypt." In Susanne Bickel and Antonio Loprieno (eds), *Basel Egyptology Prize 1: Junior Research in Egyptian History, Archaeology, and Philology*, 75–97. Basel: Schwabe.

———. 2008. "Lunar Intercalations and "Cattle Counts" During the Old Kingdom: The Hebsed in Context." In Miroslav Bárta and Hana Vymazalová (eds), *Chronology and Archaeology in Ancient Egypt (the Third Millennium B.C.)*, 44–60. Prague: Czech Institute of Egyptology, Faculty of Arts, Charles University in Prague.

Nour, Mohammed Z., Zaki Iskander, Mohammed S. Osman, and Ahmed Y. Moustafa. 1960. *The Cheops Boats*. Cairo: General Organization for Government Printing Offices.

Nuzzolo, Massimiliano. 2020. "La pierre de Palerme et les fragments associés: nouvelles découvertes sur les plus anciennes annales royales égyptiennes." *Bulletin de la Société Française d'Égyptologie* 202: 55–82.

———. 2021. "The Palermo Stone and Its Associated Fragments: New Discoveries on the Oldest Royal Annals of Ancient Egypt." *Journal of Egyptian Archaeology* 107: 58–78.

Nuzzolo, Massimiliano, Jaromír Krejčí, Mohamed Osman, and Kathryn E. Piquette. 2021. "Royal Annals of Ancient Egypt: Recent Investigations on the Palermo Stone and Its Associated Fragments." In Massimiliano Nuzzolo and Jaromír Krejčí (eds), *The Rise and Development of the Solar Cult and Architecture in Ancient Egypt*, 71–102. Wiesbaden: Harrassowitz.

O'Mara, Patrick F. 1979. *The Palermo Stone and the Archaic Kings of Egypt: Studies in the Structural Archaeology of Ancient Egypt*. La Canada, CA: Paulette.

Pätznick, Jean-Pierre. 2005. *Die Siegelabrollungen und Rollsiegel der Stadt Elephantine im 3. Jahrtausend v. Chr.: Spurensicherung eines archäologischen Artefaktes*. British Archaeological Reports International Series 1339. Oxford: Archaeopress.

———. 2007. "L'Horus Qahedjet: souverain de la 3e dynastie?." In Jean-Claude Goyon and Christine Cardin (eds), *Proceedings of the Ninth International Congress of Egyptologists: Grenoble, 6-12 septembre 2004* vol. 2, 1455–1473. Leuven: Peeters.

Petrie, William M. F. 1910. *Meydum and Memphis (III)*. British School of Archaeology in Egypt and Egyptian Research Account 18. London: British School of Archaeology in Egypt.

———. 1923. *A History of Egypt. From the Earliest Kings to the XVIth Dynasty*. A History of Egypt 1. London: Methuen & Co. Ltd.

Posener-Kriéger, Paule. 1975. "Les papyrus de Gébélein: remarques préliminaires." *Revue d'égyptologie* 27: 211–221.

———. 1991. "Graffiti on the Revetment Blocks of the Pyramid." In Geoffrey T. Martin (ed.), *Meidum*. The Australian Centre for Egyptology Reports 3, 17–21. Sydney: The Australian Centre for Egyptology.

———. 2004. *I papiri di Gebelein: scavi G. Farina 1935*. Studi del Museo Egizio di Torino: Gebelein 1. Torino: Ministero per i Beni e le Attività Culturali, Soprintendenza al Museo delle Antichità Egizie.

Redford, Donald B. 1986. *Pharaonic King-Lists, Annals and Day-Books: A Contribution to the Study of the Egyptian Sense of History*. SSEA Publications 4. Mississauga: Benben.

Reeves, C. Nicholas. 1979. "A Fragment of Fifth Dynasty Annals at University College London." *Göttinger Miszellen* 32: 47–51.

Regev, Johanna, Israel Finkelstein, Matthew J. Adams, and Elisabetta Boaretto. 2014. "Wiggle-matched 14C Chronology of Early Bronze Megiddo and the Synchronization of Egyptian and Levantine Chronologies." *Ägypten & Levante* 24: 243–266.

Regev, Johanna, Pierre de Miroschedji, and Elisabetta Boaretto. 2012. "Early Bronze Age Chronology: Radiocarbon Dates and Chronological Models from Tel Yarmuth (Israel)." *Radiocarbon* 54: 505–524.

Regev, Johanna, Pierre de Miroschedji, Raphael Greenberg, Eliot Braun, Zvi Greenhut, and Elisabetta Boaretto. 2012. "Chronology of the Early Bronze Age in the Southern Levant: New Analysis for a High Chronology." *Radiocarbon* 54: 525–566.

Regev, Johanna, Sarit Paz, Raphael Greenberg, and Elisabetta Boaretto. 2020. "Radiocarbon Chronology of the EB I–II and II–III Transitions at Tel Bet Yerah, and Its Implications for the Nature of Social Change in the Southern Levant." *Levant* 51,1: 1–22.

Regev, Johanna, Lior Regev, Eugenia Mintz, and Elisabetta Boaretto. 2017. "Radiocarbon Assessment of Early Bronze Arad: The 20 Year Lifespan of Stratum II." *Tel Aviv* 44: 165–177.

Reimer, Paula J., William E. N. Austin, Edouard Bard, Alex Bayliss, Paul G. Blackwell, Christopher Bronk Ramsey, Martin Butzin, Hai Cheng, R. Lawrence Edwards, Michael Friedrich, Pieter M. Grootes, Thomas P. Guilderson, Irka Hajdas, Timothy J. Heaton, Alan G. Hogg, Konrad A. Hughen, Bernd Kromer, Sturt W. Manning, Raimund Muscheler, Jonathan G. Palmer, Charlotte L. Pearson, Johannes van der Plicht, Ron W. Reimer, David A. Richards, E. Marian Scott, John R. Southon, Christian S. M. Turney, Lukas Wacker, Florian Adolphi, Ulf Büntgen, Manuela Capano, Simon M. Fahrni, Alexandra Fogtmann-Schulz, Ronny Friedrich, Peter Köhler, Sabrina Kudsk, Fusa Miyake, Jesper Olsen, Frederick Reinig, Minoru Sakamoto, Adam Sookdeo, and Sahra Talamo. 2020. "The IntCal20 Northern Hemisphere Radiocarbon Age Calibration Curve (0-55 Cal kBP)." *Radiocarbon* 62: 725–757.

Reisner, George A. Unpublished. *A History of the Giza Necropolis II. Unpublished 1942 Manuscript.* http://giza.fas.harvard.edu/unpubdocs/40797/full/, accessed 27 October 2021.

———. 1931. *Mycerinus: The Temples of the Third Pyramid at Giza.* Cambridge, MA: Harvard University Press.

———. 1942. *A History of the Giza Necropolis, Volume I.* Cambridge, MA: Harvard University Press.

Renfrew, Colin and Paul Bahn. 2019. *Archaeology: Theories, Methods, and Practice.* London: Thames & Hudson Ltd.

Rotem, Yael, Yorke M. Rowan, Felix Höflmayer, and Mark Iserlis. 2019. "Tel Yaqush – An Early Bronze Age Village in the Central Jordan Valley, Israel." *Bulletin of the American Schools of Oriental Research* 381: 107–144.

Roth, Ann M. 1991. *Egyptian Phyles in the Old Kingdom: The Evolution of a System of Social Organization.* Studies in Ancient Oriental Civilization 48. Chicago: University of Chicago Press.

Ryholt, Kim. 2004. "The Turin King-List." *Ägypten & Levante* 14: 135–155.

———. 2006. "The Turin King-List or So-Called Turin Canon (TC) as a Source for Chronology." In Erik Hornung, Rolf Krauss, and David A. Warburton (eds), *Ancient Egyptian Chronology.* Handbuch der Orientalistik 83, 26–32. Leiden, Boston: Brill.

Salvador, Chiara. 2020. "Graffiti." In Vanessa Davies and Dimitri Laboury (eds), *The Oxford Handbook of Egyptian Epigraphy and Palaeography*, 434–447. New York: Oxford University Press.

Schäfer, Heinrich. 1902. *Ein Bruchstück altägyptischer Annalen.* Abhandlungen der Preußischen Akademie der Wissenschaften zu Berlin 1902. Berlin: Verlag der Akademie der Wissenschaften.

Seidlmayer, Stephan J. 2006. "The Relative Chronology of Dynasty 3." In Erik Hornung, Rolf Krauss, and David A. Warburton (eds), *Ancient Egyptian Chronology.* Handbuch der Orientalistik 83, 116–123. Leiden, Boston: Brill.

Sethe, Kurt. 1903. *Urkunden des Alten Reichs [I,1-152].* Urkunden des Ägyptischen Altertums 1. Leipzig Hinrichs.

———. 1905. *Beiträge zur ältesten Geschichte Ägyptens.* Untersuchungen zur Geschichte und Altertumskunde Aegyptens 3. Leipzig Hinrichs.

Shortland, Andrew J. and Christopher Bronk Ramsey (eds). 2013. *Radiocarbon and the Chronologies of Ancient Egypt*. Oxford: Oxbow Books.

Smith, William S. 1952. "Inscriptional Evidence for the History of the Fourth Dynasty." *Journal of Near Eastern Studies* 11,2: 113–128.

Spalinger, Anthony. 1994. "Dated Texts of the Old Kingdom." *Studien zur Altägyptischen Kultur* 21: 275–319.

Stadelmann, Rainer. 1987. "Beiträge zur Geschichte des Alten Reiches: die Länge der Regierung des Snofru." *Mitteilungen des Deutschen Archäologischen Instituts, Abteilung Kairo* 43: 229–240.

———. 1993. "Dahschur." *Deutsches Archäologisches Institut Kairo, Rundbrief 1993*: 10–13.

———. 2004. "Dahschur. Knickpyramide und Taltempel des Snofru." *Deutsches Archäologisches Institut Kairo, Rundbrief 2004*: 15–18.

Steindorff, Georg 1906. *Tagebuch der Grabung an den Pyramiden von Gizeh Frühjahr 1906*. http://www.giza-projekt.org/Archivalien/1906/Ab_Tgb_06.pdf#Tgb_06.pdf, accessed 23 January 2023.

Stewart, Harry M. 1979. *Egyptian Stelae, Reliefs and Paintings from the Petrie Collection Part Two: Archaic Period to Second Intermediate Period*. Warminster: Aris & Phillips.

Strudwick, Nigel. 1985. *The Administration of Egypt in the Old Kingdom: The Highest Titles and Their Holders*. London: KPI.

Swelim, Nabil M. A. 1983. *Some Problems on the History of the Third Dynasty*. Archaeological & Historical Studies 7. Alexandria: Archaeological Society of Alexandria.

Tallet, Pierre. 2013. "Les papyrus de la Mer Rouge (Ouadi el-Jarf, Golfe de Suez)." *Comptes rendus des séances de l'Académie des Inscriptions & Belles-Lettres* 2013,2: 1015–1024.

———. 2014. "Des papyrus du temps de Chéops au ouadi el-Jarf (golfe du Suez)." *Bulletin de la Société Française d'Égyptologie* 188: 25–49.

———. 2017. *Les papyrus de la mer Rouge I: Le "journal de Merer" (Papyrus Jarf A et B)*. Mémoires publiés par les membres de l'Institut français d'archéologie orientale 136. Le Caire: Institut Français d'Archéologie Orientale.

Theis, Christoffer. 2014. "Zu den an der Pyramide Lepsius XIII gefundenen Namen: die Frage nach *Nfr-k3* und *B3-k3*." *Studien zur Altägyptischen Kultur* 43: 423–438.

Tumolo, Valentina and Felix Höflmayer. 2020. "Khirbet ez-Zeraqon and Early Bronze Age Chronology Revisited." In Suzanne Richard (ed.), *New Horizons in the Study of the Early Bronze III and Early Bronze IV of the Levant*, 249–264. University Park: Eisenbrauns.

Valloggia, Michel. 1997. "La descenderie de la pyramide de Radjedef à Abu Rawash." In Catherine Berger and Bernard Mathieu (eds), *Études sur l'Ancien Empire et la nécropole de Saqqâra dédiées à Jean-Philippe Lauer* vol. 2, 417–428. Montpellier: Université Paul Valéry-Montpellier III.

———. 2011. *Abou Rawash 1: le complexe funéraire royal de Rêdjedef*. Fouilles de l'Institut Français d'Archéologie Orientale 63. Le Caire: Institut Français d'Archéologie Orientale.

van der Moezel, Kyra V. J. 2016. *Of Marks and Meaning. A Palaeographic, Semiotic-Cognitive, and Comparative Analysis of the Identity Marks from Deir el-Medina*. Leiden: Universiteit Leiden.

Vandier, Jacques. 1968. "Une stèle égyptienne portant un nouveau nom royal de la troisième dynastie." *Comptes rendus des séances de l'Académie des Inscriptions & Belles-Lettres* 112,1: 16–22.

Verhoeven, Ursula. 2015. "Stand und Aufgaben der Erforschung des Hieratischen und der Kursivhieroglyphen." In Ursula Verhoeven (ed.), *Ägyptologische „Binsen"-Weisheiten I–II: Neue Forschungen und Methoden der Hieratistik. Akten zweier Tagungen in Mainz im April 2011 und März 2013*, 23–63. Stuttgart: Franz Steiner.

Verner, Miroslav. 1992. *Abusir II: Baugraffiti der Ptahschepses-Mastaba*. Excavations of the Czech Institute of Egyptology. Praha: Universitas Carolina Pragensis.

———. 2001. "Archaeological Remarks on the 4th and 5th Dynasty Chronology." *Archív Orientální* 69,3: 363–418.

———. 2006. "Contemporaneous Evidence for the Relative Chronology of Dyns. 4 and 5." In Erik Hornung, Rolf Krauss, and David A. Warburton (eds), *Ancient Egyptian Chronology*. Handbuch der Orientalistik 83, 124–143. Leiden, Boston: Brill.

———. 2008. "The System of Dating in the Old Kingdom." In Miroslav Bárta and Hana Vymazalová (eds), *Chronology and Archaeology in Ancient Egypt (the Third Millennium B.C.)*,

23–43. Prague: Czech Institute of Egyptology, Faculty of Arts, Charles University in Prague.

Waddell, William G. 1948. *Manetho*. Loeb Classical Library 350. London, Cambridge, MA: Harvard University Press.

Warden, Leslie A. 2015. "Centralized Taxation during the Old Kingdom." In Peter Der Manuelian and Thomas Schneider (eds), *Towards a New History for the Egyptian Old Kingdom: Perspectives on the Pyramid Age*, 470–495. Leiden, Boston: Brill.

Wildung, Dietrich. 1969. *Die Rolle ägyptischer Könige im Bewusstsein ihrer Nachwelt: Teil I: Posthume Quellen über die Könige der ersten vier Dynastien*. Münchner Ägyptologische Studien 17. Berlin: Hessling.

Wilkinson, Toby H. A. 1999. *Early Dynastic Egypt*. London, New York: Routledge.

———. 2000. *Royal Annals of Ancient Egypt: the Palermo Stone and Its Associated Fragments*. Studies in Egyptology. London, New York: Kegan Paul International.

———. 2014. "Dynasties 2 and 3." In Wolfram Grajetzki and Willeke Wendrich (eds), *UCLA Encyclopedia of Egyptology*. Los Angeles: eScholarship. https://escholarship.org/uc/item/1hb1s3pn, accessed 27 October 2021.

Yoshimura, Sakuji and Hiromasa Kurokochi. 2012. "Ein Schiff für die Ewigkeit: die bisherigen Forschungen am zweiten Boot des Königs Cheops." *Sokar* 25: 6–17.

Ziegler, Christiane. 1990. *Catalogue des stèles, peintures et reliefs égyptiens de l'Ancien Empire et de la Première Période Intermédiaire vers 2686-2040 avant J.-C.* Paris: Réunion des musées nationaux.

Черезов, Евгений В. 1960. "Древнейшая летопись „Палермский камень" и документы Древнего царства Египта." In Василий В. Струве (ed.), *Древний Египет: сборник статей*, 261–272. Москва: Издательство Восточной литературы.

Notes

1 This contribution is based on data collected as part of the ERC Starting Grant 'Challenging Time(s) – A New Approach to Written Sources for Ancient Egyptian Chronology' (GA № 757951), which has received funding from the European Research Council under the European Union's Horizon 2020 research and innovation programme at the Austrian Archaeological Institute (Department of Classical Studies) of the Austrian Academy of Sciences. The results published are solely within the author's responsibility and do not necessarily reflect the opinion of the funding agencies or host institution, which must not be held responsible for either contents or their further use. The author would like to express his gratitude to Annik Wüthrich, Charlotte Dietrich, Roman Gundacker, Frank Simons, and Julian Posch for many helpful corrections and suggestions that significantly improved the quality of this contribution. All remaining errors and inconsistencies are those of the author.

2 The number of academic publications in this field is legion. For current discussions, cf. the following publications with further references: Höflmayer and Streit 2019; Garfinkel et al. 2019; Boaretto et al. 2019; Asscher and Boaretto 2019; Mazar and Streit 2020; Finkelstein 2020.

3 Manning et al. 2014; Manning 2014; Manning et al. 2020; Bietak 2013; Bietak 2021.

4 Höflmayer 2022a; Höflmayer and Manning 2022; Bietak 2021; Höflmayer 2022b; Bruins and van der Plicht 2019; Ben-Tor 2016; Höflmayer 2017a.

5 Regev, de Miroschedji, and Boaretto 2012; Regev, de Miroschedji, Greenberg et al. 2012.

6 Regev et al. 2014; Höflmayer et al. 2014; Falconer and Fall 2016; Regev et al. 2017; Falconer and Fall 2017; Rotem et al. 2019; Tumolo and Höflmayer 2020; Regev et al. 2020; Fall et al. 2021.

7 Höflmayer 2017c.

8 Greenberg 2019.

9 Höflmayer 2016; Bonani et al. 2001; Hassan and Robinson 1987.

10 Bronk Ramsey et al. 2010; Shortland and Bronk Ramsey 2013.

11 Regev et al. 2020; Höflmayer 2017b.

12 Cf., e.g., Beckerath 1997, 3–4.

13 Ca. 3032/3982–2707/2657 BCE according to Beckerath 1997, 187, or 2900–2545 BCE according to Hornung et al. 2006a, 490. For a historical overview of this period, see Wilkinson 1999.

14 Ca. 2707/2657–2170/2120 BCE according to Beckerath 1997, 187–188, or 2543–2120 BCE according to Hornung et al. 2006a, 490. For a historical overview of this period, see Blumenthal 2019.

15 Cf. Beckerath 1997, 160; Seidlmayer 2006, 116–117; see also especially Wilkinson 1999, 66–105 and Gundacker 2015, 85–108.

16 The question as to whether the 8th dynasty should be regarded as part of the Old Kingdom is debated (cf. Blumenthal 2019, 38–40 with further bibliography). For the sake of this article, the dividing line will be drawn with the end of the 6th dynasty, assuming the 7th dynasty to be either a short interregnum of a few weeks/months, or entirely fictitious (cf. Beckerath 1997, 151; Bárta 2017, 3. 12).

17 Wilkinson 1999—on this question, see especially pages 60–61.

18 Cf. Wilkinson 2014, 2.

19 Gundacker 2013.

20 Gundacker 2015.

21 On the multipartite titulary of the Egyptian kings, see in general Beckerath 1999, 1–33 and Leprohon 2013, 7–19. As during the 3rd dynasty, the king's Horus Name was arguably still the most important one out of the royal titulary, the primary challenge to philological and chronological research on this period is (a) to determine the number and the order of attested distinct Horus Names and (b) to link other royal names to the known set of Horus Names of a specific dynasty. In the following table, only the most common versions of the respective names are listed.

22 On both these source(group)s, cf. above, section 3.

23 On theories concerning the Egyptian source of this Greek rendering, see especially Gundacker 2015, 122–123.

24 On the names of the kings of the 3rd dynasty, see Gauthier 1907, 48–59, Beckerath 1999, 48–51, Leprohon 2013, 31–34 and Gundacker 2015, 95–108; for a broader compilation and an overview of the then-recent state of research, Swelim 1983, 4–13. Nowadays, Djoser = Netjerykhet is widely accepted as the first king of the 3rd dynasty (cf. Dreyer 1998, Kitchen 1999, 246, Wilkinson 1999, 94–95, Seidlmayer 2006, 118, Ćwiek 2008, 91, Wilkinson 2014, 2–3, Blumenthal 2019, 85), Djosertety = Sekhemkhet being considered his immediate successor. For the recent hypothesis of Nebka, not Djoser, being the first king of the 3rd dynasty, which has been put forward by Ilaria Incordino, see Incordino 2007, Incordino 2008, and Incordino 2010. The order of the subsequent kings Khaba and Sanakht, however, is less certain (cf. Wilkinson 1999, 94–95, Seidlmayer 2006, 118–121, Wilkinson 2014, 3). Following Seidlmayer 2006, 117–118, the alleged royal names *Zꜣ* and *Bꜣ* are excluded from the present study.

25 The term *Nomen* is used here to designate what would later become the *Njswt-bj.tj* Name and the *Zꜣ-Rꜥw* Name, which cannot in all cases be differentiated, especially since the *Zꜣ-Rꜥw* Name, originally a royal epithet, is attested only from the reign of Radjedef onwards (cf. Beckerath 1999, 25–26).

26 It should be noted that the name **Ḏsr* 'Djoser' is not attested in contemporaneous sources. The identification of the cartouche name *Ḏsr* with the Horus Name *Nṯr.j-ḫ.t* is based solely on later inscriptions (on these, see Wildung 1969, 57–93)—cf. Wilkinson 1999, 95–96.

27 The Gold Name in question consists of a single circular sign, see Beckerath 1999, 49, no. 2, G2–3.

28 Pätznick 2005, 76 proposes the *Nb.tj* Name '*Nb.ty ḥtp rn*[…]' (**Ḥtp-rn-Nb.tj*?) for Sekhemkhet.

29 For the 3rd king of the 3rd dynasty, the name **Nfr-kꜣ* 'Neferka' has been proposed (cf. Dreyer 1998, 34; Gundacker 2015, 104; see also Theis 2014), but so far, this proposition remains conjectural due to a lack of unequivocal contemporaneous attestations of that name.

30 The Gold Name in question consists of a single falcon-on-perch sign (see Kaplony 1963, vol. 3, 132, no. (805)); for the logographic value of this sign, cf. below, endnote 34.

31 Pätznick 2005, 79 assigns the *Nb.tj* Name '*Nb.ty ḏsr.t ꜥnḫ*' to Sanakht.

32 Note, however, that Pätznick 2007 (among others) rejects the unprovenanced stela Paris Louvre E 25982 attesting the Horus Name *Qꜣi-ḥḏ.t* as a product of the 18th dynasty (first published and attributed to Huni or Nebka by Vandier 1968; on this object, see also Ziegler 1990, 54–57).

33 On the names of kings of the 4th dynasty, see Gauthier 1907, 61–103, Beckerath 1999, 52–55, Leprohon 2013, 34–37, and Gundacker 2013.

34 The Gold Name of Radjedef has mostly been read *Bjk.w-nbw*, 'Falcons of Gold' (thus, e.g., Beckerath 1999, 52 and Leprohon 2013, 36 [the latter, however, giving the alternative reading *Nṯr.w*]), but it should be noted that, unlike the Gold Names of Sneferu and Khufu, Radjedef's Gold Name is written either 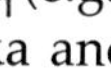 (e.g., Kuhlmann 2005, 256, fig. 16–17, Nishisaka and Takahashi 2016, 6, fig. 6, no. 6–7) or 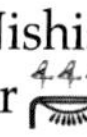 (e.g., Abubakr and

Mustafa 1971, 10–11, Nishisaka and Takahashi 2016, 6, fig. 6, no. 10; Beckerath 1999, 53, no. 3, G has , but this is incorrect, cf. Chassinat 1921, 63, fn. 2.), i.e., with the falcon-on-perch sign Gardiner G7 , which, just like the sign of the flag wrapped around a pole (Gardiner R8), may bear the phonetic value *nṯr* (cf. Wb 2, 358, Hornung 2005, 35)–instead of the 'simple' falcon Gardiner G5 . This suggests that the reading *Nṯr.w-nbw*, 'Gods of Gold', for Radjedef's Gold Name is in any case to be preferred over **Bjk.w-nbw* (but see also Kuhlmann 2005, 254, fn. 22, who treats terms like 'Gods', 'Falcons', and 'Forces' as synonyms, at least within the Gold Names of the Old Kingdom).

35 The so-far only contemporaneous evidence for this king's *Nomen* was found in workers' inscriptions on architectural elements of the unfinished pyramid of Zawiyet el-Aryan, and has been published as sketches by Alexandre Barsanti (see Barsanti 1907). Several hypotheses have been put forward regarding the reading of the disputed first hieratogramme; for an overview of the discussion, see Gundacker 2013, 79-80, fn. 325, and Theis 2014, 428-429. From a palaeographical point of view, the reading *nfr* seems most preferable (cf. particularly the shape of the respective sign within the name of king Sneferu from a workers' inscription in the Bent Pyramid at Dahshur in Fakhry 1959, pl. 21, a), but definitely needs further critical investigation. Meanwhile, the more or less well-established name '*Bꜣ-kꜣ(=j)*' shall be retained here.

36 On contemporaneous evidence for an immediate succession of Shepseskaf and Userkaf, cf. Dorman 2002, 109 and Gundacker 2015, 138–139. But see also Reisner 1931, 246, Beckerath 1997, 159, and Verner 2006, 136, all of whom treat Thamphthis as a historical king.

37 Named after the Egyptian priest Manetho (1st half of the 3rd century BCE); his work survives only as epitomized in the writings of other Classical authors. For modern editions of his main work *Αἰγυπτιακά*, see Waddell 1948, Jacoby 1958, Mosshammer 1984; for a general overview, see Gundacker 2018. Because of the very specific challenges that this Graeco-Roman-Armenian tradition poses onto research, it is largely excluded from the following considerations. For an *in extenso* treatment of the 3rd and 4th dynasties within the Manetho epitomes, see Gundacker 2015.

38 On this text genre in general, see Redford 1986; also Gozzoli 2006.

39 On pTurin Cat. 1874 in general, see (among others) Farina 1938, Gardiner 1959, Ryholt 2004, and Ryholt 2006; also https://collezionepapiri.museoegizio.it/en-GB/document/97/?inventoryNumber=1874. A comprehensive new edition is currently being prepared by Kim Ryholt.

40 On the dating, cf. Hornung et al. 2006b, 19–20. Attempts to date the surviving fragments stretch from the 4th (Черезов 1960) and 5th (e.g., Fischer 1976, 48 and Wilkinson 2000) down to the 25th dynasty (Helck 1970); those deviating from the Old Kingdom date adhered to in this paper should not uncritically be rejected. In any case, a thorough art-historical as well as philological examination of the surviving fragments still is necessary in order to narrow down the extant dating options.

41 The most important editions are Schäfer 1902 (on the main fragment 'PS'; Regional Archaeological Museum Palermo, inventory no. 1028), Gauthier 1915 (on Cairo fragments ('CF') 1–4 = Egyptian Museum Cairo J(ournal d')E(ntrée) 44859, 39735, 39734, and 44860), Cenival 1965 (on CF 5 = Egyptian Museum Cairo T(emporary) R(egisters) 15/1/75/2.), Stewart 1979, 6, pl. 3, no. 1 (*recto*) and Reeves 1979 (*verso*) (on the London Fragment ('LF') = UCL 15508), and Wilkinson 2000 (including an extensive further bibliography). On the numbering and terminology, see Wilkinson 2000, 13. A new edition of the individual fragments based on 3D scans is currently being prepared by Massimiliano Nuzzolo (Prague); meanwhile, see the preliminary studies Nuzzolo 2020, Nuzzolo 2021, and Nuzzolo et al. 2021.

42 Kim Ryholt proposes at least five different sources for the composition of the 'original' manuscript (cf. Ryholt 2004, 145–147; Ryholt 2006, 28–30).

43 Cf. (among others) Gundacker 2015, 137.

44 Cf. Gundacker 2015, 142.

45 Schäfer 1902, pl. 1; Wilkinson 2000, fig. 1.

46 Gauthier 1915, pl. 24; Wilkinson 2000, fig. 4. According to Wilkinson 2000, 209, who bases his assumptions on the width of the missing portion between PS and CF 1 (cf. Wilkinson

2000, 203), the compartments of the first reign do still belong to the reign of Netjerykhet ~ Djoser, the subsequent (rather short) reign, hence, to Sekhemkhet ~ Djosertety.

47 Schäfer 1902, pl. 1; Wilkinson 2000, fig. 1.

48 Schäfer 1902, pl. 2; Wilkinson 2000, fig. 3.

49 Gauthier 1915, pl. 30, fig. 1; Wilkinson 2000, fig. 7.

50 Gauthier 1915, pl. 31; Wilkinson 2000, fig. 9.

51 Cf. Fischer 1976, 48.

52 Cf. Redford 1986, 65–68, Clagett 1989, 47.

53 Edition by Dreyer 1987; see also Kahl et al. 1995, 168–171.

54 For an overview, see Ćwiek 2008, 87–88.

55 Cf. Baud 2002, 58–59; see also Stadelmann 1987, 230. 233.

56 Cf. Hornung et al. 2006a, 45.

57 I.e., the 'Counting of Gold and Fields' (*ṯnw.t nbw sḫ.wt*; PS r.V.3 and 5 (Schäfer 1902, pl. 1; Wilkinson 2000, fig. 1), LF r.I.1 (Stewart 1979, pl. 3, no. 1; Wilkinson 2000, fig. 11)), the 'Counting of Cattle' (*ṯnw.t jḥ(.w)*; PS v.II.2 (Schäfer 1902, pl. 2; Wilkinson 2000, fig. 3), CF 1 v.I.1 (Gauthier 1915, pl. 27; Wilkinson 2000, fig. 6) cf. above, section 4.1), and an undifferentiated 'Counting' (*ṯnw.t*; passim).

58 For a recent overview, see Warden 2015, who argues against a possible connection of taxation and 'Following of Horus'.

59 As absolute dates for the end and the beginning of the 4th dynasty depend not only on internal calculations, but also on external factors like the length of the following periods, those dates are not necessarily elaborated in every single one of the models mentioned here.

60 Giving a general overview, Beckerath 1997, 10 presumes a regular biennial census cycle for the period in question, only to revoke this later on (cf. Beckerath 1997, 158) for the reign of Sneferu with respect to PS r.VI.3–4 and the date *dipinti* from Meidum. As for the rest of the 4th dynasty, Jürgen von Beckerath more or less confines himself to the numbers of the Turin Canon.

61 According to Nolan 2003, 92–93, due to the necessity of intercalating a month in order to harmonize the lunar and solar calendars, every third—occasionally every other—census year (*rnp.t zp*) would have entailed an after-census year (*rnp.t m-ḫt zp*), thus arriving at a ratio of 1.7155 (*zp*) to 1 (*m-ḫt zp*), or, *realiter*, 20.88 ≈ 21 % fewer years after the count than years of the count. On this, see also Ciavatti 2019, 12, fig. 2.

62 This figure being construed according to the formula $x = 2(\mathrm{N}max) - \frac{1000(\mathrm{N}max)}{2088}$ (derived from Nolan's model, cf. endnote above) for each 4th dynasty king, respectively (N*max* = highest known count number—for recent data thereon, cf. section 5).

63 Hornung et al. 2006a, 45–46 assume a biennial rhythm throughout the Early Dynastic Period and the Old Kingdom but, like von Beckerath, make an exemption (at least) for the reign of Snofru on the grounds of PS r.VI.3–4. In the same volume, Miroslav Verner (Verner 2006, 127) proposes a reasonable model for calculating a reign length minimum (N*max* + ∑*Nm-ḫt*; *Nm-ḫt* representing a securely attested year after the count) that will also be adhered to in the course of this paper as far as it concerns minimal regnal lengths (cf. section 5). This strictly positivistic approach is of course especially prone to alterations induced by new archaeological discoveries.

64 Comprehensive collections of the relevant dated inscriptions are to be found in Smith 1952, Spalinger 1994, 281–294, Verner 2001, 365–385, Verner 2006, 128–136, and Verner 2008, 24–30.

65 For general information on this source group, see Arnold 1990 and van der Moezel 2016. In the following, the term *dipinti* (sg.: *dipinto*) is used for inscriptions painted with ink, as proposed by Ursula Verhoeven (cf. Verhoeven 2015, 30), whereas inscriptions incised into a surface are called *graffiti* (on the distinction, see also Salvador 2020, 434–435). As well as the dated construction *dipinti*, there are also a few specimens of dated construction *graffiti* from this period: (see Smith 1952, 118, fig. 6. 120, fig. 8. 127, no. 5; 7. 128, no. 12 (Boston MFA 25-3-310); 13 (JE 54940 = SR 2/15420); also Reisner unpublished, 720, (4), no. 3, and 720 (alternate version), (4), no. 4)).

66 Besides the better-known 4th dynasty papyrus *corpora* (e.g., the Gebelein or the Wadi el-Jarf papyri), for the sake of the present paper a few *ostraca* (most probably used as 'mummy tags' [cf. Fischer 1960, 188, fn. 2 and Haring 2020, 94]) are also subsumed under this category.

67 The correct reading of the logogram 𓆳 (Gardiner M4) within dates is somewhat debated (for a brief overview of the discussion, see Fecht 1985 and Castle 1994, 188, fn. 2). Throughout this paper, the reading *rnp.t* will be employed.

68 I.e., the respective king's accession year which covered the rest of the calendar year from his predecessor's demise to the next New Year's Day. This term was in use from at least the 1st to the 8th dynasties (cf. Hornung et al. 2006a, 45); for a 4th dynasty example of such a 'short' accession year (reign of Shepseskaf), see PS v.I.3 (Schäfer 1902, 32, pl. 2; Wilkinson 2000, fig. 3). The integer represented by *N* always refers to the *N*th count of a single king's reign and is reset to zero with every change in sovereign.

69 For a 4th dynasty example of almost the entire formula (in slightly different word order), see e.g. expedition *graffito* II at the 'Oasis Bypath' near Dakhla (from the reign of Khufu; ed. Kuhlmann 2005, 248, fig. 5).

70 Nolan 2003 and Nolan 2008 proposed a purely cultic function, whereas Gundacker 2006, 320–322, considering textual evidence from the 6th dynasty as well as administrative necessities, argued in favour of the count having an actual economical and administrative relevance. Also opting in favour of a fiscal character of the count is Brovarski 2016, 78–80.

71 On this question, see Gundacker 2006, 331–338.

72 Thus, e.g., Posener-Kriéger 1991, 19, Spalinger 1994, 318, Verner 2001, 372, Verner 2006, 124, Verner 2008, 24, Gundacker 2015, 91–92. Regarding the corpus of construction *dipinti*, Gundacker 2015, 92, however, also points out a double imbalance: 'It is not only the case that attested even years (*rnp.t sp* XY) outnumber attested odd years (*rnp.t m-ḫt sp* XY), but also in those biennia for which either year is attested, the numbers of attestations of the even year (*rnp.t sp* XY) usually outnumber the attestations of the odd year (*rnp.t m-ḫt sp* XY) significantly.' Accordingly, this corpus should be treated with additional caution.

73 Schäfer 1902, pl. 1; Wilkinson 2000, fig. 1.

74 See Smith 1952, 124, Arnold 1981, 27, Stadelmann 1987, 236, Krauss 1996, 47, Ciavatti 2019, 10; for an overview of the discussion up until 2006, see Gundacker 2006, 323.

75 E.g., Sethe 1905, Gardiner 1945, Stadelmann 1987, Baud 2000, Gundacker 2006, and, most recently, Gundacker 2015.

76 Nolan 2003 and Ciavatti 2019.

77 Spalinger 1994, Krauss 1996, Krauss 1997, Krauss 1998, Beckerath 1997, Hornung et al. 2006a, Verner 2006, and Verner 2008.

78 An extensive comparison of all of the substantiated models existing to date is highly desirable, but far beyond the scope of the present paper.

79 Gundacker 2006.

80 A further revision of the Meidum material on a larger scale will be part of the objective of the MERYT project (https://www.ifao.egnet.net/archeometrie/anr-meryt/). A preliminary study on this topic by Aurore Ciavatti (2022) has appeared in *BIFAO*. We would like to express our gratitude to her for providing us with the necessary information on this project's scope.

81 Above all Petrie 1910, pl. 5, no. 6 (from 'year 17(?)' (Petrie 1910, 9, no. 6 / 'Year of the 15th occurrence' (Spalinger 1994, 282, no. (6)) / *'15'* (Verner 2001, 366, Verner 2006, 129, Verner 2008, 25) to *rnp.t (m-)ḫt zp 15*) and Posener-Kriéger 1991, pl. 7, no. A.3 ('year of the 16th occurrence' (Spalinger 1994, 319, no. (3)) / *'16'* (Verner 2001, 366, Verner 2006, 129, Verner 2008, 25) to *rnp.t m-ḫt zp 16*). These insights have so far not quite received the attention they deserve; neither Verner 2008 nor Nolan 2008 mention the proposed readings or their implications, e.g. on the census regularity. The palaeographical details of Gundacker's readings are, among others, to be discussed *in extenso* in the future.

82 Arnold 2017.

83 As we fail to discern edges, breaks, abrasions, etc. in many of the drawings in Posener-Kriéger 1991 and photographic material is not yet published, only a minority of them can be securely ascribed to a specific regnal year until the necessary revision is completed. Hence, the following table remains (at the very least) provisional insofar as it draws from Meidum material.

84 E.g., Posener-Kriéger 1991, 19, Spalinger 1994, 283, Verner 2001, 367, Verner 2006, 130, Gundacker 2006, 54, Verner 2008, 26.

85 Stadelmann 1987, 240, fig. 4.

86 Also frequently cited as an attestation of Sneferu's 24th count (e.g., Stadelmann 1987, 235, and, following Stadelmann's reconstruction, Spalinger 1994, 282–283, Verner 2001, 367, Verner 2006, 130, Gundacker 2006, 54, Verner 2008, 26), but with all reasonable certainty a scientific *chimaera*, is a Dahshur *dipinto* briefly mentioned and sketched by Carl R. Lepsius (Lepsius 1859, Text, 1, 206) after Georg G. Erbkam (Erbkam unpublished, I, 85). Erbkam's rendering is only

a rough sketch, not a *bona fide facsimile*, and also differs from the version printed in Lepsius 1859. The traces do not support Rainer Stadelmann's proposition; rather, the *dipinto* as reproduced by Lepsius and Stadelmann should be turned clockwise by 90°—as had already been done by Sethe 1905, 85 and Maystre 1935, 96—the traces hence be read […] *ꜣbd 1 šmw sw 24* '[…] month 1 of the Shemu season, day 24' instead of *(*rnp.t zp*) *24 ꜣbd 3 ꜣḫ.t* […], '(year of the count) 24, month 3 of the Akhet season […]' (thus also Arnold 2021, 80, fn. 182). We are very grateful to Silke Grallert (BBAW, Berlin) for providing us with a digital scan of the relevant pages from Erbkam's sketchbook.

87 Cf. Verner 2001, 368, Verner 2006, 131, Verner 2008, 26. For yet another attestation model and a ratio of 4 (*zp*) : 6 (*m-ḫt zp*), see Gundacker 2006, 377–378. Considering the still-extant imbalance of single attestations, Paule Posener-Kriéger's suggestion of only occasional distinctions between *zp* and *m-ḫt zp* in the writing (cf. Posener-Kriéger 1991, 19) seems all the more plausible (cf. also Gundacker 2015, 92–93).

88 Spalinger 1994.

89 Verner 2001, Verner 2006, and Verner 2008.

90 See Tallet 2013, Tallet 2014, and Tallet 2017.

91 For further preliminary reports on this boat pit, see Nishisaka et al. 2011, Yoshimura and Kurokochi 2012, Kurokochi and Yoshimura 2013. For the first boat pit, see especially Nour et al. 1960.

92 Nishisaka and Takahashi 2016.

93 The attestation of a *rnp.t zp 14* for Khufu is apt to shed new light on the supposed inscription from the '17th year' that Petrie claims to have recognized in one of the relieving chambers of the Great Pyramid (cf. Petrie 1923, 60; on this *dipinto*, see also the article 'Dig's Days. The Secret Five Chambers' on the personal web page of Zahi Hawass: http://guardians.net/hawass/articles/secretchambers.htm). As Petrie's choice of words is ambiguous—'17th year' might point to **rnp.t zp 8* as well as **rnp.t zp 17*—and neither photographs nor facsimiles of the inscription are published, this supposed attestation remains dubious (see also Verner 2001, 373–374). In contrast, the Turin Canon might be read in support of 14 counts in the reign of Khufu. Column x+III, line 10 gives a number of 23+x regnal years for Sneferu's successor, with the papyrus breaking off after the 3rd stroke of the ones digit: . Due to the structure of hieratic numerals in general as well as in the Turin Canon in particular (numbers higher than 4 and lower than 10 are expressed by ligatures rather than by a single row of distinct strokes, cf. Möller 1909, 59, nos 618–622), either *none* or exactly *one* further stroke may be reconstructed here. In the latter case, it would be possible to assume (a) that the scribe mistook Khufu's number of *counts* (*14) for his number of *regnal years* (similarly maybe already for Sneferu's reign, cf. Gundacker 2006, 65–67), and (b) that there occurred an error in the tens digit (*14→*24), which was apparently quite common in the later Manethonian tradition and maybe happened already to the account of Djoser's reign within the Turin Canon (cf. Gundacker 2015 *passim*, and 147, fn. 280; in general see also Ryholt 2004, 151, § 33), but in sum, this string of assumptions would be purely conjectural, of course.

94 This observation had already been made by Gundacker 2006, 329–330, but could not be substantiated further because of the previously insecure attribution of the date *dipinto* in the first boat pit.

95 The central question is whether the date *dipinto* belongs to the reign or Khufu or that of his successor Radjedef. For an overview of the discussion and general considerations on the construction history of the boat pits, see Verner 2001, 375–377 and Jánosi 2005, 71–72.

96 Verner 2001, 375–377, Verner 2006, 132, and Verner 2008, 27.

97 For the CF 4 inscriptions, see Gauthier 1915, pl. 31; Wilkinson 2000, fig. 9.

98 The two compartments following the one mentioning the 2nd count as well as the one following the compartment mentioning the 8th count are still visible and can be differentiated, but due to the loss of bigger portions of text within them, no proposition can be made as to whether or not they contained count numbers.

99 For the PS inscriptions, see Schäfer 1902, pl. 1; Wilkinson 2000, fig. 1.

100 No count is recorded in PS r.VI.2, but the compartment is immediately succeeded by another one mentioning the 7th count. Since on the Palermo Stone there is no hint as to two (or more) years after the count immediately

following each other, this attestation is regarded as the year after the 6th count, here.

101 The instances of *zp 13* and *14* are especially uncertain.

102 Although the hieratic writing is unambiguous in this case, this inscription from the first boat pit at the Great Pyramid has not been translated correctly in any of the major chronological studies on Old Kingdom inscriptions (exceptions being Valloggia 1997, 419 and Gundacker 2006, 85. 328, fn. 1738. 329): Spalinger 1994, 284, no. (8) reads '[y]ear of the 11th occurrence', Verner 2001, 375, '*rnpt sp* (or *m-ḫt sp* ?) *11* (or *10* ?)' (implicitly favouring *zp 11*), Verner 2006, 132, '*rnpt zp* 11 (or 10 ?)' (without alternative), and Verner 2008, 27, '*rnpt sp* (or *m-ḫt sp* ?) *11* (or *10* ?)' (again implicitly favouring *zp 11*). The traces of paint to the left of the number ten can hardly be anything else than the remains of a single stroke indicating a 1. Further traces to the left of this sign are neither recorded nor—due to the configuration and the alignment of the *dipinto*—to be expected, hence the reading *11* for the census number is reasonably secure. As the *dipinti* of the cover stones of the first boat pit have vanished since the 1971 publication of Abdel Moneim Abubakr and Ahmed Y. Mustafa (cf. Roth 1991, 127), the chances of verifying their facsimile in the future seem rather slim. On the pertinence of this inscription, see below.

103 Following Reisner 1942, 73, this inscription—as well as another one mentioning a year of the 13th count (Smith 1952, 119, fig. 7, 2nd row, left side, cf. above on Table 3)—has usually been ascribed to the reign of Khafre (thus, e.g., by Smith 1952, 127–128, no. 11 (a), Spalinger 1994, 286, no. (2), Verner 2001, 378, Verner 2006, 133, or Verner 2008, 28), but according to Flentye 2007, 294–295. 303, the respective tomb G 7650 should be dated to the later reign of Khufu (cf. also Jánosi 2005, 71) due to its architectural features.

104 Pierre Tallet's hieroglyphic transcription of the hieratic original suggests a year *after* the 13th count (*rnp.t* (*m-*)*ḫt zp 13*), but the traces above the number *13* belong to the sign 𓊗 (*zp*, Gardiner O50), not to 𓆱 (*ḫt*, Gardiner M3). Given the layout of the papyrus, the preposition *m-ḫt* is not to be expected above the *zp* sign, so the reading *rnp.t* ⌜*zp*⌝ *13* seems reasonably sure.

105 Cf. Jánosi 2005, 71. However, cf. Verner 2001, 376 *contra*.

106 Cf. Nishisaka and Takahashi 2016, 9–12.

107 See Nishisaka and Takahashi 2016, 6, fig. 6, no. 8 According to Nishisaka and Takahashi, this earlier phase comprised the breaking of the stones in the quarry and their temporary storage in a repository before being brought to their final destination. In this phase, the Northern and Southern sides of the stones would have been inscribed with date *dipinti*.

108 Cf. Arnold 1990, 19, Verner 1992, 184, Nishisaka and Takahashi 2016, 11–12, and Arnold 2017, 395.

109 For an overview, see Verner 2006, 125 and Gundacker 2006, 321–322. The latter also gives plausible suggestions regarding the mechanisms of the choice of year designations.

110 This results in the necessity of subtracting 1 year from the respective sum of ∑dyn. 3 + ∑dyn. 4 in each model.

111 This figure according to the Turin Canon, x+III,5 (king (*Ḏsr-jt*)).

112 This figure according to the Turin Canon, x+III,6 (king (*Ḏsr-jt*)).

113 This figure according to the Turin Canon, x+III,7 (king *[*(*Ḥw-]*⌜*ḏ*⌝*[f] <ꜣ>*)).

114 The Turin Canon, x+III,4 gives a number of 19 regnal years for king (*Nb-kꜣ[-…]*), which might be influenced by the (erroneous?) 19 years assigned to (*Ḏsr-jt*) (cf. Gundacker 2015, 108–109). Assuming a deliberately extreme point of view, it is possible to argue that these 19 years might be the result of a scribal error in the tens digit (on this phenomenon, cf. above, endnote 93), thus arriving at an original number of *9 years.

115 If the jar inscription *rnp.t šms.w-Ḥrw zp 11 ḥsb Jwnw pr-zr* 'Year of the following of Horus; 11th occurrence of the "calculation" of Heliopolis, (namely) the House of the Ram' (Dreyer 1987, 99, fig. 1b, Kahl et al. 1995, 168, D3/E/I) is attributed to Huni, as has been done by Dreyer 1987, 103, one should assume at least 11 regnal years for this king.

116 The highest date securely attributable to Radjedef is *rnp.t zp 1 ꜣbd 3 pr*[*.t …*] 'Year of the count 1, month 3 of the Per[et] season, […]' from the substructure of his pyramid complex at Abu Rawash (Valloggia 1997, 426, fig. 8 and Valloggia 2011, II, 111, fig. 178). As the

actual pyramid must have been completed to a considerable degree (cf. Valloggia 2011, I, 6–7), it seems inappropriate to limit Radjedef's minimal regnal length to the figure of this single inscription. Hence, the 8 years of the Turin Canon, x+III,11 are applied here.

117 If the so-called 'will of Nikaura' and the Gebelein papyri are attributed to other rulers (cf. below, endnote 119), the highest date reasonably securely attributable to Khafre is *rnp.t zp 10 ꜣbd 4 šmw sw 24* 'Year of the count 10, month 4 of the Shemu season, day 24' from oLeiden J 429 (Goedicke 1968, pl. 5, no. 4). From three other *ostraca* from Helwan (cf. Verner 2006, 134) and a *dipinto* from the tomb of Meresankh III (G7530-7540) erroneously attributed to Khafre's year of the count 7, but actually dating from the year after the 10th (or, less probably, 2nd) count (photograph HUMFA_A4622_NS), three distinct years after the count are known.

118 For this ephemeral king, no date inscriptions mentioning regnal years are known.

119 If the date *rnp.t zp 12 jp.t* 'Year of the count 12' from the 'will of Nikaura' (from Giza tomb LG 87 = G 8158, Lepsius 1859, II, 15, a, Sethe 1903, 16–17, Goedicke 1970, pl. 3) is assigned to Menkaura, this would be the highest known count of this king. Adding three (cf. Verner 2006, 135) distinct years after the count, the result would be a minimal regnal length of 15 years. Assuming further that the tens digit of the figure of the Turin Canon is not to be reconstructed to **20*, an actual minimal regnal length of 18 years for Menkaura may be proposed.

120 This figure is taken from the Turin Canon. The highest contemporary date of Shepseskaf is *rnp.t m-ḫt zp tp.j* 'year after the first count' from the edict for the pyramid of Menkaura (Reisner 1931, pl. 19, b; Goedicke 1967, 17, fig. 1), which differs by only two years from the figure of the Turin Canon, so it seems reasonable to accept the latter as the minimal regnal length.

121 Assuming a scribal error in the tens digit in the Turin Canon, as is possibly indicated by the Old Kingdom annals (cf. Wilkinson 2000, 53, Hornung et al. 2006b, 22, Gundacker 2015, 108, fn. 106).

122 If the numbers of 19 years from the Turin Canon, x+III,4 and 5 do not refer to Sanakht ~ Nebka and Netjerykhet ~ Djoser, but instead to the first two kings of the 3rd dynasty, i.e., Netjerykhet ~ Djoser and Sekhemkhet ~ Djoserty, then the second instance (x+III,5), if taken at face value, may possibly be attributed to the latter.

123 Assuming that the 6 years given by the Turin Canon, x+III,7 are a scribal error in the tens digit for an original *16 complete regnal years, possibly with a few additional months of an incomplete last regnal year. Although suffering from an extensive re-interpretation of the names, the Manethonian tradition around the 3rd dynasty might support this number with the 17 years attributed to king *Μέσωχρις* by Sextus Julius Africanus and George Syncellus (cf. Waddell 1948, 42–43; Gundacker 2015, 87).

124 Manethonian tradition (according to Sextus Julius Africanus and George Syncellus) has 28 regnal years for king *Νεχερώφης* (cf. Waddell 1948, 40–41; Gundacker 2006, 86). Note, however, that this—fictitious though the 'maximal' model may be—would only function if Manetho's graecized name *Νεχερώφης* is *not* identified with king *(Nb-kꜣ[-...]]* from the Turin Canon, x+III,4 (since the 19 regnal years of the latter have been attributed to Netjerykhet ~ Djoser in this model), but only with the contemporaneously attested king Sanakht ~ Nebka, and has independently been misplaced at the onset of the 3rd dynasty.

125 The Turin Canon, x+III,8 attributes 24 (+1?) years to king *(Ḥwi[...]]*, while Manethonian tradition (according to Sextus Julius Africanus and George Syncellus) has 42 years for king *Ἄχης* (cf. Waddell 1948, 42–43; Gundacker 2015, 87)—which might, however, be the result of a 'psychological' error (cf. Helck 1956, 56; Barta 1981, 21; Gundacker 2015, 109–110).

126 Assuming that the immediate succession of the 7th and the 8th counts as displayed on the Palermo Stone is a scribal error (cf. O'Mara 1979, 94).

127 Based on the highest known contemporaneous count (*rnp.t zp 14* 'year of the count 14', cf. above), not the Turin Canon.

128 The figure of 8 counts being taken from the Turin Canon, x+III,11.

129 If the date *rnp.t m-ḫt zp 11* 'Year after the count 11' of pGebelein IV (Posener-Kriéger 2004, pl. 30) is assigned to Khafre's reign (the Gebelein papyri do not mention a specific king's name and are dated to the reign of Menkaura only on grounds of the palaeography and the dates

themselves, cf. Posener-Kriéger 1975, 216), his highest known regnal year would be the 22nd in this model. This figure may then be rounded up to arrive at the *26 regnal years which has been proposed as the basis of later traditions around Khafre's reign (cf. Helck 1956, 52; Beckerath 1997, 158; Gundacker 2015, 126–127).

130 This figure according to Helck 1956, 53 and Gundacker 2015, 129. 148, both of whom reference Manethonian tradition.

131 Assuming that the tens digit of the number of regnal years from the Turin Canon, x+III,14 is to be reconstructed to *20*.

132 If the number of 4 regnal years from the Turin Canon, x+III,15 is interpreted as mistaken for 4 census cycles in a regular biennial system, with the last regnal year of Shepseskaf being a year after the 4th count.

133 The Turin Canon, x+III,6 gives a number of 6 years (king (*Ḏsr-jt*]). However, if the incomplete reign CF 1 r.V.11–13 is to be attributed to Sekhemkhet ~ Djosertety and the royal titulary (including the Horus Name, the *Nomen*, and the Gold Name as well as king's mother's name, with a width of approximately 7 year compartments (cf. CF 1 r.II–III)) is, as is the case with the account of Semerkhet's reign (1st dynasty; CF 1 r.III.4–10 *supra*), centred above the regnal-year compartments, then a total of *7 year compartments may be reconstructed.

134 The number of 6 years taken from the Turin Canon, x+III,7 (king *[(Ḥw-]⌜ḏ⌝[f] <ꜣ>*]). Immediately following this number, there is a lacuna, but traces of black ink that might well conform to an entry on months are still visible.

135 Assuming that the number of 19 regnal years from the Turin Canon, x+III,4 is a scribal error for an original *9 (thus aligning the number with Netjerykhet ~ Djoser's (erroneous?) 19 years), which itself might be derived from a roundup of *8 years and x months (cf. Gundacker 2015, 142. 147, fn. 280).

136 Since the highest probable year designation for Qahedjet ~ Huni may be an '11th occurrence of calculating' (indirectly attesting 11 distinct regnal years; cf. above, endnote 115) and the Turin Canon, x+III,8 has 24 regnal years for king (*Ḥwi[…]*], the latter may with all due caution be considered a scribal error in the tens digit for an original *14 regnal years (cf. Gundacker 2015, 142).

137 Assuming that the immediate succession of the 7th and 8th counts on the Palermo Stone has to be taken seriously.

138 The year designation *rnp.t* [*zp*] *12* from the 'will of Nikaura' being attributed to Menkaura in this model (cf. Gundacker 2010, 32–33).

139 This is mostly due to the rather 'conservative' approach of the editors, but it must also be noted that the part of the chronological table concerning the 3rd and 4th dynasties that is given in Hornung, Krauss and Warburton, 490–491 suffers from certain inconsistencies in comparison to the contribution from Miroslav Verner in the same volume (Verner 2006): the latter, e.g., attributes 14+x regnal years to Menkaura (cf. Verner 2006, 127), whereas the former assume an improbably low number of 5 years for the same king.

140 Cf. (among many others) Jánosi 2005, 51, fn. 134.

141 E.g., by Henige 1981, Beckerath 1997, 28, Gundacker 2006, 103–314, or Bierbrier 2006.

142 But see for the Old Kingdom, e.g., the overviews provided by Baer 1960 and Strudwick 1985.

143 Bronk Ramsey et al. 2010.

144 Bronk Ramsey 1995; Bronk Ramsey 2001; Bronk Ramsey 2009b; Bronk Ramsey 2009a; Reimer et al. 2020.

145 Manning, Kromer, Cremaschi et al. 2020; Manning, Wacker, Büntgen et al. 2020; Höflmayer and Manning 2022.

146 Dee 2013.

147 Regev, de Miroschedji, and Boaretto 2012.

148 Greenberg 2019.

149 Regev, de Miroschedji, and Boaretto 2012.

150 Rotem et al. 2019.

151 Tumolo and Höflmayer 2020.

152 Regev et al. 2014.

153 Regev et al. 2020.

154 Höflmayer et al. 2014.

155 Nigro et al. 2019.

156 Fall et al. 2021.

157 Fall et al. 2021.

158 Höflmayer et al. 2014.

159 Regev et al. 2020.

160 Regev et al. 2014.

161 Tumolo and Höflmayer 2020.

162 Nigro et al. 2019.

163 Renfrew and Bahn 2019.

164 Tumolo and Höflmayer 2020.

Journal of Ancient Egyptian Interconnections

"There's no Place Like Home"? Representing Travel and Return from the Old to the Middle Kingdom

Dr. Anna-Latifa Mourad
Macquarie University

Abstract
The representation of travel beyond the established borders of Egypt has been conceived as one of many markers of literary fictionality. One of the few texts that showcase this is the Middle Kingdom Tale of Sinuhe. Many have examined the Tale's literary qualities through its portrayal of characters and activities associated with border traversal. But how novel was its representation of travel to the northeast? This paper focuses on travel and travellers as portrayed mainly in Old to Middle Kingdom textual material relating to Egyptian-Near Eastern relations. Examining similarities and differences across time, it questions whether Old Kingdom transregional agents and activities, as well as their representations, influenced the emergence of tropes on transborder movement. It also discusses how periods of increased long-distance connectivity may have shifted concepts of travel, likely contributing to an emphasis on the pertinence of a safe return to Egypt.

Keywords
Old Kingdom; Middle Kingdom; Egypt, Levant; Western Asia; travel; transregionalism; Sinuhe

Introduction

The Tale of Sinuhe is among the most well-known cultural artifacts of the Middle Kingdom. Several linguistic and literary analyses of this text have been written, including its representation of Egyptian and Levantine society, culture, and politics. This paper adds to a handful of other studies exploring its representation of travel.[1] It offers a brief preliminary yet theoretically informed exploration into whether and how records of transregional agents and activities from the Old to the Middle Kingdom influenced the emergence of motifs on travel and cross-border movements. The focus is on the portrayal of travel from Egypt to Western Asia, including the Sinai Peninsula. Material on travel to the Eastern Desert, the Red Sea coast, and other regions of Africa is not included, nor is that concerning non-Egyptians traveling to the Nile Valley, albeit these topics are of interest for further research.

The term 'transregionalism' and its derivatives are utilized here to refer to aspects of 'transnationalism,' or the processes of sustaining social existences, reproductions, and relations of individuals and groups involved in various facets of border crossing.[2] While transnationalism typically focuses on non-state actors and activities, incorporating those tied to the state is necessary when examining Old and Middle Kingdom Egyptian agents and activities.[3] This is due to the nature of the preserved evidence, most of which concerns the upper echelons of society, and the consequent apparent high degree of connectedness between state and non-state actors and activities. To facilitate the latter, shared physical and social spaces were likely employed, including those that offered the required infrastructure, such as routes or harbors, or the required resources and social ties, such as cultic or administrative institutions.[4] Examples of these are preserved in the Tale of Sinuhe.

In short, the Tale of Sinuhe presents a first-person account of Sinuhe, an *ir.y-pꜥ.t ḥꜣ.ty-ꜥ sꜣb ꜥḏ-mr ḏꜣt.t ity m tꜣ.w St.tyw* "hereditary prince, count, dignitary, administrator of the sovereign's estates of the lands in the *St.tyw*," as he travels to and from the Levant.[5] The text covers his flight from Egypt, purportedly after hearing about the attempted assassination of the pharaoh Amenemhat I. It then describes his seemingly aimless movements across the Egyptian border to the Levant, where he takes refuge. Eventually, and within the discretion of a Levantine ruler of Upper *Rṯnw*, Ammunenshi,[6] Sinuhe himself became a ruler of a land called *Iꜣꜣ*. Then, after several achievements, he returned to Egypt at the behest of the succeeding pharaoh, Senwosret I, who granted him a burial befitting for a highly respected member of society in Egypt.

As the most frequently attested composition of the pharaonic period, the fictional Tale of Sinuhe has survived on at least five papyri from the Middle Kingdom and over 30 papyri and ostraca from the New Kingdom.[7] The earliest surviving copy thus far known is Papyrus Berlin 3022 (B), which can be assigned to the second half of Dynasty 12.[8] It was purchased along with other Middle Kingdom texts believed to have been composed around the reign of Amenemhat III.[9] Due to its degree of preservation, it is thought to have been retrieved from a Theban burial.[10] The second major copy is Papyrus Berlin 10499 (R), with the Tale of Sinuhe on its verso and that of The Eloquent Peasant on its recto. It was found with other artifacts and papyri with magico-medical, literary, administrative, and instructional texts.[11] All were placed in a box and deposited in a late Middle Kingdom burial located beneath the Ramesseum of Thebes.[12] The association of both papyri with such a variety of texts insinuates a connection with learned, literate readers, or at least individuals who appreciated the value of the written word.

The Tale also displays, to varying degrees, several literary aspects that parallel those of the other texts with which it was discovered. Indeed, it is widely acknowledged that the Tale incorporates various genres,[13] displaying intertextuality as part of a dynamic so-called 'universe of texts.'[14] From beginning to end, the Tale is framed as a biography, a genre that seems to have emerged by the Fifth Dynasty in the funerary sphere.[15] This self-portrait offered a means to present achievement, whether of the expected social obligations of a respected member of Egyptian society and/or involvement in significant, illustrious events typically commissioned by the pharaoh.[16] Bearing in mind that the surviving material remains incomplete, some Old and Middle Kingdom biographies embrace aspects from other literary forms or styles, such as letters[17] or the use of direct speech.[18] These provide glimpses of a corpus of texts that could have offered antecedents or a "cognate forerunner," as Baines suggests, to Middle Kingdom narratives, such as that of Sinuhe.[19] Biographies also offer insights into decorum, social experience and social relations through their representation of entities, repeated motifs and/or cliches.[20] Examples of the latter include mention of Sinuhe giving water to the thirsty (line B96), as attested in Old and Middle Kingdom biographies,[21] or hosting passers-by and directing travellers (lines B95-97), as in First Intermediate Period and Middle Kingdom attestations.[22]

By the Sixth Dynasty, the use of different genres, styles, motifs, and cliches also emerge in additional types of texts. Significant here is that of the expedition inscription, which offered officials further opportunities for self-presentation. For example, the Sixth Dynasty Graffito of Anusu at Bir Mueilha in the Eastern Desert mentions that he gave water to the thirsty and bread to the hungry,[23] while the Twelfth Dynasty inscription of Horwerra at Serabit el-Khadim adds direct speech.[24] This development highlights the links between commemorating achievements in funerary or sacred places within officials' communities and commemorating expedition experiences as achievements in distant places, some of which could also be sacred.

In both contexts, self-presentation still largely remained in line with decorum. However, in the Middle Kingdom, such precepts could be subverted or questioned in less normative works, which may today be considered 'fictional' or 'literary' narratives.[25] As with the Tale of Sinuhe, these could be framed in a particular style or variably employ different genres but could also add self-referentiality, narrative structure, character development, use third-person narration, and include unfavorable events.[26] With regard to this paper's topic, some identify the use of an established 'travel/traveling abroad' motif of narrative fiction in the Tale,[27]

Dyn.	Reign	Individual	Findspot(s)	Location(s) reached in Western Asia	Reference(s)
6	Teti–Merenra	Weni	Façade(?), tombs, Abydos and Saqqara	*Sbꜣ-n.y-Ꞽyꞽ-m-ḥtp*; *Wꜥr.t-n.t-Ḥr.w-nb-mꜣꜥ.t*; land of the *Ḥr.yw-šꜥ*; *Šr.t-tp-wnḏ.w*	*Urk.* I, 98–110; Collombert 2015
	Pepy I(?)	Khnumhotep	Pillar in chapel, tomb of Khui (QH34e), Qubbet el-Hawa	*Kbn*	*Urk.* I, 140–141; Espinel 2004, 15–18; Edel, Seyfried and Vieler 2007, 467
	Pepy I–II	Iny	(?)	*ꜥmꜣꜣw*; *Ḫnty-š*; *Pꜣws*[…]; *Kbny*	Marcolin and Espinel 2011
	Pepy II	Pepynakht-Heqaib	Chapel, tomb QH35, Qubbet el-Hawa	Foreign land of the *ꜥꜣm.w*	*Urk.* I, 131–135
11	Mentuhotep II	Henenu	Vestibule, tomb TT313, Deir el-Bahri	Foreign land of the *Ḥr.yw-šꜥ* (?); *Ḫ*[*tyw*]-*ꜥš*	Hayes 1949
11–12	(?)	Khety	Tomb 65, Asasif	*Bꞽꜣ.w*; foreign lands of *Ṯnht*; *pr.w-Ḥr.w-n(.y)-ḫ.t-*[*mfkꜣ.t*]; *pr.w-Šmꜣ*; *ḥṯ.t-Ḥr.w*	Gardiner 1917, 33–35; Schenkel 1965, 283–284 [Nr. 477]
12	Senwosret III	Khusobek	Tomb 11, Cemetery E, Abydos	*St.t*; *Skmm*; *Rṯnw*	Garstang 1901; Peet 1914; Baines 1987; Goedicke 1998
		Khnumhotep (III)	Façade, tomb, Dahshur	*Kbny*; [*Rṯnw*]; possibly *Wꜣṯꞽ* and [*Rm*]*nn*	Allen 2008

Table 1: Biographical texts from the Old to the Middle Kingdom that mention travel to one or more destinations in Western Asia.

with Moers recognizing it among a select number of 'travel narratives' that embrace concepts and perhaps precepts regarding social and physical border transgression.[28] With this in mind, the next section discusses extant representations of travel from the Old to the Middle Kingdom and explores whether Old Kingdom transregional agents and activities, as well as their representations, influenced the emergence of this travel motif and tropes on trans-border movements and foreign entities.

Representing Travel to Western Asia

Extant Texts

A limited but significant number of texts from different contexts and of various styles include the motif of travel to or from Western Asia. These may offer some insight into the existing 'universe of texts' or cultural repertoire that could have inspired later works concerned with transregional agents and activities. Excluding texts mentioning toponyms of unverified locations, the compositions may be heuristically categorized into biographical, expeditionary, literary, or administrative texts.

The surviving biographical texts from the Old and Middle Kingdoms that specifically refer to travel to Western Asia date to the 6th, 11th and 12th Dynasties (Table 1). Those of the Sixth Dynasty include the inscriptions of Weni from his tombs at Saqqara and Abydos, describing activities conducted during the reigns of Teti to Merenra; the likely early Sixth Dynasty text of Khnumhotep, as preserved in the tomb of Khui at Qubbet el-Hawa, near Aswan; the biography of Ini, mentioning expeditions organized from the reigns of Pepy I to II; and the biography of Pepynakht-Heqaib from his tomb at Qubbet el-Hawa detailing an expedition during the reign of Pepy II. From the Eleventh Dynasty are the Theban texts of Henenu, dated to Mentuhotep II's reign, and that of Khety, possibly of the late Eleventh Dynasty. Dating to the Twelfth Dynasty are two texts assigned to the reign of Senwosret III: the biography of Khnumhotep III from a tomb at Dahshur, and the stela of Khusobek at Abydos.

Concerning expedition inscriptions, all those from the Old and Middle Kingdom attested in the Sinai Peninsula and mentioning the Egyptian administration may conceivably be regarded as the

Dyn.	Reign	Findspot(s)	Nr.*	Expedition Leader	Expression(s)	Reference(s)
5	Menkauhor	Wadi Maghara	12	[Not preserved]	*wp.t iri.t in* [...] "expedition performed by [...]"	Gardiner and Peet 1952, pl. 7; Černý 1955, 60
	Djedkara-Isesi	Wadi Maghara	13	Neankh-khentykhtay	*wp.t nsw.t h3b ḥnʿ*..."royal expedition sent with ..."	Gardiner and Peet 1952, pl. 7; Černý 1955, 60–61
			14	[Not preserved]	*wp.t nsw.t h[3b]* ... "royal expedition [sent] ..."	Gardiner and Peet 1952, pl. 8; Černý 1955, 61–62
			15	[Not preserved]	*wp.t iri.t in* ... "expedition performed by..."	Gardiner and Peet 1952, pl. 4; Černý 1955, 62
			19	Sobekhotep(?)	*wp.t iri.t in* [...] "expedition performed by [...]"	Gardiner and Peet 1952, pl. 9; Černý 1955, 65
6	Pepy I	Wadi Maghara	16	Meryra-ankh	*wp.t iri.t in* ... "expedition performed by ..."	Gardiner and Peet 1952, pl. 8; Černý 1955, 62–63
	Pepy II	Wadi Maghara	17	Hepy	*wp.t nsw.t h3b.t ḥnʿ*... "royal expedition which was sent with ..."	Gardiner and Peet 1952, pl. 9; Černý 1955, 64
12	Amenemhat III	Wadi Maghara	23	Khentykhety-hotep-Khnumsu	*m3ʿ... r ini.t mfk3.t ḥsmn...* "dispatched... to bring turquoise and copper..."	Gardiner and Peet 1952, pl. 10; Černý 1955, 66–67
			25	Hornakht	*iw d3.n=(i) nnw ḥr šps.w m wp.t Ḥr.w* ... "I traversed the *nn*-water laden with precious things on the mission of Horus ..."	Gardiner and Peet 1952, pl. 10; Černý 1955, 68
		Serabit el-Khadim	53	Sobek-herhab	*iyi.n ḥmw.t mḥ.t r-ḏr=sn* ... "the craftsmen arrived in their full whole..."	Gardiner and Peet 1952, pl. 17; Černý 1955, 79–80
			54	Ptahwer	*ini ḏr.w ẖ3s.wt... hbhb in.wt št3.wt ini pḥ.w tmm.t rḫ* "reaching the boundaries of the foreign lands ... traversing the mysterious valleys, reaching the total end of the unknown"	Gardiner and Peet 1952, pl. 18; Černý 1955, 80
			86	Ini	*m3ʿ ḥm=f* ... "his majesty dispatched..."	Gardiner and Peet 1952, pl. 26; Černý 1955, 94
			87	Si-Inpu	*i[yi...] mḥ r-ḏr=sn* "[... arrived] in their full whole"	Gardiner and Peet 1952, pl. 24; Černý 1955, 95
			90	Horwerra	*m3ʿ ḥm=f... r bi3 pn spr t3 pn m 3bd 3 pr.t...* "his majesty dispatched... to this mining area. This land was reached in month 3 of *pr.t* ..."	Gardiner and Peet 1952, pls. 25A, 26; Černý 1955, 97–99
			91	Sneferu	*[ḳ3b.n]=i iyi nb r st tn* "I [doubled] any travel to this place"	Gardiner and Peet 1952, pl. 33A; Černý 1955, 99
			92	Kemsiu(?)	*im.w rn n(.y) ḏ3ḏ3.t=f iyi.t ḥnʿ=f...* "name list of his company who came with him ..."	Gardiner and Peet 1952, pl. 27; Černý 1955, 100
			115	Renef-Inpu	*[iyi.n=f] m ḥtp ḥnʿ mšʿ[=f]* "[he arrived] in peace with his expedition"	Gardiner and Peet 1952, pl. 39; Černý 1955, 118–119
			117	[Not preserved]	*rḫ.t mšʿ iyi(.w) r bi3 pn* "list of the expedition which came to this mining area"	Gardiner and Peet 1952, pl. 40; Černý 1955, 121

Table 2: Expedition texts from the Old to the Middle Kingdom (MK) mentioning the arrival or dispatch of expeditions and other travel-specific expressions. Inscription Numbers (*) accord to Gardiner and Peet 1952; Černý 1955.

Dyn.	Reign	Findspot(s)	Nr.*	Expedition Leader	Expression(s)	Reference(s)
(MK)	[Uncertain]	Serabit el-Khadim	140	Sneferu	*iyi=i ḥmw.t [mḥ.t r]-ḏr=sn* …. "my craftsmen arrived in their full whole…"	Gardiner and Peet 1952, pl. 51; Černý 1955, 138–139
			141	Amenemhat	*mꜣꜥ ḥm n(.y) nṯr pn* … "the majesty of this god dispatched…"	Gardiner and Peet 1952, pl. 52; Černý 1955, 139–140
			411	Khetysenbem	[…] *sbi.t* […] *wḏ.yt nb.t r St.t r ini.t* … "'[…] travel […] every expedition to *St.t* to bring…"	Gardiner and Peet 1952, pl. 86; Černý 1955, 208

Table 2: (cont.) Expedition texts from the Old to the Middle Kingdom (MK) mentioning the arrival or dispatch of expeditions and other travel-specific expressions.

Date	Text	Main Copy(ies)	Location(s) mentioned in Western Asia	Reference
MK	Tale of Sinuhe	Papyrus Berlin 3022 Papyrus Berlin 10499	*Ptn*; *Kmwr*; *Kp(n)*; *Ḳdm*; *(R)tnw (ḥr.t)*; *Iꜣꜣ*; *Ḫnty-kšw*; lands of the *Fnḫ.w*	Koch 1990
	Satire of Trades	Papyrus Sallier II	-	Helck 1970
MK?	Admonitions of Ipuwer	Papyrus Leiden I.344	[*Kp*]*ny*	Enmarch 2005

Table 3: 'Literary' texts of the Middle Kingdom (MK) mentioning travel or the lack thereof to one or more destinations in Western Asia.

product of travelers. Those selected for this analysis and listed in Table 2 specifically note aspects of travel to or from different sites in the Sinai Peninsula, including mention of expeditions sent by the king. The table excludes inscriptions with wishes to return home.[29] Texts dating from the Old Kingdom refer to travel to Wadi Maghara and are assigned to the reigns of Djedkara-Isesi, Pepy I, and Pepy II, where preserved. Those from the Middle Kingdom are mostly attested at Serabit el-Khadim, with a few examples from Wadi Maghara. Inscriptions retaining regnal dates or names are predominantly assigned to the reign of Amenemhat III.

A small number of literary texts also represent aspects of travel (Table 3). Apart from the Tale of Sinuhe, these are all preserved on New Kingdom papyri. They include the Teaching of Duaf's son Khety or the so-called Satire of Trades and the Admonitions of Ipuwer.

Another text from the Middle Kingdom, the Daybook of Amenemhat II, provides an entirely different perspective. It records the administrative dispatch of expeditions to different locales believed to be in Western Asia.[30]

The Old Kingdom

Each journey typically comprises a motivation, a voyage, and a destination. The extant texts from the Sixth to the Twelfth Dynasties represent travel as a movement *toward* a distant location and/or as a *return* from this location. When mentioned in Sixth and Twelfth Dynasty biographical and expedition inscriptions, motivations for travel to Western Asia are always tied to a royal commission.

This is clearly represented in the first known detailed description of travel to Western Asia, preserved in the biography of Weni from his tombs at Abydos and Saqqara.[31] As is apparent from the Abydos version, the text was likely presented on the façade of the tomb.[32] It first describes Weni's duties under king Teti, followed by his exceptional achievements and the privileges granted to him under Pepy I's reign. When Pepy I "took action against the *ꜥꜣm.w Ḥr.yw-šꜥ*,"[33] he placed Weni, then an *im.y-rꜣ ḫn.tyw-š pr ꜥꜣ* "overseer of guards of the Great House,"[34] at the front of a sizeable coalition of officials of various ranks and troops of diverse origin (lines 13–19). The biography then describes how Weni planned and led them on a clearly defined route, likely to the Sinai Peninsula (lines 21–22):[35] "to the Northern Island (*iw-mḥ.ty*)[36] then to the Gate of Imhotep (*Sbꜣ-n.y-Iyi-m-ḥtp*)[37] and to the District of Horus Lord of Truth (*Wꜥr.t-n.t-Ḥr.w-nb-mꜣꜥ.t*)."[38] The so-called Song of Victory follows, emphasizing the army's achievements in returning safely (*iyi.n mšꜥ pn m ḥtp*) after destroying and flattening the land of the *Ḥr.yw-šꜥ* (lines 22–28). It mentions tearing down its forts, cutting its figs and vines, setting it to fire, killing its thousands of troops, and bringing some back as captives. Five times the *Ḥr.yw-šꜥ* rebelled, so five times Weni successfully led the coalition. The text also describes another campaign for which Weni led his troops over sea and land to quash a rebellion at the elusive Nose of Gazelle's Head (*Šr.t-tp-wnḏ.w*),[39] again returning with success (lines 29–32). It continues with other achievements Weni completed for Merenra, this time while he held the title of *ḥꜣ.ty-ꜥ im.y-rꜣ šmꜥ.w* "count, overseer of Upper Egypt."[40] Although such royal privileges for an individual of seemingly modest rank may appear peculiar, they are not unique.[41] Yet, in Weni's case, his tomb indeed contains evidence of his promotion to the office of vizier.[42] This adds to extra-biographical material that attests to the individual's high position in Egyptian society, with links to a powerful family in Abydos, possible ties with the capital, and access to interregional trade networks.[43] These ties, however, are not emphasized in the description of Weni's experiences as an expedition leader. Instead, his accomplishments in planning the expeditions and leading the troops across the routes are highlighted, as is the return in safety.

During the same reign as Weni's campaigns against the *ꜥꜣm.w Ḥr.yw-šꜥ*, Khnumhotep and Iny were sent to the Levant. The text of the *ḫrp sḥ* "director of the dining-hall"[44] Khnumhotep merely mentions that he went forth to Byblos with Tjejti and to Punt with Khui an unpreserved number of times and that he returned successfully (*iyi.k(i) m ḥtp*).[45] Limited in length, the inclusion of this first-person account in another individual's tomb showcases both the importance of such expeditions for all those involved, as well as the significance of noting return from travel to distant lands.[46]

In contrast, the biography of Iny provides hints as to the motivation for such travel. As reconstructed by Marcolin and Espinel, the biography is preserved on both a large and minor inscription.[47] According to the large inscription, Iny is described as one valued before Djedkara-Isesi (line x+2). His special treatment eventuated in Iny's ascription with a new name, *ꞽInn(.w)-dfꜣ.w*, literally "the one who brings provisions" (line x+4).[48] It was likely also associated with Iny's involvement in six campaigns to Western Asia. Four were conducted during the reign of Pepy I to *ꜥmꜣꜣw*, *Ḫnty-š* and *Pꜣws*[...], from which Iny brought back silver and every good produce (*inw*) (lines x+5–6). One expedition was sent to Byblos under the reign of Merenra, and returned with *Kbn.wt* "Byblos-type boats", alongside desired commodities from a range of sources, including lapis lazuli, lead/tin, silver, *sfṯ*-oil, and every good product (lines x+7–9). For his achievements in this campaign, Iny was praised, specifically in the court, and rewarded with gold (lines x+9–10). The minor inscription mentions the last campaign sent to *Ḫnty-š* during Pepy II's reign, from which one *Kbn.t* "Byblos-type boat" and a number of cargo boats were sent to Egypt alongside silver as well as *ꜥꜣm* men and women (lines x+2–4). Consequently, Iny was ushered to the court, had conferred upon him the titles *smr wꜥ.ty ḥr.y-ḥb sḏꜣ.wty-nṯr* "sole companion, lector priest, god's sealer,"[49] and was honored by eating a meal at the court (lines x+5–7). Regarding the path of the voyage, only one detail in the large inscription notes that Iny descended to Byblos from *Rꜣ-ḥꜣ.t*, after which it is directly mentioned that he returned safely (*iyi.k(i) im m ḥtp*; line x+10–11).

The importance of the safe return is all the more evident in the last Old Kingdom biographical text dealing with travel to Western Asia: the biography of Pepynakht-Heqaib.[50] According to his epithets, this official was *inn(.w) ḫr.t ḫꜣs.wt n nb=f* "one who brings the products of foreign lands to his lord"[51] and *dd(.w) nrw Ḥr.w m ḫꜣs.wt* "one who instils the fear of Horus in the foreign lands."[52] He is represented as an experienced expedition leader, already having mounted a campaign to *Wꜣwꜣt* and *ꞽrṯt* in Nubia prior to his journey to the foreign land of the *ꜥꜣm.w*. Pepynakht-Heqaib was sent to the latter to bring back the body of the official Anankhti, who had been constructing a *Kbn.t* "Byblos-type boat" when he was attacked by *ꜥꜣm.w n.w Ḥr.yw-š* (lines 11–12). The exact location of the campaign is not given, as it was likely not considered the target of the voyage. Instead, the actual target was the murderers, rather than all *ꜥꜣm.w*, who were successfully driven away by the official (line 15).

All in all, Old Kingdom representations of travel effectively showcase officials' achievements and affiliation with the ruling pharaohs. Framed by decorum, missions were evidently all commissioned by the state, as indeed corroborated by the preserved expedition inscriptions at Wadi Maghara noting travel by officials. Both Iny and Weni were portrayed as specially chosen by the king for the expeditions, while at least Weni may have also been in the king's personal service as "overseer of guards of the Great House." Any privileges acquired due to connections to powerful families, who in Weni's case were in very strategically positioned towns, are not attested. The officials' conduct beyond borders were as representatives of the king. Thus, they could 'instill the fear' of the ruling pharaoh in these regions. Mentions of paths leading away from Egypt are immediately followed by expressions noting safe returns, while destinations are framed in association with the purposes of the campaigns. The latter were either of bellicose nature, targeting rebellious *ꜥꜣm.w Ḥr.yw-šꜥ*; or of commercial nature, bringing back desired commodities and individuals, likely for their specialized skills. Mention of direct personal encounters with foreigners is absent. As rewards, officials could be welcomed at the court before the king, promoted, and, in Iny's case, presented with gold.

The Middle Kingdom

Some of these aspects continue to be attested in preserved early Middle Kingdom texts noting travel to Western Asia. Two assigned to the late Eleventh Dynasty remain, both from Thebes. One was collected in fragments from the vestibule of Theban Tomb 313 at Deir el-Bahri and is dated to the reign of Mentuhotep II.[53] It records how the *im.y-rꜣ pr.w ꜥꜣ* "chief steward"[54] Henenu conducted an expedition to, perhaps, a place with *Ḥr.yw-š*, brought back products, and then possibly travelled to *Ḫtyw-ꜥš*.[55] In comparison, the text of Khety is preserved on a stela from his tomb at Asasif.[56] Possibly dating to the late Eleventh Dynasty or the early Twelfth Dynasty, the text opens with an offering formula followed by a first-person account of the *sḏꜣ.wty nṯr m sid.t ḫꜣs.wt* "god's sealer[57] in making powerless the foreign lands" who, when in the *biꜣ.w* "mining region",[58] inspected it and travelled around the foreign lands of *Ṯnht*, most feasibly the Sinai Peninsula (lines 2–3).[59] He then sealed treasuries (perhaps storehouses), and collected turquoise from mines in the area (lines 3–4). As emissary of the king, and like Old Kingdom officials, he held a special place in the king's heart (lines 6–7). Accordingly, he drove off (*ḫsf*) the *ꜥꜣm.w*, adding that it was the fear of the pharaoh in foreign lands that made them respect Khety (lines 7–8). The official then notes his return in peace to the palace (*iyi.n(=i) m ḥtp r ꜥḥ=f*), bringing *tp.yw ḫꜣs.wt* "the best of the foreign lands", with a range of minerals uniquely listed alongside their sources (lines 9–12), possibly located in the Sinai Peninsula, the Eastern Desert and/or the Gulf of Suez.[60]

And indeed, such lists of goods have survived on the Mit Rahina block of Amenemhat II.[61] While an administrative text, the formula of the dispatch of an expedition, and its return with cargo is repeated. Three main expeditions were sent, one to *Ḫnty-š*, bringing back a variety of products and *ꜥꜣm.w*, like in Iny's biography, but *ꜥš*-wood rather than Iny's *Kbn.wt* "Byblos-type boats" (lines M7; M18–21). Another expedition from the Turquoise Terraces returned with minerals (dispatch not preserved; lines M13–14), while a third was sent to *Ꞽwꜣ* to hack up *St.t* (line M8), returning from *Ꞽwꜣ* and *Ꞽꜣsy* with products and captives (lines M16–18). There is no mention of routes, of the fear of the king, of losses, or of the names of involved officials, although the inscription does mention the giving of rewards, including gold (M21–26).

Significant differences are then attested in representations of travel from the reigns of Senwosret III and Amenemhat III. They are more personalised and more expansive in form, detail and content. Two biographical inscriptions have survived. The stela of Khusobek provides perspective of the *ꜣṯw ꜥꜣ n(.y) nw.t* "great intendant of the city" as he accompanied Senwosret III on his campaigns to Nubia to overthrow the *Ꞽwn.tyw*[*-Sty*] and to Western Asia to overthrow the *Mnṯ.w* of *St.t*.[62] In each, the official highlights one significant personal encounter with a foreigner that emphasises his achievements. In reference to the campaign that reached *Skmm* in the north (lines C1–4), Khusobek describes how he bravely fought against a *ꜥꜣm*. Likely because of this, he was awarded a sheathed dagger by the king (line C5).

Closer to the literary narrative structure is the fragmentary biography of Khnumhotep III that likely originally adorned the façade of a mastaba tomb at Dahshur.[63] As reconstructed by Allen, the text begins with the titles of the official, *ir.y-pꜥ.t ḥꜣ.ty-ꜥ sḏꜣ.wty bi.ty* "hereditary prince, count, sealer of the king of Lower Egypt"[64] and *im.y-rꜣ pr.w wr* "chief steward", followed by an offering formula.[65] Then, the biography presents the experiences of an *im.y-rꜣ mšꜥ n(.y) sḳd.w* "overseer of the expedition of sailors" (lines 1C1–2). Uniquely, this appears to be composed in narrative style and in third person, possibly for reasons of decorum.[66] The name of the overseer is also either suppressed or not preserved. The motive for travel was to evidently source *ꜥš*-wood, the expedition docking at Byblos where the overseer meets with the city's ruler *Mꜣki* to discuss his intentions to reach *Wꜣṯi* (lines 1C2–3; 1D1–4, 2A2–3). The diplomatic event unravels using direct speech between the ruler and the overseer. As negotiations ensue, letter correspondence with the Egyptian Residence is mentioned (lines 3P6–10), and Egyptian militaristic intervention has been posited (lines 3D2–4).[67] As with Old Kingdom texts, Khnumhotep III appears as a representative of the king. Like Weni, the fragments preserve no evidence of the privileges and training he may have been afforded as a likely member of an affluent elite family from the Oryx nome, again with well-established connections with Western Asia.[68] Based on the surviving fragments, his achievements in the expedition were instead the focus of the composition. Unlike these earlier pieces, however, the successes involved more direct, personal encounters with named people and specific places beyond the borders of Egypt.

Such personalised experiences are further attested in expedition inscriptions by the reign of Amenemhat III (Table 2). A small number include details on the traversal of routes. The inscription of the *ỉr.y-ꜥ.t n(.y) pr-ḥḏ* "hall-keeper of the treasury"[69] Hornakht at Wadi Maghara records: *ỉw dꜣ.n=(ỉ) nnw ḥr šps.w m wp.t Ḥr.w nb ꜥḥ* "(I) traversed the *nn*-water carrying precious things on the mission of Horus, lord of the palace".[70] That of the *ỉm.y-rꜣ ꜥẖn.wty wr n(.y) pr ḥḏ* "chief chamberlain of the treasury"[71] Ptahwer at Serabit el-Khadim mentions him *ỉnỉ ḏr.w ḫꜣs.wt m rd.wy=f hbhb ỉn.wt štꜣ.wt ỉnỉ pḥ.w tmm.t rḫ* "reaching the boundaries of the foreign lands with his two feet, traversing the mysterious valleys, reaching the total end of the unknown".[72] Perhaps, these travellers themselves were influenced by a more literary trope of boundary traversal at this time. Indeed, another inscription at Serabit el-Khadim for the *sḏꜣ.wty nṯr ỉm.y-rꜣ ꜥẖn.wty ẖrp sk.w* "god's sealer, chamberlain, controller of troops"[73] Horwerra describes the challenging task of searching for turquoise seemingly at the wrong time, during *tr pn ḳsn n(.y) šmw* "this difficult season of summer" (line 12).[74] The official persevered to successfully overcome the adversity with the will of the king in his heart (lines 13–8), and then directly instructs those who would search for the mineral not to lose hope but pray to Hathor who would assure success (lines 19–21). While the text mentions that his expedition arrived in its entirety with no loss (line 15), it remains uncertain if this refers to the expedition's arrival at Serabit el-Khadim,[75] or its return to Egypt as the end of the text is not preserved. Nevertheless, the return is commonly attested in other Middle Kingdom inscriptions at Serabit el-Khadim, some of which add that they would be ushered before the king upon their awaited arrival.[76]

Travel and Safe Return in the Tale of Sinuhe and other Middle Kingdom Literary Texts

Against the background of the Old and Middle Kingdom representations of travel to Western Asia, it is apparent that the Tale of Sinuhe shares similarities as well as differences with earlier and contemporaneous compositions. From the beginning of Sinuhe's narration of his journey, the Tale subverts established motivations for travel beyond the Nile Valley and introduces a third type of travel: flight *away* from a location.[77] As Moers writes, this emphasises the withdrawal from the ideal in the travel narrative.[78]

Yet like Weni, the Tale notes specific landmarks that were passed as he was crossing the borders of Egypt at the Walls of the Ruler (lines B11–23). He took a barge and headed eastwards from the quay of *Ngꜣw*, crossing east of the stone quarry above the Mistress-of-the-Red-Mountain (Gebel Ahmar) to then travel north until he reached the Walls.[79] After crossing this boundary, he reached *Ptn* and stopped at *Kmwr*, believed to be at the east of the Wadi Tumilat, before thirst, or "the taste of death" struck him. This physical or perhaps physiological reaction echoes a passage in the so-called Satire of Trades, wherein a trader who sets out to foreign lands would be *snḏ.w ḥr mꜣỉ.w ḥnꜥ ꜥꜣm.w rḫ=f sw r=f ỉw=f ḥr Km.t* "fearful of lions and *ꜥꜣm.w*, he knows himself (only) when he is in Egypt" (line 7.7).[80] The representation of such emotion is not found in any of the other surviving texts detailing travel to Western Asia. Perhaps the closest parallel is in the description of the very different lands of the *ḫsỉ* "miserable" *ꜥꜣm* as described in the Middle Kingdom Teachings of Merikara, with it being troubled[81] with water, forested and difficult to traverse (lines 91–92).[82]

In Sinuhe's case, it was his heart that gave him strength, and the *St.tyw* who gave him water (lines B23–28). What follows is a much-discussed passage mentioning Sinuhe's travels from foreign land to foreign land, setting out for Byblos and reaching *Ḳdm*, where a ruler of Upper *Rṯnw*, Ammunenshi fetched him (lines B28–31).[83] The inclusion of Byblos here perhaps evoked cultural knowledge of the region as a well-known commercial partner with Egypt. Focussing only on the textual repertoire mentioning travel (Table 1), Byblos appears as a destination in the Sixth Dynasty texts of Iny and Khnumhotep, as well as the Twelfth Dynasty biography of Khnumhotep III. It is additionally attested in the Admonitions of Ipuwer, which, in line with its portrayal of a disordered world, claims that no one sails to Byblos any more (lines 3.6–7).[84] If combined with other attestations of the toponym in Old and Middle Kingdom texts from Egypt, as well as the archaeological material at the site of Byblos, it is clear that this harbour city had strong commercial, diplomatic, and cultural ties with central Egyptian administrations, especially in the Sixth Dynasty and the mid-Twelfth to Thirteenth Dynasties.[85] Hence, by the Middle Kingdom, Byblos would have been well-recognised by several high officials in the Egyptian administration, especially those who embarked on expeditions to the Levant.

Another toponym mentioned in the Tale is *Rṯnw*. Unlike Byblos, however, *Rṯnw* clearly emerges in the Middle Kingdom cultural geography with most attestations dating to the mid-Twelfth Dynasty.[86] As recorded in the stela of Khusobek, the Egyptians engaged in hostile relations with a district in its area with a one-on-one clash between Khusobek and a *ꜥꜣm* (line C2). However, inscriptions from Serabit el-Khadim point to an alliance(s) that spanned over 20 years involving men from *Rṯnw* that likely travelled with the Egyptians to Serabit el-Khadim.[87] Interestingly, both of these portrayals are presented in the Tale of Sinuhe, with the violent encounter with a strong man of *Rṯnw* who challenges Sinuhe (lines B109–146), and in the supportive figure of the ruler of Upper *Rṯnw* Ammunenshi, knowledgeable in Egyptian affairs and acquiescent towards the needs of Egyptians (lines B30–35). Therefore, perhaps Sinuhe's encounters align with the emergent representation of direct personal engagements with Levantines, both peaceful and violent, that are attested from the second half of Dynasty 12, as well as the contemporaneous representations of *Rṯnw*.

Still, Sinuhe's more personal encounters remain unique for Egyptian texts in their details. Indeed, it should be borne in mind that Sinuhe's character development is the Tale's focal point; so, the description of foreign lands, groups and individuals is subordinate to and dependent on his own experiences.[88] Several works have explored their representation and characterisation: instances concerning the king showcase a more bellicose treatment that emphasise the foreigners' subjugation, thereby agreeing with earlier representations of idealised relations between pharaohs and foreigners; while those concerning direct engagements with non-Egyptians offer more nuanced and individualised portrayals.[89] Sinuhe's conduct abroad is also in line with Egyptian precepts: he did not divulge details of circumstances in the palace to Ammunenshi,[90] he gave water to the thirsty (line B96), he conducted Egyptian messengers (lines B94–95), and he was courageous in battle and excellent in plans (lines B98–106). Despite the years spent abroad, Egyptian customs continued to be adhered to and favoured.[91] Therefore, upon the king's request via letter correspondence, a means of communication also mentioned in Khnumhotep III's biography, Sinuhe returned to Egypt (lines B238–245).

Before arriving at the court, he was greeted at the boundary. This detail occurs in an earlier Old Kingdom biography mentioning travel, but to the south of Egypt: the biography of Harkhuf at Qubbet el-Hawa mentions that the count, sole companion, and overseer of the two cool rooms, Khuni, was sent to greet him upon his return with ships laden with wine, cakes, bread and beer.[92] For Sinuhe, the overseer of the palace's fieldworkers was sent with ships laden with gifts for the *St.tyw* who helped him on his journey home (lines B243–245).

Sinuhe was then presented to the court, the story concluding with his reinstatement into Egyptian society and the provision of a burial by the king (lines B286–308), fit for an Egyptian of high status. This agrees with the common trope attested in texts on the importance of returning from travel, or managing the safe arrival of expedition members in peace or with no loss.[93] Upon return, successful travellers could be presented to the court, like Sinuhe, and offered great rewards, which could include the provision of resources for a tomb.[94] Also aligned with the return and with this provision is the well-identified importance of being buried according to Egyptian burial practices, which is also attested in the Sixth Dynasty biography of Pepynakht-Heqaib who was sent to bring the body of a deceased person back to Egypt.[95]

No Place Like Home

Representations of travel in the Tale of Sinuhe preserve and transform earlier portrayals of the motivation, the journey, and the return from travel. Some details parallel Old Kingdom antecedents, but some appear closer to those of the Twelfth Dynasty.

However, as a composition that was likely recited and certainly copied,[96] the Tale's motif of border-crossing would have served additional purposes. As Moers notes with respect to the travel narrative, it allowed for the metaphorical equivalence of the "transgression of socially-defined boundaries" and cultural norms.[97] Several have observed that the incorporation of encounters with the foreign sharpened representations and perhaps perceptions of Egyptian identity.[98] Yet, of further importance is the trope of the return home. With this, local identity is retained and maintained. Thus, the Tale's inclusion of border traversal also reflects the tensions between the Egyptian and the Other, or the local and the supra-local, which are otherwise commonly attested in periods of increased connectivity.[99]

Hypothetically, if the Tale of Sinuhe was read and heard by scribes and other high officials of the late Twelfth Dynasty, then perhaps its commentary on travel and life abroad may have been accessible to those most likely involved in travel and transregional activities, including scribes and literate officials. Indeed, Darnell has identified texts at Wadi el-Hol that closely parallel excerpts from Sinuhe: one probably of Amenemhat III's reign is attributed to the priest Dedusobek who was travelling to participate in a festival at Deir el-Bahri and lists deities similar to those in Sinuhe (lines B206–210); and another is of the late Middle Kingdom to Second Intermediate Period and is a literary text.[100] If such travelling individuals encountered the Tale, one may offer a further interpretation that can be added to the many others proposed for its function and reception: perhaps it offered a treatise on transregionalism itself. Accordingly, it features details on the socially accepted conduct of Egyptians abroad, the pitfalls of the transregional experience, the state of affairs between the central Egyptian administration and key foreign groups and places, and the role of the state in ensuring the return and appropriate reward for Egyptians who travelled abroad.

In line with previous representations, the Tale further emphasises the importance of the 'return home' and the ability to re-join the Egyptian social structure securely and successfully, no matter the time and level of integration in non-Egyptian communities. This, in turn, suits well the period when the Tale was composed and copied as one of increasing connectivity, when transregional agents were likely required to be motivated to travel and to return, in accordance with the central administration's ideals.[101] As Kristiansen writes in reference to Bronze Age trade, such compositions helped create "a mental template of cognitive geographies that makes distance and dangers, routes and destinations familiar to the traveler".[102] The travel-abroad motif and the representation of its aspects as exemplified in the Tale of Sinuhe would have thus made not only the foreign familiar; it also raised awareness of the concept of travel and traversing liminal borders. Perhaps, this is one of the many reasons for the Tale's enduring popularity across history.

Acknowledgments

Funding for this work was supported by a Macquarie University Research Fellowship for the project "The Ties that Bind: Negotiating Foreign Relations in the Second Millennium BC". The paper was first presented at the "Egypt and the Mediterranean World from the Late Fourth through the Third Millennium BCE" conference. I am grateful to its organisers, Dr. Karin Sowada and Dr. Matthew J. Adams for the invitation to present at this engaging event, as well as the opportunity to contribute to this volume. I also thank Dr. Sowada for stimulating discussions regarding the Tale of Sinuhe in a retrospective view of Old Kingdom contacts with the Near East that prompted some of the ideas herein. Thanks are also due for the two reviewers who offered helpful comments on this paper.

Abbreviation

Urk. *Urkunden des Ägyptischen Altertums. Abteilung I–VIII.* Leipzig—Berlin: Hinrichs, 1903–1988.

References

Aḥituv, Shmuel. 1984. *Canaanite Toponyms in Ancient Egyptian Documents*. Jerusalem: Magnes Press, Hebrew University.

Ahrens, Alexander. 2020. *Aegyptiaca in der nördlichen Levante: Eine Studie zur Kontextualisierung und Rezeption ägyptischer und ägyptisierender Objekte in der Bronzezeit.* Orbus Biblicus et Orientalis 41. Leuven–Paris–Bristol: Peeters.

Allen, James P. 1996. "Some Theban Officials of the Early Middle Kingdom." In Peter der Manuelian and Rita E. Freed (eds.), *Studies in Honor of William Kelly Simpson*, 1–26. Boston: Museum of Fine Arts.

———. 2008. "The Historical Inscription of Khnumhotep at Dahshur: Preliminary Report." *Bulletin of the American Schools of Oriental Research* 352: 29–39.

Altenmüller, Hartwig. 2015. *Zwei Annalenfragmente aus dem frühen Mittleren Reich*. Hamburg: Helmut Buske Verlag.

Altenmüller, Hartwig and Ahmed M. Moussa. 1991. "Die Inschrift Amenmhets II. aus dem Ptah-Tempel von Memphis. Ein Vorbericht." *Studien zur Altägyptischen Kultur* 18: 1–48.

Baines, John. 1982. "Interpreting Sinuhe." *The Journal of Egyptian Archaeology* 68: 31–44.

———. 1987. "The Stela of Khusobek: Private and Royal Military Narrative and Values." In Jürgen Osing and Günter Dreyer (eds.), *Form und Mass: Beiträge zur Literatur, Sprache und Kunst des alten Ägypten. Festschrift für Gerhard Fecht zum 65. Geburtstag am 6. Februar 1987*, 43–61. Ägypten und Altes Testament 12. Wiesbaden: Kommission bei O. Harrassowitz.

———. 1999a. "Forerunners of Narrative Biographies." In Anthony Leahy and John Tait (eds.), *Studies on Ancient Egypt in Honour of H. S. Smith*, 23–37. Occasional Publications 13. London: Egypt Exploration Society.

———. 1999b. "Prehistories of Literature: Performance, Fiction, Myth." In Gerald Moers (ed.), *Definitely, Egyptian Literature. Proceedings of the Symposium "Ancient Egyptian Literature: History and Forms"*, 17–41. Lingua Aegyptia – Studia Monographica 2. Göttingen: Hubert & Co.

———. 2004. *Die Bedeutung des Reisens im Alten Ägypten*. Siegfried-Morenz-Gedächtnis-Vorlesung 13. Leipzig: Ägyptisches Museum der Universität.

———. 2007. "Travel in Third and Second Millennium Egypt." In Colin Adams and Jim Roy (eds.), *Travel, Geography and Culture in Ancient Greece, Egypt and the Near East*. Leicester Nottingham Studies in Ancient Society 10. Oxford: Oxbow Books.

———. 2013. *High Culture and Experience in Ancient Egypt*. Sheffield–Bristol: Equinox.

———. 2020. "Ancient Egyptian Biographies: From Living a Life to Creating a Fit Memorial." In Julie Stauder-Porchet, Elizabeth Frood, and Andréas Stauder (eds.), *Ancient Egyptian Biographies. Contexts, Forms, Function*, 47–83. Atlanta: Lockwood Press.

Bárta, Miroslav. 2003. *Sinuhe, the Bible, and the Patriarchs*. Prague: Czech Institute of Egyptology.

Bárta, Miroslav and Jiří Janák. 2021. "Sinuhe: Popular Hero, Court Politics, and the Royal Paradigm." In Alejandro Jiménez-Serrano and Antonio J. Morales (eds.), *Middle Kingdom Palace Culture and Its Echoes in the Provinces. Regional Perspectives and Realities*, 101–118. Leiden–Boston: Brill.

Berg, Patricia. 2014. *Perspectives on Mobility and Travelling: A Study of References to Functionally-Bound Forms of Individual Movement in Non-literary Texts from New Kingdom Deir El-Medina*. PhD Dissertation, University of Helsinki.

Bietak, Manfred. 2010. "From Where Came the Hyksos and Where Did They Go?" In Marcel Marée (ed.), *The Second Intermediate Period (Thirteenth–Seventeenth Dynasties). Current Research, Future Prospects*, 139–181. Orientalia Lovaniensia Analecta 192. Leuven–Paris–Walpole: Peeters.

Blackman, Aylward. 1930. "A New Translation of the Inscription of Herwerre at Serabit el-Khadim." *Bulletin de l'institut français d'archéologie orientale* 30: 97–101.

Blumenthal, Elke 1984. *Altägyptische Reiseerzählungen. Die Lebensgeschichte des Sinuhe. Der Reisebericht des Wen-Amun*. Reclams Universal-Bibliothek 928. Leipzig: Reclam.

Bommas, Martin. 2014. "Sinuhes Flucht. Zu Religion und Literatur als Methode." *Zeitschrift für Ägyptische Sprache und Altertumskunde* 14/1: 15–23.

Bunbury, Judith and Jeffreys, David. "Real and Literary Landscapes in Ancient Egypt." *Cambridge Archaeological Journal* 21/1: 65–75.

Burkard, Gunter. 1977. *Textkritische Untersuchungen zu ägyptischen Weisheitslehren des Alten und Mittleren Reiches*. Ägyptologische Abhandlungen 34. Wiesbaden: Harrassowitz.

Burkard, Gunter and Hans-Werner Fischer-Elfert. 1994. *Ägyptische Handschriften* vol. 4. Verzeichnis der orientalischen Handschriften in Deutschland 19.4. Stuttgart: Franz Steiner.

Campagno, Marcelo 2015. "Egyptian Boundaries in the Tale of Sinuhe." In Hans Amstutz, Andreas Dorn, Matthias Müller, Miriam V. Ronsdorf, and Sami Uljas (eds.), *Fuzzy Boundaries. Festschrift für Antonio Loprieno* vol. 1, 335–346. Hamburg: Widmaier Verlag.

Černý, Jaroslav. 1955. *The Inscriptions of Sinai* vol. 2. *Translations and Commentary*. London: Oxford University Press.

Clavin, Patricia. 2005. "Defining Transnationalism." *Contemporary European History* 14 (4): 421–439.

Clère, Jacques Jean and Jacques Vandier. 1948. *Textes de la Première Période Intermédiaire et de la XIeme Dynastie* vol. 1. Bibliotheca Aegyptiaca 10. Brussels: Éditions de la Fondation égyptologique Reine Elisabeth.

Collombert, Philippe. 2015. "Une nouvelle version de l'autobiographie d'Ouni." In Rémi Legros (ed.), *Cinquante ans d'éternité. Jubilé de la Mission archéologique française de Saqqâra*, 145–157. Mission archéologique française de Saqqâra 5; Bibliothèque d'étude 162. Cairo: Institut français d'archéologie orientale.

Colonna, Angelo. 2018. "Gods in Translation. Dynamics of Transculturality between Egypt and Byblos in the III Millennium BC." *Studi de Materiali di Storia delle Religioni* 84 (1): 65–90.

Cooper, Julien Charles. 2020. *Toponymy on the Periphery. Placenames of the Eastern Desert, Red Sea and South Sinai in Egyptian Documents from the Early Dynastic until the End of the New Kingdom*. Probleme der Ägyptologie 39. Leiden–Boston: Brill.

Coulon, Laurent. 2020. "Clichés in Ancient Egyptian Autobiographies." In Julie Stauder-Porchet, Elizabeth Frood, and Andréas Stauder (eds.), *Ancient Egyptian Biographies. Contexts, Forms, Function*, 205–223. Atlanta: Lockwood Press.

Darnell, John Coleman. 1997. "A New Middle Egyptian Literary Text from the Wadi el-Ḥôl." *Journal of the American Research Center in Egypt* 34: 85–100.

———. 2002. *Theban Desert Road Survey in the Egyptian Western Desert* vol. 1: *Gebel Tjauti Rock Inscriptions 1–45 and Wadi el-Hôl Rock Inscriptions 1–45*. Oriental Institute Publication 119. Chicago: Oriental Institute Press.

Di Biase-Dyson, Camilla. 2013. *Foreigners and Egyptians in the Late Egyptian Stories*. Probleme der Ägyptologie 32. Leiden–Boston: Brill.

Edel, Elmar, Karl J. Seyfried, and Gerd Vieler. 2007. *Die Felsgräbernekropole der Qubbet el-Hawa bei Assuan I: Die Architektur, Darstellungen, Texte, archäologischer Befund und Funde der Gräber QH 24–QH 209* vol. 1. Paderborn: Schöningh.

Eder, Christian. 1995. *Die ägyptischen Motive in der Glyptik des östlichen Mittelmeerraumes zu Anfang des 2. Jts. v. Chr.* Orientalia Lovaniensia Analecta 71. Leuven: Peeters.

Enmarch, Roland. 2005. *The Dialogue of Ipuwer and the Lord of All*. Oxford: Oxford Institute.

Eriksen, Thomas Hylland. 2007. "Creolization in Anthropological Theory and in Mauritius." In Charles Stewart (ed.), *Creolization: History, Ethnography, Theory*, 153–177. Walnut Creek: Left Coast Press.

Espinel, Andrés Diego. 2002. "The Role of the Temple of Ba'alat Gebal as Intermediary between Egypt and Byblos during the Old Kingdom." *Studien zur Altägyptischen Kultur* 30: 103–119.

———. 2004. "Minima epigraphica." *Discussions in Egyptology* 59: 7–20.

———. 2015–2016. "Bringing Treasures and Placing Fears: Old Kingdom Epithets and Titles Related to Activities Abroad." *Isimu* 18–19: 103–146.

Eyre, Christopher. 1994. "Weni's Career and Old Kingdom Historiography." In Christopher Eyre, Anthony Leahy, and Lisa Montagno Leahy (eds.), *The Unbroken Reed: Studies in the Culture and Heritage of Ancient Egypt in Honour of A. F. Shore*, 107–124. Egypt Exploration Society Occasional Publications 11. London: Egypt Exploration Society.

———. 2013. "The Practice of Literature: The Relationship between Content, Form, Audience, and Performance." In Roland Enmarch and Verena M. Lepper (eds.), *Ancient Egyptian Literature: Theory and Practice*, 101–142. Proceedings of the British Academy 188. Oxford: Oxford University Press.

Faist, Thomas. 2004. "The Border-Crossing Expansion of Social Space: Concepts, Questions and Topics." In Thomas Faist and Eyüp Özveren (eds.), *Transnational Social Spaces*, 1–34. London–New York: Routledge.

Fischer, Henry George. 1968. *Dendera in the Third Millennium B.C. down to the Theban Domination of Upper Egypt*. New York: J.J. Augustin.

Flammini, Roxana. 2010. "Elite Emulation and Patronage Relationships in the Middle Bronze: The Egyptianized Dynasty of Byblos." *Tel Aviv* 37: 154–168.

Fox, Robin Lane. 2008. *Travelling Heroes. Greeks and their Myths in the Epic Age of Homer*. London: Allen Lane.

Galán, José M. 2005. *Four Journeys in Ancient Egyptian Literature*. Lingua Aegyptia Studia Monographica 5. Göttingen: Hubert & Co.

Gardiner, Alan H. 1914. "New Literary Works from Ancient Egypt." *The Journal of Egyptian Archaeology* 1 / 1: 20–36.

———. 1917. "The Tomb of a Much-Travelled Theban Official." *The Journal of Egyptian Archaeology* 4: 28–38.

———. 1947. *Ancient Egyptian Onomastica*. Oxford: Oxford University Press.

Gardiner, Alan H. and T. Eric Peet. 1952. *The Inscriptions of Sinai* vol. 1: *Introduction and Plates*. 2nd edition. London: Egypt Exploration Fund.

Garstang, John. 1901. *El-Arábah: A Cemetery of the Middle Kingdom Survey of the Old Kingdom Temenos Graffiti from the Temple of Sety*. London: Bernard Quaritch.

Gnirs, Andrea M. 1996. "Die ägyptische Autobiographie." In Antonio Loprieno (ed.), *Ancient Egyptian Literature: History and Forms*, 191–241. Probleme der Ägyptologie 10. Leiden–New York–Köln: Brill.

Goedicke, Hans. 1957. "The Route of Sinuhe's Flight." *The Journal of Egyptian Archaeology* 43: 77–85.

———. 1962. "The Inscription of *Ḥr-wr-rʿ*." *Mitteilungen des Deutschen Archäologischen Instituts Abteilung Kairo* 18: 14–25.

———. 1984. "The Riddle of Sinuhe's Flight." *Revue d'Égyptologie* 35: 95–103.

———. 1992. "Where did Sinuhe stay in "Asia"? (Sinuhe B 29-31)." *Chronique d'Égypte* 67: 28–40.

———. 1998. "Khu-u-Sobek's Fight in 'Asia'." *Ägypten und Levante* 7: 33–37.

Golénischeff, Wladimir Semenovich. 1916. *Les papyrus hiératiques nos. 1115, 1116A et 1116B de l'Ermitage impérial à St-Pétersburg*. Saint Petersburg: Papiers de l'état.

Green, Michael. 1983. "The Syrian and Lebanese Topographical Data in the Story of Sinuhe." *Chronique d'Égypte* 58: 38–59.

Gundacker, Roman. 2017. "The Significance of Foreign Toponyms and Ethnonyms in Old Kingdom Text Sources." In Felix Höflmayer (ed.), *The Late Third Millennium in the Ancient Near East. Chronology, C14, and Climate Change*, 333–426. Oriental Institute Seminars 11. Chicago: The University of Chicago.

El-Hawary, Amr. 2014. "Sinuhe und die / das Fremde." In Harold M. Hays, Frank Feder, and Ludwig D. Morenz (eds.), *Interpretations of Sinuhe. Inspired by Two Passages. Proceedings of a Workshop held at Leiden University, 27–29 November 2009*, 15–22. Leiden–Leuven: Nederlands Institut voor het Nabije Oosten–Peeters.

Hayes, William C. 1949. "Career of the Great Steward Ḥenenu under Nebḥepetrēʿ Mentuḥotpe." *The Journal of Egyptian Archaeology* 35: 43–49.

Helck, Wolfgang. 1970. *Die Lehre des Dw3-Ḫtjj*. Wiesbaden: Harrassowitz.

Helck, Wolfgang. 1989. "Ein Ausgreifen des Mittleren Reiches in den Zypriotischen Raum?" *Göttinger Miszellen* 109: 27–30.

Hofmann, Tobias. 2002. "Die Autobiographie des Uni von Abydos." *Lingua Aegyptia* 10: 225–237.

Iversen, Eric. 1984. "The Inscription of Herwerrēʿ at Serâbit-al-Kādim." In *Studien zu Sprache und Religion Ägyptens zu Ehren von Wolfhart Westendorf überreicht von seinen Freunden und Schülern* vol. 1: *Sprache*, 507–519. Göttingen: F. Junge.

Jones, Dilwyn. 2000. *An Index of Ancient Egyptian Titles, Epithets and Phrases of the Old Kingdom*, 2 vols. British Archaeology Reports 866. Oxford: Archaeopress.

Kahl, Jochem. 1998. "Es ist vom Anfang bis zum Ende so gekommen, wie es in der Schrift gefunden worden war. Zur Überlieferung der Erzählung des Sinuhe." In Manfred Dietrich and Ingo Kottsieper (eds.), *"Und Mose schrieb dieses Lied auf". Studien zum Alten Testament und zum Alten Orient. Festschrift für Oswald Loretz zur Vollendung Seines 70. Lebensjahres mit Beiträgen von Freunden, Schülern und* Kollegen, 383–400. Münster: Ugarit-Verlag.

Kanawati, Naguib. 2003. *Conspiracies in the Egyptian Palace. Unis to Pepy I*. London–New York: Routledge.

Kanawati, Naguib and Linda Evans. 2016. *Beni Hassan* vol. 3: *The Tomb of Amenemhat*. Oxford: Aris & Phillips.

Kitchen, Kenneth A. 1967. "Byblos, Egypt, and Mari in the Early Second Millennium B.C." *Orientalia* 36: 39–54.

Kloth, Nicole. 2002. *Die (auto-)biographischen Inschriften des ägyptischen Alten Reiches: Untersuchung zur Phraseologie und Entwicklung*. Studien zur Altägyptischen Kultur Beihefte 8. Hamburg: Buske.

Knoblauch, Christian. 2010. "Preliminary Report on the Early Bronze Age III Pottery from Contexts of the 6th Dynasty in the Abydos Middle Cemetery." *Ägypten und Levante* 20: 243–261.

Koch, Roland. 1990. *Die Erzählung des Sinuhe*. Bibliotheca Aegyptiaca 17. Brussels: Éditions de la Fondation égyptologique Reine Elisabeth.

Kopetzky, Karin. 2018. "Tell el-Dabʿa and Byblos: New Chronological Evidence." *Ägypten und Levante* 28: 309–358.

Kopetzky, Karin and Manfred, Bietak. 2016. "A Seal Impression of the Green Jasper Workshop from Tell el-Dabʿa." *Ägypten und Levante* 26: 357–375.

Köpp, Heidi. 2008a. "Reisen in prädynastischer Zeit und Frühzeit." In Eva-Maria Engel, Vera Müller, and Ulrich Hartung (eds.), *Zeichen aus dem Sand. Streiflichter aus Ägyptens Geschichte zu Ehren von Günter Dreyer*, 401–412. Wiesbaden: Harrassowitz Verlag.

———. 2008b. "Weibliche Mobilität: Frauen in Sänften und auf Streitwagen." In Carsten Peust (ed.), *Miscellanea in Honorem Wolfhart Westendorf*, 34–44. Göttingen: Seminar für Ägyptologie und Koptologie der Universität.

Köpp-Junk, Heidi. 2013. "Travel." In Elizabeth Frood and Willeke Wendrich (eds.), *UCLA Encyclopedia of Egyptology*. Los Angeles. https://escholarship.org/uc/item/3945t7f7.

———. 2015. *Reisen im Alten Ägypten. Reisekultur, Fortbewegungs- und Transportmittel in pharaonischer Zeit*. Wiesbaden: Harrassowitz Verlag.

———. 2016. "Pharaonic Prelude – Being on the Move in Ancient Egypt from Predynastic Times to the End of the New Kingdom." *Journal of Ancient Egyptian Interconnections* 12: 21–40.

Kristiansen, Kristian. 2018. "Theorizing Trade and Civilization." In Kristian Kristiansen, Thomas Lindkvist, and Janken Myrdal (eds.), *Trade and Civilisation. Economic Networks and Cultural Ties, from Prehistory to the Early Modern Era*, 1–24. Cambridge: Cambridge University Press.

Kristiansen, Kristian and Thomas B. Larsson. 2005. *The Rise of Bronze Age Society. Travels, Transmissions and Transformations*. Cambridge: Cambridge University Press.

Kurth, Dieter. 1996. "Der Erfolg des Harurrê in Serabit el-Chadim." *Göttinger Miszellen* 154: 57–64.

Landgrãfová, Renata. 2011. *It is My Good Name that You Should Remember. Egyptian Biographical Texts on Middle Kingdom Stelae*. Prague: Faculty of Arts, Charles University in Prague.

Lichtheim, Miriam. 1973. *Ancient Egyptian Literature. A Book of Readings* vol. 1: *The Old and Middle Kingdoms*. Berkeley–Los Angeles–London: University of California Press.

———. 1988. *Ancient Egyptian Autobiographies Chiefly of the Middle Kingdom: A Study and an Anthology*. Orbis Biblicus et Orientalis 84. Göttingen: Vandenhoeck & Ruprecht.

Loprieno, Antonio (ed.). 1996a. *Ancient Egyptian Literature: History and Forms*. Probleme der Ägyptologie 10. Leiden–New York–Köln: Brill.

———. 1996b. "Defining Egyptian Literature: Ancient Texts and Modern Theories." In Antonio Loprieno (ed.), *Ancient Egyptian Literature: History and Forms*, 39–58. Probleme der Ägyptologie 10. Leiden–New York–Köln: Brill.

———. 2003. "Travel and Fiction in Egyptian Literature." In David O'Connor and Stephen Quirke (eds.), *Mysterious Lands. Encounters with Ancient Egypt*. 31–51. London: UCL Press, Institute of Archaeology.

Marcolin, Michele and Andrés Diego Espinel. 2011. "The Sixth Dynasty Biographic Inscriptions of Iny: More Pieces to the Puzzle." In Miroslav Bárta, Filip Coppens, and Jaromír Krejãí (eds.), *Abusir and Saqqara in the Year 2010/1*, 570–615. Prague: Czech Institute of Egyptology, Faculty of Arts, Charles University in Prague.

Marcus, Ezra S. 2007. "Amenemhet II and the Sea: Maritime Aspects of the Mit Rahina (Memphis) Inscription." *Ägypten und Levante* 17: 137–190.

Miniaci, Gianluca. 2020. *The Middle Kingdom Ramesseum Papyri Tomb and its Archaeological Context*. Kitab; Egyptology in Focus; Material Culture of Ancient Egypt and Nubia 1. Westoning: Nicanor Books.

Moers, Gerald (ed.). 1999a. *Definitely, Egyptian Literature. Proceedings of the Symposium "Ancient Egyptian Literature: History and Forms"*. Lingua Aegyptia Studia Monographica 2. Göttingen: Hubert & Co.

Moers, Gerald. 1999b. "Travel as Narrative in Egyptian Literature." In Gerald Moers (ed.), *Definitely, Egyptian Literature. Proceedings of the Symposium "Ancient Egyptian Literature: History and Forms"*, 43–61. Lingua Aegyptia Studia Monographica 2. Göttingen: Hubert & Co.

———. 2001. *Fingierte Welten in der ägyptischen Literatur des 2. Jahrtausends v. Chr.: Grenzüberschreitung, Reisemotiv und Fiktionalität*. Probleme der Ägyptologie 19. Leiden: Brill.

Montet, Pierre. 1928. *Byblos et l'Égypte*. Bibliothèque archéologique et historique 11. Paris: Libraire Orientaliste Paul Geuthner.

Morales, Antonio J., Sebastian Falk, Mohamed Osman, Raùl Sánchez Casado, Hazem Shared et al. 2016. "The Middle Kingdom Theban Project: Preliminary Report on the Freie Universität Mission to Deir el-Bahari, First and Second Seasons (2015-2016)." *Studien zur Altägyptischen Kultur* 45: 257–282.

Morales, Antonio J., Rawda Abd el-Hady, Kelly Accetta, Sergio Alarcón, Teresa Bardaji et al. 2017. "The Middle Kingdom Theban Project: Preliminary Report on the University of Alcalá Expedition to Deir el-Bahari, Third Season (2017)." *Studien zur Altägyptischen Kultur* 46: 153–190.

Morales, Antonio J., Rawda Abd el-Hady, Kelly Accetta, Marta Arranz, Teresa Bardaji et al. 2018. "The Middle Kingdom Theban Project: Preliminary Report on the University of Alcalá Expedition to Deir el-Bahari, Fourth Season (2018)." *Studien zur Altägyptischen Kultur* 47: 183–221.

Moreno García, Juan Carlos. 2020. "The Social Context of Biographies (Old and Middle Kingdom)." In Julie Stauder-Porchet, Elizabeth Frood, and Andréas Stauder (eds.), *Ancient Egyptian Biographies. Contexts, Forms, Function*, 251–268. Atlanta: Lockwood Press.

Morenz, Ludwig D. 1996. *Beiträge zur ägyptischen Schriftlichkeitskultur des Mittleren Reiches und der Zweiten Zwischenzeit*. Ägypten und Altes Testament 29. Wiesbaden: Harrassowitz Verlag.

———. 2013. "Egyptian Life, by and with Literary Texts." In Roland Enmarch and Verena M. Lepper (eds.), *Ancient Egyptian Literature: Theory and Practice*, 227–250. Proceedings of the British Academy 188. Oxford: Oxford University Press.

Morschauser, Scott. 2000. "What Made Sinuhe Run: Sinuhe's Reasoned Flight." *Journal of the American Research Center in Egypt* 37: 187–198.

Mourad, Anna-Latifa. 2013. "Remarks on Sinuhe's Qedem and Yaa." *Göttinger Miszellen* 238: 69–84.

———. 2015. *Rise of the Hyksos. Egypt and the Levant from the Middle Kingdom to the Early Second Intermediate Period*. Archaeopress Egyptology 11. Oxford: Archaeopress.

———. 2017. "The Asiatic *St.t* and the *St.tyw* from the Early Dynastic Period to the Middle Kingdom." In Camilla Di Biase-Dyson and Leonie Donovan (eds.), *The Cultural Manifestations of Religious Experience. Studies in Honour of Boyo G. Ockinga*, 297–310. Ägypten und Altes Testament 85. Münster: Ugarit Verlag.

———. 2020. "Foreigners at Beni Hassan: Evidence from the Tomb of Khnumhotep I (No. 14)." *Bulletin of the American Schools of Oriental Research* 384: 105–132.

———. Forthcoming. "Foreigners meeting Foreigners: Sustaining Cross-Border Social Relations in the Middle Kingdom."

Müller, Christel. 2016. "Globalization, Transnationalism, and the Local in Ancient Greece." Oxford Handbooks Online. https://doi.org/10.1093/oxfordhb/9780199935390.013.42.

Obsomer, Claude. 1995. *Sésostris Ier. Étude chronologique et historique du Règne*. Connaissance de l'Egypte Ancienne 5. Brussels: Safran.

———. 1999. "Sinouhé l'Égyptien et les raisons de son exil." *Le Muséon* 112: 207–271.

Pantalacci, Laure. 1996. "Un été à Sérabit el-Khadim (encore sur l'inscription de Horrourê, Sinaï n°90)." *Göttinger Miszellen* 150: 87–91.

Parkinson, Richard B. 1996. "Individual and Society in Middle Kingdom Literature." In Antonio Loprieno (ed.), *Ancient Egyptian Literature: History and Forms*, 137–155. Probleme der Ägyptologie 10. Leiden–New York–Köln: Brill.

———. 1997. *The Tale of Sinuhe and Other Ancient Egyptian Poems, 1940–1640 BC*. Oxford–New York: Clarendon Press.

———. 1999. "The Dream and the Knot. Contextualizing Middle Kingdom Literature." In Gerald Moers (ed.), *Definitely, Egyptian Literature. Proceedings of the Symposium "Ancient Egyptian Literature: History and Forms"*, 63–82. Lingua Aegyptia Studia Monographica 2. Göttingen: Hubert & Co.

———. 2002. *Poetry and Culture in Middle Kingdom Egypt. A Dark Side of Perfection*. London: Equinox.

———. 2009. *Reading Ancient Egyptian Poetry Among Other Histories*. Malden–Oxford–Chichester: Wiley-Blackwell.

Peet, Thomas Eric. 1914. *The Stela of Sebek-Khu. The Earliest Record of an Egyptian Campaign in Asia*. Manchester: Sherratt & Hughes.

Pérez-Accino, José-Ramón. 2011. "Text as Territory: Mapping Sinuhe's Shifting Loyalties." In Fredrik Hagen, John Johnston, Wendy Monkhouse, Kathryn Piquette, John Tait, and Martin Worthington (eds.), *Narratives of Egypt and the Ancient Near East. Literary and Linguistic*

Approaches, 177–194. Orientalia Lovaniensia Analecta 189. Leuven–Paris–Walpole: Peeters.

Pratt, Catherine E. 2009. "Minor Transnationalism in the Prehistoric Aegean? The Case of Phoenicians on Crete in the Early Iron Age." *Diaspora* 18 (3): 305–335.

Purdy, Struther. 1977. "Sinuhe and the Question of Literary Types." *Zeitschrift für Ägyptische Sprache und Altertumskunde* 104: 112–127.

Quibell, James. 1898. *The Ramesseum*. Egyptian Research Account 1896. London: Bernard Quaritch.

Quirke, Stephen. 1996. "Narrative Literature." In Antonio Loprieno (ed.), *Ancient Egyptian Literature: History and Forms*, 263–276. Probleme der Ägyptologie 10. Leiden–New York–Köln: Brill.

Rainey, Anson F. 1972. "The World of Sinuhe." *Israel Oriental Studies* 2: 369–408.

———. 1994. "Review: Remarks on Donald Redford's "Egypt, Canaan, and Israel in Ancient Times"." *Bulletin of the American Schools of Oriental Research* 294: 81–85.

Redford, Donald B. 1986. "Egypt and Western Asia in the Old Kingdom." *Journal of the American Research Center in Egypt* 23: 125–143.

———. 1992. *Egypt, Canaan, and Israel in Ancient Times*. Princeton: Princeton University Press.

Richards, Janet. 2002. "Text and Context in Late Old Kingdom Egypt: The Archaeology and Historiography of Weni the Elder." *Journal of the American Research Center in Egypt* 39: 75–102.

———. 2005. *Society and Death in Ancient Egypt. Mortuary Landscapes of the Middle Kingdom*. Cambridge: Cambridge University Press.

Ritner, Robert Kriech. 1993. *The Mechanics of Ancient Egyptian Magical Practice*. Studies in Ancient Oriental Civilization 34. Chicago: The University of Chicago.

Roth, Ann Macy. 1995. *A Cemetery of Palace Attendants including G 2084–2099, G 2230+2231, and G 2240*. Giza Mastabas 6. Museum of Fine Arts: Boston.

Scharff, Alexander. 1936. *Der historische Abschnitt der Lehre für König Merikarê*. Munich: Verlag der Bayerischen Akademie der Wissenschaften in Kommission bei der C.H. Beck'schen Verlagsbuchhandlung.

Schenkel, Wolfgang. 1965. *Memphis - Herakleopolis - Theben: Die epigraphischen Zeugnisse der 7-11. Dynastie Ägyptens*. Ägyptologische Abhandlungen 12. Wiesbaden: Otto Harrassowitz.

Schneider, Thomas. 2002. "Sinuhes Notiz über die Könige: Syrisch-anatolische Herrschertitel in ägyptischer Überlieferung." *Ägypten und Levante* 12: 257–272.

Seibert, Peter. 1977. *Die Charakteristik: Untersuchungen zu einer altägyptischen Sprechsitte und ihren Ausprägungen in Folklore und Literature* vol. 1: *Philologische Bearbeitung der Bezeugungen*. Ägyptologische Abhandlungen 17. Wiesbaden: Harrassowitz Verlag.

Sethe, Kurt 1903–1988. *Urkunden des Ägyptischen Altertums. Abteilung I–VIII*. Leipzig—Berlin: Hinrichs, 1903–1988.

Seyfried, Karl-Joachim. 1981. *Beiträge zu den Expeditionen des Mittleren Reiches in die Ost-Wüste*. Hildesheimer Ägyptologische Beiträge 15. Hildesheim: Gerstenberg Verlag.

Smith, William Stevenson. 1969. "Influence of the Middle Kingdom of Egypt in Western Asia, especially in Byblos." *American Journal of Archaeology* 73 (3): 277–281.

Sowada, Karin. 2009. *Egypt in the Eastern Mediterranean during the Old Kingdom: An Archaeological Perspective*. Orbus Biblicus et Orientalis 237. Fribourg–Göttingen: Academic Press Fribourg–Vandenhoeck & Ruprecht.

Spalinger, Anthony. 1998. "Orientations on Sinuhe." *Studien zur Altägyptischen Kultur* 25: 311–339.

Stauder, Andréas. 2014. "Linguist Dissonance in *Sinuhe*." In Harold M. Hays, Frank Feder, and Ludwig D. Morenz (eds.), *Interpretations of Sinuhe. Inspired by Two Passages. Proceedings of a Workshop held at Leiden University, 27–29 November 2009*, 173–188. Leiden–Leuven: Nederlands Institut voor het Nabije Oosten–Peeters.

Stauder-Porchet, Julie. 2017. *Les autobiographies de l'Ancien Empire égyptien: étude sur la naissance d'un genre*. Orientalia Lovaniensia Analecta 255. Leuven: Peeters.

———. 2020a. "Genres and Textual Prehistories of the Egyptian Autobiography in the Old Kingdom." In Julie Stauder-Porchet, Elizabeth Frood, and Andréas Stauder (eds.), *Ancient Egyptian Biographies. Contexts, Forms, Function*, 87–116. Atlanta: Lockwood Press.

———. 2020b. "Harkhuf's Autobiographical Inscriptions. A Study in Old Kingdom Monumental Rhetoric. Part I. Texts, Genres, Forms." *Zeitschrift für Ägyptische Sprache und Altertumskunde* 147 (1): 57–91.

———. 2020c. "Harkhuf's Autobiographical Inscriptions. A Study in Old Kingdom Monumental Rhetoric. Part II. The Inscribed Facade." *Zeitschrift für Ägyptische Sprache und Altertumskunde* 147 (2): 197–222.

Stauder-Porchet, Julie, Elizabeth Frood, and Andréas Stauder (eds.). 2020. *Ancient Egyptian Biographies. Contexts, Forms, Function.* Atlanta: Lockwood Press

Strudwick, Nigel. 2005. *Texts from the Pyramid Age.* Leiden–Boston: Brill.

Tallet, Pierre. 2018. *La zone minière pharaonique du Sud-Sinaï* vol. 3: *Les expéditions égyptiennes dans la zone minière du Sud-Sinaï du prédynastique à la fin de la XXe dynastie.* Mémoires publiés par les membres de l'institut français d'archéologie orientale du Caire 138. Cairo: Institut français d'archéologie orientale.

Tufnell, Olga and William A. Ward. 1966. "Relations between Byblos, Egypt and Mesopotamia at the End of the Third Millennium B.C.: A Study of the Montet Jar." *Syria* 43: 165–241.

Vernus, Pascal. 2020. "Autobiography versus Biography in the Second Person and Biography in the Third Person: Textual Formats, Authorship, and Apocryphal/Pseudoepigraphic Works." In Julie Stauder-Porchet, Elizabeth Frood, and Andréas Stauder (eds.), *Ancient Egyptian Biographies. Contexts, Forms, Function*, 225–247. Atlanta: Lockwood Press.

Vertovec, Steven. 2009. *Transnationalism.* London–New York: Routledge.

Vinson, Steve. 2004. "The Accent's on Evil: Ancient Egyptian "Melodrama" and the Problem of Genre." *Journal of the American Research Center in Egypt* 41: 33–54.

Ward, William A. 1971. *Egypt and the East Mediterranean World 2200–1900 B.C.: Studies in Egyptian Foreign Relations during the First Intermediate Period.* Beirut: American University of Beirut.

———. 1982. *Index of Egyptian Administrative and Religious Titles of the Middle Kingdom.* Beirut: American University of Beirut.

Winand, Jean. 2014. "The Tale of Sinuhe. History of a Literary Text." In Harold M. Hays, Frank Feder, and Ludwig D. Morenz (eds.), *Interpretations of Sinuhe. Inspired by Two Passages. Proceedings of a Workshop held at Leiden University, 27–29 November 2009,* 215–243. Leiden–Leuven: Nederlands Institut voor het Nabije Oosten–Peeters.

Zamacona, Carlos Gracia. 2019. "Imagining Henenu." *Near Eastern Archaeology* 82 (2): 75–81.

Notes

1 For more on travel in ancient Egypt, see Baines 2004; 2007; Köpp 2008a; 2008b; Köpp-Junk 2013; 2015; Berg 2014.

2 Eriksen 2007, 172; Clavin 2005, 422; Vertovec 2009, 2.

3 For those of the Middle Kingdom, see Mourad, forthcoming.

4 See Faist 2004; Vertovec 2009; Pratt 2009, 311–312, 314.

5 For the Tale and its translation, see Koch 1990; Parkinson 1997, 21–53. For more on *St.t* and the *St.tyw*, see Mourad 2017.

6 For suggested interpretations of this Semitic-sounding name, see Rainey 1972, 373; Lichtheim 1973, 234, n. 4; Mourad 2013, 71.

7 Baines 1982, 32; Parkinson 1997, 26; 2002, 296–297. For more on the transmission of the text, see Winand 2014.

8 Burkard and Fischer-Elfert 1994, 110–111 [Nr. 167]; Obsomer 1999, 208.

9 The papyrus also comprises A Man and his Ba, and The Eloquent Peasant. Parkinson 2002, 72.

10 For an overview of proposed findspots, see Parkinson 2002, 72.

11 Other texts include the Dramatic Papyrus, the Onomasticon, expedition accounts regarding Nubian fortresses, and other teachings and maxims. See Quibell 1898, 3; Gardiner 1947, 6; Ritner 1993, 222–232; Morenz 1996, 144–147; Parkinson 2002, 71–72; Miniaci 2020.

12 Quibell 1898, 3; Miniaci 2020.

13 The definition of 'genre' in assessments of Egyptian texts is not without issue. It is approached here as a variable category of texts classified according to similarities in content as well as formal aspects. Parkinson 2002, 32–36; Vinson 2004; Di Biase-Dyson 2013, 50–54.

14 Loprieno 1996b, 51–52; Moers 2001, 106–154; Parkinson 2002, 60–63; Stauder 2014.

15 For more on ancient Egyptian biographies, see Lichtheim 1988; Gnirs 1996; Baines 1999a; Kloth 2002; Stauder-Porchet 2017; Stauder-Porchet, Frood and Stauder 2020.

16 Stauder-Porchet 2020a.

17 Baines (1982, 38) refers to the praise to Sahura in the biography of Niankhsekhmet (*Urk.* I, 39–40) and letters from kings in the biographies

of Rashepses (Djedkara-Isesi; *Urk.* I, 179–180) and Harkhuf (Pepy II; *Urk.* I, 128–131). See also Baines 1999b, 29–31; Stauder-Porchet 2020a, 108.

18 Examples may be found in the biography of Kaiemtjennet at Saqqara of Djedkara-Isesi's reign (*Urk.* I, 180–186) or the stela of Djari of Intef II's reign (Clère and Vandier 1948, 14 [§18]). See also Stauder-Porchet 2020a, 108.

19 Baines 1999b, 30–31.

20 Parkinson (2002, 91–98) considers recurrent thematic elements of decorum that permeated time, contexts, and genres, such as matters of the heart, vices, and death; all could be subverted or questioned in Middle Kingdom literary texts. For more on cliches in biographies, see Coulon 2020. See also Lichtheim 1988, 6–7.

21 Examples may be found in the Old Kingdom biographies of Harkhuf (line 5; *Urk.* I, 122), Pepynakht-Heqaib (line 2; *Urk.* I, 133), or Idu Seneni (lines 4–5; Kloth 2002, 9 [Nr. 16]). In the First Intermediate Period, the expression "bread to the hungry and clothes to the naked" is, for instance, attested on the false door of Neferyu (line C.1–2; Fischer 1968, 206, pl. 25) or the stela of Seneni (line B.1; Fischer 1968, 209, fig. 43, pl. 26). See also Coulon 2020.

22 This can perhaps be compared with the conduct recorded by Egyptian officials in, for instance, the First Intermediate Period stela of Seneni ("I ferried across the stranded man in my boat. [I did not say?] "go away" to one who came to me, and conducted the traveller," lines B.2–4; Fischer 1968, 209, fig. 43, pl. 26; Lichtheim 1988, 34), or the biography of Beni Hassan's Amenemhat ("the (one) who offers a welcome to everyone travelling downstream or upstream," south jamb, line 2; Kanawati and Evans 2016, 25, pls. 3, 82b).

23 Strudwick 2005, 149; Stauder-Porchet 2017, 15–16, n. 34; Vernus 2020, 172; Coulon 2020, 208.

24 Inscription Nr. 90. Gardiner and Peet 1952, pls. 25A, 26; Pantalacci 1996.

25 For more on approaches to literature, fictionality and narrativity in ancient Egypt, see Loprieno 1996a; 2003; Moers 1999a; 2001; Parkinson 2002.

26 Purdy 1977; Baines 1982, 34; Moers 1999b, 50; Parkinson 1999, 72–74, 76–79.

27 Baines 1982, 33; Loprieno 2003; Galán 2005, 15; Köpp-Junk 2013. See also Blumenthal 1984.

28 Moers 1999b; 2001.

29 See below, n. 93.

30 See Helck 1989; Redford 1992, 79, n. 47; Eder 1995, 191; Marcus 2007, 143–145; Mourad 2015, 78–79; Altenmüller 2015.

31 For the Abydos inscription, see *Urk.* I, 98–110; Richards 2002; Hofmann 2002. For that at Saqqara, see Collombert 2015.

32 Richards 2002, 82.

33 The term *aAm.w* is usually translated as "Asiatic." It more broadly refers to individuals from several regions north(east) of Egypt during the Old and Middle Kingdoms (Mourad 2015, 194–196). Suggestions for its derivation include the Semitic *ʿm/glm* "people" or the Egyptian *ʿmʿꜣ* "throwstick." On the other hand, *Ḥr.yw-šʿ* can be literally translated to "those who are on / across the sand". Combined, the terms possibly identify individuals encountered in or across the desert regions north(east) of Egypt. For further discussion, see Rainey 1994, 81–82; Redford 1986, 127, n. 19; Espinel 2006, 123–126; 145; Gundacker 2017, 349–352.

34 The title *ḫn.tyw-š* is typically translated as "land-tenant" or "tenant landholder" (Jones 2000, 189 [710]). Roth (1995, 1) favors "palace attendant," which aligns well with the activities attested for officials bearing this title. The translation favored here follows Kanawati (2003, 14–24).

35 For a thorough discussion of the toponyms in the biography, see, with references, Gundacker 2017.

36 For suggestions that the "Northern Island" is likely in the Delta, see Goedicke 1957, 81; Gundacker 2017, 355.

37 For the suggestion that the "Gate of Imhotep" may be located near the Isthmus of Suez, see Gundacker 2017, 355.

38 For suggestions that the "District of Horus Lord of Truth" may be at or near the Eastern Delta or in the north of the Sinai Peninsula, see, with references, Gundacker 2017, 355; Cooper 2020, 141–142 [Nr. 16].

39 For suggestions on the location of the "Nose of Gazelle's Head" in the Sinai Peninsula or the southern Levant, see, with references, Gundacker 2017, 355–361; Cooper 2020, 249–254 [Nr. 68.1].

40 Jones 2000, 246 [896].

41 For examples of activities conducted by holders of the title *ḫn.tyw-š*, and royal favors bestowed

to them in the Old Kingdom, see Kanawati 2003: 15–24.

42 Richards 2002, 93, fig. 15.

43 See Eyre 1994; Knoblauch 2010.

44 Jones 2000, 736–737 [2682].

45 Espinel 2004, 15–18; Edel, Seyfried and Vieler 2007, 467.

46 Baines 2013, 251–252; 2020, 55.

47 Marcolin and Espinel 2011.

48 Marcolin and Espinel 2011, 589.

49 Jones 2000, 767 [2791], 781 [2848], 892 [3268]. For the reading *sḏꜣ.wty* instead of *ḫtm.ty*, see Ward 1982, 169 [1468].

50 *Urk.* I, 131–135; Kloth 2002, 13–14 [Nr. 25].

51 Jones 2000, 306 [Nr. 1116].

52 Jones 2000, 1009 [Nr. 3739]. For more on these epithets in the Old Kingdom, see Espinel 2015–2016.

53 Hayes 1949; Morales et al. 2016, 280–282; 2017, 155–165; 2018, 184–194; Zamacona 2019.

54 See Ward 1982, 22 [Nr. 140]; Allen 1996, 11.

55 Hayes 1949.

56 JE 45058. Gardiner 1917, 33–35; Schenkel 1965, 283–284 [Nr. 477]; Landgrãfová 2011, 57–58 [Nr. 18].

57 Ward 1982, 171 [Nr. 1480].

58 For more on this term, see Cooper 2020, 222–225 [Nr. 55].

59 For more on this toponym, see Cooper 2020, 254–256 [Nr. 69].

60 See Cooper 2020, 153–155 [Nr. 21.4], 199–202 [Nr. 44.1], 213–215 [Nr. 51.1], 222–225 [Nr. 55.1], 229–230 [Nr. 57.1], 231–234 [Nr. 59.1], 234–235 [Nr. 60.1], 236–237 [Nr. 61.1], 237 [Nr. 62.1], 240–242 [Nr. 64.9], 254–256 [Nr. 69.1]. 261–265 [Nr. 73.1].

61 Altenmüller and Moussa 1991; Altenmüller 2015. See also Marcus 2007.

62 Manchester 3306. Garstang 1901; Peet 1914; Baines 1987; Goedicke 1998; Landgrãfová 2011, 211–213 [Nr. 63]; Mourad 2015, 100–101, 281, fig. B.2.

63 Allen 2008.

64 Ward 1982, 102 [Nr. 850], 104–105 [Nr. 864], 170 [Nr. 1472].

65 Allen 2008, 32, pl. 1.

66 See also Baines 1999b, 30; Eyre 2013, 131–132; Vernus 2020, 189.

67 Allen 2008, 35–36.

68 See Mourad 2020; forthcoming.

69 Ward 1982, 59 [477].

70 Inscription Nr. 25. Gardiner and Peet 1952, pl. 10; Černý 1955, 68.

71 Ward 1982, 16 [80].

72 Inscription Nr. 54. Gardiner and Peet 1952, pl. 18; Černý 1955, 80.

73 Ward 1982, 14–15 [72], 136 [1173], 171 [Nr. 1480].

74 Inscription Nr. 90. Blackman 1930; Gardiner and Peet 1952, pls. 25A, 26; Černý 1955, 97–99; Goedicke 1962; Iversen 1984; Pantalacci 1996; Kurth 1996.

75 Goedicke (1962, 21 [u]) argues that the destination to which the expedition's safe arrival (*iyi*) alludes is Serabit el-Khadim rather than the Nile Valley.

76 Inscriptions Nrs. 112 and 405. Černý 1955, 114, 205.

77 For more on Sinuhe's flight, see Purdy 1977; Goedicke 1984; Spalinger 1998, 312; Obsomer 1999; Moers 1999b, 53–54; 2001, 252–255; Morschauser 2000; Parkinson 2002, 151–156.

78 Moers 1999b, 53–54; 2001, 252–253.

79 For explorations of the route, see Goedicke 1957; Bunbury and Jeffreys 2011, 69–71.

80 Helck 1970.

81 Although some translate *ꜣhw m mw* as "lacking in water" (Lichtheim 1973, 108, n. 14; Parkinson 1997, 223), the translation here follows Gardiner (1914, 30) and Ward (1971, 29), with *ꜣhw* instead referring to "misery, trouble, injury, or pain".

82 Golénischeff 1913, pls. 11–12. The dating of the text is uncertain. Some ascribe it to the First Intermediate Period (Scharff 1936, 53; Ward 1971, 22; Lichtheim 1973, 97), some to the Eleventh Dynasty (Burkard 1977, 6) and others to the Twelfth Dynasty (Seibert 1967, 88).

83 See, for instance, Rainey 1972; Green 1983; Aḥituv 1984, 158; Goedicke 1992; Parkinson 1997, 44, n. 15; Schneider 2002; Mourad 2013.

84 Enmarch 2005, 27, 69.

85 See, for instance, Montet 1928; Kitchen 1967; Tufnell and Ward 1966; Smith 1969; Espinel 2002; Sowada 2009, 128–141; Flammini 2010; Mourad 2015, 165–171, 197, fig. 7.9; Colonna 2018; Kopetzky 2018; Ahrens 2020, 211–233.

86 See Mourad 2015, 199, fig. 7.9; Kopetzky and Bietak 2016, 371–372.

87 *Rṯnw* is mentioned in Inscription Nrs. 85, 87, 92, 114, 115 and 120. Gardiner and Peet 1952, pls. 23 [85], 24 [87], 27 [92], 36 [114], 38 [114], 39 [115], 43 [120]; Černý 1955, 92–94 [85], 95 [87], 100 [92], 116–118 [114], 118–119 [115]; 122–124

[120]; Seyfried 1981, 159–163 [9–10], 165 [13], 167 [16], 177–179 [31], 180–181 [35]; Bietak 2010, 147; Mourad 2015, 136–137; forthcoming; Tallet 2018, 38–42.

88 Moers 2001.

89 See, for instance, Loprieno 1988, 41–59, 83; Parkinson 2002, 157; Pérez-Accino 2011; el-Hawary 2014; Campagno 2015.

90 As identified in Bárta and Janák 2021, 107.

91 See Bárta 2003, 52; Galán 2005, 93–94; Bárta and Janák 2021, 112–114.

92 Biography of Harkhuf, left of the entrance, line 9. *Urk.* I, 127 [13–15]. See also Stauder-Porchet 2020b; 2020c.

93 For instance, the text of Khnumhotep and the biography of Weni, as discussed in this paper, or the First Intermediate Period stela of Fegu ("the overseer of priests, Weser, sent me on all kinds of missions, and I returned safely"; Lichtheim 1988, 35) and the biography of Amenemhat ("I returned following him (Senwosret I) as an alert one; no loss occurred in my army"; south thickness of entrance, lines 10–11; Kanawati and Evans 2016, 26, pls. 5, 84b). Other Middle Kingdom texts at Wadi Maghara, Serabit el-Khadim and Rod el-'Air attest to the desire to reach (*pḥ*) home safely (Inscriptions Nrs. 28, 36, 40, 48, 53, 115, 142, 401, 413, 510–511, 516; Gardiner and Peet 1952, pls. 12 [28], 13 [40], 14 [36], 16 [48], 17 [53], 39 [115], 53 [142], 83 [401], 88 [413], 94 [510–511], 95 [516]; Černý 1955, 69 [Nr. 28]; 72 [36], 73 [40], 77 [48], 79 [53], 119 [115], 142 [142], 204 [401], 209 [413], 219 [510–511], 220 [516]).

94 The east face of Inscription Nr. 112 at Serabit el-Khadim also mentions how an expedition leader's arrival was awaited in the palace, where he will be ushered in to see the king (Gardiner and Peet 1952, pl. 37; Černý 1955, 114). For more on the significance of attendance at court, see Baines 2020, 54–55.

95 Lines 10–15; *Urk.* I, 134–135. This is also mentioned in the biography of Sabni at Qubbet el-Hawa, who travelled to Wawat to return the body of his father for proper burial (lines 1–2; *Urk.* I, 135–136; Kloth 2002, 203–207 [Nr. 66]). For more on the return for burial in Egypt, see Köpp-Junk 2016, 27; Gundacker 2017, 346–347; Stauder-Porchet 2020b, 71.

96 For more on the reception of texts, see Parkinson 1996, 140–145; 1999, 64–66; Richards 2005, 19–31; Eyre 2013; Morenz 2013; Winand 2014.

97 Moers 1999b, 53. See also Campagno 2015.

98 Loprieno 2003, 32; Köpp-Junk 2013; Campagno 2015.

99 In reference to ancient Greek poleis, Müller (2016) recognises that "localism and the idea of the local are a byproduct of globalism, a reaction to connectivity".

100 Inscription Nr. 5. Darnell 1997; 2002, 99–101 [WHRI 5], 107–119 [WHRI 8]; Parkinson 2002, 73; 2009, 125–126. See also Moreno García 2020, 254–255, 263.

101 See Baines 2007, 19; Kristiansen 2018, 4.

102 Kristiansen 2018, 4. Kristiansen refers to examples from Greek mythology (Odysseus) and oral traditions (Pytheas). For more on this, see also Kristiansen and Larsson 2005, 32–61; Fox 2008.

Journal of Ancient Egyptian Interconnections

The Egyptian Enclaving of Southern Canaan during the Late Fourth Millennium BCE – Some Theoretical, Cultural, and Spatial Aspects

In memoriam of Prof. Ram Gophna

Yitzhak Paz
Israel Antiquities Authority

Abstract
Egyptian presence in the Southern Levant during the late fourth millennium BCE (Early Bronze Age IB, henceforward EB IB), centered in southwestern Israel, is an issue thoroughly studied for several decades. These studies covered every aspect of material culture, relative and absolute chronology, socio-political and economic implications, and more. Scholars characterized this Egyptian presence in different ways: from a military or colonial occupation focusing on the establishment of Egyptian enclaves within local settlements, to a minimal, purely commercial activity with almost no physical Egyptian presence. The current paper will attempt to outline theoretical, cultural, and spatial aspects of encounters between Egyptians and the local Canaanite population based on old and new data from sites like Tel Maaḥaz, Tel Lod, and Al-Maghar. The results of the study of various settlements between the Besor and Yarkon River basins where Egyptians physically resided may point toward a short-term foreign presence with variable influence on the local Canaanite population not always reflected in Canaanite material culture. At the same time, the 'enclaving' process led by Egyptian state institutions probably prompted hostility that may have resulted in resistance leading, in turn, to the demise of Egyptian enclaves.

Keywords
Egyptian colony; group agency; colonial encounters; resistance; Early Bronze Age

Introduction: Some Notes on the Theory of Migration, Colonies, and Colonial encounters

The current paper does not aim to cover all theoretical aspects of colonial phenomena but to outline some nodes in the relevant theoretical research that may have implications for our discussion on Egyptian presence in the southern Levant during the late fourth millennium BCE.

In his article dealing with the theory of migration, Anthony,[1] aware of the complications scholars face when defining and identifying immigrating groups in the archaeological record, created a model including various types of migrations. Aspects common to migrations are push and pull factors: a movement of individuals and groups in two directions (both into the new place and back to their homeland), a variety in the distance made by migrants to their new destiny, and the employment of scouts to detect the best places and opportunities in the new place, sometimes establishing the first bases for the migrant population. Push factors are represented by elements such as population pressure, violence, or the exhaustion of resources in the land of origin, while pull factors are the benefits that await in the new place.[2] Anthony also notes that migration movements may be characterized by 'leapfrogging,' reflected in the landscape as 'islands' separated from one another, or by 'migration streams' represented by continuous settlement patterns along main routes, water sources, and others.[3]

Numerous theoretical models analyzing migration and migrating groups focus on the bilateral agency between migrating groups (newcomers) and indigenous populations (hosts). Most interesting is a new model, posed by McSparron and others, describing four agency scales—low, medium, high, and very high. Very high and high group agency represent situations where the migrant group has a technological and quantitative advantage over the host community. In these situations, a migrant group with very high group agency would not need to differentiate between external and internal domains since their dominance across society would be complete. Indeed, it may well be the host community members who must begin to differentiate their lives into internal and external domains. Moreover, high group agency of migrating groups will possibly press a host community into accepting aspects of the culture and technology of the newcomers, although it may also cause the opposite reaction, that of resistance.[4] Medium and low group agency represent situations where newcomers are forced to respond to their new environment through adaptation and adjustment to their local host community. The model described above is most valid to our attempt to understand the agency Egyptian colonial entities had on Canaanite settlements and *vice versa*, based on our estimation of the scale of bilateral agency.

Focusing our lens on colonial aspects of migration, it seems that 'world system' and acculturation theories[5] that tend to adhere to unilinear models by which colonies established by the messengers of state societies are the only influential side, while host communities are passive, are no longer applicable.[6] Not for nothing has the new scholarly focal point shifted from the description of colonies and colonization to the archaeological manifestation, in material culture, of aspects such as symbolic power between regions[7] and, more generally, to the analysis of 'colonial encounters.'[8]

In his study, Stein—acknowledging the many types of settlements that can be referred to as 'colonies'—offers the following general definition of a colony and how it can be identified in the archaeological record: "A colony can be provisionally defined as an implanted settlement established by one society in either uninhabited territory or the territory of another society."[9] And then "in general, one can identify as colonies those settlements whose architecture, site plan, and material culture assemblage are identical to those of another region but are located as spatially discrete occupations surrounded by settlements of the local culture."[10] Going one step further, Stein tries to show how colonial encounters can be traced in the archaeological record through a close examination that should be conducted at household levels in settlements where a colonial existence is suspected. In her research about the Chinese enclave at Market Street, San Hoze, Voss describes several aspects of material culture that can shed light on the complex nature of these encounters. It turns out the Chinese population in Market Street preferred Asian-made pottery and Chinese culinary habits while adopting western ways reflected in butchery methods, thus showing no resistance to western culture.[11] Stein tried to define foreign population behavior, at the domestic level, as living together in a spatially contiguous area, separated from a host community, and employing practices that differ from local patterns in the host community while resembling the cultural practices of the homeland.[12] At the same time, a continuous interaction between newcomers and host populations in the same settlement can be seen in the emergence of new, creolized, or hybridized identities, artifactual styles, and forms of social organization.[13]

Some Scholarly Notions of Egyptian Presence in Southern Canaan in the Fourth millennium BCE

In an analysis of Egyptian presence in the land of Israel, Miroschedji, and Sadek[14] portray three main strategies reflected in settlement patterns and the spatial distribution of Egyptian material culture traits. Another suggestion for a hierarchy of Egyptian influence was made by van den Brink and Braun, who divided settlement sites into four 'tiers' according to the volume of Egyptian presence.[15]Sites with Egyptian or Egyptianized finds can be roughly divided, as proposed by Miroschedji, into three main categories:

1. Settlements that reflect direct domination and control by the Egyptian governing apparatus, which was concentrated in a 'hardcore' area

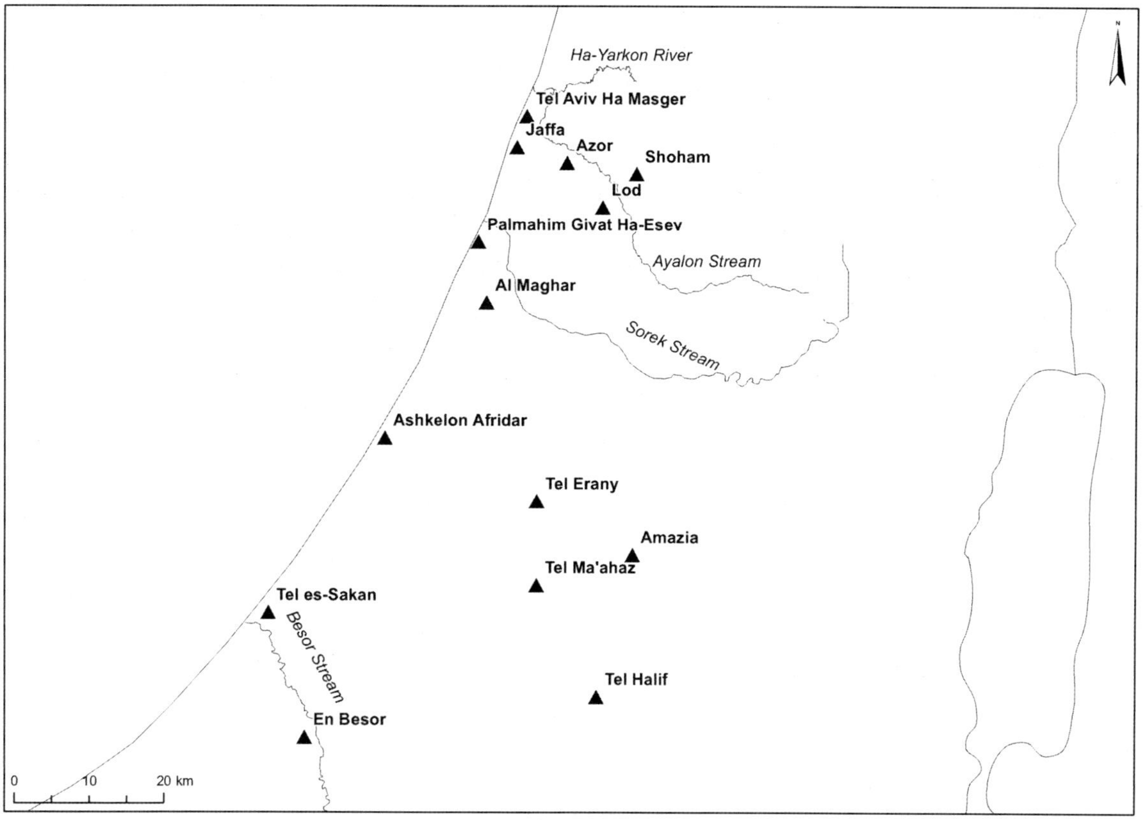

FIGURE 1: Sites mentioned in the text.

of the Besor stream basin and manifested in Egyptian outposts. In these settlements, Tel Sakan and 'En Besor, the vast majority of the material culture traits (architecture, pottery, administrative paraphernalia) are Egyptian.[16]

2. Settlements located between the Besor basin and the Yarkon River, where Egyptians physically resided within the local Canaanite population (e.g., Tel Lod, Al-Maghar). In these settlements, Egyptian pottery, especially kitchenware, flint artifacts, and in some cases royal *'serekhs,'* could identify the foreign enclave residents from host populations. Numerous sites that relate to this type have already been excavated and thoroughly studied.[17]

3. Settlements located north of the Yarkon River, where Egyptian (or Egyptianized) pottery and artifacts were found, reflecting trading relations rather than the physical presence of Egyptians (sites like 'En Esur and Tell Abu Al-Kharaz).[18]

It should be stressed that the current paper will only focus on the second settlement category (FIG. 1), where Egyptian 'enclaves' were found within the indigenous Canaanite population. Also, the discussion only relates to the latest EB IB horizon (EB IB2),[19] the period when Egyptian presence in the land of Israel reached its zenith, in the days of Dynasty 0, Naqada IIIb–c1. Thus, this paper will focus on selected sites where colonial encounters can be traced and plausibly characterized, such as Tel Maaḥaz, Al-Maghar, and Tel Lod.[20]

The controversy around the exact nature of Egyptian presence in southern Canaan is still going on and is clearly connected to the interpretation given by various scholars regarding Egyptian interests in the southern Levant. The current study does not aim to describe the full scholarly debate on this issue but focuses on potential evidence of the nature of colonial encounters between the local population and the Egyptian foreigners.

First, it is revealing to compare the spatial distribution of Egyptian outposts and sites where extensive Egyptian presence between the late fourth millennium BCE and the Late Bronze Age (henceforward LBA) was detected. Although it is a well-known difference between the two remote periods that the LBA was characterized by the full-fledged direct control of the Egyptian New Kingdom over the southern Levant (clearly not the situation in the fourth millennium BCE), it is still interesting that the headquarters of Egyptian presence were located at virtually the same location in both periods. These headquarters were situated adjacent to the outlet of the Besor stream (at Gaza of the LBA and Tell Sakan of the EB IB), a point that most probably monitored both land and maritime routes along the coastal plain from south to north.[21] The same can be said about other 19th-Dynasty bases sharing the same general location with late fourth-millennium Egyptian outposts: Tell el-Farah (S) and 'En Besor, Tel Shera' and Tel Maaḥaz.[22]

The archaeological record in the 'hardcore' area of Egyptian presence presents Egyptian-style masonry, kitchenware, culinary habits, and traces of an administrative system, as well as a military presence in Sinai.[23] Also, Yekutieli suggested that Egyptian locations were remote from the origins of natural resources and, therefore, had a political rather than an economic goal, aiming at the prosperous Canaanite settlements.[24] The Egyptian strategic plan was conducted, according to Yekutieli,[25] in two stages:

1. The first stage included plundering and the occupation of new territory. Miroschedji ascribed a 'colonial situation' to the exploitation of southern Canaanite resources by the bearers of the Naqada culture, dating it to the period ending around 3150 BCE (Naq. IIc–d to IIIa).[26]
2. The second stage was the creation of a colony that exploited Canaanite resources. This stage should probably be dated to the late EB IB (Naq. IIIb–c1).[27] During this stage, Egyptian presence in the land of Israel expanded northward toward the Yarkon River and reached a zenith defined by the three settlement categories described above.

Characterizing Egyptian–Canaanite Colonial Encounters in the Southern Levant

In order to try and characterize Canaanite-Egyptian interactions, it will be sufficient to outline the main possible scenarios for such interaction between host and newcomers' communities.

In their study on acculturation attitudes in plural societies, Berry and others define four divergent strategies by which newcomer groups engage host societies: assimilation, integration, separation, and marginalization. The first two strategies represent a successful social interaction between the groups, and they differ from one another by the extent to which original cultural traits of the new group (customs, clothing, culinary habits, and others) are maintained within the larger societal framework. Assimilation means that none of the original cultural traits are maintained, while integration points to the preservation of some original traits alongside the actions made by the group to become an integral part of a larger societal framework.[28]

When no positive interactions with the larger society are present, that is, when accompanied by the preservation of ethnic identity and traditions, another scenario is in place. Depending on which group (the dominant or non-dominant) controls the situation, this scenario may take the form of either segregation or separation, the model being imposed by the dominant group.

Classic segregation tends to keep people "in their place," with group maintenance of a traditional way of life outside full participation in the larger society deriving, perhaps, as in the case of a separatist society, from a group's desire to lead an independent existence.[29]

Egyptian presence within Canaanite settlements can be evaluated given the above-discussed issues, and the main questions to be asked should relate to the level of agency Egyptian residents had on the local population,[30] and which of the four strategies suggested by Berry and others can be valid for this colonial encounter. I will try to address these questions by examining the available information from selected sites located between the Besor stream and the Yarkon River (see Fig. 1).

The results of the limited excavations at Tel Maaḥaz may hint at a horizontal rather than vertical relation between Strata II and I at the site, both dated to the late EB IB. Moreover, these strata may actually represent two contemporaneous occupations within the same settlement: a five-dunam Canaanite occupation, and a smaller one dominated by Egyptian ceramics (with an incised *serekh* amongst these) concentrated at the center of the site.[31] The uniqueness of the Egyptian presence at Tel Maaḥaz rests upon its location – on the western edge of the Judean Shephelah, where a vast Canaanite population inhabited numerous settlements,[32] testifying, perhaps, to an Egyptian attempt to expand its influence in this direction. The limited data from Tel Maaḥaz hint at a short-lived Egyptian occupation that ceased to exist by the late EB IB, whereas the local Canaanite occupation continued well into the third millennium BCE.[33]

It seems that colonial encounters between Egyptians and Canaanites at Tel Maaḥaz lacked any 'positive' traits of assimilation or integration and can instead be classified as segregation. While we cannot establish which population dominated the situation, we can still see no signs of a creolized culture emerging during the late EB IB at the site. On the contrary, each community maintained its material culture and spatial location within the settlement.

Another site with an extensive Egyptian presence and where bilateral encounters can be examined is Tel Ḥalif Terrace (Naḥal Tillah). Here, quite a different picture emerges compared to Tel Maaḥaz. The excavated areas reflect a similar distribution of Egyptian and local pottery (found on the same floors), and it seems there was no distinct or separated Egyptian quarter at the site. These finds may reflect a high degree of integration between both communities, where each group kept its material culture and habits and did not assimilate into one another or create a 'creolized' culture. The finds may also represent a reality where social-cultural boundaries between the groups were fluid and flexible.[34]

The EB IB settlement of Amaziah, located c. 15 km north of Tel Ḥalif, encompassed an extensive storage facility comprising at least eleven silos, their capacity clearly exceeding the village's need. The silos, probably reflecting a centralized administrative-economic system, were dated by local and Egyptian pottery to the EB IB.[35] The Egyptian vessels found at the site included storage jars, cylindrical vessels, and bread molds. These molds were not considered by the excavators as evidence for the physical existence of Egyptians at the site but rather as vessels used by the local population to bake bread for Egyptian customers.[36] However, I believe that an alternative suggestion seems preferable, based upon the possible relation of Amaziah to Tel 'Erani, located northwest, where a significant Egyptian population resided in the last centuries of the fourth millennium BCE, after the demise (or destruction) of the early EB IB fortified city.[37] Thus, it can be suggested that the Egyptian colony situated at Tel 'Erani was one of the customers (but not necessarily the only one) for grains and other commodities stored at Amaziah. Consequently, a group of Egyptians (soldiers?) would have been stationed at Amaziah to obtain and secure the flow of these commodities. Furthermore, it can even be suggested that the silos were reused as an Egyptian initiative to supply Egyptian residents in southwestern Canaan. In this sense, the Egyptians exploited the fertile lands of the Shephelah, where Amaziah is located, and it can be speculated that the commodities stored in the silos were used by both the local Canaanite population and the Egyptian foreigners. Furthermore, the Egyptian colonial apparatus may have taxed and even implemented corvee work on the local population.

The site of Al-Maghar is located on the easternmost Kurkar ridge parallel to the coastal plain of Israel, close to the western flank of the Soreq stream. Al-Maghar was thoroughly surveyed (but not excavated), and it seems to have been an extensive settlement during the EB IB, its size estimated at c. 7 ha.[38] During the survey of the site, numerous Egyptian vessels were found, amongst them wine jars, cylindrical vessels, and many fragments of bread molds. Petrographic analysis conducted by M. Iserlis on three molds suggests that they originated in the vicinity of 'En Besor or Tell Sakan.[39] Thus, and as the site was located on the highway leading northward toward the Yarkon–Ayalon settlement cluster, it would appear that the Egyptian presence at Al-Maghar was much further 'state-oriented,' initiated and equipped by formal administrative outposts.[40] However, it is not possible to reconstruct the exact relationship between Egyptians and Canaanites within this settlement since the site was not excavated.

Located c. 10 km north of Al-Maghar, Palmahim Giv'at Ha-Esev, where an Egyptianized vessel was found, may reflect a small navigational landmark for sailors that may testify to Egyptian efforts to secure and maintain maritime activity during the EB IB.[41]

Tel Lod, one of the major sites in the eastern Yarkon-Ayalon basin (estimated size between four and five ha),[42] was excavated by several expeditions, each of which detected complex stratigraphy for the Early Bronze Age. In the current paper, I will refer to the excavations carried out by Yannai and Marder; van den Brink; Paz, Rosenberg, and Nativ; and Golani.[43] The published results from these excavations reveal that the Egyptian presence was detected in all the excavated areas (save the not yet studied northwestern side) and is reflected in a wide array of pottery types—lotus-shaped bowls, cylindrical vessels, wine jars, many bread molds—as well as Egyptian originating flint tools and objects.[44] The nature and derivation of the Egyptian occupation at Tel Lod are by no means clear. No exclusive 'Egyptian' quarters or structures were reported in any of the excavations. Also, Egyptian pottery and finds were found together with local Canaanite pottery, sometimes in pits. Moreover, the share of Egyptian/Egyptianized pottery compared to the local one was negligible (no more than 2% of the assemblage in Paz, Rosenberg, and Nativ's excavation).[45]

Despite the above, several points may reflect a 'state-oriented' Egyptian presence. First, the petrographic analysis of bread molds (made by M. Iserlis),[46] clearly shows that these were brought from the vicinity of 'En Besor-Tell Sakan, just like those from Al-Maghar (see above), meaning that the settlers of the Tel Lod colony were equipped through the state facilities at the Besor basin. Second, the seven incised majestic *serekhs* found at the northeastern side of the settlement[47] may hint at a more formalized existence, maybe even one with a facility for wine jars.

At any rate, the Egyptian presence at Tel Lod was probably very limited in time, at least at the southeastern and southwestern sides of the site (Golani; van den Brink; Paz, Rosenberg, and Nativ's excavations).[48] This can be mainly deduced from the stratigraphy of the three excavations mentioned above, which report a pre-Egyptian phase, dated to the EB IB: Stratum IVb in van den Brink's excavation, Stratum VI in Paz, Rosenberg and Nativ's excavation, and Stratum VII in Golani's excavation (mixed Neolithic, Chalcolithic and EB IB remains). Two out of the three excavations report post-Egyptian strata, where Egyptian finds are rare or completely lacking, which should still be dated within the late EB IB: Stratum III in Paz, Rosenberg, and Nativ's excavation,[49] and Strata III–II in Golani's excavation (note that Golani first dated Strata III–II to the EBII, but a thorough examination of the pottery related to these strata, conducted by Golani and Paz, resulted in the belief that the pottery and the strata should be dated to the EB IB).

Thus, the Egyptian presence at Tel Lod, 'sandwiched' between pre- and post-colony local EB IB settlements, seems to have been short-lived. Also, its spatial distribution throughout the site remains unclear. We may try to reconstruct a process by which this encounter with the local population was initially peaceful, as Egyptians were able to settle in various points within the local population. However, it seems that already during the late EB IB, with the rise of Egyptian exploitation of Canaanite resources, the local population expressed growing signs of hostility that may have led Egyptians toward separation in a restricted location, finally abandoning the site.

Tel Aviv Ha-Masger Street is probably the northernmost point where Egyptian kitchenware was found. It should be pointed out that several excavations conducted at the site have mainly exposed an EB IA settlement characterized by the employment of large rock-cut pits. The EB IB occupation at the site, which includes stone-built architecture, was seemingly more or less restricted to the center of the site and was only revealed in one excavation[50] At any rate, a notable relic of this small settlement was two large fragments of basins used for beer making in Egyptian settlements.[51] Being the only remnants of possible Egyptian-oriented activity, one may speculate that there was only a restricted Egyptian presence at Ha-Masger Street during the EB IB. The motivation behind this presence may be a possible relation with the nearby Jaffa, a natural anchorage point that was probably of importance for maritime activity during the EBA, as evidenced by sherds found during excavations.[52]

Discussion: Some Spatial Observations and Evidence of Canaanite Resistance

Egyptian presence in the land of Israel was probably multi-faceted and characterized by more than one interest group (besides official state institutions), as already suggested by Kansa and Levy for (at least) Naḥal Tillah.[53]

It can be stated that the spatial deployment of Egyptian enclaves in the study area is by no means accidental and was planned in order to gain maximal efficiency and control over land and maritime routes, economic resources, and agricultural lands. Thus, Tell Sakan was located where it could command maritime activity heading northwards, probably aided by the small post of Giv'at Ha-Esev towards Jaffa. The Egyptian colonial apparatus 'planted' an enclave in each major Canaanite settlement system. Each enclave was planted in the largest and most powerful settlement and probably monitored some aspects of socio-political activities within each settlement cluster. A good example can be seen in the eastern Yarkon-Ayalon basin, with settlements like Lod, Shoham North, and Azor. Tel Lod, the largest and probably most crowded and strong settlement, was chosen as the host of the implanted enclave in the area.

Egyptian physical presence seems to have created two levels of control: direct control—through state-level administration—and indirect control, maybe powered by other interest groups. Direct control can be seen in the spatial deployment of the Egyptian colonization apparatus. At least one site with Egyptian presence existed along each of the main streams that transverse the c. 90 km long area between 'En Besor and the Yarkon River, staffed and equipped by the state administration and the facilities stationed and built along the Besor stream (Tell Sakan and 'En Besor). Along the Soreq stream, the site of Al-Maghar, which yielded kitchenware equipped from 'En Besor, may have operated the small beacon/observation point of Palmahim Giva'at Ha-'Esev. Also, along the Yarkon-Ayalon River system, the site of Tel Lod, which again yielded kitchenware equipped from 'En Besor, may have been somehow connected with Jaffa and Ha-Masger Street, and maybe also Azor. Also of note is the Egyptian effort to establish a physical presence on the western edges of the Shephelah, which was probably fertile enough to be economically exploited. Thus, we see Egyptians residing at Tel Ḥalif Terrace, Tel Maaḥaz, and Amaziah, all three sites located in this region.

Although Egyptian presence in southern Canaan was multi-faceted, and commercial and economic considerations were definitely present, a violent aspect still seems to have affected local resistance to this alien presence. As was suggested by Yekutieli,[54] there is evidence of a considerable Egyptian military presence in northern Sinai and possible destruction of the early EB IB city of Tel 'Erani and the village of Afridar (probably during the first stage of Egyptian intrusion, see above).

Another intriguing issue is that numerous fortified settlements were present in Canaan during the late EB IB as part of an early urbanization process.[55] The mere fact is that none of these fortified settlements was located south of the Yarkon River. In fact, the study area—between the Yarkon and the Besor basin—was completely devoid of fortified settlements, with only one exception: Tell Sakan, the Egyptian stronghold in southwestern Canaan. Moreover, no fortifications were found even at Tel Lod, a large flourishing Canaanite settlement, while at the same period, Tel Aphek, located c. 20 km north of Tel Lod, was fortified with a 2.8 m wide wall.[56] One can only wonder whether the pre-planned implanted Egyptian enclave, equipped through existing state-level facilities and expressing power symbols (such as the *serekh* incised vessels) within Tel Lod has something to do with this fact. It would seem that during the later stage of Egyptian colonial presence, the re-enforcement of the fortifications at Tell Sakan and, possibly, also the deposit of the Kfar Monash hoard may all point toward military activity related to a Canaanite resistance and even a threat to Egyptian presence. The LBA Egyptian fortress at Jaffa, which was attacked, destroyed, and rebuilt several times during the LBA, can illustrate this point.[57] A physical threat due to hostility may have been the reason for the short-lived enclave of Tel Lod and maybe of other settlements as well, where segregated Egyptians had explicitly boasted symbols of power and dominance. However, at other sites, like Tel Ḥalif Terrace, where distinctions between Egyptians and Canaanites were less pronounced and lower agency and patronage were expressed by the foreigners, hostilities were probably minimal.

Other aspects of Canaanite resistance to Egyptian presence during the late fourth millennium BCE that characterize this colonial encounter may be viewed in light of post-colonial archaeological finds.[58] One form of this resistance may have been the symbolic destruction of Egyptian power symbols, as observed in the Stratum XIX Temple at Megiddo.[59] It can also be speculated that the fact that no Egyptian material-culture traits were adopted by Canaanite society may reflect a traumatic aspect of this colonial encounter. This rejection of Egyptian traits is seen in many domains; at the domestic level, the employment of brewing and baking vessels left no manifestations in the local EB IB–EBII material culture. The employment of organic inclusions for ceramic manufacture was rare in Canaanite pottery-making. In architecture, mudbrick structures were not adopted. Most of all, the Egyptian administrative, record-keeping, and writing systems, all vehicles of control and power during the colonies' life, were rejected and were not adopted by Canaanite society. This rejection seems to reflect a bipolar reaction to colonial encounters where one side (the newcomers) has higher agency than the other side (the host community). We can thus suggest that some Egyptian enclaves (probably at sites like Tel Maaḥaz and Tel Lod) had high or very high agency over the local population. Power symbols were explicitly projected by the Egyptian population (incised *serekhs*, the majestic bull) in the loci of interaction between Canaanites and Egyptians, and some aspects of material culture reflect hybridization and imitation of Egyptian pottery.[60] At the same time, other enclaves (such as Tel Ḥalif Terrace) may have had a bilateral, low- to medium-level agency with the Canaanite population within a flexible socio-political relationship.

Conclusion

The current paper has outlined several nodes deduced from available data on several spatial, theoretical, and socio-political aspects of an 'enclaving' process employed by the newly established Egyptian state during the late fourth millennium BCE. This process was multi-faceted and probably operated by more than one agent, which may have resulted in several types of encounters between the Canaanite host populations and the Egyptian newcomers. However, there is reason to believe that this 'enclaving' process was pre-planned and spatially deployed in a way that would have secured Egyptian socio-economic and political interests. The exploitation of Canaanite resources by the Egyptians eventually triggered resistance and hostility from the host population and may have been one of the reasons for the withdrawal of Egypt from Canaan by the end of the fourth millennium BCE.

References

Algaze, Guillermo. 1993. *The Uruk World System: The Dynamics of Expansion of Early Mesopotamian Civilization.* Chicago: University of Chicago Press.

Amiran, Ruth and Edwin C. M. van den Brink. 2002. "The Ceramic Assemblage from Tel Ma'ahaz, Stratum I (Seasons 1975- 1976)." In Edwin C. M. van den Brink and Thomas Evan Levy (eds.), *Egypt and the Levant, Egyptian-Canaanite Interaction: From the 4th Through Early 3rd Millennium B.C.E.*, 273–279. London: Leicester University Press.

Anthony, David W. 1990. "Migration in Archeology: The Baby and the Bathwater." *American Anthropologist* New Series 92(4): 895–914.

Barkan, Diego and Duaa Abu-Salah. 2017. "Tel Aviv, Ha-Masger Street." *Hadashot Arkheologiyot. Excavations and Surveys in Israel* 129. https://www.hadashot-esi.org.il/report_detail_eng.aspx?id=25319&mag_id=125, accessed 4 January 2021.

Beit-Arieh, Itzhak and Ram Gophna. 1999. "The Egyptian Protodynastic (Late EB I) Site at Tel Ma'ahaz: A Reassessment." *Tel Aviv* 26: 191–207.

Berry, John. W., Uichol Kim, S. Power, and M. Young. 1989. "Acculturation Attitudes in Plural Societies." *Applied Psychology: An International Review* 38: 185–206.

Braun, Elliot. 2002. "Egypt's First Sojourn in Canaan." In Edwin C.M. van den Brink and Thomas Evan Levy (eds.), *Egypt and the Levant: Interrelations from the 4th through the Early 3rd Millennium BCE*, 173–189. London: Leicester University Press.

van den Brink, Edwin C.M. 2002. "An Egyptian Presence at the End of the Late Early Bronze Age I at Tel Lod, Central Coastal Plain, Israel." In Edwin C. M. van den Brink and Thomas Evan Levy (eds.), *Egypt and the Levant, Egyptian-Canaanite Interaction: From the 4th Through Early 3rd Millennium B.C.E.*, 286–305. London: Leicester University Press.

van den Brink, Edwin C.M. and Elliot Braun. 2003. "Egyptian Elements and Influence on the Early Bronze Age I of the Southern Levant. Recent Excavations, Research and Publications." *Archeo-Nil* 13: 77–91.

Burke, Aaron A., Martin Peilstöcker, Amy Karoll, George A. Pierce, Krister Kowalski, and Nadia Ben-Marzouk. 2017. "Excavations of the New Kingdom Fortress in Jaffa, 2011–2014: Traces of Resistance to Egyptian Rule in Canaan." *American Journal of Archaeology* 121: 85. DOI: 10.3764/AJA.121.1.0085.

Dietler, Michael. 1998. "Consumption, Agency, and Cultural Entanglement: Theoretical Implications of a Mediterranean Colonial Encounter." In James Cusick (ed.), *Studies in Culture Contact: Interaction, Culture Change and Archaeology*, 288–315. Carbondale, Southern Illinois University Press.

Fischer, Peter. M. 2002. "Egyptian-Transjordanian Interaction during Predynastic and Protodynastic Times: The Evidence from Tell Abu al-Kharaz, Jordan Valley." In Edwin C.M. van den Brink and Thomas Evan Levy (eds.), *Egypt and the Levant, Egyptian-Canaanite Interaction: From the 4th Through Early 3rd Millennium B.C.E.*, 323–333. London: Leicester University Press.

Gal, Zvi and Moshe Kochavi. 2000. "Area B: Stratigraphy, Architecture and Tombs." In Moshe Kochavi, Pirhiyah Beck, and Esther Yadin (eds.), *Aphek-Antipatris I, Excavations of Areas A and B, the 1972–1976 Seasons*, 59–92. Tel Aviv: The Institute of Archaeology, Tel Aviv University.

Getzov, Nimrod, Yitzhak Paz, and Ram Gophna. 2001. *Shifting Urban Landscapes during the Early Bronze Age in the Land of Israel*. Tel Aviv: Ramōt.

Given, Michael. 2004. *The Archaeology of The Colonized*. London: Routledge.

Golani, Amir. 2013. "Lod, Remez Neighborhood." *Hadashot Arkheologiyot. Excavations and Surveys in Israel* 125. http://www.hadashot-esi.org.il/report_detail_eng.aspx?id=2282&mag_id=120, accessed 21 March 2017.

Gophna, Ram. 1995. *Excavations at 'En Besor*. Tel Aviv: Ramōt.

———. 2002. "Elusive Anchorage Points along the Israel Littoral and the Egyptian-Canaanite Maritime Route during the Early Bronze Age I." In Edwin C.M. van den Brink and Thomas Evan Levy (eds.), *Egypt and the Levant, Egyptian-Canaanite Interaction: From the 4th Through Early 3rd Millennium B.C.E.*, 418–421. London: Leicester University Press.

Gophna, Ram, Yitzhak Paz, and Itamar Taxel. 2010. "Al-Maghar: An Early Bronze Age Walled Town in the Lower Soreq Valley and the EB IB–II Sequence in the Central Coastal Plain of Israel." *Strata* 28: 9–38.

Gosden, Chris. 2004. *Archaeology and Colonialism: Cultural Contact from 5000 BC to the Present*. Cambridge: Cambridge University Press.

Ilan, Ornit. 2002. "Egyptian Pottery from Small Tel Malhata and the Interrelations between the Egyptian 'Colony' in Southwest Palestine and the 'Canaanite' Arad Basin and Central Highlands." In Edwin C.M. van den Brink and Thomas Evan Levy (eds.), *Egypt and the Levant, Egyptian-Canaanite Interaction: From the 4th Through Early 3rd Millennium B.C.E.*, 306–332. London: Leicester University Press.

Kanias, Zah. 2011. "Tel Aviv, Ha-Masger Street." *Hadashot Arkheologiyot. Excavations and Surveys in Israel* 123. https://www.hadashot-esi.org.il/Report_Detail_Eng.aspx?id=1719&mag_id=118, accessed 20/07/2011

Kansa, Erik and Thomas E. Levy. 2002. "Ceramics, Identity and the Role of the State: The View from Naḥal Tillah." In Edwin C.M. van den Brink and Thomas Evan Levy (eds.), *Egypt and the Levant, Egyptian-Canaanite Interaction: From the 4th Through Early 3rd Millennium B.C.E.*, 190–212. London: Leicester University Press.

McSparron, Cormac, Colm Murphy, Eileen Murphy, and Jonny Geber. 2019. "Migration, Group Agency, and Archaeology: A New Theoretical Model." *International Journal of Historical Archaeology* 24: 219–232.

Milevski, Ianir, Eliot Braun, Daniel Varga, and Yigal Israel. 2016. "On Some Possible Implications of a Newly Discovered Early Bronze Age Large Scale Silo Complex at Amaziah, Naḥal Lachish (Israel)." In Linda R. Manzanilla and Mitchell S. Rothman (eds.), *Storage in Ancient Complex Societies, Administration, Organization and Control*, 61–83. New York and London: Routledge.

Miroschedji, Pierre de. 2002. "The Socio-Political Dynamics of Egyptian-Canaanite Interaction in the Early Bronze." In Edwin C.M. van den Brink and Thomas Evan Levy (eds.), *Egypt and the Levant, Egyptian-Canaanite Interaction: From the 4th Through Early 3rd Millennium B.C.E.*, 39–54. London: Leicester University Press.

Miroschedji, Pierre de and Mouein Sadek. 2000. "Tell es-Sakan 2000." *Orient Express* 4: 98–101.

Morris, Ellen Fowles. 2005. *The Architecture of Imperialism: Military Bases and the Evolution of Foreign Policy in Egypt's New Kingdom*. Probleme der Ägyptologie 22. Leiden: Brill.

Paz, Yitzhak. 2002. "Fortified Settlements of the EBIB and the Emergence of the First Urban System." *Tel Aviv* 29: 238–261.

———. Forthcoming. "The Early Bronze Age Pottery from Jaffa." In: Zeev Herzog and Lilly Singer-Avitz (eds.), *Excavations at Tell Jaffa 1999*.

Paz, Yitzhak, Itai Elad, and Anat Cohen-Weinberger. 2021. "Three Egyptian Serekh-Like Incisions Found on One Vessel at the Early Bronze Age IB City of 'En Esur, Israel." *Journal of Ancient Egyptian Interconnections* 29: 52–66.

Paz, Yitzhak, Danny Rosenberg, and Assaf Nativ. 2005. "Excavations at Lod: Neolithic and Chalcolithic Remains and an Egyptian Presence in the Early Bronze Age." *Salvage Excavation Reports* 2: 114–158.

Stein, Gil. J. 2005. "The Comparative Archaeology of Colonial Encounters." In Gil J. Stein (ed.), *The Archaeology of Colonial Encounters*, 1–29. Santa Fe: School for Advanced Research Press.

Voss, Barbara L. 2005. "The Archaeology of Overseas Chinese Communities." *World Archaeology* 37: 424–439.

Yannai, E. and Ofer Marder. 2000. "Lod." *Hadashot Arkheologiyot. Excavations and Surveys in Israel* 112: 63*–65*.

Yegorov, Dimitri and Ianir Milevski. 2017. "Tel'Erani." *Hadashot Arkheologiyot. Excavations and Surveys in Israel* 129. https://www.hadashot-esi.org.il/Report_Detail_Eng.aspx?id=25179&mag_id=125, accessed 1/03/2017.

Yekutieli, Yuval. 1998. *The Early Bronze Age I of North Sinai: Social, Economic and Spatial Aspects.* Ph.D. dissertation, Ben Gurion University of the Negev, Beersheba (Hebrew, with English summary).

———. 2000. "Early Bronze Age I Pottery in Southwestern Canaan." In Graham Philip and Douglas Baird (eds.), *Ceramics and Change in the Early Bronze Age of the Southern Levant*, 129–152. Sheffield: Sheffield University.

———. 2007. "The Relationship Between Egypt and Canaan During the Early Bronze Age I as Viewed from South-West Canaan." *Qadmoniot* 40: 66–74 (Hebrew).

Notes

1 Anthony 1990.
2 Anthony 1990: 900–902.
3 Anthony 1990: 902–904.
4 McSparron et al. 2019, 228–229.
5 See, e.g., Algaze 1993.
6 See, e.g., Dietler 1998.
7 Gosden 2004, 3.
8 Stein 2005.
9 Stein 2005, 8.
10 Stein 2005, 12.
11 Voss 2005, 431–435.
12 Stein 2005, 13.
13 Stein 2005, 21.
14 Miroschedji and Sadek 2000.
15 van den Brink and Braun 2003, 78–85.
16 See also Gophna 1995; Miroschedji and Sadek 2000; Braun 2002.
17 E.g., Naḥal Tillah (Kansa and Levy 2002); Tel Maaḥaz (Amiran and van den Brink 2002); small Tel Malhata (Ilan 2002); Tel Lod (van den Brink 2002).
18 Paz, Elad and Cohen-Weinberger 2021; Fischer 2002.
19 See Yekutieli 2000.
20 Gophna, Paz, and Taxel 2010; van den Brink 2002; Yannai and Marder 2000; Golani 2013.
21 See Morris 2005, Fig. 21.
22 See Miroschedji 2002, Fig. 2.4; Morris 2005, Fig. 21.
23 Yekutieli 1998, 213.
24 Yekutieli 1998, 221.
25 Yekutieli 1998, 222–223.
26 Miroschedji 2002, 41–44, Table 2.1.
27 See, e.g., Miroschedji 2002, table 2.1.
28 Berry et al. 1989, 187–188.
29 Berry et al. 1989, 188.
30 McSparron et al. 2019.
31 See Beit-Arieh and Gophna 1999, 195; Amiran and van den Brink 2002.
32 Beit-Arieh and Gophna 1999, 205–206.
33 See Beit-Arieh and Gophna 1999, 197.
34 Kansa and Levy 2002, 201–205.
35 Milevski et al. 2016, 67–69.
36 Milevski et al. 2016, 75.
37 See, e.g., Yegorov and Milevski 2017.
38 Gophna, Paz, and Taxel 2010, 11.
39 See Gophna, Paz, and Taxel 2010, 20, Fig. 9.
40 See also Gophna, Paz, and Taxel 2010, 30.
41 See Gophna 2002.
42 See, e.g., Getzov, Paz, and Gophna 2001, 48; Golani 2013, Fig. 1.
43 See Yannai and Marder 2000; van den Brink 2002; Paz, Rosenberg, and Nativ 2005; Golani 2013.
44 See, e.g., Paz, Rosenberg, and Nativ 2005, 147–149, Fig. 28; Yannai and Marder 2000.
45 Paz, Rosenberg, and Nativ 2005, 147.
46 See Paz, Rosenberg, and Nativ 2005, 147–148.
47 Yannai and Marder 2000.
48 See Golani 2013, Fig. 1.
49 Paz, Rosenberg, and Nativ 2005, 139.
50 IAA Permit 5538, see Barkan and Abu-Salah 2017, Fig. 1; Kanias 2011; a full publication of Kanias' excavation is being prepared by Y. Paz.
51 See Barkan and Abu Salah 2017, fig. 7.
52 Paz, Forthcoming.
53 Kansa and Levy 2002, 203–206.
54 Yekutieli 1998, 222; 2007, 73–74.
55 See, e.g., Getzov, Paz, and Gophna 2001, 22–24; Paz 2002; Paz, Elad, and Cohen-Weinberger 2021, 54–58.
56 See Gal and Kochavi 2000, 63.
57 Burke et al. 2017.
58 Given 2004.
59 Yekutieli 2007, 74.
60 See, e.g., Yekutieli 2007, 72–74.

Journal of Ancient Egyptian Interconnections

Applied Potmarks between Lebanon and Egypt in the Early Bronze Age

Metoda Peršin
Freie Universität Berlin

Abstract

Although potmarks were discovered at many archaeological sites in the Near East and Egypt, interpretations of their functions vary. Despite the diversity of techniques used in potmark production (e.g. incised, painted, impressed, applied), applied potmarks were especially neglected in research, and attracted attention mostly through the so-called ram's head applications. A recent systematic study of potmarks from the Bronze Age contexts in Lebanon has revealed not only that applied marks do exist, but they appear frequently and come in a variety of forms and combinations. Contacts between the Levant and Egypt in the Bronze Age are known both from written sources and analysis of archaeological material. The latter includes ceramic vessels imported to Egypt, some of which bear applied potmarks. This paper investigates the Early Bronze Age applied potmarks in Lebanon through a contextual lens, as well as applied potmarks found on imported vessels in Egypt. As a result, this paper offers new insights on the function of applied potmarks and the exchange practices between Egypt and Lebanon in the Early Bronze Age.

Keywords

Potmarks, Early Bronze Age, Lebanon, Egypt

Introduction

Potmarks have been found at numerous archaeological sites and interpreted in many different ways. They may have been related to the manufacturing process of the vessels,[1] or used to identify a workshop,[2] a family,[3] gender or age,[4] ownership,[5] the destination of the vessel,[6] or its origin.[7] Furthermore, their functions could be related to the content of the vessels,[8] branding,[9] administrative purposes,[10] exchange process,[11] funerary practices,[12] or libation.[13] Although these interpretations vary considerably from one another, it is highly likely that potmarks acquired different roles across different areas and in different time periods, meaning that any of these interpretations may be plausible at a certain point in time at a certain place.

Potmarks are in general defined as isolated signs incised, excised, painted, or impressed on ceramic vessels.[14] Applied potmarks are rarely mentioned in literature,[15] on the one hand due to the fact that potmark application was not the most frequent potmarking technique, and, on the other, since such applications are sometimes not recognized as potmarks. An applied potmark is created by forming a small piece of clay into the desired form and attaching it to the vessel before firing. This is in contrast to other potmarking techniques that allow mark creation after firing, as in the case of painted or incised marks.

One of the most known groups of applied potmarks are the so-called ram's head applications. They were documented at several sites in Lebanon,[16] in the Southern Levant[17] and in Egypt.[18] Their interpretations often vary in publications; sometimes they were considered as decoration,[19] other times as part of a marking system.[20] This paper considers ram's heads applications as potmarks that were part of a marking system in use in the Early Bronze Age and reveals that the ram's head applications are far from being the only type of applied potmarks in Lebanon. Although marked vessels are very rare compared to unmarked vessels in general and applied potmarks are not attested as frequently as other types of potmarks, a recent systematic study of Bronze Age marks from Lebanon unveils that there is a substantial amount of such marks present in the area and that they materialize in many different shapes and combinations. The results presented in this paper are preliminary thoughts on Early Bronze Age potmarking practices in Lebanon and will be discussed in more detail in the author's Ph.D. dissertation that analyzes potmarks from Bronze Age contexts in Lebanon.[21]

In addition to the applied potmarks found in Lebanon, three applied potmarks discovered in Egypt and believed to be of Lebanese origin are included in this study. All three of these marks originate from cemeteries in Giza, which provides very different contextual information to the applied marks documented in Lebanon. They were included in this study both to add fresh data to the analysis of the functions of potmarks in Lebanon and to investigate their meaning in their final deposition place, the Egyptian tombs.

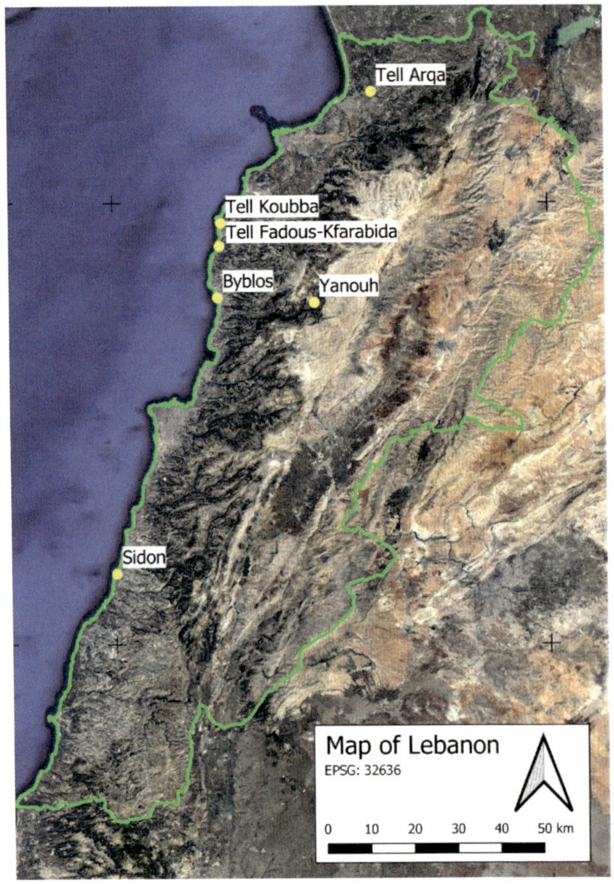

Figure 1: Sites in Lebanon where applied potmarks were found (map by author).

Applied Potmarks in Lebanon

Applied potmarks in Lebanon were found at six sites (Fig. 1), namely Tell Arqa, Tell Koubba, Tell Fadous-Kfarabida, Yanouh, Byblos, and Sidon. A total of 160 individual potmarks bearing an application were analysed for this paper and the signs can be classified in 28 groups. Some of the signs appear more frequently while some are attested only once. The five most common signs are: ram's head application (see Fig. 2:6), one applied knob (see Fig. 2:7), one incised line with an applied knob next to it (see Fig. 2:8), snake application (see Fig. 3:1), and one incised line with two applied knobs on each side (see Fig. 3:2).

Applied potmarks from Lebanon can generally be dated to the Early Bronze Age II and III. They are rarely attested in Middle Bronze Age contexts and no applied marks from Lebanon dating to the Late Bronze Age are known to the author. All the Early Bronze Age examples from Lebanon come from settlements, where they are related to domestic and public buildings. It should be noted here that there are hardly any documented Early Bronze Age II–III burials in Lebanon,[22] which may be the reason for a skewed picture of the extent of applied marks.

One of the more common groups of applied marks are simple applied individual knobs. They consist of a small round piece of clay that measures around 5 mm in diameter, but may reach over 1 cm, especially if the vessel is large. One of the common locations where these knobs are applied are handles, either at their top or at their bottom. Potmarks located at the top of the handle are well known in archaeological literature; in contrast, marks located at the bottom are not frequent. Single applied knobs located at the bottom of the handles (see Fig. 3:3) are restricted to jugs; such examples were found at Tell Fadous-Kfarabida and Sidon.

When the single applied knob is located at the top of the handle, its precise location may vary from one vessel to another. All of the examples discovered at Tell Fadous-Kfarabida have the knob located in the center of the handle (see FIG. 2:7), whereas the vast majority of the examples from Sidon tend to have the knob applied on the left side of the handle (see FIG. 3:4).

Applied knobs are the most frequently used applications appearing in combination with a variety of incised signs. A factor that seems to have played an important role is where exactly the applied knob is located in relation to the incision(s). Different potmarks may consist of the same individual elements positioned in different structured combinations. One such example is the use of one incised line in combination with two applied knobs. In the first case, the vertical incised line is flanked by two knobs (see FIG. 3:2). The second design consists of the same elements, a line and two applied knobs, but with the knobs located at the top and bottom of the line (see FIG. 3:8). Some potmarks made of a combination of incisions and applications bear an applied knob positioned directly on top of the incised sign (see FIG. 3:6, 7).

While most potmarks from Lebanon were located in visible places on the vessels, a new group of potmarks was identified in this study that breaks with this tradition. In this case, the potmarks are located on the round bases (see FIG. 3:5) of vessels usually interpreted as cooking pots. The examination of the wares of these vessels confirms that they were indeed used for cooking.[23]Although potmarks have been previously identified on cooking pots in Lebanon,[24] they were always located in prominent positions, mostly around the rims. Examples of the new potmark variant, located at the base of cooking vessels, have so far been documented at Tell Koubba and Sidon. They appear in a variety of shapes and encompass both incised and applied marks. They are most frequently attested in Sidon where they make up about 10% of all the Early Bronze Age potmarks. Sign types, however, are not limited only to the bases of vessels, cooking pots, or even to the site. For example, the potmark consisting of an incised line with two applied knobs at its ends attested several times on the bases of cooking pots in Sidon (see FIG. 3:5) appears also on the neck of a storage jar at Tell Fadous-Kfarabida (FIG. 3:8). Other signs located on the bases of cooking pots in Sidon were documented at other sites in Lebanon and located in other positions on different types of vessels.

APPLIED POTMARKS IN EGYPT

Although only three applied potmarks found in Egypt and believed to be of Lebanese origin (Sowada personal communication) are included in this study, they add important information to the Lebanese assemblage. First, their contextual information differs greatly from the ones excavated in Lebanon. Second, the large distance between their production and subsequent excavation spots triggers questions related to the connectivity between Lebanon and Egypt, and whether it was only physical objects that travelled across space or were the conceptual ideas behind such potmarks transferred as well.

All three potmarks from Giza discussed here are on storage jars combed on the outside. They are in well visible places, either on the shoulder of the vessel or on its upper body. Even though these three marks differ from each other, they all have parallels in Lebanon. Combed vessels found in Egypt are mostly associated with tombs of royalty or high officials.[25] Since such vessels were highly valued, would that mean that the potmarks they bore also had a similar important role? Also, if the vessels coming from Lebanon were not only treasured for their content but reused and circulated after they had been emptied of their original content,[26] does that also give a special meaning to the potmark on the vessel, or did the potmark just make it to Egypt as a by-product?

The first mark,[27] which represents a curved applied form (FIG. 2:1), can be dated to the mid-Fourth Dynasty. It is not complete, but the preserved part allows for a comparison with complete examples found in Lebanon. One such potmark from Tell Fadous-Kfarabida was applied at the top of the jug handle (FIG. 2:2). Other marks of the same type were also found on storage jars at Tell Fadous-Kfarabida, as well as Sidon. The applied mark from Egypt has its high visibility in common with the same types of marks from Lebanon, yet the locations of these marks on the vessels from Lebanon may vary. As in the case of the jug mentioned above, such marks may appear at the top of the handle; in other cases they are located on the neck or shoulder area of the vessel. The find contexts of these marks in Lebanon are associated with domestic buildings.

The second example of an applied mark found in Egypt[28] is represented by two knobs, the lower

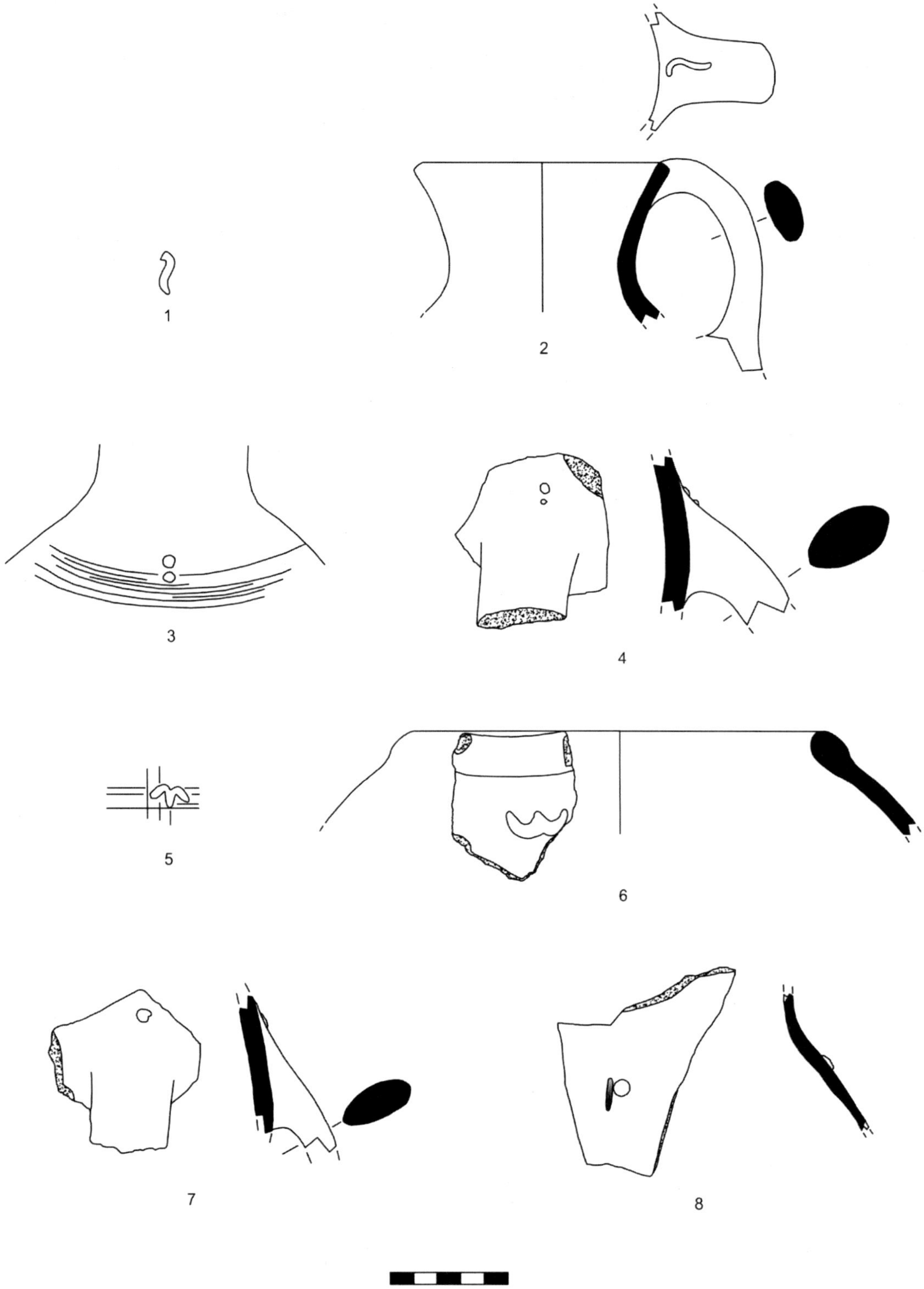

Figure 2: Selected applied potmarks from Lebanon and Giza. 1. Drawn after a photograph of MFA 37.2725 © Museum of Fine Arts, Boston. 3. Drawn after a photograph of KH 8029 © Kunsthistorisches Museum Wien. 5. Drawn after a photograph of MFA 37.1319 © Museum of Fine Arts, Boston; all photographs provided by Karin Sowada).

smaller than the upper one (FIG. 2:3), located on the neck of a storage jar from Giza dated to the Fifth Dynasty. In Lebanon, two knobs can be applied in several different ways—vertically, horizontally or diagonally—and may be of equal size or, as in the case of the mark from Egypt, may consist of a larger and a smaller knob. Only one potmark from Lebanon closely parallels the Egyptian example in both size and position (FIG. 2:4). This potmark comes from Tell Fadous-Kfarabida and the mark is applied at the top of the handle of a vessel.

The third example from Giza is an applied ram's head[29] located on the upper body of a storage jar, at the level of the handles (FIG. 2:5). The vessel is dated to the middle- to late-Fourth Dynasty. Applied ram's heads are one of the most frequent groups of potmarks in Lebanon when it comes to the applied forms. They were found at several sites, yet the majority of them come from Sidon. These applications are sometimes located at the top of the handle, but in most cases these are on the body of the vessel. Although they are most frequently attested on storage jars and jugs, they also appear on cooking pots (FIG. 2:6). They can also be applied upside down, as seen in the example.

DISCUSSION

Despite the meager number of applied potmarks discovered in Egypt, their general characteristics show the importance of certain traits. All the discussed examples are located on storage jars. As these are appropriate vessels for transportation, it is not surprising that these are the ones bearing potmarks. On the other hand, all of these potmarks have prominent locations on the vessels and were intended to be well visible to the user of the vessel. It is not possible to say with certainty if the marks and their visibility played a role directly related to trade, but as a high number of vessels coming to Egypt from Lebanon are marked in a very visible location, the marks' location might have been significant.

The applied potmarks found in Lebanon show that the marks may have had various functions. Potmarks are not restricted to storage jars and are not always well visible. In cases of storage jars and jugs, they tend to have a visible placement, associated with the handles or the neck and shoulder area of the vessel. A number of marks, however, are attested on the rounded bases of cooking pots, which are vessels not very suitable for transportation. The signs appearing on these bases have counterparts at different sites in Lebanon, and are located in different places on the vessels of different types. It would seem therefore that the marks on these vessels were not necessarily related to trade. Furthermore, as the same types of marks appear on vessels of different sizes, they certainly do not relate to the volume of the vessel.

In Lebanon, many applied potmarks come from domestic dwelling contexts and their use in a domestic environment is furthermore supported by the marks located on cooking pots. Whereas a pre-firing potmark on a storage jar may have lost its original meaning if the jar is reused, most cooking pots were likely originally intended to end up in their find spots. It seems, therefore, that the potmarks were understood and intended to be understood by a variety of users. The fact that the same signs appear on cooking pots used in a domestic setting at one site, as well as on storage jars that may have taken part in trade and are located at sites where such marks are not present on cooking pots, points to a diversified and rather wide audience of the potmarking system.

The Early Bronze Age sites along the Lebanese coast are not large in size and may, in cases such as Tell Fadous-Kfarabida, cover an area as small as 1.5 ha.[30] Given that over 80 different types (including applied and incised examples) of potmarks were discovered at this site, it does not seem likely that the marks would denote specific potters or workshops. The evidence against such an interpretation is also provided by the locations of the specific applied marks. Whereas simple applied knobs for instance, when associated with handles of vessels, are at Tell Fadous-Kfarabida always located in the center of the handle, their preferred placement in Sidon is to the left of the handle. In both cases the signs are very well visible, however their specific location would indicate that they were produced by different workshops who chose the locations of the marks individually. At the same time, as the signs are of the same type, their meaning is expected to remain the same at both sites and to both (groups) of producers.

The variety of combinations of incised marks and applications show that the system of applied potmarks is quite complex and as it is not related to specific vessel types, wares, locations on the vessels, or archaeological contexts and sites, the reasons for marking the vessels should be sought elsewhere. The use of specific elements within the repertoire of

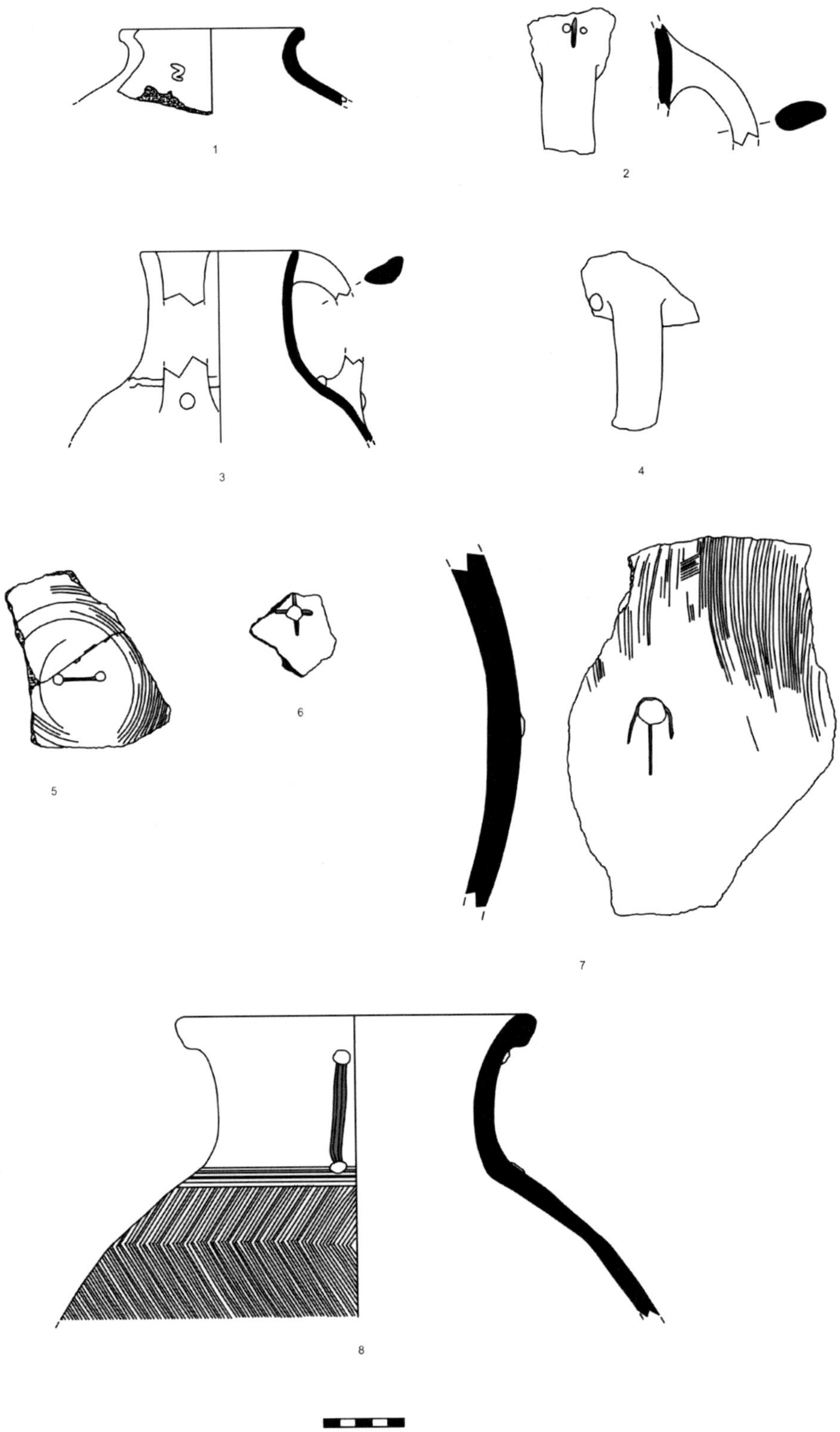

Figure 3: Selected applied potmarks from Lebanon.

the applied marks seems to follow certain rules and represents a specific graphic system. As the marks from all the studied sites follow a specific code, it seems that the sites were integrated into a common marking system that was in use in Lebanon in the Early Bronze Age.

Analyzing potmarks in Lebanon is still work in progress, and the discussed assemblage of applied marks represents only about one third of all the Early Bronze Age potmarks and about one sixth of all the Bronze Age potmarks from Lebanon studied in the Ph.D. dissertation of the author. Some general interpretations of potmark functions can already be omitted based on the sample included in this paper. Potmarks do not seem to represent a potter, workshop, merchant, volume, point of origin or destination of a vessel. It seems therefore, that the role of potmarks found in Egypt was not directly related to transportation or the final destination of the vessel. Since imported vessels were quite frequently marked, it may be possible that just as the imported vessel was considered a prestigious object, the foreign mark on it would enhance its meaning as an exotic item. The remaining question is whether the potmarking audience in Egypt actually recognized the meaning of such applied marks, conceived at the place of their production. A systematic analysis of contextual data of a larger sample of potmarks both from Lebanon and Egypt, conducted as part of the forthcoming Ph.D. dissertation, will no doubt shed more light on the functions of such potmarks in the Near East, yet some of the questions may remain unanswered.

One of the main questions in studying applied potmarks that cannot yet be answered properly, is why applications were sometimes located on top of incised marks, therefore sealing them in a way. It is clear that any application was produced at the place of origin of the vessel, in contrast to incised marks that could have been created after the vessel was fired and possibly not related to its area of production in any way. Is it then possible that an applied mark certified the origin of the vessel and its content, similar to the concept of branding, well known in the Near East in the Bronze Age,[31] in contrast to the post-firing incised marks, that could have been forged somewhere on the way.

Conclusion

Potmarks studies are often limited to a descriptive level, which is inevitable when dealing with small assemblages and a lack of contextual data. The possible interpretations of the potmark uses are often deduced from excluding the different possibilities to reach different conclusions. At the same time, it is highly likely that different marking systems were in use in different spatial and temporal contexts and it is therefore not to be expected that a uniform explanation of the functions of marks could be reached. In this paper, the author presents a small assemblage of Egyptian applied potmarks of Lebanese origin, as well as a substantial amount of applied potmarks excavated in Lebanon. Through the study of this assemblage, this paper provides new insights on the distribution of applied potmarks, that have been with a few exceptions mostly overlooked in the past, further offers some thoughts about the use of potmarks in general, and highlights the importance of contextual analysis in the study of potmarks.

Acknowledgements

This study was funded by the Elsa-Neumann-Stipend, Berlin. I am grateful to the directors of the excavations who shared with me applied potmarks from their projects: Hermann Genz (Tell Fadous-Kfarabida), Claude Doumet-Serhal (Sidon), and Kamal Badreshany, Graham Philip, and Hélène Sader (Tell Koubba). A special thanks goes to Karin Sowada for providing the information on the applied marks from Egypt.

References

Aston, David A. 2009. "Theban Potmarks – Nothing Other than Funny Signs? Potmarks from Deir el-Medineh and the Valley of the Kings." In Ben J. J. Haring, Olaf Ernst Kaper, and Ceest van Zoest (eds.), *Pictograms or Pseudo Script?: Non-Textual Identity Marks in Practical Use in Ancient Egypt and Elsewhere. Proceedings of a Conference in Leiden, 19 - 20 December 2006)*, 45–61. Leiden: Nederlands Instituut voor het Nabije Oosten.

Bréand, Gaëlle. 2005. "Les marques et graffiti sur poteries de l'Egypte pré- et protodynastique. Perspectives de recherches à partir de l'exemple d'Adaïma." *Archéo-Nil* 15: 17–30.

Doumet-Serhal, Claude, Dafydd Griffiths, Emmanuelle Vila, and Corine Yazbeck. 2006. *The Early Bronze Age in Sidon: "College Site"*

Excavations (1998–2000–2001). Bibliothèque archéologique et historique 178. Beyrouth: Institut français du Proche-Orient.

Feldbacher, Rainer and Peter M. Fischer. 2008. "Potmarks on Ceramic Containers from Early Bronze Age Tell Abu Al-Kharaz". In Peter M. Fischer (ed.), *Tell Abu al-Kharaz in the Jordan Valley. Volume 1: The Early Bronze Age*, 391–398. Vienna: Verlag der Österreichischen Akademie der Wissenschaften.

Gallorini, Carla. 1998. *Incised Marks on Pottery and Other Objects from Kahun Systems of Communication in Egypt during the Late Middle Kingdom*. Ph.D. Dissertation, University of London.

Genz, Hermann. 2001. "Early Bronze Age Potmarks from Khirbat az-Zayraqūn: Some Aspects Concerning their Meaning." *Studies in the History and Archaeology of Jordan* 7: 217–228, http://publication.doa.gov.jo/Publications/ViewChapterPublic/1461.

2014. "The Northern Levant (Lebanon) during the Early Bronze Age." In A. E. Killebrew and M. Steiner (eds.), *The Oxford Handbook of the Archaeology of the Levant: c. 8000–332 BCE*. Oxford: Oxford University Press. DOI: 10.1093/oxfordhb/9780199212972.013.021.

Genz, Hermann and Hélène Sader. 2007. "Excavations at the Early Bronze Age Site of Tell Fadous-Kfarabida: Preliminary Report on the 2007 Season of Excavations." *Bulletin d'archéologie et d'architecture libanaises* 11: 7–16.

Genz, Hermann, Riva Daniel, Alison Damick, Alexander Ahrens, Sireen El-Zaatari, Felix Höflmayer, Walter Kutschera and Eva M. Wild. 2010. "Excavations at Tell Fadous-Kfarabida: Preliminary Report on the 2010 Season of Excavations." *Bulletin d'archéologie et d'architecture libanaises* 14: 241–273.

Hirschfeld, Nicolle E. 2002. "Marks on Pots: Patterns of Use in the Archaeological Record at Enkomi." In Joanna S. Smith (ed.), *Script and Seal Use on Cyprus in the Bronze and Iron Ages*. Colloquia and Conference Papers 4, 49–109. Boston, MA: Archaeological Institute of America.

———. 2004. "Eastwards via Cyprus? The Marked Mycenaean Pottery of Enkomi, Ugarit and Tell Abu Hawam." In Jacuqeline Balensi, Jean-Yves Monchambert, and Sylvie Müller-Celka (eds.), *La céramique mycénienne de l'Égée au Levant: Homage à Vronwy Hankey*, 97–104. Travaux de la Maison de l'Orient et de la Méditerranée 41. Lyon: Maison de l'Orient et de la Méditerranée-Jean Pouilloux.

———. 2006. "Vases Marked for Exchange: The Not-So-Special Case of Pictorial Pottery." In Eva Rystedt and Berit Wells (eds.), *Pictorial Pursuits: Figurative Painting on Mycenaean and Geometric Pottery. Papers from Two Seminars at the Swedish Institute at Athens in 1999 and 2001*, 83–96. Stockholm: Swedish Institute at Athens.

———. 2012. "Appendix IV: Potmarks." In Vassos Karageorghis and Yannis Violaris (eds.), *Tombs of the Late Bronze Age in the Limassol Area, Cyprus (17th–13th Centuries BC)*, 289–299. Nicosia: Municipality of Limassol.

Junker, Hermann. 1926. *Vorläufiger Bericht über die vierte Grabung bei den Pyramiden von Gizeh vom 4. Januar bis 9. April 1926*. Wien: Akademie der Wissenschaften.

Mazzoni, Stefania. 1987. "The Diffusion of the Palestinian Combed Jars." In Shawqi Shaath (ed.), *Studies in the History and Archaeology of Palestine. Proceedings of the First International Symposium on Palestine Antiquities*, Vol. II, 145–158. Aleppo: Aleppo University Press.

Orton, Clive, Paul Tyres and Alan Vince 1993. *Pottery in Archaeology*. Cambridge Manuals in Archaeology. Cambridge: Cambridge University Press.

Paz, Sarit. 2014. "The Small Finds." In Raphael Greenberg (ed.), *Bet Yeraḥ: The Early Bronze Age Mound. Volume II: Urban Structure and Material Culture. 1933–1986 Excavations*, 235–298. Israel Antiquities Authority Reports 54. Jerusalem: Israel Antiquities Authority. https://www.jstor.org/stable/j.ctt1fzhfbz.

Peršin, Metoda. Forthcoming. "Potmarks." In Hermann Genz, Alison Damick, Zuzanna Wygnańska, Martin Makinson, Marshall Woodworth, Mahmoud Mardini, Naseem Raad, A. Rutter, Jana Alameh, Berj Wanessian, S. Rempel, J. Baldi, Marta D'Andrea, Metoda Peršin, Karin Kopetzky, Ziad El Morr, Canan Çakırlar, F. Slim, Youri van den Hurk, Francis Koolstra, M. Price, Cheryl Makarewicz, Michiel Vanhecke, Rachel M. Winter, Willemien de Kock, Chris Stantis, Nina Maaranen, J. Peterkin, Geoff Nowell, Colin MacPherson, and Holger Schutkowski, "Excavations at Tell Fadous-Kfarabida: Preliminary Report on the 2016 Season of Excavations." *Bulletin d'archéologie et d'architecture libanaises*.

———. Submitted. *Potmarking Practices in the Bronze Age Lebanon: The Lebanon Potmark Database*. PhD dissertation, Freie Universität Berlin.

Sconzo, P. 2013. *Final Reports of the Syrian-German Excavations at Tel el-'Abd. Volume II: Tell el-'Abd II. Pottery and Potmarks at an Early Urban Settlement of the Middle Euphrates River Valley, Syria*. Altertumskunde des Vorderen Orients 16/2; Archäologische Studien zur Kultur und Geschichte des Alten Orients. Münster: Ugarit Verlag.

Sowada, Karin. 2009. *Egypt in the Eastern Mediterranean during the Old Kingdom: an archaeological perspective*. Orbis Biblicus et Orientalis 237, Fribourg: Academic Press.

Sowada, Karin. Mary Ownby and Anna Wodzińska. 2020. "The Petrography of Imported Levantine Combed Vessels from Early Old Kingdom Giza." *Levant* 52: 197–214. DOI: 10.1080/00758914.2019.1664197.

Tassie, Geoffrey J., Fekri A. Hassan, Joris van Wetering, and Bram Calcoen. 2008. "Corpus of Potmarks from the Protodynastic to Early Dynastic Cemetery at Kafr Hassan Dawood, Wadi Tumilat, East Delta, Egypt." In Béatrix Midant-Reynes, Yann Tristant, Joanne Rowland, and Stan Hendrickx (eds.), *Egypt at Its Origins 2: Proceedings of the International Conference "Origin of the State, Predynastic and Early Dynastic Egypt", Toulouse (France), 5th–8th September 2005*. Orientalia Lovaniensia Analecta 172, 201–234. Leuven & Dudley, MA: Peeters.

Wengrow, David. 2008. "Prehistories of Commodity Branding." *Current Anthropology* 49(1): 7–34. DOI: 10.1086/523676.

Wodzińska, Anna. 2009. "Potmarks from Early Dynastic Buto and Old Kingdom Giza: Their Occurrence and Economic Significance." *British Museum Studies in Ancient Egypt and Sudan* 13: 239–261.

Notes

1 Gallorini 1998, 259; Hirschfeld 2004, 99.
2 Sconzo 2013, 283–311.
3 Aston 2009, 55.
4 Bréand 2005, 23.
5 Wodzińska 2009, 245, 246.
6 Wodzińska 2009, 246.
7 Tassie et al. 2008, 210.
8 Genz 2001, 226.
9 Wengrow 2008.
10 Gallorini 1998, 260, 261.
11 Hirschfeld 2006, 86, 88.
12 Hirschfeld 2002, 83.
13 Hirschfeld 2012, 289, 290.
14 Sconzo 2013, 223.
15 Feldbacher and Fischer 2008.
16 Doumet-Serhal et al. 2006, pl. 174.5–7; Genz and Sader 2007, fig. 13; Genz et al. 2010, pl. 6.3.
17 Paz 2014, fig. 6.9.41–42.
18 Sowada et al. 2019, 9 b.
19 Paz 2014, 250.
20 Mazzoni 1987, 148.
21 Peršin, Forthcoming.
22 Genz 2014, 300, 301.
23 Orton et al. 1993, 220.
24 Doumet-Serhal et al. 2006, pl. 125.1; Peršin, Forthcoming.
25 Sowada et al. 2020, 197.
26 Sowada et al. 2020, 200.
27 Sowada 2009, 59, fig. 8, pl.1.
28 Junker 1926, 75.
29 Sowada 2009, 59, fig. 8, pl. 1.
30 Genz et al. 2010, 241.
31 Wengrow 2008.

Journal of Ancient Egyptian Interconnections

Reconsidering Egyptian–South Levantine Interaction: Evidence from Early Bronze Age II Contexts at Tell es-Sultan and Tell el-Far'ah North

Maura Sala
Faculty of Theology of Lugano – Università della Svizzera italiana

Abstract
In recent decades, evidence of a two-way relationship between First Dynasty Egypt and the Early Bronze Age II communities of southern Levant progressively emerged. The ongoing investigation hints at a branched network of exchanges between Egypt and the Levant, which was operational at the dawn of the earliest Levantine urbanization and involved multiple Levantine centers. While a complete reassessment of Egyptian–south Levantine relations in the EB II / ESL 4 is beyond its scope, this paper reviews evidence from two key south-Levantine sites: Tell es-Sultan and Tell el-Far'ah North. The paper examines the amount, range, and find context of the Egyptian and Egyptian-style objects from Tell es-Sultan and Tell el-Far'ah North, and seeks to assess their role in these early urbanized societies.

Keywords
Egyptian–south Levantine interaction; Early Bronze II; Tell es-Sultan; Tell el-Far'ah North; Egyptian and Egyptian-style objects; social differentiation

1. Introduction
Interactions between Egypt and the southern Levant in the late 4th/early 3rd millennium BCE have been reconsidered in recent scholarly literature. The growing identification of Egyptian material at south Levantine sites (e.g., Tel Beth Yerah, Tell Abu al-Kharaz, Tel Yarmuth, Tell es-Sultan) on the one hand, and archaeometric studies on imported ceramics from royal tombs at Abydos on the other, have corroborated the existence of a two-way relationship between First Dynasty Egypt and the south Levantine communities during the Early Bronze Age (henceforth EB) II. While a complete reassessment of First Dynasty–EB II relations is beyond its scope, the paper seeks to review evidence from two key sites: Tell es-Sultan and Tell el-Far'ah North (Fig. 1). These sites belonged to different trade networks (including Egypt) operating in the northern and southern areas of the country: Tell es-Sultan took part in the Egyptian–Levantine trade because of its strategic position and proximity to raw materials of the Dead Sea basin, while Tell el-Far'ah North was the leading center in the area between the central hills and the Jordan Valley. The paper examines the Egyptian and Egyptian-style objects from Tell es-Sultan and Tell el-Far'ah North, their amount, and finding contexts, and seeks to assess their role in these early urbanized societies.

2. Egyptian–South Levantine Contacts in the EB II/ESL 4: A Targeted Interaction Strategy
Following the establishment of a pack-donkey route running from the Nile Delta to the southern Levant via northern coastal Sinai,[1] contacts between Egypt and the southern Levant gradually increased from the mid-4th millennium BCE onward. The scope

of such interregional exchanges rose throughout the EB IB/Naqada IID–IIIA period, with a peak of imported ceramics presence in Egypt.[2] In the late 4th millennium (late EB IB/ESL 3b/Naqada IIIB), the Egyptian demand for Levantine products and the need to organize their supply prompted an on-the-ground Egyptian presence in the southern coastal plain.[3] Yet, Egyptian implants were short-lived and were evacuated before the onset of south Levantine EB II. Adjacent local settlements were abandoned as well, whereas a number of fortified centers arose in the territory. While Egyptian presence withdrew, local polities exercising a stronger territorial control emerged, within a process of political realignment, settlement coalescence, and social (corporate) reorganization that affected the country.[4] The use of the trans-Sinaitic caravan route along the coast was also resized, alongside the intensification of Egyptian maritime activity toward the central Levant.[5] However, copious south Levantine ceramic imports from First Dynasty royal and elite tombs in Egypt and, in turn, Egyptian material at EB II south Levantine sites confirm the persistence of exchanges, while marking a turning point in Egyptian–south Levantine relations. Contacts did not cease after the Egyptian retreat. During the EB II, direct exploitation through on-the-ground presence was replaced by a new, targeted product acquisition strategy, likely implemented by Egyptian agents who accomplished trade and diplomatic tasks with the new local urban elites, procurers of the coveted commodities.[6]

Expanding maritime activity along the Levantine seaboard, moreover, intensified the exchange of commodities like coniferous resins, vegetable oils, and other,[7] from the northern part of the country (such as the upper and central Jordan Valley). Pottery containers were purposely manufactured to package and transport these liquid commodities via land and sea;[8] this is the case of well-fired jugs and loop-handled jars (some belonging to the metallic ware category[9]). New optical mineralogy and pXRF studies of Levantine ceramics from First Dynasty royal tombs at Abydos showed that some containers originated in northern Canaan, many of them at the site of Tel Beth Yerah.[10] Egyptian finds from the EB II town of Tel Beth Yerah complement this picture.[11] Some of the Egyptian–Levantine interactions for the trade in Levantine container-based products may thus have been centered at this site.[12]

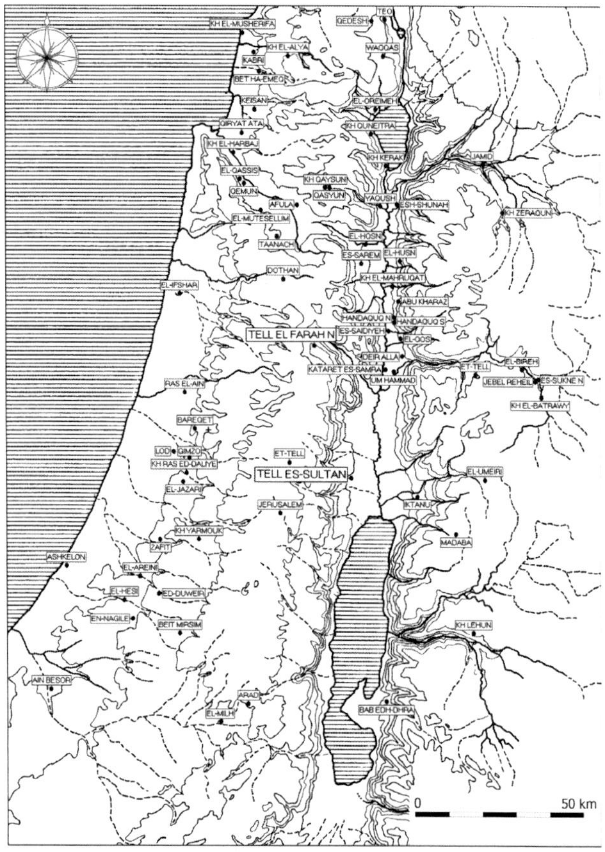

Figure 1: Map of EB II sites in the southern Levant (Nigro 2010, fig. 1.2).

Vessels from southerly areas (e.g., the southern hills or northern Negev) do not seem to be present in First Dynasty royal tombs. Although their presence cannot be excluded,[13] they were unlikely to be a significant component of imported pottery. In fact, the nature of commodities (asphalt and salt (?) from the Dead Sea, metals, foodstuffs, and livestock)[14], and the modes of overland transport operating in this part of the country, probably required a different kind of containers, like bags, baskets, or panniers made of organic materials.[15]

What south Levantine communities received in exchange for the exported goods remains to be clarified. Egyptian prestige objects were part of the trade flow. They could be obtained by various means, such as a return for exported commodities or diplomatic gifts, not ruling out that some of them could be acquired down-the-line via merchants or inter-community exchanges. Raw materials such as shells and stones, and possibly perishable products like textiles, foodstuffs, and livestock, were also part of the trading.[16]

Figure 2: Tell es-Sultan. Plan of the EB II dwelling quarter on the northern plateau (later phase; Nigro 2010, fig. 4.45).

2.1. The Corpus of Aegyptiaca from EB II southern Levant

Fine stone vessels characterize the repertoire of Egyptian prestige objects from EB II sites in southern Levant.[17] During the late EB IB–EB II, stone vessel manufacture in southern Levant was limited to a few rough limestone bowls (except for basalt vessels).[18] Egyptian stone vessels are recognizable for their material, shape, and high-quality production technique. Stone bowls dominate, imported not as containers, but for their own value. Contexts of retrieval differ, but Egyptian vessels often come from household (elite?) contexts. In the following EB III, the association with ceremonial (cultic and palatial) structures becomes prominent, as the finds from ʻAi and Tel Yarmuth may indicate.[19]

Egyptian stone palettes may have been sought for their inherent meaning and function; besides their exotic value, they could reproduce Egyptian cosmetic habits. During the EB II, Egyptian prototypes inspired local artisans to manufacture palette-like objects, probably intended to satisfy local consumption by newly created urban elites. This occurrence can be observed in EB II–III contexts at Tell es-Sultan (see below) and Bab edh-Dhraʻ.[20] Local items differ from Egyptian palettes in shape, technology, and material;[21] they are roughly rectangular with rounded edges, plain, with a hole drilled in the top center, and made of regional stones.

Maceheads, in local and non-local stones (e.g., marble, granite, diorite, travertine, calcite, limestone) and resembling Egyptian specimens, also occur. Originally developed for warfare, Egyptian maceheads assumed a ritual function throughout the Predynastic period and later became a symbol of power for the king and his courtiers.[22] In the southern Levant, maceheads were adopted as ceremonial objects and status-related insignia. Their manufacture has a long tradition dating back to the Chalcolithic; therefore, when lacking a precise identification of raw material, it is difficult to establish if these were imported or locally produced. Also, raw stones may have been imported from Egypt and worked in the country.[23] In some cases, Egyptian origin has been suggested on technological and stylistic grounds.[24]

Personal ornaments made of non-local stones and frit/faience, and Nilotic shells (used, for example, as cosmetic containers), are also attested.

3. Egyptian and Egyptian-Style Objects from EB II Contexts at Tell es-Sultan

The present study began with a reassessment of Egyptian imports and Egyptian-style objects from Tell es-Sultan/Jericho, attested at the site throughout the EB I–III. The rise of the EB II urban center at Tell es-Sultan may be related to various factors:[25] the favorable environment of the oasis, with abundant fresh water and cultivable land that produced substantial food supplies accumulation, but also the exploitation of Dead Sea resources, such as asphalt,[26] salt, and sulfur. Tell es-Sultan/Jericho's strategic location, which controlled the routes along the Jordan Valley, and the site's proximity to the raw materials of the Dead Sea basin, put it at the center of an extended trade network that included Egypt. Regional and interregional exchanges enhanced the role of the town as a trading center and triggered the development of a complex, urbanized society. A ruling elite, controlling the town, the oasis, and trade, progressively emerged, as did the ideological apparatus supporting the new organizational model.[27]

The attestation of *aegyptiaca* at Tell es-Sultan starts in the late EB IA, increases in the EB IB,

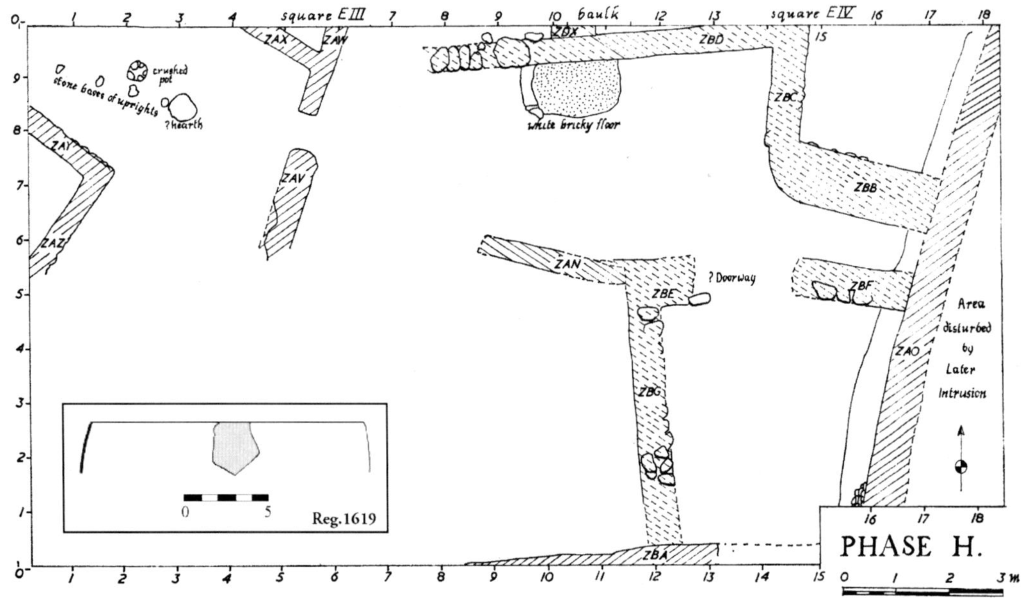

Figure 3: Tell es-Sultan. Plan of the EB II dwelling units in Kenyon's Squares EIII–IV (earlier phase; Kenyon 1981, pl. 316b), where stone bowl Reg. 1619 was retrieved (Dorrell 1983, fig. 229:17).

and continues in the EB II, when the imitation of Egyptian objects also began, likely to meet the demand by the emerging urban elite.[28] If compared to the EB I,[29] the presence of Egyptian material in the EB II town seems to decrease. However, it should be considered that south-Levantine EB II was a short-lived phase[30] and that the attestation of *aegyptiaca* continues into the EB III.[31]

Egyptian and Egyptian-style objects from EB II contexts come from the northern dwelling quarter (Fig. 2); in addition, an Egyptianizing palette is ascribed to the EB II occupation in Tomb D12 in the necropolis.

3.1. A Stone Bowl

A bowl fragment of likely Egyptian origin was retrieved during Kenyon's excavations in Squares EIII–IV, in an early stage of the EB II northern dwelling quarter (Kenyon's Phase H; Fig. 3). It consists of the incurved rim of a bowl made of fine, polished limestone (Reg. No. 1619).[32] Although the heirloom value of Egyptian vessels, sometimes handed down through the centuries, has to be considered, this does not seem the case for this vessel since the two superimposed EB IB and EB II settlements in Squares EIII–IV are separated by a severe destruction (Phase M):[33] the item would have therefore come from its primary context.

3.2. Stone Palettes

No Egyptian palettes have been attributed so far to the EB II occupation,[34] but a group of Egyptianizing palettes was documented. Four specimens come from Kenyon's excavations in the northern dwelling quarter and the necropolis: Reg. No. 1197 from Squares EIII–IV, Phase Fi;[35] Reg. No. 2630 from Trench II, Phase XVI.liv–lv;[36] and Reg. No. 2632 from Trench II, Phase XVI.lviii (roughly finished and thicker);[37] Reg. No. 353 from Tomb D12. Three of these are published here (Fig. 4). [38] The material the palettes were made of was not recorded, but the distinctive greenish gray to gray-black stone from Wadi Hammamat used in the production of Egyptian palettes can be excluded (see note 21). Moreover, local copies exhibit a plain rectangular shape with slightly rounded edges and contrast with the Protodynastic Egyptian palettes retrieved at Tell es-Sultan itself in EB I layers, which show a sharp square or rectangular shape and are decorated with two incised lines parallel to the edge on one side.[39]

3.3. A Stone Macehead

Half of a well-worked barrel-shaped macehead (Reg. No. 1449), made of an unidentified black stone, was retrieved in Squares EIII–IV, Phase K–J (Fig. 5).[40] Although only the analysis of the stone can settle the question of its type, the description

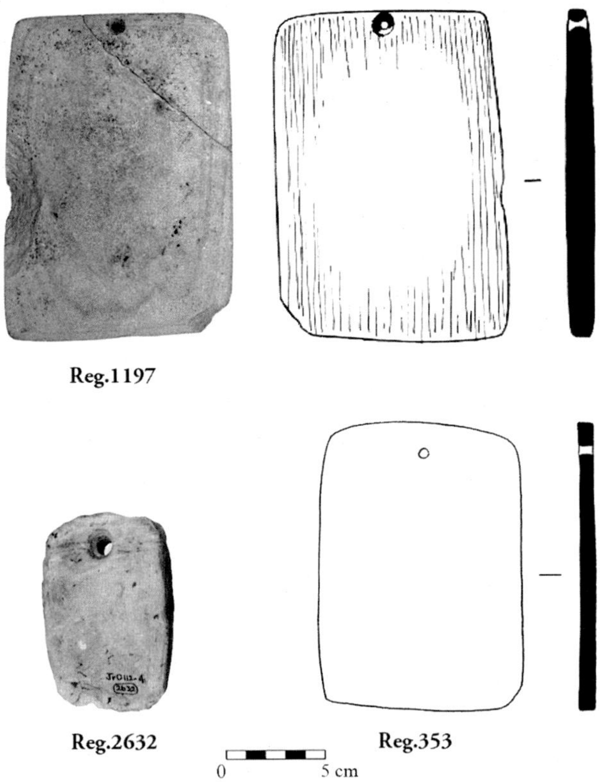

Figure 4: Tell es-Sultan. Three of the four Egyptian-style palettes from Kenyon's excavations: Reg. No. 1197 (Dorrell 1983, fig. 230: 12), Reg. No. 2632 (Dorrell 1983, pl. 21: c), and Reg. 353 (Kenyon 1960, fig. 40:3).

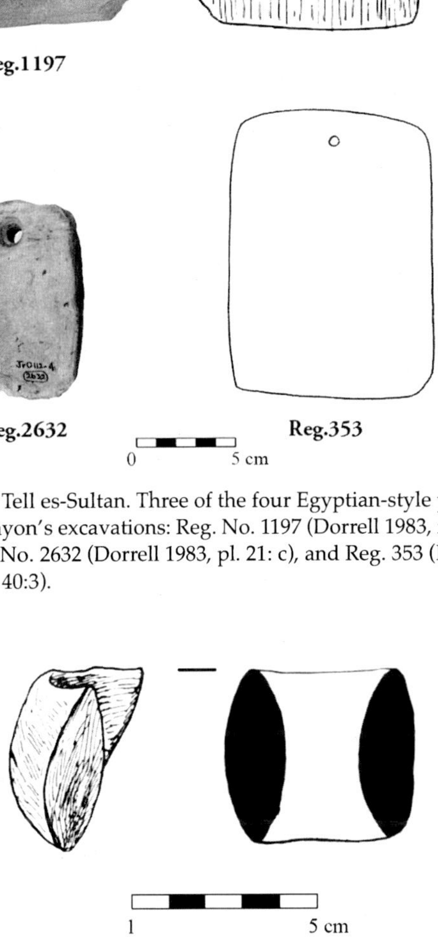

Figure 5: Tell es-Sultan. Half of a barrel-shaped macehead (Reg. No. 1449) from Kenyon's Squares EIII–IV (Wheeler 1982, fig. 256: 2).

may point to a material unusual for the region,[41] perhaps suggesting that either the macehead or the material was imported. Egyptian maceheads produced in non-local stones (e.g., marble, granite, diorite, travertine, calcite) are attested in the country throughout the EB II–III urban era. At Tell es-Sultan itself, a group of eleven maceheads can be ascribed to the EB III town; when raw material is not specified,

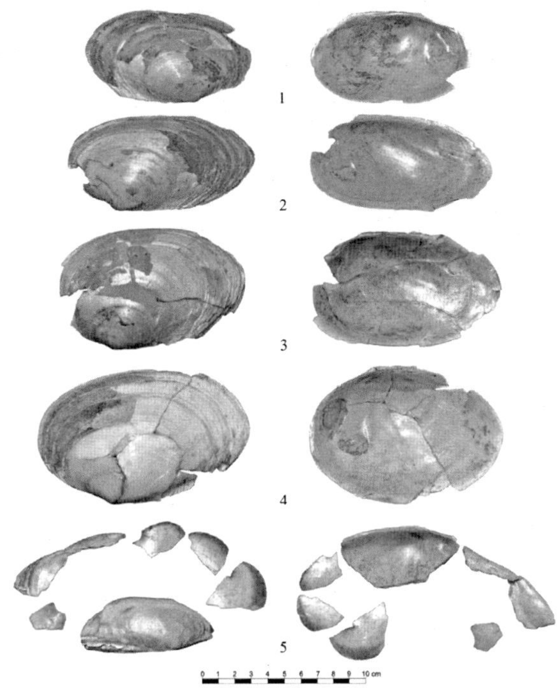

Figure 6: Tell es-Sultan. The five *Chambardia rubens* shells from the northern dwelling quarter (Nigro et al. 2018, fig. 7).

the style and manufacturing technique may point to an Egyptian origin or strong Egyptian emulation for most of them.[42]

3.4. Beads

Disk and barrel-shaped beads made of frit/faience, carnelian, calcite, and rock crystal, retrieved in EB II–III tombs, may also represent Egyptian imports. This is the case of beads from EB II Tomb A127 and EB III Tombs F2 and F3.[43] As for carnelian and frit/faience beads, the question of provenance remains uncertain. Small carnelian and faience objects are widespread at EB II–III south Levantine sites and they should not be considered Egyptian imports unless chemical and technological evidence confirms this. Sources of carnelian were present in the country and may have provided the raw material for a local bead-making industry.[44] Likewise, faience production centers are thought to have existed in both Egypt and the ancient Near East during the 3rd millennium BCE.

3.5. Organic Materials: Nilotic Shells

A hoard of five Nilotic shells (*Chambardia rubens*), found in an EB II domestic unit in the northern

Egyptian and Egyptian-style objects from Tell es-Sultan		
Archaeological Period	Egyptian objects	Egyptian-style objects
mature EB IB	1 palette 5 maceheads* (4 from the tell and 1 from the necropolis) stone and frit/faïence beads	1 palette (from the latest EB IB layer in Trench III)
EB II	**1 stone vessel** **1 macehead** **five Nilotic shells (*Chambardia rubens*)** **stone and frit/faïence beads**	**4 palettes**
EB III	11 maceheads* (10 from the tell and 1 from the necropolis) 1 pedant made of *Chambardia rubens* stone and frit/faïence beads	1 palette

Table 1: Summary table of Egyptian and Egyptian-style objects from Tell es-Sultan.
* Raw materials are not always specified, but many maceheads were made of calcite or marble

dwelling quarter, represents an Egyptian import (Fig. 6).[45] During the EB II, specimens of *Chambardia rubens* are attested at 'Ain Assawir (Tomb 40), 'Arad, and Bab edh-Dhra'; numerous *Chambardia rubens* were also found in the Megiddo temple area dated to the EB I–III.[46] Due to their iridescent inner surface, *Chambardia rubens* shells were considered luxury goods and used both in the manufacture of personal items and as containers for cosmetics. Scanning Electron Microscopy examination revealed that the shells retrieved at Tell es-Sultan contained manganese dioxide, a substance obtained from malachite/azurite/oxidized copper (presumably quarried from mines in the Sinai), which was a basic pigment for cosmetics in ancient Egypt. The five imported shells were thus probably used as cosmetic containers. They may be related to elite individuals who were in contact with Egypt and chose Egyptian cosmetic habits as a means of demonstrating rank.[47] Likewise, Egyptianizing palettes could be associated with Egyptian-influenced cosmetic habits. At Tell es-Sultan, *Chambardia rubens* is attested also in the necropolis in EB III Tomb F4 as a double-holed trapezoidal pedant.[48]

3.6. Conclusions

Egyptian and Egyptian-style items from EB II contexts at Tell es-Sultan hint at trade and cultural contacts with Egypt. Although Egyptian imports could have arrived through indirect or down-the-line trade, the strategic location and the access to important resources suggest direct interconnections between Egypt and the site. Meanwhile, local artisans started a production of Egyptian-inspired objects (as attested by the Egyptianizing palettes), likely to satisfy increasing demand by high-ranking people.

The presence of Egyptian items in the EB II–III town would also point to the persistence of an exchange path between Egypt and the southern part of the country throughout the first half of the 3rd millennium BCE, while Egyptian interests moved northward. Interesting from this point of view is the recent isotopic analysis on a sacrificial donkey from an EB III deposit at Tell es-Safi providing evidence of the movement of pack animals between Old Kingdom Egypt and EB III southern Levant, and indicating that overland transport via donkey caravans across north Sinai continued somehow into the EB III.[49] Tell es-Sultan participated, to varying degrees, in this branch of the Egyptian–south Levantine exchange network throughout the EB I–III.

4. Egyptian and Egyptian-Style Objects from EB II Contexts at Tell el-Far'ah North

Tell el-Far'ah North is located in the western part of the fertile Wadi Far'ah Valley, on a main thoroughfare that connected the central hills with the Jordan Valley. Thanks to the presence of two close springs ('Ain Far'ah and 'Ain Daleib), the proximity to agricultural areas, and the strategic position, occupation at the mound developed in the late 4th millennium BCE, until an urban center arose at the dawn of the EB II.

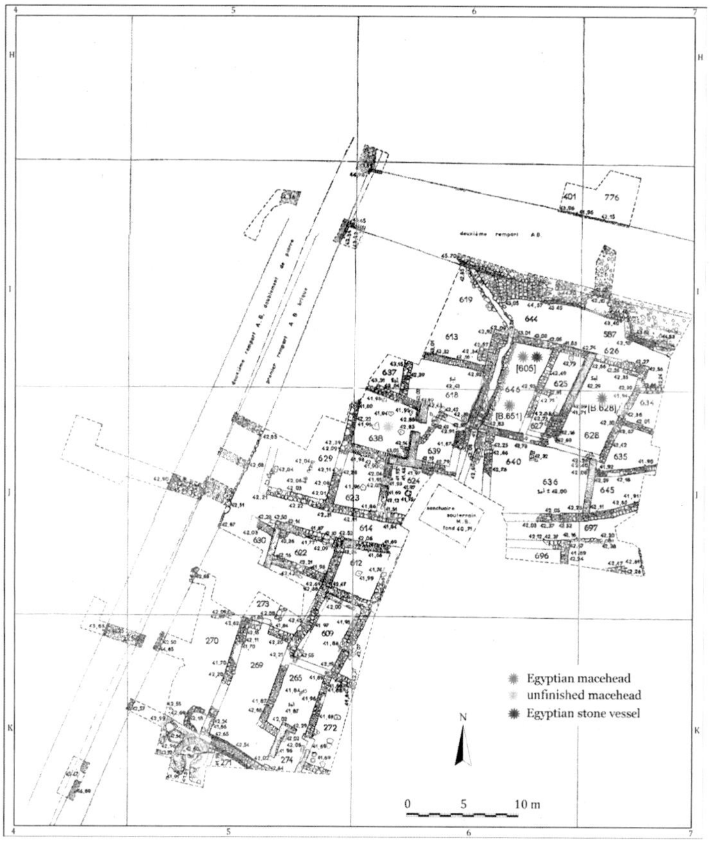

FIGURE 7: Tell el-Far'ah North. Plan of the EB II northwestern dwelling quarter (mid-EB II,Vaux's period 3; modified afterVaux 1961, pl. XXXIV). Loci in brackets, where Egyptian items were found, belong to different (upper or lower) dwelling reconstructions.

The central hill country underwent a period of settlement peak and intensified activity during the EB IB: the area was one of the most suitable districts for the horticulture-based economy that brought about a dramatic demographic and economic growth.[50] Horticulture products were produced not only for local consumption but also for export to adjacent regions, including Egypt, where the demand for wine and olive oil intensified from the Naqada IID–IIIA period onward. Intra- and interregional exchanges spurred agricultural activities and settlement expansion, and triggered the development of political and social complexity.[51] Tell el-Far'ah North was one of the thriving settlements in this process and became the leading town in the district during the EB II.

Palynological analysis based on the Sea of Galilee pollen record would indicate a decline in olive horticulture in the EB II; the latter has been explained as a consequence of the cessation of intensive interaction with Egypt.[52] Nevertheless, the identification of Tel Beth Yerah as a hub of interregional commodity trading, with evidence for direct contacts with Egypt (see above), points to enduring Egyptian–south

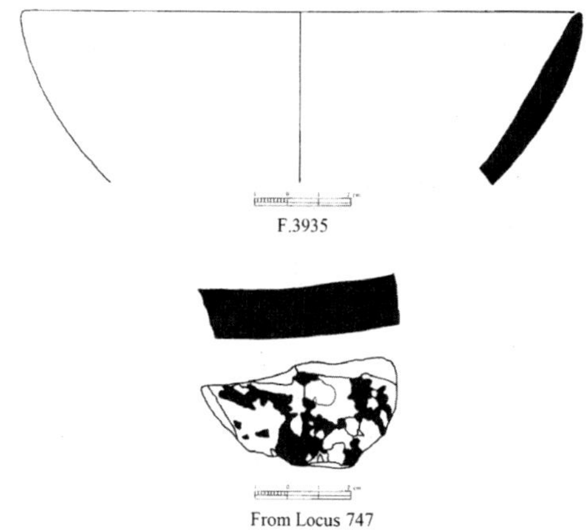

FIGURE 8: Tell el-Far'ah North. Egyptian stone vessels from the EB II town (Sowada 2009, fig. 4a–b).

Levantine interconnections throughout the EB II and centered in the northern Jordan Valley. The central hill country could be one of the procurers,[53] with its vineyard and olive products channeled to a network of long-distance exchanges.

The connection with Egypt is hinted by some Egyptian and Egyptian-style objects retrieved in the EB II urban center of Tell el-Far'ah North.[54] Items come from superimposed phases of EB II dwellings in the northwestern dwelling quarter (FIG. 7); an unfinished macehead comes from the northern sector.[55]

4.1. STONE VESSELS

Two Egyptian stone vessels were found in the EB II town (FIG. 8): a finely polished travertine bowl fragment (from L.605; F.3935), which finds parallels primarily in First Dynasty specimens, and the body sherd of a thick-walled black and white porphyry spheroidal jar (without registration number), from Trench L.747, which finds parallels between the late First and the Third Dynasty.[56]

4.2. STONE MACEHEADS

Two maceheads made in non-local stones were found in the northwestern dwelling quarter. Despite their summary description and the need for their further scientific study, the stone types may suggest an Egyptian origin or imported

Egyptian and Egyptian-style objects from Tell el-Far'ah North		
Archaeological Period	Finds	
	Egyptian objects	Egyptian-style objects
EB IB	1 palette (from Tomb 12) [2 maceheads]	
EB II	**2 stone vessels** **3 maceheads**	**2 (unfinished) maceheads**

Table 2: Summary table of Egyptian and Egyptian-style objects from Tell el-Far'ah North.

raw materials. A cylindrical macehead with hourglass perforation (F.3897) in travertine was retrieved in L.605; while a fragment of a macehead (F.4101) in diorite was found below L.628 (Fig. 7). A small pear-shaped macehead (F.4210) in hematite was found below L.651.[57] Two unfinished maceheads, both incompletely drilled, may represent local copies and provide evidence for macehead production: a spherical macehead (from L638; F.4074) in white limestone;[58] and half of an ovoid-shaped macehead (F.62) in polished limestone(?) from Square 4, in the northern sector of the site.[59]

4.3. Conclusions

The case of Tell el-Far'ah North is interesting for both the finds and the contexts of retrieval. The presence of Egyptian prestige objects across the EB II dwellings illustrates the wealth achieved by some segments of the population. This may hint at emerging social groups within the EB II community and may be related to the development of an urban elite. Sebag (2005) has suggested that some larger multi-room houses might be identified as elite residences ('patrician houses') in view of their size and the quality of their construction—this would point to the dwellers' higher social status and offer evidence of social differentiation.[60]

The surplus of horticulture products prompted intra- and interregional exchanges. *Aegyptiaca* at Tell el-Far'ah North may have arrived via mediators or resulted from internal exchanges, but they may also reveal interactions (direct or mediated) between the town and Egyptian agents based somewhere in the country.[61] In any case, Egyptian material reached the site within the framework of the active interconnections between Egypt and northern Canaan in the EB II.

5. Concluding Remarks

Contrary to the literature pointing to a drop in Egyptian–south Levantine interaction during the EB I–II shift, the case studies of Tell es-Sultan and Tell el-Far'ah North contribute to the ongoing reevaluation of the topic. The two sites document the presence of Egyptian and Egyptian-style objects in EB II contexts and point to Egyptian contacts in the initial urbanizing phase.

During the EB I–II transition, Egypt's engagement in southern Levant was reorganized, aiming at a different goal both in terms of commodities and procurement modes: a two-way relationship between Egypt and its immediate northeastern neighbor was set up. Exchanges were likely achieved through the action of Egyptian agents who developed relations with local elites, possibly addressing some key centers (e.g., Tel Beth Yerah). The Egyptian–south Levantine interaction included diversified networks of both sea and land routes, in the north and south, and involved several centers located as far as the inland, depending on the different commodities Egypt was looking for.

Egyptian prestige objects were involved in the exchange mechanism. These exotic items may have been acquired by individuals of local elites. Personal equipment and bodily adornment were, in fact, one of the distinguishing features of emerging groups: the restricted access to certain forms of personal display contributed to social differentiation. Local elites likely aimed at acquiring exotic prestige goods to enhance their social status, and contacts with Egypt provided these elites some form of status involving the display of Egyptian objects.[62] While exporting local commodities, the elites of Tell es-Sultan and Tell el-Far'ah North may thus have acquired, among other things, exotic prestige objects, as well as exotic grooming habits, and may have used them to emphasize their status by means of display.[63] The contexts of retrieval—across the dwellings of the EB II towns—seems also to indicate the request and consumption of such luxury goods by emerging social groups. Hence, although evidence is still patchy, trade and cultural relations between Egypt and the earliest urban organizations of the southern Levant are undergoing reevaluation in the light of new data. The reassessment of data from old and new excavations at Tell es-Sultan and Tell el-Far'ah North offers new insights contributing to the ongoing investigation.

References

Amiran, R. 1974. "The Painted Pottery Style of the Early Bronze II Period in Palestine." *Levant* 6: 65–68.

———. 1985. "Canaanite Merchants in Tombs of the Early Bronze I at Azor." *'Atiqot* 17: 190–192.

Amiran, R., U. Paran, Y. Shiloh, R. Brown, Y. Tsafrir, and A. Ben-Tor. 1978. *Early Arad. The Chalcolithic Settlement and Early Bronze City. Vol. I. First–Fifth Seasons of Excavations, 1962–1966*. Judean Desert Studies. Jerusalem: Israel Exploration Society.

Arnold, E. R., G. Hartman, H. J. Greenfield, I. Shai, L. E. Babcock, and A. M. Maeir. 2016. "Isotopic Evidence for Early Trade in Animals between Old Kingdom Egypt and Canaan." *PLoS ONE* 11(6). DOI: 10.1371/journal.pone.0157650.

Badreshany, K., G. Philip, and M. Kennedy. 2020. "The development of integrated regional economies in the Early Bronze Age Levant: new evidence from 'Combed Ware' jars." *Levant* 52(1–2): 160–196.

Bar, S. 2014. *The Dawn of the Bronze Age. The Pattern of Settlement in the Lower Jordan Valley and the Desert Fringes of Samaria during the Chalcolithic Period and Early Bronze Age I*. Culture and History of the Ancient Near East 72. Leiden & Boston: Brill.

Bar-Yosef Mayer, D. E. 2000. "Mollusc Shells." In I. Finkelstein, D. Ussishkin, and B. Halpern (eds.), *Megiddo III. The 1992–1998 Seasons*. Monograph Series 18, 478–486. Tel Aviv: Emery and Claire Yass Publications in Archaeology.

———. 2002. "Egyptian-Canaanite Interaction during the Fourth and Third Millennia BCE: The Shell Connection." In E.C.M. van den Brink and T.E. Levy (eds.), *Egypt and the Levant. Interrelations from the 4th through the Early 3rd Millennium B.C.E.*, 129–135. London & New York: Leicester University Press.

Bar-Yosef Mayer, D. E., and I. Baruch. 2006. "Mollusc Shells." In I. Finkelstein, D. Ussishkin, and B. Halpern (eds.), *Megiddo IV. The 1998–2002 Seasons*. Monograph Series 24, 497–504. Tel Aviv: Emery and Claire Yass Publications in Archaeology.

Braun, E. 2011. "Early Interactions between Peoples of the Nile Valley and the Southern Levant." In E. Teeter (ed.), *Before the Pyramids. The Origins of Egyptian Civilization*. Oriental Institute Museum Publications 33, 105–122. Chicago: The Oriental Institute of the University of Chicago.

Brink, E. C. M. van den and E. Braun. 2002. "Wine Jars with Serekhs from Early Bronze Lod: Appellation Vallée du Nil Contrôlée, but for Whom?" In E. C. M. van den Brink and E. Yannai (eds.), *In Quest of Ancient Settlements and Landscapes: Archaeological Studies in Honour of Ram Gophna*, 167–192. Tel Aviv: Ramot Publishing/Tel Aviv University.

Connan, J., A. Nissenbaum, and D. Dessort. 1992. "Molecular Archaeology: Export of Dead Sea Asphalt to Canaan and Egypt in the Chalcolithic–Early Bronze Age (4th–3rd Millennium BC)." *Geochimica et Cosmochimica Acta* 56(7): 2743–2759.

Czarnowicz, M. 2014. "Egyptian Mace-Heads from The Southern Levant." In M. A. Jucha, J. Dębowska-Ludwin, and P. Kołodziejczyk (eds.), *Aegyptus Est Imago Caeli. Studies Presented to Krzysztof M. Cialowicz on His 60th Birthday*, 195–201. Kraków: Institute of Archaeology, Jagiellonian University in Kraków.

Dorrell, P. G. 1983. "Appendix A. Stone Vessels, Tools, and Objects." In K.M. Kenyon and T.A. Holland, *Excavations at Jericho. Volume Five. The Pottery Phases of the Tell and Others Finds*, 485–575. London: British School of Archaeology in Jerusalem.

Finkelstein, I. and R. Gophna. 1993. "Settlement, Demographic, and Economic Patterns in the Highlands of Palestine in the Chalcolithic and Early Bronze Periods and the Beginning of Urbanism." *Bulletin of the American Schools of Oriental Research* 289: 1–22.

Fischer, P. 2002. "Egyptian-Transjordanian Interaction during Predynastic and Protodynastic Times: The Evidence from Tell Abu al-Kharaz,

Jordan Valley." In E. C. M. van den Brink and T. E. Levy (eds.), *Egypt and the Levant. Interrelations from the 4th through the Early 3rd Millennium B.C.E.*, 323–333. London & New York: Leicester University Press.

Garstang, J., I. Ben-Dor, and G. M. Fitzgerald. 1936. "Jericho: City and Necropolis (Report for the Sixth and Concluding Season, 1936)." *Liverpool Annals of Archaeology and Anthropology* 23: 67–100.

Geraty, L. T., L. G. Herr, Ø. S. LaBianca, J. R. Battenfield, R. G. Boling, D. R. Clark, J. I. Lawlor, L. A. Mitchel, and R. Younker. 1986. "Madaba Plains Project: A Preliminary Report of the 1984 Season at Tell el-'Umeiri and Vicinity." *Bulletin of the American Schools of Oriental Research, Supplementum* 24: 117–144.

Getzov, N. 2006. *The Tel Bet Yerah Excavations, 1994–1995*. IAA Reports 28. Jerusalem: Israel Antiquities Authority.

Gilbert, G. P. 2004. *Weapons, Warriors and Warfare in Early Egypt*. BAR International Series 1208. Oxford: BAR.

Greenberg, R. 2019. *The Archaeology of the Bronze Age Levant. From Urban Origins to the Demise of City-States, 3700–1000 BCE*. Cambridge World Archaeology. Cambridge: Cambridge University Press.

Greenberg, R., and E. Eisenberg. 2002. "Egypt, Bet Yerah and Early Canaanite Urbanization." In E.C.M. van den Brink and T.E. Levy (eds.), *Egypt and the Levant. Interrelations from the 4th through the Early 3rd Millennium B.C.E.*, 213–222. London & New York: Leicester University Press.

Greenberg, R. and M. Iserlis. 2014. "The Early Bronze Age Pottery Industries." In R. Greenberg (ed.), *Bet Yeraḥ – The Early Bronze Age Mound, Vol. II: Urban Structure and Material Culture, 1933–1986 Excavations*. IAA Reports 54, 53–150. Jerusalem: Israel Antiquities Authority.

———. 2020. "A Note on First Dynasty Egypt, Tel Bet Yerah, and the Origins of Commodity Exchange on the Levantine Seaboard." *Journal of Ancient Egyptian Interconnections* 27: 38–50.

Greenberg, R., S. Paz, D. Wengrow, and M. Iserlis. 2012. "Tel Beth Yerah: Hub of the Early Bronze Age Levant." *Near Eastern Archaeology* 75: 88–107.

Greenberg, R., D. Wengrow, and S. Paz. 2010. "Cosmetic Connections? An Egyptian Relief Carving from Early Bronze Age Tel Bet Yerah (Israel)." *Antiquity* (Project Gallery) 324(84), http://www.antiquity.ac.uk/projgall/greenberg324/.

Greenfield, H. J., T. L. Greenfield, E. Arnold, I. Shai, S. Albaz, and A. M. Maeir. 2020. "Evidence for Movement of Goods and Animals from Egypt to Canaan during the Early Bronze of the Southern Levant: A View from Tell Eṣ-Sâfi/Gath." *Ägypten und Levante* 30: 377–397.

Hartung, U. 2001. *Umm el-Qaab II, Importkeramik aus dem Friedhof U in Abydos (Umm el-Qaab) und die Beziehungen Ägyptens zu Vorderasien im 4. Jahrtausend v. Chr*. Archäologische Veröffentlichung 92. Mainz: Philipp von Zabern.

Hartung, U., C. E. Köhler, V. Müller, and M. F. Ownby. 2015. "Imported Pottery from Abydos: A New Petrographic Perspective." *Ägypten und Levante* 25: 295–333.

Hendrickx, S. and L. Bavay. 2002. "The Relative Chronological Position of Egyptian Predynastic and Early Dynastic Tombs with Objects Imported from the Near East and the Nature of Interregional Contacts." In E.C.M. van den Brink and T.E. Levy (eds.), *Egypt and the Levant. Interrelations from the 4th through the Early 3rd Millennium B.C.E.*, 58–80. London & New York: Leicester University Press.

Holland, T. A. 1982. "Appendix C. Figurines and Miscellaneous Objects." In K. M. Kenyon and T.A. Holland, *Excavations at Jericho. Volume Four. The Pottery Type Series and Other Finds*, 551–563. London: British School of Archaeology in Jerusalem.

———. 1983. "Appendix M. Stone Maceheads." In K. M. Kenyon and T. A. Holland, *Excavations at Jericho. Volume Five. The Pottery Phases of the Tell and Others Finds*, 804–813. London: British School of Archaeology in Jerusalem.

Hübner, U. 2011. "Die archäologische Expedition 2011 in die Region um Petra: Ausgrabungen auf Umm Saysabān." *Natur und Mensch. Jahresmitteilungen der Naturhistorische Gesellschaft Nürnberg* 2011: 157–168.

Iserlis, M., D. Steiniger, and R. Greenberg. 2019. "Contact between First Dynasty Egypt and Specific Sites in the Levant: New Evidence from Ceramic Analysis." *Journal of Archaeological Science: Reports* 24: 1023–1040.

Jacobs, P. F. 1996. "A Cosmetic Palette from Early Bronze Age III at Tell Halif." In J.D. Seger (ed.), *Retrieving the Past: Essays on Archaeological Research and Methodology in Honor of Gus W. van Beek*, 123–134. Winona Lake, IN: Eisenbrauns.

Jacobs, P. F. and J. D. Seger. 2017. *Lahav VI: Excavations in Field I at Tell Halif, 1976–1999. The Early Bronze III to Late Arabic Strata*. Reports of the Lahav Research Project/Excavations at Tell Halif, Israel, VI. Winona Lake, IN: Eisenbrauns.

Kansa, E. and T. E. Levy. 2002. "Ceramics, Identity, and the Role of the State: The View from Nahal Tillah." In E. C. M. van den Brink and T. E. Levy (eds.), *Egypt and the Levant. Interrelations from the 4th through the Early 3rd Millennium B.C.E.*, 190–212. London & New York: Leicester University Press.

Kenyon, K. M. 1960. *Excavations at Jericho. Volume One. The Tombs Excavated in 1952–1954*. London: British School of Archaeology in Jerusalem.

———. 1981. *Excavations at Jericho. Volume Three. The Architecture and Stratigraphy of the Tell*. London: British School of Archaeology in Jerusalem.

Klemm, R. and D. D. Klemm. 2008. *Stones and Quarries in Ancient Egypt*. London: The British Museum Press.

Kroeper, K. 1996. "Minshat Abu Omar: Burials with Palettes." In J. Spencer (ed.), *Aspects of Early Egypt*, 70–92. London: British Museum Press.

Ktalav, I. 2013. "Mollusc Shells." In I. Finkelstein, D. Ussishkin, and E. H. Cline (eds.), *Megiddo V. The 2004–2008 Seasons*, vol. III. Monograph Series 31, 1215–1219. Winona Lake, IN: Eisenbrauns.

Langgut, D., M. J. Adams, and I. Finkelstein. 2016. "Climate, Settlement Patterns and Olive Horticulture in the Southern Levant during the Early Bronze and Intermediate Bronze Ages (c. 3600–1950 BC)." *Levant* 48(2): 117–134.

Loud, G. 1948. *Megiddo II. Seasons of 1935–39*. Oriental Institute Publications 62. Chicago: The University of Chicago Press.

Marcus, E. 2002. "Early Seafaring and Maritime Activity in the Southern Levant from Prehistory through the Third Millennium BCE." In E. C. M. van den Brink and T. E. Levy (eds.), *Egypt and the Levant. Interrelations from the 4th through the Early 3rd Millennium B.C.E.*, 403–417. London & New York: Leicester University Press.

Milevski, I. 2011. *Early Bronze Age Goods Exchange in the Southern Levant. A Marxist Perspective*. London: Routledge.

Milevski, I., O. Marder, and A.N. Goring-Morris. 2002. "The Circulation of Asphalt in Southern Canaan and Egypt during the Early Bronze I." In E. C.M. van den Brink and E. Yannai (eds.), *In Quest of Ancient Settlements and Landscapes. Archaeological Studies in Honour of Ram Gophna*, 219–236. Tel Aviv, Ramot Publishing.

Miroschedji, P. de. 2002. "The Socio-Political Dynamics of Egyptian-Canaanite Interaction in the Early Bronze Age." In E.C.M. van den Brink and T.E. Levy (eds.), *Egypt and the Levant. Interrelations from the 4th through the Early 3rd Millennium B.C.E.*, 39–57. London & New York: Leicester University Press.

———. 2015. "Les relations entre l'Égypte et le Levant aux IVe et IIIe millénaires à la lumière des fouilles de Tell es-Sakan." *Comptes rendus de l'Académie des Inscriptions et Belles-Lettres* 2015 (avril–juin): 1003–1038.

———. 2018. "The Urbanization of the Southern Levant in Its Near Eastern Setting." *Origini. Prehistory and Protohistory of Ancient Civilizations* 42: 109–148.

Müller, V. 2014. "Relations between Egypt and the Near East during the 1st Dynasty as Represented by the Royal Tomb of Den in Umm el-Qaab/Abydos." In F. Höflmayer and R. Eichmann (eds.), *Egypt and the Southern Levant in the Early Bronze Age: C14, Chronology, Connections*. Orient-Archäologie 31, 241–258. Rahden/Westf: M. Leidorf.

Nigro, L., with contributions by M. Sala. 2010. *Tell es-Sultan/Jericho in the Early Bronze II (3000–2700 BC): the rise of an early Palestinian city. A synthesis of the results of four archaeological expeditions*. Rome "La Sapienza" Studies on the Archaeology of Palestine & Transjordan 5. Rome: "La Sapienza" Expedition to Palestine & Jordan.

Nigro, L. 2019. "Tell es-Sultan/ancient Jericho in the Early Bronze Age II–III." In E. Gallo (ed.), *Conceptualizing Urban Experiences: Tell es-Sultan and Tall al-Ḥammām Early Bronze Cities across the Jordan*. Rome "La Sapienza" Studies on the Archaeology of Palestine & Transjordan 13, 79–108. Rome: "La Sapienza" Expedition to Palestine & Jordan.

Nigro, L., L. Calcagnile, J. Yasin, E. Gallo, and G. Quarta. 2019. "Jericho and the Chronology of Palestine in the Early Bronze Age: A Radiometric Re-assessment." *Radiocarbon* 61(1): 211–241.

Nigro, L., E. Gallo, R. Gharib, F. Mura, M. Macrì, and T. Rinaldi. 2020. "An Egyptian Green Schist Palette and an Amazonite Gemstone from the "Palace of the Copper Axes" at Batrawy, Jordan." *Vicino Oriente* 24: 1–26.

Nigro, L., D. Montanari, F. Mura, J. Yasine, and T. Rinaldi. 2018. "A Hoard of Nilotic Nacreous Shells from Egypt to Jericho (Early Bronze II, 3000–2800 BCE): Their Finding, Content and Historical Archaeological Implications." *Palestine Exploration Quarterly* 150(2): 110–125.

Nissenbaum, A., A. Serban, R. Amiran, and O. Ilan. 1984. "Dead Sea Asphalt from the Excavations in Tel Arad and Small Tel Malhata." *Paléorient* 10: 157–161.

Paz, S. 2014. "The Small Finds." In R. Greenberg (ed.), *Bet Yeraḥ – The Early Bronze Age Mound, Vol. II: Urban Structure and Material Culture, 1933–1986 Excavations*. Israel Antiquity Authority Reports 54, 235–298. Jerusalem: Israel Antiquities Authority.

Portugali, J. and R. Gophna. 1993 "Crisis, Progress and Urbanization: The Transition from Early Bronze I to Early Bronze II in Palestine." *Tel Aviv* 20: 164–185.

Rast, W. E. and R. T. Schaub. 1989. *Bâb edh-Dhrâ': Excavations in the Cemetery Directed by Paul W. Lapp (1965–67)*. Reports of the Expedition to the Dead Sea Plain, Jordan 1. Winona Lake, IN: Eisenbrauns.

———. 2003. *Bâb edh-Dhrâ': Excavations at the Town Site (1975–1981). Part 1: Text, Part 2: Plates and Appendices*. Reports of the Expedition to the Dead Sea Plain, Jordan 2. Winona Lake, IN: Eisenbrauns.

Regev, J., P. de Miroschedji, R. Greenberg, E. Braun, Z. Greenhut, and E. Boaretto. 2012. "Chronology of the Early Bronze Age in the southern Levant: new analysis for a high chronology." *Radiocarbon* 54(3–4): 525–566.

Rowan, Y. M. and T. E. Levy. 2011. "Transitions in Macehead Manufacture in the Ancient Levant: A Case Study from Nahal Tillah (Tel Halif Terrace), Israel." In M. S. Chesson (ed.), *Daily Life, Materiality, and Complexity in Early Urban Communities of the Southern Levant. Papers in Honor of Walter E. Rast and R. Thomas Schaub*, 199–218. Winona Lake, IN: Eisenbrauns.

Sala, M. 2008. *L'architettura sacra della Palestina nell'età del Bronzo Antico I–III*. Contributi e Materiali di Archeologia Orientale 13. Rome: Università degli Studi di Roma "La Sapienza".

———. 2012. "Egyptian and Egyptianizing Objects from EB I–III Tell es-Sultan/Ancient Jericho." *Vicino Oriente* 16: 277–303.

———. 2014. "EB II–III *Aegyptiaca* East of the Jordan: A Reevaluation of Trade and Cultural Interactions between Egypt and the Transjordanian Urban Centres." *Vicino Oriente* 18: 65–81.

Sarret, M., P. Adam, P. Schaeffer, Q. Ebert, J. Perthuison, and G. Pierrat-Bonnefois. 2017. "Organic Substances from Egyptian Jars of the Early Dynastic Period (3100–2700 BCE): Mode of Preparation, Alteration Processes and Botanical (Re)Assessment of "Cedrium"." *Journal of Archaeological Science: Reports* 14: 420–431.

Sebag, D. 2005. "Les habitats au Bronze Ancien au Levant sud." *Bulletin du Centre de recherche français à Jérusalem* 16: 20–44.

Sellin, E. and C. Watzinger. 1913. *Jericho. Die Ergebnisse der Ausgrabungen*. Wissenschaftliche Veröffentlichung der Deutschen Orient-Gesellschaft 22. Leipzig: J.C. Hinrichs.

Serpico, M. 2000. "Resins, Amber and Bitumen." In P.T. Nicholson and I. Shaw (eds.), *Ancient Egyptian Materials and Technology*, 430–474. Cambridge: Cambridge University Press.

Serpico, M., and R. White. 1996. "A Report on the Analysis of the Contents of a Cache of Jars from the Tomb of Djer." In J. Spencer (ed.), *Aspects of Early Egypt*, 128–139. London: British Museum Press.

Sowada, K. N. 2000. "Egyptian Palettes in the EB II and EB III Canaan." In P. Matthiae, A. Enea, L. Peyronel, and F. Pinnock (eds.), *Proceedings of the First International Congress on the Archaeology of the Ancient Near East*, 1527–1540. Rome: Università degli Studi di Roma "La Sapienza".

———. 2009. *Egypt in the Eastern Mediterranean during the Old Kingdom. An Archaeological Perspective*. Orbis Biblicus et Orientalis 237. Fribourg & Göttingen: Academic Press Fribourg & Vandenhoeck & Ruprecht.

———. 2014. "Never the Twain Shall Meet? Synchronising Egyptian and Levantine Chronologies in the 3rd Millennium BC". In F. Höflmayer and R. Eichmann (eds.), *Egypt and the Southern Levant in the Early Bronze Age: C14, Chronology, Connections*. Orient-Archäologie 31, 293–313. Rahden/Westf: M. Leidorf.

———. 2018a. "Hidden Exports: A Likely Early Bronze Age Exchange in Egyptian Cattle to the Levant." *Bulletin of the Australian Centre for Egyptology* 26: 71–78.

———. 2018b. "Stone Vessels." In M. Lebeau (ed.), *ARCANE Interregional Vol. II. Artefacts*, 245–276. Turnhout: Brepols.

———. 2020. "Perspectives on Egypt in the Southern Levant in Light of the High Early Bronze Age Chronology." In S. Richard (ed.), *New Horizons in the Study of the Early Bronze III and Early Bronze IV of the Levant*, 149–168. Winona Lake, IN: Eisenbrauns.

Sowada, K. N., M. Ownby, and A. Wodzińska. 2020. "The Petrography of Imported Levantine Combed Vessels from Early Old Kingdom Giza." *Levant* 52(1–2): 197–214.

Thalmann, J. P. and K. Sowada. 2014. "Levantine "Combed Ware"." In M. Lebeau (ed.), *ARCANE Interregional Vol. I. Ceramics*, 323–345. Turnhout: Brepols.

Vaux, R. de. 1951. "La troisième campagne de fouilles à Tell el-Far'ah près Naplouse: rapport préliminaire (suite)." *Revue Biblique* 58(4): 566–590.

———. 1961. "Les fouilles de Tell el-Far'ah, rapport préliminaire sur les 7e, 8e, 9e campagnes, 1958–1960." *Revue Biblique* 68(4): 557–592.

Vaux, R. de and A. M. Steve. 1947. "La première campagne de fouilles à Tell el-Far'ah, près Naplouse." *Revue Biblique* 54(3): 394–433, 573–589.

———. 1949. "La deuxième campagne de fouilles à Tell el-Far'ah près Naplouse: rapport préliminaire (suite)." *Revue Biblique* 56(1): 102–138.

Wengrow, D. 2006. *The Archaeology of Early Egypt: Social Transformation in North-East Africa, 10,000–2650 BC*. Cambridge: Cambridge University Press.

Wheeler, M. 1982. "Appendix F. Loomweights and Spindle Whorls." In K. M. Kenyon and T. A. Holland, *Excavations at Jericho. Volume Four. The Pottery Type Series and Other Finds*, 623–637. London: British School of Archaeology in Jerusalem.

Wilkinson, A. 1989. "Objects from the Early Bronze II and III Tombs." In W. E. Rast and R. T. Schaub, *Bâb edh-Dhrâ': Excavations in the Cemetery Directed by Paul W. Lapp (1965–67)*. Reports of the Expedition to the Dead Sea Plain, Jordan 1, 444–470. Winona Lake, IN: Eisenbrauns.

Yannai, E. 2002. "Imported Finds from the 'Ein Assawir Tombs (Israel) and Their Significance in Understanding the Chronological Synchronization between Israel, Egypt, and Eastern Anatolia." In E. C. M. van den Brink and T. E. Levy (eds.), *Egypt and the Levant. Interrelations from the 4th through the Early 3rd Millennium B.C.E.*, 334–345. London & New York: Leicester University Press.

Yekutieli, Y. 2002. "Settlement and Subsistence Patterns in North Sinai during the Fifth to Third Millennia BCE." In E. C. M. van den Brink and T. E. Levy (eds.), *Egypt and the Levant. Interrelations from the 4th through the Early 3rd Millennium B.C.E.*, 422–433. London & New York: Leicester University Press.

———. 2004. "Landscape of Control: An Early Bronze Age Ascent in the Southern Judean Desert." *Ancient Near Eastern Studies* 41: 5–37.

Notes

1 Yekutieli 2002, 430–431; Braun 2011, 108–111. Terracotta figurines of laden donkeys retrieved in EB I sites along the coastal plain (Bat Yam, Azor, Ras el-'Ain/Aphek, 'Ain Assawir: Milevski 2011, 187–188), as well as the high rate of equid remains from this area (Milevski 2011, 179–184, 214–215), may be related to the use of donkey caravan routes.

2 They are represented first and foremost by some 700 imported vessels retrieved in Tomb U-j at Abydos (Naqada IIIA1; Hartung 2001). The main incentive for these trade activities was the procurement of Levantine commodities lacking in Egypt at the time: wine, first of all (Müller 2014, note 14), but also olive oil, resins, timber, and copper. Already by c. 3300 BCE, these products played an important role in local patterns of elite consumption, ritual, and funerary display (Wengrow 2006, 137–140).

3 Some speak of 'Egyptian colonial territory' in the late EB IB, for example Miroschedji 2002, 41–44; 2015, 1018–1025; Braun 2011, 112–117; Greenberg 2019, 57–64; *contra* Kansa and Levy 2002, 199, 203–206; Hartung et al. 2015, 325–326, who point out that Egypt at that time was not yet a single territorial state, but home to many regional, probably competing, polities. Also, Czarnowicz and Braun this volume.

4 Miroschedji 2018, 110–123, 130; Greenberg 2019, 71–94. This came along with a definitive assertion of the Egyptian state and national identity in the Nile Valley. South Levantine EB II is currently considered contemporary with

the First Dynasty of Egypt, from the reign of Djer (Sowada 2020, 153–154).

5 Miroschedji 2002, 45–46; Marcus 2002, 407–409. In keeping with the results of the north Sinai surveys that found no EB II–III remains, the pack-donkey route from southern Levant to Egypt via north Sinai was dismissed for the end of the EB I (Yekutieli 2002, 423–425). However, a recent isotopic analysis on a sacrificial donkey from an EB III deposit at Tell es-Safi proves the movement of pack animals between Egypt and the southern districts of the country still during the EB III (see below).

6 Sowada 2009, 36–37, 241–244; Miroschedji 2015, 1026–1028. These agents could be Egyptians coming from the homeland or Egyptian traders who lived in Canaan. At Tel Beth Yerah, the presence of Egyptian emissaries directly at the site has been assumed (Greenberg and Eisenberg 2002, 214–221; Greenberg and Iserlis 2020, 43–44).

7 In the Predynastic period, wine was presumably the main container-based commodity exported to Egypt, until Egyptians introduced wine making in the country during the Protodynastic period (Brink and Braun 2002, 168–170; Hendrickx and Bavay 2002, 70, 75; Hartung et al. 2015, 298–302). In the Early Dynastic (ED) period, coniferous resins and vegetable oils, used for ritual activities, became the dominant traded commodities (Sowada 2009, 43–44, 191–192, 198–200; Müller 2014, 244–246; Hartung et al. 2015, 324). This is confirmed by residue analyses on pottery containers from First Dynasty royal tombs at Abydos (Serpico and White 1996; Sarret et al. 2017). Recent studies on sealing practices in Egypt, however, would demonstrate that special wines continued to be imported, albeit on a smaller scale, for specific purposes (Müller 2014, 247–248).

8 Marcus 2002, 409–411.

9 Badreshany, Philip, and Kennedy 2020; Greenberg and Iserlis 2020.

10 Iserlis, Steiniger, and Greenberg 2019, 1028–1036; Greenberg and Iserlis 2020, 40–44.

11 Greenberg and Eisenberg 2002. Egyptian finds from EB II contexts include: a locally made jug bearing a hieroglyphic graffito incised after firing (Greenberg and Iserlis 2014, 66, fig. 3.43:4); an Egyptian jar, dated on typological grounds to the ED period (Greenberg and Iserlis 2014, 67, fig. 3.45:8); Egyptian jar sherds (Getzov 2006, 76) and seven faience beads (Getzov 2006, 100) from Getzov's excavations; the fragment of a siltstone bowl (Paz 2014, fig. 6.39:204); the relief-carved fragment of a siltstone palette (although from a secondary depositional context: Greenberg, Wengrow, and Paz 2010; Greenberg et al. 2012, 96). These finds point to active contacts between the site, its urban elite, and Egypt during the EB II.

12 Data point to the broad region (including Lebanon and Syria) for Egyptian–Levantine interactions throughout the EBA. Archaeometric analyses on ceramic imports in Egypt suggest that Egypt developed interregional contacts with both the southern and central Levant since the late Predynastic period (Naqada IID–IIIA: Hartung et al. 2015, 298–304, 322–324). A variety of procurement networks were operational during the ED period (Hartung et al. 2015, 308–322, 324–325; Iserlis, Steiniger, and Greenberg 2019, 1035–1037). At this stage, the importation of north Canaanite vessels to First Dynasty Egypt played a key role. The situation is not clear for the Second and Third Dynasties (Sowada 2014, 297); however, by the 4th Dynasty the 'Byblos run' became the focus of Egyptian maritime commerce and container-based products from central Levant became customary. This is confirmed by both typological observations (Thalmann and Sowada 2014, 361, 365, 369–372) and petrographic studies (Sowada, Ownby, and Wodzińska 2020).

13 The presence of white-slipped, red-painted vessels possibly associated to local southern assemblages (e.g., from Arad: Amiran 1974) has been registered and might suggest the existence of additional ways to Egypt.

14 Sowada 2020, 157.

15 See, for example, Amiran 1985, 192; Milevski 2011, 190–191.

16 Sowada 2009, 204–206; 2018a, Arnold et al. 2016; Greenfield et al. 2020, 384–386, 390.

17 For a summary presentation: Sowada 2009, 48–50. For different items from EB II contexts: Paz 2014, 290–291, fig. 6.39:204 (Tel Beth Yerah); Loud 1948, pl. 258:1 (Megiddo); Yannai 2002, 338, fig. 22.1:21 ('Ain Assawir); Sowada 2009, 49–50, figs. 4c, 5a (Tel Yarmuth); Amiran et al. 1978, 57, pl. 77:1–2 (Arad).

18 Sowada 2018b, 256–258.

19 'Ai and Tel Yarmuth were key EB III centers in southern Canaan. At 'Ai, in particular, Egyptian stone vessels likely represented diplomatic gifts or endowments to a temple (Sala 2008, 302–303; Sowada 2009, 104–119, 216–218).

20 Along with Egyptian palettes (two from Field XVI, Reg. 2924 and 1262, Rast and Schaub 2003, 294, fig. 10.39:2, 400, fig. 12.6:3–4; two from Charnel Houses A22, Reg. 1900 and 3364, Sowada 2000, 1529–1530, fig. 1c, 1e; one from Charnel Houses A21,Rast and Schaub 1989, 343; Wilkinson 1989, 455–456, fig. 261:7; and one from Charnel Houses A51,Rast and Schaub 1989, 384–385; Wilkinson 1989, 454, fig. 261:3; see also Sowada 2009, 96–97, fig. 18, pl. 13), some Egyptian-style items made of local stones were retrieved in the EB II–III tombs in the necropolis: three from Charnel Houses A51 (Wilkinson 1989, 452–454, fig. 261:1–2, 4) and two from Charnel Houses A41 (Wilkinson 1989, 454–455, fig. 261:5–6).

21 Besides their shape and fine manufacture technique, Egyptian-imported palettes are recognizable from the stone they are made of: almost exclusively the greenish grey to gray-black stone from the Wadi Hammamat, alternatively indicated as siltstone, graywacke, or schist (Klemm and Klemm 2008, 306–309).

22 Gilbert 2004, 35–41.

23 Czarnowicz 2014, 195–196; Sowada 2009, 232–233; 2014, 297.

24 See, for example, Fischer 2002, 330; *contra* Rowan and Levy 2011, 208. Indeed, the higher attestation of maceheads in the southern part of the country (at Tell es-Sultan itself: eleven maceheads, plus a possible specimen from Sellin and Watzinger's excavations of the EB I remains; Sala 2012, 282–283) may suggest an Egyptian influence in the spread of these items (Rowan and Levy 2011, 210–212).

25 Nigro 2019, 80–83.

26 Historical sources indicates that asphalt was a major economic asset of the Dead Sea region. Discoveries from EB I levels at Site H/Wadi Gaza, Afridar, Small Tel Malhata, Tel Halif Terrace, Tel Erani, Horvat Illin Tahtit, Nizzanim, Palmahim, and Lod, where asphalt lumps were found, testify that export and trade of Dead Sea asphalt in the southern part of the country began as early as the late 4th millennium BCE (Nissenbaum et al. 1984; Connan, Nissenbaum, and Dessort 1992; Milevski, Marder and Goring-Morris 2002; Milevski 2011, 164–169). The export of Dead Sea asphalt to Egypt in the late 4th millennium BCE is attested from Maadi (Connan, Nissenbaum, and Dessort 1992, 2755–2758; Serpico 2000, 456). In the EB II, asphalt was possibly one of the commodities traded by the center of Arad, whose exchange network reached Egypt via north Sinai (Connan, Nissenbaum, and Dessort 1992, 2758; Sowada 2009, 44–45; and Yekutieli 2004 on the possible existence of a route connected with asphalt distribution).

27 Nigro 2010, 1–5.

28 Sala 2012, 284–285.

29 Sala 2012, 281–284.

30 Regev et al. 2012, 558–559, pp. 552–553 referring to Tell es-Sultan; *contra* Nigro et al. 2019. Considering the latter (Nigro et al. 2019, 225–227), it should be noted that no samples from late EB II (EB IIB) contexts come from the new excavations, whereas samples from Kenyon's excavations come from unsecure contexts [BM-551], cover an extremely long-time range [BM-1783R and BM-550], or give quite different 14C ages [BM-1780N and BM-552].

31 Sala 2012, 285–286.

32 Rim diameter 16 cm, thickness 0.3 cm (Dorrell 1983, 554, 556, fig. 229:17). Conversely, the oval limestone bowl with two or three lug handles (Reg. 1507: Dorrell 1983, 554, pl. 19a) probably is of local production.

33 Possibly ascribed to an earthquake (Kenyon 1981, 325, pl. 315a).

34 Two Egyptian rectangular palettes, with two incised lines parallel to the edge, were retrieved in the EB I settlement (see note 39).

35 Dorrell 1983, 559, fig. 230:12. Dimensions: length 16.5 cm × width 11.5 cm × thickness 1.5 cm. Reg. 1197 was bigger and finely made, with a smoother, worn-down area in the center of each face.

36 Dorrell 1983, 559 (not illustrated).

37 Dorrell 1983, 559, pl. 21:c. Dimensions: length 10 cm × width 6.5 cm × thickness 2 cm.

38 Kenyon 1960, 125, fig. 40:3. Dimensions: length 14.1 cm × width 10.2 cm × thickness 0.8 cm.

39 Two Egyptian palettes belonging to this type, typical of the Protodynastic period (Naqada IIIB) up to the First Dynasty (Kroeper 1996, 74–79, 81, figs. 3–5, 8), were found in the EB I

settlement (Sala 2012, 281–282; respectively: Reg. 3678 from Garstang's excavations in the North-Eastern Trench, Level VII, late EB IA (Garstang, Ben-Dor, and Fitzgerald 1936, pl. XXXVI:26) and Reg. 1955 from Kenyon's excavations in Trench III, phase XV.liia, late EB IB (Holland 1982, 559, fig. 226:16). The EB I contexts of retrieval are consistent with the general production date of this type in Egypt. Similar Egyptian palettes continue to be attested throughout the EB II–III period, when they were no longer produced in Egypt (on this topic see Sowada 2000, 1531–1533). They have been retrieved at Tel Beth Yerah (Paz 2014, 291, fig. 6.40), 'Ain Assawir (Tomb 40: Yannai 2002, 338, fig. 22.1:22), Tel Halif (Jacobs 1996; Jacobs and Seger 2017, 87–88, fig. 2.B.26.), Tell el-Umeiri (Geraty et al. 1986, 135), Numeira (Sowada 2000, 1528–1529, fig. 3b), Bab edh-Dhra' (see note 20), Umm Saysabān in the region of Petra (Hübner 2011, 162–164, fig. 14), till the recent finds from Khirbet al-Batrawy (Sala 2014, 68–69; Nigro et al. 2020, 4–5). An additional item (Reg. 1874) from Kenyon's excavations in Trench III, from the latest EB IB layer (phase XVI.lxi–lxiia), represents a local palette-like object (Dorrell 1983, 559, fig. 230:13).

40 Wheeler 1982, 630, fig. 256:2. Dimensions: 5 cm × 4.5 cm. Reg. 1449 was published as a spindle whorl, together with Reg. 1116 (Wheeler 1982, fig. 256:1). Both items were later recatalogued as maceheads (Holland 1983, 811). The shape (shorter) and perforation (wider) of Reg. 1449 are quite unusual and make this artefact a variant form of barrel-shaped macehead.

41 As it happens elsewhere: see e.g., Czarnowicz 2014, 198–199

42 Sala 2012, 286. Ten maceheads from the tell (Holland 1983, 804–806, fig. 365:3–5, 7, 10–11, 13; Wheeler 1982, 630, fig. 256:1), and one from the necropolis (Kenyon 1960, 171, fig. 66:4) were retrieved during Kenyon's excavations. To these, a pear-shaped macehead from Sellin and Watzinger's excavations may be added (Sellin and Watzinger 1913, fig. 110).

43 Respectively (Kenyon 1960, 91–92, fig. 28; 155–156, fig. 55; 173–174, fig. 65). Actually, for a number of beads stone types are not indicated.

44 Sowada 2009, 94; Milevski 2011, 169–173; Greenfield et al. 2020, 389.

45 Nigro et al. 2018, 111–116.

46 Respectively, Bar-Yosef Mayer 2002, 131, table 7.1; Yannai 2002, note 4 ('Ain Assawir); Amiran et al. 1978, pls. 118:2–6, 119:2 (Arad); Wilkinson 1989, 456, fig. 262:1 (Bab edh-Dhra'); Bar-Yosef Mayer 2000, 480; Bar-Yosef Mayer and Baruch 2006, 501, 503; Ktalav 2013, 1216 (Megiddo temple area, along with Red Sea shells).

47 Nigro et al. 2018, 119–121.

48 Kenyon 1960, 146, fig. 48:4, pl. VII:4 (no. 273); Bar-Yosef Mayer 2002, 130, table 7.12.

49 Arnold et al. 2016; Greenfield et al. 2020, 384–386. Given the nature of the finds, the domestic neighborhood where the sacrificial donkey was found has been associated with merchant families involved in regional and interregional exchanges (Greenfield et al. 2020, 390–391).

50 Finkelstein and Gophna 1993, 6, 9–14. In the Wadi Far'ah and the surrounding highlands of Samaria, most of the settlements were newly established during the EB I, and mainly in the EB IB phase (Bar 2014, 410–415). In this period, the exploitation of new districts (e.g., the western Wadi Far'ah) and the economic transition toward a more intensive exploitation of orchard crops took place. Settlement and demographic growth in the area might also be linked to the inroad and/or relocation of new people from the outside attracted by a favorable environment (Bar 2014, 454–455).

51 Langgut, Adams, and Finkelstein 2016, 124–125.

52 Langgut, Adams, and Finkelstein 2016, 125–127.

53 Population size and horticulture kept increasing in the central hills during the EB II (Portugali and Gophna 1993, 173–178; Bar 2014, 130–133), despite a decrease in site number.

54 As for the EB IB occupation, a travertine palette is recorded from Tomb 12 (F.2103: Vaux 1951, pl. 27b.4; Sowada 2009, 228). Two stone maceheads (both half-preserved) are also registered: one made of limestone from Tomb 3 (F.794; Vaux and Steve 1949, 108), the other one from the tell (F.1208; unpublished), but their origin cannot be determined. Finally, a number of 'iridescent' shells, and carnelian and frit/faience beads, were retrieved in the EB I tombs (Tombs 2, 3, 5 and 8: Vaux and Steve 1949, 108–109, 122, 126, 133–134, pls. IV,a,7–8, IV,b,17–18, VI,b,4–5; Tombs 9, 11 and 12: Vaux 1951, 572, 574, pls. XXVI,a,3, XXVI,b,17, XXVII,b,1).

55 Excavations of the EB I–II settlements at Tell el-Far'ah North, carried out by Roland de

Vaux between 1946 and 1960 on behalf of the École Biblique et Archéologique Française de Jérusalem (EBAF), were published only through preliminary reports. Most of the materials remain unpublished. Some Egyptian and Egyptian-style objects were identified from a preliminary survey through the original handwritten object inventories ('Catalogues des objets') kept in the EBAF archives.

56 Sowada 2009, 49, fig. 4a–b.

57 Registered in the unpublished handwritten inventory (EBAF archives): *Fouilles de Tell el-Far'ah, Septième campagne 1958, Catalogue des objets*, pp. 47 (F.3897), 90 (F.4101), 112 (F.4210). Hematite piriform maceheads could be Egyptian imports, although hematite was rarely used in the manufacture of maceheads in Egypt (Czarnowicz 2014, 198).

58 Registered in the unpublished handwritten inventory (EBAF archives): *Fouilles de Tell el-Far'ah, Septième campagne 1958, Catalogue des objets*, p. 85.

59 Registered in the unpublished handwritten inventory (EBAF archives): *Fouilles de Tell el-Far'ah, Première Saison 1946, Catalogue des objets*, p. 16.

60 Sebag 2005, 32, fig. 7; Miroschedji 2018, 126–127. Some of the elite dwellings yielded evidence of feasting or storage activities, such as the so-called 'Maison des Jarres' (Vaux and Steve 1947, 403–404, pls. XI [Trench V], XVII).

61 An indirect or down-the-line trade in Egyptian exotica through merchants or inter-community exchange was operational in the country. However, this does not seem to be the case with the Egyptian finds from Tell el-Far'ah North, where the regional setting and complementary evidence (e.g., from Tel Beth Yerah) suggests an Egyptian connection.

62 Even east of the Jordan, Egyptian objects are increasingly attested in the EB II–III period (Sala 2014), when some Transjordanian settlements achieved the status of urban centers and were able and eager to trade local commodities in exchange for exotic goods. The EB III collection of Egyptian and Egyptian-style objects found at Khirbet al-Batrawy (Nigro et al. 2020), at the edges of the Syro-Arabic Desert, illustrates these interregional exchanges.

63 Greenberg and Iserlis 2020, 44.

Journal of Ancient Egyptian Interconnections

Contents, Status, and Symbolism: The Study of Residues from Imported Jars at Old Kingdom Giza

Karin Sowada
Macquarie University

Wilma Wetterstrom
Harvard University and Ancient Egypt Research Associates

Geraldine Jacobsen
Centre for Accelerator Science, ANSTO, Sydney

Fiona Bertuch
Centre for Accelerator Science, ANSTO, Sydney

Margaret Serpico
University College London

Abstract

Throughout the 4th to 6th Dynasties of the Old Kingdom (c. 2613–2181 BCE), liquid commodities were imported in ceramic combed jars made in workshops in the Byblos region, enabling proximal geographic identification of the original contents. Results of scientific, archaeometric, and archaeological research on a large corpus of jars found in elite tombs at Giza, now in the Museum of Fine Arts, Boston, reveal a complex story of the use and reuse of the jars and that very little remains of the original and even secondary contents. Rather, from the moment of production, the jars had a complex itinerary. At different times, jars were invested with diverse meanings that included their original use as a transport and product container, a symbol of royal power, an elite status symbol, and, more recently, a 20th-century museum artifact. It is argued that a number of jars were used more than once before final deposition in elite tombs, where they were provided as gifts to high officials and royal family members. The jars acquired the significance of prestige markers in the status framework of Egyptian elites, signifying proximity to royal grace and favor. As a result of ancient use and modern interventions, the original contents of the jars are difficult to discern, with wider implications for how to characterize the liquid commodities trade with the region.

Keywords

Egypt; Lebanon; Old Kingdom; resins; trade; Giza; ceramics; residues; radiocarbon dating

Introduction

Identification of liquid commodities traded between Egypt and the Levant during the Old Kingdom (c. 2686–2181 BCE) has largely eluded discovery for decades. Debate has involved the study of textual evidence on the one hand and, on the other, speculation based on very limited archaeological data and scientific analysis. Recent multi-proxy analyses of remaining residues in the large corpus of imported combed jars from Giza held in the Museum of Fine Arts in Boston (MFA) reveal that few jars contain traces of contents visible to the naked eye. Indeed, on examination, a number of jars revealed evidence of having been used more than once and prepared especially for burial as items in their own right. Archaeological observations suggest that the jars had a more complex itinerary than simply as containers for liquid commodities, and once received in Egypt, moved through the palace economy to final interment with different perceived identities along the way. Moreover, modern handling of the jars has contributed further complexity through interventions such as cleaning.

This paper examines the reception and archaeology of the jars themselves: their condition on deposition, the presence or absence of contents, evidence of stoppers, and various ancient and modern interventions. A case study using macroscopic, microscopic, and archaeometric methods on contents associated with jar MFA 47.1662 demonstrates the nature of the problems encountered in identifying the contents and analyzing legacy archaeological data. Using an object itinerary approach, these data also help reveal the complex journey of the jars, their significance, and meaning at different points along the way.

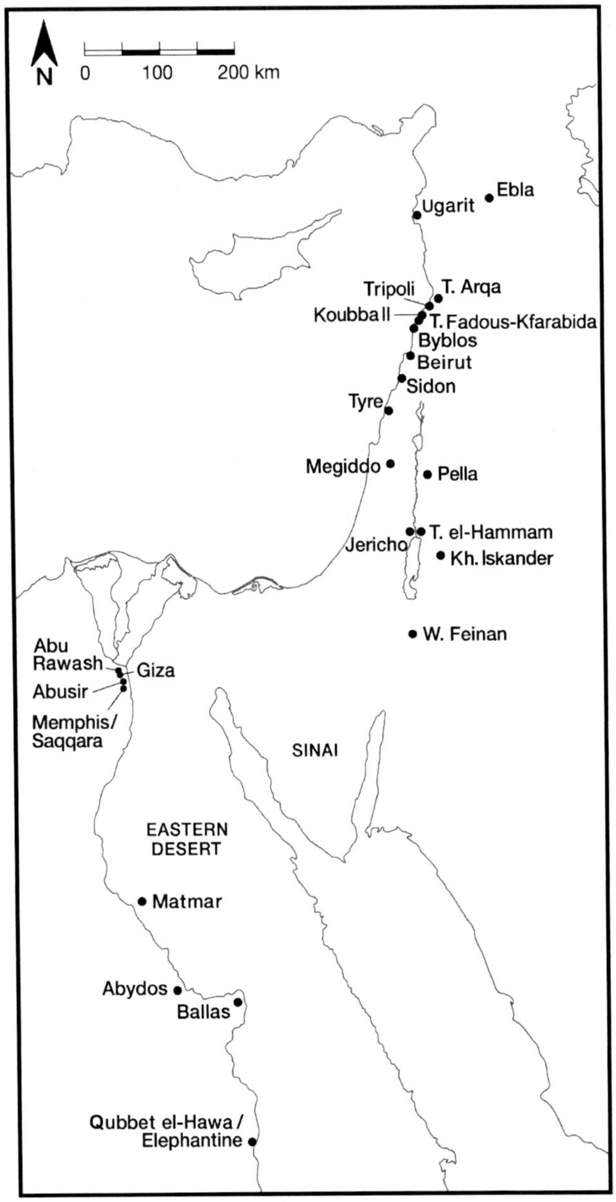

FIGURE 1: Map of Egypt and the Levant, showing sites mentioned in the text.

Imported Combed Jars in Egypt and the 'Contents Problem'

During the 4th to 6th Dynasties, the two-handled combed jar was the primary Levantine imported transport container for shipping liquid commodities to Egypt.[1] Results of thin-section petrography on jars from Giza reveal that vessels were produced in the Central Levant, between Beirut and Tripoli; recent geochemical results identified the Byblos region itself as the place of manufacture during the 4th Dynasty, a pattern which likely continued for much of the Old Kingdom (FIG. 1).[2] The dominance of this type and the uniform nature of the vessels over a long period indicates a standardized production regime in northern Lebanon that served the requirements of Egyptian state maritime trade in a highly efficient manner.[3] This arrangement was so successful that it lasted for over 350 years.[4]

While many jars have been studied from the perspective of ceramic production and technology, little attention has been paid to their contents and the archaeology of the jars themselves. To date, the contents of only three jars have been scientifically examined with conclusions published, and even this

Figure 2: (a) Upper body and body sherd of jar MFA 13.5671, showing calcium carbonate residue. Giza Tomb G 4440, early–mid Fourth Dynasty (Photographs K. Sowada, used courtesy © Museum of Fine Arts, Boston); (b) Interior view of jar MFA 13.2829a showing drip marks on the wall (Photograph 2022 © Museum of Fine Arts, Boston).

was done many decades ago. Little detail is known of the scientific method used, and only two of the three examined jars yielded informative results.[5] A current program of multi-proxy analysis is seeking to unravel the 'contents problem,' but even this has proved more complex than initially anticipated.[6]

This complexity prompted a detailed assessment of the archaeology and object itinerary of the jars themselves. The MFA holds an important corpus of 29 imported jars from G.A. Reisner's excavations at Giza, conducted from 1902 to 1942 on behalf of the Harvard University–MFA Egyptian Expedition. Five are one-handled jugs, and the remaining 24 are combed jars. All the vessels come from tombs belonging to the kings' extended family and senior officials and date from the early 4th to the late 6th Dynasty.[7] This is the largest group of such vessels outside Egypt. Thanks to George Reisner's recording, a great deal is known about the archaeological setting and modern recording of this material, not only through primary publication data but also through his original field notes and photographs, now publicly available.[8] This enables construction of a general life history of imported jars and thus contributes to understanding how they were used at different times, the associated significance attributed to them at different points, and possible reasons for the overall paucity of contents.

(A) The Impact of 20th-Century Excavation and Museum Methods

The collated examination of the MFA jars and the original field records enables several key observations. First, few jars have obvious visible residues on the interior walls, rims, or dribbling down the exterior and interior surfaces. Over a two-year period commencing in November 2017, the jars were examined multiple times by the writers, and samples of any remaining residues were taken, repeatedly observing how little was visible to the naked eye. Access to interior surfaces for examination and taking samples also varied and was controlled by museum procedures: eight jars were still in fragments, so all surfaces were accessible; six jars were completely restored from sherds, so the interiors were difficult to inspect; and a further thirteen were intact but likewise hard to examine internally, especially where the neck was narrow. Very few vessels had either loose or adhering residues on the interior walls that could be sampled, even around the base where an accumulation would be expected (Fig. 2a; Table 3 at the end of this chapter). Recent photographs taken by the Museum from inside several large intact jars using a suspended camera revealed 'drip' marks on the walls and limited adhering residues (Fig. 2b).

The lack or loss of residues can be partially explained by post-excavation and museum conservation practices. Examination of original Giza field photographs suggests that external surfaces were

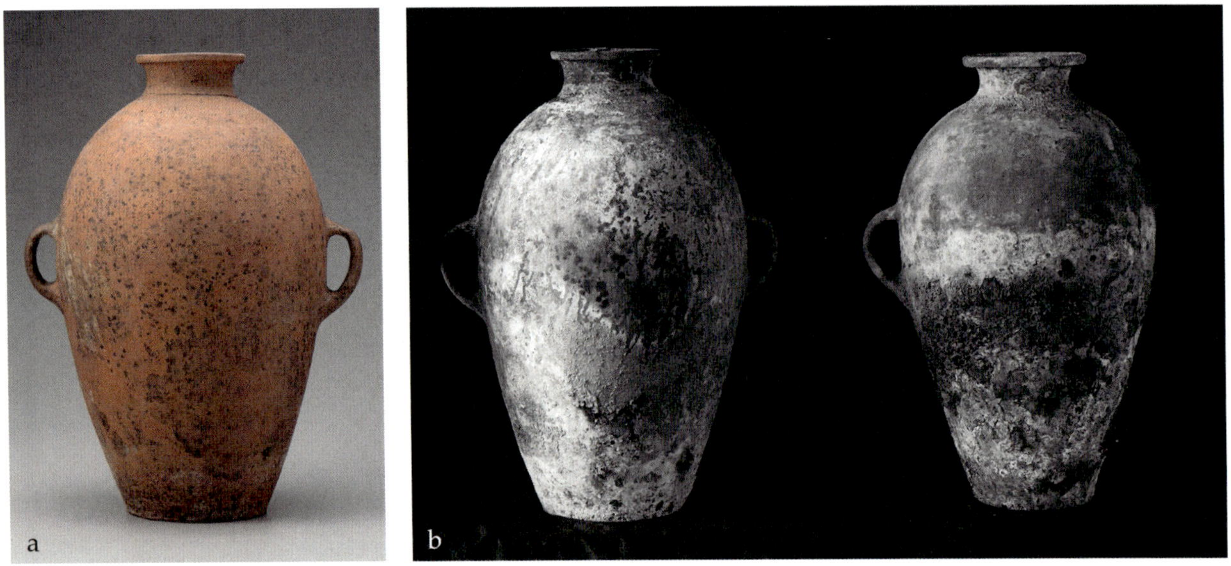

Figure 3: Jars from Tomb G 2381A, late Sixth Dynasty. (a) Current photo of jar MFA 13.2930 showing loss of original accretions. Height 48.3cm (b) Original field photograph. Note surface accretions on MFA 13.2930 (left). The remains of the stopper, visible in Fig. 6, is missing. MFA 13.2929 is on the right. Photo dated 01/25/1913 (Photographs 2021 © Museum of Fine Arts, Boston).

Figure 4: (a) Stopper from jar 86-12/HH/2000, showing traces of a plaster stopper under local unfired Nile silt (right). From the tomb complex of Qar Junior, Abusir, Sixth Dynasty (photo courtesy M. Bárta); (b) Jar MFA 13.2929, showing traces of white plaster (diagonal arrow) and the 'shadow' of a plaster stopper across the shoulder. Comparison with the field photograph in Figs 3b and 6 indicates post-excavation removal of accretions (Photograph 2021 © Museum of Fine Arts, Boston).

often 'cleaned up' for photography (Fig. 3). Further cleaning evidently occurred at the Museum over the ensuing years, especially when intact jars were prepared for display or sherds for restoration. Even ancient 'kill holes' were 'restored' by plastering over the 'damage' in modern times: jug MFA 20.1904 had three kill holes near the base, all plastered over during restoration.[9] Indeed, this latter category—jars restored from sherds—was likely the most extensively desalinated and cleaned, inside and out, in accordance with standard museum practices. Nowadays, there is an emerging realization of data loss through excavation practice and post-excavation handling of ceramics. The result is that field strategies are shifting to ensure the retention of micro-datasets for future analysis.

FIGURE 5: (a) Jar MFA 13.2928a-b; (b) Underside of stopper MFA 13.2928b showing several layers of material. (Photographs 2022 © Museum of Fine Arts, Boston).

(B) THE REMAINS OF NILE MUD STOPPERS OR SEALINGS AND THE ARCHAEOLOGICAL SETTING

Many jars were used anciently more than once, shown by the extant remains of multiple plaster and Nile mud stoppers on some jars. Whereas Nile mud indicates vessels resealed in Egypt, when and by whom plaster stoppers were used requires a cautious assessment. Possibly the traces of a white shadow on the upper shoulder of many jars are remains of the first or second stopper. The nature of the original sealing in Lebanon is also not known: it may have been clay, textile and string, or maybe plaster; elemental analyses on plaster samples are required to resolve this.

From the late Old Kingdom, a combed jar from Giza and one from Matmar were found with Nile mud stoppers, whereas no less than seven late 6th Dynasty jars from Abusir are likewise sealed, some with contents still inside.[10] One Abusir jar had a Nile mud stopper placed *over* remnants of an earlier cream-colored plaster stopper, a piece of which is visible on the shoulder. Under this are traces of another white coating on the rim and neck (FIG. 4a).[11] The Nile mud stoppers from Abusir and Giza are impressed with an inscribed seal. The Matmar jar was found with a broken rim sealed with a clay sherd lid held in place with a leather strap and secured by a Nile mud stopper with no reported seal impression.[12] MFA 13.2930 likewise appears to have been originally sealed with a piece of leather, part of which was still in situ on discovery (FIG. 6 inset left). The presence of mud stoppers made from Egyptian Nile clay not only points to a late Old Kingdom date, since such stoppers are confined to that period but also demonstrates that some jars were resealed locally at least once prior to interment.

Examination of original field photographs and object registration notes show that when discovered, many vessels lacked a stopper altogether (Table 3).[13] The Giza fieldnotes only mention a stopper, or the substantial remains of such, if it was present when the vessel was originally recorded. One must, of course, account for the method of field recording that was a product of its time and different people. Many of the field entries are brief and lacking detail, thus the modern reader is captive to what was thought worthy of documenting at the time. That said, where extensive remnants of a stopper remained *in situ* or was stabilized in the field, it was evidently conserved and recorded.[14] Most of the Giza jars now in Boston are uncapped, but examination of the surface reveals that all vessels were anciently sealed with white plaster at some point, as noted above (e.g., FIGS. 3b, 4–8).[15]

In this respect, the collection of jars from late 6th Dynasty Giza tomb G 2381 A is instructive. An original photograph of the burial chamber shows four jars behind the coffin, three with stoppers and one leaning over with a broken stopper.[16] A fifth jar, MFA 13.2929, likely fell over and is not shown. FIG. 6 shows MFA 13.2930 (left) with a mostly missing stopper, yet the field photograph shows none (FIG. 3a, right), indicating that it had fallen off during excavation or was cleaned off for photography. The

Figure 6: Intact burial chamber of Giza Tomb G 2381 A, belonging to Impy, reign of Pepy II, Sixth Dynasty. Note four combed jars alongside the coffin, MFA 13.2929 is not visible. Remains of the earlier plaster stopper of MFA 13.2930 are on the shoulder; along the neck are remains of a mud stopper or piece of leather (?). Photo dated 12/31/1912. (Photograph 2021 © Museum of Fine Arts, Boston).

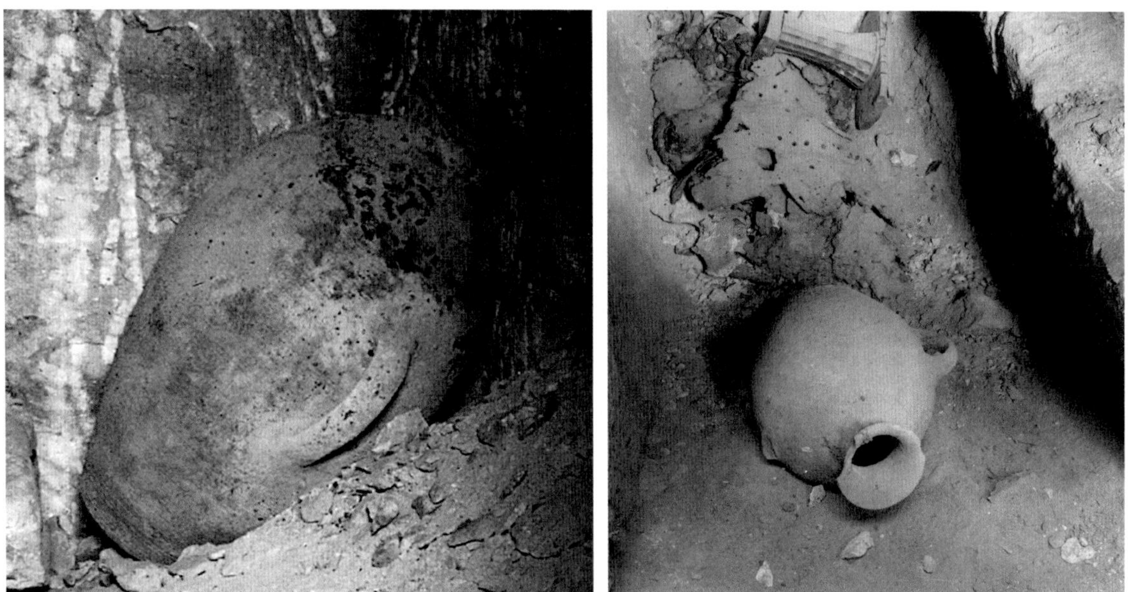

Figure 7: (a) Jar MFA 20.1903 from Giza Tomb G 1031 A *in situ*: the neck and rim are seen with no visible stopper. Photo dated March 1904; (b) Jar MFA 47.1662 from Giza Tomb G 2350 L, shown *in situ* inside the coffin but likely moved from its original position during ancient robbing. The jar was missing a handle and the rim was broken (note sherds near the mouth), the stopper was also fully absent. Photo dated 05/02/1940 (Photographs 2021 © Museum of Fine Arts, Boston).

broken neck of MFA 13.2928a–b reveals multiple sealings which may or may not be local. Close inspection of the original photo showing the jar *in situ* reveals that the neck and stopper had already broken off (see the black void on the left-hand side) and may indeed have been re-positioned for the picture or moved in ancient times (FIG. 6 detail). As many as three possible layers of different materials on the stopper can be discerned: a primary layer of clay which does not appear to be Nile silt or mud, and two subsequent layers of plaster. Each layer likely represents separate acts of closure (FIG. 5b).[17]

Yet, from field notes and photographs, it seems likely that stoppers were *absent* from many other jars on discovery. Some jars from earlier tombs were found *not sealed*. For example, 4th Dynasty jar MFA 20.1903 from plundered Tomb G 1031 A was missing its stopper completely and appeared 'cleaned up' (FIG. 7a).[18] Jar MFA 47.1662 from plundered Fifth Dynasty Giza Tomb G 2350 L shows the stopper almost completely absent (FIG. 7b).[19] The rim likewise appears 'cleaned up' anciently, as loose fragments lying nearby bear only small patches of surface plaster and few if any residues are visible on the rim, even though the field notes record residues in the jar (further discussed below). The point here is that the lack of stoppers in the field photos and notes, combined with a general lack of actual substantive contents, even in small quantities for most jars, indicate that many vessels appear to have been unsealed, maybe partially filled, possibly emptied, and indeed anciently 'cleaned up' prior to deposition. Some vessels were also ritually 'killed,' some close to the base where any contents would have seeped out.

Case Study: The Problematic 'Contents' of Combed Jar MFA 47.1662

The conundrum of 'empty' jars and the general lack of visible residues cannot be easily explained. In the case of the Giza jars, contents could have been robbed out anciently, used in a funerary ritual, have been of a kind that did not leave extensive visible remains or deteriorated/evaporated, *or* the jars were extensively cleaned prior to burial and/or extensively cleaned post-excavation. Funerary rites or tomb robbing could offer an explanation: robbers could have climbed out with a container for stolen liquids, such as a goatskin slung over the body or simply taken the jar from the tomb.[20] For some interred jars, contents may have been already crystalline, facilitating removal in a sack or bag.

FIG. 8: Jar MFA 47.1662. Height 31.0cm. Mid-5th Dynasty (Photograph 2021 © Museum of Fine Arts, Boston).

To help assess this issue, jar MFA 47.1662 (FIG. 8) with associated loose contents MFA OP.1.47.1662 was investigated to evaluate the nature and relationship of the material to the jar in light of possible multiple ancient and modern interventions. The jar was found in the burial chamber of Giza Tomb G 2350 L (= G 5290), dated to the Fifth Dynasty. Visual inspection of the clay fabric on a crack through the rim revealed that it was made of P200, the main fabric for Old Kingdom imports originating in the Byblos area.[21] Slight traces of yellowish plaster were visible on the neck and rim, but the overall surface had been thoroughly cleaned. The field photo shows the jar lying on its side in the stone sarcophagus, near a pile of robbed bones and objects (FIG. 7b). The rim had minor pieces missing, and there was a small amount of residual material adhering to the neck, but for the most part, the neck and rim looked relatively clean. Field notes record that the jar 'contains dried oil, shiny black color, cf Lucas analysis of 32-12-18' [i.e., MFA 47.1661],[22] but did not state if this was loose or adhering to the vessel walls, and it was not analyzed at the time. Two samples from the interior wall of the jar were taken in 2021, and analysis is in progress.

Loose Contents MFA OP.1.47.1662

The MFA holds a small plastic bag of loose contents labeled as having been removed from this jar. The date of transfer from the jar is not certain and is nowhere stated in the MFA records. No loose contents were mentioned in the field notes and Reisner recorded no other contents, yet residues *were* adhering to the walls, as evidenced by the observations of Lucas (see above) and the samples taken in 2021. That said, the relationship of at least some of the bag contents to jar MFA 47.1662 is possible but cannot be verified with certainty. Indeed, as we will see below, there is clear evidence of material not related to the original contents in the bag, which includes modern remains, but perhaps not all of the same age (Fig. 9).

The nature of this situation will be familiar to anyone who works with museum objects obtained from an old archaeological excavation. The MFA accession date of the jar is signaled by the prefix '47,' indicating that the Museum accessioned this and other objects in that year. A number of objects were secured in the Harvard Camp storeroom at Giza up until 1947, when they were transferred to the United States. Former Chair of the Department of Ancient Art at the MFA, Dr. Rita Freed, recounted a conversation long ago with Dr. Dows Dunham, who was a member of the team that closed the Camp. According to Dr. Freed (pers. comm. 1 July 2021), Dunham reflected that 'there was a lot to do in a very short time.' Thus, working under time pressure, quick decisions about material were likely needed, and without several key people who were present during the original fieldwork.[23]

The contents of the bag, approximately 100 ml, was partially sorted by Dr. Wilma Wetterstrom in the Scientific Research Laboratory of the MFA Boston over four visits between April and August 2019. Much of the contents was sediment and dust (Fig. 9a). The remainder was a curious collection of botanical, faunal, and unidentified material, and most of it almost certainly was not in the jar when excavated by Reisner (Table 1).[24] The most abundant items were small pieces of dark matte and 'resinous'-looking material. Some pieces adhered to ceramic flakes, which could have spalled off the walls of

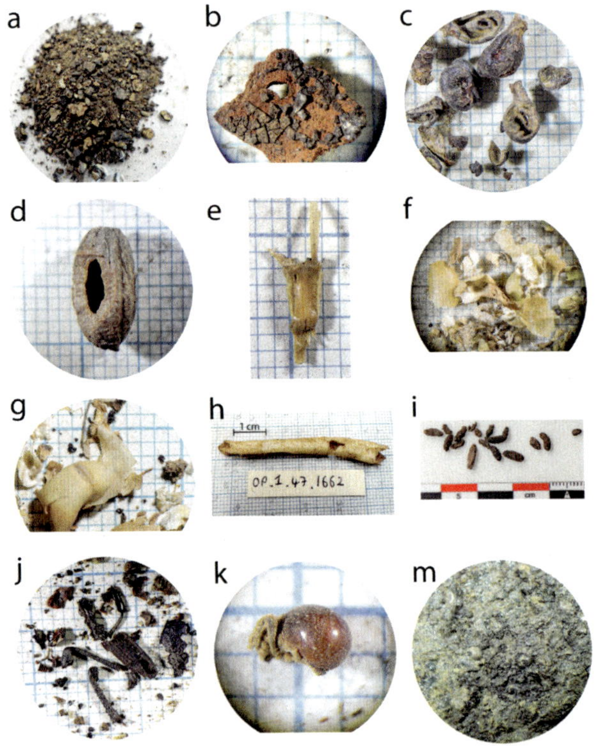

Fig. 9: Contents of bag MFA OP.1.47.1662. (a) Loose contents.; (b) Ceramic fragment with resinous adhesions; (c) Grape pips and pip fragments; (d) Olive stone; (e) Barley rachis; (f) Botanical material; (g) Detail of (f), showing flax fragment; (h) Animal bone; (i) Rodent droppings; (j) Insect carapace and fragments; (k) Spider beetle; (m) Spider beetles embedded in resinous material (Photographs W. Wetterstrom, used courtesy Museum of Fine Arts, Boston). Grid squares = 1 mm.

the jar (Fig. 9b). Five representative samples were taken from the bag for analysis (see above), and two additional samples were submitted for AMS dating (see below).

The most abundant identifiable botanical material was grape (*Vitis vinifera* L.) pips and pip fragments (Fig. 9c). The specimens consist of the tough testa (seed coat) with no traces of the endosperm or embryo, indicating degrading as could be expected in old specimens. A sample submitted for AMS dating proved to be a few hundred years old (180±20 years) (Appendix 1). The bag contents also included one small olive stone (*Olea europaea* L.), bearing a hole gnawed by rodents, undoubtedly seeking the seed inside (Fig. 9d). It would not have been in the jar at the time of discovery. If it had, it is unlikely that Reisner would have missed it, given that olive stones are easily recognized and large enough to spot by the naked eye. In addition, the

Identification	Latin name	Count, description	Comments
PLANT MATERIAL			
Olive	*Olea europaea* L.	1 stone	Hole with rodent gnaw marks
Grape	*Vitis vinefera* L.	Numerous seed (pip) fragments At least 7 pips counted based on "necks" of the seed	Pips consist only of the seed coat, with desiccated soft tissue of the fruit adhering to some
Barley	*Hordeum vulgare* L.	1 rachis internode	In very good condition. Color slightly darker than fresh material. Hairs intact. Shiny appearance.
Cereal chaff and straw		Some fragments	Degraded. Unidentifiable
Legume	*Fabaceae* family	Some seed coat fragments	One fragment has hilum characteristic of legumes
Legume	*Fabaceae* family?	Stem/pod/ leaf fragments	Problaby legume
Fibers, string		Small mass	Fibers are very fine, possibly flax
String		1 piece of fine string	Possibly flax
Wood		1 small fragment	Degraded
FAUNAL MATERIAL			
Bone		1	Hollow, possibly from a bird
Insect parts		Numerous legs, carapaces, jaws	Possible grain pests, such as the grain weevil.
Spider beetles	*Gibbium*?	Numerous loose specimens with thorax, abdomen, and some legs intact	Many spider beetles embedded in a piece of 'resin'
OTHER			
Unidentifiable		Minute fragments	

Table 1: Summary of observations from MFA OP.1.47.1662, bag of loose contents. Notes: 1. Fragments cannot be quantified, except very subjectively as some, numerous, etc. Weight would be the only objective measure for quantity, but not useful here given the uncertainty of the source and date of the material. 2. For dimensions see photos. Most specimens are seen on grid paper with 1 mm grid squares.

earliest examples of olive-stone finds in Egypt date to Middle Kingdom deposits at Memphis, so this would have been noticed at the time.[25]

The other identifiable botanical specimen is a segment of barley (*Hordeum vulgare* L.) rachis (Fig. 9e), the central axis of the cereal head. Its shiny surface, intact fine hairs, and color, only slightly darker than a fresh rachis, suggest that the specimen is not ancient. Other botanical material included bits of chaff, probably derived from cereals; unidentifiable fragments of plant tissue, most of which were degraded (Fig. 9f); and a deteriorating fragment of wood. Bits of seed testa probably belong to the legume family, as indicated by one fragment that displays a hilum (scar left from where a stalk connected the seed to the pod) (Fig. 9g) characteristic of legumes. A small mass of fine fibers and a thread in the bag may be derived from plants, such as flax (Fig. 9f).

The faunal material included a small hollow bone, possibly from a bird (Fig. 9h). Rodent droppings, roughly 4 to 6 millimeters long, were abundant and modern as per AMS dating (215 cal AD ± 25) (Fig. 9i; Table 2). Insect carapaces, legs, and jaws were numerous (Fig. 9j). These may derive from grain storage pests. The most abundant insect was the spider beetle (Fig. 9k), recognizable because many examples were preserved with the thorax, abdomen,

ANSTO Code	Sample Type	MFA Museum No.	δ(^{13}C) (‰)	Percent of Modern Carbon (pMC, 1σ error)	Conventional Radiocarbon Age (years BP, 1σ error)	Calibrated Age Ranges (cal BCE/cal CE, 95.4% CI)	Median Calibrated Age (cal BCE/CE)
OZY543	Plant matter including possible resinous pieces	OP.1.47.1662	−23.2±01	61.50±0.20	3,905±30	2469–2296 cal BCE (95.4%)	2392 BCE
OZY544	Plant matter including possible resinous pieces	OP.1.47.1662	−22.8±0.1	63.66±0.18	3,630±25	2127–2093 cal BCE (8.1%) 2041–1920 cal BCE (85.3%) 1915–1900 cal BCE (2.1%)	1992 BCE
OZY550	Rodent droppings	OP.1.47.1662	−23.7±0.2	97.37±0.25	215±25	1644 –1684 cal CE (35.1%) 1735–1804 cal CE (53.4%) 1929 – ….. cal CE (7.0%)	1763 CE
OZY551	Grape seed	OP.1.47.1662	−25.8±0.1	97.80±0.22	180±20	1661 – 1693 cal CE (19.5%) 1726 – 1810 cal CE (56.6%) 1919 – ….. cal CE (19.3%)	1765 CE

Table 2: C14 dates from selected contents of bag MFA OP.1.47.1662.

and some legs intact. The beetle infests foodstuffs and has been found in mummies and archaeological settlement sites in Egypt.[26]

One spider beetle was attached to a rodent dropping, apparently feeding on it at the time of death. Other rodent droppings bore holes that may have been dug by beetles, which might be a species known to tunnel in human feces and eat foodstuffs.[27] This species has not been recovered from archaeological sites,[28] but is the one found in Egypt today, suggesting that the spider beetles in the bag are modern, as does the beetles' association with the AMS-dated rodent droppings. Curiously, a great mass of spider beetles were embedded in a piece of the resinous material (Fig. 9m), suggesting that they were in a container with the resin when the material was soft enough to entrap the beetles, such as during the blistering hot days of Egyptian summers.

To ascertain the relationship of the material to the jar, samples of different materials were selected from the bag for radiocarbon dating (Appendix 1). The results revealed a 'mixed bag' of dates, with only Sample OZY543 returning the date 2469–2296 cal BCE (95.4%), which is coeval with a date in the 5th Dynasty. The other three samples were later, including two dating from the early modern era. The mixed dating of the samples from bag OP.1.47.1662 indicates that a significant amount, with the likely exception of resin fragments with ceramic attached (Fig. 9b), does not belong to the jar and was collected in modern times.

Discussion

As revealed by the case study of MFA 47.1662 and MFA OP.1.47.1662, considering the 'life cycle' of the jars is required when assessing possible ancient contents. MFA 47.1662 demonstrates, on the one hand, the difficulties of working with legacy data, and museum material and the nature of preserved residues on the other.

A general reconstruction of the object itinerary of combed jars in Egypt—from point-of-manufacture to the 21st century—helps segment ancient and modern interventions. These interventions are linked to the jars' changing purpose and semiotic journey. Various approaches are needed to examine the nature of cultural entanglement, the shifting use, circulation, meaning and symbolism, remains of the contents (if any), and the validity and complexity of the scientific results obtained from remaining residues, visible and microscopic. An object itinerary is thus proposed here for the early Old Kingdom, recognizing that in the later Old Kingdom, shifts in royal power mean that elite officials may have enjoyed more direct control and access to commodities from foreign expeditions resulting in different interventions. Moreover, the

Old Kingdom spans over 350 years; thus, an object itinerary for combed jars cannot be considered homogeneous for the duration of this era.

(a) Starting with the clay raw materials, jars were made by local potters in workshops in the Byblos region as a specialized production for maritime transport to Egypt. This must have occurred through negotiation between Egyptian and Byblite elites and concomitant direction to, and experimentation by, local pottery workshops. Elsewhere in Lebanon, combed jars appear to have been made for local use and not traded between sites in the Central Levant; thus, the involvement of other centers remains to be established.[29] Once in the hands of this specialized production, the combed jar acquired a different purpose in that it was exclusively reserved for the Egyptian state. From its point of manufacture, it was a commoditized article of international trade and economic value, set apart from a local utilitarian function and with technically different properties. That the Egyptians did not request a distinctive shape and used an existing local type may stem from familiarity with two-handled jars from previous eras; it may also reflect a certain economy and efficiency in size and workshop production.[30] Between the Byblite producers and the Egyptian 'purchasers,' different perceptions of the jars were apparently underpinned by 'deeply divergent perceptions of the value of the objects being exchanged,' as will be seen below.[31]

(b) Jars were filled and locally stoppered, then shipped by boat from Byblos with other commodities under the auspices of Egyptian agents acting on behalf of the king.[32] Supply and shipping was facilitated by local Byblite suppliers and elites.[33] Once on the ship, a cultural reconstruction began at the hands of Egyptian agents, sailors, and possibly Byblite representatives.[34] Vessels assumed the identity of cargo, with the main priority being minimal breakage and safe delivery.

(c) On docking at the Giza harbor, the cargo was probably received and disembarked with great pomp and ceremony. To Egyptian eyes, the strange pottery shape denoted non-Egyptian 'otherness,' hallmarking the exotic contents. Importantly, the fleet's arrival signaled not only the success of the king's expedition in material terms but also evidence of his divine triumph and domination over the forces of chaos, represented by the sea and unknown threats of 'the foreign.'[35] Thus, the jars, while maintaining the aura of *exotica* owing to their shape and contents, became entangled in the ideology of kingship and reached the most visible and important stage of their cultural transformation.

(d) At some point, the jar stoppers were removed and the primary contents decanted. Possibly, this was also accompanied by a ceremony. Empty jars may have been washed inside and out and remains of stoppers cleaned off, then stored for future use, possibly in the Treasury at Giza.

(e) Having been 'commissioned' through their journey into royal hands, jars may have been reused more than once for ritual and ceremonial purposes or re-purposed for the palace economy. Each of these points involved the possibility of cleaning and reusing with different contents and resealing. This proposition helps explain the presence of combed jars in the Heit el-Ghurab worker's settlement at Giza.[36] The use of such jars at HeG also suggests that its inhabitants were people of status in the pecking order of pyramid workers and officials, owing to access and use of foreign jars linked to activities of the divine king.[37] The rich provisioning of victuals for particular settlement areas also points to this status.

(f) Occasionally, jars passed beyond the palace economy, evidenced by several jars in non-royal contexts.[38] One example is the jar from intact Grave 3209 of an unnamed person at Matmar (BM EA 63698), found with a small number of modest grave goods and dated to the late 5th–early 6th Dynasty.[39] The jar 'escaped' the palace economy into the common realm of the 'unwritten dead.'[40] The jar is an outlier in terms of its final ownership, as most are found in elite tombs. The Matmar vessel is disconnected from its royal origins and must have been considered a great prize by the tomb owner and the family, having been repaired for burial. Possibly, it was gifted by a local elite as a reward for service or was at some point the product of robbing.

(g) Finally, most extant jars passed into the hands of male high officials or their families for interment in tombs. Jars would have been visible to everyone in the funeral procession and may have played a role in the burial ritual.

Extensive robbing of many tombs means that the original location and position of the jars can only be conjectured; yet it appears that most were placed in the burial chamber (e.g., FIG. 6, 7, Table 3). This is the likely stage at which some jars were 'killed.' Jars, along with other burial goods, passed into the realm of the dead.

(h) Ancient robbing disturbed many vessels: any contents may have been removed, vessels were shifted around the tomb, some may have been removed altogether; others were broken during robbing and left in fragments around the tomb and its environs. Through this activity, jars and any contents had a new value, that of a commodity capable of being exchanged for other goods.

(i) Further robbing may have taken place during the 19th and 20th centuries AD. Jars were excavated by various missions in the 20th century and were fully or partially cleaned up in the field and photographed. Many were sent to overseas museums or placed in on-site storerooms and museums in Egypt. A number were restored. At this final stage, jars—particularly intact vessels—regained a different form of value through their age, rarity, as evidence of past human activity from ancient Egypt, and a tangible link to antiquity. A near-complete disassociation from the original place of manufacture is complete.

Conclusions

The preceding analysis demonstrates that unraveling the nature of imported liquid commodity imports during the Old Kingdom is a difficult task. To assess the contents and other aspects of imported jars, an object itinerary approach helps to examine the materiality of its manufacture and subsequent handling, the archaeological context, and modern interference. Analysis of contents thought to be from MFA 47.1662, including radiocarbon dating, demonstrates the complex archaeological questions and complications of legacy data in a museum context. All these elements inform the data obtained from multi-proxy analyses of the residues. A similar approach could be used with ceramic containers of any period.

At Giza, the absence of jar stoppers and contents on discovery suggests that at least some jars were interred empty or with a minimal deposit of loose material, perhaps representing a symbolic or magical offering. Thus, rather than holding the original imported or even a secondary commodity, the jar itself could be the burial item: "the exchange [and its political and economic context] was the source of value."[41] It signaled the privilege and status of the owner and even the social control of the royal house.[42] Their value as markers of status or social mobility indicated proximity to royal power, esteem, and access—real, imagined, or symbolic—to their exotic contents. Owning imported pottery was a social and political statement.

Due to their place in the palace economy, imported ceramic containers could continue in circulation beyond their initial arrival in Egypt and were likely washed out and used multiple times before interment. In their journey from Byblos to their ultimate destination in an elite tomb or royal establishment, the purpose and symbolism of the jars underwent a cognitive shift in the hands of the Egyptian consumers—from container to status item. The nature of cultural entanglement involved in this shift meant that while the jars were eventually embraced as funerary equipment, they never lost their 'otherness.' In fact, this quality was their appeal, a visual and symbolic reminder of proximity to the king and his divine qualities embodied in the projection of Egypt's power beyond its borders, even if they bore little content.

Appendix 1: Results of Radiocarbon Dating Samples from MFA OP.1.47.1662

Due to the uncertainty regarding the date of the contents from MFA OP.1.47.1662, and the relationship of the material to jar MFA 47.1662, four different samples were selected and subjected to AMS radiocarbon dating at the Australian Nuclear Science and Technology Organisation (ANSTO) facility at Lucas Heights in Sydney, Australia.[43] Sample selection was based on the nature and quantity of each sample type so as to ensure material was left for future analysis.

Because of the nature and uncertainty of potential contamination sources, extensive pre-treatment was performed on all samples. Plant material, rodent droppings, and grape seeds were washed with acetone (45°C, 1hr) x2, methanol (45°C, 1hr) x2, thoroughly rinsed with high-purity water, and oven-dried at 60°C. Samples were then treated with 2M HCl (60°C, 1hr), 0.1M NaOH (RT, 1hr), 2M HCl (RT, 1hr), and rinsed thoroughly with high-purity water and oven-dried at 60°C.

Degraded plant material (i.e., dissolved with the methods used for plant material) was washed with acetone (45°C, 1hr) x2, methanol (45°C, 1hr) x2, thoroughly rinsed with high-purity water, and then oven-dried at 60°C. Samples were then treated with 2M HCl (60°C, 1hr), rinsed thoroughly with high purity-water and oven-dried at 60°C. All samples were then processed to graphite in the AMS chemistry laboratories.[44]

Delta (13C) values relate solely to the graphite derived from the fraction that was used for the radiocarbon measurement. Sometimes, the delta (13C) of this fraction is not the same as that of the bulk material. Measurements are determined using EA-IRMS. Some delta (13C) values may not have an associated uncertainty due to the limited number of determinations. The Conventional Radiocarbon ages were rounded following Stuiver and Polach (1977). The definition of percent Modern Carbon and Conventional Radiocarbon age can also be found in this publication. The calibration of the conventional radiocarbon ages was performed against the latest international radiocarbon calibration curve for the northern hemisphere (IntCal20).[45] Calibrations of the two modern samples were performed against the Post-bomb atmospheric Northern Hemisphere Zone 2 Calibration curve.[46] All calibrations were performed using the OxCal 4.4 calibration software.[47]

Results revealed wide variations in the dates of the four samples (Table 2). Sample OZY550 (rodent droppings) and OZY551 (grape seed) were identified as modern. In contrast, the third sample (OZY544, of plant matter) returned a date of 2151–2034 cal BCE (78.7% probability), placing it in the First Intermediate Period. This latter result is much later than the 5th Dynasty date of the tomb in which it was found. A fourth sample (OZY543, also of plant matter, with some resinous pieces) returned a date broadly consistent with the tomb. This and other similar resinous pieces, including loose pieces attached to ceramic, likely belong to the original phases of the life-cycle of the jar. The other results suggest two possibilities, either the likely contamination of ancient material or that the contents of the bag were gathered together in modern times from several ancient and modern sources, which may have included ancient residues from the jar.

Acknowledgments

We thank the Museum of Fine Arts, Boston, for permission to study the jars and sample the contents; in particular, the Head of Scientific Research, Dr. Richard Newman, the Head of the Department of Ancient Art, Dr. Rita Freed, Curator Dr. Denise Doxey, and Dr. Susan Allen, who provided all the support for the on-site work. In addition, we are grateful to Dr. Geraldine Jacobsen and her team from the Centre for Accelerator Science at the Australian Nuclear Science and Technology Organisation (ANSTO) at Lucas Heights (Sydney, Australia) for undertaking the radiocarbon dating. Dr. Alice McClymont, Anthony Dakhoul, and Nathaniel Lowe provided additional editing and graphic support in preparing illustrations.

Funding Sources

This work was funded by an Australian Research Council Future Fellowship held by Karin Sowada, 'Pyramids, Power and the Dynamics of States in Crisis' (Project FT170100288) at the Department of History & Archaeology, Macquarie University, Sydney; the radiocarbon dating was funded by ANSTO Grant No. 12203 'Toward a radiocarbon chronology of Egypt during the Pyramid Age (c. 2600–2180 BCE).' We also acknowledge the financial support for the Centre for Accelerator Science at ANSTO, through the Australian National Collaborative Research Infrastructure Strategy (NCRIS).

Table 3: Summary of observations from the original field notes, registration, photographs, museum records, and observations made on the jars between November 2017and July 2019. The Photo ID # refer to the image numbers recorded on www.gizapyramids.org; the original field records were also available on the site.

Museum no. / Field Registration no.	Pottery Type	Provenance (owner's name noted if preserved)	Date	Vessel Condition	Field Notes (www.gizapyramids.org)	Photo Observations (www.gizapyramids.org)
MFA 13.5638 / Reisner Field # 13-11-64	Combed jar	Western Cemetery Pit G 4240 A Sneferu-seneb (plundered)	Early 4th Dynasty	Body, neck, and rim mended from fragments with some pieces missing	No indication of contents or stopper (Photo ID # OR02_p035)	No indication of contents or stopper in vessel photo (Photo ID # C5384_NS)
MFA 13.5639 / 13-11-65	Combed jar	Western Cemetery Pit G 4240 A (plundered)	Early 4th Dynasty	In fragments	No indication of contents or stopper (Photo ID # OR02_p035)	No photos in archive
MFA 13.5671 / 13-11-106	Combed jar	Western Cemetery Pit G 4440 A, shaft (plundered)	Probably early-mid 4th Dynasty	Body mended from fragments; neck and rim intact	No indication of contents or stopper (Photo ID # OR02_p047)	No indication of contents or stopper in vessel photo (Photo ID # C5410_NS; Fig. 2a)
MFA 13.5672 / 13-11-107	Combed jar	Western Cemetery Pit G 4440 A, shaft (plundered)	Probably early-mid 4th Dynasty	Neck, rim, and shoulder mended from fragments; body missing	No indication of contents or stopper (Photo ID # OR02_p048)	No indication of contents or stopper in vessel photo (Photo ID # C5424_NS, left)
MFA 13.5673 / 13-11-108	Combed jar	Western Cemetery Pit G 4440 A, shaft (plundered)	Probably early 4th Dynasty	Body mended from fragments with some pieces missing; neck, rim, and shoulder missing	No indication of contents or stopper in field notes (Photo ID # OR02_p048)	No indication of contents or stopper in vessel photo (Photo ID # C5424_NS, right)
MFA 37.2729; Peabody 43-42-50/5887, 43-42-50/5887.1 & 2 / 35-8-11	Combed jar	Western Cemetery Mastaba G 5020-Annex From top of mastaba and pit	4th Dynasty	Body mended from fragments with some pieces missing; neck and rim intact	No indication of contents or stopper (Photo ID # OR27_p1279)	No indication of contents or stopper in vessel photos (Photo ID # B8594_NS, right; # SC139372)
MFA 37.2725 / 35-8-8	Combed jar	Western Cemetery Mastaba G 5020-Annex From top of mastaba and pit	4th Dynasty	Body, neck, and rim mended from fragments with some pieces missing	No indication of contents or stopper (Photo ID # OR27_p1278)	No indication of contents or stopper in vessel photos (Photo ID # B8594_NS, left; # SC183712)
MFA 37.1319 / 34-6-17j	Combed jar	Eastern Cemetery Pit G 7330 A, debris of pit (plundered)	4th Dynasty	Body mended from fragments with some pieces missing; neck and rim intact	No indication of contents or stopper (Photo ID # OR25_p1216)	No indication of contents or stopper in vessel photos (Photo ID # C13432_NS; # C13433_NS; # SC183702)
MFA 13.5593 / 13-10-29	Combed jar	Western Cemetery Pit G 4340 A, debris in shaft (plundered) Pottery found at the bottom of Shaft G 4340 A and in the burial chamber, precise findspot of vessel not stated	4th Dynasty	Body mended from fragments with some pieces missing; neck and rim intact	No indication of contents or stopper; "burnt black inside" but this is crossed out and "with grey interior" is written above (Photo ID # OR02_p007; OR02_p008)	No indication of contents or stopper in vessel photo (Photo ID # B2092_NS, bottom left)
MFA 20.1881 / 14-1-82	Combed jar	Western Cemetery Pit G 4530 A (plundered) Pottery found at the bottom of Shaft G 4530 A and in the burial chamber, precise findspot is not stated	4th Dynasty- early 5th Dynasty	Body mended from fragments with some pieces missing; neck and rim intact	No indication of contents or stopper (Photo ID # OR02_p087)	No indication of contents or stopper in vessel photo (Photo ID # C5578_NS)

Museum no. / Field Registration no.	Pottery Type	Provenance (owner's name noted if preserved)	Date	Vessel Condition	Field Notes (www.gizapyramids.org)	Photo Observations (www.gizapyramids.org)
MFA 19.1456 / 14-1-10	Combed jar	Western Cemetery Pit G 4630 A chamber Medew-nefer (plundered)	Late 4th-early 5th Dynasty	Body and neck intact; part of rim missing	No indication of contents or stopper (Photo ID # OR02_p059; # OR02_p070)	No indication of contents or stopper in excavation photo (Photo ID # C5486_NS) or vessel photos (Photo ID # C5518_NS; SC139330)
MFA 20.1889 / 14-1-14	Combed jar	Western Cemetery Pit G 4630 A shaft (plundered)	Late 4th-early 5th Dynasty	Body mended from fragments with some pieces missing; neck intact with part of rim missing	No indication of contents or stopper (Photo ID # OR02_p069; # OR02_p070)	No indication of contents or stopper in vessel photos (Photo ID # C5547_NS; # SC139340)
MFA 20.1914 / 14-3-67	Combed jar	Western Cemetery Pit G 4620 A of Kanefer, probably from burial chamber, found in fragments (plundered)	5th Dynasty	Egyptian imitation. See Sowada 2018, *Bulletin de liaison de la céramique Égyptienne* 28, 117–122.	Not seen	No indication of contents or stopper in vessel photos (Photo ID C5752_NS) No contents visible on MFA photo
MFA 47.1661 / 32-12-18	Combed jar	Western Cemetery Pit G 2140 A, debris of chamber (plundered) Found in burial chamber at bottom of shaft	Mid 4th-early 5th Dynasty	Body intact; part of neck and rim missing	No indication of contents or stopper (Photo ID # OR24_p1158)	Heavy accretions on exterior visible on vessel photos (Photo ID # B9313_NS, bottom middle right; # SC139375)
MFA 20.1903 / No number	Combed jar	Western Cemetery Pit G 1031 A (intact tomb)	4th-early 5th Dynasty (?)	Body intact but with 'kill hole' and heavy accretions on upper part; neck intact but part of rim missing	No field notes in archive	Possible residues on upper body but no stopper visible in vessel photos; neck and rim completely cleaned (Photo ID # C10232_OS, # C13023_OS; # 13024_OS; # 13031_OS; # C5375_NS; SC139344)
MFA 13.5132 / 13-1-506	Combed jar	Western Cemetery Pit G 2175 B Khnum-nefer (plundered?)	Late 4th-5th Dynasty	Vessel seen amidst coffin debris in excavation photo with broken neck nearby (Photo ID # C3268_NS) but mended and in place in vessel photo (Photo ID # B1682_NS); now in fragments	No indication of contents or stopper (Photo ID # OR01_p076)	No indication of contents or stopper in excavation photo (Photo ID # C3268_NS) or vessel photo (Photo ID # B1682_NS, bottom left)
MFA 47.1662 / 40-5-7	Combed jar	Western Cemetery Pit G 2350 L (= G 5290) (chamber plundered) Vessel found lying on its side inside sarcophagus near body	5th Dynasty	Body and neck intact; part of rim missing	'contains dried oil, shiny black color cf. Lucas analysis of 32-12-18'; no indication of stopper (Photo ID # OR30_p1590)	No indication of contents or stopper in excavation photo (Photo ID # B9276_NS; Fig. 8) or vessel photos (Photo ID # B9294_NS, bottom middle; # SC139376)
MFA 37.2724 / 35-7-41	Combed jar	Western Cemetery Pit G 2370 B Senedjem-ib Inty Precise findspot not known; field notes mention 'broken pottery' near sarcophagus but no other detail	Mid-late 5th Dynasty	Body, neck, and rim mended from fragments with some pieces missing	No indication of contents or stopper (Photo ID # OR27_p1274)	No indication of contents or stopper in vessel photos (Photo ID # C13649_NS; SC183711)
MFA 37.2723 / 35-7-41	Combed jar	Western Cemetery Pit G 2387 A, main shaft of G 2385, chamber	6th Dynasty	Body mended from fragments; neck and rim not visible	'plaster (gypsum) jar cover, cover not complete' with pencil drawing; no indication of contents (Photo ID # OR27_p1266)	Broken plaster stopper in place in vessel photos (Photo ID # C13647_NS; # SC183710)

Museum no. / Field Registration no.	Pottery Type	Provenance (owner's name noted if preserved)	Date	Vessel Condition	Field Notes (www.gizapyramids.org)	Photo Observations (www.gizapyramids.org)
MFA 13.2928a–b / 12-12-573	Combed jar & stopper	Western Cemetery Pit G 2381 A, burial chamber Impy, also known as Merptah-ankhmeryre (intact tomb)	Late 6th Dynasty, reign of Pepy II	Body intact; neck broken off	'broken off at neck in antiquity fibrous ball in neck small amt [sic] organic matter' (Photo ID # OR01_p072). Organic matter now numbered MFA OP.1.13.2928.	Plaster stopper intact but not attached to vessel in excavation photo (Photo ID # B1612_NS, Fig. 2b, 5-6); broken plaster stopper in place in vessel photo (Photo ID # B1680_NS, right)
MFA 13.2929 / 12-12-569	Combed jar	Western Cemetery Pit G 2381 A, burial chamber (intact tomb) Vessel found standing alongside coffin	Late 6th Dynasty, reign of Pepy II	Body, neck, and rim intact	No indication of contents or stopper (Photo ID # OR01_p071). Organic matter now numbered MFA OP.1.13.2929 may be misnumbered and actually belong to MFA 13.2930 (below).	No indication of contents or stopper in vessel photos (Photo ID # B1681_NS, right; SC183586 Fig. 6)
MFA 13.2930 / 12-12-571	Combed jar	Western Cemetery Pit G 2381 A, burial chamber (intact tomb) Presumably found alongside coffin	Late 6th Dynasty, reign of Pepy II	Body, neck, and rim intact	'contains organic matter' (Photo ID # OR01_p072); no indication of stopper. Organic matter now numbered OP.1.13.2929 may be misnumbered and actually belong to this vessel.	Possible remains of a leather stopper on neck (Photo ID # B1612_NS, Fig. 6 left) but no indication of contents in excavation photo or vessel photo (Photo ID # B1681_NS, left, Fig. 3a)
MFA 13.2931 / 12-12-572	Combed jar	Western Cemetery Pit G 2381 A, burial chamber (intact tomb) Vessel found standing alongside coffin	Late 6th Dynasty, reign of Pepy II	Body intact; neck and rim not visible	'large lime-plaster stopper. Unopened.' (Photo ID # OR01_p072)	Plaster stopper intact and in place in excavation photo (Photo ID # B1612_NS) and vessel photos (Photo ID # B1680_NS, left; # SC183588, Fig. 6)
MFA 13.2932 / 12-12-570	Combed jar	Western Cemetery Pit G 2381 A, burial chamber (intact tomb) Vessel found standing alongside coffin	Late 6th Dynasty, reign of Pepy II	Body intact; neck and rim not visible	'large mud stopper sealed with cyl. seal' (Photo ID # OR01_p072)	Nile mud stopper intact and in place in excavation photo (B1612_NS) and vessel photos (Photo ID # C3363_NS; # SC183589)
MFA 20.1899 / 13-10-25	One-handled jug	Western Cemetery Pit G 4340 A Pottery fragments found amongst debris in shaft and in burial chamber; precise findspot is not stated	4th Dynasty	Body and neck mended from fragments with some pieces missing; rim and top of handle missing	No indication of contents or stopper (Photo ID # OR02_p005; # OR02_p006)	No indication of contents or stopper in vessel photos (Photo ID # B2092_NS, bottom right; # SC139342)
MFA 13.5615 / 13-10-68	One-handled jug	Western Cemetery Pit G 4340 A Pottery fragments found amongst debris in shaft and in burial chamber; precise findspot is not stated	4th Dynasty	Body mended from fragments, in two parts; neck intact but rim missing	No indication of contents or stopper (Photo ID # OR02_p018; # OR02_p019)	No indication of contents or stopper in vessel photo (Photo ID # B2092_NS, top left & middle)

Museum no./ Field Registration no.	Pottery Type	Provenance (owner's name noted if preserved)	Date	Vessel Condition	Field Notes (www.gizapyramids.org)	Photo Observations (www.gizapyramids.org)
MFA 20.1904 / No number	One-handled jug with trefoil mouth	Western Cemetery Pit G 1233, Annex A (intact burial)	Early–mid 4th Dynasty	Body intact but with 'kill hole' on lower part	No indication of stopper; possible mention of contents, but hard to read (Photo ID # E011192)	No indication of stopper or contents in excavation photo (Photo ID # A10923_OS) but white accretions on neck, rim, and shoulder visible in original vessel photos (Photo ID # C13022_OS; # C13032_OS) suggest that one was present. Vessel now heavily cleaned (Photo ID # SC125197)
MFA 20.1905 / No number	One-handled jug	Western Cemetery Pit G 1233, Annex A (intact burial) Found west of coffin lying on its side	Early–mid 4th Dynasty	Body intact but with 3 'kill holes' on upper and lower body (Photo ID # C13026_OS); neck intact but part of rim missing	No field notes in archive	No indication of stopper or contents in excavation photo (Photo ID # C11399_OS) but traces of white plaster around the neck and handle in vessel photos (Photo ID # C13027_OS; # SC139345) suggest that one was present.
MFA 33.721 / 32-12-13	One-handled jug	Western Cemetery Pit G 2170 A (plundered) Vessel found in debris of chamber	Late 4th to early 5th Dynasty	Body mended from fragments with some pieces missing; neck, rim and top of handle missing	No indication of contents or stopper (Photo ID # OR24_p'157)	No indication of contents or stopper in vessel photos (Photo ID # A7065_NS, middle right; # SC139360)

References

Appadurai, Arjun. 2013. "Introduction: Commodities and the politics of value." In Arjun Appadurai (ed.), *The Social Life of Things: Commodities in cultural perspective*, 3–61. Cambridge: Cambridge University Press. https://hdl.handle.net/2027/heb.32141.

Badreshany, Kamal, Karin Sowada, Mary Ownby, Mathilde Jean, Michel De Vreeze, Alice McClymont, and Graham Philip. 2022. "The characterisation of ceramic production from the central Levant and Egyptian trade in the Pyramid Age." *Journal of Archaeological Science: Reports* 41: 1–16. DOI: 10.1016/j.jasrep.2021.103309.

Badreshany, Kamal, Graham Philip, and Melissa Kennedy. 2020. "The Development of Integrated Regional Economies in the Early Bronze Age Levant: New Evidence from "Combed-Ware" Jars." Levant 52: https://doi.org/10.1080/00758914.2019.1641009.

Bárta, Miroslav, Aleš Bezděk, Viktor Černý, Salima Ikram,Petr Kočár, Roman Křivánek, Martina Kujanová, Petr Pokorný,Colin Reader, Zdenka Sůvová, Petra Vlčková. 2009. *Abusir XIII. Abusir South 2: Tomb Complex of the Vizier Qar, his sons Qar Junior and Senedjemib, and Iykai*. Prague: Czech Institute of Egyptology.

Biga, Maria G. and Piotr Steinkeller. 2021. "In search of Dugurasu." *Journal of Cuneiform Studies* 73: 1–70.

Borchardt, Ludwig. 1910–1913. *Das Grabdenkmal des Königs S'aḥu-Re*, I–II. Leipzig: Hinrichs. https://digi.ub.uni-heidelberg.de/diglit/borchardt1910ga.

Brunton, Guy. 1948. *Matmar. British Museum expedition to Middle Egypt 1929–1931*. London: Bernard Quaritch Ltd.

Esse, Douglas L. 1991. *Subsistence, Trade, and Social Change in Early Bronze Age Palestine*. Studies in Ancient Oriental Civilization 50. Chicago: Oriental Institute, The University of Chicago.

Fink, David, Michael Hotchkis, Quan Hua, G. E. Jacobsen, A. M. Smith, U. Zoppi, David P. Child, C. Mifsud, H.A. Van der Gaast, A.A. Williams, and M. Williams. 2004. "The ANTARES AMS facility at ANSTO." *Nuclear Instruments and Methods in Physics*

Research Section B 223–224: 109–115. https://doi.org/10.1016/j.nimb.2004.04.025.

Gerisch, Rainer, Wilma Wetterstrom, and Mary Ann Murray. 2008. "Egypt's Oldest Olive." *AERAGRAM* 9(2): 3. https://www.aeraweb.org/wp-content/uploads/2015/01/aeragram9_2.pdf

Hartung, Ulrich. 2001. *Umm el-Qaab I:. Importkeramik aus dem Friedhof U in Abydos (Umm el-Qaab) und die Beziehungen Ägyptens zu Vorderasien im 4. Jahrtausend v. Chr.* Archäologische Veröffentlichungen 92. Mainz: Philipp von Zabern.

Hartung, Ulrich, E. Christiana Köhler, Vera Müller, and Mary F. Ownby. 2015. "Imported pottery from Abydos: a new petrographic perspective." *Ägypten und Levante* 25: 295–333.

Hassan, Selim. 1936. Excavations at Giza 2: 1930–1931. Cairo: Faculty of Arts of the Egyptian University & Government Press.

Hua, Quan, Mike Barbetti, and Andrzej Rakowski. 2013. "Atmospheric Radiocarbon for the Period 1950–2010." *Radiocarbon* 55(4), 2059–2072. DOI: 10.2458/azu_js_rc.v55i2.16177.

Helck, Wolfgang. 1971. *Die Beziehungen Ägyptens zu Vorderasien im 3. und 2. Jahrtausend v. Chr.* 2nd ed. Wiesbaden: O. Harrassowitz.

Junker, Hermann. 1929. *Gîza 1. Die Mastabas der IV. Dynastie auf dem Westfriedhof.* Vienna and Leipzig: Hölder-Pichler-Tempsky. http://giza.fas.harvard.edu/pubdocs/214/full/.

Knapp, Arthur B. 1991. "Spice, Drugs, Grain and Grog: Organic Goods in Bronze Age East Mediterranean Trade." In Noël H. Gale (ed.), *Bronze Age Trade in the Mediterranean. Papers presented at the Conference held at Rewley House, Oxford, in December 1989,* 21–68. Studies in Mediterranean Archaeology 90. Jonsered: P. Åström.

Knoblauch, Christian. 2010. "Preliminary Report on the Early Bronze Age III Pottery from Contexts of the 6th Dynasty in the Abydos Middle Cemetery." *Ägypten und Levante* 20: 243–261.

Krauss, Rolf. 1999. "Nh(h)-Öl=Oliveöl." *MDAIK* 55: 293–298.

Lehner, Mark . 2015. "Labor and the Pyramids. The Heit el-Ghurab "Workers Town" at Giza." In Piotr Steinkeller and Michael Hudson (eds.), *Labor in the Ancient World, International Scholars Conference on Ancient Near Eastern Economies 5,* 397–520. Dresden: ISLET-Verlag.

Lucas, A. (Alfred). 1931. ""Cedar" – tree products employed in mummification." *The Journal of Egyptian Archaeology* 17: 13–20.

Lucas, A. (Alfred), and John R. Harris. 1989. *Ancient Egyptian Materials and Industries.* 4th ed. London: Histories and Mysteries of Man.

Marcolin, M. and Diego Espinel, A. 2011. "The Sixth Dynasty Biographic Inscriptions of Iny: More Pieces to the Puzzle." In Miroslav Bárta, Filip Coppens, and Jaromir Krejcí (eds.), *Abusir and Saqqara in the Year 2010/1,* 570–615. Prague: Czech Institute of Egyptology.

Marcus, Ezra. 2002. "Early Seafaring and Maritime Activity in the Southern Levant from Prehistory through the Third Millennium BCE." In Edwin C.M. van den Brink and Thomas E. Levy (eds.), *Egypt and the Levant: Interrelations from the 4th through the Early 3rd Millennium B.C.E.,* 403–417. London and New York: Leicester University Press.

Miroschedji, P. de. 2021. On Early Bronze Age Levantine combed vessels: the view from the south, *Levant* 53, 30–68. https://doi.org/10.1080/00758914.2021.1917814.

Murray, Mary Anne. 1992. "Archaeobotany." In Lisa Giddy and David Jeffreys, "Memphis, 1991." *The Journal of Egyptian Archaeology* 78: 1–11. https://doi.org/10.1177/030751339207800102.

Panagiotakopulu, Eva. 2001. "New Records for Ancient Pests: Archaeoentomology in Egypt." *Journal of Archaeological Science* 28: 1235–1246. DOI: 10.1006/jasc.2001.0697.

Ramsey, Christopher B. 2009. "Bayesian Analysis of Radiocarbon Dates." *Radiocarbon* 51(1): 337–360.

Reimer, Paula J., Edouard Bard, Alex Bayliss, J. Warren Beck, Paul G. Blackwell, Christopher Bronk Ramsey, Caitlin E. Buck, Hai Cheng, R. Lawrence Edwards, Michael Friedrich, Pieter M. Grootes, Thomas P. Guilderson, Haflidi Haflidason, Irka Hajdas, Christine Hatté, Timothy J. Heaton, Dirk L. Hoffmann, Alan G. Hogg, Konrad A. Hughen, K. Felix Kaiser, Bernd Kromer, Sturt W. Manning, Mu Niu, Ron W. Reimer, David A. Richards, E. Marian Scott, John R. Southon, Richard A. Staff, Christian S. M. Turney, Johannes van der Plicht 2013. "IntCal13 and Marine13 Radiocarbon Age Calibration Curves 0–50,000 Years Cal BP." *Radiocarbon* 55(4): 1869–1887.

Reisner, George A. 1915. "Accessions to the Egyptian Department during 1914." *Bulletin of the Museum of Fine Arts, Boston* 13(76): 29–36.

Reisner, George A. 1942. *A History of the Giza Necropolis 1*. Cambridge, MA: Harvard University Press.

Reisner, George A. and William Stevenson Smith. 1955. *A History of the Giza Necropolis, 2*. Cambridge, MA: Harvard University Press.

Richards, Janet. 2005. *Society and Death in Ancient Egypt. Mortuary Landscapes of the Middle Kingdom*. Cambridge: Cambridge University Press.

Seidlmayer, Stephan J. 1990. *Gräberfelder aus dem Übergang vom Alten zum Mittleren Reich: Studien zur Archäologie der Ersten Zwischenzeit*. Heidelberg: Heidelberger Orientverlag.

Serpico, Margaret. 2000. "Resins, Amber and Bitumen." In Paul T. Nicholson and Ian Shaw (eds.), *Ancient Egyptian Materials and Technology*, 430–474. Cambridge: Cambridge University Press.

Serpico, Margaret and Raymond White. 1996. "A Report on the Analysis of Contents of a Cache of Jars from the Tomb of Djer." In Jeffrey Spencer (ed.), *Aspects of Early Egypt*, 128–139. London: British Museum Press.

———. 2000. 'Oil, Fat and Wax." Paul T. Nicholson and Ian Shaw (eds.), *Ancient Egyptian Materials and Technology*, 390–429. Cambridge: Cambridge University Press.

Sowada, Karin. 2009. *Egypt in the Eastern Mediterranean during the Old Kingdom: An Archaeological Perspective*. Orbis Biblicus et Orientalis 237. Fribourg/Göttingen: Academic Press/Vandenhoeck & Ruprecht.

———. 2020. Foreign Trade and Heit el-Ghurab, *AERAGRAM* 20(2): 22–23.

Sowada, Karin, Mary Ownby, and Anna Wodzińska. 2020. "The Petrography of Imported Combed Vessels from Early Old Kingdom Giza." *Levant* 52(1-2): 197–214. https://doi.org/10.1080/00758914.2019.1664197 (accessed 30 October 2019).

Stager, L.E. 1992. "The Periodization of Palestine from Neolithic through Early Bronze Age Times." In Robert W. Ehrich (ed.), *Chronologies in Old World Archaeology*, 22–41. Chicago: The University of Chicago Press.

Stuiver, Minze and Henry A. Polach. 1977. "Discussion Reporting of ^{14}C Data." *Radiocarbon* 19(3): 355–363. https://doi.org/10.1017/S0033822200003672

Thalmann, Jean-Paul and Karin Sowada. 2014. "Levantine "Combed Ware"." In Marc Lebeau (ed.), *Associated Regional Chronologies for the Ancient Near East and the Eastern Mediterranean, ARCANE Interregional, Vol. I: Ceramics*, 355–78. Turnhout: Brepols.

Ward, William A. 1991. "Early Contacts between Egypt, Canaan, and Sinai: Remarks on the Paper by Amnon Ben-Tor." *Bulletin of the American Schools of Oriental Research* 281: 11–26.

Notes

1 Reisner and Smith 1955, 74–76; Helck 1971, 28–34; Esse 1991, 110–124; Stager 1992; Marcus 2002; Sowada 2009, 154–182; Bárta et al. 2009, 243–271; Knoblauch 2010; Thalmann and Sowada 2014; Badreshany et al. 2020. It is assumed that such jars were imported during the 3rd Dynasty, but none have survived.

2 Sowada, Ownby and Wodzińska 2020; Sowada, Ownby and Bárta, 2021; Badreshany et al. 2022.

3 Badreshany et al. 2020.

4 Sowada, Ownby and Bárta 2021.

5 Sowada 2009, 64–65, Fig. 10; Reisner and Smith 1955, 75; Knapp 1991, 30; Sowada 2009, 62, Fig. 9 Pl. 13, MFA 47.1661; Lucas and Harris 1989, 319–320; Serpico and White 1996, 132–133; Hassan 1936, 145–147.

6 The results of the analyses are being prepared for publication, led by Dr. Margaret Serpico (University College London) and Dr. Sophia Aharonovich (Australian Catholic University) as part of ARC Project FT170100288.

7 Reisner and Smith 1955, 73–76; Helck 1971, 28–34; Thalmann and Sowada 2014, 369–374; Sowada 2009, 55–74, 154–182.

8 Reisner 1942; Reisner and Smith 1955; www.gizapyramids.org accessed 23 April 2020.

9 For curatorial details, see Sowada 2009, 71 [55], Fig. 12, Pl. 7. The modern treatment was observed on examination of the jug by the writer in July 2019.

10 Reisner and Smith 1955, pl. 52g, d (MFA 13.2932); Brunton 1948, 29, 45, pl. 37; Bárta et al. 2009, 243–271. Two sealed jars from Tomb G 2381 A, MFA 13.2831 (weighed 7.27 kg) and MFA 13.2932 are heavier than jars from the same tomb without stoppers (e.g., MFA 13.2929 = 5.188 kg). The weight of the sealed jars indicates that the contents are still inside (Sowada 2009, 162). The identity of the contents is not known.

11 Bárta et al. 2009, 349, Pl. 32.5; Sowada, Ownby and Bárta 2021, Fig. 10a. The underlying white coating may represent the original jar sealing.

[12] Brunton 1948, 29, 45,pl. 37; Seidlmayer 1990, Fig. 81; Sowada 2009, 83 [95], Fig. 14.

[13] The field records and original photographs in Table 3 were examined online by the writer in 2019, but the images could not be viewed online at the time of writing due to a web software issue.

[14] See, for example, the broken plaster stopper of jar MFA 37.2723 from Giza Tomb G 2387 (Sowada 2009, Pl. 5[47]).

[15] See also Figs 3, 5, and 7 in Sowada, Ownby and Wodzinska 2020.

[16] Reisner and Smith 1955, 76; Sowada 2009, 68–69 and references.

[17] Evidence of multiple plaster stoppers may represent reuse in Lebanon prior to export. We are grateful to Dr. Christian Knoblauch (University of Swansea) for this observation.

[18] Reisner 1915, no. 76; Reisner 1942, fig. 299, Pl. 63d; Reisner and Stevenson Smith 1955, 76; Sowada 2009, 60–61, Fig. 9, Pl. 2.

[19] Formerly Tomb G 2350 L; for the jar, see Sowada 2009, 65–66 and references therein.

[20] Some combed jars are small and could have been removed: jar MFA 47.1661 is only 27.6 cm high, see Sowada 2009, 62, pl. 3{25]. Reisner also reported that sherds of several combed jars were found in street debris outside the mastabas, see Reisner 1942, 462–465, 477.

[21] Sowada, Ownby and Wodzinska 2020; Reisner and Smith 1955, 76, Fig. 97, Pl. 52f; Sowada 2009, 65–66 [39], 171.

[22] A sample of the contents from MFA 47.1661 was analyzed by A. Lucas and found to be 'true resin of the coniferous tree' (Reisner and Smith 1955, 75; Lucas and Harris 1989, 320).

[23] Archaeological excavations were wound back in 1940 as war pressed in. Reisner died in 1942, and by 1947, the region was still recovering from World War 2.

[24] Sowada and Wetterstrom decided it was not worthwhile to continue sorting the contents after AMS dating determined that only one of the submitted samples was within the age range of the jar. However, Dr. Wetterstrom assessed the unsorted contents on the final MFA visit and saw no materials other than what had been already identified.

[25] Murray 1992, 10–11. The AERA Giza Expedition reported the discovery of olive wood charcoal dated to the 4th Dynasty (Gerisch, Wetterstrom and Murray 2008, 3). Olive wood or olive fruit is not otherwise attested in Old Kingdom Egypt, although there has been speculation based on the textual record (e.g., Krauss 1999).

[26] Panagiotakopulu 2001, 1238.

[27] Panagiotakopulu 2001, 1238.

[28] Panagiotakopulu 2001, 1238.

[29] Badreshany et al. 2022.

[30] This can be contrasted to the imported bottle shape from Naqada IIIA1 tomb U-j, which have few direct parallels in the Levantine archaeological record and appear to have been 'made to order' for the tomb owner: see, for example, Ware Group 1 in Hartung 2001, 71-125; Hartung et al. 2015, 298-299.

[31] Appadurai 2013, 12.

[32] See, for example, the 'seal-bearer of the god [ie king], Iny': Marcolin and Diego Espinel 2011.

[33] See, for example, the Levantine-Egyptian relationships discussed in Biga and Steinkeller 2021.

[34] Appadurai 2013, 29.

[35] On this, see the row of foreign jars depicted on the causeway of Sahure: Borchardt 1910-13: Pl. 3.

[36] Lehner 2015, 413-315; 455-460; Sowada et al. 2020.

[37] Lehner 2015, 407-411.

[38] See jars from Ballas and sherds from Elephantine, summarised in Sowada 2009, 84-85. Jars found outside the capital zone of Abu Rawash to Dashur tend to date to the mid-Fifth to Sixth Dynasty. See also n. 12.

[39] For curatorial information and references, see Sowada 2009, 83, Fig. 14.

[40] Richards 2005, 134, quoting S. Quirke.

[41] Appadurai 2013, 56.

[42] Appadurai 2013, 57.

[43] Fink et al. 2004.

[44] Procedure as per Hua et al. 2001.

[45] Reimer et al. 2013.

[46] Hua, Barbetti, and Rakowski 2013.

[47] Ramsey 2009.

Journal of Ancient Egyptian Interconnections

The "Combed Ware" Storage and Transport Vessels from Khirbet ez-Zeraqon: A Reappraisal of the EB II–III Evidence in Light of Recent Petrographic Studies

Valentina Tumolo
Durham University

Kamal Badreshany
Durham University

Abstract
The present study offers new petrographic data on selected pottery from the EB II-III site of Khirbet ez-Zeraqon in northern Jordan, which includes storage and transport vessels with combed surfaces traditionally grouped under the label "Combed Ware." The results contribute to our understanding of the role played by these vessels in relation to the wider ceramic production documented at the site. On a larger scale, and thanks to the recent chronological reassessment of Khirbet ez-Zeraqons's stratigraphic sequence, our study provides further evidence for evaluating the developments of the broad phenomenon of Levantine combed vessels.

Keywords
Early Bronze Age Levant; Khirbet ez-Zeraqon; Combed Ware vessels; petrographic analyses; ceramic production

1. Introduction[1]

The investigation of the role played by the Levantine pottery manufacture is central to understand the socio-economic trajectories that characterized the Levant and the southeastern Mediterranean during the Early Bronze Age (henceforth EBA or EB; Fig. 4).[2] In this sense, the study of the material from the site of Khirbet ez-Zeraqon, in northern Jordan, contributes to the examination of the transformations that occurred in the area between the end of the fourth and the first centuries of the third millennium BCE. The reappraisal of the evidence brought to light by the excavations conducted at the site in the 1980s and 1990s establishes the life of the main EB settlement within a short time frame mostly falling within the local EB II.[3] As suggested by recent research, the site did not adapt to the changes at the transition to the EB III and, after some decades of decline, was completely abandoned at the beginning of this latter phase.

Our petrographic study, conducted on selected samples that include combed storage and transport vessels, offers new information on ceramic manufacture at the site. The evidence that emerges from this analysis is consistent with a revised understanding of the regional pattern of Levantine pottery industries during the late fourth and third millennium BCE and their change through time, connected to both internal socio-economic trajectories and the dynamics of short- and long-distance exchange. More specifically, the repertoire of combed storage and transport vessels at Khirbet ez-Zeraqon provides further support for the definition of a broad central and southern Levantine horizon. Around 2900/2800 BCE, a change occurred in the ceramic industry associated with these types of containers, shifting from specialized and nucleated manufactures to small-scale ones that made use of locally available raw materials.

2. The Archaeological Context: Khirbet ez-Zeraqon

Khirbet ez-Zeraqon (lat/long: 32.58638/35.948439) lies in the northern Transjordanian plateau, on a hilltop rising above the Wādī eš-Šellāle.[4] This area was characterized by an average rainfall between 300 and 400 mm per year during the fourth and the third millennium BCE.[5] This would have been sufficient for supporting rain-fed agriculture, but additional water supply could have been necessary in more arid years.[6]

The archeological site consists of a mound that covers an area of about 8 ha, which was the subject of systematic excavations conducted between 1984 and 1994 under the direction of Siegfried Mittmann (Biblisch-Archäologisches Institute of the Eberhard Karls University of Tübingen, Germany) and Moawiyah Ibrahim (Institute of Archaeology and Anthropology of the Yarmouk University of Irbid, Jordan).[7] These investigations revealed a major occupation dated by excavators to the local EB II–III.

The settlement was established in a single phase of construction at the beginning of EB II, creating a well-defined outline of a town surrounded by a massive defense wall, with a lower city on the south and an upper city on the north (Fig. 1). Through time, this plan underwent only slight modifications due to some secondary rebuilding and adjustments primarily pertaining to the city gates and the reinforcement of the city wall.[8] The upper town (Fig. 2), on the northern side of the mound, was dominated by two main architectural complexes: the "temple complex," comprising what are believed to be cult buildings, a circular altar and subsidiary structures;[9] and the "palace complex," which was a large unit formed by at least four juxtaposed sectors characterized by different layouts and likely served diverse functions, such as administrative, economic-industrial, and representative.[10] Among these sectors, building B0.8 included small irregular rooms with installations for food-processing and stockpiling, with a pottery repertoire largely composed of storage vessels.[11] In the lower city

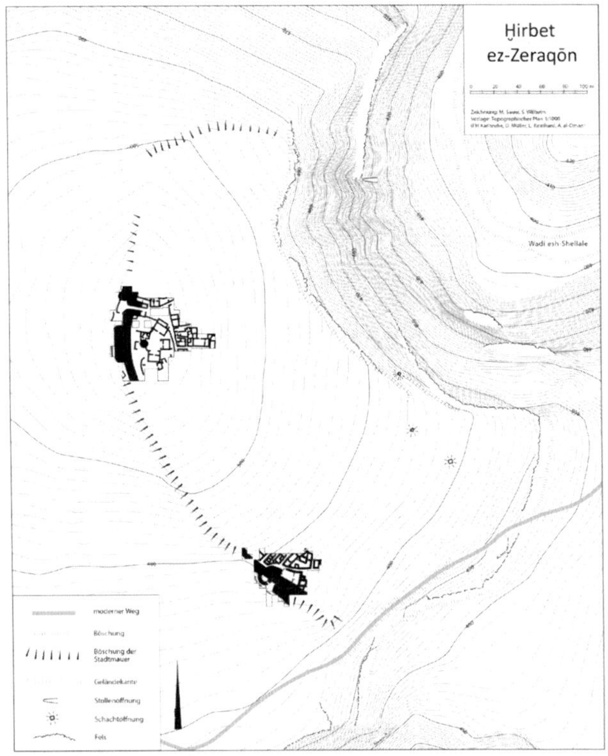

Figure 1: Khirbet ez-Zeraqon, topographic plan (courtesy of the Khirbet ez-Zeraqon archeological expedition).

(Fig. 3), most of the revealed buildings were residential,[12] while the function of Building B1.3—whether private or collective—remains unclear.[13]

Within the occupational sequence of this settlement, three main chronological stages have been identified based on their distinctive pottery assemblages and defined, for this reason, as "ceramic horizons," respectively named "early horizon," "middle horizon," and "late horizon."[14] Each of these broad periods is associated with stratigraphic phases, sub-phases, and architectural activities. The foundation of the town took place in the early horizon and, after some reconstructions, the last phase of occupation was characterized by signs of instability: the city gates were reinforced, and the entrances were blocked. At the same time, some sectors of the city were no longer kept in repair, such as parts of the defense wall in the lower town that had started to collapse into the open B1.5 space.[15] After this stage of decline, the site was completely abandoned, with no evidence of destruction. Following a gap of about four hundred years, the site was reoccupied in the EB IV, probably by small groups of temporary settlers, as suggested

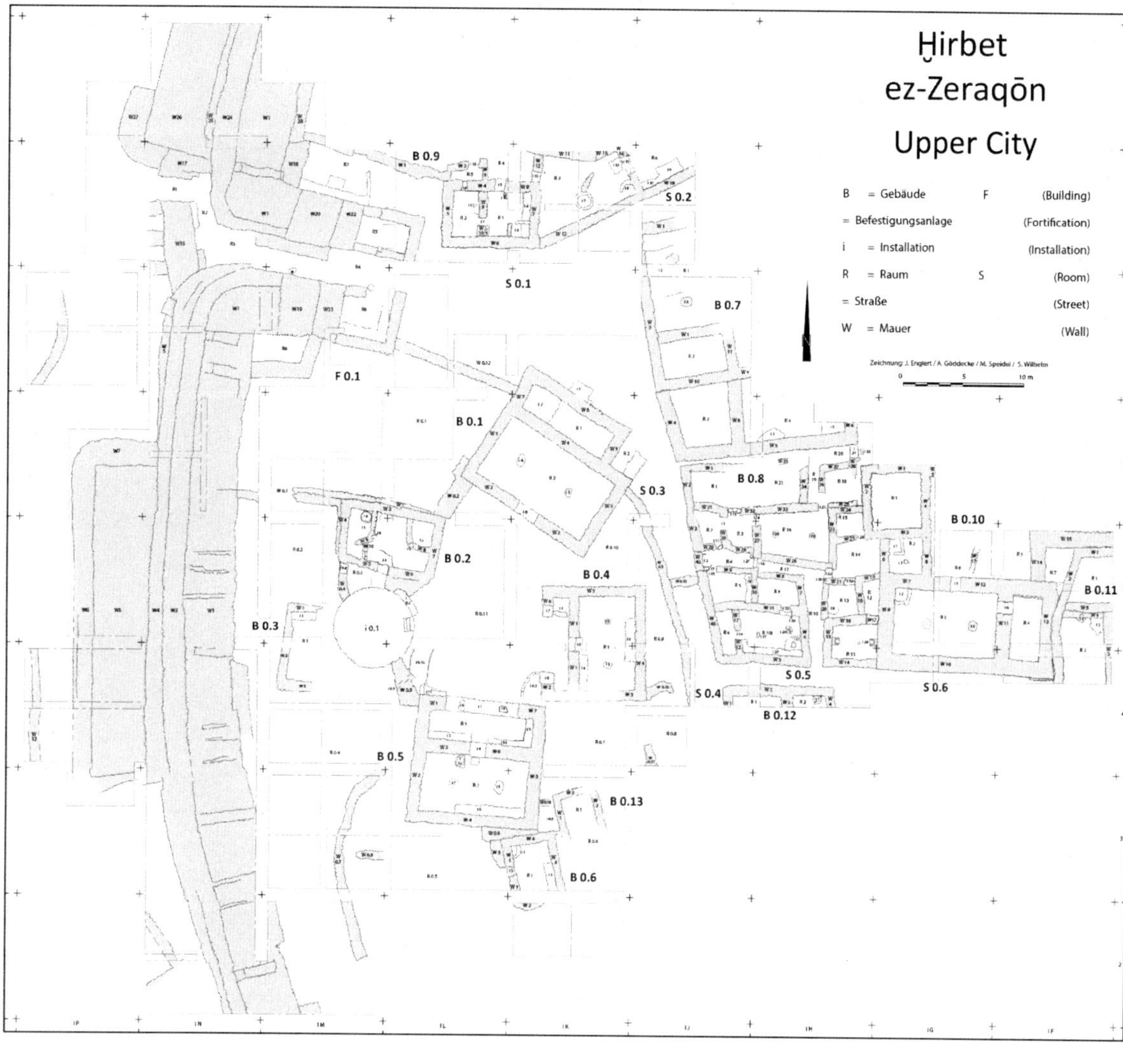

Figure 2: Khirbet ez-Zeraqon, upper city plan (courtesy of the Khirbet ez-Zeraqon archeological expedition).

by scattered ceramics and small structures such as stone-lined silos, which partly reused the ruins of the previous buildings.[16]

Based on comparisons with ceramic inventories of the northern Transjordan and Cisjordan, and the upper and middle Jordan Valley, the three EB II–III chronological horizons have been ascribed respectively to the EB II, the EB II/III transition, and the EB III.[17] More specifically, the early horizon can be set in the EB II, as suggested by ceramic comparisons from Phase C of Tel Bet Yeraḥ[18] and Strata XIIC-A and XIIE-D at Tel Qashish.[19] The same appears to apply to the middle horizon, which can be assigned to the late EB II or the EB II/III transition. For the late horizon, it is possible to suggest an attribution to the EB II/III transition or the early EB III, since the repertory finds strong analogies with Period C and early Period D at Tel Bet Yeraḥ, while later EB III shapes, such as oversized platters that are characteristic of the late Period D of Tel Bet Yeraḥ and Megiddo level J-6, are instead absent.[20] As found in the very earliest EB III stages at Tel Bet Yeraḥ, the ceramic repertoire of this horizon includes only a few Khirbet Kerak Ware sherds.[21]

The relative chronological assessment made on the base of the stratified ceramic repertoires is supported by radiocarbon data, which suggest a date of ca. 3100/3050–3000 cal. BCE for the early horizon, ca. 3000–2950 cal. BCE for the middle horizon, and ca. 2950–2850 cal. BCE for the late horizon (Fig. 4).[22] These absolute dates concur with recent proposals on high absolute chronologies

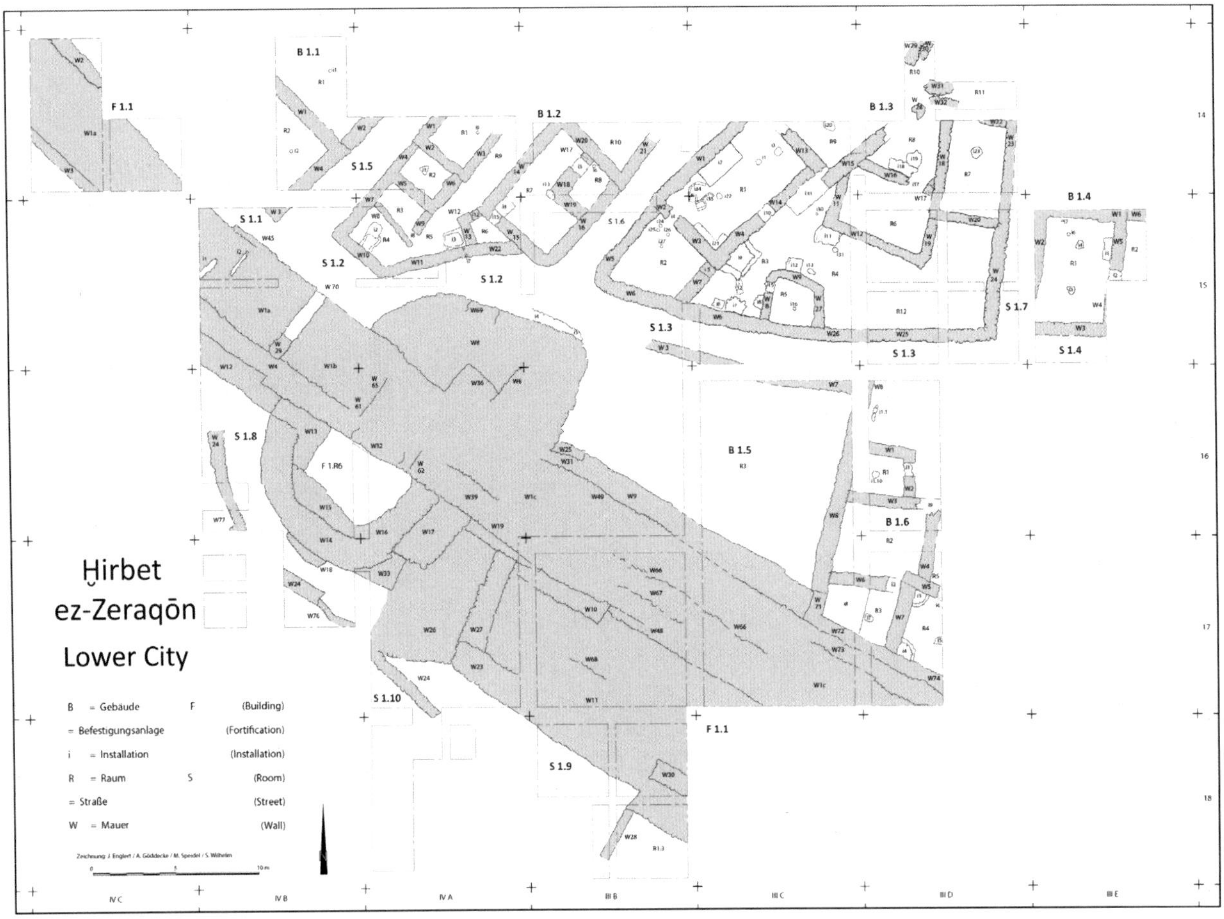

Figure 3: Khirbet ez-Zeraqon, lower city plan (courtesy of the Khirbet ez-Zeraqon archeological expedition).

for the EBA in the southern Levant,[23] and hint at a length of the settlement at Khirbet ez-Zeraqon of about two or three hundred years. This occupation mostly corresponds to the EB II, or Early Southern Levant 4 (henceforth ESL) according to the new Arcane periodization and is contemporary with the First Dynasty in Egypt;[24] its abandonment took place at the end of the transition between EB II and EB III, or the very beginning of the EB III (EB IIIA or ESL 5a).

The life of Khirbet ez-Zeraqon's settlement appears consistent with the socioeconomic trajectories that characterized the northern part of the southern Levant during the EB II, when sites were rebuilt or newly founded, intense inter-sites exchanges were established, and a simplification and standardization of material culture took place, also embodied by new ceramic technologies.[25] The location of the site along the middle Wādī eš-Šellāle,[26] placed along major east-west and north-south routes,[27] had a strategic significance in relation to the regional networks of connectivity.

The abandonment of the site after only a few hundred years of occupation implies the town did not survive the broader transformations which affected the settlements across the upper Jordan Valley, the Galilee and the Golan. The sense of instability that characterized the end of the EB II is testified by the reinforcement of the defense system during the latest phase of occupation of Khirbet ez-Zeraqon, by the thickening of the city walls and blocking the gates' entrances. As suggested by Greenberg, this situation might have resulted from structural transformations of EBA society that brought about the abandonment of several EB II settlements. Such changes were underlined by the contraction of exchange networks and manufacturing industries, which resulted in the reduction in scale and the loss of specialization of craft activities.[28] On the other hand, due to the location of the site in close

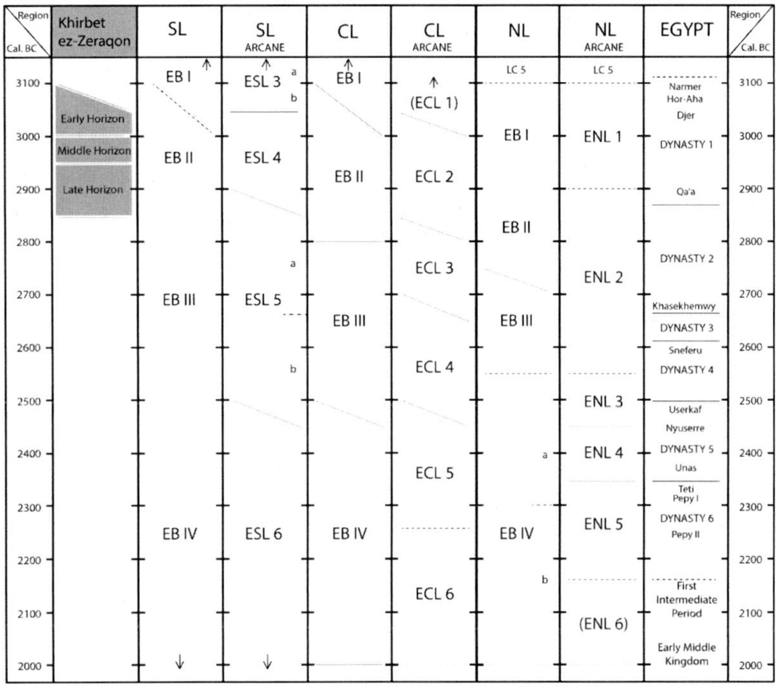

Figure 4: Chronological setting of the early, middle and late horizons occupation at Khirbet ez-Zeraqon, in relation with third millennium Levantine and Egyptian regional chronologies, based on the traditional Early Bronze Age and the ARCANE terminologies (after Lebeau and de Miroschedji 2013: xi), and Sowada's proposal for Egyptian-Levantine synchronization (after Sowada 2020; Sowada *et al.* 2021). SL = Southern Levant; CL = Central Levant; NL = Northern Levant.

proximity to an area characterized by fluctuating ecological conditions, environmental aspects may have played a role in its abandonment.[29]

3. The Levantine Combed Ware and the Combed Vessels at Khirbet ez-Zeraqon

3.1. Levantine Combed Ware

The definition of "Combed Ware" has been traditionally used to designate a variety of storage and transport vessels—jars and pithoi—but also vats with combed treatment on the external (and sometimes internal) surface, characteristic of the EBA Levant. Due to both for their physical features and their presence in Egyptian elite funerary contexts, these vessels have been interpreted as containers for high-value liquid products, such as oil and wine.[30] Besides the exact nature of the content(s), the central role played by the combed jars in the exchanges between the Levant and Egypt is unquestionable.

The combing treatment on the surface has been variously interpreted as a form of decoration, a distinctive "branding" of vessels, or a functional treatment aimed at reducing porosity and, consequently, the evaporation of the liquids contained.[31] On the other hand, the combing can be considered the result of technological actions comprised in—and developed together with—the manufacturing process, aimed at reinforcing the structure of the vessels and, at the same time, helping to join and mask the coils of the handmade bodies. This primary technical—and not esthetical—purpose would explain the application of combing also on the inner surfaces of vessels, as documented from the coastal Levant.[32]

From a chronological and spatial viewpoint, vessels with combed surfaces represented a broad and complex Levantine phenomenon, which had a long duration and diverse regional characteristics. Combed vessels first appeared in the northern part of the southern Levant at the end of the fourth millennium BCE, in the local EB II (ESL 4) (Fig. 4), sometimes already at the EB I/EB II transition[33] (ESL 3, c. 3150–3100/3050 BCE), and they continued during the EB III (ESL 5). In the central Levant, combed vessels also appeared during the local EB II (Early Coastal Levant 2, henceforth ECL), around the same time as in the south, possibly slightly later.[34] During this stage, such containers were documented to the south of Tell 'Arqa, where they began to be attested for only from the EB II/III transition.[35] In contrast to the southern Levant, the production continued after 2500 BCE, in the EB IVA (ECL 5) and EB IVB (ECL 6) and, contemporarily to these stages, vessels with combed surfaces appeared in the northern Levant as well, particularly along the coast and, to a lesser extent, in the inland.

In Egypt, combed containers have been uncovered at several sites.[36] Vessels of this type found in contexts of the Dynasty 0 and First Dynasty might originate from both the southern and the central Levant.[37] After a gap in the documentation for the 2nd and 3rd Dynasties, the containers found in contexts dated from the 4th Dynasty are more uniform than before, consisting of vessels originating in the central Levant, which was the main economic partner for Egypt as a supplier of Levantine products in this period.[38] Seafaring became the prevalent mode of transport, and the containers assumed shapes more suitable for maritime shipping than the earlier southern Levantine items, which were instead clearly designated for terrestrial transport.[39]

As already stressed by several scholars,[40] the unitary definition of Combed Ware is misleading as these vessels were neither part of a single production nor manufactured using a single fabric. Under this label are grouped vessels that shared the combed treatment on their surfaces but characterized by heterogeneous fabrics, manufacturing techniques and formal features, thus showing regional and chronological differences.[41] They were in fact produced by several similar—but differentiated—ceramic industries active across the Levant showing various degrees of independent development, each also manufacturing other vessel types, both open and close shapes showing diverse surface treatments, such as burnishing.[42] Among these larger manufactures, the North Canaanite Metallic Ware[43] and similar Metallic Ware types with burnished surfaces on the Lebanese coast are included.[44] Further combed vessels made of local fabrics were widespread in the Levant,[45] such as the South Canaanite Lime-Coated Ware, a production typical of the central and southern part of the southern Levant during the EB III and characterized by vessels mostly distinguished by a lime coating applied after firing.[46]

Regarding the fabrics used, it is apparent that the ceramic industries producing combed vessels in the Levant can be divided into two broad groups, both already documented from the EB II: one using shale-derived clay sources, and the other employing calcareous clays. Within the shale-derived fabric groups, which seems to be mostly related to the EB II, falls the North Canaanite Metallic Ware and some Lebanese manufactures. Conversely, during the EB III, combed vessels were made of calcareous clays derived from numerous sources available close to their loci of production.[47]

3.2. The Combed Pottery from Khirbet ez-Zeraqon

At Khirbet ez-Zeraqon, combed jars and pithoi are present in the ceramic repertoire throughout the three phases of occupation, while the spouted vats with two vertical loop handles and combed surface are absent in the earliest stage.[48] Through time, the absolute number of stratified vessels and sherds with combed surface increases from the earlier to the later stage of occupation.[49] From the restorable vessels uncovered, two types of combing treatments can be recognized: a vertical combed pattern and a horizontal-plus-vertical one; the latter consists of horizontal strips of combing interrupted by patches of vertical combing.[50] These two distinct patterns show a clear association with specific vessel-types (Fig. 5): the vertical pattern is exclusively applied to pithoi with flat base and out-flared rim (type L),[51] while the horizontal-plus-vertical style of combing characterizes handled jars with a flat base (type K)[52] and the outer surface of the spouted vats with two vertical loop handles (type D).[53]

Vessels with combed surfaces are associated at the site with three out of the thirteen ware types identified by Genz on the base of macroscopic inspection: Ware g, Ware c and Ware d.[54] Broadly speaking, these wares are polyvalent at the site; in addition to combed vessels, they are also associated with open (bowls, platters) and close forms of different types (jars, pithoi, jugs, and juglets).[55] As a whole, Ware c is the most frequent in the repertoire of diagnostic pottery from the three phases, making up almost 50% of the corpus, while Ware g makes up only about the 12%, and Ware d 6%.[56] From a chronological viewpoint, Ware g decreases through time, as does Ware d, while Ware c increases dramatically from the early to the late horizon.[57]

Ware g is a highly fired ware, made of a fine orange to reddish and gray fabric, with many small mineral inclusions (0.2–2 mm); the thicker sherds have a reduced gray core. This ware has been considered as corresponding to the North Canaanite Metallic Ware as defined by Greenberg and Porat (1996),[58] and at the site it is associated with diverse functional types, especially pithoi, and platters (type B), but not with vats.[59] Pithoi with vertical combing associated with Ware g are documented through the entire occupation of the site, as well as jars with a horizontal-plus-vertical combed surface.[60] Ware

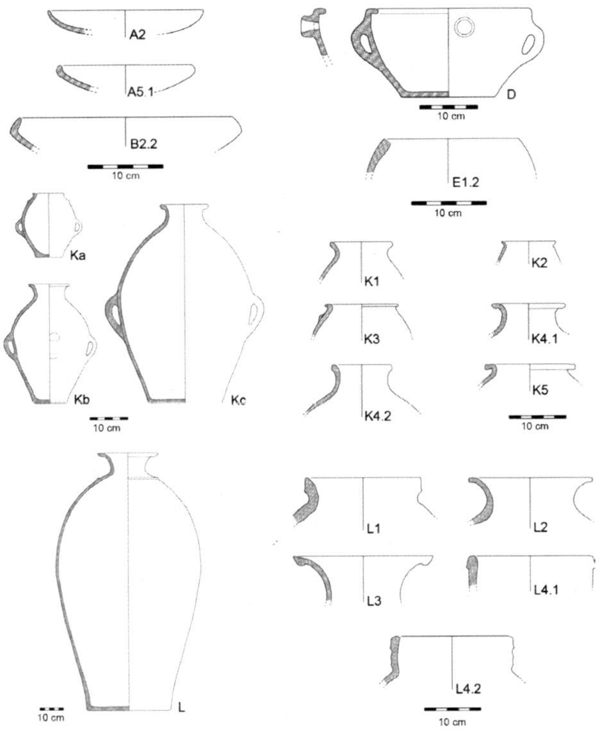

Figure 5: Main ceramic types from Khirbet ez-Zeraqon, as mentioned in the text (after Genz 2002).

c is a highly fired beige to red fabric with many fine mineral inclusions (0.2–1 mm); Ware d is very similar, sometimes grayish with many medium-fine mineral inclusions (0.5–1 mm).[61] Ware c has been considered as largely associated with open shapes, vats,[62] and closed shapes such as pithoi, especially those with vertical combing and applied plastic rope decoration, and with a vast number of jars, some showing horizontal-plus-vertical combing[63] as documented by items found *in situ* below the late horizon collapse layers.[64] Similarly, Ware d jars, some with a combed surface, mostly came from contexts of the last stage of occupation of the site.[65]

4. Petrographic Analysis of Selected Early Bronze Age II–III Pottery from Khirbet ez-Zeraqon

4.1. Materials

For the present study, analysis was undertaken on 45 selected samples from the site, including both complete/restorable vessels and single pottery sherds[66] consisting mostly of jars and pithoi. Examples of bowls, platters, and one holemouth pot were also included, characterized by surface treatments other than combing, such as burnishing and painting (Table 1, at the end of this chapter). The jars and pithoi comprised in the study are correlated with Genz's Wares g, c, and d, all the open shapes with Ware g, except for one holemouth jar, correlated with Ware j2,[67] a type that is never associated with combing at the site. This full repertory was examined to contextualize the combed containers within the broader spectrum of ceramic production documented at the site. These include eight restorable examples, as well as twelve rim sherds of pithoi that, from a typological viewpoint (Type L3), are likely to have derived from vessels with combed surface.[68]

As for the find contexts, most of the analyzed material (26 samples), including all the restorable vessels, is dated to the late horizon, and comes both from the upper and the lower city, being found either *in situ* or collected from tumble layers. All the items associated with the early/middle horizon were recovered from fill or tumble layers of the palace and the temple area, while those attributed to the middle horizon belonged to various contexts in the lower city.

4.2. Aims

Petrographic analysis of the selected samples was undertaken to reassess the conclusions on their typological/macroscopic study along three specific lines of enquiry. The goals of these analyses were as follows:

(1) To better our understanding of raw material preferences, manufacturing processes, firing temperature, degrees of standardization and the production centralization level of these vessels during the EB II and EB III. A key aspect of this study was to gain an understanding of how ware variability, as observed macroscopically, can be linked to the wares composition. Furthermore, this study offers evidence allowing to investigate the changes observed between EB II–III and EB IV ceramics from the site through the analysis of petrographic sections.

(2) To suggest possible production location(s) for the various ware groups based on their petrographic characteristics.

(3) To investigate the features of the combed storage and transport vessels at the site and place their development within the wider regional context of the Levantine Combed Ware industries.

4.3. Analytical Methods

The samples were first studied by transmitted light using a Leitz petrographic microscope. Light micrographs were taken with a Leica EC3 digital camera mounted on the microscope. The thin-sections were described using terminology and values proposed by Stoops (2003), Quinn (2013), and Klein and Philpotts (2013).[69] The measurement and quantification of the aplastic fraction of each sample and grain measurements were completed using the digital image analysis software, Jmicrovision.[70] Tiled images of an area on each thin-section measuring 1 cm^2 were produced for this purpose.

4.3.1. *A Note on Nomenclature*

It should be noted that the petro-fabric nomenclature presented here is integrated with that of the EB IV assemblage.[71] As that study was published first, the fabric groups 1–5 date to the EB IV. For the EB IV, fabric group 1 was further divided into three sub-fabrics (1A, B, and C). Fabric 1 also occurs during the EB II–III and represents the only overlap between the two periods at Khirbet ez-Zeraqon. The main Group 1 EB II–III sub-fabrics are labeled 1D and 1E, reflecting the disparity in preparation between the EB II–III and EB IV fabrics. One EB II–III sample (termed Fabric 1A) represents the only petrographic overlap between the two periods.

4.4. Petrographic Analysis Results

The petrographic analysis of the EB II–IIIA ceramic materials shows the existence of two distinct categories of petro-fabrics and preparations: a quartz-calcareous-basalt fabric, and a shale-derived fabric. Variations of the latter are commonly found in the central and northern part of the southern Levant during the EB II and EB II/III transition.[72] At Khirbet ez-Zeraqon, the most common fabrics utilized were quartz and limestone rich, with fragments of Pliocene basalts, rich in silty quartz along with unrelated coarser calcareous and shale derived fabrics. During the EB IV, the most common fabric is similarly quartz and limestone rich, with fragments of Pliocene basalts, though notably lacking in silty quartz. Also, shale fabrics are no longer found. Thus, the common EB II and EB IIIA fabrics at Khirbet ez-Zeraqon are distinct from those of the EB IV, suggesting a significant break with later ceramic traditions at the site, even when vessels were sometimes manufactured using similar locally available materials.[73]

Fabric 1: The Quartz-Limestone-Basalt Fabric

The dominant fabric in the EB II–III samples is Fabric 1, which can be described broadly as a Quartz-Limestone-Basalt Fabric, in most cases dominated by silty quartz (Fig. 6). Fabric 1 was used for jars and pithoi and on the whole it maps mostly onto the main macroscopic Ware groups c and d. Most samples of this fabric date to the late horizon, though a good number date to the middle horizon. Fabric 1 consists of a clay-rich matrix with a fine texture. The ground mass is brown to reddish-brown in plane polarized light, indicating firing, at least at some stage, in an oxidizing atmosphere. The groundmass is rich in microcrystalline calcite and, in some cases, an optically active crystallic b-fabric is observed. The groundmass is sometimes well-sintered and elongate channel voids can occur. Fabric 1 samples are composed of a similar suite of aplastic inclusions. Three sub-fabrics were identified (1A, 1D, and 1E); these can be distinguished by differences in the texture and frequency of particular inclusions. Texturally, the samples present aplastic inclusions that are subangular to subhedral. Less commonly, rounded spherical and elongate grains are noted. Equant grains of very fine to medium sand-sized micritic limestone occur most commonly (5–10%). Fossiliferous chalks occur occasionally. Fine to medium sand-sized grains of basalt occur commonly (3–5%). These are mostly subangular to subhedral and, rarely, rounded with finer texture. The basalts are composed of plagioclase feldspar, augite, olivine and opaque metal oxide phases (probably Fe-Ti). Fabric 1 is also composed of silt to fine sand-sized grains of quartz to varying degree, occurring rarely (1–2%) in a few cases, but commonly 10–20%. Fine sand-sized grains of chert (1–2%) can also occur. Grains of fine sand-sized calcite occur rarely, often exhibiting zoning. Rarely, rounded red optically active fine sand-sized grains occur, which are in high relief. These bodies are clay rich and are likely glauconite, chlorite, or some form of iddingsite.

Sub-fabric 1A is represented by only one sample. It is relatively coarse but contains very little silty quartz when compared to 1D and 1E. The sample, similar to the most common EB IV fabric, represents the only potential petrographic overlap between the EB II–III and EB IV. Fabrics 1D and 1E are quite similar to each other and the groupings should be regarded more as part of a spectrum than a clear division. They are the most common sub-fabrics

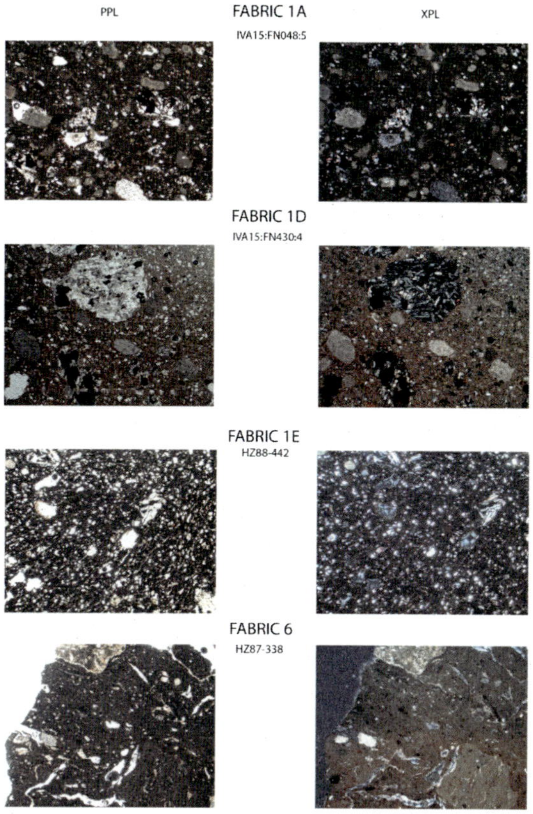

Figure 6: Photomicrographs of samples from Fabrics 1A, 1D, 1E and 6 in plane polarized light (PPL) and cross polars (XPL). Field of view is 2 × 2 mm for each photomicrograph. The image of 1A shows a number of limestone grains, fragments of basalt, fragments of chert, and silty quartz. 1B details large sand-sized grains of basalt and a few limestone fragments along with silty to fine sand-sized quartz. The image of 1C depicts frequent grains of silty to fine sand-sized quartz along with a few fragments of basalt. The image of Fabric 6 shows a large grain of limestone (top-left) and a large grain of white (kaolinite-rich) shale (bottom-right).

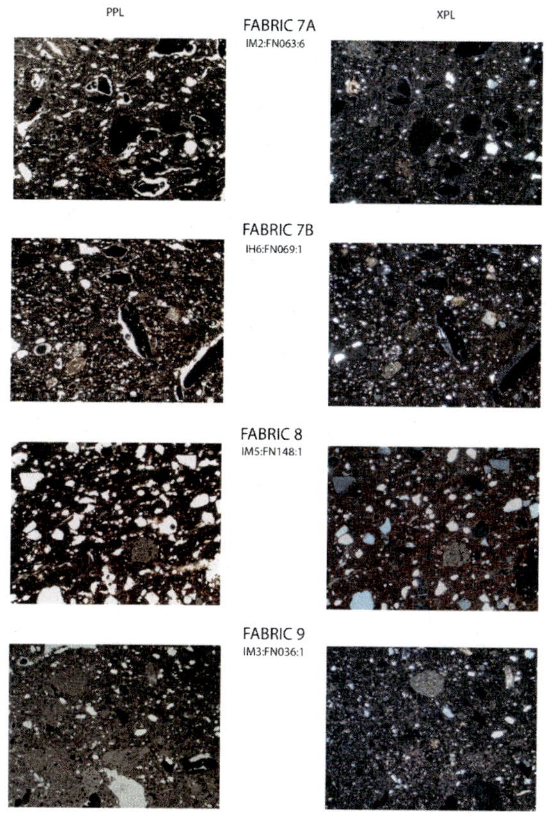

Figure 7: Photomicrographs of samples from Fabrics 7A, 7B, 8 and 9 in plane polarized light (PPL) and cross polars (XPL). Field of view is 2 × 2 mm for each photomicrograph. The image of 7A details frequent shale fragments and a few grains of fine to medium sand-sized quartz. 7B shows shale fragments and frequent silt and fine-sand sized grains of quartz. The image of Fabric 8 illustrates that it is dominated by fine to large grains of quartz. The image of Fabric 9 shows silty quartz and a fragment of fine-grained basalt.

during the middle and late horizons at the site. Both contain large amounts of silty quartz, differentiating them from 1A and the EB IV fabrics. Fabric 1D samples are coarser grained and the samples of fabric 1E tend to be finer grained relative to the other two fabrics.

Fabric Groups 6 and 7: Shale Fabrics

Shale fabrics consist of a clay–rich matrix with a fine texture. As mentioned above, fabrics of this type are relatively common during the EB II and EB II/III transition throughout the central and the northern part of the southern Levant, generally disappearing during the EB III. The groundmass is mostly well-sintered, sometimes vitrified, and optically inactive. Elongate channel voids occur. The samples belonging to this petro-fabric are composed of closely related materials but can be divided into two main fabrics: 6 and 7. Fabric 6 (Fig. 6), represented by only three samples, consists of white firing shales. Fabric 7 (Fig. 7), composed of reddish-firing shales, is represented by 11 samples; it can be divided into two quite similar sub-fabrics (7A and 7B), with 7B presenting much more fine-sand and silty quartz (similar in quantity to Fabric 1E).

All the samples belonging to these fabrics contained fine-grained moderate to coarse sand-sized shales or argillaceous rock fragments (ARFs), occurring moderately in the samples (10–25%). They are most commonly highly rounded and elongate, often containing silt to fine sand-sized quartz grains and sometimes carbonates and Fe-Ti oxide phases. They are most commonly Fe rich, though composed of variable amounts. SEM-EDS analysis on several samples showed that an iron content of 5–10% is frequent.[74] A fraction of non-iron bearing shales, probably composed of kaolinite, can be found in some samples, though these are dominant only in Fabric 6. These fragments can be identified as they are white even in partially oxidized or reduced zones. Overall, these shales are poorly compacted and poorly lithified, as further indicated by splitting along the long axis of many of the elongated ARFs. The elongated shales often show a preferred orientation. Well-rounded grains of quartz found in both spherical and more elongated shapes occur occasionally to moderately in the shales. Within the matrix of the samples, quartz most commonly occurs in silt to medium sand-sized grains that are anhedral, although some larger grains also occur. Many samples contain larger fragments of quartz-rich sandstones. Pieces of micritic lime mudstone and siltstones occur in varying amounts but are generally rare (1–5%); they occur in medium or coarse sand-sized grains. Some finer rounded grains of fine sand sized calcite occur in trace amounts.

Fabric group 6 is represented by three samples: two pithoi and a holemouth pot. The 11 samples of fabric group 7 are mostly pithoi, with only one jar and two bowls amongst them. All the samples dated from the EB II–IIIA; the items from late-horizon contexts are residual sherds and one restorable pithos, which might be a long-lived heirloom. However, if those four items were actually produced during the late horizon, vessels made of Fabrics 6 and 7 from Khirbet ez-Zeraqon may represent one of the few clear examples of the continued use of shale-wares for large jar forms during the very earliest stage of the EB III in the southern Levant. Most evidence suggests shale wares are concentrated in the EB II throughout the Levant, yet they are found, to a much lesser degree, in the central Levant at least, at Tell 'Arqa and Tell Koubba in EB III phases, although their usage is restricted to fine-ware jugs.[75]

Fabric Group 8: Quartz-Calcareous

Fabric 8 can be described as a Quartz-Calcareous fabric with all samples exhibiting a similar suite of non–plastic inclusions (Fig. 7). Fabric group 8 is represented by 10 samples and largely used for bowls and platters, though the samples also include two jars and one pithos. The fabric occurs throughout the EB II–IIIA at the site. All the samples of this fabric are composed of a clay-rich groundmass rich in microcrystalline calcite that in most cases has an optically active crystallic b–fabric. Less commonly, a highly sintered optically inactive fabric is noted, indicating a relatively high firing temperature. The samples are composed of a clay-rich matrix with elongate and channel voids which occur rarely. The aplastic inclusions are always poorly sorted but can exhibit a bimodal distribution. The grains exhibit a high to moderate sphericity. Larger grains are sometimes subangular. Rarely, grains are elongated. Pieces of carbonate rock, micritic mudstone (dunham classification) or fossiliferous chalks occur occasionally (1–5%) in the samples.

Rounded to subangular fine to coarse sand-sized grains of quartz with a moderate to high sphericity occur occasionally to moderately in the samples (10–20%). Quartz most commonly occurs in fine to medium sand-sized grains that are anhedral. Carbonate rocks occur in fine to coarse sand-sized grains. Rarely, some samples are silty in texture. Medium to coarse sand-sized grains of cryptocrystalline rocks, including chert, and discrete bodies dominated by phyllosilicates (in some cases kaolinites as determined by EDS) occur rarely. Sandstones and rounded grains of fine sand-sized calcite occur rarely. Trace amounts of microcline are present. Fine-grained moderate to coarse sand-sized shales and other discrete iron oxide bodies occur rarely in the samples; they were most commonly elongate and highly rounded, and they often contain coarse silt sized quartz and carbonate grains. Trace amounts of silt-sized grains of zircon occur in some samples.

Fabric 9: Silty Quartz—Calcareous-Fine-Grained Basalt Fabric

Fabric 9 is represented only by one jar sherd from the tumble layer associated with the abandonment of the site. The fabric is similar in description to Fabric 8 but dominated by silty quartz (Fig. 7). The sample also contains a number of carbonate fragments rich in iron oxide bodies and fine-grained basalt fragments. Hopefully, more examples of this fabric will be discovered in the future so that it can be better defined.

4.5. Provenance, Comparative Petrography and Technological Considerations

The petrographic analyses demonstrate that most samples were made using a similar set of ingredients—calcareous clays and limestone, basalt, and fine-sand and silty quartz tempers. Shale-wares were also used during the site's occupation, placing the site of Khirbet ez-Zeraqon within the sphere of shale-ware distribution characteristic of the central Levant during the EB II and EB II/III transition. The results, showing relatively few fabrics and a general lack of sub-fabrics, suggest high-degree centralization in the dominant production modes used to make these vessels during the EB II–IIIA. Most fabrics are represented by several samples, with only one 'petro-loner' ascribed to Fabric 9. This differs from the EB IV ceramic repertory, which showed a larger number of minor fabrics, although these were mostly associated with cooking pots.[76]

In terms of provenance, Fabric 1 is consistent with materials available in the area surrounding Khirbet ez-Zeraqon[77] and a similar fabric was used during the EB IV, suggesting that the fabric reflects local production (see below for discussion). The precise production location, in the absence of kilns, remains unclear, as the raw materials can be found across the Irbid Plateau and in many locations in the nearby Jordan Valley. The fabrics are, for example, similar to some EB II–III examples described at Tel Bet Yeraḥ, although they occur less commonly at that site.[78] A larger programme of geo-prospection around Khirbet ez-Zeraqon and petrographic and geochemical analyses focused on EB II–IIIA may shed further light on the production location and distribution of Fabric 1.

Fabrics 6 and 7 are composed of shales, typically ascribed to Lower Cretaceous outcrops, which are not found near Khirbet ez-Zeraqon, and thus represent either imported vessels or raw materials. The samples are petrographically identical to the Fabrics 1B, 1D, and 1E as described in Badreshany et al. 2020, showing also that these shared a geochemical signature. Badreshany et al. proposed itinerant production modes for these shale-derived wares to explain the distribution of very large vessels made in this material, which occur at quite some distance from the required clay sources.[79] The evidence from Khirbet ez-Zeraqon might support this interpretation as the most common type of vessel made using shale fabrics is the pithos, which is difficult to transport safely over large distances. This study reinforces the notion that during the EB II sites across the central and northern part of the southern Levant were linked, at least, by communities of ceramic practice that drew upon similar materials to supply vessels to important centers.

Fabric 8, documented through the entire development of the site, is dominated by quartz. It is difficult to assign a provenance, but, given the technological departure from the most common fabric (1) during the EB II–III and IV, it can be suggested that either the vessels or the material used are non-local. Unlike the pithoi made of shale, most vessels produced of Fabric 8 are smaller bowls and platters that could have been transported more easily over a distance. Another feature of Fabric 8 vessels are the well-rounded fragments of quartz used as temper, which suggests beach sand from a coastal, lacustrine, or riparian environment. Quartz-rich fabrics are described at Tell el-Farah,[80] dating to the EB II, but these present quartz grains that are finer in texture than the samples from Khirbet ez-Zeraqon and, typically, the quartz is more angular. Fabric 8 is somewhat similar to the dominant fabrics of the EB III on the northern Lebanese coast,[81] yet the latter often exhibit foraminifera which were not noted in samples from Khirbet ez-Zeraqon.

Firing temperatures were found to be relatively low, not exceeding 800–850 C in most cases, though a vitrified ground mass was noted on some samples in all fabric groups, indicating that some vessels may have been fired toward the higher end of this spectrum. These temperatures are in line with those noted by other commentators studying ceramics of the period.[82]

The trajectory of EB ceramic development as noted at Khirbet ez-Zeraqon involves the appearance, during the EB II, of vessels made of non-local materials (represented by Fabrics 6, 7 and 8) and, in a lesser quantity, of a class of ceramics made of locally available materials (Fabric 1), this latter increasing in quantity through time and becomes more common into the EB III. This mirrors the trajectory described for the central[83] and the southern Levant,[84] where ceramics produced using locally available materials are present alongside shale-rich fabrics from an early point in the EB II, with the former becoming more prominent over time. In a central Levantine context, Badreshany et al.[85] explain this trajectory as indicative of a "local-capture" of ceramic production for vessels intended to hold products of economic value as these became increasingly important to emerging regional political economies. The petrographic analysis of materials from Khirbet ez-Zeraqon suggests a similar process where local production ramps up considerably after the initial EB II phases.

4.6. Association with Types, Surface Treatments, and Wares

From the material analyzed, it is apparent that no exclusive uses of ceramic fabrics for specific pottery shapes and surface treatments existed at the site, although certain preferences can be noted. The local Fabric 1 is mostly employed for jars, followed by pithoi. Of the two sets of non-local materials, the shale-rich fabrics (Fabrics 6 and 7) were prevalently used for storage and—less often—for transport vessels, with relatively few open shapes,[86] while the quartz-rich fabric (Fabric 8) was largely employed for bowls and platters with burnished surfaces (Table 1).

Surface treatments seem to be more associated with shapes than with the fabric types and applied independently from the latter. The vessels with burnished surface—including all the open shapes and two jars—are mostly made of the quartz-rich Fabric 8 and to a lesser extent from shale-derived fabrics (Fabrics 7A and 7B). In contrast, most jars and pithoi are mostly divided between the local Fabric 1 and the shales-derived Fabrics 7 and 6, the latter being used also for the holemouth pot HZ87-338. The ceramic industry that used local clays was especially active in the production of storage and transport jars largely characterized by pattern combing, as it appears from the complete items. Moreover, combing was also applied on pithoi made of shale fabrics. Therefore, our results suggest that the containers with combed surface were produced by using two sets of raw materials, one consisting of local clays and one of non-local origins. These might have been associated with different ceramic industries. On the other hand, the strong typological and technological similarity of combed vessels made of both local and shale-derived fabrics—as also suggested by the presence of silty quarts—hints at one same ceramic tradition which developed through time, with a shift in preference toward more locally available raw materials.

The petrographic analysis also suggests that the items associated with Genz's Ware c and d—including all the restorable jars and pithoi with combed surface and a jar with painted surface—are made of the Quartz-Limestone-Basalt local Fabric 1. As for the materials associated with Ware g, these can be mostly divided between close forms, which were predominantly produced using the shale Fabrics 7 and 6, and open shapes made of the quartz-calcareous Fabric 8. These results agree with Genz's classification, which pinpointed that Ware g was prevalently associated with pithoi and bowls,[87] but also suggest that his Ware g incorporates at least two different production types, both using non-local materials, namely the shales (Fabrics 6 and 7) and the quartz-rich (Fabric 8) fabrics.

4.7. Chronological and Spatial Patterns

The earliest sherds included in our dataset—assigned to the early/middle horizon—belong mainly to the shale-rich Fabrics 7 and, to a lesser extent, the quartz-rich Fabric 8, while only one sample is associated with the quartz–limestone–basalt local Fabric 1E. In contrast, most of the items dated to the middle horizon belong instead to the fabric group 1, which is also used for a large number of items, both sherds and restorable vessels, associated with the late horizon. This testifies to a growing use of the local fabrics over time. On the other hand, both quartz-rich Fabric 8 and shale Fabrics 6 and 7 continued to be present in the later stage, although some samples might be residual sherds or heirlooms. This might be the case, for example, of the large pithos IM2:FN034:22, which could have been in use for several generations before the abandonment of the site leading to its burial beneath the collapse of the city.[88]

5. Discussion: The Combed Vessels within the EB II–III Ceramic Industries at Khirbet ez-Zeraqon and in Levantine Context

In line with other recent studies, the petrographic analyses of the ceramic repertoire from Khirbet ez-Zeraqon revealed that the combed vessels formed part of larger pottery productions that included diverse shape types and surface treatments. Most of the analyzed restorable combed containers were made of the local quartz-and-limestone rich Fabric 1, in the most common variant 1E. Combed pithoi were also produced from shale-rich clays, which were used to manufacture vessels characterized by other surface treatments as well, such as burnishing. This might suggest that surface treatments were linked more to shapes than fabrics. In any case, it is apparent that there was not a unique relationship between fabrics and surface treatments.

Contextualizing the data regionally, the developments through time identified by the petrographic characterization of the combed containers from Khirbet ez-Zeraqon can be linked to—and fits within—the dynamics documented elsewhere in the central and the southern Levant during the EB II–III. At Khirbet ez-Zeraqon, storage and transport jars with combed surface are associated with two main fabric groups, both employed for other ceramic types as well: one using shale-rich clays, the other using locally available raw materials. In the central and northern part of the southern Levant, for the local/calcareous fabrics, the diverse petrographic aspects and geochemical data point to the use of many and distinct local outcrops in the various subregions.[89] In contrast, at least two different main sets of shale-rich clays, from the Lower Cretaceous outcrops of the Lebanon and Anti-Lebanon Mountains and surrounding areas,[90] were used respectively in the Bekaa area and along the coastal Lebanon and Jordan Valley.[91] The shale group of this latter region matches the sub-fabric 7B at Khirbet ez-Zeraqon, characterized by fine-sand and silty quartz.[92] This composition supports the production of vessels with high-quality technological features, as well as further types of shale clays, which create hard and durable vessels that can be fired to higher temperatures than those made by using calcareous fabrics. On the other hand, the activities surrounding the transport of the shale-rich clays from the specific outcrops would have been time-consuming in terms of their logistical arrangements, while the pottery production would have required high artisanal skills. As such, the entire *chaîne opératoire*, from the clay mining and transport to the final production, was likely associated with specialized producers. These might have been active close to the few locations of the shale clays outcrops,[93] or they might have operated in an itinerant way[94] (see above).

From a chronological viewpoint, the earliest ceramic samples from Khirbet ez-Zeraqon are mostly associated with the shale Fabric 7, together with the non-local quartz-rich Fabric 8, while the local Fabric 1 became increasingly prevalent through time, being largely present in association with the last stage of life of the site. A comparable dynamic characterized the EB II–III ceramic inventory of the near site of Tel Bet Yeraḥ, which finds great similarities to that of Khirbet ez-Zeraqon.[95] At Tel Bet Yeraḥ, the shale clays, broadly present in the local Period C and used for the same type of vessels as the calcareous fabrics—including combed containers[96]—were almost completely replaced by the latter fabrics in the following Period D.[97] This does not seem to happen at Khirbet ez-Zeraqon, perhaps due to the nature of the remains analyzed, which consisted of residual single sherds and a complete pithos that could have been an heirloom from previous generations (see § 4.7). On the other hand, such evidence might be attributed to the chronological setting of the site. In fact, the presence of the shale fabrics among the remains of the last stage of occupation is not surprising considering the short duration of the EBA settlement and its abandonment at the beginning of the EB IIIA.[98] On a broader level, the decrease over time in shale fabrics, and the concomitant increase in those made using locally available material, is consistent with patterns visible across much of Levant, with shale-rich fabrics being mostly used during the EB II in relatively centralized modes of production, while diverse local fabrics becoming progressively more predominant in the EB III.[99] At northern sites of the southern Levant, such as Dan, most of the EB II ceramic assemblage consisted of vessels made of shale fabrics,[100] and at Tell Koubba and Fadous-Kfarabida, the calcareous fabrics predominated in EB III.[101] At Tell 'Arqa, combed jars were not documented during the EB II (Phase T – ECL2), and their production began during the EB II/III transition (Phase S – ECL3), using exclusively limestone fabrics. They represented the only type of jars and pithoi produced at the site from this phase onward.[102] The gradual replacement of the shale fabrics by calcareous ones was not associated in central Levant with any technological change. In fact, the manufacturing process was characterized by a certain continuity, consistent with the existence of specialized potters, or at least a well-defined body of ceramic knowledge. The shift, observed consistently between sites, is a change in preferences in raw material sources, which could be a consequence of changes in the organisation and/or the *loci* of productions. This happened together with a transformation of the formal typological repertoire, which can be associated with a general trend towards greater technological homogeneity.[103] In the northern part of the southern Levant, the decline of the shale-derived ceramic industries at the end of the EB II and the predominance of the local ceramic fabrics, linked to the diversification of local productions, might be associated with a reduction in the specialized manufactures that characterized the transition to the EB III.[104] The different trajectories of southern and central Levantine ceramic manufactures and the diverse roles played by the two regions in the exchange with Egypt are mirrored by the origin of the Levantine containers found in Predynastic, Proto-Dynastic and Early Dynastic contexts.[105]

6. Conclusions

During the late fourth and third millennia BCE, Levantine ceramic manufacturing associated with combed vessels underwent transformations, with the gradual replacement of shale-rich fabrics by locally sourced material and the multiplication of production centers, also further south than in the early stages.[106] The evidence from Khirbet ez-Zeraqon concurs with this broader scenario.

The petrographic analyses conducted on selected samples from the site suggest that most of the jars and pithoi with combed surface were made of two main fabric types, using shale-rich clays and quartz-and-limestone ones, respectively. As in the rest of the Levant, these fabric types were not limited to the production of vessels with combed surface but were also used for other vessel types with diverse surface treatments, such as burnishing. Moreover, the presence of fine sand-sized quartz associated with both fabric groups suggests a technological similarity among different industries. The silty quartz shale sub-fabric matches petrographically with evidence from several sites in coastal Lebanon, Beqaa and northern Transjordan, placing Khirbet ez-Zeraqon at the southern borders of a larger phenomenon of related productions that mostly developed to the north.

From a diachronic viewpoint, it is possible to suggest that the use of the shale fabrics at the site decreased though time and the locally available clays became more frequent during the last stages of occupation. This is consistent with the broad development of ceramic production in the Levant. Moreover, comparing the EB II–III materials from Khirbet ez-Zeraqon to those of the EB IV yields an overlap suggesting that some aspects of production developed around similar locally available materials, though not necessarily reflecting a direct continuity in production.

Further extensive studies on the use of raw materials through time, combined with strong stratigraphic sequences and short interval radiocarbon determinations, are needed to better evaluate the regional patterning of technological changes in relation to the combed storage and transport jars, and to fully understand the role played by the diverse productions of these containers within the broader scenario of eastern Mediterranean economy. This discussion of the new data from Khirbet ez-Zeraqon, when considered in light of the broader regional context, offers a further step in our understanding of the puzzling phenomenon of the combed vessels and the diverse roles played by the various regions of the Levant in the production, distribution, and consumption of these containers across a variety of spatial scales.

Acknowledgements

The authors would like to acknowledge with great appreciation the directors of the excavation at Khirbet ez-Zeraqon, Siegfried Mittmann and Mohawiah Ibrahim, for entrusting us with the study of the materials from the site. A special thanks goes to Jens Kamlah for his continuous support of these investigations. We wish to warmly thank Karin Sowada and Matthew J. Adams for kindly inviting us to join the Egypt & the Mediterranean World conference and publication. We wish to express our gratitude to Graham Philip, Dan Lawrence, and the two anonymous reviewers for their valuable comments and suggestions. The work of Valentina Tumolo was supported by the CLaSS Project (the CLaSS project has received funding from the European Research Council under the European Union's Horizon 2020 research and innovation programme, grant agreement No 802424, award holder Dan Lawrence).

Table 1: List and description of samples analyzed in the study.

Sample ID	Shape	Type	Part	Preservation	Surface	Ware	Petrofabric	Find Context	Chronological Horizon	Chronological Attribution	Reference
IM5:FN148:1	Bowl	A, A2	Rim	Sherd	Burnished inside	Ware g	8	R0.2	Early/Middle horizon	EB II/EB II–III trans.	Genz 2002, Taf. 14:8
IH6:FN039:6	Bowl	A, A2	Rim	Sherd	Burnished	Ware g	8	Palace complex; B0.8	Late Horizon	EB IIIA	Genz 2002, Taf. 43:2
IH6:FN020:1	Bowl	A, A2	Rim	Sherd	Burnished inside	Ware g	8	Palace complex; B0.8	Late Horizon	EB IIIA	Genz 2002, Taf. 45:1
IM5:FN146:1	Bowl	A, A2	Rim	Sherd	Burnished inside	Ware g	7B	R0.2	Early/Middle horizon	EB II/EB II–III trans.	Genz 2002, Taf. 14:7
IM3:FN034:2	Bowl	A, A5.1	Rim	Sherd	Burnished	Ware g	7A	R0.4	Late Horizon	EB IIIA	Genz 2002, Taf. 15:12
IM2:FN034:25	Platter	B, B2.2	Rim	Sherd	Burnished	Ware g	8	Palace complex; B0.8	Late Horizon	EB IIIA	Genz 2002, Taf. 41:11
IM2:FN034:26	Platter	B, B2.2	Rim	Sherd	Burnished	Ware g	8	R0.2	Late Horizon	EB IIIA	Genz 2002, taf. 13:5
IM2:FN034:24	Platter	B, B2.2	Rim	Sherd	Burnished inside	Ware g	8	Palace complex; B0.8	Late Horizon	EB IIIA	Genz 2002, Taf. 44:2
IM2:FN034:27	Platter	B, B2.2	Rim	Sherd	Burnished inside	Ware g	8	B1.2	Middle Horizon	EB II–III trans.	Genz 2002, Taf. 78:5
IIIC15:FN207:4	Close shape	-	Body sherd	Sherd	-	Ware c	1E	B1.3	Late Horizon	EB IIIA	-
HZ87-338	Holemouth Jar	E1.2	Rim	Restorable vessel	Pre-firing incised mark	Ware j2	6	B1.2	Late Horizon	EB IIIA	Genz 2002, Taf. 72:2
IVA15:FN482:1	Jar	K, K1	Rim	Sherd	-	Ware d	1D	F1.1	Middle Horizon	EB II-III trans.	-
IH6:FN111:16	Jar	K, K1	Rim	Sherd	-	Ware g	1E	Palace complex; B0.8	Early/Middle horizon	EB II/EB II–III trans.	Genz 2002, Taf. 44:12
IVA15:FN315:3	Jar	K, K1	Rim	Sherd	-	Ware c	1E	F1.1	Middle Horizon	EB II–III trans.	-
IVA15:FN048:5	Jar	K, K4.1	Rim	Sherd	-	Ware d	1A	S1.2	Late Horizon	EB IIIA	-
IVA15:FN121:1	Jar	K, K4.1	Rim	Sherd	-	Ware c	1E	S1.2	Late Horizon	EB IIIA	-
IM2:FN034:6	Jar	K, K4.1	Rim	Sherd	Burnished	Ware g	7B	R0.4	Early/Middle horizon	EB II/EB II–III trans.	Genz 2002, Taf. 19:7
IH6:FN099:160	Jar	K, K4.2	Rim	Sherd	-	Ware g	8	Palace complex; B0.8	Early/Middle horizon	EB II/EB II–III trans.	Genz 2002, Taf. 47:1
IM3:FN036:1	Jar	K, K4.2	Rim	Sherd	-	Ware g	9	R0.4	Late Horizon	EB IIIA	Genz 2002, Taf. 16:12
IVA15:FN155:15	Jar	K, K4.2	Rim	Sherd	-	Ware c	1E	S1.2	Mixed phases	-	-
IVA15:FN296:1	Jar	K, K4.2	Rim	Sherd	-	Ware d	1E	F1.1	Middle Horizon	EB II–III trans.	-
IVA15:FN179:11	Jar	K, K4.2	Rim	Sherd	-	Ware d	1E	S1.2	Middle Horizon	EB II–III trans.	-
IH6:FN046:1	Jar	K, K5	Rim	Sherd	Burnished	Ware g	8	Palace complex; B0.8	Late Horizon	EB IIIA	Genz 2002, Taf. 43:11
IVA15:FN430:4	Jar	K, K5	Rim	Sherd	-	Ware c	1D	F1.1:R4	Middle Horizon	EB II–III trans.	-

Sample ID	Shape	Type	Part	Preservation	Surface	Ware	Petrofabric	Find Context	Chronological Horizon	Chronological Attribution	Reference
HZ88-506	Jar	Kb	Base + body + handles	Restorable vessel	Pattern combed; pre-firing incised mark	Ware c	1E	Palace complex; B0.8	Late Horizon	EB IIIA	Genz 2002, Taf. 29:1
HZ88-442	Jar	Kb K4.2	Complete	Restorable vessel	Large irregular painted strips	Ware d	1E	B1.4:R1	Late Horizon	EB IIIA	Genz 2002, Taf. 108:3
HZ88-508	Jar	Kc	Base + body + handles	Restorable vessel	Pattern combed	Ware c	1E	B0.8	Late Horizon	EB IIIA	Genz 2002, Taf. 34:3
HZ91-789	Jar	Kc	Base + body + handles	Restorable vessel	Pattern combed	Ware c	1E	Palace complex; B0.8	Late Horizon	EB IIIA	Genz 2002, Taf. 29:4
IM2:FN034:7	Pithos	L	Base + body	Restorable vessel	Vertically combed	Ware c	1E	R0.11	Late Horizon	EB IIIA	Genz 2002, Taf. 8:1
IM2:FN034:8	Pithos	L	Base + body	Restorable vessel	Vertically combed	Ware c	1E	B1.3	Late Horizon	EB IIIA	Genz 2002, Taf. 85:1
IM2:FN034:9	Pithos	L	Base + body	Restorable vessel	Vertically combed	Ware c	1E	Palace complex; B0.8	Late Horizon	EB IIIA	Genz 2002, Taf. 31:1
IM2:FN034:10	Pithos	L	Base + body + neck	Restorable vessel	Vertically combed; plastic rope application	Ware c	1E	B1.3	Late Horizon	EB IIIA	Genz 2002, Taf. 84:1
IM2:FN034:22	Pithos	L	Complete	Restorable vessel	Vertically combed	Ware g	7B	B1.6	Late Horizon	EB IIIA	Genz 2002, Taf. 126:1
IM2:FN034:11	Pithos	L, L3	Rim	Sherd	Combed?	Ware g	6	S1.2	Late Horizon	EB IIIA	-
IM2:FN034:12	Pithos	L, L3	Rim	Sherd	Combed?	Ware g	6	S1.2	Middle Horizon	EB II–III trans.	-
IM2:FN034:13	Pithos	L, L3	Rim	Sherd	Combed? Pre-firing incised mark	Ware g	8	R0.4	Early/Middle horizon	EB II/EB II–III trans.	Genz 2002, Taf. 19:12
IM2:FN034:14	Pithos	L, L3	Rim	Sherd	Combed?	Ware g	1E	R0.2	Late Horizon	EB IIIA	Genz 2002, Taf. 14:4
IM2:FN034:15	Pithos	L, L3	Rim	Sherd	Combed?	Ware g	1E	S1.2	Middle Horizon	EB II-III trans..	-
IM2:FN034:16	Pithos	L, L3	Rim	Sherd	Combed?	Ware g	7A	R0.4	Early/Middle horizon	EB II/EB II–III trans.	Genz 2002, Taf. 19:10
IM2:FN034:17	Pithos	L, L3	Rim	Sherd	Combed?	Ware g	7A	R0.4	Early/Middle horizon	EB II/EB II–III trans.	Genz 2002, Taf. 19:11
IM2:FN034:18	Pithos	L, L3	Rim	Sherd	Combed?	Ware g	7A	R0.4	Late Horizon	EB IIIA	Genz 2002, Taf. 17:7
IM2:FN034:19	Pithos	L, L3	Rim	Sherd	Combed?	Ware g	7A	R0.4	Late Horizon	EB IIIA	Genz 2002, Taf. 17:6
IM2:FN034:20	Pithos	L, L3	Rim	Sherd	Combed?	Ware g	7B	Palace complex; B0.8	Early/Middle horizon	EB II/EB II–III trans.	Genz 2002, Taf. 44:1
IM2:FN034:21	Pithos	L, L3	Rim	Sherd	Combed?	Ware g	7B	R0.1	Early/Middle horizon	EB II/EB II–III trans.	Genz 2002, Taf. 13:2
IM2:FN034:23	Pithos	L, L3	Rim	Sherd	Combed?	Ware g	7B	R0.4	Late Horizon	EB IIIA	Genz 2002, Taf. 17:3

References

Badreshany, Kamal, Graham Philip, and Melissa Kennedy. 2020. "The Development of Integrated Regional Economies in the Early Bronze Age Levant: New Evidence from 'Combed Ware' Jars." *Levant* 52(1-2): 160–196.

Badreshany, Kamal, Sowada, Karin, Ownby, Mary, Jean, Mathilde, de Vreeze, Michel, McClymont, Alice and Philip, Graham. 2022. "The Characterisation of Ceramic Production from the Central Levant and Egyptian Trade in the Pyramid Age." *Journal of Archaeological Science: Report* 41: 103309. https://doi.org/10.1016/j.jasrep.2021.103309.

Ben–Tor, Amnon, and Ruhama Bonfil. 2003. "The Stratigraphy of the Early Bronze Age II–III." In Amnon Ben–Tor, Ruhama Bonfil, and Sharon Zuckerman (eds.), *Tel Qashish: A Village in the Jezreel Valley; Final Report of the Archaeological Excavations (1978–1987)*, 61–124; Qedem Reports 5. Jerusalem: The Israel Exploration Society.

Botticelli, Michela, Silvano Mignardi, Caterina De Vito, Maura Sala, Giacomo Mazzotta, Leticia Da Silva Gondim, and Laura Medeghini. 2022. "The 'Metallic Ware' from Tell el Far'ah North (West Bank): Petrography, Technology, and Provenance of a Hidden Ceramic Industry." *Ceramics International* 48:1: 1366–1374. https://doi.org/10.1016/j.ceramint.2021.09.222.

D'Andrea, Marta. 2020. "The Religious Complexes of Megiddo and Khirbet ez-Zeraqon and the Early Bronze Age Interregional Connectivity." *Studa Eblaitica* 6: 1–39.

D'Andrea, Marta, Khaled Douglas, Hermann Genz, and Kamal Badreshany. 2022. "The 'Post-Urban' Occupation at Hirbet ez-Zeraqon, Jordan: New Insights into the Early Bronze Age IV on the Northern Plateau." *ZDPV* 138.

Deckers, Katleen, Simone Riehl, Valentina Tumolo, Hermann Genz, and Dan Lawrence. 2021. "Intensive olive production at Levantine sites. New data from Fadous-Kfarabida and Khirbet-ez Zeraqon." *Journal of Archaeological Science: Report*: https://doi.org/10.1016/j.jasrep.2021.102841.

de Miroschedji, Pierre. 2021. "On Early Bronze Age Levantine combed vessels: the view from the south." *Levant* 53(1): 30–68.

Douglas, Khaled. 2007. *Die Befestigung der Unterstadt von Ḫirbet ez–Zeraqōn im Rahmen der frühbronzezeitlichen Fortifikation in Palästina.* ADPV 27.3. Wiesbaden: Harrassowitz Verlag.

———. 2011. "Beyond the City Walls: Life Activities Outside the City Gates in the Early Bronze Age in Jordan; Evidence from Khirbet ez–Zeraqon." In Meredith S. Chesson, Walter Aufrecht, and Ian Kuijt (eds.), *Daily Life,Materiality, and Complexity in Early Urban Communities of the Southern Levant: Papers in Honor of Walter E. Rast and R. Thomas Schaub*, 3–21. Winona Lake, IN: Eisenbrauns.

Genz, Hermann. 2001. "Early Bronze Age Potmarks from Khirbat az-Zayraqūn: some aspects concerning their meaning." *Studies in the History and Archaeology of Jordan* VII: 217–228.

———. 2002. *Die frühbronzezeitliche Keramik von Ḫirbet ez-Zeraqōn. Mit Studien zur Chronologie und funktionalen Deutung frühbronzezeitlicher Keramik in der südlichen Levante.* ADPV 27.2; Wiesbaden: Harrassowitz Verlag.

———. 2010. "Thoughts on the Functions of 'Public Buildings' in the Early Bronze Age Southern Levant." In Bolger, Diane and Louise. C. Maguire (eds.), *Development of Pre-State Communities in the Ancient Near East: Studies in Honour of Edgar Peltenburg.* BANEA Monograph Series, Vol. 2, 46–52. Oxford: Oxbow Books.

Genz, Hermann, Riva Daniel, Konstantin E. Pustovoytov, and Marshall Woodworth. 2011. "Excavations at Tell Fadous-Kfarabida. Preliminary Report on the 2011 Season of Excavations." *BAAL* 15: 151–174.

Greenberg, Raphael. 2011. Travelling in (World) Time: Transformation, Commoditization, and the Beginnings of Urbanism in the Southern Levant. In Toby C. Wilkinson, Susan Sherratt and John Bennet (eds.), *Interweaving Worlds. Systemic Interactions in Eurasia, 7th to 1st Millennia BC. Papers from a conference in memory of Professor Andrew Sherratt*, 231–242. Oxford: Oxbow Books.

———. 2017. "No Collapse: Transmutations of Early Bronze Age Urbanism in the Southern Levant." In Felix Höflmayer (ed.), *The Late Third Millennium in the Ancient Near East. Chronology, C14, and Climate Change.* The Oriental Institute of the University of Chicago, Oriental Institute Seminars 11, 73–85. Chicago: University of Chicago.

Greenberg, Raphael, and Mark Iserlis. 2014. "The Early Bronze Age Pottery Industries." In Raphael Greenberg (ed.), *Bet Yerah, The Early Bronze Age Mound, Volume II: Urban Structure and Material Culture 1933–1986 Excavations*, 53–149; IAAR 54. Jerusalem: Israel Antiquities Authority.

———. 2020. "A Note on First Dynasty Egypt, Tel Bet Yerah, and the Origins of Commodity Exchange on the Levantine Seaboard." *Journal of Ancient Egyptian Interconnections* 27: 38–50.

Greenberg, Raphael, Sarit Paz, David Wengrow, and Mark Iserlis. 2012. "Tel Bet Yerah: Hub of Early Bronze Age Levant". *Near Eastern Archaeology* 75: 88–107.

Greenberg, Raphael, and Naomi Porat. 1996. "A Third Millennium Levantine Pottery Production Center: Typology, Petrography, and Provenance of the Metallic Ware of Northern Israel and Adjacent Regions." *BASOR* 301: 5–24.

Hartung, E. Ulrich, Christiana Köhler, Vera Müller and Mary F. Ownby. 2015. "Imported Pottery from Abydos: a new Petrographic perspective." Ägypten *und Levante / Egypt and the Levant* Vol. 25: 295–333.

Hewett, Zarina, Michelle de Gruchy, Daniel Hill, and Dan Lawrence. 2022. "Raincheck: A new diachronic series of rainfall maps for Southwest Asia over the Holocene". *Levant* 54(1): 5–28.

Höflmayer, Felix, Michael W. Dee, Hermann Genz, and Simone Riehl. 2014. "Radiocarbon Evidence for the Early Bronze Age Levant: Tell Fadous-Kfarabida (Lebanon) and the End of the Early Bronze III Period." *Radiocarbon* 56: 529–42.

Ibrahim, Muawiyah M., and Siegfried Mittmann. 1987. "Tell el–Mughayyir and Khirbet Zeiraqoun." *Newsletter of the Institute of Archaeology and Anthropology, Yarmouk University Irbid* 4: 3–6.

———. 1988. "Khirbet ez-Zeraqon Excavations." *Newsletter of the Institute of Archaeology and Anthropology, Yarmouk University Irbid* 6/2: 7–9.

———. 1989. "Zeiraqun (Khirbet el)." In Denyse Homès–Fredericq and John Basil Hennessy (eds.), *Archaeology of Jordan: II 2; Field Reports; Sites L–Z*. Akkadica Supplement 8, 641–46 Leuven: Peeters.

———. 1991." Excavations at Khirbet ez-Zeraqoun 1991." *Newsletter of the Institute of Archaeology and Anthropology, Yarmouk University Irbid* 12: 3–5.

———. 1994. "Excavations at Khirbet ez-Zeraqon, 1993." *Newsletter of the Institute of Archaeology and Anthropology, Yarmouk University Irbid* 16: 11–15.

———. 1997. "Zeiraqun, Khirbet el." In Eric M. Meyers (ed.), *The Oxford Ecyclopedia of Archaeology in the Near East* Vol. 5, 388–89. Oxford: Oxford University Press.

Iserlis, Mark, Daniel Steiniger, and Raphael Greenberg. 2019. "Contact between first dynasty Egypt and specific sites in the Levant: New evidence from ceramic analysis." *Journal of Archaeological Science: Reports* 24: 1023–1040.

Jean, Mathilde. 2020. "Pottery production at Tell Arqa (Lebanon) During the 3rd Millennium BC: Preliminary results of Petrographic Analysis." *Levant* 52(1-2): 136–159.

Kamlah, Jens. 2000. *Der Zeraqōn–Survey 1989–1994. Mit Beiträgen zur Methodik und geschichtlichen Auswertung archäologischer Oberflächenuntersuchungen in Palästina*. Abhandlungen in des Deutschen Palästina–Vereins 27,1. Wiesbaden: Harrassowitz Verlag.

Klein, Cornelius, and Philpotts, Anthony. 2013. *Earth Materials. Introduction to Mineralogy and Petrology*. Cambridge: Cambridge University Press.

Lawrence, Dan, Graham Philip, and Michelle de Gruchy. 2021. "Climate Change and Early Urbanism in Southwest Asia: A Review." *WIREs Climate Change*, e741. https://doi.org/10.1002/wcc.741.

Lebeau, Marc, and de Miroschedji, Pierre. 2013. "Foreword." In Marc Lebeau (ed.), *Arcane Interregional. Ceramics*. Arcane Interregional vol. I, ix–xi. Turnhout: Brepols.

Medeghini, Laura, Maura Sala, Caterina De Vito. and Silvano Mignardi. 2019. "A forgotten Centre of cCeramic Production in Southern Levant: Preliminary Analytical Study of the Early Bronze Age Pottery from Tell el-Far'ah North (West Bank)." *Ceramics International* 45(9): 11457–11467. https://doi.org/10.1016/j.ceramint.2019.03.013.

Mittmann, Siegfried. 1970. *Beiträge zur Siedlungs- und Territorialgeschichte des Nördlichen Ostjordanlandes*. Abhandlungen des Deutschen Palästina–Vereins 2. Wiesbaden: Harrassowitz Verlag.

———. 1994. "Hirbet ez–Zeraqon: Eine Stadt der frühen Bronzezeit in Nordjordanien." *Archäologie in Deutschland* 2: 10–15.

Mohd, Bassem Khalil. 1997. *Geological Map of Irbid 3155 II 1:50000*. Hashemite Kingdom of Jordan: Natural Resources Authority Geological Directorate.

Quinn, Patrick Sean. 2013. *Ceramic Petrography. The Interpretation of Archaeological Pottery and Related Artefacts in Thin Section*. Oxford: Archaeopress.

Regev, Joanna, Pierre de Miroschedji, Raphael Greenberg, Eliot Braun, Zvi Greenhut, and Elisabetta Boaretto. 2012a. "Chronology of the Early Bronze Age in the Southern Levant: New Analysis for a High Chronology." *Radiocarbon* 54: 525–66.

Regev, Johanna, Pierre de Miroschedji, and Elisabetta Boaretto. 2012b. "Early Bronze Age Chronology: Radiocarbon Dates and Chronological Models from Tel Yarmuth (Israel)." *Radiocarbon* 54: 505–24.

Regev, Johanna, Sarit Paz, Raphael Greenberg, and Elisabetta Boaretto. 2020. "Radiocarbon chronology of the EB I–II and II–III transitions at Tel Bet Yerah, and its implications for the nature of social change in the southern Levant." *Levant*. DOI: 10.1080/00758914.2020.1727238.

Riehl, Simone, Reid Bryson, Konstantin E. Pustovoytov. 2008. "Changing Growing Conditions for Crops During the Near Eastern Bronze Age (3000-1200 BC): The Stable Carbon Isotope Evidence." *Journal of Archaeological Science* 35: 1011–1022.

Roudit, Nicholas. JMicroVision: un logiciel d'analyse d'images pétrographiques polyvalent. Genève.

Sowada, Karin. 2020. "Perspectives on Egypt in the Southern levant in Light of the High Early Bronze Age Chronology." In Suzanne Richard (ed.), *New Horizons in the Study of the Early Bronze III and Early Bronze IV in the Levant*, 149–168. University Park, Pennsylvania: Eisenbrauns.

Sowada, Karin, Mary Ownby, and Anna Wodzińska. 2020. "The petrography of imported Levantine Combed vessels from early Old Kingdom Giza." *Levant* 52(1–2): 197–214.

Sowada, Karin, Mary Ownby, and Miroslav Bárta, 2021. "The Origin of Imported Jars from 6th Dynasty Abusir: New Light on Early Bronze Age Egyptian-Levantine Relations." *Bulletin of the American Society for Overseas Research* 386: 221–236.

Stoops, Georges. 2003. *Guidelines for Analysis and Description of Soil and Regolith Thin Sections*. Madison: Soil Science Soc. of America.

Thalmann, Jean-Paul. 2013. "Le Lion, la Chèvre et le Poisson. À propos d'une Jarre à empreintes de sceaux-cylindres de Tell Arqa (Liban)." *Syria* 90: 255–312.

Thalmann, Jean-Paul, and Karin Sowada. 2013. "Levantine "Combed Ware." In Marc Lebeau (ed.), *Arcane Interregional. Ceramics*. Arcane Interregional Vol. I, 323–346. Turnhout: Brepols.

Tumolo, Valentina. 2019. "The Early Bronze Age Seal Impressions on Jars from Ḫirbet ez–Zeraqōn. Preliminary Remarks on Pottery and Images." *Studia Eblaitica* 5: 35–56.

Tumolo, Valentina, and Felix Höflmayer. 2020. "Khirbet ez–Zeraqon and Early Bronze Age chronology revisited". In Suzanne Richard (ed.), *New Horizons in the Study of the Early Bronze III and Early Bronze IV in the* Levant, 249–264. University Park; Pennsylvania: Eisenbrauns.

Vacca, Agnese, and Marta D'Andrea. 2020. "The Connections Between the Northern and the Southern Levant During Early Bronze Age III: Reevaluations and New Vistas in Light of New Data and Higher Chronologies." In Suzanne Richard (ed.), *New Horizons in the Study of the Early Bronze III and Early Bronze IV in the* Levant, 120–145. University Park; Pennsylvania: Eisenbrauns.

Welton, Lynn, Emily Hammer, Michelle de Gruchy, and Dan Lawrence. Forthcoming. "A Multi-Proxy Reconstruction of Anthropogenic Land Use in Southwest Asia at 6 kya: Combining Archaeological, Ethnographic and Environmental Datasets". *Holocene*.

Zuckerman, Sharon. 2003. "The Early Bronze Age II–III Pottery." In Amnon Ben-Tor, Ruhama Bonfil, and Sharon Zuckerman (eds.), *Tel Qashish: A Village in the Jezreel Valley; Final Report of the Archaeological Excavations (1978–1987)*, 130–164; Qedem Reports 5. Jerusalem: The Israel Exploration Society.

Notes

[1] This article is the result of a joint work. V. Tumolo has written the introduction, the archaeological context of Khirbet ez-Zeraqon, the overview on the Levantine Combed Ware (sections 1-3), the assessment of materials and results (sections 4.1, 4.6-4.7), and the discussion (section 5). K. Badreshany has addressed the petrographic analysis (sections 4.2-4.4). Section 4.5 and the conclusions (section 6) have been jointly written.

[2] The chronological framework for the Levant used in this paper follows the proposals on high absolute dates recently suggested by

several scholars for the specific subregions and supported by radiocarbon determinations (see Höflmayer et al. 2014; Regev et al. 2012a; Regev et al. 2012b; Regev et al. 2014; Regev et al. 2020; Tumolo and Höflmayer 2020; Vacca and D'Andrea 2020) and by the ARCANE project (Lebeau and de Miroschedji 2013, xi). The synchronization between Egypt and the Levant is based on the proposals of Sowada 2020 and Sowada et al. 2021.

3 Tumolo and Höflmayer 2020.

4 Ibrahim and Mittmann 1987, 3; 1988, 7; 1989, 642; 1991, 3; 1994, 11–12; 1997, 388; Genz 2002, 7, Abb. 1; Douglas 2007, 3.

5 Hewett et al. 2022.

6 Riehl et al. 2008, 1015, 1017–1018; Deckers et al. 2021.

7 Ibrahim and Mittmann 1987, 3; 1988, 7; 1989, 643; 1991, 3; 1994, 11–12; 1997, 388; Mittmann 1994, 12; Genz 2002, 7; Douglas 2007, 4.

8 Douglas 2007; 2011.

9 Mittmann 1994, 13–14; Genz 2002, 95–96; Genz 2010, 48; D'Andrea 2020.

10 Ibrahim and Mittmann 1994, 14; Mittmann 1994, 14; Genz 2002, 96–98.

11 Genz 2002, 96, 102–104, Tab. 71, Taf. 24–47; 2010b, 49. Vats were also uncovered, possibly employed for processing liquid products (Genz 2002, 92, 104).

12 Building B1.1, on the north–western limits of the excavated area, was only very partially exposed (see Genz 2002, 99).

13 Mittmann 1994, 14–15; Ibrahim and Mittmann 1994, 15; Genz 2002, 100, Tab. 67, Taf. 80–10.

14 Genz 2002, 39–49, 79–84.

15 Genz 2002, 13, 101.

16 Ibrahim and Mittmann 1987, 6; 1989, 645; 1997, 388; Kamlah 2000, 193; Genz 2002, 10; D'Andrea et al. 2022.

17 Genz 2002, 39–49, 77–88, 221.

18 Greenberg and Iserlis 2014, 70–76, 110–125.

19 Ben-Tor and Bonfil 2003, figs 24–36, 46–51; Zuckermann 2003, 134–142.

20 Tumolo and Höflmayer 2020, 253–254 with references therein.

21 Genz 2002, 30, 44; Regev et al. 2020, 19.

22 Tumolo and Höflmayer 2020, 255–259.

23 Regev et al. 2012.

24 Lebeau and de Miroschedji 2013: xi; Sowada 2020, 149–154. The same applies to the EB II of Tel Bet Yeraḥ (Greenberg and Iserlis 2020, 40 with references therein). The radiocarbon data recently published by Regev and colleagues for Tel Bet Yeraḥ set the transition between the Period D and Period C between 2902 and 2888 BC (Regev et al. 2020, 16–18), contemporary with part of the late horizon at Khirbet ez-Zeraqon.

25 Greenberg 2017, 34.

26 Mittmann 1970, 11–15; Kamlah 2000, 189–192.

27 D'Andrea 2020, 12.

28 Greenberg 2017, 35, 48–50; see also D'Andrea 2020, 13.

29 Wilkinson et al. 2014, 53, 88–91; Deckers et al. 2021; Lawrence et al. 2021. Although the site was placed in an area potentially suitable for rainfed agriculture and arboriculture, it was in close proximity with the zone characterized by values of annual rainfall lower than 300 mm (M. De Gruchy personal communication; Welton et al. forthcoming).

30 Badreshany et al. 2020, 162; de Miroschedji 2021, 61 with references therein. See Genz et al. 2011, 161–163 for Organic Residue Analysis.

31 Badreshany et al. 2020, 173 with references therein. De Miroschedji considered hardly convincing that combing could have been considered as a branding, because many of the vessels exported to Egypt were only lightly combed and some were covered by lime coating (de Miroschedji 2021, 43, contra Badreshany et al. 2020, 173). The combing could have had the advantage of providing tactile grip, rendering the surface less slippery.

32 Jean 2020, 141–143 with references therein; de Miroschedji 2021, 44–48, 57 with references therein.

33 De Miroschedji 2021, 50.

34 Although the nature and length of the EB I cultural facies of the central Levant have not been clarified yet, the beginning of the local EB II can be placed around 3100/3000 BC (Thalmann 2013, 258, Fig. 1; Jean 2020, 139, Tab. 1). De Miroschedji suggested that there is no strong evidence unequivocally supporting the chronological priority of southern Levantine productions that used shale–rich fabrics over the central ones (de Miroschedji 2021, 55 with references therein).

35 Phase S ca. 2800–2700/2650 = ECL3 (Jean 2020, 141–142).

36 Thalmann and Sowada 2013, 337.

37 Levantine ceramic made of both calcareous and shale fabrics is already documented in Predynastic Egypt, as in the Tomb U–j at Abydos, and this concurrence characterized also contexts of the 1st Dynasty (Hartung et al. 2015, 316–324), synchronized with the EB II /ESL4 / ECL2 from the reign of Djer onward (Sowada 2020, 153–154). According to Greenberg and Iserlis, the material from Abydos included both ceramic of the South Levantine Metallic Ware and southern potter fabrics from Tel Bet Yeraḥ (2020, 43).

38 Sowada 2020, 155; Sowada et al. 2020; Sowada et al. 2021. Following the abandonment of the Egyptian on-the-ground presence in Sinai and on the southern coastal plain of the southern Levant, although the central Levant became the major economic partner for Egypt, the relationship between Egypt and the southern Levant continued after the 1st Dynasty (Iserlis et al. 2019; Greenberg and Iserlis 2020, 46; Sowada 2020, 153–154, 164).

39 Badreshany et al. 2020, 162; Badreshany et al. 2022; Greenberg and Iserlis 2020, 44, 46; de Miroschedji 2021, 63 with references therein.

40 Thalmann and Sowada 2013, 323–238; Badreshany et al. 2020, 160–163; de Miroschedji 2021, 30–31.

41 Badreshany et al. 2020, 172; de Miroschedji 2021, 46–60.

42 Badreshany et al. 2020, 162 with references therein.

43 Greenberg and Porat 1996.

44 Badreshany et al. 2020, 162.

45 Thalmann and Sowada 2013; 356–358; Badreshany et al. 2020, 165; de Miroschedji 2021, 63.

46 De Miroschedji 2021, 32–44, 48–54. The prevalent use of jars with ledge–handles, instead of loop–handles, would confirm that the southern EB III vessels were not involved in long–distance trades (de Miroschedji 2021, 60).

47 Badreshany et al. 2020, 174 with references therein.

48 Vats with combed surfaces are documented from the middle horizon and are mostly associated with the late stage of occupation of the site (Genz 2002, 41–43). Combed vessels are characterized also by the presence of incised pot marks and seal impressions applied before firing (Genz 2001; Genz 2002, 109–117; Tumolo 2019).

49 Genz 2002, 47–49.

50 Genz 2002, 33–35.

51 With several subtypes, having an average volume between 112 and 141 liters (Genz 2002, 27, Abb.7, 12). Examples often show parallel smooth narrow strips horizontally or diagonally arranged on the body, which are possible impressions created by the ropes that helped hold the vessels together before firing (Genz 2002, 36).

52 Type K, subtypes Kb and Kc, with two loop handles at the mid body and a volume between 4.5 and 9 liters, and 20.5 and 28 liters (Genz 2002, 27, Abb. 6, 11).

53 The latter are characterized by combing only on the outer surface (Genz 2002, 26, 32, Abb.5, Tab. 8).

54 Genz 2002, 29-31.

55 Genz 2002, 31.

56 Genz 2002, 30, Tab. 6.

57 Genz 2002, 44–46, Tabb. 51–53.

58 Genz 2002, 30.

59 Genz 2002, 31, Tab. 7.

60 e.g., Genz 2002, Taf. 32:3. Jars made of Ware g are also characterized by red slip and polished surfaces, or painted strips (e.g., Genz 2002, Taf. 99:7; Taf. 75:1).

61 Genz 2002, 30.

62 A large part of the numerous vats made of Ware c is characterized by horizontal-plus-vertical combing (Genz 2002, 31, Tab. 7, 34, Tab. 10), while they only rarely have other types of decoration (e.g., red painted large strips: Genz 2002, Taf. 108:2).

63 Ware c jars dated to the late horizon can be covered by red slip or strips of red painting (e.g., Genz 2002, Taf. 74:2, Taf. 82:4).

64 Genz 2002, Taf. 8:1a; Taf. 25:3, Taf. 26:1, Taf. 31:2–3, Taf. 36:1, 37:1; Taf. 52:1.

65 Genz 2002, 31, Tab. 7; 34, Tab. 10; 44–46.

66 Five items were included in the study conducted by Badreshany et al. 2020, 165 and Tab. 2.

67 Genz 2002, 30.

68 Differently from other surface treatments, at Khirbet ez-Zeraqon as at other sites (e.g., de Miroschedji 2021, 47), combing did not extend to the neck of jars and pithoi. All the rim sherds of pithoi analyzed in the present study belong to Genz's type L3 (Genz 2002, 21, Abb. 12) that is largely - although not exclusively - associated with combing at the site.

69 Stoops 2003; Quinn 2013; Klein and Philpotts 2013.

70 Roduit 2007 (www.jmicrovision.com).

71 D'Andrea et al. 2022.

72 Badreshany et al. 2020; Jean 2020; Greenberg and Porat 1996.

73 D'Andrea et al. 2022.

74 Badreshany 2013; Badreshany et al. 2020.

75 Jean 2020.

76 D'Andrea et al. 2022.

77 Mohd 2000.

78 Greenberg and Iserlis 2014.

79 Badreshany et al. (2020) suggest that the production was made by itinerant potters, transporting the powdered shale-clays with them. This would also be supported, according to de Miroschedji, by the fact that the productivity of full–time potters, whose expertise would have been necessary for the shale–derived industries such as the North Canaanite Metallic Ware, would have exceeded the needs of a single community of central and southern Levant (de Miroschedji 2021, 60–61). On the other hand, it can be suggested that the clays were sourced and transported to multiple stable production centers in the region, organized through centralized systems that exploited the strong communication networks active in the EB II.

80 Botticelli et al. 2022.

81 Badreshany et al. 2020; Jean 2020.

82 Medeghini et al 2019; Botticelli et al. 2022.

83 Badreshany et al 2020; Badreshany et al. 2022; Jean 2020.

84 de Miroschedji 2021, 31; Greenberg and Iserlis 2020.

85 Badreshany et al 2020.

86 Shale fabrics were used for bowls and platters also at Tel Bet Yeraḥ (Greenberg and Isserlis 2014, 59-50).

87 Genz 2002, Tab. 7.

88 The pithos HZ88-430 presents some ad-hoc perforations, too large to be aimed at a repair using metal clips, and likely hinting at a secondary reuse of the vessel (Genz 2002, 106).

89 Such as the Jurassic and Upper Cretaceous outcrops of northern Lebanon associated to central Levantine manufactures (Badreshany et al. 2020, 190–191).

90 Greenberg and Porat 1996.

91 Badreshany et al. 2020, 188. The industries of the Jordan Valley area possibly included the North Canaanite Metallic Ware tradition (de Miroschedji 2021, 50).

92 Group 1D of Badreshany et al. (2020, 182).

93 Greenberg and Iserlis 2020, 39.

94 Greenberg and Porat 1996; Badreshany et al. 2020, 189–190.

95 See, among others, Tumolo and Höflmayer 2020, 235.

96 In the earliest EB II phase at Tel Bet Yeraḥ, the North Canaanite Metallic Ware/South Levantine Metallic Ware repertoire, made with shale-rich clay, was limited to a restricted number of types, and expanded in the successive stages, including diverse shapes (Greenberg and Iserlis 2020, 40–41, 44). Evidence of a ceramic manufacturing area at the southern side of the settlement revealed that local fabrics were used during Phase C for fashioning types similar to those associated with the North Canaanite Metallic Ware (Greenberg et al. 2012, 95).

97 Greenberg and Iserlis 2014, 76.

98 On the base of absolute dates, the entire life of the settlement of Khirbet ez-Zeraqon (ca. 3100/3050–2850 cal. BC) mostly corresponds to the EB II at Tel Bet Yeraḥ, which spans from ca. 3150 to 2902/2888 BC (Greenberg and Iserlis 2020, 40; Regev et al. 2020, 16–18).

99 Badreshany et al. 2020, 174, 184–188.

100 Greenberg and Porat 1996, 11.

101 Badreshany et al. 2020, 187.

102 This development was part of a broader process that affected the entire ceramic manufacture at the site, with strong changes taking place during the EB II-III (Phase S – ECL3), when the shale fabrics that were used in Phase T (EB II – ECL2) were abandoned. Shale-rich Fabrics 5 and 6, documented only in phase T, were not associated with any specific type. Jars were vertically burnished during phase T, while pattern combing started from phase S. In Phase R, also horizontal combing appeared, which is the only combed treatment known for jars in the following phase P. From phase S, storage vessels were made of Fabrics 2 and 3, the latter being a multi–purpose fabric that survived into the EB IV (Phase P), when it became the predominant fabric, suggesting a general tendency toward homogenization in the ceramic production (Jean 2020, 141–142, 147–153).

103 Jean 2020, 151 with references therein.

104 Greenberg and Isserlis 2014, 59–60; Greenberg 2017, 46.

105 The petrographic analyses conducted by Sowada and colleagues on materials from the settlement of Heit el-Ghurab and the Giza necropolis suggested that the combed jars belonged to a specialised production of made with iron-rich calcareous clays originating from the area around Byblo. Similarly, combed vessels from the 6th Dynasty tomb complex of Qaar at Abusir appear to have been imported from the northern part of the Lebanese coast (Sowada et al. 2020; Sowada et al. 2021).

106 De Miroschedji 2021.

Made in the USA
Middletown, DE
08 July 2023

34734516R00186